Series in Machine Perception and Artificial Intelligence – Vol. 73

T0336004

PROGRESS IN
COMPUTER VISION
AND
IMAGE ANALYSIS

Editors

Horst Bunke
University of Bern, Switzerland

Juan José Villanueva
Gemma Sánchez
Xavier Otazu
Computer Vision Center/UAB, Spain

NEW JERSEY · LONDON · SINGAPORE · BEIJING · SHANGHAI · HONG KONG · TAIPEI · CHENNAI

Published by

World Scientific Publishing Co. Pte. Ltd.

5 Toh Tuck Link, Singapore 596224

USA office: 27 Warren Street, Suite 401-402, Hackensack, NJ 07601

UK office: 57 Shelton Street, Covent Garden, London WC2H 9HE

British Library Cataloguing-in-Publication Data
A catalogue record for this book is available from the British Library.

PROGRESS IN COMPUTER VISION AND IMAGE ANALYSIS
Series in Machine Perception and Artificial Intelligence — Vol. 73

Copyright © 2010 by World Scientific Publishing Co. Pte. Ltd.

ISBN-13 978-981-283-445-4
ISBN-10 981-283-445-1

Printed in Singapore.

PROGRESS IN
COMPUTER VISION
AND
IMAGE ANALYSIS

PREFACE

An image is worth more than ten thousand words - and for that reason Computer Vision has received enormous amounts of attention from several scientific and technological communities in the last decades. Computer Vision is defined as the process of extracting useful information from images in order to be able to perform other tasks.

An image usually contains a huge amount of information that can be utilized in various contexts. Depending on the particular application, one may be interested, for example, in salient features for object classification, texture properties, color information, or motion. The automated procedure of extracting meaningful information from an input image and deriving an abstract representation of its contents is the goal of Computer Vision and Image Analysis, which appears to be an essential processing stage for a number of applications such as medical image interpretation, video analysis, text understanding, security screening and surveillance, three-dimensional modelling, robot vision, as well as automatic vehicle or robot guidance.

This book provides a representative collection of papers describing advances in research and development in the fields of Computer Vision and Image Analysis, and their applications to different problems. It shows advanced techniques related to PDE's, wavelet analysis, deformable models, multiple classifiers, neural networks, fuzzy sets, optimization techniques, genetic programming, among others. It also includes valuable material on watermarking, image compression, image segmentation, handwritten text recognition, machine learning, motion tracking and segmentation, gesture recognition, biometrics, shadow detection, video processing, and others.

All contributions have been selected from the peer-reviewed international scientific journal ELCVIA (http://elcvia.cvc.uab.es). The contributing authors (as well as the reviewers) are all established researchers in the field and they provide a representative overview of the available techniques and applications of this broad and quickly emerging field.

v

The aim of this book is to provide an overview of recent progress in methods and applications in the domains of Computer Vision and Image Analysis for researchers in academia and industry as well as for Master and PhD students working in Computer Vision, Image Analysis, and related fields.

H. Bunke
J.J. Villanueva
G. Sanchez
X. Otazu

CONTENTS

CHAPTER 1

AN APPEARANCE-BASED METHOD FOR PARAMETRIC
VIDEO REGISTRATION

Xavier Orriols, Lluis Barceló and Xavier Binefa

Computer Vision Center, Universitat Autònoma de Barcelona
08193 Bellaterra, Spain
E-mail: xavier.binefa@uab.es

In this paper, we address the problem of multi-frame video registration using an appearance-based framework, where linear subspace constraints are applied in terms of the appearance subspace constancy assumption. We frame the multiple-image registration in a two step iterative algorithm. First, a feature space is built through and Singular Value Decomposition (SVD) of a second moment matrix provided by the images in the sequence to be analyzed, where the variabilities of each frame respect to a previously selected frame of reference are encoded. Secondly, a parametric model is introduced in order to estimate the transformation that has been produced across the sequence. This model is described in terms of a polynomial representation of the velocity field evolution, which corresponds to a parametric multi-frame optical flow estimation. The objective function to be minimized considers both issues at the same time, i.e., the appearance representation and the time evolution across the sequence. This function is the connection between the global coordinates in the subspace representation and the parametric optical flow estimates. Both minimization steps are reduced to two linear least squares sub-problems, whose solutions turn out to be in closed form for each iteration. The appearance constraints result to take into account all the images in a sequence in order to estimate the transformation parameters. Finally, results show the extraction of $3D$ affine structure from multiple views depending on the analysis of the surface polynomial's degree.

1.1. Introduction

The addition of temporal information in visual processing is a strong cue for understanding structure and $3D$ motion. Two main sub-problems appear when it comes to deal with motion analysis; *correspondence* and *reconstruction*. First issue (correspondence) concerns the location analysis of which elements of a frame correspond to which elements in the following images of a sequence. From elements correspondence, reconstruction corresponds to $3D$ motion and structure recovery of the observed world. In this paper, we focus on the first issue, and, more specifically, the problem is centered on the observed motion in static scenes onto the image plane which is produced by camera motion: *ego-motion*. In previous work, dense[1,2] and sparse[3-5] methods to estimate the motion field have been used to this end. Sparse methods strongly rely on the accuracy of the feature detector and not all the information available in the image is employed. Dense methods are based on optical flow estimation which often produces inaccurate estimates of the motion field. Moreover the analysis is instantaneous, which means that is not integrated over many frames. Many authors[6-10] focus on this registration problem in terms of $2D$ parametric alignment, where the estimation process is still between two frames. Thus, taking into account that the second step, *reconstruction*, requires that all the transformations must be put in correspondence with a certain frame of reference, the accumulation error can be present in these computations.

Authors in[11] introduce the notion of *subspace constancy assumption*, where visual prior information is exploited in order to build a views+affine transformation model for object recognition. Their starting point is that the training set has to be carefully selected with the aim of capturing just appearance variabilities; that is, the training set is assumed to be absent of camera (or motion) transformations. Once the learning step is performed, the test process is based on the computation of the affine parameters and the subspace coefficients that map the region in the focus of attention onto the closest learned image. However, in this paper, the topic that we deal with has as input data the images of a sequence that include a camera (or motion) transformations.

In this paper, we address the problem of multi-frame registration by means of an *eigenfeatures* approach, where linear subspace constraints are based on the assumption of constancy in the appearance subspace. We frame the multiple-image registration in a two-step iterative algorithm. First, a feature space is built through and SVD decomposition of a second moment matrix provided by the images in the sequence to be analyzed. This technique allows us to codify images as points capturing the *intrinsic degrees of freedom* of the appearance, and at the same time, it yields compact description preserving visual semantics and perceptual similarities.[12-14]

Second, a parametric model is introduced in order to estimate the transformation that has been produced across the sequence. This model is described in terms of a polynomial representation of the velocities field evolution. Polynomial coefficients are related with $3D$ information. For instance, in the specific case of affine transformations of a planar surface, the linear terms (0 and 1 degree) will contain information about its translations and rotations, the quadratic terms will explain the projective behavior, and so forth. Each step is utilized as the input entry to the next step; that is, once the eigen-subspace is computed, we show how the transformations are estimated, therefore, images are registered according to these estimates and again the eigen-subspace is built with the registered images in the previous step. These two step are iterated until the error function converges under a certain degree of tolerance.

The outline of the paper is as follows: section 2 frames the idea of using the eigenfeatures approach and its relation with the parametric model of transformations. More specifically, we analyze how such an appearance subspace is built according to a previously selected frame of reference. Therefore, a polynomial model is introduced in order to link the appearance constraints to the transformations that occurred across the sequence. In the experimental results, section 3, we show a new manner of encoding temporal information. We point out that when parallax is involved in the problem of video registration, the temporal representation gives a visual notion of the depth in the scene, and therefore it offers the possibility of extracting the affine $3D$ structure from multiple views. The relation between the surface polynomial's degree and $3D$ affine structure is also illustrated. In section 4, the summary and the conclusions of this paper are shown.

1.2. Appearance Based Framework for Multi-Frame Registration

In this section, we present an objective function which takes into account appearance representation and time evolution between each frame and a frame of reference. In this case, temporal transformations estimation is based on the fact that images belonging to a coherent sequence are also related by means of their appearance representation.

Given a sequence of F images $\{I_1, \ldots, I_F\}$ (of n rows and m columns) and a selected frame of reference I_0, we can write them in terms of column vectors $\{y_1, \ldots, y_F\}$ and y_0 of dimension $d = n \times m$. Both pictures *pixel-based* I_i and *vector-form* y_i of the i-th image in the sequence are relevant in the description of our method. The first representation I_i is useful to describe the transformations that occurred to each pixel. The vector-form picture is utilized for analyzing the underlying appearance in all the sequence.

Under the assumption of brightness constancy, each frame in the sequence I_i can be written as the result of a Taylor's expansion around the frame of reference I_0:

$$I_i(\vec{x}) = I_0(\vec{x}) + \nabla I_0(\vec{x})^T \vec{\omega}_i(\vec{x}) \qquad (1.1)$$

This is equivalent, in a vector-form, to:

$$y_i = y_0 + t_i \qquad (1.2)$$

where t_i is the vector-form of the second summand $\nabla I_0(\vec{x})^T \vec{\omega}_i(\vec{x})$ in eq. (1.1). First description is exploited in section 1.2.2, where the parametric polynomial model to describe the velocity field estimates is applied. The vector-form description in eq (1.2) is employed in the following section 1.2.1 to develop the appearance analysis respect to a chosen reference frame.

1.2.1. *Appearance Representation Model*

First of all, we need to define a space of features where images are represented as points. This problem involves finding a representation as a support for analyzing the temporal evolution. To address the problem of appearance representation, authors in[12-14] proposed Principal Component Analysis as redundancy reduction technique in order to preserve the semantics, i.e. perceptual similarities, during the codification process of the principal features. The idea is to find a small number of causes that in combination are able to reconstruct the appearance representation.

One of the most common approaches for explaining a data set is to assume that causes act in linear combination:

$$y_i = W\xi_i + y_0 \qquad (1.3)$$

where $\xi_i \in \Re^q$ (our chosen reduced representation, $q < d$) are the causes and y_0 corresponds to the selected frame of reference. The q-vectors that span the basis are the columns of W ($d \times q$ matrix), where the variation between the diferents images y_i and the reference frame is encoded.

With regard to equation (1.2), and considering the mentioned approximation in (1.3), we can see that the difference t_i between the frame of reference y_0 and each image y_i in the sequence is described by the linear combination $W\xi_i$ of the vectors that span the basis in W. Notice that in the usual PCA techniques y_0 plays the role of the sample mean. In recognition algorithms this fact is relevant, since there is assumed that each sample is approximated by the mean (ideal pattern) with an added variation which is given by the subspace W. However, in our approach, each image y_i tends to the frame of reference y_0 with a certain degree of variation, which is represented as a linear combination of the basis W.

Furthermore, from eq. (1.1), the difference t_i, that relies on the linear combination of the appearance basis vectors, can be described in terms of the parametric model which defines the transformation from the reference frame y_0 and each image y_i. This parametric model is developed in the following section 1.2.2.

Besides, from the mentioned description in terms of a subspace of appearance, we can see the form that takes the objective function to be minimized. Indeed, the idea is to find: a basis W, a set of parameters $\{p_1, ..., p_r\}$, (that model the temporal transformations), and a set of registered images where the squared distance between the difference obtained through the taylor's expansion t_i and the projected vector in the appearance subspace $W\xi_i$ is minimum, i.e.:

$$\mathcal{E}(W, ..., p_1^i, ..., p_r^i, ...) = \sum_{i=1}^{F} |t_i(p_1^i, ..., p_r^i) - W\xi_i|^2 \qquad (1.4)$$

The minimization of this objective function requires of a two-step iterative procedure: first it is necessary to build an appearance basis, and therefore, to estimate the parametric transformations that register the images in the sequence. In the following sections introduce closed forms solutions for each step.

1.2.2. Polynomial Surface Model

In this section we present a polynomial method to estimate the transformation between de reference frame I_0 and each frame I_i in the sequence. To this end we utilize the pixel-based picture. From equation (1.1) we can see that the difference between a frame I_i and the frame of reference I_0 relies on the velocities field $\vec{\omega}_i(\vec{x})$. A s-degree polynomial model for each velocity component can be written as follows:

$$\vec{w}_i(\vec{x}) = \mathcal{X}(\vec{x})\vec{P}_i \qquad (1.5)$$

where $\mathcal{X}(\vec{x})$ is a matrix that takes the following form:

$$\mathcal{X}(\vec{x}) = \left[\begin{array}{c|c} \Omega(\vec{x}) & 0 \\ \hline 0 & \Omega(\vec{x}) \end{array} \right]$$

with

$$\Omega(\vec{x}) = \left[1 \; x \; y \; xy \; x^2 \; ... \; (x^l y^k) \; ... \; y^s \right]$$

where $\Omega(\vec{x})$ is a $d \times 2r$, ($r = (s+1)(s+2)$), matrix that encodes pixel positions, and $\vec{P}_i$ is a column vector of dimension $r = (s+1)(s+2)$, which corresponds to the number of independent unknown parameters of the transformation. In matrix language $\mathcal{X}(\vec{x})$ is a matrix $2d \times r$, $\vec{P}$ has dimensions $r \times 1$, and the velocities corresponding to each pixel can be encoded in a matrix $\vec{w}_i(\vec{x})$ of dimensions $2d \times 1$. The gradient expression in the linear term of the taylor's expansion (1.1) can be written in a diagonal matrix form as follows:

$$
G_x = \begin{bmatrix} g_x^1 & 0 & \cdots & 0 \\ 0 & g_x^2 & \cdots & 0 \\ \vdots & & \ddots & \vdots \\ 0 & \cdots & \cdots & g_x^d \end{bmatrix} \qquad G_y = \begin{bmatrix} g_y^1 & 0 & \cdots & 0 \\ 0 & g_y^2 & \cdots & 0 \\ \vdots & & \ddots & \vdots \\ 0 & \cdots & \cdots & g_y^d \end{bmatrix}
$$

Stacking horizontally both matrices we obtain a matrix G of dimensions $d \times 2d$: $G = [G_x \mid G_y]$. Therefore, according to the vector-form in eq (1.2), the difference t_i between the i-th frame y_i and the frame of reference y_0, is expressed in terms of the polynomial model through:

$$
t_i(\vec{x}, \vec{P_i})_{d \times 1} = G_{d \times 2d} \mathcal{X}(\vec{x})_{2d \times r} \vec{P_i} \mid_{r \times 1} \tag{1.6}
$$

Given that the term $G_{d \times 2d} \mathcal{X}(\vec{x})_{2d \times r}$ is computed once for all the images in iteration, we re-name it as $\Psi_{d \times r} = G_{d \times 2d} \mathcal{X}(\vec{x})_{2d \times r}$. Notice that even when images are highly dimensional, (e.g. $d = 240 \times 320$), the computation of Ψ can be perfomed easily in *Matlab* by means of the operator ".*", without incurring in an out of memory.

1.2.3. *The Algorithm*

Given the parametric model for the transformations of the images in a sequence, the objective function (1.4) can be written explicitly in terms of the parameters to be estimated:

$$
\mathcal{E}(W, \vec{P_1}, \ldots, \vec{P_F}) = \sum_{i=1}^{F} \mid \Psi \vec{P_i} - W \xi_i \mid^2 \tag{1.7}
$$

In order to minimize this objective function, we need a two step procedure: first given a set of images, the subspace of appearance W is computed, and secondly, once the parameters $\vec{P_i}$ that register each frame y_i to the frame of reference y_0 are obtained, the images are registered in order to build again a new subspace of appearance.

a. Appearance Subspace Estimation. Consider an intermediate iteration in the algorithm, thus, the set of registered images to be analyzed are: $\{\phi_1(y_1, \vec{P_1}), \ldots, \phi_F(y_F, \vec{P_F})\}$. From this set and the reference frame y_0, the appearance subspace can be performed by means of an Singular Value Decomposition of the second moments matrix[a]:

$$\Sigma = \sum_{i=1}^{F}(\phi_i(y_i, \vec{P_i}) - y_0)(\phi_i(y_i, \vec{P_i}) - y_0)^T \tag{1.8}$$

The column vectors of W correspond to the q first eigenvectors of (1.8), that have been previously ordered from the largest eigenvalues to the smallest one. The projected coordinates onto the appearance subspace are: $\xi_i = W^T(\phi_i(y_i, \vec{P_i}) - y_0)$.

b. Transformation Parameters Estimation. Setting derivatives to zero in eq. (1.7) respect to the transformation parameters, they are computed as follows:

$$\vec{P_i} = \left[\Psi^T\Psi\right]^{-1}\Psi^T W \xi_i \tag{1.9}$$

Note that the matrix $\left[\Psi^T\Psi\right]^{-1}$ has manageable dimensions $r \times r$, i.e. in the linear polynomial case $r = 3$, in the quadratic case $r = 12$, etc. We can see that while the appearance (global information) is codified in W, the local infomation which is related to the pixels in the images is encoded in Ψ. With this, we can see that their combination in eq. (1.9) gives a relation between each image's subspace coordinates ξ_i and the parameters that register each frame to the frame of reference. Moreover, this method considers the contribution of all the frames in the sequence to the estimation of each single set of transformation parameters. From these estimates, we compute a new set of registered images $\{\phi_1(y_1, \vec{P_1}), \ldots, \phi_F(y_F, \vec{P_F})\}$ and repeat step a. These two steps are iterated until a certain degree of tolerance in the value obtained through the error function eq. (1.7).

1.3. Experimental Results

In order to see the range of applications of this technique, we deal with two sort of problems. First, we study a camera movement, where it is shown the different results that appear when it comes to deal with a specific selected frame of reference. In particular, this camera movement is a zoom that can be interpreted in terms of registration as zoom-in or zoom-out operations depending on the selection of the reference frame. Secondly, the significance of the polynomial's degree is analyzed through a sequence that includes a moving object due to a parallax effect.

---

[a]This can be performed following the idea introduced in.[14]

Fig. 1.1.   Some selected frames (1st, 3rd, 5th) from a sequence: 1,41,81 form the original one.

1.3.1. Selecting a Reference Frame. Consequences in the Registration

This topic is about camera operations with a single planar motion. Figure 1.1 shows three frames from a sequence of 100 frames, where a zoom-in is originally perfomed. In this particular case, we selected 5 frames ($1^{st}, 21^{st}, 41^{st}, 61^{st}, 81^{st}$) from the original sequence to perform this analysis. This was motivated in order to exploit the fact that the images have not to be taken continuously; the key point is that they are related by the same underlying appearance. Here, we analyze three cases depending on the selection of the reference frame: zoom-in registration fig.1.2 and zoom-out registration fig.1.3.

Figure 1.2 shows a zoom-in registration that has been obtained selecting as reference frame the left side image in fig. 1.1. To this end, we utilized a linear polynomial model (1 degree), and the subspace of appearance has been built using just one eigenvector, given that appearance is mainly conserved in the sequence. The point is that the dimension not only depends on the error reconstruction as in a recognition problem,[12–14] but also relies on the selection of the frame of reference.

Figure 1.2 (a) shows a time evolution of the registered sequence images, while figure 1.2(d) the registration picture also explains the module of the velocity field in each pixel. Latter figure gives a notion of the situation of the camera's center. This is highly useful to perform an analysis of camera operations from this registration technique. Figures 1.2(b) and (c) show the estimate optical flow field, which is computed respect to the reference frame, in some frames of the sequence. When it comes to register from this vector field, we have to take the inverse direction that is indicated in each arrow.

Besides, even though the sequence evolution showed a zoom-in camera operation, we can register selecting as reference frame the last frame, (see right side image in fig. 1.1). The main difference between the registrations in figure 1.2 and figure 1.3 is the size of the final mosaic (top views of fig. 1.2(a) and fig. 1.3(a)).

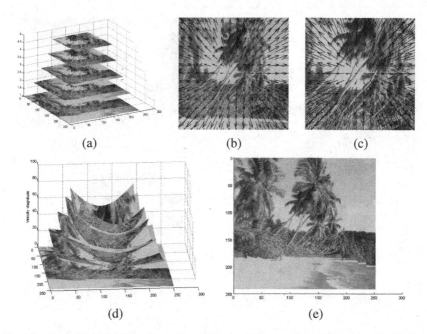

Fig. 1.2.   Zoom in: (a) Registered images according to a 1 degree polynomial model, where the first frame has been taken as reference frame. Optical flow field corresponding to the third frame (b), and to the last frame (c). (d) Velocity field module representation of the sequence of images. (e) Top view of (d).

Actually, the size of the final mosaic selecting as reference frame the first frame is equal to the reference frame. However, taking as reference frame the last frame (case fig1.3) the size of the final mosaic is bigger than the size of the reference frame. This is clearly reflected in the module representations of the sequence registration, figures 1.2(d) and 1.3(d).

1.3.2. Analyzing the Complexity in the Polynomial Model. Towards 3D Affine Reconstruction

In order to get an insight into the relation between the complexity of the polynomial estimation of the velocity field and the $3D$ affine structure which is encoded in the image sequence, we deal with three sort of experiments. The idea is to see the variety of possibilities that the polynomial surface model offers in this registration framework. Three cases present different relative motions across the image sequence.

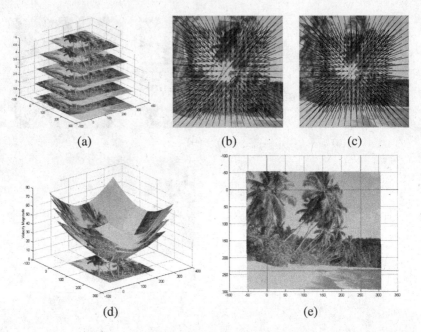

Fig. 1.3.   Zoom out: (a) Registered images according to a 1 degree polynomial model, where the last frame has been taken as reference frame. Optical flow field corresponding to the third frame (b), and to the first frame (c). (d) Velocity field module representation of the sequence of images.(e) Top view of (d), where the red lines show the original size of the reference frame.

First sequence of images corresponds to a camera panning operation, where the target is an object with different depths respect to the camera position. This fact produces a parallax effect onto the image plane, which means that the affine model (degree 1) to estimate the velocities field is not sufficient. Figure 1.4 shows three frames of a sequence of ten images, which have been used to perform the first analysis of $3D$ motion. To estimate the introduced parametric optical flow, we used a third degree polynomial model, which according to eq. (1.5) represents 20 parameters in the estimation process.

Registration results are shown in figure 1.5 (a) and (b), where the first frame has been taken as reference frame. First one is a velocity field module representation of the image sequence, where is can be seen that the edge between the dark region and the light one is in the same pixel reference coordinate position in each frame. We use the method described in[15] to estimate the $3D$ affine structure from the registered images. To this end we utilized all the pixels in the images to perform the factorization method. This fact is present in the $3D$ reconstruction results (see figs. 1.5(c) and (d)) since the union edges between planes are smoothly re-

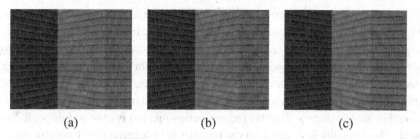

Fig. 1.4.   Three frames of a sequence of ten images. First image (a) corresponds to the first frame, (b) is the fifth and (c) is the tenth.

produced. To reproduced properly these mentioned high frequency regions, it is necessary to consider hard constraints in the $3D$ recovery step. This topic remains a task for our future research.

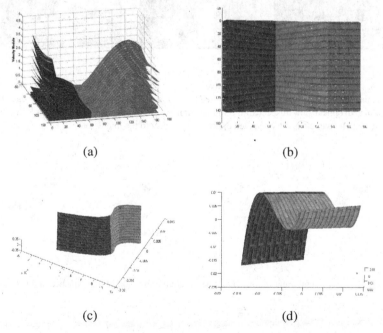

Fig. 1.5.   Velocity field module representation (a) of the registered images, where 2 eigenvectors of appearance and a polynomial model of 3rd degree have been used to this estimation. Fig. (b) is the top view of (a). Two views, (c) and (d), of the $3D$ affine structure of the sequence.

Second experiment is centered on a rotating object in front of a static camera. Figure 1.6 shows three frames of a sequence of five in the performance of this experiment. We selected the middle frame as reference frame. This figure also shows the optical flow respect to the reference frame. In this case we used a fourth degree polynomial model and 3 eigenvectors of appearance. The complexity of this sequence is shown in figure 1.7, where different views of the $3D$ affine reconstruction are illustrated. The $3D$ reconstruction method is obtained through[15] as well. The difficulty here relies on the fact that the background is basically static. Therefore, it should be appropriate a previous segmentation of the moving object. This is the reason of a significantly high degree polynomial model.

Fig. 1.6.   Three frames of a sequence of five images, where 3 eigenvectors of appearance and a polynomial model of 4th degree have been used to the registration process. Right side image shows the estimated optical flow respect to the middle frame (which corresponds to the third one in the sequence). Left side one is the computed optical flow respect to the middle one.

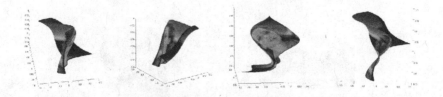

Fig. 1.7.   Different views of the $3D$ affine structure estimation of the sequence in fig. 1.6.

Third experiment deals with a translational camera motion. Two main motion layers are present in this sequence due to a parallax effect. Figure 1.8 shows three frames of a sequence of five, where the tree belongs to a different motion layer than the background (houses). Apparently, the sequence can be interpreted as a moving object with moving background as well. Nevertheless, the cause is the difference in depth that the tree is situated from the background, and, moreover, the specific movement of the camera. The registration has been performed using 2 eigenvectors of basis appearance and a 3rd degree polynomial model for the motion field. The result of this can be seen in figures 1.9 (a) and (b). More specifically, figure 1.9 (a) gives a certain notion of the relative depth among different regions in the images, due to the module representation of the velocity field; regions with higher velocity module are meant to be nearer the camera than regions with a lower module. Figure 1.9 (b) shows a top view of (a), where the result of registering is regarded in terms of a mosaic image. Finally, figure 1.9(c) shows the $3D$ affine structure estimation using,[15] where all the images pixels in the sequence have been employed. With this, we can see that the final $3D$ smooth surface shows this mentioned depth difference due to parallax.

Fig. 1.8.   Three frames of a sequence of five images. These images correspond to $1^{st}, 3^{st}$ and 5st (from right side to left side).

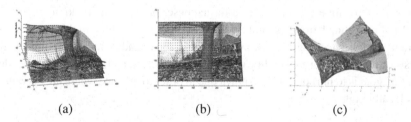

(a)   (b)   (c)

Fig. 1.9.   Velocity field module representation (a) of the registered images, where 2 eigenvectors of appearance and a polynomial model of 3rd degree have been used to this estimation. Fig. (b) is the top view of (a). A view (c) of the $3D$ affine structure of the sequence.

1.4. Summary and Conclusions

The problem of multi-frame registration has been presented through an *eigenfeatures* approach, where linear subspace constraints are based on the assumption of constancy in the appearance subspace. One of the main contributions of the appearance subspace encoding is that the appropriate scale in each problem is captured from the images themselves, i.e., robust time derivatives of the optical flow are obtained from eigenfeatures. As mentioned in section 2.1, this fact is due to the consideration of both pictures, *pixel-based* and *vector-form*, into the same formulation. First picture exploits local information, while the vector-form is utilized for global information purposes. The aim of this is to point out that image time derivatives are computed coupling the linear combination of the eigenfeature basis and the spatial information which is provided by the polynomial surface model (pixel-based picture). This coupling is performed in a objective function that is minimized in order to obtain the registration of a sequence.

This approach is combined with a polynomial model for estimating the transformation that has been produced across the sequence. Although the objective function, that corresponds to the connection between the global coordinates in the subspace representation and the parametric optical flow estimates, requires a two step procedure, the minimization steps have been reduced to linear least squares subproblems, whose solutions turned out to be in a closed form for each iteration.

We dealt with a variety of experiments in order to analyze the range of applications of this registration technique. One of the purposes is to see that the contribution of a parametric multiframe optical flow estimation provides a smooth reconstruction of the $3D$ affine structure the is imaged in the sequence, where all the pixels information is employed. Besides, from section 3.2, the relation between the polynomial model and the $3D$ reconstruction has been observed qualitatively. It is a task of future work to give a formal description of this relation. Also, the idea of including hard constraints to the reconstruction method in this polynomial framework is encouraging. The purpose is to keep the advantageous motion analysis estimation in terms of a few number of parameters, and, at the same time, the future goal is to introduce prior knowledge in order to indicate where the curvature is locally higher.

Acknowledgments

This work was supported by CICYT grant TEL99-1206-C02-02.

References

1. M. Irani, B. Rousso, and S. Peleg, Recovery of ego-motion using region alignment, *IEEE trans. on P.A.M.I.* **19**(3), (1997).
2. H. Heeger and A. Jepson, Simple method for computing 3D motion and depth, *ICCV.* pp. 96–100, (1990).
3. F. Lustman, O. Faugeras, and G. Toscani, Motion and structure from motion from point and line matching, *ICCV.* pp. 25–34, (1987).
4. B. Horn, Relative orientation, *IJCV.* pp. 58–78, (1988).
5. R. Chipolla, Y. Okamoto, and Y. Kuno, Robust structure from motion using motion parallax, *ICCV.* pp. 374–382, (1993).
6. J. Wang and E. Adelson, Layered representation for motion analysis, *CVPR.* pp. 361–366, (1993).
7. S. Ayer and H. Sawhney, Layered representation of motion video using robust maximum-likelihood estimation of mixture models and mdl encoding, *ICCV.* pp. 777–784, (1995).
8. H. Sawhney and S. Ayer, Compact representation of videos through dominant and multiple motion estimation, *IEEE Trans. on PAMI.* **18**, 814–829, (1996).
9. J. Bergen, P. Anandan, K. Hanna, and R. Hingorani, Hierarchical model-based motion estimation, *ECCV.* pp. 237–252, (1992).
10. S. Ju, M. Black, and A. Jepson, Multilayer, locally affine optical flow, and regularization with transparency, *CVPR.* pp. 307–314, (1996).
11. M. Black and A. Jepson, Eigentracking: Robust matching and tracking of articulated objects using a view-based representation, *ECCV.* pp. 329–342, (1996).
12. M. Turk and A. Pentland, Eigenfaces for recognition, *Journal of Cognitive Neuroscience.* **3**(1), 71–86, (1991).
13. A. Pentland, B. Moghaddam, and T. Starner, View-based and modular eigenspaces for face recognition, *IEEE Conference on Computer Vision and Pattern Recognition.* (1994).
14. H. Murase and S. Nayar, Visual learning and recognition of 3d objects from appearance, *IJVC.* **14**(5), 5–24, (1995).
15. C. Tomasi and T. Kanade, Shape and motion from image streams under orthography: a factorization method, *IJCV.* **9**, 137–154, (1992).

CHAPTER 2

AN INTERACTIVE ALGORITHM FOR IMAGE SMOOTHING AND SEGMENTATION

M. C. de Andrade

Centro de Desenvolvimento da Tecnologia Nuclear - CDTN, P.O. BOX 941, Belo Horizonte, MG, Brazil

This work introduces an interactive algorithm for image smoothing and segmentation. A non-linear partial differential equation is employed to smooth the image while preserving contours. The segmentation is a region-growing and merging process initiated around image minima (seeds), which are automatically detected, labeled and eventually merged. The user places one *marker* per region of interest. Accurate and fast segmentation results can be achieved for gray and color images using this simple method.

1. Introduction

Image denoising and segmentation play an important role in image analysis and computer vision. Image denoising reduces the noise introduced by the image acquisition process, while image segmentation recovers the regions associated to the objects they represent in a given image. Image segmentation typically relies on semantically poor information, directly obtained from the image around a spatially restrained neighborhood and, for this reason, is broadly classified as a *low-level* treatment [6].

Image segmentation often requires pre- and post-processing steps, where user judgment is fundamental and feeds information of highly semantic content back into the process. Pre-processing is an essential step, in which specialized filters smooth the image, simplifying it for the subsequent segmentation step. Interactive segmentation allows the user to intervene directly in the segmentation process thus contributing to its success. Additionally, post-processing may be required to complete the task, if the segmentation itself fails to produce the desired results.

Image segmentation is an application-oriented problem. There is no general-purpose segmentation method. The choice of a particular technique depends on the nature of the image (non-homogeneous illumination, presence of noise or texture, ill-defined contours, occlusions), post-segmentation operations _ (shape recognition, interpretation, localization, measurements), primitives to be extracted (contours, straight segments, regions, shapes, textures) and on physical limitations (algorithmic complexity, real-time execution, available memory) [6]. Moreover, other important issues concerning fundamental aspects of image segmentation methods such as, initialization, convergence, ability to handle topological changes, stopping criteria and over-segmentation, must be taken into account. Therefore, the performance of a segmentation method can not be evaluated beforehand, its quality can only be evaluated by the results obtained from the treatments using the extracted primitives. However, many of the difficulties found in image segmentation can be reduced by adequately smoothing the image during the pre-processing step.

Segmentation by *deformable models - DM* describes contours, which evolve under a suitable energy functional. The pioneer work of Kass et. al. [12], the *snakes method* uses image forces and external constraints to guide the evolution of the *DMs* by minimizing the energy of spline curves and surfaces. Former versions of this method required the initialization to be done close to the boundaries of the objects, to guarantee proper convergence and to avoid being trapped by local minima. The *gradient vector flow* [28], an improved version of the *snakes method*, largely solved the poor convergence problem. The *balloon method* [7] adds an inflation force to the *snakes*, to move the initialized model into the neighborhood of the edges, avoiding local minima. However, the inflation force often pushes the contour over weak edges.

Modeling the contours in the level set framework [20, 21], easily solves the topological problem, i.e., merging of the non-significant regions (or curves enveloping them). The *active contours method* presented by Caselles et. al. [5] and the *front propagation method* introduced by Malladi et. al [13, 14], for example, greatly simplify the topological problem but do not address the initialization and convergence issues. Initialization is usually difficult and time-consuming requiring the manual introduction of polygons around the features of interest. Convergence is also difficult since some models are still evolving while others have finished the evolution or, worse, have leaked through weak boundaries. The geometrical version of the *active contours method* is stable and retrieves simultaneously several contours but do not retrieves angles [5]. The *bubbles method* [23] simplifies the initialization process by allowing, for instance, contours to be initialized at the image minima or at predefined grid cells having homogeneous statistical properties. However, *bubbles method* requires fine tuned parameters in order to achieve simultaneous convergence of bubbles. Moreover, it is slow as compared to *watershed-based* methods [25, 16].

Conventional *region-growing and merging* methods work well in noisy images but are sensitive to seed initialization and produce jagged boundaries. For example, the s*eeded-region-growing method - SRG* [1, 15], introduces a competition between regions by ordering all pixels according to some suitable criteria, a property inherited from the *non-hierarchical watershed method - NHW* [25, 26]. This global competition ensures that the growth of regions near weak or diffuse edges is delayed until other regions have the chance to reach these areas. However, SRG does not incorporate any geometric information and hence can leak through narrow gaps or weak edges. Another approach, the *region competition method – RC* [30] combines the geometrical features of the DM and the statistical nature of *SRG*. This method introduces a local competition that exchange pixels between regions, resulting in a decrease in energy, thus allowing recovery from errors. However, *RC* produces jagged boundaries and depends on seed initialization, which eventually might lead to leakage through diffuse boundaries, if the seeds are asymmetrically, initialized [19].

The *non-hierarchical watershed method* as proposed by Vincent [25, 26] – *NHW*, treats the image as a 3D surface, starts the region growing from the surface minima, and expands the regions inside the respective *zone of influence* of each minimum. The region-growing process evolves all over the image, stopping where adjacent regions get into contact. At these points *barriers* are erected. This solution provides a powerful stopping criterion, difficult to achieve in the PDE-based level set framework. However, *NHW* may leads to a strong over-segmentation if proper image smoothing is not provided. There are solutions to the over-segmentation problem like CBMA [2] and Characteristics Extraction [24], however, they depend on interactively tuning parameters related to geometric features of the regions of interest. The *watershed method* as proposed by Meyer- *MW* [16] starts the region-growing process from markers. *MW* is optimal since each pixel and its immediate neighborhood are visited only once. However, highly specialized filters are required to extract the markers. Finally, the *skeletally coupled deformable models method - SCDM* [19] combines features of curve evolution deformable models, such as *bubbles* and *region-competition* methods and introduces an inter-seed skeleton to mediate the segmentation. However, it requires an elaborated sub-pixel implementation [19, 22].

Not intended as a comparison but only as an illustration, Figure 1 shows some of the main issues of the above mentioned image segmentation methods. This microscopic image shows bovine endothelial corneal cells acquired through a CCD camera attached to a microscope. The original 256 gray-scale image is depicted in (a). The simultaneous convergence problem can be observed in (b) using the *bubbles method* with bubbles initialized at image minima and in (c) using the front-propagation method with 36 seeds initialized by hand. Notice that while some bubbles are still evolving, some have converged and others are being merged. Another problem, "leaking" can occur through weak or diffuse edges, as can be observed in (d) and (e), with *seeded region-growing method* and *CBMA* [2] respectively. Over-segmentation (f) results from the excessive number of local minima and occurs in *watershed method* if appropriate denoising is not provided.

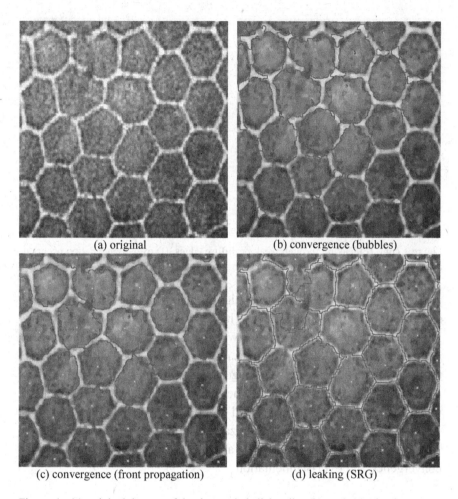

(a) original   (b) convergence (bubbles)

(c) convergence (front propagation)   (d) leaking (SRG)

Figure 1. (a) original image of bovine endothelial cells. (b) and (c) simultaneous convergence problem. (d) leaking through weak or diffuse edges.

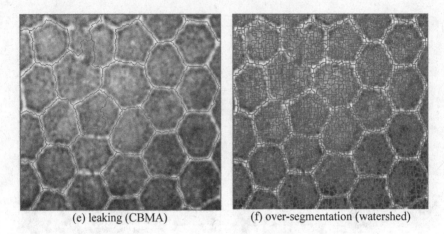

| (e) leaking (CBMA) | (f) over-segmentation (watershed) |

Figure 1 cont. (e) leaking through weak or diffuse edges. (f) over-segmentation occurs if appropriate denoising is not provided.

In this paper, an interactive algorithm for image smoothing and segmentation – ISS is introduced. This approach overcomes some of the limitations of previous methods, while retaining some of their most attractive features. ISS combines a noise removal step, which preserve the edges with an interactive image segmentation step, resulting in a robust and easy-to-use technique where higher level knowledge about the image can readily be incorporated in the segmentation process. ISS simplifies the problem of initialization, and provides an integrated solution to the problems of automatic stopping, simultaneous convergence and over-segmentation.

2. The interactive image smoothing and segmentation algorithm - ISS

ISS treats the image as a 3D surface in evolution. This construction serves a dual purpose. At first, implemented in the PDE-based level set framework [20, 21], an edge preserving smoothing algorithm removes noise by constraining the surface to evolve according to its vertically projected mean curvature [29, 27]. Secondly, inspired in the watershed transformation [26] and implemented in the Mathematical Morphology framework [3, 4, 16, 17, 25, 26, 2, 8, 9], a fast and robust algorithm segments the image simulating an immersion on its surface. In this context, segmentation can be described as a *region growing and merging* process starting from surface local minima. To deal with the over-segmentation problem, ISS merges non-significant regions as the immersion simulation takes place. The immersion obeys an order of processing selected by the user according to a criterion based on the image characteristics. All image pixels are previously sorted according to the selected criterion. Sorting provides an order of processing and assures that pixels lying around the edges have their processing postponed. Previously sorting all image pixels in ascending order also provides a way to make detection and labeling of the surface *minima* fully automatic. A detailed explanation of the different sorting criteria can be found in Section 2.3. ISS segments the image into as many regions as the number of *markers* interactively placed by the user. This means that one and only one *marker* per region-of-interest is required. Simple rules guide the merging process: two adjacent regions, growing around local minima, are blindly merged if they do not have *markers*, or if only one of them has a *marker*. Hence, merging is only prevented when two adjacent regions already having *markers,* get into contact. At this point an edge has been found. These rules assure that the topological changes required to reduce the over-segmentation be easily handled through this merging mechanism.

Figure 2 illustrates the steps in the evolution of the ISS algorithm for a sample of rock. Figure 2a shows a 256 gray-scale microscopic image of a polished rock after applying the PDE based denoising filter for 10 iterations. This particular image presents sharp transitions between regions presenting homogeneous but different intensities. A convenient processing order can be established, in this case, by sorting pixels according to the difference between the maximum and minimum gray-levels (morphological gradient) inside the pixel neighborhood $N(p)$. Since this difference is higher around the edges, sorting all image pixels in ascending order according to this criterion will assure that pixels lying around the edges will be the last ones to be processed. Figure 2b shows the morphological gradient image. Figure 2c shows the minima of Figure 2b (white spots) superimposed on it. These minima constitute the set of *seeds,* which are automatically detected and labeled by the ISS algorithm as the evolution takes place. Figure 2d shows the 52 *markers* placed by the user (colored squares) and associated to each region-of-interest. By comparing Figures 2d and 2p it is clear that there is a one-to-one correspondence between each *marker* and each region extracted by the ISS algorithm. Figures 2d to 2o show snap-shots of the region-growing evolution. Finally, Figure 2p shows the ISS segmentation result superimposed on the original image, after all non-significant regions have been merged.

As an interactive segmentation algorithm, ISS requires manual inclusion and exclusion of *markers*. The user repeats the process until satisfactory results are achieved. Interactivity improves the segmentation results by allowing high-level information about the image to be fed back into the process.

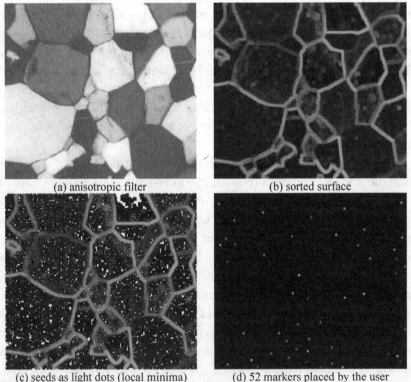

(a) anisotropic filter   (b) sorted surface

(c) seeds as light dots (local minima)   (d) 52 markers placed by the user

Figure 2. ISS algorithm in action: (a) anisotropic filter, (b) sorted image, (c) seeds, (d) markers.

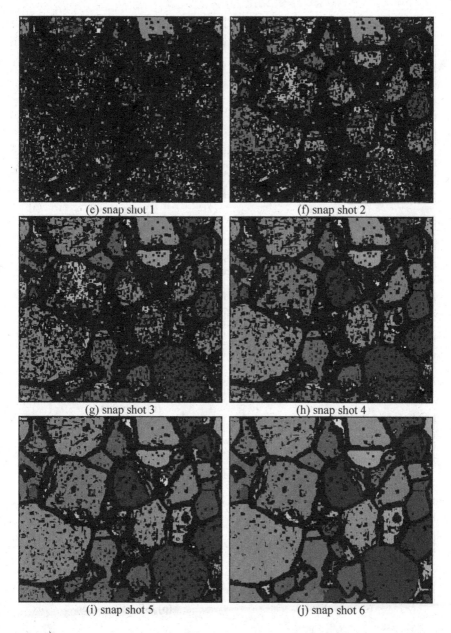

Figure 2 cont. ISS algorithm in action: (e to h) sequence of snap shots showing region growing.

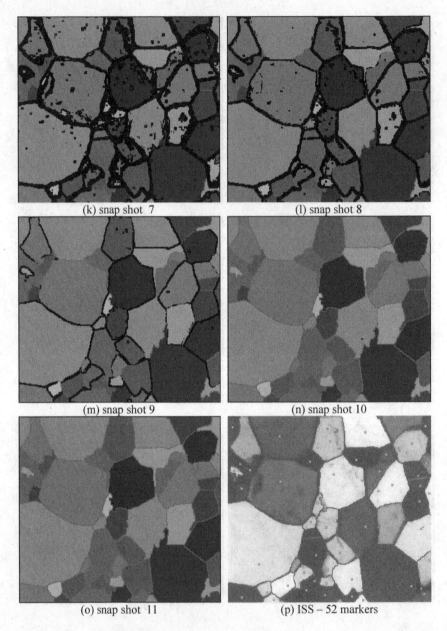

(k) snap shot 7 (l) snap shot 8

(m) snap shot 9 (n) snap shot 10

(o) snap shot 11 (p) ISS – 52 markers

Figure 2 cont. ISS algorithm in action: (o) last snap-shot showing final segmentation, (p) edges and markers superimposed on the original image.

2.1. Edge preserving smoothing under controlled curvature motion

Surface evolution under partial differential equations (PDEs) based level set framework has successfully been used to perform both image denoising and image segmentation. For the purpose of image denoising, PDEs can be utilized to modify the image topology and implement an edge preserving smoothing under controlled curvature motion [29].

By treating the image $I(x,y,z(t))$ as a 3D time-dependent surface and selectively deforming this surface based on the vertical projection of its mean curvature, effectively removes most of the non-significant image extrema. For smoothing purposes, the surface height z at the point $p(x,y)$ is initialized as the value of the local gray-level. The local surface deformation is computed from the local mean curvature κ expressed by the following relation between the second derivatives of I:

$$\kappa = \frac{I_{xx}(1+I_y^2)-2I_xI_yI_{xy}+I_{yy}(1+I_x^2)}{2(1+I_x^2+I_y^2)^{3/2}} \quad (1)$$

To evolve the image I as a surface under this modified level set curvature motion is equivalent to repeatedly iterate the following edge-preserving anisotropic filter:

$$I_{t+1}=I_t+\kappa \quad (2)$$

Appendices A and B present ISS pseudo-code and ISS execution time for test-images, respectively.

2.1.1. Stopping criteria for curvature based denoising

The decision regarding when to stop the iterative process depends on the image characteristics and on the regions to be extracted. At each step, the image is slightly "flattened" according to its local curvature. It is important to notice that repeatedly applying this filter may "erase" the image, therefore user judgement is crucial in deciding when to stop. If features being extracted are relatively homogeneous a slight denoising may be sufficient to remove noise allowing good segmentation. Images presenting inhomogeneous regions may require more iterations, while some images may be segmented without smoothing at all.

Figure 3 illustrates an example of image denoising using Equation 2. The original RGB image of a butterfly is shown in Figure 3a.

(a) original

(b) ISS denoising after 40 iterations

Figure 3. (a) original RGB image of a butterfly.

(c) ISS denoising after 80 iterations

(d) median filter

Figure 3 cont. (c) denoising after 80 iterations. (d) median filter.

Figures 3b and 3c illustrate the results of applying the anisotropic filter on the original image during 40 and 80 iterations, respectively. It can be observed that as the number of iteration increases, regions become more homogeneous at the expenses of loosing some fine detail. For the purpose of comparison, Figure 3d shows the median filter applied on the original image.

2.1.2. Effect of denoising on the ISS

Denoising increases region homogeneity by removing or reducing local extrema. This is translated into smoother and better-localized edges after segmentation. Usually, the effort spent on denoising varies depending on image characteristics. The effect of denoising on the ISS segmentation can be perceived on Figure 4. Figure 4a shows a 256 gray-scale MRI image of a brain slice. Figures 4b and 4c show the result of applying the anisotropic filter described by Equation 2, for 40 and 80 iterations, respectively. Figures 4d, 4e and 4f show the ISS segmentation result for the corresponding filtered and non-filtered images. Notice that 40 iterations were insufficient to extract the edges. However, after 80 iterations regions became sufficiently homogeneous. It can also be perceived that after denoising edges became less jagged and more precisely localized.

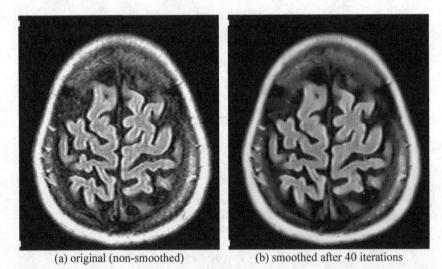

(a) original (non-smoothed)   (b) smoothed after 40 iterations

Figure 4. Effect of denoising on ISS segmentation result.

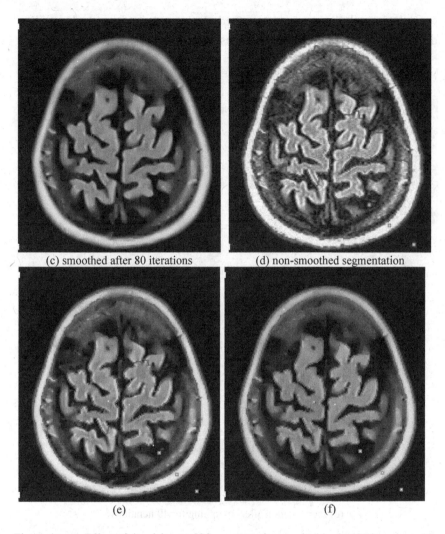

(c) smoothed after 80 iterations   (d) non-smoothed segmentation

(e)   (f)

Figure 4 cont. Effect of denoising on ISS segmentation result, (c) after 80 iterations, (d) to (f) segmentation results for (a) to (b).

Another example of the effect of denoising on the ISS segmentation can be observed in the aerial image of Figure 5. In this image denoising had little effect on segmentation, since the original non-smoothed image already presented highly homogeneous regions and sharp transitions between them. Comparing segmentation results in Figure 5b (non-smoothed) and Figure 5c (smoothed during 40 iterations) shows that denoising slightly improved the edges.

(a) original (non-smoothed)　　　　　　(b) non-smoothed segmentation

(c) segmentation after smoothing for 40 iterations

Figure 5. Effect of denoising on ISS segmentation, aerial image.

2.2. *The interactive region growing and merging step*

In region-growing methods, the regions are expanded around *seeds* obeying a given *processing order*. Usually, the regions grow in successive layers until the growing process finally stops thus defining the location of the edges. From this perspective, the most important pixels are precisely those located in a narrow-band around the final location of the edges. Sorting all image pixels according to a convenient relation between each pixel $p(x,y)$ and its neighborhood $N(p)$ is, in most cases, sufficient to impose such *processing order*, deferring the processing of the pixels on the edges. Many useful relations can be used to sort the pixels. This ordering can be established, for instance, by defining a *3D* surface whose height z, at each point $p(x,y)$, is given by this relation. Sorting the $z's$ in ascending order allows the region-growing process to automatically start from the minima of the sorted surface. The following relations, for instance, were implemented in the ISS:

- In its simplest form, to z is assigned the value of the image gray levels themselves; or
- z could be computed as the difference between a pixel and mean value in $N(p)$ as in the *SRG method*;
- z computed as the difference between the maximum and the minimum values in $N(p)$; It's equivalent to compute the morphological gradient;
- z as the mean curvature at $p(x,y)$ as expressed by equation 2.

The first relation is useful when the image characteristics are such that the gray-levels already dictate a natural processing order. In the example shown in Figure 2a, the regions already have edges at *higher* elevations than their inner parts. The second relation is useful for images having homogeneous textures. The third relation is useful, for instance, in images having discrete transitions between the regions having homogeneous gray-levels, as shown in Figure 4a. In this case, taking the difference between the maximum and the minimum in $N(x)$, forces higher values at the edges and, also has the additional benefit of closing small gaps at the borders.

Finally, by adding a merging mechanism, controlled by user-placed seeds, the region-growing and merging process is complete. A correspondence table, as shown below, can be used to merge the regions. This table is initialized as a sequence of integers from 1 to N, where N is the number of minima present in the image. N is updated according to the temporal sequence of absorptions. If, for instance, the region having label = 1 absorbs the region having label = 3, the merging table is updated as shown below:

before	1	2	3	4	5	...	i	...	N
after	1	2	1	4	5	...	i	...	N

2.3. The ISS algorithm steps

Apply the edge preserving anisotropic filter, described by Equation 2 to the image. Repeatedly applying this filter can erase most of the significant information present in the image. Thus, the iterative process has to be stopped after a reasonable result is achieved. User judgment and the application requirements should be taken into account to decide when to stop. See Appendix A for a pseudo-code of this algorithm.

1. By using a mouse, place one *marker* per region, labeling them from 1 to N. N is the total number of markers. A marker may be a single point or a set of points of arbitrary shape.

2. Sort all image pixels in ascending order, by the address calculation technique presented by Issac et. al. [11], according to one of the criteria listed below:

- gray level of the current pixel;
- difference between the maximum and minimum values in the neighborhood $N(p)$ of the current pixel;
- difference between a pixel and the average of it's neighbors;
- mean curvature at the current pixel;
- any other criteria which can be used to defer the processing of the edges.

3. For each pixel p extracted from the sorted list, find how many positive labeled pixels exist in its neighborhood $N(p)$. The three possible outcomes are:

- There is no positive labeled pixel in $N(p)$. The current pixel receives a new label and starts a new region. New regions receive labels starting from $N+1$. Notice that labels from 1 to N are reserved for user placed *markers*. Labels starting from $N+1$ are reserved to *seeds*.

- There is only one labeled pixel in $N(p)$. The current pixel receives this label and is integrated into the corresponding neighbor region.
- There are 2 or more positive labeled pixels in $N(p)$. If 2 or more neighbors have *markers* labels (label $<= N$), a border has been found, mark the current pixel as a "border", say a -1 label. Otherwise merge all neighbors into one region (the one having the smaller label; i.e., the first labeled in $N(p)$) and add the current pixel to it. If there are 2 labeled pixels in $N(p)$ and one has *marker* label and the other a *seed* label, the one having a *marker* label absorbs the one having a *seed* label.

4.By using a merging table, re-label all pixels to reflect the absorption they have undergone.

5.Draw the segmented image according to the newly assigned labels.

Appendix A and B present ISS pseudo-code and ISS execution time for test-images, respectively.

3. Applications

This section illustrates some practical results obtained with the ISS algorithm for different classes of image and also the segmentation obtained with other methods. Figures 6, 7 and 8 present ISS segmentation for microscopic images of ceramic, geological and medical images. Figure 9 illustrates the performance of ISS and other segmentation methods on different kind of image. In the segmented images, user selected *markers* are shown as green dots and the extracted edges are shown as red lines. Figure 6a presents a micrograph of ceramic material containing grains (dark gray) separated by thin gaps (light gray). Observing that pixels on the edges are lighter than inside grains, they were sorted and processed according to the original intensity of the gray levels, i.e., from darker to lighter. Figure 6b shows the ISS segmentation result. Figure 7a shows a color micrograph of a geological sample containing several grains. As this image presents homogeneous regions and discrete transitions between them, pixels were sorted in ascending order and processed according to the intensities of the morphological gradient (difference between maximum and minimum gray in $N(p)$), thus delaying the processing of the pixels around the edges. Figure 7b shows the ISS segmentation result. Figure 8a shows the micrograph of a cross-section of a human renal glomerulus containing the Bowman's capsule, the vascular pole, and surrounding structures. Figure 8b shows the ISS segmentation result. Again, the morphological gradient was used to sort and process these pixels. Notice that even barely perceptible edges were precisely extracted in these images.

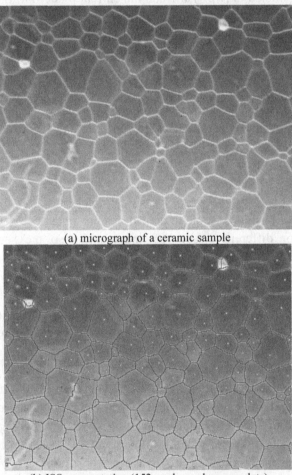

(a) micrograph of a ceramic sample

(b) ISS segmentation (152 markers, shown as dots)

Figure 6. ISS segmentation result for a ceramic sample micrograph.

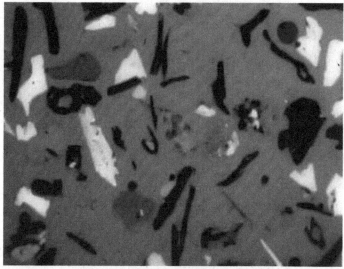

(a) micrograph of a geological sample

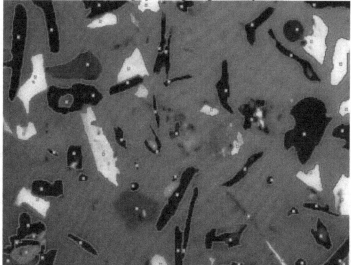

(b) ISS segmentation result (75 markers, shown as dots)

Figure 7. ISS segmentation result for a geological sample micrograph.

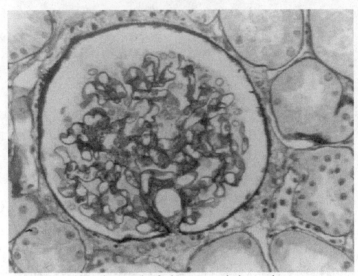

(a) micrograph of a human renal glomerulus

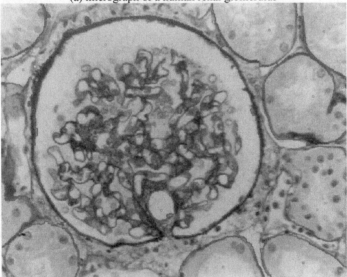

(b) ISS segmentation result (15 markers, shown as dots)

Figure 8. ISS segmentation result for a human renal glomerulus micrograph.

Comparing the performance of image segmentation methods is not easy, since many variables are involved in the task and the methods often have different theoretical foundations. However, peculiarities of each method can be observed if they are applied to a set of images having characteristics such as irregular illumination, occlusions, reflexes, noisy or smoothed regions, sharp or diffuse edges and regions compound of more than one homogeneous regions. Figure 9 shows a set of images coming from specialized application fields such as medicine (finger x-ray and corneal endothelial cells), geology (microscopic hematite grains) as well as from ordinary scenes (peppers and flower) which present such peculiar characteristics. They have been chosen to briefly illustrate some of the problems above mentioned and how they can influence current image segmentation methods as those based on Deformable Models (Front Propagation - FP and Bubbles - BUB), Statistical Region Growing (Seeded Region Growing – SRG) and Immersion Simulation (ISS). Appearing in the first column of Figure 9 are the original non-filtered images. Second, third and fourth columns show segmentation produced by FP or BUB, SRG and ISS, respectively. Each image was segmented employing the same set of markers, with the exception of Figure 9j, which do not make use of markers. Markers appear as green squares and models - the set of points enveloping a region in evolution - as contours in red.

Homogeneous regions and sharp transitions between them often simplify the segmentation task. By comparing segmentation results in Figure 9 it becomes clear that simultaneous convergence of all models presents more difficulties to DM based methods because regions often do not present sufficient homogeneity and sharp transitions. The speed of a model depends on region homogeneity and its displacement is often delayed or even stopped by discontinuities. From the practical point of view this may result in models being pushed beyond some edges while others are still evolving, see images (b), (f) and (r). Due to stronger noise in image (f) model propagation is more difficult in than in image (n), for example. Homogeneity also plays an important role in statistical based methods like SRG, where the region growing process depends on the average intensity of each region. SRG may be trapped by the presence of more than one homogeneous sub-region inside a region-of-interest. SRG segmentation of petals image shown in image (o) illustrates this problem. Occlusion of two regions having similar intensities often lead to leaking. Leaking can be observed on the two peppers situated on the first plane in ISS segmentation image (s) and SRG segmentation (t) for peppers image and also in SRG segmented image (o). Compare segmentation results of SRG (o) to FP (n) and ISS (p). Initialization also plays an important role in most image segmentation methods. Usually models are initialized by hand inside and/or outside the features of interest. In SRG seed size and position may change region initial average intensity thus interfering in the way model progress.

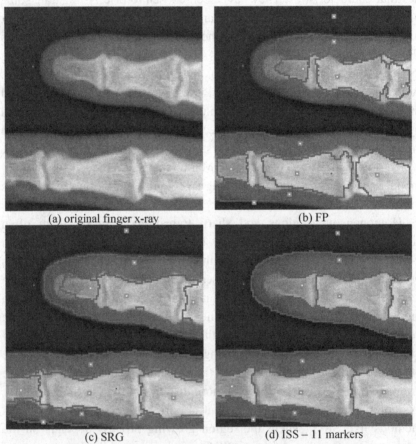

| (a) original finger x-ray | (b) FP |
| (c) SRG | (d) ISS – 11 markers |

Figure 9. Segmentation results for Deformable Models (FP and BUB), SRG and ISS applied to a finger x-ray image.

Automatically initializing models at image minima or at preferential points as done by BUB simplifies the initialization. However, simultaneous evolution of models inside and outside regions often results in double edge, see image (j). Initialization in ISS is automatically done at image minima and because regions not having markers are blindly merged, ISS presents low sensitivity on seed size, position and noise. ISS fails if sorting do not effectively postpone the processing of pixels lying on the edges of the features of interest. Otherwise, ISS will produce segmentations of very good quality as can be observed in Figure 9.

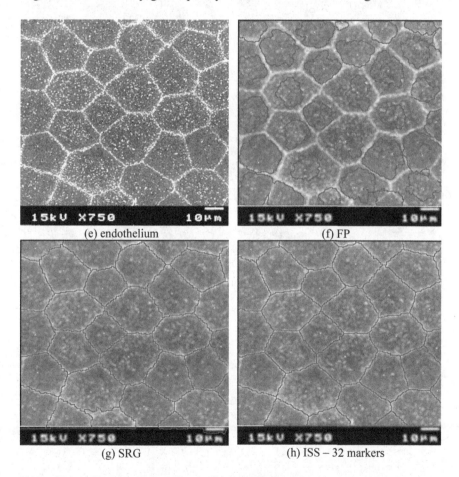

(e) endothelium (f) FP

(g) SRG (h) ISS – 32 markers

Figure 9 cont. Segmentation results for Deformable Models (FP and BUB), SRG and ISS applied to a micrograph of corneal endothelial sample.

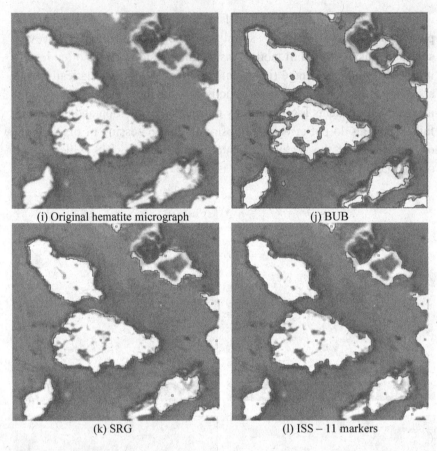

(i) Original hematite micrograph   (j) BUB

(k) SRG   (l) ISS – 11 markers

Figure 9 cont. Segmentation results for Deformable Models (FP and BUB), SRG and ISS applied to a micrograph of hematite.

(m) flower

(n) FP

(o) SRG

(p) ISS- 44 markers

Figure 9 cont. Deformable Models (FP and BUB), SRG and ISS applied to the flower image.

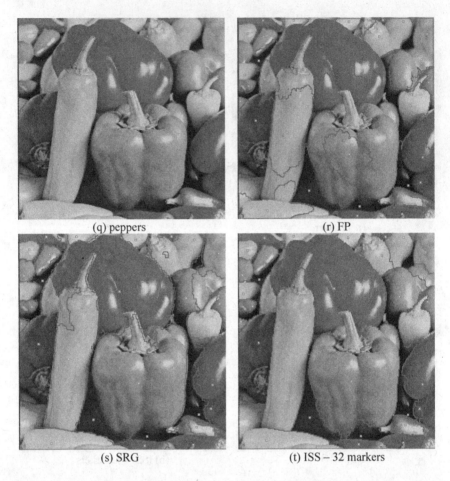

(q) peppers

(r) FP

(s) SRG

(t) ISS – 32 markers

Figure 9 cont. Deformable Models (FP and BUB), SRG and ISS applied the peppers image.

4. Conclusions and Outlook

The ISS combines some valuable features of known image smoothing and segmentation methods developed in the Mathematical Morphology and in the PDE-based level set frameworks, for instance:

• efficient edge preserving smoothing guided by PDEs, typical of surface evolution methods;

- ability to automatically detect all image minima and to make the regions grow inside the respective zones of influence, a property inherited from the *watershed transformation* (NHW);
- ability to automatically stop the growing process whenever two user labeled regions get into contact, a characteristic difficult to implement in the PDE based level set framework;
- global competition between all image pixels according to a pre-defined sorting criterion;
- ability to change the image topology by using a simple merging mechanism, thus dramatically reducing over-segmentation and the need of pre-processing;
- recovery from errors mediated by a user-guided segmentation;
- relatively low sensitivity to seed positioning;
- execution time directly proportional to image size;
- no need of tuning parameters;
- applicable to color or gray-scale in any number of dimensions.

However, ISS is not applicable to situations requiring automatic segmentation, like video segmentation. As other flooding simulation algorithms, ISS is sensitive to broken edges and may "leak" through *gaps* resulting in wrong segmentation results. Color attributes could be used to improve the segmentation algorithm.

Acknowledgments

The author would like to acknowledge the CNPq - Conselho Nacional de Desenvolvimento Científico e Tecnológico of Brazil and FAPEMIG – Fundação de Amparo à Pesquisa de Minas Gerais, for the financial support and the CISE - Computer and Information Sciences and Engineering of the University of Florida, for the technical support

Appendix A. ISS Pseudo-code

Pseudo code for denoising gray-scale images. For RGB images apply the code below to each channel.

```
step = n;  // number of iterations.
For each step do {
 For each row do {
  For each column do {
    Compute central difference differentials dx, dy, dxx, dyy, dxy, dx2
    and dy2 in the neighborhood N(p) of the central pixel p using
    floating point arithmetic;
    /* slightly modifies p at each step. */
    p = (int) (p + (dxx*(1+dy2) + dyy*(1+dx2)- 2*dx*dy*dxy) /
      (1+dx2+dy2) )
  }
 }
}
```

Pseudo-code for ISS segmentation.

```
MaxNumOfLabels = MNL;  // Maximum number of labels
Obs: Labels 1 to N are reserved for markers; labels from N+1 to MNL are reserved
for seeds.
Initialize a merging table vector with labels 1 to MNL;
Place one marker per region-of-interest labeling them from 1 to N;
Sort all pixel in ascending order by the address calculation technique [11], according
to a chosen criterion, which postpone the processing of pixels lying around the edges.
For each pixel extracted from the sorted list do {
  Find how many different positive label exist in N(p);
  If (there is no positive labeled pixel in N(p) )
    Current pixel receives a new label starting a new temporary region;
  Else if (there is only one positive labeled pixel in N(p) )
    Current pixel receives this label;
  Else if (there is 2 or more positive labeled pixels in N(p) )
    If (2 or more positive labels <= N)
      Current pixel receives a "EDGE" label;
    Else {
      Merge all neighbors into one region; the one having the smallest positive label
in N(p);
      Current pixel receives this label;
    }
}
```

By using the merging table, relable all pixel to reflect the absorption they have undergone.

Appendix B. ISS Execution time for known test-images

IMAGE	SIZE	TIME* (ms) Denoising	TIME* (ms/iteration)	TIME* (ms) Segmentation
LENA	127x127	440	15	22
	256x256	1540	51	86
	512x512	5270	176	286
	1024x1024	17850	595	1098
PEPPERS	127x127	440	15	22
	256x256	1650	55	88
	512x512	5770	192	330
	1024x1024	19770	659	1154
BOAT	127x127	390	13	22
	256x256	1540	51	76
	512x512	5820	194	308
	1024x1024	20050	668	1154
* Figures for 30 iterations on Pentium IV class machine 1.7GHz, 768MB RAM, Windows XP				

References

1. R. Adams, et. al. Seeded region-growing. *IEEE Trans. Pattern Analysis and Machine Intelligence,* 16, 6, 641-647, 1994.
2. M. C. Andrade, et. al. Segmentation of microscopic images by flooding simulation: a catchment basins merging algorithm. *Proceedings of SPIE Nonlinear Image Processing VIII,* San Jose, USA, 3026, 164—175, 1997.
3. S. Beucher. *Segmentation d'image et morphologie mathematique.* École Nationale Supérieure de Mines de Paris, PhD thesis, 1990.
4. S. Beucher. Watershed, hierarchical segmentation and waterfall algorithm. *Mathematical Morphology and its Applications to Image Processing,* Kluwer Academic Publishers, 69—76, 1994.
5. F. Caselles, et al. Image selective smoothing and edge detection by nonlinear diffusion. *SIAM Journal on Numerical Analysis,* 29, 1, 183—193, 1992.
6. J. P. Cocquerez, S. Philipp. *Analyse d' images: filtrage et segmentation.* Masson, Paris, 1995.
7. L. D. Cohen, at. al. Finite element methods for active contours models and balloons for 2D and 3D images. *IEEE Trans. Pattern Analysis and Machine Intelligence,* 15, 1131—1147, 1993.
8. M. Grimaud. La geodesie numerique en morphologie mathematique. Application a la detection automatique de microcalcifications en mammographie numerique, École Nationale Supérieure de Mines de Paris, PhD thesis, 1991
9. M. Grimaud. A new measure of contrast: the dynamics. *Proceedings of SPIE. Image Algebra and Morphological Image Processing,* 1769, 292-305, 1992.
10. G. Guo et. al.. Bayesian learning, global competition and unsupervised image segmentation. *Pattern Recognition Letters,* 21, 107-416, 2000.
11. J. Isaac, et al. Sorting by Address Calculation. *Journal of the ACM,* 169—174, 1954.
12. M. Kass, et. al. Snakes active contour models. *International Journal of Computer Vision, 1,* 321-331, 1988.
13. R. Malladi, et al. Shape modeling with front propagating: a level set approach. *IEEE Trans. Pattern Analysis and Machine Intelligence,* 17, 2, 158—175, 1995.
14. R. Malladi, et al. A fast level set based algorithm for topology-independent shape modeling. *Journal of Mathematical Vision,* 6, 269-289, 1996.
15. A. Mehnert, et. al. An improved seeded region-growing algorithm. *Pattern Recognition Letters 18,* 106-1071, 1997.
16. F. Meyer. Un algorithme optimal de ligne de partage des eaux. VIII Congrès de *Reconaissance de Forme et d'Intelligence Artificielle.* Lyon, France, 847-857, 1991.
17. F. Meyer, S. Beucher.. Morphological segmentation. Journal of Visual Communication and Image Representation, 1, 1, 21-46, 1990.
18. P. Perona, et. al. Scale-space and edge detection using anisotropic diffusion. *IEEE Trans. Pattern Analysis and Machine Intelligence.* 12, 7, 629—639, 1990.

19. T. Sebastian, et. al. Segmentation of carpal bones from a sequence of 2D CT images using skeletally coupled deformable models. www.lem.s.brown.edu, 2000.
20. J. A. Sethian. Tracking Interfaces with Level Sets. *American Scientist*. May-jun, 1997.
21. J. A. Sethian Level Set Methods and Fast Marching Methods. Cambridge Press, 2nd ed, 1999.
22. K. Siddiqi, et. al. Geometric shock-capturing ENO schemes for sub-pixel interpolation, computation and curve evolution. *Graphical Models and Image Processing*, 59, 5, 278—301, 1997.
23. H. Tek, et. al. Volumetric segmentation of medical images by three-dimensional bubbles. *Computer Vision and Machine Understanding*, 65, 2, 246—258, 1997.
24. C. Vachier. Extraction de Caracteristiques, Segmentation et Morphology Mathematique. École Nationale Supérieure des Mines de Paris. PhD. Thesis, 1995.
25. L. Vincent. Algorithmes morphologiques a base de files d'attente et de lacets. Extension aux graphes.. École Nationale Supérieure de Mines de Paris, PhD thesis, 1990.
26. L. Vincent, P. Soille. Watersheds in digital spaces: An efficient algorithm based on immersion simulations. IEEE Trans. Pattern Analysis and Machine Intelligence, 13, 6, 583—598, 1991.
27. J. Weickert. Anisotropic diffusion in image processing. B.G. Teubner Stuttgart, Deutschland, 1998.
28. C. Xu, J. L. Prince. Snakes, Shapes , and Gradient Vector Flow. IEEE Trans. on Image Processing. 7, 3, 359—369, 1988.
29. A. Yezzi. Modified curvature motion for image smoothing and enhancement. IEEE Trans. on Image Processing, 7, 3, 345-352, 1998.
30. S. C. Zhu, et al. Region competition: unifying snakes, region-growing, and bayes/MDL for multiband image segmentation, IEEE Trans. Pattern Analysis and Machine Intelligence, 18, 9, 880—900, 1996.

CHAPTER 3

RELEVANCE OF MULTIFRACTAL TEXTURES IN STATIC IMAGES

Antonio Turiel*

Air Project - INRIA. Domaine de Voluceau BP105
78153 Le Chesnay CEDEX. France

In the latest years, multifractal analysis has been applied to image analysis. The multifractal framework takes advantage of multiscaling properties of images to decompose them as a collection of different fractal components, each one associated to a singularity exponent (an exponent characterizing the way in which that part of the image evolves under changes in scale). One of those components, characterized by the least possible exponent, seems to be the most informative about the whole image. Very recently it has been proposed an algorithm to reconstruct the image from this component, just using physical information conveyed by it. In this paper, we will show that the same algorithm can be used to assess the relevance of the other fractal parts of the image.

3.1. Introduction

Edge detection and texture classification are two main tasks in image processing, recognition and classification.[1] Extraction of edges provides information about the objects composing the scene, sometimes allowing segmentation; edges are thus the main source of information in the image and serve well also for classifying purposes. Texture information is more subtle, concerning the patterns and regularities inside the objects, light rendering and similar features. They also provide an important amount of information and they are specially useful in classification and segmentation tasks.

One of the reasons to introduce the multifractal formalism in image processing was to provide a unified, reasonable way to deal with edges and textures at the same time.[2] The multifractal classification splits the image in edge-like and texture-like sets, which are arranged according to their properties under changes

---

*Present affiliation: Physical Oceanography Department. Institut de Cincies del Mar - CMIMA (CSIC). Passeig Martim de la Barceloneta, 37-49. 08003 Barcelona. Spain.

in scale (that is, under zooms). This approach is specially well adapted to certain types of images (for instance, those of turbulent or chaotic nature, as multifractality arose to explain the statistical properties of turbulent flows), but a great variety of real world scenes seem to be well described in this framework.[3]

There is another reason to use the multifractal formalism: due to some statistical properties, one of the fractal components issued from the multifractal classification allows reconstructing the whole image. The implementation of the reconstruction algorithm has been recently proposed.[4] That reconstruction algorithm was designed to work over the most edge-like of the fractal components (reconstructing from edge-like structures has been explored in several contexts from scale-space theory[5] to wavelet analysis[6]). The key point is that the same algorithm can potentially be applied to the other components of the multifractal decomposition. The goal of this paper is to use this algorithm to evaluate the relative importance of each one of those fractal components.

The paper is structured as follows: in Section 3.2, the theoretical fundations of the multifractal framework are briefly explained and the main implications discussed. Section 3.3 shows how to apply the formalism in practice, in particular to produce the multifractal decomposition. In Section 3.4 the reconstruction algorithm is presented and its properties are discussed; next, in Section 3.5 we will make use of it to obtain an assessment about the relevance of each fractal component. Finally, in Section 3.6 the conclusions of our work are presented.

For the purposes of illustration, we will make use of Lena's picture (Figure 3.1) and we will apply our techniques on it. The image presents remarkable deviations from the multifractal scheme (for instance, it has fuzzy edges in out of focus objects and numerous coding and processing artifacts), but however it is rather well described as a multifractal object.

3.2. Multifractal framework

The multifractal formalism was developed first in the study of turbulent flows,[7] as a way to explain the properties under changes of scale of very turbulent systems. It has been applied to the study of different types of images by several authors,[2,8] as images have some properties which resemble to those of turbulent flows. We briefly sketch here the basic concepts in the approach we are going to use; for further details the reader is referred to.[2]

We will denote any image by $c(\vec{x})$ where $\vec{x}$ denotes the vector coordinates of the referred pixel and it is normalized so that its average over the image vanishes, $\langle c(\vec{x}) \rangle_{\vec{x} \in \text{image}} = 0$. According to[2] we define a positive measure μ as follows: for any subset $\mathcal{A}$ of the image, its measure $\mu(\mathcal{A})$ is given by:

Fig. 3.1. Lena's image.

$$\mu(\mathcal{A}) = \int_{\mathcal{A}} d\vec{y} \, |\nabla c|(\vec{y}) \tag{3.1}$$

that is, the measure assigns a weight to the set $\mathcal{A}$ equal to the sum of the absolute variations of the image over it. Texturized areas will contribute with larger weights to the measure μ than flatly illuminated, smooth surfaces. In fact we will not be interested in the value of the measure over sets of fixed size, but in its evolution under changes in scale (resolution) around each point. Given a collection of balls $B_r(\vec{x})$ of radii r and center $\vec{x}$, we will say that the measure μ is multifractal if:

$$\mu(B_r(\vec{x})) \approx \alpha(\vec{x}) \, r^{2+h(\vec{x})} \tag{3.2}$$

for r's small enough. The exponent $h(\vec{x})$ is called the local singularity exponent, and characterizes the way in which image behaves under changes in the size parameter r at the particular point $\vec{x}^{\mathrm{a}}$. As we consider small r's, the largest values of the measures $\mu(B_r(\vec{x}))$ correspond to the smallest values of the exponents $h(\vec{x})$. For that reason, we will be specially interested in negative singularity exponents, which are found at pixels which contribute strongly to the measure by themselves (take into account that we consider very small radii). One of the advantages of this definition is that what determines the value of $h(\vec{x})$ is not the absolute variation of $c(\vec{x})$ at the point $\vec{x}$, but its relative importance compared to the variations at the surrounding points: multiplying $c(\vec{x})$ by a constant modifies $\alpha(\vec{x})$ in eq. (3.2), but lefts $h(\vec{x})$ unchanged. The classification of points accordingly is local, in opposition with global thresholding techniques.

Natural images, that is, real word scenes of "natural" objects are of multifractal character,[2,9] what has been tested for a large variety of scenes[3] and even with color images.[10] This property is far from trivial, and accounts for a special arrangement of edges and textures in images. In the following, we will only discuss on this type of images, although the same methods could be applied to other as well. Assessment of multifractality on real, digitized images can not be easily performed by a direct application of eq. (3.2) because of several technical reasons: some interpolation mechanism should be devised to take into account non-integer radii, for instance (there may be also undesiderable long-range effects which should be filtered; see[2] for a full discussion). In order to obtain a good evaluation of the singularity exponents, singularity analysis via wavelet analysis[11] should be performed. Wavelet analysis is a quite straightforward generalization of the scaling measurements in eq. (3.2): insted of applying the measure over finite size balls of radii r, a convolution of the measure μ with a scaled version of a wavelet Ψ is computed. More precisely, the wavelet projection $T_\Psi\mu(\vec{x}, r)$ of the measure μ at the point $\vec{x}$ and the scale r is defined as:

$$T_\Psi\mu(\vec{x}, r) = \int d\vec{y} \, |\nabla c|(\vec{y}) \frac{1}{r^2} \Psi(\frac{\vec{x}-\vec{y}}{r}) \tag{3.3}$$

The measure μ is multifractal (in the sense of eq. (3.2)) if and only if:

$$T_\Psi\mu(\vec{x}, r) \approx \alpha_\Psi(\vec{x}) \, r^{h(\vec{x})} \tag{3.4}$$

for small scale parameters r. Notice that α_Ψ is in general dependent of the wavelet

---

[a]The prefactor (2 in our case) in the definition of the singularity exponent, eq. (3.2), is conventionally set to the dimension of the embedding space. This normalization allows to compare results from subspaces of different dimensions: the value of $h(\vec{x})$ becomes independent of the dimension of the space.

Ψ and the measure μ, but the scaling exponent $h(\vec{x})$ has exactly the same value than in eq. (3.2) and does only depend on μ, that is, on the image $c(\vec{x})^{\text{b}}$.

From the theoretical point of view, the choice of the particular wavelet Ψ is irrelevant for the determination of the exponents $h(\vec{x})$; it can be even chosen as a positive function[c]. However, in practical grounds there are wavelets which resolve better the finer structures than other. In Figure 3.2 we show the representations of the multifractal classifications for four different wavelets. We will discuss further about the choice of the wavelet in Section 3.3.

Multifractal classification of points is the first stage for multifractal decomposition of images (what justifies the name "multifractal" for the method). Points in the image can be arranged in fractal components, each one associated to a value for the singularity exponent. Namely, the fractal component F_{h_0} associated to the exponent h_0 is given by:

$$F_{h_0} = \{ \vec{x} \in \text{image} \mid h(\vec{x}) = h_0 \} \tag{3.5}$$

As the measure verifies to be multifractal, every point in the image can be associated a particular singularity exponent, so the image can be decomposed as the union of all its fractal components. They are indeed fractal sets,[2] their dimensions being connected with statistical properties of images.[12] The most interesting of those fractal components is the Most Singular Manifold (MSM),[9] which is the fractal component associated to the least possible exponent. This set is usually related to the edges present in the image.[2] The least possible exponent is usually denoted h_∞ and its associated manifold F_{h_∞} is generally denoted F_∞ in short.

3.3. Multifractal decomposition

A correct determination of the MSM F_∞ implies a good multifractal decomposition, according to what was explained in Section 3.2. The main point concerns the choice of the analyzing wavelet Ψ. Once the wavelet is fixed, the singularity exponents are computed at every point in the image. The exponents are obtained by means of a log-log regression applied to eq. (3.4) at every point, in a range of scales typically going from 1 to 8 pixels non uniformly sampled (see[2]). Once every point is assigned a singularity exponent, the value of h_∞ is estimated. A usual way to do this consists of taking the average between the values associated to the 1% and the 5% most singular points.[2] The dispersion around this value is

---

[b]Let us remark that the normalization in the wavelet Ψ elliminates the prefactor 2 in the exponent.
[c]Positive functions are not proper (admissible) wavelets (an admissible wavelet has zero mean[11]). Recall that the admissibility condition is necessary for signal representation (reconstruction), but not for signal analysis.

conventionally fixed depending on the application. In Figure 3.2 we present the functions $h(\vec{x})$ for four different wavelets. Let us define them. Let $\vec{x} = (x_1, x_2)$ be the position vector, $r = \sqrt{x_1^2 + x_2^2}$ its modulus. We will make use of the following wavelets $\Psi_i(\vec{x})$, $i = 1, 2, 3, 4$:

(1) Lorentzian wavelet:

$$\Psi_1(\vec{x}) = \frac{1}{1 + r^2}$$

(2) First radial derivative of Lorentzian wavelet:

$$\Psi_2(\vec{x}) = \frac{d\Psi_1}{dr}(\vec{x}) = \frac{-2r}{(1 + r^2)^2}$$

(3) Gaussian wavelet:

$$\Psi_3(\vec{x}) = e^{-\frac{1}{2}r^2}$$

(4) Second radial derivative of gaussian wavelet:

$$\Psi_4(\vec{x}) = \frac{d^2\Psi_1}{dr^2} = (r^2 - 1)e^{-\frac{1}{2}r^2}$$

Each one of those wavelets fits the best for a particular application. Lorentzian wavelet (Ψ_1) is a possitive wavelet of slow decay at infinity. It is very good to resolve sharp (negative) singularities in the measure μ (good spatial localization), but it has the backdraw of being unable to distinguish all the singularities beyond $h = 0$ (it returns the value $h = 0$ for all of them); besides, it cannot be used to analize the signal $c(\vec{x})$ directly (a certain number of vanishing moments would be required[2,13]). The gaussian wavelet (Ψ_3) cannot be either used over the signal itself, as it is positive also, but having fast decaying tails it is able to resolve the whole range of singularities (typically between -1 and 2, see[2]); the backdraw is a worse spatial localization, specially for the MSM. The second derivative of the gaussian (Ψ_4) is, from the theoretical point of view, the best possible choice for analyzing signals: it resolves the whole range of values of $h(\vec{x})$ and it can be even used over the signal itself, without necessity of constructing a measure. However, in practice it has very poor spatial localization, associated to an inner minimum scale of several pixels, necessary to separate positive from negative extrema in wavelet projections. The best choice in practice is then the derivative of

Fig. 3.2. Multifractal decompositions on Lena's image for Lorentzian wavelet and its derivative (top) and Gaussian wavelet and its second derivative (bottom) (see Section 3.5). The smaller is the singularity exponent, the brighter is the point.

Lorentzian wavelet (Ψ_2), which arrives to a compromise in range of detected singularities, localization and applicability over the full signal. It is not well adapted for any one of those tasks (it truncates the range of singularities above $h = 1$, it blurs localization, it has not enough number of vanishig moments), but it is able to provide meaningful results in every context.

In Figure 3.3 several different fractal manifolds for our image are represented, every column showing the sets associated to each one of the wavelets discussed above. The first step is to compute h_∞ as described at the beginning of this Section, obtaining the different values for the different wavelets: $h_\infty = -0.47$ for Ψ_1, $h_\infty = -0.32$ for Ψ_2, $h_\infty = -0.43$ for Ψ_3 and $h_\infty = -0.68$ for Ψ_4. As a general remark, wavelets with higher orders of derivative are more imprecise in the determination of this value, while positive wavelets throw more similar results.

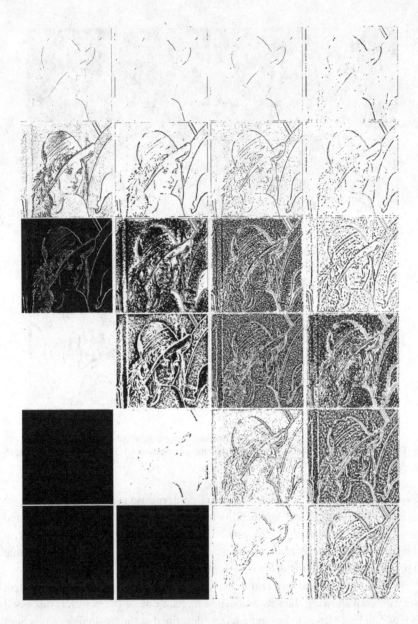

Fig. 3.3. Multifractal decompositions on Lena's image. From left to right: Lorentzian wavelet, its derivative, Gaussian wavelet and its second derivative. From top to bottom: excluded manifolds, MSMs, second MSMs, third MSMs, fourth MSMs and fifth MSMs.

Once the value of h_∞ has been obtained, we isolate the MSM, defining it as the set of points $\vec{x}$ for which $h_\infty - \Delta h \leq h(\vec{x}) < h_\infty + \Delta h$ with a conventionally fixed value of the dispersion Δh; in the following we take $\Delta h = 0.15$. We represent also the other fractal manifolds according to the given dispersion, so the nth MSM will be the set of points $\vec{x}$ for which $h_\infty + (2n-3)\Delta h \leq h(\vec{x}) < h_\infty + (2n-1)\Delta h$ (the MSM itself is the first MSM). Finally, we define the manifold of excluded points or excluded manifod as the set of points $\vec{x}$ such that $h(\vec{x}) < h_\infty - \Delta h$, that is, which are more singular than expected. Those events are generally associated to the borders of the image and some particular events, which happen to have singularities close to -1, typical to isolated edges.[2] In Figure 3.3, we show all those manifolds.

3.4. Reconstructing from edges

Recently, an algorithm to reconstruct the whole image from the most singular of its fractal components has been proposed.[4] We will not go into details about the reconstruction algorithm; we will just present the final formula and discuss it. The reader is referred to the original paper.

The reconstruction formula intends to reproduce the whole image from the value of the gradient field over the MSM. First, let us define the essential gradient over a general set F. We define it as a vector function which is only different from zero over the set F, namely:

$$\vec{v}_F(\vec{x}) \equiv \nabla c(\vec{x}) \, \delta_F(\vec{x}) \qquad (3.6)$$

where the symbol δ_F stands for a delta function on the set F. The reconstruction algorithm is given by the following expression:

$$c(\vec{x}) = \vec{g} \otimes \vec{v}_{F_\infty}(\vec{x}) \qquad (3.7)$$

where $\otimes$ stands for the convolution and the reconstructing kernel $\vec{g}$ is given in the Fourier space by the following expression:

$$\hat{\vec{g}}(\vec{f}) = i\frac{\vec{f}}{f^2} \qquad (3.8)$$

In the above expression, the symbol $\hat{\ }$ stands for the Fourier transform, $\vec{f}$ is the spatial frequency (the variable in the Fourier domain) and $i \equiv \sqrt{-1}$. The reconstruction formula states that it is possible to retrieve the image from the essential gradient associated to the MSM F_∞. Note, however, that the formula could be applied to any set F; we will denote by c_F the image retrieved from the essential gradient associated to the set F; namely:

$$c_F(\vec{x}) = \vec{g} \otimes \vec{v}_F(\vec{x}) \qquad (3.9)$$

We will call eq. (3.9) the generalized reconstruction formula. In this language, the reconstruction formula states that $c_{F_\infty} = c$. The generalized reconstruction formula has some nice properties.

- *It is linear in the reconstructing data:* If the set F is the disjoint union of two sets F_1 and F_2 (i.e., $F = F_1 \cup F_2$, with $F_1 \cap F_2 = \emptyset$), then $c_F = c_{F_1} + c_{F_2}$. This comes from the fact that $\vec{v}_{F_1 \cup F_2} = \vec{v}_{F_1} + \vec{v}_{F_2}$ if the sets are disjoint, and the associativity of the convolution product.
- *It always exists a set from which reconstruction is perfect:* If $F = \Re^2$, that is, the whole image, $\vec{v}_F = \nabla c$, but as $\hat{\nabla} c(\vec{f}) = -i \vec{f} \hat{c}(\vec{f})$ and taking into account the definition of $\vec{g}$, trivially $c_F = c$.

Taking into account both remarks, we conclude that if F^c is the complementary set of a set F, $c_F + c_{F^c} = c$, which can also be expressed as $c - c_F = c_{F^c}$, that is, the reconstruction from the complementary of F is equivalent to the error image (the difference between the reconstruction and the actual image). The reconstruction formula states that there exists a rather sparse set F_∞ from which the reconstruction is perfect (equivalently, the reconstruction error is zero). In practice, however, a good determination of F_∞ is sometimes difficult. In such cases, the generalized reconstruction formula allows measuring how relevant the points not included in that set are, for instance just measuring the PSNR's for the reconstructed images. Due to linearity, the same measure can be interpreted as the decrease in the error associated to the inclusion of those points in the estimate of F_∞. We apply those ideas in the next section to interpret the importance of the different fractal components extracted according different wavelet projections.

3.5. Relevance of the fractal manifolds

We will make an assess about the relative importance of the fractal manifolds by means of the generalized reconstruction formula. In Figure 3.4 we show the different images reconstructed from the manifolds presented in Figure 3.3 using eq. (3.9); in Table 3.1 the associated PSNRs can be found. We see that the MSM provides always the greatest amount of information about the image, which is reflected both by visual inspection and the values of the PSNR. However, the second manifold contains a significant amount of information, which reflects in the recogniscible structures which are reconstructed from it and still significant values of PSNR (in the case of the Lorentzian wavelet (first column), the second MSM contains all the other points, because it is not able to distinguish singularities above $h = 0$ and they are truncated to that value). The other manifolds (when they can be distinguished, that is, when considering wavelets other that Lorentzian) contain significantly very few information.

The excluded manifold deserves a particular comment. It contains very sharp edges and it accounts for global illumination conditions (for instance, more light over the hat or the shoulder, the global focus on the right of the image,...). It should be included in any reasonable reconstructing set, even if their statistical properties (due to boundary conditions or strong fluctuations) may constitute a deviation from the multifractal model (as they more singular than what is predicted by the model).

The relative importance of each fractal part can be better understood looking at Figure 3.5, in which images in Figure 3.4 are progressively summed up from top the column to the bottom; due to linearity of eq. (3.9), the resulting images are equivalent to the result of reconstructing from the succesive union of manifolds in Figure 3.3. It is obvious from visual inspection that after the second manifold very few information is incorporated in the successive additions, a fact also evidenced by the associated PSNRs, Table 3.2.

3.6. Conclusions

In this paper we have recalled the multifractal formalism, which stands to be a method for classifying points in images according to their singular character. We have seen that this rather mathematical characterization (the singularity exponent) has an interpretation in terms of relative informative relevance: the most singular points are the most informative about the scene. This characterization of the informational content is made by means of the reconstruction algorithm,[4] which was proposed as a way to reconstruct images from edges, derived from simple, general assumptions. The properties of the reconstruction algorithm allow to isolate the contribution of every point in the final reconstructed image. We have made use of it to assess the qualities as reconstructing sets of the different fractal components spawned in the multifractal scheme.

The method proposed here could be used to determine which properties (edges, textures) are important to keep in order to have a good visual performance in compressed images and which ones could be removed without affecting significantly the quality. It is a rather natural technique, as it is based on physical

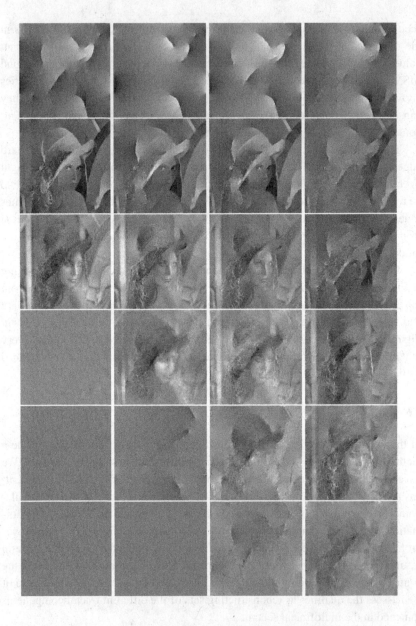

Fig. 3.4.   Reconstruction images from the sets represented in Figure 3.3.

properties of images. It is important to notice that the reconstruction algorithm
can be considered an edge-detection based coding scheme, much in the way of

Table 3.1. PSNRs (in dB) for the reconstructed images represented in Figure 3.4.

Ψ_1	Ψ_2	Ψ_3	Ψ_4
14.54	14.40	14.26	14.27
17.22	15.48	16.19	14.45
14.76	14.31	15.25	14.73
13.32	13.30	13.47	15.17
13.32	13.30	13.24	14.09
13.32	13.32	13.29	13.46

the modern techniques of ridgelets and curvelets,[14] which have been shown to be very efficient for image coding.

In order to implement compressing techniques using the reconstruction algorithm, high performance reconstructing sets should be extracted from images. The technique of singularity classification is a good first approach to obtain that set,

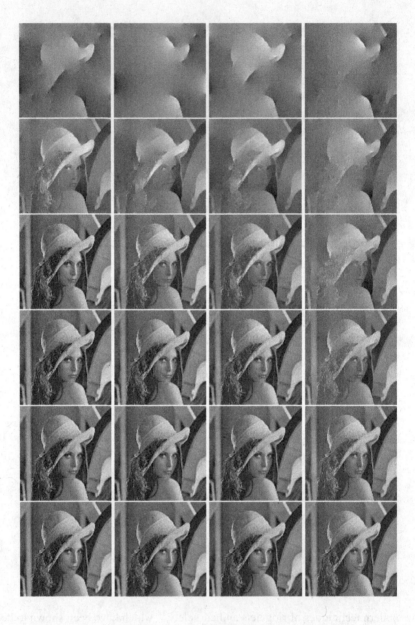

Fig. 3.5.   Accumulated reconstructed images, from the reconstructed images in Figure 3.4.

but the multifractal model is just approximate for general real word images (it was derived for a subset of so-called natural scenes) and so the MSM is just an

Table 3.2.   PSNRs (in dB) for the accumulated reconstructed images represented in Figure 3.5.

Ψ_1	Ψ_2	Ψ_3	Ψ_4
14.54	14.40	14.26	14.27
17.66	15.89	15.49	14.86
70.42	26.66	22.46	15.86
70.80	52.04	31.52	20.73
70.80	70.80	43.01	27.27
70.80	70.80	48.85	35.52

approximation to the best reconstructing set. Besides, singularity detection is a complicated technique, which requires fine tuning in the choice of the analyzing wavelet. In spite of all those backdraws, it is possible to obtain good performance just using singularity analysis (see Figure 3.6). From a more general perspective, however, other methods for the extraction of the reconstructing set need to be devised.

Fig. 3.6. Left: MSM with Lorentzian wavelet, $h_\infty = -0.5 \pm 0.2$. Right: reconstructed image (PSNR=24.52 dB).

Acknowledgements

During the ellaboration of this work, A. Turiel was financially supported by a post-doctoral grant from INRIA. I am grateful to J. Grazzini for his comments and suggestions.

References

1. D. Marr, *Vision*. (W.H. Freeman and Co., New York, 1982).
2. A. Turiel and N. Parga, The multi-fractal structure of contrast changes in natural images: from sharp edges to textures, *Neural Computation*. **12**, 763–793, (2000).
3. A. Nevado, A. Turiel, and N. Parga, Scene dependence of the non-gaussian scaling properties of natural images, *Network*. **11**, 131–152, (2000).
4. A. Turiel and A. del Pozo, Reconstructing images from their most singular fractal manifold, *IEEE Trans. on Im. Proc.* **11**, 345–350, (2002).
5. R. Hummel and R. Moniot, Reconstructions from zero crossings in scale space, *IEEE Trans. on Acoustics, Speech and Signal Processing*. **37**(12), 2111–2130 (December, 1989).
6. S. Mallat and S. Zhong. Wavelet transform maxima and multiscale edges. In ed. R. M. B. et al, *Wavelets and their applications*. Jones and Bartlett, Boston, (1991).
7. U. Frisch, *Turbulence*. (Cambridge Univ. Press, Cambridge MA, 1995).

8. J. Lévy-Véhel. Introduction to the multifractal analysis of images. In ed. Y. Fisher, *Fractal Image Encoding and Analysis*. Springer Verlag, (1998).

9. A. Turiel, G. Mato, N. Parga, and J. P. Nadal, The self-similarity properties of natural images resemble those of turbulent flows, *Physical Review Letters*. **80**, 1098–1101, (1998).

10. A. Turiel, N. Parga, D. Ruderman, and T. Cronin, Multiscaling and information content of natural color images, *Physical Review E*. **62**, 1138–1148, (2000).

11. I. Daubechies, *Ten lectures on wavelets*. CBMS-NSF Series in App. Math., (Capital City Press, Montpelier, Vermont, 1992).

12. G. Parisi and U. Frisch. On the singularity structure of fully developed turbulence. In eds. M. Ghil, R. Benzi, and G. Parisi, *Turbulence and Predictability in Geophysical Fluid Dynamics. Proc. Intl. School of Physics E. Fermi*, pp. 84–87, Amsterdam, (1985). North Holland.

13. A. Arneodo, F. Argoul, E. Bacry, J. Elezgaray, and J. F. Muzy, *Ondelettes, multifractales et turbulence*. (Diderot Editeur, Paris, France, 1995).

14. E. J. Candès and D. L. Donoho. Curvelets, multiresolution representation, and scaling laws. In eds. A. Aldroubi, A. F. Laine, and M. A. Unser, *Wavelet Applications in Signal and Image Processing VIII*, vol. 4119, *Proc. SPIE*, (2000).

CHAPTER 4

POTENTIAL FIELDS AS AN EXTERNAL FORCE AND ALGORITHMIC IMPROVEMENTS IN DEFORMABLE MODELS

A. Caro [†], P.G. Rodríguez [†], E. Cernadas [‡],
M.L. Durán [†] and T. Antequera [§]

[†] *Departamento de Ingeniería de Sistemas Informáticos y Telemáticos,
Escuela Politécnica, Universidad de Extremadura, E-10071 Cáceres, Spain
E-mail: {andresc, pablogr, mlduran}@unex.es*
[‡] *Departamento de Electrónica e Computación,
Universidade de Santiago de Compostela, Spain
E-mail: cernadas@dec.usc.es*
[§] *Departamento de Produccin Animal y Ciencia de los Alimentos,
Universidad de Extremadura, Cáceres, Spain
E-mail: tantero@unex.es*

Deformable Models are extensively used as a Pattern Recognition technique. They are curves defined within an image domain that can be moved under the influence of internal and external forces. Some trade-offs of standard deformable models algorithms are the selection of image energy function (external force), the location of initial snake and the attraction of contour points to local energy minima when the snake is being deformed. This paper proposes a new procedure using potential fields as external forces. In addition, standard Deformable Models algorithm has been enhanced with both this new external force and algorithmic improvements. The performance of the presented approach has been successfully proved to extract muscles from Magnetic Resonance Imaging (MRI) sequences of Iberian ham at different maturation stages in order to calculate their volume change. The main conclusions of this paper are the practical viability of potential fields used as external forces, as well as the validation of the algorithmic improvements developed. The feasibility of applying Computer Vision techniques, in conjunction with MRI, for determining automatically the optimal ripening time of the Iberian ham is a practical conclusion reached with the proposed approach.

4.1. Introduction

Active Contours (or snakes) are a low-level processing technique widely used to extract boundaries in many pattern recognition applications.[1] In this paper, an improved snake is proposed to recognise muscles in MRI sequences of Iberian ham in different maturation stages. In the next subsections, an overview of the Active Contours is presented, and the relationship with the field of Food Technologies is exposed. In addition, the algorithm design is presented in section 2, and the obtained results are discussed in section 3. Conclusions are shown in section 4.

4.1.1. *Overview on Active Contours*

Deformable models are curves defined within an image domain that can be moved under the influence of internal forces, which are defined within the curve or surface itself, and external forces, which are computed from the image data. The internal forces are designed to keep the model smooth during deformation. The external forces are defined to move the model toward an object boundary or other desired features within an image.[2]

Energy-minimising Active Contour models were proposed by Kass et al.[3] They formulated a model using an energy function. They developed a controlled continuity spline which can be operated upon by internal contour forces, images forces, and external forces which are supplied by an interactive user, or potentially by a higher level process. The goal was to obtain a local minimum that seems most useful to that process or user. An algorithmic solution involves derivation of this objective function and optimisation of the derived equation for finding an appropriate solution. However, in general, variational approaches do not guarantee global optimality of the solution.[4]

Amini et al.[4] also proposed a dynamic programming algorithm for minimising the functional energy that allows addition of hard constraints to obtain a more desirable behaviour of the snakes. However, the proposed algorithm is slow, having a great complexity $O(nm^3)$, where n is the number of points in the contour and m is the size of the neighbourhood in which a point can move during a single iteration.[4,5]

Cohen[5] proposed an additional force that made the curve behave like a balloon which is inflated by this new force. On the other hand, Williams and Shah[6] developed a Greedy algorithm which has performance comparable to the Dynamic Programming and Variational Calculus approaches. They presented different formulations for the continuity term, and they examined and evaluated several approximations for the curvature term. The proposed approach was compared to the original Variational Calculus method of Kass et al. and the Dynamic Programming method developed by Amini et al. and found to be comparable in the final results, while having less computational cost than Dynamic Programming (lower complexity) and being more stable and flexible for including hard constraints than the Variational Calculus approach.

Kichenassamy[7] presented a new Active Contour and surface model based on novel gradient flows, differential geometry and curve and surface evolutions. This led to a novel snake paradigm in which the feature of interest may be considered to lie at the bottom of a potential well.

In addition, Radeva et al.[8] proposed new approaches incorporating the gradient orientation of image edge points, and implementing a new potential field and external force in order to provide a deformation convergence, and attraction by both near and far edges.[9]

McInerney and Terzopoulos[10] also developed a parametric snake model that had the power of an implicit formulation by using a superposed simplicial grid to quickly and efficiently reparameterise the model during the deformation process.

To reduce the problems caused by convergence to local minima, some authors have proposed simulated annealing as well as multiscale methods.[11] Prez et al.[12] presented a new technique to construct Active Contours based on a multiscale representation using wavelet basis. Another approach to deal with this problem was proposed by Giraldi et al.[13] They presented the Dual Active Contour Model, which consisted basically in comparing one contour that expands from inside the target feature, and another one which contracts from the outside. The two contours were interlinked to drive the contour out of local minima, making the solution less sensitive to the initial position.

Caselles et al.[14] proposed a Geodesic Active Contour model based on energy minimisation and geometric Active Contours based on the theory of curve evolution. They proved that a particular case of the classical energy snake model is equivalent to finding a geodesic or minimal distance path in a Riemannian space with a metric derived from the image content. This means that under a specific framework, boundary detection can be considered equivalent to finding a path of minimal weighted length via an Active Contour model based on geodesic or local minimal distance computation. Nevertheless, no method has been proposed for finding the minimal paths within their Geodesic Active Contour model.[15] Goldenberg et al.[16] proposed a new model, using an unconditionally stable numerical scheme to implement a fast version of the geodesic Active Contour model.

Xu and Prince[17] developed a new external force for Active Contours, which they called Gradient Vector Flow. This new force was computed as a diffusion of grey-level gradient vector of a binary edge map derived from the image. The corresponding snake was formulated directly from a force balance condition rather than a variational formulation.[18]

Ballerini[19] proposed an energy minimisation procedure based on Genetic Algorithms. These Genetic Algorithms operate on the position of the snake, and their fitness function is the total snake energy. A modified version of the image energy was used, considering both the magnitude and the direction of the gradient and the Laplacian of Gaussian, though the region of interest is defined by an external user.

Park and Keller[20] presented a new approach that combines Dynamic Programming and the watershed transformation, calling it the Watersnake. The watershed transformation technique is used to decide what points are needed, in order to eliminate unnecessary curves while keeping important ones.

4.1.2. Scope and purpose of the research

Image segmentation is a very important aspect of the Computer Vision techniques. It could be applied in the field of Food Technology to determine some features of this kind of images. Particularly, Iberian ham images were processed in this research in order to find out some characteristics and reach conclusions about this excellent product. The Iberian pig is a native animal bred from the south-western area of Spain, and dry-cured ham from Iberian pig is a meat product with a high sensorial quality and first-rate consumer acceptance in our country. The ripening of Iberian ham is a lengthy process (normally 18-24 months).

Physical-chemical and sensorial methods are required to evaluate the different parameters in relation with quality, being generally tedious, destructive and expensive.[21] Traditionally, the maturation time is fixed, when the weight loss of the ham is approximately 30%.[22] So, other methodologies have long been awaited by the Iberian ham industries.

The use of image processing to analyse Iberian products is quite recent. Some researches[23-25] have processed flat images taken by a CCD camera from Iberian ham slices for different purposes. They estimated some parameters in Iberian ham like intramuscular fat content[25] and marbling[23] or classified various types of raw Iberian ham.[24] The obtained results are very encouraging and suggestive to its application for the systematic inspection of Iberian products. However, although Computer Vision is essentially a non-destroying technique, ham pieces must be destroyed to obtain images using these techniques.

MRI (Magnetic Resonance Imaging) offers great capabilities to non-invasively look inside the bodies. It is widely used in medical diagnosis and surgery. It provides multiples planes (digital images) of the body or piece. Its application to the Food Technology is still recent and it is confined for researching purposes.

Cernadas et al.[26–28] analyse MR images of raw and cured Iberian loin to classify genetic varieties of Iberian pigs and to predict the intramuscular fat content. The results are promising to its application to ham.

The loin is an uniform and simple muscle, and this is a very important advantage, comparing with the great number and complex distribution of muscles of the ham, being this one a significant drawback.

In a previous work,[31] classical snakes (mainly the greedy algorithm) have been applied to ham MRI sequences to extract boundaries of the Biceps Femoris muscle. Although the obtained results were nearly satisfactory, the method suffers from robustness for others muscles. This is one of the reasons because of the Quadriceps muscle has been studied in this paper too. An enhanced Active Contour approach is proposed, based on the use of potential fields as external force and the improvements of the standard greedy algorithm for taking into account the peculiarities of the particular environment.

This new method is applied over a database of specific MR images from Food Technology, particularly Iberian ham images obtained at four different maturation stages (raw, post-salting, semi-cured and cured ham). Deformable Models are used to achieve the extraction of different muscles (Biceps Femoris and Quadriceps), studying their volume changes during the ripening of Iberian ham. The verification of the presented approach is shown examining these muscles, and the obtained practical results may allow us to design a methodology to optimise the ripening process.

4.2. Algorithm Design

A standard Active Contours overview is presented in section 2.1. In section 2.2, some particular problems and algorithmic improvements are presented. The enhanced algorithm is used in conjunction with real MR images (section 2.3).

4.2.1. *Standard Deformable Models*

Deformable Models (Active Contours, or Snakes), are curves that can be moved due to the influence of internal and external forces.[1] These forces are defined so that the snake can detect the image objects in which we are interested.[29] Active Contours are defined by an energy function. By minimising this energy function, the contour converges, and the solution is achieved.

An Active Contour is represented by a vector, v, which contains all of the n points of the snake. The functional energy of this snake is given by:

$$E = \int [E_{int}(v(s)) + E_{image}(v(s))]ds$$

$$= \int [\alpha(s)E_{cont}(v(s)) + \beta(s)E_{curv}(v(s)) + \gamma(s)E_{image}(v(s))]ds \qquad (4.1)$$

E_{int} is the internal energy of the contour. It consists in continuity energy (E_{cont}) plus curvature energy (E_{curv}). E_{image} represents the proper energy of the image, which is very different from one image to another.

α, β and γ are values that can be chosen to control the influence of the three terms.[30,31] For example, a large value of γ means that the energy image is more significant than the rest. When a discontinuity occurs at a point, α is zero. β is zero in corners of the image (null curvature energy).[33,34]

The algorithm is iterative, and during each of the iterations, energy of the m neighbours is computed for each one of the n points of the snake. This point is moved to the neighbour having the lowest energy of the neighbourhood.

The continuity energy attempts to minimise the distance among points of the snake. The algorithm uses the difference between the average distance among points, d, and the distance between the two points under consideration: $d - |v_i - v_{i-1}|$.

The curvature energy could be computed in many forms. We used the expression $|v_{i-1} - 2v_i + v_{i+1}|^2$, which uses the distance between one point and the previous one, and so on.

The image energy is a gradient magnitude.[17,18,32] At each point in the image, gradient magnitude has a normalised value in $0 - 255$, in order to have the same range as the other energy terms.

In our particular case, the points of the image with higher gradient values are located in edges. Therefore, points with small gradient measures are situated in the center of some image object delimited by edges.

The image energy is the only information that the algorithm has about the image on which it is working.[32,35] The other terms of energy (E_{cont} and E_{curv}) in the general equation to minimise are based on distances among points of the snake, but they do not use any specific information of the image. Then, it is extremely relevant to find a good image energy function,[17] in order to control the correct evolution of the Active Contour. It is the only way the algorithm has to get information about the image.

4.2.2. The new approach for Deformable Models

The internal forces of Deformable Models are designed to hold the curve together (elasticity forces, i.e. E_{cont}) and to keep it from bending too much (bending forces, i.e. E_{curv}). Typically, the external forces are defined as a gradient of a potential function. Both internal and external forces attempt to drive the curve toward the edges (object boundary) or other desired features within an image. Unfortunately, the initial snake often needs to be placed near to the searched border. Furthermore, Active Contours have difficulties progressing into concave boundary. Then, selecting correct external forces that solve these problems is highly recommended.

One of the proposed ideas in this work consists in creating potential fields, using them instead of traditional external forces. The purpose of building these potential fields is to move the points of the contours toward the object boundary, not only when they are situated close to the borders, but even when they are not located near to the edges. A traditional potential force cannot attract distant points or either moves them into concave boundary regions, being these two key difficulties with standard Active Contour algorithms. A potential field is developed for solving these problems, and it is presented in this section. Capture range for snakes has been extended, and concave regions could be explored using this new field. These are the main advantages of using this field as an external force for the Active Contour.

The potential fields are computed in a two steps algorithm. The algorithm is described as follows:

As a first stage, edge map images are necessary before computing the potential field, in order to determine the object initial boundary. These primary borders will be used to increasingly grow the potential field.

A $7x7$ Gausian filter has been used to smooth the images. The filter size is either $13x13$ or $15x15$. The goal is to smooth the images converting similar textures in homogeneous grey levels, avoiding dissimilarities. A $3x3$ Sobel operator is applied, obtaining the edge images.

Although the edge images apparently seem to be almost black (except for edges, which are shown in a light white colour), they contain a great variety of data. This extra information is found in dark grey levels, and needs to be equalized to obtain an adequate binary image. The equalisation process converts the grey levels of the edges to values close to 255. After that, the images are converted to binary using a threshold. This value is calculated considering the grey level which divides the histogram in two parts: the black colour (80% of the total pixels) and the white colour (the other 20%).

This bi-level image is used as an edge map to grow the potential field, so removing all the groups of isolated pixels is desirable. These groups of noisy pixels can seriously affect the potential field, producing a local convergence for the snake algorithm (global minimum would not be assure). Eliminating islands of pixels is a remarkable task in the pre-processing stage. A recursive process based on a growing seed is developed for finding islands of pixels with a size (number of pixels) lower than a given value (48 or 96 pixels, depending on the image).

Therefore, the original image has been filtered, equalized, converted to binary level and processed to eliminate the undesirable noise, just before the potential field is computed (see Figure 4.1).

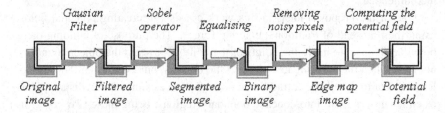

Fig. 4.1.   Obtaining the potential field.

As a second step, the potential field is calculated as a degradation (diffusion) of the binary edge map derived from the image. Considering the bi-level image has white edges (level 255) and black background (level 0), the developed algorithm produces a colour degradation (potential field) in the background points between points of boundaries, as Figure 4.2 shows.

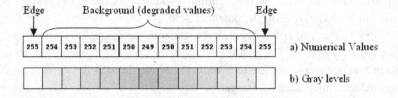

Fig. 4.2.   The calculated potential fields between two points of boundaries.

In this way, images containing potential field magnitudes have been calculated. For each point of the image, the potential field is computed, obtaining a new image, with the same dimensions as the original, which contains the potential field value for each one of the image points.

Contour initialisation is one of the main problems of the Deformable Models. The snake must be developed to find the object searched for. An automatic algorithm has been developed to place an initial contour inside the images.

For its realisation, the potential field image is known. Searching inside the images in order to find the points with the smallest values is required. The key is to distribute all the points of the contour surrounding all those points of the image with smallest potential field values. In this manner, it is ensured that the snake will evolve towards the edges of the object, searching for points with levels of energy smaller than the energy values of the points in the initial snake.

While the contour is being deformed another difficulty could arise: some points of the contour could be attracted to the same place and cross over their trajectories (Figure 4.3.a). This is highly undesirable, because great amounts of nodes situated near by do not have significant information in the recognition task.

Moreover, contours with dots that cross over their trajectories (Figure 4.3.b) would be useless. The goal is to distribute all the nodes of the snake in such a way that they determine the object contour in the best way possible. A procedure has been added to eliminate the nearest knots and aggregate new points between the most distant nodes (Figure 4.3.c).

Figure 4.3 shows a 7-point contour. Points 3 and 4 cross over their trajectories during the evolution of the curve (Figure 4.3.a), producing a non-desirable snake (Figure 4.3.b). The algorithmic improvement remove one of this two points when they are getting closer (Figure 4.3.c), adding a new point in the middle of the largest segment (between the points 1 and 7 from the initial situation is added a new one, renaming all the points).

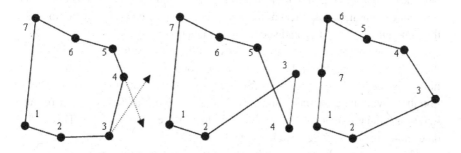

Fig. 4.3. One of the developed algorithmic improvements.

A serious effort in the pre-processing stage is necessary to ensure successful object recognition using Deformable Models. The image processing phases (pre-processing stage) could be considered as algorithmic improvements, due to the final program deal with processed images, instead of the original ones.

4.2.3. A practical application: Deformable Models on Iberian ham MRI

The evolution study of the Iberian ham muscles during the ripening process could
be one of the goals to confirm the practical viability of using the proposed approach. Muscle recognition could be used for determining the fat content and
its distribution, as well as for studying how the hams evolve in their maturation
process.

The presented research is based on MRI sequences of Iberian ham images.
One of the images of these sequences is shown in figure 4.4.a. A technique to
recognise the main muscle structures (Biceps Femoris and Quadriceps) is employed. Four Iberian hams have been scanned, in four stages during their ripening
time.

The images have been acquired using an MRI scan facilitated by the "Infanta
Cristina" Hospital in Badajoz (Spain). The MRI volume data set is obtained from
sequences of T1 images with a FOV (field-of view) of $120x85$ mm and a slice
thickness of $2mm$, i.e. a voxel resolution of $0.23x0.20x2mm$. The total number
of images of the obtained database is 336 for the Biceps Femoris, and 448 for the
Quadriceps muscle.

As a previous step, a pre-processing stage is introduced, in order to compute
the potential field values (Figure 4.4.b and 4.4.c). Therefore, images containing
potential field magnitudes have been calculated.

In addition, the initial snakes for the central images of the sequence have been
previously calculated too (Figure 4.4.d). When the final snake for this image has
been achieved, this final contour is automatically modified, and a scaled version
(the same contour, but smaller) of the final snake is selected as the fist contour for
the immediately preceding and succeeding images.

Once the complete database of images and the initial values of the snakes for
these images are set, the application of Active Contours to compute the area of the
muscle is needed. The greedy algorithm runs over the central image. The snake is
initialised with the computed values, and next, the algorithm finishes after further
iterations, and the final snake is reached for this image (Figure 4.4.e). This snake
determines the area of the muscle over the image.

The next step is based on applying this final snake for the central image as
an initial snake for the following image, as it was previously mentioned. In such
a manner, the final snake that could be used as initial for the next image of the
sequence is obtained. Similarly, the final snake achieved in the central image
could be used as an initial snake for the previous image, and so on.

The final step computes areas and volumes for the extracted muscles (Figure 4.4.f). Calculating the surface of the final obtained snake for each image is

possible to determine the volume for the muscle.

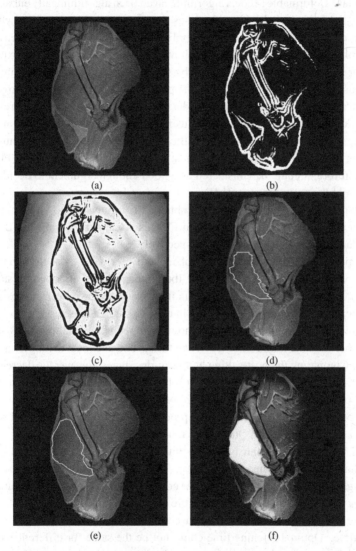

Fig. 4.4.ᐟ Algorithm design for the practical application. (a) Original image. (b) Map image. (c) Potential field. (d) Initial snake. (e) Final snake. (f) Area of the muscle.

4.3. Practical Results and their Discussion

The standard Deformable Models algorithm haven been algorithmically enhanced, and potential fields have been employed as external forces. A new approach has been successfully proved in a practical application, using these two key ideas.

The obtained practical results show how the potential field, used as external forces for Deformable Models, seems to be an acceptable solution for finding patterns (muscles in the proposed practical application). It is not necessary to place the initial snake near to the searched border, and all the difficulties in progressing into concave boundary have been solved using potential fields in conjunction with all the algorithmic improvements. Both Biceps Femoris and Quadriceps muscles have been satisfactorily recognised for most of the images of the database (Figure 4.5). Therefore, it could be considered as a good enough argument to decide the validation of the proposed algorithm.

A comparison of the muscles size (obtained using the proposed technique) during the maturation stages is shown in Figures 4.6.a and 4.6.b for the Biceps Femoris and the Quadriceps muscles, respectively.

The practical application of the enhanced Deformable Models algorithm shows how the volume reduction of the Iberian ham during its ripening stages. Both new external forces and algorithmic improvements have been successfully proved, reaching suitable results equally in the two studied muscles.

The results presented in Figure 4.6 show a size reduction of almost 10% as an average, between the initial stage (raw) and the second one (post-salting), for both muscles. Comparing the post-salting and semi-dry stages, the average decrease is about 20%, and the size reduction produced between the semi-dry and cured-dry stages is of nearly 15% as an average, for both muscles. The approximate average ratio is 45% at the end of the maturation process, 21 months after the initial stage, for both Biceps Femoris and Quadriceps muscles.

Food Technology specialists have estimated the total weight decrease in the Iberian ham during the same time at 30%. This way, a relationship between the ham weight (30%) and muscle size (45%) could be established for the maturation time, as a first approximation. Thus, a more complete study is necessary.

These weight decreases could be caused by the loss of water during the maturation time. Optimal ripening time could not be the same for different Iberian pig hams. By studying the percentage rate of volume during the ripening process, it was possible to predict the optimal maturation moment. So, the new proposed approach could be considered as alternative to the traditional methods, proving not only the validation of the presented technique as another option to the conventional processes, but the appropriate use of potential fields as external forces

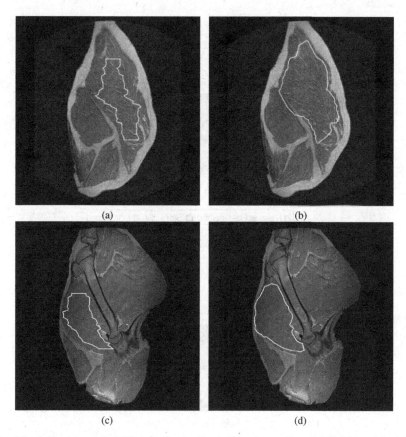

Fig. 4.5. Initial (a) and final (b) snake for the Biceps Femoris muscle, and initial (c) and final (d) snake for the Quadriceps muscle.

in Deformable Models, as well as the practical efficiency of the algorithmic improvements.

4.4. Conclusions

Using potential fields as external forces is a suitable solution for Deformable Models. It is allowed to initialise snakes far from the searched border, combining this new external force with algorithmic improvements. The redistribution of the snake points during the snake deformation stage, the elimination of groups of isolated pixels in the pre-processing stage and the utilisation of scaled versions of the final snakes used as initial snakes for consecutive images suppose important and valid

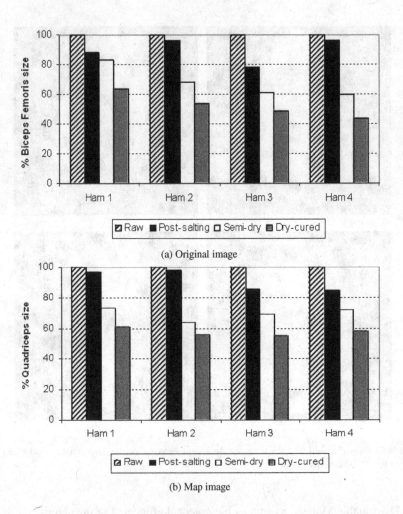

Fig. 4.6.   Biceps Femoris (a) and Quadriceps (b) muscle size evolution during the ripening time.

algorithmic improvements. These significant enhances allow snakes evolve into concave boundary too. The practical feasibility of applying Computer Vision techniques, in conjunction with MRI, to automatically determine the optimal ripening time for the Iberian ham, is another conclusion obtained from this work. Therefore, great perspectives for the pork industry are offered by this new approach, to improve the efficiency in the ripening process in the future.

Acknowledgements

The authors are grateful to the Denominacin de Origen "Dehesa de Extremadura", the Hermanos Alonso Roa company from Villar del Rey (Badajoz), and the Infanta Cristina Hospital (Badajoz). In addition, we wish to express our gratitude to the Ministerio de Educación y Ciencia (Spain's Government Board - Research Project number TIN2005-05939) and the Junta de Extremadura (Local Government), under the IPR98A03P, 2PR01C025 and 3PR05B027 projects, for the support and collaboration to the realization of this work.

References

1. A. Blake and M. Isard, Active Contours. Springer, London - UK (1998).
2. C. Xu, D.L. Pham and J.L. Prince, Medical Image Segmentation Using Deformable Models, Handbook of Medical Imaging: Medical Image Processing and Analysis, 2:129-174, SPIE Press (2000).
3. M. Kass, A. Witkin and D. Terzopoulos, Snakes: Active Contour models, Proceedings of First International Conference on Computer Vision, 1:259-269 (1987).
4. A.A. Amini, T.E. Weymouth and R. Jain, Using Dynamic Programming for Solving Variational Problems in Vision, IEEE Transactions on Pattern Analysis and Machine Intelligence, 12:855-867 (1990).
5. L.D. Cohen, On Active Contour Models and Balloons, Computer Vision, Graphics and Image Processing: Image Understanding, 53(2):211-218 (1991).
6. D.J. Williams and M. Shah, A Fast Algorithm for Active Contours and Curvature Estimation, Computer Vision, Graphics and Image Processing: Image Understanding, 55:14-26 (1992).
7. S. Kichenassamy, A. Kumar, P. Olver, A. Tannenbaum and A. Yezzi,, Gradient Flows and Geometric Active Contour Models, Proc. International Conference on Computer Vision (1995).
8. P. Radeva and J. Serrat, Rubber Snake: Implementation on Signed Distance Potencial, Proc. International Conference SWISS Vision, 1:187-194 (1993).
9. P. Radeva, J. Serrat and E. Mart, A Snake for Model-Based Segmentation, 5th International Conference on Computer Vision (1995).
10. T. McInerney and D. Terzopoulos, Topologically Adaptable Snakes, Proc. Fifth International Conference on Computer Vision, 1:840-845 (1995).
11. F. Leymarie and M.D. Levine, Tracking deformable objects in the plane using an Active Contour Model, IEEE Transactions on Pattern Analysis and Machine Intelligence, 15(6):617-634 (1993).
12. F. Prez and A. Falcn, Active Contours with Wavelet Basis, V Ibero American Symposium on Pattern Recognition, 1:423-432 (2000).
13. G.A. Giraldi, L.M. Gonalvez and A.F. Oliveira, Dual Topologically Adaptable Snakes, Proceedings of the Third International Conference on Computer Vision, Pattern Recognition, and Image Processing, 1:103-106 (2000).

14. V. Caselles, R. Kimmel and G. Sapiro, Geodesic Active Contours, International Journal of Computer Vision, 22(1):61-79 (1997).

15. C. Han, T.S. Hatsukami, J.N. Hwang and C. Yuan, A Fast Minimal Path Active Contour Model, IEEE Transactions on Image Processing, 10(6):865-873 (2001).

16. R. Goldengerg, R. Kimmel, E. Rivlin and M. Rudzsky, Fast Geodesic Active Contours, IEEE Transactions on Image Processing, 10(10):1467-1475 (2001).

17. C. Xu and J.L. Prince, Gradient Vector Flow: A New External Force for Snakes, IEEE Proc. On Computer Vision and Pattern Recognition, 1:66-71 (1997).

18. C. Xu and J.L. Prince, Snakes, Shapes, and Gradient Vector Flow, IEEE Transactions on Image Processing, 1:359-369 (1998).

19. L. Ballerini, Genetic snakes for medical images segmentation, Lectures Notes in Computer Science, 1596:59-73 (1999).

20. J. Park and J.M. Keller, Snakes on the Watershed, IEEE Transactions on Pattern Analysis and Machine Intelligence, 23(10):1201-1205 (2001).

21. T. Antequera, C.J. Lpez-Bote, J.J. Crdoba, C. Garca, M.A. Asensio, J. Ventanas and Y. Daz, Lipid oxidative changes in the processing of Iberian pig hams, Food Chemical, 54:105 (1992).

22. R. Cava and J. Ventanas, Dinmica y control del proceso de secado del jamn ibrico en condiciones naturales y cmaras climatizadas, Tecnologa del jamn ibrico, Ed. Mundi Prensa, 1:260-274 (2001).

23. E. Cernadas, M.L. Durn and T. Antequera, Recognizing Marbling in Dry-Cured Iberian Ham by Multiscale Analysis. Pattern Recognition Letters (2002).

24. M.L. Durn, E. Cernadas, A. Caro and T. Antequera, Clasificacin de distintos tipos de jamn ibrico utilizando Anlisis de Texturas, Revista Electrnica de Visin por Computador, 5 (2001).

25. M.L. Durn, A. Caro, E. Cernadas, A. Plaza and M.J. Petrn, A fuzzy schema to evaluate fat content in Iberian pig meat images, V Ibero American Symposium on Pattern Recognition, 1:207-216 (2000).

26. E. Cernadas, M.L. Durn, P.G. Rodrguez, A. Caro, E. Muriel and R. Palacios, Estimating intramuscular fat content of cured Iberian loin using statistical analysis of its magnetic resonance images, Portuguese Conf. on Pattern Recognition (2002).

27. E. Cernadas, A. Plaza, P.G. Rodrguez, M.L. Durn, J. Hernndez, T. Antequera, R. Gallardo and D. Villa, Estimation of Dry-Cured Iberian Ham Quality Using Magnetic Resonance Imaging, The 5th International Conference on Applications of Magnetic Resonance in Food Science, 1:46-47 (2000).

28. E. Cernadas, T. Antequera, P.G. Rodrguez, M.L. Durn, R. Gallardo and D. Villa, Magnetic Resonance Imaging to Classify Loin from Iberian Pigs, Magnetic Resonance in Food Science - A View to the Next Century, 1:239-254. Ed. The Royal Society of Chemistry (2001).

29. J.M. Bonny, W. Laurent, R. Labas, R. Taylor, P. Berge and J.P. Renou, Magnetic Resonance Imaging of connective tissue: a non-destructive method for characterising muscle structure, Journal of the Science of Food and Agriculture, 81:337-341 (2000).

30. S. Ranganath, Contour Extraction from Cardiac MRI Studies Using Snakes, IEEE Transactions on Medical Imaging, 14:328-338 (1995).

31. A. Caro, P.G. Rodrguez, E. Cernadas, M.L. Durn, E. Muriel and D. Villa, Computer Vision Techniques Applying Active Contours to Muscle Recognition in Iberian Ham

MRI, Proc. International Conference on Signal Processing, Pattern Recognition and Aplications, 1:62-66 (2001).

32. D. Suter and F. Chen, Left Ventricular Motion Reconstruction Based on Elastic Vector Splines, IEEE Transactions on Medical Imaging, 19:295-305 (2000).

33. S. Ranganath, Analysis of the effects of Snake Parameters on Contour Extraction, Proceedings of the 2nd International Conference on Automation, Robotics, and Computer Vision, CV4.5.1-CV4.5.5 (1992).

34. O.V. Larsen, P. Radeva and E. Mart, Guidelines for Choosing Optimal Parameters of Elasticity for Snakes, Proceedings of International Conference on Computer Analysis and Image Processing, 1:106-113 (1995).

35. K.P. Ngoi and J.C. Jia, A new colour Image Energy for Active Contours in Natural Scenes, Pattern Recognition Letters, 17:1271-1277 (1996).

CHAPTER 5

OPTIMIZATION OF WEIGHTS IN A MULTIPLE CLASSIFIER HANDWRITTEN WORD RECOGNITION SYSTEM USING A GENETIC ALGORITHM

Simon Günter and Horst Bunke

Department of Computer Science, University of Bern,
Neubrückstrasse 10, CH-3012 Bern, Switzerland
E-mail: sguenter@iam.unibe.ch, bunke@iam.unibe.ch

Automatic handwritten text recognition by computer has a number of interesting applications. However, due to a great variety of individual writing styles, the problem is very difficult and far from being solved. Recently, a number of classifier creation methods, known as ensemble methods, have been proposed in the field of machine learning. They have shown improved recognition performance over single classifiers. For the combination of these classifiers many methods have been proposed in the literature. In this paper we describe a weighted voting scheme where the weights are obtained by a genetic algorithm.

5.1. Introduction

The field of off-line handwriting recognition has been a topic of intensive research for many years. First only the recognition of isolated handwritten characters was investigated,[1] but later whole words[2] were addressed. Most of the systems reported in the literature until today only consider constrained recognition problems based on small vocabularies from specific domains, e.g. the recognition of handwritten check amounts[3] or postal addresses.[4] Free handwriting recognition, without domain specific constraints and large vocabularies, was addressed only recently in a few papers.[5,6] The recognition rate of such systems is still low, and there is a need to improve it.

The combination of multiple classifiers has become a very active area of research recently.[7,8] It has been demonstrated in a number of applications that using more than a single classifier in a recognition task can lead to a significant improvement of the system's overall performance. Hence multiple classifier systems seem to be a promising approach to improve the recognition rate of current handwriting recognition systems. Concrete examples of multiple classifier systems in handwriting recognition include.[9-16]

To build a multiple classifier system, one needs a number of basic classifiers first. Very often, the design of these basic classifiers is guided by intuition and heuristics. Sometimes, different sources of information, which are redundant or partly redundant to each other, are exploited, for example, zip code and city name in address reading,[4] or legal and courtesy amount in bankcheck processing.[3] Recently, a number of procedures for classifier generation, called ensemble creation methods, were proposed in the field of machine learning. A summary of these methods is given in.[17] They are characterized by the fact that they produce several classifiers out of one given base classifier automatically. Given a base classifier, an ensemble of different classifiers can be generated by changing the training set,[18] the input features,[19] the input data by injecting randomness[20] or the parameters and architecture of the base classifier.[21]

In a multiple classifier system for handwriting recognition, each of the basic classifiers first generates, as its output, one or several hypotheses about the identity of the unknown word to be recognized. Next, these outputs need to be appropriately combined to derive the final recognition result. There are many ways to combine the results of a set of classifiers, depending on the type of the classifiers' output.[22,23] If the output is only the best ranked class then majority voting can be applied. More sophisticated voting schemes also look at the probability of the classification error for a specific class (Bayesian Combination Rule[24]), or dependencies between the classifiers (Behavior-Knowledge Space[25]). Some classifiers have a ranked list of classes as output. In this case often Borda count[26] or related methods are used. In the most general situation, a classifier generates a score value for each class. Then the sum, product, maximum, minimum, or the median of the scores of all classifiers can be calculated and the class with the highest value is regarded as the combined result.[24] It is also possible to first weight each classifier according to its individual performance and then apply a combination rule.[27]

Automatic classifier ensemble generation methods together with related combination schemes have rarely been applied in the field of cursive handwriting recognition until now. In this paper we propose a framework where the individual base classifiers are given by hidden Markov Models (HMMs).[28] This kind of classifier has shown superior performance over other approaches in many handwriting recognition tasks. The proposed multiple classifier system is distinguished from many other classifiers described in the literature in that it has to deal with a large number of classes. (In the experiments described in Section 5.6 a recognition problem with over 2000 words, i.e. pattern classes, was considered.) This restricts the number of possible classifier combination schemes. For example, considering class specific error rates in the combination method, as it was proposed in,[23] is no longer feasible because of its low reliability in case of a high number of classes. Further constraints on possible combination schemes are imposed by the use of HMMs as base classifiers. In our framework, only the class on the first rank together with its score is returned by each individual HMM classifier. Therefore, Borda count, as well as sum, product, and median rule can't be applied. Yet weighted voting is feasible for this problem. It is, in fact, the most general form of classifier combination available in the proposed framework.

In weighted voting, each classifier has a single vote for its top ranked class, and this vote is given a weight. To derive the final decision in a multiple classifier system using weighted voting, the weights assigned to each class by the different classifiers are summed up and the class with the highest score is selected as the final result. Under a weighted voting scheme, the weights assigned to the individual classifiers are free parameters. Sometimes these weights are chosen proportional to the recognition performance of individual classifiers. In this paper, we apply a more general approach where the weights are considered as parameters which are to be selected in such a way that the overall performance of the combined system is optimized. A genetic algorithm is used to actually determine an optimal (or suboptimal) combination of weight values. Also in[29] a genetic algorithm was used for weight optimization in a multiple classifier system. However, an easier recognition problem was considered there, i.e. the application was the recognition of handwritten digits and the combined classifiers were not created by an ensemble creation method, but were each separately designed by hand. In[30] a genetic algorithm was used for the selection of a subset of classifiers from an ensemble, which is equivalent to weight optimization using only the weights 0 and 1. Another application of a genetic algorithm in a multiple classifier framework has been proposed in.[16] In this work, a genetic algorithm was used to select individual classifiers from a pool for the different modules of a multiple classifier framework.

The remainder of this paper is organized as follows. In Section 5.2 our base classifier, which is a handwritten word recognizer based on hidden Markov Models (HMMs), is introduced. The following section describes the methods used to produce classifier ensembles from the base classifier. Then the classifier combination schemes used in this work are introduced in Section 5.4. The genetic algorithm for the calculation of the weights applied in the weighted voting combination scheme is described in Section 5.5. In Section 5.6 experimental results comparing genetic weight optimization with other combination schemes are presented. Finally the last section draws conclusions from this work.

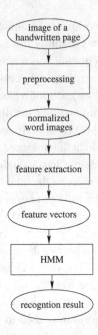

Fig. 5.1.   System overview.

5.2. Handwritten word recognizer

The basic handwritten text recognizer used in the experiments of this paper is similar to the one described in.[6] It follows the classical architecture and consists of three main modules (see Fig. 5.1): the preprocessing, where noise reduction and normalization take place, the feature extraction, where the image of a handwritten text is transformed into a sequence of numerical feature vectors, and the recognizer, which converts these sequences of feature vectors into a word class.

The first step in the processing chain, the preprocessing, is mainly concerned with text image normalization. The goal of the different normalization steps is to produce a uniform image of the writing with less variations of the same character or word across different writers. The aim of feature extraction is to derive a sequence of feature vectors which describe the writing in such a way that different characters and words can be distinguished, but avoiding redundant information as much as possible. In the presented system the features are based on geometrical measurements. At the core of the recognition procedure is an HMM. It receives a sequence of feature vectors as input and outputs a word class. In the following these modules are described in greater detail. In the Appendix a small subset of

Fig. 5.2. Preprocessing of the images. From left to right: original, skew corrected, slant corrected and positioned. The two horizontal lines in the right most picture are the two baselines.

the words used in the experiments described in Section 5.6 are shown.

5.2.1. *Preprocessing*

Each person has a different writing style with its own characteristics. This fact makes the recognition task complicated. To reduce variations in the handwritten texts as much as possible, a number of preprocessing operations are applied. The input for these preprocessing operations are images of words extracted from the database described in.[31,32] In the presented system the following preprocessing steps are carried out:

- Skew Correction: The word is horizontally aligned, i.e. rotated, such that the baseline is parallel to the x-axis of the image.
- Slant Correction: Applying a shear transformation, the writing's slant is transformed into an upright position.
- Line Positioning: The word's total extent in vertical direction is normalized to a standard value. Moreover, applying a vertical scaling operation the location of the upper and lower baseline are adjusted to a standard position.

An example of these normalization operations is shown in Fig. 5.2. For any further technical details see.[6]

5.2.2. *Feature extraction*

To extract a sequence of feature vectors from a word, a sliding window is used. The width of the window used in the current system is one pixel and its height is equal to the word's height. The window is moved from left to right over each word. (Thus there is no overlap between two consecutive window positions.) Nine geometrical quantities are computed and used as features at each window position. A graphical representation of this sliding window technique is shown in Fig. 5.3.

The first three features are the weight of the window (i.e. the number of black pixels), its center of gravity, and the second order moment of the window. This set

Window

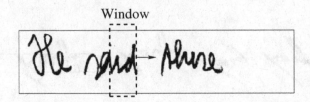

Fig. 5.3.   Illustration of the sliding window technique. A window is moved from left to right and features are calculated for each position of the window. (For graphical representation purposes, the window depicted here is wider than one pixel.)

characterizes the window from the global point of view. It includes information about how many pixels in which region of the window are, and how they are distributed. The other features represent additional information about the writing. Features four and five define the position of the upper and the lower contour in the window. The next two features, number six and seven, give the orientation of the upper and the lower contour in the window by the gradient of the contour at the window's position. As feature number eight the number of black-white transitions in vertical direction is used. Finally, feature number nine gives the number of black pixels between the upper and lower contour. Notice that all these features can be easily computed from the binary image of a text line. However, to make the features robust against different writing styles, careful preprocessing, as described in Subsection 5.2.1, is necessary.

To summarize, the output of the feature extraction phase is a sequence of 9-dimensional feature vectors. For each word to be recognized there exists one such vector per pixel along the x-axis, i.e. along the horizontal extension of the considered word.

5.2.3. Hidden Markov models

Hidden Markov models (HMMs) are widely used in the field of pattern recognition. Their original application was in speech recognition.[33] But because of the similarities between speech and cursive handwriting recognition, HMMs have become very popular in handwriting recognition as well.[34]

When using HMMs for a classification problem, an individual HMM is constructed for each pattern class. For each observation sequence, i.e.· for each sequence of feature vectors, the likelihood that this sequence was produced by an HMM of a class can be calculated. The class whose HMM achieved the highest likelihood is considered as the class that produced the actual sequence of observations.

An HMM consists of a set of states and transitions probabilities between those

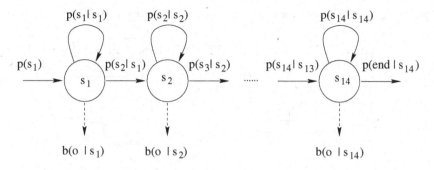

Fig. 5.4.   HMM for a single character with linear transition structure.

states. One or several of the states are defined as final states. For each state a like-lihood value for each possible observation is defined. If there is a finite number of observations then a probability for each observation, i.e. feature vector, is defined, but if we have continuous observation vectors a probability distribution is used. A valid sequence of states for a observation sequence $o_{seq} = o_1, o_2, \ldots, o_n$ is $s_{seq} = s_1, s_2, \ldots, s_n$ where s_n is a final state. Note that the number of states in s_{seq} is the same as the number of observations in o_{seq}. The likelihood of the sequence of states s_{seq} is the product of the likelihoods of observing o_i in state s_i for all observations, multiplied by the probabilities of the transitions from state s_i to s_{i+1} for all $i \in \{1, \ldots, n - 1\}$. There are two possibilities to define the likelihood of an observation sequence o_{seq} for a given HMM. Either the highest likelihood of all possible state sequences is used (Viterbi recognition), or the sum of the likelihoods of all possible state sequences is considered as the likelihood of the observation sequence (Baum-Welch recognition). In the system described in this paper the first possibility is used. For details see,[33] for example.

In word recognition systems with a small vocabulary, it is possible to build an individual HMM for each word. But for large vocabularies this method doesn't work anymore because of the lack of enough training data. Therefore, in our system an HMM is build for each character. The use of character models allows us to share training data. Each instance of a letter in the training set has an impact on the training and leads to a better parameter estimation.

To achieve high recognition rates, the character HMMs have to be fitted to the problem. In particular the number of states, the possible transitions and the type of the output probability distributions have to be chosen. In our system each character model consists of 14 states. This number has been found empirically. (The rather high number can be explained by the fact that the sliding window used for feature extraction is only one pixel wide and that many different writing

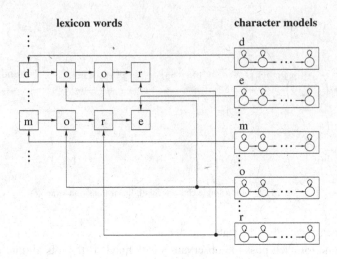

Fig. 5.5.   Concatenation of character models yields the word models.

styles are present in the used database.) Because of the left to right direction of writing, a linear transition structure has been chosen for the character models. From each state only the same or the succeeding state can be reached. (A graphical representation of the HMMs used in our system is shown in Fig. 5.4.) Because of the continuous nature of the features, probability distributions for the features are used. Each feature has its own probability distribution and the likelihood of an observation in a state is the multiplication of the likelihoods calculated for all features. This separation of the elements of the feature vector reduces the number of free parameters, because no covariance terms must be calculated. The probability distribution of all states and features are assumed to be Gaussians, so that only two free parameters per distribution exist, namely, the mean and the variance. The initialization of the models is done by Viterbi alignment to segment the training observations and recompute the free parameters of the models, i.e. the mean and variance of each probability distribution and the transition probabilities between the states. To adjust these free parameters during training, the Baum-Welch algorithm[33] is used.

To model entire words, the character models are concatenated with each other. Thus a recognition network is obtained (see Fig. 5.5). Note that this network doesn't include any contextual knowledge on the character level, i.e., the model of a character is independent of its left and right neighbor. In the network the best path is found with the Viterbi algorithm.[33] It corresponds to the desired recognition result, i.e., the best path represents the sequence of characters with maximum probability, given the image of the input word. The architecture shown in Fig. 5.5 makes it possible to avoid the difficult task of segmenting a word into individual characters. More details of the handwritten text recognizer can be found in.[6]

5.3. Ensemble creation methods

In this section the ensemble creation methods used in this paper are described. Each ensemble creation method takes a base classifier and a training set as input and returns a number of trained instances of the base classifier as a result. In the first subsection general aspects of ensemble creation are discussed. Then details of the various methods are given.

5.3.1. *Issues in ensemble creation*

A good performing ensemble creation method should have at least two properties. First, the method should create diverse classifiers, which means that the misclassification of patterns should have a low correlation across different classifiers (or in other words, the recognition rate of a classifier C_i on the patterns misclassified by another classifier C_j should be close to the average recognition rate of C_i). In the ideal case independent classifiers are created, but this is almost impossible in real world applications. The diversity of classifiers is crucial, because all of the known combination rules can only increase the performance of single classifiers if they are used with an ensemble of diverse classifiers. It is well known that a high correlation between the errors committed by individual classifiers may lead to a decreasing performance of the ensemble when compared to the best individual classifier. For a more detailed discussion of classifier diversity the reader is referred to.[35]

The second requirement is that an ensemble creation method should produce individual classifiers whose recognition rate is not much lower than that of the trained base classifier. It is obvious that the recognition rate of an ensemble using a combination rule depends on the performance of its individual members. There are some ensemble creation methods that have the potential of creating classifiers which outperform the best base classifier. But if many members of an ensemble have a poor performance they may eventually become dominant over the well-performing classifiers. To avoid performance degradation an ensemble creation method should particularly avoid to overfit the training data.

In the following, four ensemble creation methods, namely, Bagging, AdaBoost, random subspace, and architecture variation are introduced. These methods were originally proposed in the area of machine learning. Note that their quality with regard to the two properties discussed above is application dependent and can't be guaranteed a priori.

5.3.2. *Bagging*

Bagging,[18] an acronym for **b**ootstrapping and **agg**regat**ing**, was among the first methods proposed for ensemble creation. Given a training set S of size n, bagging generates N new training sets $S_1, \ldots, S_N$, each of size n, by randomly drawing elements of the original training set, where the same element may be drawn multiple times. If the probability of being drawn is equally distributed over S, as it is the case here, about two third of all training elements are contained in each modified training set S_i, some of them multiple times. Each of the new sets S_i is used to train exactly one classifier. Hence an ensemble of N individual classifiers is obtained from N new training sets.

5.3.3. *AdaBoost*

Similarly to Bagging, AdaBoost[36] modifies the original training set for the creation of the ensemble. To each pattern of the training set a selection probability is assigned, which is equal for all elements of the training set in the beginning. Then elements for a new training set are randomly drawn from the original training set taking the selection probabilities into account. The size of the new training set is equal to the size of the original one. After the creation of a new training set, a classifier is trained on this set. Then the new classifier is tested on the original training set. The selection probabilities of correctly classified patterns in the original training set are decreased and the selection probabilities of misclassified patterns are increased. During the execution of the AdaBoost procedure the selection probabilities are dynamically changing. Hence, unlike Bagging, where the classifiers are created independently, the classifiers generated by AdaBoost are dependent on selection probabilities, which in turn depend on the performance of previously generated classifiers.

The main idea of AdaBoost is to concentrate the training on "difficult" patterns. Note that the first classifier is trained in the same way as the classifiers in Bagging. The classical AdaBoost algorithm can only be used for two-class problems, but AdaBoost.M1,[36] a simple extension of AdaBoost, can cope with multiclass problems. Consequently, AdaBoost.M1 was applied in the system described in this paper.

5.3.4. *Random subspace method*

In the random subspace method[19] an individual classifier uses only a subset of all features for training and testing. The size of the subset is fixed and the features are randomly chosen from the set of all features.

For the handwritten text recognizer described in Section 5.2 the situation is special in the sense that the number of available features is rather low. (As described in Section 5.2, only nine features are extracted at each position of the window.) Therefore, the features are not completely randomly chosen. If the number of classifiers which use feature f_i is denoted by $n(f_i)$, then the following relation holds: $\forall i, j \ |n(f_i) - n(f_j)| \ <= 1$. This means that each individual feature is used in approximately the same number of classifiers. Therefore, all features have approximately the same importance. By means of this condition it is enforced that the information of every feature is exploited as much as possible. By contrast, when choosing completely random feature sets, it is possible that certain features are not used at all.

In the experiments described in Section 5.6, always subsets of six features were used. This number was experimentally determined as a suitable value. The whole training set with feature vectors of reduced dimensionality was used for the training of each individual classifier.

5.3.5. *Architecture variation*

Another way to create an ensemble out of a base classifier is to vary its architecture. In a feed-forward neural network, for example, one may change the number of hidden layers or the number of neurons in each layer.[21] Similar possibilities exist for HMM. Our base classifier was changed as follows.

First, the linear topology was replaced by the Bakis model (see Fig. 5.6). This topology allows more flexibility in the decoding process by skipping certain states. Next, two additional architectures were implemented. The HMM models used in our base classifier don't include any ligature states[a]. But the transition from one character to the next is often context dependent. Therefore, if certain character pairs are not sufficiently well represented in the training set, misalignments at the beginning and at the end of a character model during decoding may be expected. To account for this kind of problem, the semi-jumpin and semi-jumpout architecture shown in Fig. 5.6 were introduced. Here the first or last $\frac{n-4}{2}$ states of a linear model may be skipped (with n denoting the total number of states of the considered HMM).

---

[a]Here the term ligature denotes a connection stroke between two consecutive characters

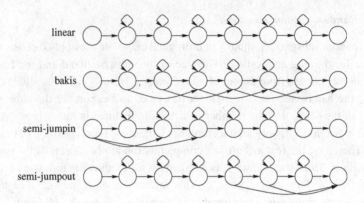

Fig. 5.6. HMM topologies (for a small HMM with 6 emitting states. Note that the HMMs of the classifier in Section 5.2 have 14 emitting states.)

Normally the columns of a word image are read form left to right. Another possibility is to read them from right to left. Because the Viterbi search used in the decoding phase is a suboptimal procedure that prunes large portions of the search space, the results of a forward and a backward scan of the word are not necessarily the same. To implement a right-to-left scan of the image, only the concatenation of character HMMs needs to be changed appropriately.

Apparently, left-to-right as well as right-to-left scanning can be combined with any of the architectures shown in Fig. 5.6. Therefore, a total of eight different classifiers were generated. Each of these classifiers was trained on the full training set.

5.4. Combination schemes

In this section the combination schemes used in our multiple classifier system for handwriting recognition are described.

5.4.1. *Maximum score rule*

In this scheme the word class with the highest score among all word classes and all classifiers is the output of the combined classifier. This combination scheme is denoted as *max* in the following.

5.4.2. *Performance weighted voting*

In the weighted voting combination scheme a weight is assigned to each classifier. For all word classes the sum of the weights of the classifiers which output this class is calculated and the combined result is the word class that has the largest sum of weights. In the performance weighted voting scheme, which is denoted as *perf voting* in the following, the weight of the classifier is equal to the classifier's performance (i.e. recognition rate) on the training set. The system described in Section 5.2 was found to have a good generalization power, i.e. the results on the training set allow a good estimation of the behavior of the system on test data. So the training set was used for the evaluation of the performance of the classifiers. For other classifiers it may be necessary to use a separate validation set to evaluate the performance of the created classifiers. (The Nearest-Neighbor classifier, for example, has always a recognition rate of 100 % on its training set.)

5.4.3. *Weighted voting using weights calculated by a genetic algorithm*

Using the performance of a classifier as its weight is based on the intuitive assumption that classifiers with a high recognition rate are more trustworthy than classifiers that perform poorly. However, there is no objective proof that this strategy is optimal. Under a more general approach, one considers the set of weights as free parameters in a multiple classifier system, and tries to find the combination of values that lead to the best performance of the whole system. Out of many possible optimization procedures it was decided to use a genetic algorithm[37] for weight optimization. Among the reasons to favor a genetic approach over other methods was the simplicity and elegance of genetic algorithms as well as their demonstrated performance in many other complex optimization problems.[38–40]

The training set used to find the individual classifiers was also used to derive the optimal combination of weights, assuming that the obtained values lead to a good performance on the test set as well. The genetic algorithm for weight optimization will be described in Section 5.5 in greater detail. In the following this algorithm will be denoted as *ga voting*.

5.4.4. *Voting with ties handling*

Under this scheme a normal voting procedure is executed first, i.e., if the occurrence of a class among the results of the classifiers is higher than the occurrence of any other class then this class is output as the combined result. A tie occurs if no unique result is obtained. For some applications it may be sufficient to just reject a pattern if a tie occurs, but here we use a more general approach. In case of a tie we focus our attention on those classes that compete under the tie and apply one the above mentioned combination schemes. So there is voting with tie handling by maximum score rule, by performance weighted voting, and by weighted voting using weights calculated by a genetic algorithm. Theses schemes are denoted as *ties max*, *ties perf voting*, and *ties ga voting*, respectively.

5.5. Genetic algorithm for the calculation of the weights used by weighted voting

First proposed in,[37] genetic algorithms have been found to be robust and practical optimization methods. In a genetic algorithm a possible solution of the problem under consideration is represented by a chromosome. In the initialization step of the algorithm a set of chromosomes is created randomly. The actual set of chromosomes is called the population. A fitness function is defined to represent the quality of the solution given by a chromosome. Only the chromosomes with the highest values of this fitness function are allowed to reproduce. In the reproduction phase new chromosomes are created by fusing information of two existing chromosome (crossover) and by randomly changing them (mutation). Finally the chromosomes with the lowest values of the fitness function are removed. This reproduction and elimination step is repeated until a predefined termination condition is become true. In the following we describe the genetic algorithm that is used in our multiple classifier system in more details.

5.5.1. *Chromosome representation and fitness*

The representation of a set of weights for the individual classifiers by a chromosome is straightforward. Each chromosome is represented by an array of real numbers between 0 and 1. The i-th position of the array corresponds to the weight of the i-th classifier of the ensemble. The number of elements in the array is equal to the number of classifiers. The fitness of a chromosome is defined as the recognition rate of the ensemble when using weighted voting with the weights represented by the chromosome. Note that by using the performance of the whole ensemble as fitness the diversity of the individual classifiers is also taken into account.

5.5.2. *Initialization and termination*

A population of size 50 was used in the algorithm. All positions of the chromosomes are set to random real values between 0 and 1 at the beginning of the algorithm. If the fitness value of the ten best chromosomes is the same the algorithm is terminated. Alternatively, if this condition doesn't become true, the algorithm is terminated after 100 generations. The weights of the chromosome with the highest fitness value encountered during all generations (not only the last one) are the final result and are used for the weighted voting combination.

5.5.3. *Crossover operator*

A normal one point crossover operator is used. First a position i in the chromosome is randomly selected. Then the values the first parent chromosome from position 1 to position i are copied to the corresponding positions in the first child chromosome. Moreover, the values of the remaining positions of the first parent chromosome are copied to the corresponding positions of the second child chromosome. Then the positions of the children chromosomes not yet defined are set to the corresponding values of the second parent chromosome. The probability of the crossover was set to 90 %.

5.5.4. *Mutation operator*

The mutation operator is applied to all new chromosomes produced by the crossover operator. This operator changes only one random position of the array in the following manner. The value at this position is changed by a constant multiplied with a random number between 0 and 1. Under this procedure, the chance of an increase or a decrease is both equal to 50%. If the value after this modification is higher than 1 or lower than 0 it is set to 1 and 0, respectively. In the experiments the constant was set to 0.2.

5.5.5. *Generation of a new population*

First 25 chromosomes are produced by the crossover operator. Each of the 50 chromosomes of the old generation may be selected as a parent of a new chromosome. The selection probability of a chromosome is proportional to its fitness value minus the minimal fitness value of the old generation (i.e. the chromosome with the lowest fitness in the old population has a selection probability equal to 0). The mutation operator is applied to all new 25 chromosomes. Then the 50 old and the 25 new chromosomes are combined into one population. To reduce this population to the original size, the 25 chromosomes with the smallest score values are removed. Note that also newly created chromosomes may be removed.

5.6. Experiments

All ensemble creation methods discussed in Section 5.3 were implemented and tested on a part of the IAM database. This database is publicly available[b] and has been used by several research groups meanwhile.[31] The original version of the

---

[b]http://www.iam.unibe.ch/~zimmerma/iamdb/iamdb.html

database contains complete lines of text as its basic entities, without any segmentation of a line of text into individual words.[31] Meanwhile, however, part of this database has been segmented into individual words.[31,32] A subset of these words was used in the experiments described in this section.

The training set used in the experiments contains 9861 and the test set 1066 word instances over a vocabulary of size 2296. The test set was chosen in such a way that none of its writers was represented in the training set. Hence all experiments described in this paper are writer independent. The total number of writers who contributed to the training and test set is 81. A small sample of words from this database is shown in the Appendix.

Table 5.1 shows the results of the experiments. The recognition rate of the classifier with the original architecture and training set was 66.23 %. Bagging, AdaBoost and random subspace method each created 10 classifiers while the architecture variation method generated only 8 (see Subsection 5.3.5).

Table 5.1.   Recognition rates achieved by the ensemble creation methods under different combination rules. The best result for each ensemble creation method is printed in bold face.

combination	ensemble creation method			
	Bagging	AdaBoost	random subspace	architecture var.
max	65.2 %	63.51 %	62.10 %	45.97 %
perf voting	67.64 %	**68.86 %**	68.11 %	68.39 %
ga voting	**67.92 %**	68.29 %	**68.67 %**	**68.76 %**
ties max	67.35 %	68.29 %	67.54 %	66.98 %
ties perf voting	67.64 %	**68.86 %**	68.11 %	68.57 %
ties ga voting	67.82 %	68.39 %	68.01 %	68.57 %
original	66.23 %			

At first glance, the recognition performance of all systems under consideration may appear quite low. One has to keep in mind, however, that a very difficult classification problem is considered. First of all, we are faced with a pattern recognition task that involves 2296 pattern classes. Secondly, there were almost no constraints imposed on the writers. Hence all kinds of different writing styles and writing instruments are represented in the data set. Thirdly, a large number of writers contributed to the database, and all experiments were run in a writer-independent fashion, i.e. the writers of the training and validation set are disjoint from the writers of the test set.

In the following the results of the different combination schemes are discussed. Obviously the *max* combination performed rather poorly. A possible explanation of this poor performance is the different ranges of score values returned by the classifiers. Because the score is only a likelihood value, it depends on the specific

HMM, and identical score values from different HMMs don't necessarily imply that the word classes which correspond to these values have the same probability of being correct. Note that the performance of the maximum combination rule is especially poor for *architecture var* and *random subspace*, where the HMMs of the classifiers are very different. A possibility to overcome this problem is to normalize the score values for each classifier. However, this possibility has not been explored in the context of this paper and is left to future research.

All other combination schemes lead to an increase of the recognition rate for all ensemble creation methods when compared to the original classifier. The proposed *ga voting* combination was the best scheme for three out of the four ensemble creation methods considered in the tests. The quality of the other schemes relative to each other varied among the tests.

Please note that with the simple weighting mechanism of *perf voting* also good results were achieved. The superior performance of *ga voting* over *perf voting* doesn't hold true any longer for voting with tie handling. Here *ties ga voting* is outperformed by *ties perf voting* for two ensemble creation methods. The reason for this behavior is that the weights calculated by the genetic algorithm are optimized for weighted voting and not for voting with ties handling by weighted voting. Nevertheless *ties ga voting* is clearly superior to the original classifier.

To compare the different ensemble methods in more detail the average performance and the standard deviation of the performances of the individual classifiers were calculated. Those values are shown in Table 5.2.

Table 5.2. Average performance and the standard deviation of the performance of the individual classifiers. The performances of the original classifier is 66.23 %.

measure	ensemble creation method			
	Bagging	AdaBoost	random subspace	architecture var.
average	66.02 %	65.82 %	60.76 %	52.49 %
std. deviation	0.58 %	1.82 %	4.66 %	9.71 %

Bagging produced classifiers with very similar performances and which were in average almost as good as the original classifier. As the performance of the ensemble is not much higher than the performance of the original classifier in respect to the other ensemble methods it may be concluded that the diversity of the classifiers is low.

The classifiers produced by AdaBoost had a wider range of performance than Bagging. Although the average performance of the individual classifier is slightly lower than in Bagging, a much better ensemble performance was achieved. This indicates that the classifiers are quite diverse. AdaBoost was the only ensemble method were *ga voting* did not produce the best result. A possible reason for this is the following. In AdaBoost the performance of the ensemble on the training set is optimized by focusing on "difficult" patterns. Such optimization on the training set normally leads to classifiers which are much better on the training set than on the test set. As the genetic algorithm works with the results of the training set, it may overestimate the performance of some classifiers and produce suboptimal weights. This problem may be overcome by using a separate validation set for calculating the weights.

The average performance of the classifiers produced by *random subspace* was much lower the performance of AdaBoost, yet the ensemble performance was still quite good. So the diversity of classifiers increased again. For *random subspace* the best performance of *ga voting* in respect to the other combination schemes was achieved (*ga voting* had a 0.56 % higher performance than the second best scheme). An analysis of the calculated weights showed that the weights of three out of the ten classifiers were so low that in fact those classifiers were almost irrelevant for the combination. This means that *ga voting* was capable to discover the classifiers which lower the ensemble performance and to exclude them from the combination.

The classifiers produced by *architecture var.* had in average a very low performance (20.26 % lower than the performance of the original classifier). Yet good ensemble results were achieved by this method which leads to the conclusion that the classifiers must be very diverse. For all ensemble methods but *architecture var. perf voting* and *ties perf voting* produced te same results.

When using *ga voting* or *ties ga voting*, in addition to the testing of all classifiers on the training set also the genetic algorithm must be executed. Yet the time consumption of the genetic algorithm is over 1000 times lower than that of the tests on the training set so that this additional overhead is not significant.

5.7. Conclusions

In this paper the recognition of cursively handwritten words was considered. Because of the large number of classes involved and the great variations of words from the same class, which is due to the considerable number of individual handwriting styles, this is regarded a difficult problem in pattern recognition. Multiple classifier systems have demonstrated very good performance in many pattern recognition problems recently. In this paper we have explored a number of classifier ensemble generation methods and related combination schemes. As hidden Markov Models (HMMs) are considered to be one of the most powerful methods for cursive handwriting recognition today, we have focused on those classifier ensemble generation method and combination procedures that are applicable in situations where the base classifiers of a multiple classifier system are given by HMMs.

The combination schemes considered in this paper are based on the assumption that each base classifier only outputs its top-ranked class, together with a score value. Among other combination schemes, two versions of weighted voting were considered. In the first version the weight of each individual base classifier was set equal to its recognition rate on the test set. By contrast a genetic algorithm was used for weight optimization in the second version, using the recognition performance of the whole ensemble as fitness function. In a series of experiments it was shown that for all but one combination scheme all multiple classifier systems could improve the performance of the original, single HMM-based classifier. Among all combination schemes tested in the experiments, for three out of four creation methods, the highest recognition rate was obtained with weighted voting using genetic weight optimization.

The results reported in this paper confirm the suitability of genetic algorithms to find optima or near optima of functions in complex situations. Future works will address the problem of genetic weight optimization for systems including significantly more classifiers. These classifiers may be generated from a single base classifier using methods similar to those considered in the present paper. Alternatively, it is possible to produce the base classifiers by the simultaneous application of several classifier generation procedures. Topic of future work will also be the use of a separate validation set for the calculation of the weights of the classifiers to avoid overfitting problems.

Acknowledgments

The research was supported by the Swiss National Science Foundation (Nr. 20-52087.97). The authors thank Dr. Urs-Victor Marti for providing the handwritten word recognizer and Matthias Zimmermann for the segmentation of a part of the IAM database. Additional funding was provided by the Swiss National Science Foundation NCCR program "Interactive Multimodal Information Management (IM)2" in the Individual Project "Scene Analysis".

Appendix A. Handwritten Word Samples

Labour   for   Federal

discrimination   to

If   spending   yesterday

America   controlled   which

Bureau   members   approval

Commonwealth   negotiating

by   Consultative   associates

References

1. C.Y. Suen, C. Nadal, R. Legault, T.A. Mai, and L. Lam. Computer recognition of unconstrained handwritten numerals. *Proc. of the IEEE*, 80(7):1162–1180, 1992.
2. J.-C. Simon. Off-line cursive word recognition. *Proc. of the IEEE*, 80(7):1150–1161, July 1992.
3. S. Impedovo, P. Wang, and H. Bunke, editors. *Automatic Bankcheck Processing*. World Scientific Publ. Co, Singapore, 1997.
4. A. Kaltenmeier, T. Caesar, J.M. Gloger, and E. Mandler. Sophisticated topology of hidden Markov models for cursive script recognition. In *2nd Int. Conf. on Document Analysis and Recognition, Tsukuba Science City, Japan*, pages 139–142, 1993.
5. G. Kim, V. Govindaraju, and S.N. Srihari. Architecture for handwritten text recognition systems. In S.-W. Lee, editor, *Advances in Handwriting Recognition*, pages 163–172. World Scientific Publ. Co., 1999.
6. U.-V. Marti and H. Bunke. Using a statistical language model to improve the performance of an HMM-based cursive handwriting recognition system. *Int. Journal of Pattern Recognition and Art. Intelligence*, 15:65–90, 2001.
7. J. Kittler and F. Roli, editors. *1st International Workshop on Multiple Classifier Systems*, Cagliari, Italy, 2000. Springer.
8. J. Kittler and F. Roli, editors. *2nd International Workshop on Multiple Classifier Systems*, Cambridge, UK, 2001. Springer.
9. A. Bellili, M. Gilloux, and P. Gallinari. An hybrid MLP-SVM handwritten digit recognizer. In *6th International Conference on Document Analysis and Recognition*, pages 28–32, 2001.
10. A. Brakensiek, J. Rottland, A. Kosmala, and G. Rigoll. Off-line handwriting recognition using various hybrid modeling techniques and character n-grams. In *7th International Workshop on Frontiers in Handwritten Recognition*, pages 343–352, 2000.
11. Y. Huang and C. Suen. Combination of multiple classifiers with measurement values. In *Second International Conference on Document Analysis and Recognition*, pages 598–601, 1993.
12. D. Lee and S. Srihari. Handprinted digit recognition: A comparison of algorithms. In *Third International Workshop on Frontiers in Handwriting Recognition*, pages 153–162, 1993.
13. A. Rahman and M. Fairhurst. An evaluation of multi-expert configurations for the recognition of handwritten numerals. *Pattern Recognition*, 31(9):1255–1273, 1998.
14. X. Wang, V. Govindaraju, and S. Srihari. Multi-experts for touching digit string recognition. In *5.International Conference on Document Analysis and Recognition*, pages 800–803, 1999.
15. L. Xu, A. Krzyzak, and C. Suen. Methods of combining multiple classifiers and their applications to handwriting recognition. *IEEE Transactions on Systems, Man and Cybernetics*, 22(3):418–435, 1992.
16. A. Rahman and M. Fairhurst. Automatic self-configuration of a novel multiple-expert classifier using a genetic algortihm. In *Proceedings of the 7th International Conference on Image Processing and its Applications*, pages 57–61.
17. T. G. Dietterich. Ensemble methods in machine learning. In[7], pages 1–15, 2000.
18. Leo Breiman. Bagging predictors. *Machine Learning 2*, pages 123–140, 1996.

19. T. K. Ho. The random subspace method for constructing decision forests. *IEEE Trans. on Pattern Analysis and Machine Intelligence*, 20(8):832–844, 1998.

20. T.G. Dietterich and E.B. Kong. Machine learning bias, statistical bias, and statistical variance of decision tree algorithms. Technical report, Departement of Computer Science, Oregon State University, 1995.

21. D. Partridge and W. B. Yates. Engineering multiversion neural-net systems. *Neural Computation*, 8(4):869–893, 1996.

22. R. Duin and D. Tax. Experiments with classifier combination rules. In^7, pages 16–29, 2000.

23. C. Suen and L. Lam. Multiple classifier combination methodologies for different output level. In^7, pages 52–66, 2000.

24. J. Kittler, R. Duin, and M. Hatef. On combining classifiers. *IEEE Trans. on Pattern Analysis and Machine Intelligence*, 20:226–239, 1998.

25. T. Huang and C. Suen. Combination of multiple experts for the recognition of unconstrained handwritten numerals. *IEEE Trans. on Pattern Analysis and Machine Intelligence*, 17:90–94, 1995.

26. T.K. Ho, J.J. Hull, and S.N. Srihari. Decision combination in multiple classifier systems. *IEEE Trans. on Pattern Analysis and Machine Intelligence*, 16:66–75, 1994.

27. G. Houle, D. Aragon, R. Smith, M. Shridhar, and D. Kimura. A multilayered corroboration-based check reader. In J. Hull and S. Taylor, editors, *Document Analysis System 2*, pages 495–546. World Scientific, 1998.

28. L. Rabiner. A tutorial on hidden Markov models and selected applications in speech recognition. *Proc. of the IEEE*, 77(2):257–285, 1989.

29. L. Lam, Y.-S. Huang, and C. Suen. Combination of multiple classifier decisions for optical character recognition. In^{41}, pages 79–101.

30. K. Sirlantzis, M. Fairhurst, and M. Hoque. Genetic algorithms for multiclassifier system configuration: A case study in character recognition. In^8, pages 99–108.

31. U. Marti and H. Bunke. The IAM-database: an English sentence database for off-line handwriting recognition. *Int. Journal of Document Analysis and Recognition*, 5:39–46, 2002.

32. M. Zimmermann and H. Bunke. Automatic segmentation of the IAM off-line database for handwritten English text. In *Proc. of the 16th Int. Conference on Pattern Recognition*, volume 4, pages 35–39, Quebec, Canada, 2002.

33. L. Rabiner and B.-H. Juang. *Fundamentals of Speech Recognition*. Prentice Hall, 1993.

34. A. Kundu. Handwritten word recognition using hidden Markov model. In^{41}, pages 157–182.

35. A. Krogh and J. Vedelsby. Neural networks ensembles, cross validation, and active learning. In *Advances in Neural Information Processing Systems*, volume 7, pages 231–238. MIT Press, 1995.

36. Yoav Freund and Robert E. Schapire. A descision-theoretic generalisation of on-line learning and an application to boosting. *Journal of Computer and Systems Sciences*, 55(1):119–139, 1997.

37. J. Holland. *Adaption in Natural and Artificial Systems*. University of Michigan Press, 1975.

38. F.J. Ferri, V. Kadirkamanathan, and J. Kittler. Feature subset search using genetic

algorithms. In *IEE/IEEE Workshop on Natural Algorithms in Signal Processing (NASP 93)*, pages 23/1–23/7, 1993.

39. J. Morris, D. Deaven, and K. Ho. Genetic-algorithm energy minimization for point charges on on a sphere. *Physical Review B*, 53(4):1740–1743, 1996.

40. H. Zhang, B.-T. Mühlenbein. Genetic programming of minimal neural nets using Occam's razor. In S. Forrest, editor, *Proceedings of the 5th International Conference on Genetic Algorithms, ICGA-93*, pages 342–349, 1993.

41. H. Bunke and P. Wang, editors. *Handbook of Character Recognition and Document Image Analysis*. World Scientific, 1997.

CHAPTER 6

DEMPSTER-SHAFER'S BASIC PROBABILITY ASSIGNMENT BASED ON FUZZY MEMBERSHIP FUNCTIONS

A.O. Boudraa[§,†], L. Bentabet[‡,†], F. Salzenstein[+] and. L. Guillon[§]

[§]*IRENav, EA3634, Ecole Navale, 29200 Brest−Armées, France.*
[‡]*Department of Mathematics and Computers Sciences, Sherbrooke University, Canada.*
[+]*Iness, CNRS UMR 7163, ULP Strasbourg I, 67000 Strasbourg, France.*
[†]*CREATIS, CNRS UMR 5515, INSA 502, 69621 Villeurbanne, France.*
E-mail: boudra@ecole-navale.fr[*]

In this paper, an image segmentation method based on Dempster-Shafer evidence theory is proposed. *Basic probability assignment* (*bpa*) is estimated in unsupervised way using pixels fuzzy membership degrees derived from image histogram. No assumption is made about the images data distribution. *bpa* is estimated at pixel level. The effectiveness of the method is demonstrated on synthetic and real images.

6.1. Introduction

Multisensor data fusion is an evolving technology that is analogous to the ongoing cognitive process used by human to integrate data from their senses continually and make inferences about the external world.[1] The information provided by one sensor is usually limited and sometimes of low accuracy. The use of multiple sensors is an alternative to improve accuracy and provide the user with additional information of increased reliability about the environment in which the sensors operates. Applications of data fusion range from medical imaging, scene analysis, Robotics, non destructive evaluation, target tracking to airborne surveillance. Data fusion can be done at different levels of representation: signal, pixel, feature and symbolic levels. In this work we address the problem of pixel-level fusion. Different strategies have been developed for data fusion. The frameworks used for data management are Bayesian inference, Dempster-Shafer (DS) theory[2,3] and

---

[*]Corresponding author.

fuzzy logic inference. DS theory makes inferences from incomplete and uncertain knowledge, provided by different independent knowledge sources. A first advantage of DS theory is its ability to deal with ignorance and missing information. In particular, it provides explicit estimation of imprecision and conflict between information from different sources and can deal with any unions of hypotheses (clusters).[4] This is particularly useful to represent "mixed" pixels in image segmentation problems. The main limitation of Bayesian inference is that it cannot model imprecision about uncertainty measurement. The degree of belief we have on a union of clusters (without being able to discriminate between them) should be shared by all the simples hypotheses, thus penalizing the good one. DS theory handles uncertain and incomplete information through the definition of two dual non additive measures: plausibility and belief. These measures are derived from a density function, m, called *basic probability assignment (bpa)* or *mass function*. This probability assigns evidence to a proposition (hypothesis). The derivation of the *bpa* is the most crucial step since it represents the knowledge about the application as well as the uncertainty incorporates in the selected information source. *pba* definition remains a difficult problem to apply DS theory to practical applications such in image processing. For example, *bpa* may be derived, at pixel level, from probabilities[5–7] or from the distance to cluster centers.[8] In this work *bpa* is estimated in unsupervised way and using fuzzy membership functions to take into account the ambiguity within pixels. This ambiguity is due the possible multi-valued levels of brightness in the image. This indeterminacy is due to inherent vagueness rather than randomness. The number of the clusters of the image is supposed known. In[7] the *bpa* estimation is based on the assumption that the probability distribution of the gray level values (image histogram) is Gaussian model. Our estimation approach does not make any assumption about the probability distribution of the gray level histogram and is not limited to only two sources.

6.2. Dempster-Shafer theory

In DS theory, there is a fixed set of q mutually exclusive and exhaustive elements, called the frame of discernment, which is symbolized by:

$$\Theta = \{H_1, H_2, \ldots, H_q\}$$

The representation scheme, Θ, defines the working space for the desired application since it consists of all propositions for which the information sources can provide evidence. Information sources can distribute mass values on subsets of the frame of discernment, $A_i \in 2^\Theta$ (6.1). An information source assign mass values only to those hypotheses, for which it has direct evidence.

$$0 \leq m(A_i) \leq 1 \tag{6.1}$$

bpa has to fulfill the conditions: $m(\emptyset) = 0$ and $\sum_{A_i \in 2^\Theta} m(A_i) = 1$. If an information source can not distinguish between two propositions, H_i and H_j, it assigns a mass value to their union $(H_i \bigcup H_j)$. Mass distribution from different information sources, $m_j (j = 1, \ldots, d)$, are combined with Dempster's orthogonal rule (6.2). The result is a new distribution, $m(A_k) = (m_1 \oplus m_2 \oplus \ldots \oplus m_d)(A_k)$, which incorporates the joint information provided by the sources.

$$m(A_k) = (1 - K)^{-1} \times \sum_{A_1 \cap A_2 \ldots A_d = A_k} \left(\prod_{1 \leq j \leq d} m_j(A_j) \right) \tag{6.2}$$

$$K = \sum_{A_1 \cap A_2 \ldots A_d = \emptyset} \left(\prod_{1 \leq j \leq d} m_j(A_j) \right) \tag{6.3}$$

K is often interpreted as a measure of conflict between the different sources (6.3) and is introduced as a normalization factor (6.2). The larger K is the more the sources are conflicting and the less sense has their combination. The factor K indicates the amount of evidential conflict. If $K = 0$, this shows complete compatibility, and if $0 < K < 1$, it shows partial compatibility. Finally, the orthogonal sum does not exist when $K = 1$. In this case, the sources are totally contradictory, and it is no longer possible to combine them. In the cases of sources highly conflicting, the normalisation used in the Dempster combination rule can be mistaking, since it artificially increases the masses of the compromise hypotheses.[9] One may suggest as in[9] that the conflict come from the "true" assumption has been forgotten (in the set of hypotheses). However, this cannot occur under closed-world assumption, which is our case, and thus the high conflict level is rather due to the fact that one of the sources is erroneous. In such case, conflict problems should not occur provided that the source information modeling was correctly done, in particular including, when necessary, an ignorance or error term (by affecting non null masses to compound hypotheses and Θ).[10] Finally, we find a normalization process is necessary to satisfy the relations $m(\emptyset) = 0$ and $\sum_{A_i \in 2^\Theta} m(A_i) = 1$ and to preserve the associative properties of the combination rule. From a mass distribution, numerical values can be calculated that characterize the uncertainty and the support of certain hypotheses. Belief (6.4) measures the minimum or necessary support whereas plausibility (6.5) reflects the maximum or potential support for that hypothesis. These two measures, derived from mass values, are respectively defined from 2^Θ to $[0, 1]$:

$$Bel(A_i) = \sum_{A_j \subseteq A_i} m(A_j) \tag{6.4}$$

$$Pls(A_i) = \sum_{A_j \cap A_i \neq \emptyset} m(A_j) \tag{6.5}$$

The equations (6.4) and (6.5) imply that $Bel(.)$ and $Pls(.)$ are dual measures related by

$$Pls(A_i) = 1 - Bel(\neg A_i) \tag{6.6}$$

6.3. Fuzzy approach

Modeling real problems typically involves processing uncertainty of three types. Uncertainty of probabilistic nature, uncertainty due to the lack of specification and fuzziness. Traditionally nonfuzzy uncertainties are handled by probabilistic methods such as Bayesian networks and DS theory while fuzziness uncertainty is modeled by fuzzy set theory. Fuzzy uncertainty deals with situations where boundaries of the sets (clusters) under consideration are not sharply defined (partial occurrence of an event). On the other hand, for nonfuzzy uncertainties there is no ambiguity about set boundaries, but rather, about the belongingness of elements or events to crisp sets. Real data are often imprecise and contain some ambiguity caused by the way they have been obtained. Origins of this kind of ambiguity may be inaccuracy of the used devices involving an error of measurement of fuzzy nature. In image processing, images which are mappings of natural scenes are always accompanied by an amount of fuzziness due to imprecision of gray values and ambiguity created by the mapping mechanism. There are many situations where we often face at the same time fuzzy and nonfuzzy uncertainties. This suggests to combine DS and fuzzy sets frameworks. Thus, the goal of this work is to estimate *bpas* using fuzzy membership functions which capture vagueness.

Let $X = \{x_1, x_2, \ldots, x_{MN}\}$ be an image set of size $M \times N$ with L levels, $g = 0, 1, 2, \ldots, L - 1$, and x_{mn} is the gray level of a (m, n)th pixel in X. Let $\mu(X) = \{\mu(x_1), \mu(x_2), \ldots, \mu(x_{MN})\}$ be the corresponding fuzzy membership degrees derived from X. $\mu(.)$ is obtained by operating a fuzzifier on X. This fuzzifier performs a mapping from crisp data values (X) into a fuzzy set represented by $\mu(X)$. We denote by $\mu_i(x_{mn})$ the fuzzy membership degree of pixel x_{mn} to fuzzy subset (cluster) i of X. In this work, Fuzzy C-means (FCM) algorithm[11] is used as fuzzifier. FCM has an advantage of clustering data without the need for a statistical model of the data. For image fuzzification we use an histogram based gray-level fuzzification.[12] Thus, we use gray level g instead of the intensity of (m, n)th pixel x_{mn} (Figure 1). The FCM only operates on the histogram and consequently is faster than the conventional version,[11] which processes the whole data set X

6.4. Basic probability assignment

In image segmentation problem, Θ is the set of all the clusters of the image, $|\Theta| = C$ is the number of clusters and 2^C contains all the possible unions of clusters. The hypotheses considered in DS formulation are: $\emptyset$ (whose mass is null), simple hypothesis H_i and compound hypotheses $H_j \bigcup \ldots H_l$. For the choice of the *bpa* of H_k and H_l, the following strategy is used :

(1) Affecting a non null mass to $H_k \bigcup H_l$ if H_k and H_l are not discriminated on the image (not distinguishable by the sensor) (Figure 1). There is an ambiguity between H_k and H_l. In this case affecting a pixel with gray level g to cluster k or l using of fuzzy membership rule is not valuable ($\mu_k(g) \approx \mu_l(g)$).

(2) Affecting a null mass to $H_k \bigcup H_l$ if H_k and H_l are discriminated on the image. There is no or less ignorance about clusters k and l.

In performing a fuzzy clustering on image histogram[12] the intersection between two fuzzy membership degree curves $\mu_k(g)$ and $\mu_l(g)$ to two consecutive centroids V_k and V_l (Figure 1), occurs in one and only one point. This point corresponds to a high degree of ambiguity and then to maximum value of $m(H_k \bigcup H_l)$. For example, at pixel with gray level $g = 139$ information source can not distinguish between between clusters H_2 and H_3, $m(H_2 \bigcup H_3)(g = 139) \neq 0$, while at pixel with gray level $g = 50$ there is no ambiguity to affect $g = 50$ to cluster H_1 and thus $m(H_2 \bigcup H_3)(g = 50) = 0$, (Figure 1). The *bpa* are normalized such that $\sum\limits_{H_i \in 2^C} m(H_i) = 1$. Using image histogram, for each level g, and according the C values, different cases are distinguished. For more convenience, we use the following notations:

$$\beta = \max_{1 \leq i \leq C} (\mu_i(g)) \tag{6.7}$$

$$\alpha = \beta - \min_{1 \leq i \leq C} (\mu_i(g)) \tag{6.8}$$

$$I = \{1, \ldots, C\}$$

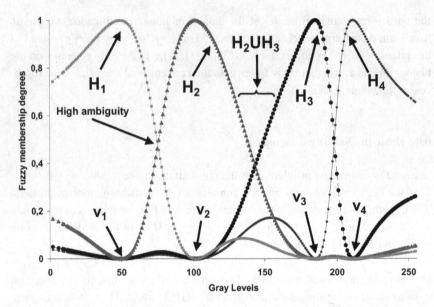

Fig. 6.1.   Plot of fuzzy membership functions generated by FCM algorithm (RX image). V_i stands for the centroid of the ith cluster.

where

$$\sum_{i=1}^{C} \mu_i(g) = 1$$

I is the set of cluster indices and its cardinal is the number of clusters, C. $\arg(\beta) = \arg(\max\limits_{1 \le i \le C} \mu_i(g))$ is the maximum fuzzy membership defuzzification rule. The pixel with gray level g is affected to cluster $\arg(\beta)$.

In the proposed fusion scheme for all C values, both simples and compound hypotheses are taken into account. In the framework of histogram based segmentation and for $C \le 3$, ambiguity can not occur between all the C classes. Thus, a null mass is affected to the union of hypotheses (Eqs. (6.12),(6.16),(6.22),(6.25)). For $C = 2$, in general there is at least one pixel where the two classes (hypotheses) are not sufficiently distinguishable form each other so that a new compound hypotheses is created with a non null mass (Eq. (6.9)). However, if the two hypotheses are well distinguishable from each other, the mass value of their union is null (Eq. (6.20)). For all C values, and for all cases (with less or high ambiguity), the mass value affected to single hypothesis proportional to the corresponding fuzzy membership degree (Eqs. (6.10),(6.13),(6.17),(6.18),(6.19),(6.23),(6.26)).

The mass value affected to compound hypotheses is proportional to the sum of their fuzzy membership degrees (Eqs. (6.11),(6.14),(6.15),(6.21),(6.24)). In each case, the normalization condition must be verified.

- If there is high ambiguity to affect a pixel with gray level g to cluster k or l:
  $| \mu_k(g) - \mu_l(g) | \leq \xi$ then

  (1) For $C = 2$

  $$m(\bigcup_{i=1}^{C} H_i)(g) = \alpha \tag{6.9}$$

  $$m(H_i)(g) = [1 - \alpha] \times \mu_i(g) \; i \in I \tag{6.10}$$

  (2) For $C = 3$

  $$m(H_k \cup H_l)(g) = \alpha \times [\mu_k(g) + \mu_l(g)] \; (k,l)_{k \neq l} \in I \tag{6.11}$$

  $$m(\bigcup_{i=1}^{C} H_i)(g) = 0 \tag{6.12}$$

  $$m(H_i)(g) = [1 - m(H_k \cup H_l)(g)] \times \mu_i(g) \tag{6.13}$$

  where $i, (k,l)_{k \neq l} \in I$

  (3) For $C > 3$

  $$m(H_k \cup H_l)(g) = \alpha \times [\mu_k(g) + \mu_l(g)] \; (k,l)_{k \neq l} \in I \tag{6.14}$$

  $$m(\bigcup_{\substack{i=1 \\ i \neq k, i \neq l}}^{C} H_i)(g) = \alpha \times \sum_{\substack{i=1 \\ i \neq k, i \neq l}}^{C} \mu_i(g) \tag{6.15}$$

  $$m(\bigcup_{i=1}^{C} H_i)(g) = 0 \tag{6.16}$$

  $$m(H_t)(g) = [1 - m(\bigcup_{\substack{i=1 \\ i \neq k, i \neq l}}^{C} H_i)(g) - m(H_k \cup H_l)(g)]$$
  $$\times \mu_t(g) \tag{6.17}$$

  where $t, (k,l)_{k \neq l} \in I$

- If there is less or no ambiguity to affect a pixel with gray level g to cluster k:
  $| \mu_k(g) - \mu_l(g) | > \xi$ then

(1) For $C = 2$

$$m(H_l)(g) = \mu_l(g) \times (\mu_k(g) - \mu_l(g)) \, (k, l)_{k \neq l} \in I \quad (6.18)$$
$$m(H_k)(g) = 1 - \mu_l(g) \times (\mu_k(g) - \mu_l(g)) \, (k, l)_{k \neq l} \in I \quad (6.19)$$
$$m(\bigcup_{i=1}^{C} H_i)(g) = 0 \quad (6.20)$$

(2) For $C = 3$

$$m(H_k \cup H_l)(g) = \alpha \times [\mu_k(g) + \mu_l(g)] \, (k, l)_{k \neq l} \in I \quad (6.21)$$
$$m(\bigcup_{i=1}^{C} H_i)(g) = 0 \quad (6.22)$$
$$m(H_i)(g) = [1 - m(H_k \cup H_l)(g)] \times \mu_i(g) \quad (6.23)$$

where $i, (k, l)_{k \neq l} \in I$

(3) For $C > 3$

$$m(\bigcup_{\substack{i=1 \\ i \neq k}}^{C} H_i)(g) = \sum_{\substack{i=1 \\ i \neq k}}^{C} \mu_i(g) \times (\beta - \mu_i(g)) \quad (6.24)$$

$$m(\bigcup_{i=1}^{C} H_i)(g) = 0 \quad (6.25)$$

$$m(H_t)(g) = (1 - m(\bigcup_{\substack{i=1 \\ i \neq k}}^{C} H_i)(g)) \times \mu_t(g) \, t \in I \quad (6.26)$$

ξ is a threshold value. We make assumption that the images are well registered. Since, images are clustered separately then a spatial correspondence between the labels of clusters of different images is necessary so that pixels representing the same physical object of the scene may be superimposed and thus to be able to correctly combine the different information sources (6.2). The label-to-label mapping strategy is described in.[13] The use of image histogram loose spatial information about pixels arrangement and the spatial correlation between adjacent pixels. Furthermore, the membership resulted from the FCM algorithm are considerably troublesome in a very noisy environment. To reduce noise effect and to improve the classification results contextual processing is performed. Thus, before *bpas* estimation, membership value of each pixel is updated by using its neighborhood contextual membership values. In this work, a 3×3 neighborhood mean and median filters are used.[13]

6.5. Results

The proposed data fusion method is first tested on synthetic images. Two images, corrupted by Gaussian noise, simulating US and RX acquisitions are shown in Figure 2. Each image contains four clusters (C=4). In the US image (Fig. 2(a)), one region (smallest thickness) is confused with the background and in the RX image (Fig. 2(b)) the greatest thickness is under-exposed and the thicker regions are not well distinguished. The aim here is to exploit, through using the proposed data fusion technique, the redundant and complementary information of the two images in order to correctly segment the image in four clusters. The maximum of plausibility is used as a decision rule. Figures 2(e) and 2(f) show the DS fusion result obtained using median and average filters respectively. ξ is set 0.05. Note that within the segmented regions, some artifacts are present (Figs. 2(e)-(f)), reflecting the influence of noise present in the initial images (Figs. 2(a)-(b)) on final segmentation. Both filters give a good segmentation result but the regions given by the average operation are more homogeneous than in the median case. The four regions are well brought out and this shows that informations provided by two images are well exploited by the fusion scheme. This result also shows that the estimated *bpas* are a good modeling of the information associated to simple and compound hypotheses. This also shows the interest of taking into account the contextual information in *bpas* estimation. In order to get a better insight into the actual ability of the DS fusion based segmentation, in comparison with conventional algorithms which exploit information only from one image, we give in Fig. 2(c) and 2(d) a comparison example. The segmentation results in Figs 2(c) and 2(d) have been obtained using the FCM algorithm. They correspond respectively to the US and RX images respectively. When segmentation is performed with one image, we observe that 23.94% and 34.94% of pixels have been mis-segmented for RX and US images respectively. Segmentation errors have been largely reduced when exploiting simultaneously the two images through the use of DS fusion approach including spatial information. Indeed, in the latter case, only 0.95% of pixels have been mis-segmented. This good performance difference between these two types of segmentation approaches can also be easily assessed by visually comparing the segmentation results. Figure 3 illustrates the application of the proposed fusion scheme to human brain Magnetic Resonance (MR) of three patients with Multiple Sclerosis (MS) lesions (Figures 3(a)-(f)). Figures 3(a)-(c) represent T_2-weighted images and Figures 3(d)-(f) the corresponding Proton Density (PD) weighted images. Each pair of images (T_2,PD) are strongly correlated and also spatially registered, and show the MS lesions as hypersignal regions. The fused images are shown in Figures 3(g)-(i). In each patient, regions such as white matter, grey matter, cerebrospinal fluid (CSF), background are correctly segmented. This is of great interest in medical applications in particular the estimation of size and volume of the brain tissues. However, the proposed scheme is not able to separate the MS lesions region from CSF (Fig. 3(g)-(i)). This is due essentially to the fact that pixels of CSF and MS lesions share the same intensities.

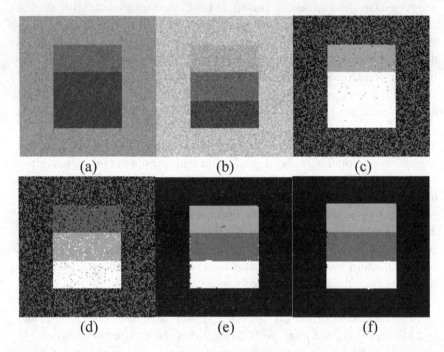

(a)   (b)   (c)

(d)   (e)   (f)

Fig. 6.2.   (a) US image. (b) RX image. (c) Fuzzy segmentation of US image. (d) Fuzzy segmentation of RX image. Fused image obtained using median value (e) and average value of the membership degrees (f).

6.6. Conclusion

In this paper, an original data fusion scheme to multisensor images segmentation based on the DS and fuzzy logic theories to take into account nonfuzzy and fuzzy uncertainties is proposed. This methodology consists in estimating basic probability assignment using fuzzy membership degrees derived from gray-level image histogram. A contextual processing is introduced to integrate the spatial correlation between adjacent pixels. The obtained results on synthetic and medical images are encouraging. In this work, we make assumption that images are well registered. The presented results are limited to only one modality. Extensive tests on real data and analysis of several decision rules are necessary in order to evaluate the robustness of the method. Only filters with 3×3 size are used. Thus, different window sizes must be tested to show their effect on the fusion results.

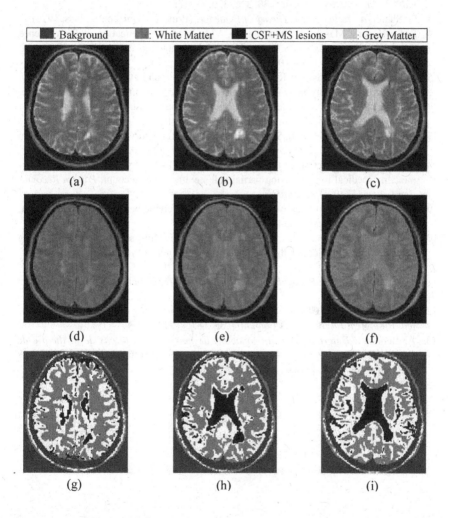

Fig. 6.3.   Segmentation result of MR images obtained in 3 patients with MS lesions. (a), (b), (c) T_2 weighted images. (d), (e), (f) PD weighted images. (g), (h), (i) DS fusion result of the three patients using average operation.

References

1. D.L. Hall, *Mathematical Techniques in Multisensor Data Fusion*. (Artech House, MA, 1992).
2. A. Dempster, Upper and lower probabilities induced by a multivalued mapping, *Annals of Mathematical Statistics* **38**, 325–339, (1967).
3. G. Shafer, *A Mathematical Theory of Evidence*. (Princeton University Press, 1976).
4. S. Le Hegarat-Mascle, I. Bloch and D. Vidal-Madjar, Application of DS evidence theory to unsupervised classification in multiple remote sensing, *IEEE Trans. Geosci. Remote Sensing*. **35**, 1018–1031, (1997).
5. T. Lee, J.A. Richards and R.H. Swain, Probabilistic and evidential approaches for multisource data analysis, *IEEE Trans. Geosci. Remote Sensing*. **25**, 283-293, (1987).
6. F. Salzenstein and A.O. Boudraa, Unsupervised multisensor data fusion approach, *Proc. IEEE ISSPA*. Kuala Lumpur, **1**, 152–155, (2001).
7. M. Rombaut and Y. M. Zhu, Study of Dempster-Shafer theory for image segmentation applications, *Image and vision computing*. **20** (1), 15–23, (2002).
8. I. Bloch, Some aspect of Dempster-Shafer evidence theory for classification of multimodality medical images taking partial volume effect into account, *Pattern Recognition Letters*. **17**, 905–916, (1996).
9. P. Smets, The combination of evidence in the transferable belief model, *IEEE Trans. Patt. Anal. Mach. Intell*. **12**, 447–458, (1990).
10. S. Le Hegarat-Mascle, D. Richard and C. Ottle Multi-scale data fusion using Demspter-Shafer evidence theory, *Integrated Computer-Aided Engineering*. **10**, 9–22, (2003).
11. J.C. Bezdek, *Pattern Recognition with Fuzzy Objective Function Algorithms*, Plenum Press, NY, (1981).
12. A.O. Boudraa and P. Clarysse, Fast fuzzy gray level image segmentation method, *Medical Biological Engineering Computing*. **35**, 686, (1997).
13. A. Bentabet, *Détermination des fonctions de masses dans le cas de la théorie de l'évidence par coalescence floue*. (MSc. Dissertation, Institut National des Sciences Appliquées de Lyon, France, 1999).

CHAPTER 7

AUTOMATIC INSTRUMENT LOCALIZATION IN
LAPAROSCOPIC SURGERY

Joan Climent and Pere Mars

Computer Eng. and Automatic Control dept. (UPC),
Pau Gargallo,5. 08028 Barcelona. Spain,
E-mail: Juan.Climent@upc.es

This paper presents a tracking algorithm for automatic instrument localization in robotically assisted laparoscopic surgery. We present a simple and robust system that does not need the presence of artificial marks, or special colours to distinguish the instruments. So, the system enables the robot to track the usual instruments used in laparoscopic operations. Since the instruments are normally the most structured objects in laparoscopic scenes, the algorithm uses the Hough transform to detect straight lines in the scene. In order to distinguish among different instruments or other structured elements present in the scene, motion information is also used. We give in this paper a detailed description of all stages of the system.

7.1. Introduction

Laparoscopic surgery is a minimally invasive surgical procedure. The surgeon inserts instruments and a laparoscope into the patient's body through multiple incisions, and performs the operation viewing the images displayed on a video screen. The main problem of such a technique lies in the difficulties of mutual understanding between the surgeon and the camera assistant. The camera assistant also gets tired in long operations and the image becomes unstable. Several robotized assistance systems have been developed to deal with these new problems.[10–12] All different approaches presented in the literature use image processing techniques to track the instrument so that it is always centered in the displayed image. Some works[13] use colour information, but because of the high variability of colours in different scenes, the instruments must be coloured with an artificial colour. Others[12] use instruments that present artificial marks. We present in this paper a system that tracks instruments that have neither been marked nor coloured. No

specific marks are needed; the system works with the usual surgical instruments.
The system is based on a sequence of different image processing techniques. The
objective of this paper is to show, in detail, the way that these techniques have
been used, and the results obtained.

7.2. System Description

A system overview is shown in Fig. 7.1.

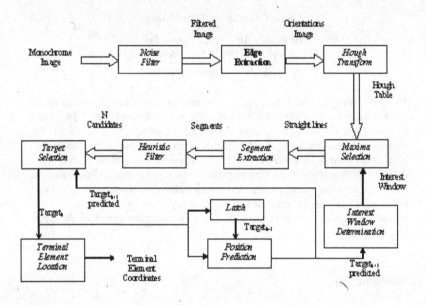

Fig. 7.1.   System Overview.

The original image is filtered in order to reduce the influence of noise. To
extract edge orientations, a classical edge extractor is applied afterwards. The
straight lines present in the image are detected using the Hough transform. The
most prominent lines are selected. All straight lines that satisfy some heuristic
criteria are considered as possible targets. According to the last position of the
instrument in the scene, the best candidate between straight lines selected is chosen, and its ending point marks the position on the terminal element. Once the
actual position of the instrument is determined, its position in the next frame will
be predicted. This position determines the location of the processing window of
the Hough table for the next frame. A description of all these stages is detailed in
the following subsections.

7.2.1. *Filtering stage*

The effects of noise on the results of the transformation are a matter of concern when dealing with real image data. Such noise may be due to random corruption of the signal during the data acquisition process or it may be a normally distributed random error in the localization of image points due to the effects of digitizing continuous data. The characterization and prediction of the effects of noise have been studied extensively.[3,4]

In order to reduce the effects of noise on the edge orientation determination, a Gaussian filter is applied to the original image in this first stage:

$$h(x, y) = \frac{1}{2\pi\sigma^2} e^{-\frac{(x^2+y^2)}{2\sigma^2}} \tag{7.1}$$

As a smoothing mask, it has optimal properties in a particular sense: it removes small-scale texture and noise as effectively as possible for a given spatial extent in the image.

Another interesting property of the Gaussian is that it is rotationally symmetric. This means that in all directions smoothing will be the same; there will not be distortion in any direction. Since we are dealing with orientations, this isotropic property is mandatory.

Finally, the Gaussian filter is separable:

$$h(x, y) = \frac{1}{2\pi\sigma^2} e^{-\frac{(x^2+y^2)}{2\sigma^2}} = \frac{1}{\sqrt{2\pi}\sigma} e^{-\frac{x^2}{2\sigma^2}} \cdot \frac{1}{\sqrt{2\pi}\sigma} e^{-\frac{y^2}{2\sigma^2}} = h_{1D}(x) \cdot h_{1D}(y) \tag{7.2}$$

A 2D Gaussian convolution can be implemented using two orthogonal 1D Gaussian convolutions. Thus, the computational cost of the filtering stage is linear instead of quadratic.

Fig. 7.2(b) shows the image output after the Gaussian filtering with a standard deviation $\sigma = 1.5$ and a kernel size of 7.

7.2.2. *Edge orientation extraction*

Edge orientations are needed to compute the Hough transform. The prior filtering stage is mandatory since the precision in the orientation of gradient operators is very sensitive to noise.

For extracting edge orientation a simple gradient operator is used. Given the filtered image f(x,y), an approximation of the gradient direction $\theta(x, y)$ is computed as:

$$\theta(x,y) = atan\frac{\Delta y}{\Delta x} \qquad (7.3)$$

where $\Delta y = f(x, y - 1) - f(x, y + 1)$ and $\Delta x = f(x - 1, y) - f(x + 1, y)$

The Sobel operator is not used in this stage. The justification is quite simple. The Sobel operator performs local smoothing. In our application there is no need of new smoothing since the image has been filtered previously. So, the computational load may be reduced by using the central difference masks instead.

The computational load is also reduced by considering only pixels whose gradient magnitude is above a certain threshold, Th. Fig. 7.2(c) shows the orientation image. Orientations have been quantified in 256 levels.

7.2.3. *Hough transform computation*

Paul Hough introduced the Hough transform in 1962.[1] It is known that it gives good results in the detection of straight lines and other shapes even in the presence of noise and occlusion.

Our vision system detects the surgical instruments using the Hough transform. Since the instruments show a structured shape, mainly straight lines, the Hough transform is a powerful tool to detect them. There can be found in the literature other tracking applications that also use the Hough transform; see, for example.[2] Other works within the medical imaging discipline that make use of the Hough transform include.[6-8]

At this stage, the normal parameterization of the Hough transform is used to extract the most significant straight lines in the scene.

$$x\cos\theta + ysin\theta = \rho \qquad (7.4)$$

where ρ and θ are the length and orientation of the normal vector to the line from the image origin. Each straight line is uniquely defined by ρ and θ, and for every point in the original image (x,y) it is possible to create a mapping from feature to the parametric space.

If we divide the parameter space into a number of discrete accumulator cells, we can collect 'votes' in the (ρ, θ) space from each data point in the (x, y) space. Peaks in (ρ, θ) space will mark the equations of lines of co-linear points in the (x, y) space.

Interested readers can find a good survey about Hough transform[5] . A book which makes easily assimilated theory and advice available to the non specialist concerning state of the art Hough transform techniques is.[9]

For every pixel in the image, the gradient direction has been determined in the last stage. Thus, the computation of distance ρ, becomes a single operation. Edge direction information made available at the edge detection stage is the most commonly used constraint on the range of parameters to be calculated.[14]

The (ρ, θ) space has been implemented using a 256x256 array of accumulators. All pixels, except those whose gradient magnitude is below the threshold Th, are mapped to one point in the (ρ, θ) space. The corresponding cells in the accumulator are incremented every time a new pixel is mapped into it. Fig. 7.2(d) shows a 3D representation of the Hough table in the (ρ, θ) space.

Peaks in the (ρ, θ) space correspond to the presence of straight lines in the scene. The maximum peak is selected as the longest straight line in the image.

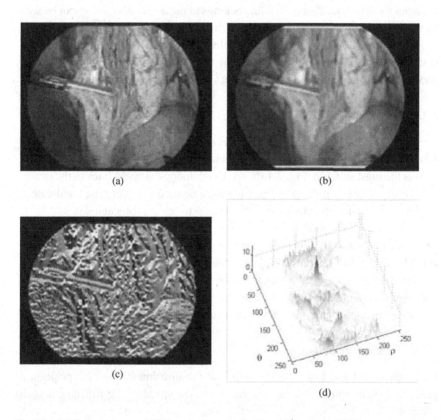

Fig. 7.2. (a) Original image. (b) Filtered image. (c) Gradient orientations. (d) 3D representation of Hough table.

7.2.4. *Segment extraction*

One useful property of the Hough transform is that the pixels that lie on the line do not need to be contiguous. On the other hand, it can also give misleading results when objects happen to be aligned by chance. Some pixels are not a part of surgeon's tool but noise pixels or some other edge with the same line components.

The tool ending is determined by the loss of continuity in gradient direction along the straight line. Pixels along the straight line are traced until their orientations present a significant change with respect to the line orientation. For every pixel on the line we compute the difference between its gradient direction and line direction. This difference is considered as a local error. Then this error is averaged along the line. Fig. 7.3(a) shows the error in the orientations of all pixels along the main straight line. Part of this line belongs to the surgeon's tool. It can be seen that the continuity in orientations is lost when the tool ends.

Fig. 7.3(b) shows, in white, pixels selected as belonging to the tool, and, in black, those belonging to the background. The tool ending can then be located once the pixels not belonging to the correct segment have been removed.

7.2.5. *Heuristic filter*

The longest line in the scene does not always belong to the instrument. Thus, some extra information is needed to decide which one among the possible candidate lines is the most suitable. Fig. 7.4 shows the ten longest straight lines in the image. A heuristic filter and motion information must be used to reject false candidates.

Some heuristic information is used in order to reject false candidates.

The length of the straight line must be greater than a minimum fixed value.

Instruments always come into scene from out of the field of view of the camera. Thus, straight lines must finish in a boundary of the scene.

Since the tracking system focuses the area of interest in the centre of the image, only radial lines are candidates to be selected as surgeon's tools.

All candidates that do not satisfy these conditions are automatically rejected.

7.2.6. *Position prediction*

Given the actual and last frame positions of the instrument, the next position is predicted. A first order model is used. First, the speed of the instrument v_k is computed from two consecutive positions x_{k-1} and x_k, with being $x_k = (\rho, \theta)$ the position in Hough table at the k-th iteration:

$$v_k = x_k - x_{k-1} \tag{7.5}$$

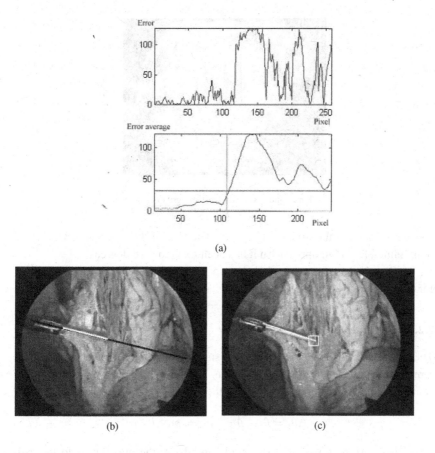

(a)

(b)   (c)

Fig. 7.3.   (a) Error line profile. (b) Segment extraction. (c) Tool ending location.

Afterwards, the next position xk+1 is estimated:

$$\hat{x}_{k+1} = x_k + v_k T \qquad (7.6)$$

where T is the sample period between two processed frames. We process a frame in 125 ms.

There must be certain continuity between the location of the peak in the (ρ, θ) space of the current frame and the location of the peak in the last frame. Thus, not all the Hough table must be computed at every iteration, we only process those pixels whose (ρ, θ) pair is within a window of acceptable values. Once the next position $\hat{x}_{k+1}$ has been estimated, the processing window is centered at this new position for the next frame. The objective of this processing window is, of

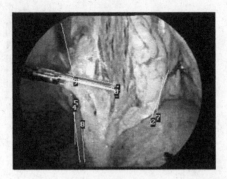

Fig. 7.4. Ten candidates, the longest straight lines in the image.

course, to increase the processing speed. The size of the processing window is programmable. In our application it has been fixed to ± 20 degrees.

The estimated position is also used to select the best target from the list of candidates.

7.2.7. *Target selection*

The position $\hat{x}_{k+1}$ estimated in the last stage, will determine which one of the remaining candidates is the most probable. The error between the positions of all candidates, and the estimated position is then computed:

$$\Delta\theta_i = \theta_i - \widehat{\theta}_T, \Delta\rho_i = \rho_i - \widehat{\rho}_T \tag{7.7}$$

Once these errors are computed for all candidates, the one closest to the estimated position and with the highest value in the Hough transform accumulator is selected. The function used is:

$$d_i = \frac{\text{valHough}_i}{max(\text{valHough})} \cdot \left(1 - \frac{|\Delta\theta_i|}{max\,|\Delta\theta_i|}\right) \cdot \left(1 - \frac{|\Delta\rho_i|}{max\,|\Delta\rho_i|}\right) \tag{7.8}$$

where max(valHough) is the absolute maximum of the Hough table values.

7.3. Results

Our vision system has been implemented on a PC system with a 1.7Ghz. Pentium III processor and a commercial image acquisition board. Processing time for the complete process is 125 ms., which is suitable for a real-time tracking application. The size of the processed images is 768x576 pixels.

Table 7.1. Parameter values.

Parameter	Description	Value
Th	Minimum gradient module	10
$max\,|\Delta\theta_i|$	Maximum variation of θ between consecutive frames	20
$max\,|\Delta\rho_i|$	Maximum variation of ρ between consecutive frames	35

Table 7.2. Static test results.

Longest lines in scene	% of correct identifications
1st	77%
2nd	11%
3rd	4%
4th	4%
5th	2%
6th	1%
7th	1%
8th	0%
9th	0%
10th	0%

Some parameters are configurable and must be tuned by the user. We show in Table 7.1 the values assigned in our application:

Table 7.2 shows the results of an experiment designed to show the percentage of cases in which the correct tool corresponds to the straight lines detected. A set of 128 images extracted from a real operation video have been used for the experiment. The experiment has been divided in two stages: the first one is a static test, and uses only the information provided by the image itself. The second one is a dynamic test, and it takes into account the information obtained from the previous images of the video sequence. The static test uses only the information given by the Hough transform. The dynamic test uses the static information plus the position prediction detailed in Sec. 7.2.6.

For each image, the ten top values of the Hough table are selected and sorted by decreasing order. The coordinates (ρ, θ) of these maxima in the Hough table correspond to ten different straight lines in the image. The objective of the experiment is to show when the correct surgeon's tool straight line corresponds with the lines detected in the Hough transform stage. The first column of Table 7.2 are the longest straight lines in the Hough transform table, the second are the probabilities that these lines correspond with the correct tool.

The dynamic test takes into account the information obtained from the previ-

ous frames in the sequence, a position prediction (described in Sec. 7.2.6) and a
target selection (described in Sec. 7.2.7) are performed in order to detect the tool.
Using dynamic information the rate of correct detections goes up to 99%. Finally,
Fig. 7.5 and Fig. 7.6 show the results obtained with other different images.

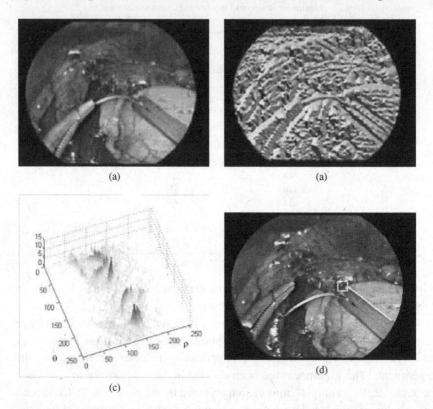

Fig. 7.5.   (a) Original image. (b) Gradient orientations. (c) 3D representation of Hough table (d) Tool
ending location.

7.4. Conclusion

We have presented a detailed description of all stages of a vision system. This
system performs a real-time tracking of the surgical tools in laparoscopic operations. The method presented uses the Hough transform to detect the presence of
structured objects in the scene. This technique has permitted the system to work
without colour restrictions or special marks on the instruments.

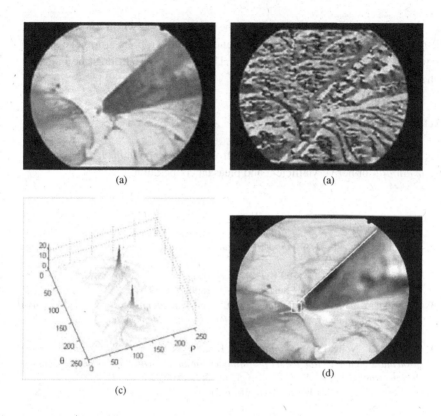

Fig. 7.6. (a) Original image. (b) Gradient orientations. (c) 3D representation of Hough table (d) Tool ending location.

The system can track tools whose orientations are within a 20 degrees interval between two consecutive frames. Since eight frames are processed per second, this means that angular speed of the tracked tool must be below 160 degrees per second.

We get some false detections in some conflictive cases, due to:

- Tool goes out of the field of view. We get a very short straight line when the tool progressively goes out from the visible area. This problem will be solved when the robotic arm closes the loop and surgeon tools are always into the visible area.

- Low contrast between the tool and the background. This problem is present in areas with bad quality illumination. These areas are not suitable to perform any surgical task.

- Sudden movements of the tool. The constraints shown in Table 7.1 must be respected. Anyway, it is not recommended that the robotic arm make sudden movements in a live surgical operation. The tracking system must be inhibited when such movements occur.

Acknowledgements

The authors thank Dr. Silvina Thevenet, from the *Universidad Nacional del Centro in Tandil*, for her very efficient and pleasant cooperation.

References

1. Hough P. V. C. (1962), *Method and Means for Recognising Complex Patterns*, (U.S. Patent No. 3069654)
2. Ermolin and.Ljustin, C. (1990) *The use of image processing in tracking, Nucl. Instrum,Methods Phys. Res.*,(Sect. A) Vol. A 289(3) pp. 592–596.
3. Grimson, W. E .L.and Huttenlochner, D. P. (1990). *On the sensitivity of the Hough transform for object recognition*, IEEE Pattern Anal. Mach. Intell, Vol. 10 pp. 25–274.
4. Hunt, D. J., Nolte, L. W., Reibman, A. R and.Ruedger,W. H. (1990) *Hough transform and signal detection theory performance for images with additive noise*, Comput. Vision Graphics Image Process. Vol. 52 pp. 386-401.
5. Leavers, V. F. (1993) *Which Hough transform?*, CVGIP: Image Unders. Vol. 58(2) pp.250-264.
6. Nixon, M. S., Hames T. K,. Martin P., Powell, S. and.de Pavia, S. (1992) *3-D arterial modelling using feature extraction in ultrasound images*, Int. Conf. on Image Processing and its Applications, (Maastricht, Netherlands), pp. 37–376.
7. Nixon, M. S and Hames, T. K. 1993 *New technique for 3D artery modelling by noninvasive ultrasound*, IEE Proc. I Commun. Speech and Vision, Vol. 140(1) pp. 8–94.
8. Thomas, A. D. H.,Davies, T. and Luxmoore, A. R. (1992) *The Hough transform for locating cell nuclei*, IEE Colloquium on Applications of Image Processing in Mass Health Screening, (London), pp. 81–84.
9. Leavers, V. F. (1992) *Shape Detection in Computer Vision Using the Hough Transform, Springer-Verlag, New* (York/Berlin)
10. Hurteau, R., DeSantios, S., Begin, E. and Gagner, M. (1994) *Laparoscopic Surgery assisted by a robotic cameraman: Concept and experimental results*, Proc.IEEE Int. Conf. Robotics and Automation , (San Diego), pp.2286-2289
11. Taylor, R. H., Funda, J., Eldridge, B.,Gomory, S. and Gruben, K. (1995) *A telerobotic assistant for laparoscopic surgery*, IEEE Engineering in Medicine and Biology, Vol. 14 (3) pp.279-288,
12. Casals, A., Amat, J., Prats, D., Laporte, E. (1995) *Vision guided robotic system for laparoscopic surgery*, Proc.Int. Conf. Advanced Robots, pp.33-36, Catalonia,

13. Wei, G., Arbter, K., Hirzinge, G. (1997) *Real-time visual servoing for laparoscopic surgery, IEEE Engineering in Medicine and Biology*, Vol. 16 (1) pp. 40–45,
14. Ballard, D. H. (1981) *Generalizing the Hough transform to detect arbitrary shapes, Pattern Recognit*, Vol. 13(2), pp. 111–122,

CHAPTER 8

A FAST FRACTAL IMAGE COMPRESSION METHOD BASED ON ENTROPY

M. Hassaballah*, M. M. Makky* and Youssef B. Mahdy [+]

*Mathematics Department, Faculty of Science, South Valley University,
Qena, Egypt
E-mail: m.hassaballah@mailer.svu.edu.eg
[+]Faculty of Computers &Information, Assuit University, Assuit, Egypt
E-mail: mahdy@aun.edu.eg

Fractal image compression gives some desirable properties like resolution independence, fast decoding, and very competitive rate-distortion curves. But still suffers from a (sometimes very) high encoding time, depending on the approach being used. This paper presents a method to reduce the encoding time of this technique by reducing the size of the domain pool based on the Entropy value of each domain block. Experimental results on standard images show that the proposed method yields superior performance over conventional fractal encoding.

1. Introduction

With the ever increasing demand for images, sound, video sequences, computer animations and volume visualization, data compression remains a critical issue regarding the cost of data storage and transmission times. While JPEG currently provides the industry standard for still image compression, there is ongoing research in alternative methods. Fractal image compression [1,2] is one of them. It has generated much interest due to its promise of high compression ratios at good decompression quality and it enjoys the advantage of very fast decompression. Another advantage of fractal image compression is its multi-resolution property, i.e. an image can be decoded at higher or lower resolutions than the original, and it is possible to "zoom-in" on sections of the image. These properties made it a very attractive method for applications in multimedia: it was adopted by Microsoft for compressing thousands of images in its Encarta multimedia encyclopaedia [3].

Despite of all the above properties of fractal image compression, the long computing in the encoding step still remains the main drawback of this technique. Because good approximations are obtained when many domain blocks are allowed, searching the pool of domain blocks is time consuming. In other word, consider an N x N image and n x n range blocks. The number of range blocks is $(N/n)^2$, while the number of the domain blocks is $(N-2n+1)^2$. The computation of best match between a range block and a domain block is $O(n^2)$. Considering n to be constant, the computation of complexity search is $O(N^4)$.

Several methods have been proposed to overcome this problem. The most common approach for reducing the computational complexity is the classification scheme. In this scheme range and domain blocks are grouped in classes according to their common characteristics. In the encoding phase, only blocks belonging to the same class are compared, thus saving a lot of computation while keeping the performance in terms of image quality quite close to that of exhaustive search. Jacquin [2] proposed a discrete feature classification scheme based on Ramamurthi and Gersho approach [4]. The domain blocks are classified according to their perceptual geometric features. Only three major types of block are differentiated: shade blocks, edge blocks, and midrange blocks. In the Fisher's classification method [5], a given image block is divided into four quadrants. For each quadrant, the average and the variance are computed. According to certain combination of these values, 72 classes are constructed. This method reduces the searching space efficiently. However, it required large amount of computations and, the arrangement of these 72 classes is complicated.

In clustering methods [6,7] the domain blocks are classified by clustering their feature vectors in Voronoi cells whose centers are designed from the test image or from a set of training images. For each range block, matches are sought in the neighboring classes only. Another discrete feature classification based on mean was proposed by Hurtgen and Stiller [8]. The feature vector is constructed by comparing the sub-block mean of each quadrant to the block's mean. In this approach the search area for a domain block is restricted to a neighborhood of the current range. All the above approaches can only reduce the factor of proportionality in O(N) the time complexity for a search in the domain pool, where N is the size of the domain pool.

A different approach is to organize the domain blocks into a tree-structure, which could admit faster searching over the linear search. This approach is able to reduce the order of complexity from O(N) to O(log N). The idea of tree-structured search to speed up encoding has long been used in the related technique of Vector Quantization [9]. Caso et al. [10] and Bani-Eqbal [11] have proposed formulations of tree-search for fractal encoding. In the feature vector approach introduced by Saupe in [12,13] a small set of d real-valued keys is devised for each domain which make up a d-dimensional feature vector. These keys are carefully constructed such that searching in the domain pool can be restricted to the nearest neighbors of a query point, *i.e.* the feature vector of the current range. Thus the sequential search in the domain pool is replaced by multi-dimensional nearest neighbor searching, which can be run in logarithmic time. Unfortunately, the feature vector dimension is very high, i.e. equal to the number of pixels in the blocks. This limits the performance of this approach as the multi-dimensionality search algorithms. Moreover large amounts of memory are required. Some attempts to solve this problem are presented in [14].

Complexity reduction methods that are somewhat different in character are based on reducing the size of the domain pool. Jacobs *et al.*'s method uses skipping adjacent domain blocks [15]. Monro [16] localizes the domain pool relative to a given range based on the assumption that domain blocks close to range block are well suited to match the given range block. Saupe's Lean Domain Pool method discards a fraction of domain blocks with the smallest variance [17]. The latest survey on the literature may be found in [18-20].

In this paper a new method to reduce the encoding time of fractal image compression is proposed. This method is based on removing the domain block with high entropy, ε from the domain pool. In this way, all the useless domains will be removed from the pool achieving a more productive domain pool. The proposed method can be extended to speed up the hybrid fractal coders and improve their performance.

The rest of this paper is organized as follows. Section 2, briefly describes fractal image coding and the baseline algorithm. In Section 3, definition of entropy and using it in the proposed method to reduce the encoding time of fractal image compression is presented, followed by experimental results and discussion in Section 4. The conclusions of the present work are summarized in Section 5.

2. Fractal Image Coding

2.1. Principle of Fractal Coding

In the encoding phase of fractal image compression, the image of size NxN is first partitioned into non-overlapping range blocks R_i, { $R_1, R_2,...R_p$ } of a predefined size BxB. Then, a search codebook (domain pool Ω) is created from the image taking all the square blocks (domain blocks) D_j, { $D_1, D_2,...D_q$ } of size 2Bx2B, with integer step L in horizontal or vertical directions. To enlarge the variation, each domain is expanded with the eight basic square block orientations by rotating 90 degrees clockwise the original and the mirror domain block. The range-domain matching process initially consists of a shrinking operation in each domain block that averages its pixel intensities forming a block of size BxB.

For a given range R_i, the encoder must search the domain pool Ω for best affine transformation w_i, which minimizes the distance between the image R_i and the image $w_i(D_i)$, (i.e. $w_i(D_i) \approx R_i$). The distance is taken in the luminance dimension not the spatial dimensions. Such a distance can be defined in various ways, but to simplify the computations it is convenient to use the Root Mean Square RMS metric. For a range block with n pixels, each with intensity r_i and a decimated domain block with n pixels, each with intensity d_i the objective is to minimize the quality

$$E(R_i, D_i) = \sum_{i=1}^{n} (sd_i + o - r_i)^2 \tag{1}$$

which occurs when the partial derivatives with respect to s and o are zero. Solving the resulting equations will give the best coefficients s and o [5].

$$s = \frac{n \sum_{i=1}^{n} d_i r_i - \sum_{i=1}^{n} d_i \sum_{i=1}^{n} r_i}{n \sum_{i=1}^{n} d_i^2 - (\sum_{i=1}^{n} d_i)^2} \tag{2}$$

$$o = \frac{1}{n}(\sum_{i=1}^{n} r_i - s \sum_{i=1}^{n} d_i) \tag{3}$$

With s and o given the square error is

$$E(R^i, D^i)^2 =$$

$$\frac{1}{n}\left[\sum_{i=1}^{n} r_i^2 + s(s \sum_{i=1}^{n} d_i^2 - 2 \sum_{i=1}^{n} d_i r_i + 2o \sum_{i=1}^{n} d_i) + o(on - 2 \sum_{i=1}^{n} r_i) \right] \tag{4}$$

If the denominator in Eq. (2) is zero, then s =0 and $o = \frac{1}{n} \sum_{i=1}^{n} r_i$.

The parameters that need to be placed in the encoded bit stream are s_i, o_i index of the best matching domain, and rotation index. The range index i can be predicted from the decoder if the range blocks are coded sequentially. The coefficient s_i represents a contrast factor, with $|s_i| \leq 1.0$, to make sure that the transformation is contractive in the luminance dimension, while the coefficient o_i represents brightness offset.

At decoding phase, Fisher [5] has shown that if the transforms are performed iteratively, beginning from an arbitrary image of equal size, the result will be an attractor resembling the original image at the chosen resolution.

2.2. Baseline Fractal Image Coding Algorithm

The main steps of the encoding algorithm of fractal image compression based on quadtree partition [5] can be summarized as follows:

Step 1: Initialization (domain pool construction)
      Divide the input image into N domains, D_j

        For $(j =1; j \leq N; j ++)$
        Push D_j onto domain pool stack Ω

Step 2: Choose a tolerance level ℓ_C;

Step 3: Search for best matches between range and domain blocks
      For (i =1 ; i $\leq$ num_range ; i ++)   {
        min_error = ℓ_C;
        For (j =1 ; j $\leq$ num_domain; j ++) {
          Compute s, o;
          If (0 $\leq$ s< 1. 0)
            If (E (R_i , D_j) < min_error) {

              min_error = E(R_i , D_j);
              best_domain[i] =j ; }
        }
        If (min_error = = ℓ_C)

          Set R $_i$ uncovered and partition it into 4 smaller blocks;
        Else ·
         . Save_coefficients(best_domain, s, o);
      }

    In this algorithm, parameter ℓ_C settles the fidelity of the decoded image and the compression ratio. By using different fidelity tolerances for the collage error, one obtains a series of encodings of varying compression ratios and fidelities. For a range block if ℓ_C is violated for all the domain blocks, that is the range block is uncovered, the range block is divided into four smaller range blocks, and one can search for the best match domains for these smaller range blocks. At the end of **step 1** the domain pool Ω has N domain (*i.e.* all domains).

3. The Proposed Method

3.1. Entropy

Assume that there exists a set of events S= $\{ x_1, x_2,... x_n \}$, with the probability of occurrence of each event $p(x_i) = p_i$. These probabilities, P= $\{ p_1, p_2,... p_n \}$, are such that each $p_i \geq 0$, and $\sum_{i=1}^{n} p_i = 1$.
The function,

$$I(x_i) = -\log p_i \tag{5}$$

is called the amount of self-information associated with event x_i. This function is a measure of occurrence of the event x_i. The function I focuses on one event at a time. In most situations, however, and certainly in the context of data compression, one has to look at the entire set of all possible events to measure content over the entire set. An important concept introduced by Shannon is *entropy* associated with a set of events, which takes the form:

$$H(p_1, p_2,...p_n) = H(s) = -\sum_{i=1}^{n} p_i \log p_i \tag{6}$$

Entropy can be defined as the average self-information that is, the mean (expected or average) amount of information for an occurrence of an event x_i. In the context of coding a message, entropy represents the lower bound on the average number of bits per input value. The function H has the following lower and the upper limits:

$$0 = H(1,0,0,...0) \leq H(p_1 p_2,...p_n) \leq H(\frac{1}{n},\frac{1}{n},...\frac{1}{n}) = \log n \tag{7}$$

In other words, if the events are equally likely, the uncertainty is the highest since the choice of an event is not obvious. If one event has probability 1 and the others probability of 0, the choice is always the same, and all uncertainly disappears.

3.2. The Entropy Based Encoded Algorithm

Equation (1) is a full search problem and as mentioned previously is computationally intensive. One of the simplest ways to decrease encoding time of this full search problem is to decrease the size of the domain pool in order to decrease the number of domains to be searched. The proposed method reduces the encoding time of fractal image compression by performing less searches as opposed to doing a faster search, by excluding many of domain blocks from the domain pool. This idea is based on the observation that many domains are never used in a typical fractal encoding, and only a fraction of this large domain pool is actually used in the fractal coding. The collection of used domains is localized in regions with high degree of structure [17]. Figure (1) shows the domain blocks of size 8x8 that are actually used in the fractal code of Lena image. As expected the indicated domains are located mostly along edges and in the regions of high contrast of the image.

Analyzing the domain pool, there is a very large set of domain blocks in the pool with high entropy, which are not used in the fractal code. Thus, it is possible to reduce the search time by discarding a large fraction of high entropy blocks, which affect only a few ranges. For these ranges a sub-optimal domains with smaller entropy may be found. In this way, the domain pool is constructed from blocks with the lowest entropy instead of all domains. In this case, the encoding time is heavily reduced

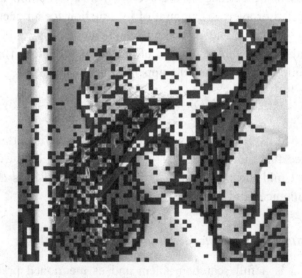

Figure 1. Domains of size 8x8 that are used for fractal coding of 512x512 Lena are shown in black.

by a priori discarding those domains from the pool, which are unlikely to be chosen for the fractal coding. Eq. (6) is used to calculate the entropy value for each domain block. According to this value a decision is taken to determine if this domain can become a part of the domain pool or not.

A parameter ε will control the domain entropy value in the implementation, with ε being a quality parameter since it determines the size of the domain pool. The proposed method can only reduce the factor of proportionality in the O(N) complexity, where N is the domain pool size. But one can use the Tree approach [21] on the resulting efficient domain pool after removing all useless domain blocks, which is able to fundamentally reduce the order of encoding time from O(N) to O(log N).

The baseline algorithm mentioned above is modified in such a way that the domain pool Ω contains only domain blocks which have a certain entropy value. The main steps of the modified encoder algorithm of fractal image compression can be summarized as follows:

Step 1: Initialization (domain pool construction)
   Choose parameter ε ;
   Divide the input image into N domains, D_j
   For $(j =1; j \leq N; j ++)$ {
      Ent =entropy (D_j);
      If (Ent $\leq \varepsilon$)
         Push D_j onto domain pool stack Ω }

Step 2: Choose a tolerance levels ℓ_C ;

Step 3: Search for best matches between range and domain blocks
   For (i =1 ; i $\leq$ num_range ; i ++) {
      min_error = ℓ_C ;
      For (j =1 ; j $\leq$ num_domain; j ++) {
      Compute **s, o**;
         If (0 $\leq$ s< 1. 0)
            If (E(R_i , D_j) < min_error) {
               min_error = E(R_i , D_j);
               best_domain[i] =j ;   }
   }

If (min_error $= = \ell_C$)

    Set R_i uncovered and partition it into 4 smaller blocks;

    Else

       Save_coefficients(**best_domain, s, o**);

}

At the end of **step 1** the domain pool has *num_domain* domain according to $\mathcal{E}$ value.

4. Experimental Results

This section presents experimental results showing the efficiency of the proposed method. The performance tests carried out for a diverse set of well-known images of size 512x512 gray levels with 8bpp, on a PC with Intel Pentium III 750 MHz CPU and 128MB memory under windows 98 operating system using Visual C++6.0 programming language and the time is measured in seconds. Moreover, the scaling coefficient (contrast) restricted to values between 0 and 1 in order to avoid searching domain pool twice (*i.e.* allowed only positive scaling factors in the gray level transformation). To ensure a compact encoding of the affine transformation, the value of contrast and brightness are quantized using 4 and 6 bits for contrast and brightness, respectively, hence the compression ratio is 95% and 89% for fixed range size and quadtree partitions respectively. This study focuses on the implementation issues and presents the first empirical experiments analyzing the performance of benefits of entropy approach to fractal image compression. First, the performance of the proposed method with fixed range size partition is examined. The size of the range block is set to be 8x8 pixel, and hence the domain size is 16x16, with domains overlapping *i.e.* the domain step L (distance between two consecutive domains) is divided by 4. The result is shown in table (1). Second, the same experiment is carried out with well-known technique of quadtree partitioning, allowing up to three quadtree levels. The average tolerated error between the original image and its uncompressed version is set to be $\ell_C = 2.0$. The results are shown in table (2).

Table 1. Performance of fixed range size coding of four test images.

ε	Lena		Peppers		Boat		Hill	
	Time	PSNR	Time	PSNR	Time	PSNR	Time	PSNR
0	124.99	36.34	119.65	37.51	122.59	28.31	119. 56	34. 93
1	106.41	36.34	111.81	37.49	100.20	28.28	115.86	34.93
1.2	100.34	36.32	110.08	37.46	92.26	28.25	105.86	34.92
1.5	87.68	36.30	98.37	37.39	79.04	28.18	86.06	34.86
1.8	76.02	36.23	86.54	37.34	64.06	27.99	65.67	34.78
2	68.56	36.12	74.99	37.29	58.77	27.98	51.77	34.65
2.5	50.36	35.98	55.01	37.23	45.42	27.76	21.67	34.37
2.8	40.45	35.95	40.03	37.08	39.55	27.73	12.38	34.23
3	32.89	35.73	31.99	36.98	35.50	27.62	8.67	33.89
3.5	18.26	35.36	13.69	36.56	22.86	27.38	5.38	33.46
3.8	10.82	34.83	6.03	35.59	15.93	27.22	4.52	33.16
4	5.80	34.39	3.01	34.50	11.56	26.89	4.16	33.15

Table 2. Performance of quadtree partition coding of four test images.

ε	Lena		Peppers		Boat		Hill	
	Time	PSNR	Time	PSNR	Time	PSNR	Time	PSNR
0	797.78	40.66	749.63	40.50	1151.26	34.23	1304.45	39.14
1	760.91	40.65	745.91	40.51	1144.31	34.12	1323.31	39.12
1.2	753.86	40.65	743.14	40.52	1201.96	34.27	1313.14	39.12
1.5	712.72	40.64	746.93	40.51	1180.62	34.23	1318.08	39.09
1.8	647.72	40.59	736.98	40.50	981.00	34.2	1192.09	39.09
2	601.98	40.56	629.49	40.49	880.75	34.27	1062.43	39.05
2.5	489.06	40.48	553.58	40.45	632.66	34.28	677.08	38.96
2.8	417.90	40.39	477.20	40.49	541.81	34.17	442.98	38.85
3	367.91	40.36	398.01	40.43	494.21	34.11	317.13	38.75
3.5	246.4	40.12	236.96	40.32	408.76	33.79	121.95	38.69
3.8	174.00	39.88	127.97	39.98	327.58	33.71	80.03	38.63
4	120.18	39.83	64.09	39.71	250.91	33.53	65.82	38.51

The results in tables (1) and (2) show that the encoding time scales linearly with ε . This is expected since the major computation effort in the encoding lies in the linear search through the domain pool. For the case without domain pool reduction ε =0 (full search) there is no savings in the encoding time as shown in Fig. (2). Also, in the case of fixed range size partition the loss in quality of the encoding in terms of fidelity is larger than for quadtree partition. This is caused by the fact that some larger range can be covered well by some domains, which are removed from the domain pool at larger values of ε (e.g. $\varepsilon \geq 2.5$). As a consequence some of these ranges are subdivided and their quadrants may be covered better by smaller domains than the larger range.

This simple entropy approach leads to very significant savings in encoding time and is similar to the approach used in [5]. With fixed range size partition, it causes only negligible or no loss in the equality of image, thereby reducing by 2 the encoding time (at ε =2.5). In the quadtree case, when ε =3.8 the encoding time of Hill image is 80.03 sec while the PSNR is 38.63 dB. For comparison, the baseline (full search) required 1304.45 sec and the PSNR achieved is 39.14 dB. This represented a speed up factor of over 16 at the expense of a slight drop of PSNR of 0.51 dB. Generally, the speed-up in terms of actual encoding time is almost 7 times while the loss in quality of the image is almost 0.83 dB. This compares well with Saupe's Lean Domain Pool Method,

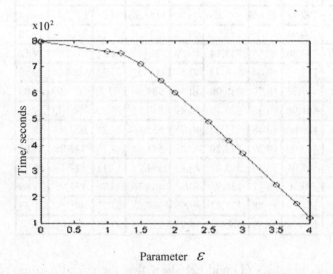

Parameter ε

Figure 2. Encoding time versus epsilon ε for 512x512 Lena image.

which achieved comparable speedup of 8.9 at the expense of a drop of 1.7dB for Lena image [18]. Also, with Chong Sze [22], which achieved a speed-up of 9.3 with 0.87 dB loss for the same image. Figures (3), and (4) show examples of reconstructed images, which were encoded using the entropy method with fixed range size and quadtree partitions.

Fixed range size partition	Quadtree partition
Encoding time: 5.8s.	Encoding time: 120.18s.
Quality: 34.39dB	Quality: 39.83 dB.

Figure 3. Lena 512x512 image.

Fixed range size partition	Quadtree partition
Encoding time: 3.01s.	Encoding time: 64.09s.
Quality: 34.50dB	Quality: 39.71dB.

Figure 4. Peppers 512x512 image.

Figure 5. Peppers 512x512 image encoded in 2.93s by the proposed method and the PSNR of the reconstructed image is 33.56dB.

Finally, the proposed method seems to be applicable in situations where extremely fast encodings are desired and some quality degradation can be tolerated (*e.g.* by choosing $\varepsilon \geq 3.8$). For example, Fig. (5) shows that the Peppers image is coded in 2.93s with a quality of 33.56 dB (while the full search encoding time is 749.63s with a quality of 40.50 dB). This means that the image fidelity is still acceptable at least for some applications where high fidelity is not an absolute requirement.

5. Conclusions

In this paper a parameterized and non-adaptive version of domain pool reduction is proposed, by allowing an adjustable number of domains to be excluded from the domain pool based on the entropy value of the domain block, which in turn reduced the encoding time. Experimental results on standard images showed that removing domains with high entropy from the domain pool have little effect on the image quality while significantly reduce the encoding time. The proposed method is highly comparable to other acceleration techniques. Next step in our research is to use the proposed method to improve the speed of hybrid coders (gaining better results than JPEG) that are based on fractal coders and transform coders so as to improve their performance.

References

1. M. Barnsley and A. Jacquin. Applications of Recurrent Iterated Function Systems to Images. *SPIE Visual Communications and Image Processing*, Vol. 1001, pp. 122-131, (1988).

2. A. E. Jacquin. Image Coding Based on a Fractal Theory of Iterated Contractive Image Transform. *IEEE trans. on Image Processing*, Vol. 1, pp. 18-30, (1992).

3. M. Barnsley and L. Hurd. Fractal Image Compression. *on Image Processing: Mathematical Methods and Applications*. Clarendon Press, Oxford, (1997).

4. B. Ramanurthi and A. Gersho. Classified Vector Quantization of Image. *IEEE Trans. Communication*, COM-34, Vol. 11, pp. 1105-1115, (1986).

5. Y. Fisher. *Fractal Image Compression: Theory and Applications*. Springer-Verlag, New York, (1994).

6. R. Hamzaoui. Codebook Clustering by Self-Organizing Maps for Fractal Image Compression. *In NATO ASI Conf. Fractal Image Encoding and Analysis*, Trondheim, July 1995. Fractals, Vol. 5, Supplementary issue, April (1997).

7. R. Hamzaoui and D. Saupe. Combining Fractal Image Compression and Vector Quantization. *IEEE Trans. on Image Processing*, 9(2), pp.197-208, (2000).

8. B. Hurtgen and C. Stiller. Fast Hierarchical Codebook Search for Fractal Coding of Still Images. *Proceeding of SPIE*, Vol. 1977, pp. 397-408, (1993).

9. L.M. Po and C.K. Chan. Adaptive Dimensionality Reduction Techniques for Tree-Structured Vector Quantization. *IEEE Trans. on Communications*, Vol. 42, No. 6, pp. 2246-2257, (1994).

10. G. Caso, P. Obrador and C.-C. Kuo. Fast Methods for Fractal Image Encoding. Proc. *SPIE Visual Communication and Image Processing*, Vol. 2501, (1995).

11. B. Bani-Eqbal. Enhancing the Speed of Fractal Image Compression. *Optical Engineering*, Vol. 34, No. 6, pp.1705-1710, (1995).

12. D. Saupe. Accelerating Fractal Image Compression by Multi-dimensional Nearest Neighbor Search. In *Proc. Data compression Conference*, March 28-30, (1995).

13. D. Saupe. Fractal Image Compression via Nearest Neighbor Searching. *In Conf. Proc. NATO ASI, Fractal Image Coding and Analysis*, Trondheim, July (1995).

14. C.S. Tong and W. Man. Adaptive Approximation Nearest Neighbor Search for Fractal Image Compression. *IEEE Trans. on Image Processing*, 11 (6), (2002).

15. E.W. Jacobs, Y. Fisher, and R.D. Boss. Image Compression: A study of the Iterated Transform Method. *Signal Process*, Vol. 29, pp. 251-263, (1992).

16. D.M. Monro and F. Dudbridge. Approximation of Image Blocks. In *Proc. Int. Conf. Acoustics, Speed, Signal Processing*, Vol. 3, pp.4585-4588, (1992).

17. D. Saupe. Lean Domain Pools for Fractal Image Compression. *Proceedings IS&T/SPIE 1996 Symposium on Electronic Imaging: Science & Technology Still Image Compression II*, Vol. 2669, (1996).

18. M. Polvere and M. Nappi. Speed-Up in Fractal Image Coding: Comparison of Methods. *IEEE Trans. on Image Processing*, Vol. 9, pp.1002-1009, (2000).

19. B. Wohlberg and G. Jager. A review of the Fractal Image Compression Literature. *IEEE Trans. on Image Processing*, Vol. 8, No. 12, pp. 1716-1729, (1999).
20. D. Saupe and R. Hamzaoui. Complexity Reduction Methods for Fractal Image Compression. *In I.M.A. Conf. Proc. on Image Processing; Mathematical methods and applications*, Sept., J.M. Blackedge (ed.), (1994).
21. X. Gharavi-Alkhansari, and T.S.Huang. Fractal Image Coding Using Rate-Distortion Optimized matching Pursuit. *Proc. SPIE*, pp. 265-304, (1996).
22. C.S. Tong, and M. Pi. Fast Fractal Encoding Based on Adaptive Search. *IEEE Trans. on Image Processing*, Vol .10, No.9, pp.1269-1277, (2001).

CHAPTER 9

ROBUSTNESS OF A BLIND IMAGE WATERMARK DETECTOR DESIGNED BY ORTHOGONAL PROJECTION

Cong Jin and Jiaxiong Peng

Department of Computer Science, Central China Normal University
Wuhan *430079*, P.R.China
E-mail: jincong@mail.ccnu.edu.cn

Digital watermarking is a key technique practical intellectual property protecting systems and concealment correspondence systems. In this paper, we discussed a blind detection method for the digital image watermark. The theories research show that the orthogonal projection sequence of a digital image is one-to-one correspondence with this digital image. By this conclusion, we designed a novel blind watermark detector. In this detector, to calculate the correlation value between the image and watermark, the intensity information of digital image is not used, and the orthogonal projection sequence of this image is used. Experiment results show that this watermark detector not only to have very strong resistant ability to translation and rotation attacks, but also to have the good robustness to Gaussian noise. Performance of this watermark detector is better than general detector designed by the intensity information directly. The conclusions of this paper are useful to the research in the future.

1. Introduction

Digital watermarking[1,2], the art of hiding information into multimedia data in a robust and invisible manner, has gained great interest over the past few years. There has been a lot of interest in the digital watermarking research, mostly due to the fact that digital watermarking might be used as a tool to protect the copyright of multimedia data. A digital watermark is an imperceptible signal embedded directly into the media content, and it can be detected from the host media for some applications. The insertion and detection of digital watermarks can help to identify the source or ownership of the media, the legitimacy of its usage, the type of the content or other accessory information in various applications. Specific operations related to the status of the watermark can then be applied to cope with different situations.

A majority of the watermarking algorithms proposed in the literature operate on a principle analogous to spread-spectrum communications. A pseudo-random sequence, which is called digital watermark, is inserted into the image. During extraction, the same pseudo-random sequence is correlated with the estimated pattern extracted from the image. The watermark is said to be present if the computed correlation exceeds a chosen threshold value. Among this general class of watermarking schemes, there are several variations that include choice of specific domain for watermark insertion, e.g. spatial, DCT, wavelet, etc; and enhancements of the basic scheme to improve robustness and reduce visible artifacts. The computed correlation depends on the alignment of the pattern regenerated and the one extracted from the image. Thus proper synchronization of the two patterns is critical for the watermark detection process. Typically, this synchronization is provided by the inherent geometry of the image, where pseudo-random sequences are assumed to be placed on the same image geometry. When a geometric manipulation is applied to the watermarked image, the underlying geometry is distorted, which often results in the de-synchronization and failure of the watermark detection process. The geometric manipulations can range from simple scaling and rotation or cropping to more complicated random geometric distortions as applied by Stirmark[3].

Different methods have been proposed in literature to reduce/prevent algorithm failure modes in case of geometric manipulations. For non-blind watermarking schemes, where the original image is available at the detector, the watermarked image may be registered against the original image to provide proper synchronization[4]. For blind watermarking schemes, where the original image is not available at the detector, proposed methods include use of the Fourier-Melin transform space that provides rotation, translation, scale invariance[5], and watermarking using geometric invariants of the image such as moments[6] or cross-ratios[7]. Hartung *et al*[8] have also proposed a scheme that divides the image into small blocks and performs correlation for rotations and translations using small increments, in an attempt to detect the proper synchronization.

In this paper, the orthogonal projective sequence of a digital image is analyzed. A blind image watermark detector is designed by using the orthogonal projective sequence of digital image. In Section 2, we first discuss definition and its properties of the orthogonal projective sequence of a digital image. A conclusion, the orthogonal projection sequence of a digital image is one-to-one correspondence with this digital image, is obtained. By this conclusion, we designed a blind watermark detector. Then, in Section 3, we present our experimental results. Experiment results show that this watermark detector not only to have very strong resistant ability to translation and rotation attacks, but also to have the good robustness to Gaussian noise. Finally, Section 4 contains our conclusions.

2. The Design Method of the Watermark Detector

We assume that the real image intensity function $I(x, y)$ is piecewise continuous, and has non-zero in a bounded domain, where $x = 0,1,\ldots,m-1;\ y = 0,1,\ldots,n-1,\ m \times n = N$.

The geometric moments[9] of order $(p+q)$ of $I(x, y)$ are defined as

$$M_{pq} = \int_{-\infty}^{+\infty} \int_{-\infty}^{+\infty} x^p y^q I(x,y) dx dy \tag{1}$$

where $p,\ q=0,1,2,\ldots,\infty$. By [10], we know that the infinite sequence $\{M_{pq}\}$ is one-to-one correspondence with image intensity function $I(x, y)$ whenever $I(x, y)$ is piecewise continuous. If the integral value is calculated by equation (1), we can add the definition $I(x, y)=0$ in the outside bounded domain.

Let H be a Hibert space, and $\{g_i(x,y)\}_{i=1}^{\infty}$ be normal orthogonal basis of H. We have

$$\iint_A g_i(x,y)g_j(x,y) dx dy = \begin{cases} 0, & i \neq j \\ 1, & i = j \end{cases}$$

Let $I(x, y) \in H$ and be square integrable function, we define

$$\alpha_i = \alpha(g_i(x,y))_A = \iint_A I(x,y)g_i(x,y)dxdy, \quad i = 1,2,... \tag{2}$$

Where, α_i is called the coordinate of $I(x, y)$ with respect to this basis, also is called the orthogonal projection.

Is it one-to-one correspondence between infinite sequence $\{\alpha_i\}_{i=1}^{\infty}$ and image function $I(x, y)$? Because the existence of function $I(x, y)$, to satisfy the equation (2), can't be guaranteed only by arbitrarily infinite sequence $\{\alpha_i\}_{i=1}^{\infty}$, this one-to-one correspondence can't exist generally. But if $\{\alpha_i\}_{i=1}^{\infty}$ satisfying the some conditions, this one-to-one correspondence may exist. This is conclusion of our Theorem.

Theorem If the function series $\sum_{j=1}^{\infty} \alpha_j g_j(x,y)$ is uniformly convergent, then there is an unique function $I(x, y)$ such that $I(x, y)$ satisfy the equation (2).

Proof Let $I(x,y) = \sum_{j=1}^{\infty} \alpha_j g_j(x,y)$. By uniformly convergent of the function series $\sum_{j=1}^{\infty} \alpha_j g_j(x,y)$, we indicate that $I(x, y)$ exists, and

$$\iint_A I(x,y)g_i(x,y)dxdy = \iint_A g_i(x,y)\{\sum_{j=1}^{\infty} \alpha_j g_i(x,y)\}dxdy, \quad i = 1,2,...$$

To exchange calculus order between the integral and sum and to use the normal orthogonality of the function systems $\{g_i(x,y)\}_{i=1}^{\infty}$, we may obtain

$$\iint_A I(x,y)g_i(x,y)dxdy = \alpha_i, \quad i = 1,2,...$$

Therefore, $I(x, y)$ satisfies the equation (2). Following, we discuss uniqueness of image $I(x, y)$.

Let $I_1(x,y) \neq I_2(x,y)$, $(x,y) \in A$, and their projection sequences are same. We notice that

$$\alpha_i = \iint_A I_1(x,y)g_i(x,y)dxdy, \quad \alpha_i = \iint_A I_2(x,y)g_i(x,y)dxdy, \quad i = 1,2,...$$

By subtraction of these two equations, we obtain

$$\iint_A g_i(x,y)\{I_1(x,y) - I_2(x,y)\}dxdy = 0, \quad i = 1,2,\ldots$$

By the completeness[10] of the basis, $I_1(x,y) = I_2(x,y)$ can be obtained, where $(x,y) \in A$. This is contradictory with assumption of Theorem, therefore $I(x, y)$ is unique.

By this Theorem we know that the orthogonal projective sequence $\{\alpha_i\}_{i=1}^{\infty}$, obtained by general normal orthogonal basis $\{g_i(x,y)\}_{i=1}^{\infty}$, is one-to-one correspondence with image intensity function $I(x, y)$ under the condition of Theorem. Therefore, the infinite sequence $\{\alpha_i\}_{i=1}^{\infty}$ is a feature sequence of digital image $I(x, y)$.

Because only finite terms can be researched in the $\{g_i(x,y)\}_{i=1}^{\infty}$, we let $S = \{g_i(x,y)\}_{i=1}^{N}$. From now, we research digital watermark is only on the S.

It is very common that the digital watermarking is embedded using multiplicative embedding method. The watermarked image data $J(x, y)$ are now formed from the digital watermarking $W(x, y)$ and the original image data $I(x, y)$ according to

$$J(x,y) = I(x,y) + \omega \cdot I(x,y) \cdot W(x,y), \quad x = 0,1,\ldots,m-1; \quad y = 0,1,\ldots,n-1 \quad (3)$$

where ω is the strength factor controlling the watermarking strength. This way of embedding digital watermarking was proposed, among others, by *Cox et.al.*[11].

We denote the finite projective sequence of digital watermarking $W(x, y)$ is $w = \{w_i\}_{i=1}^{N}$. One can attack watermarked image $J(x, y)$ by general image processing operations, such as translation, rotation, noise, etc., or by combining these operations. Attacked image $\tilde{J}(x,y)$ of $J(x, y)$ may be obtained. We denote the finite projective sequence of attacked image $\tilde{J}(x,y)$ is $\gamma = \{\gamma_i\}_{i=1}^{N}$.

Many measurements have been proposed for blind watermark detection[12]. Among them, a frequently used one is the normalized correlation measurement, which measures the cosine angle of the two feature vectors. In this paper, we let two feature vectors are w and γ respectively, by means of

$$c = \frac{\sum_{i=1}^{N} w_i \gamma_i}{\sqrt{\sum_{i=1}^{N} w_i^2} \sqrt{\sum_{i=1}^{N} \gamma_i^2}} \qquad (4)$$

To detect a watermark in a possibly watermarked image $\tilde{J}(x,y)$, we calculate the correlation between the image $\tilde{J}(x,y)$ and the $W(x, y)$. In general, $W(x, y)$ generated using different keys have very low correlation with each other. Therefore, during the detection process the correlation value will be very high for a $W(x, y)$ generated with the correct key and would be very low otherwise. During the detection process, it is common to set a threshold ρ to decide whether the watermark is detected or not. If the correlation exceeds a certain threshold ρ, the watermark detector determines that image $\tilde{J}(x,y)$ contains watermark $W(x, y)$.

Although the Fourier transformation[10] has many advantages for image signal processing, its operation speed is influenced by the real and imaginary part calculated respectively. We know that Walsh function system[13] is a complete normal orthogonal basis, therefore, it can become a basis when orthogonal projection sequence of digital image is calculated. In addition, each Walsh function value is always 1 or -1, and it is easy to obtain the kernel matrix, so the calculation is simple and operation speed can be increased.

According to arrangement order, the Walsh function can be generated by three methods. In this paper, the Walsh function is generated using the Hadamard matrix.

By the one dimensional Walsh function systems, the two dimensional Walsh function systems can be generated according to following as arrangement order

$Walsh(0, x) \ Walsh(0, y), \ Walsh(0, x) \ Walsh(1, y), \ \dots \ , \ Walsh(0, x) \ Walsh(n\text{-}1, y),$
$Walsh(1, x) \ Walsh(0, y), \ Walsh(1,x) \ Walsh(1, y), \ \dots \ , \ Walsh(1, x) \ Walsh(n\text{-}1, y),$
$\dots \qquad\qquad \dots \qquad\qquad \dots$
$Walsh(m\text{-}1,x)Walsh(0,y), Walsh(m\text{-}1,x) \ Walsh(1,y), \dots, Walsh(m\text{-}1,x)Walsh(n\text{-}1,y)$

The $m \times n$ two dimensional Walsh functions are generated altogether. For a digital image, according to the above method, we can obtain projection matrix of this digital image. The projection matrix has the same size with this digital image. Of course, if the digital image has bigger size, we can't use too many two dimensional Walsh functions. How much two dimensional Walsh functions are used, it should be decided according to actual situation.

3. Experiment Results and Discussion

In these experiments, we will investigate the robust detection problem of blind digital watermarking. Let us consider 512×512 grayscale images. Let Fig.1 be an original image. 1000 stochastic matrixes W_i (i=1, 2, ..., 1000), their elements drawn from a zero-mean Gaussian distribution, are generated randomly. Among them, the W_{500} is a digital watermarking generated with the correct key, and otherwise generated with the incorrect key. Each W_i is a $m \times n$ matrix. Fig.2 is the watermarked image for embedding W_{500} into Fig.1 using multiplicative method, when ω =0.03.

Figure 1. The original image   Figure 2. The watermarked image
                                           (ω =0.03)

3.1. *Performance Test of Two kinds of Methods*

For watermarking detection problem, the normalized correlations are computed by the intensity information of digital image (called Detector 1) and orthogonal projection sequence (called Detector 2) of this image, respectively. For a digital image, the equation (2) is rewritten following as

$$\alpha_{ij} = \sum_{k=0}^{m-1}\sum_{l=0}^{n-1} I(k,l)Walsh(i,k)Walsh(j,l), \ i = 0,1,\ldots,m-1; \ j = 0,1,\ldots,n-1$$

Fig.3(a) is output result of Detector 1, and Fig.3(b) is output result of Detector 2. We notice that the peak values of two Detectors are created all at output position 500. Therefore, two detectors can detect the watermark successfully. However, by comparing, performance of Detector 2 is better than Detector 1's. Because the threshold value choice range of Detector 2 is bigger than the Detector 1's, which can guarantee the lower false alarm probability.

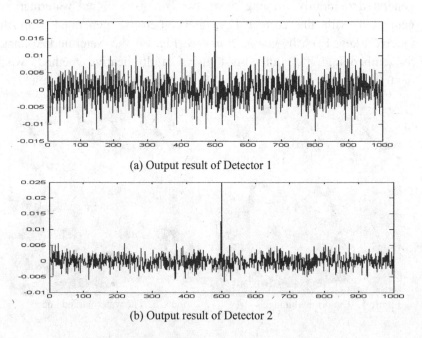

(a) Output result of Detector 1

(b) Output result of Detector 2

Figure 3. The comparison of the output results of two Detectors

3.2. Test of Anti-Noise Attack

Fig.4(a) is result image generated by zero-mean Gaussian noise with variance 0.01 adding to Fig.2.

We detect W_{500} to Fig.4(a) to use two detectors respectively, and the Fig.4(b) and (c) are their output results.

(a) The watermarked image attacked by the Gaussian noise

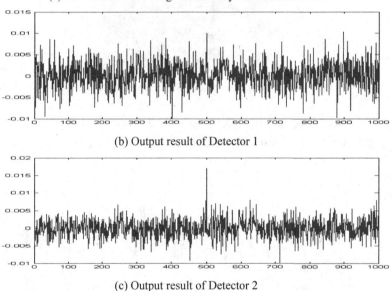

(b) Output result of Detector 1

(c) Output result of Detector 2

Figure 4. The comparison of the output results of two Detectors.

From the Fig.4(b) and (c) we know that Detector 1 can't detect W_{500} correctly, and Detector 2 can generate a higher the peak value in 500 position. This show that Detector 2 is not sensitive to noise, and it has the very strong anti-noise ability. This is because the projection characteristic of digital image is integral characteristic of this image, and integral calculus of digital image has the smooth function, therefore Detector 2 has the anti-noise attack ability.

3.3. *Test of Anti-Rotation Attack*

Fig.5(a) is a result image when Fig.2 is rotated 5 degrees.

(a) This is an image by rotating Fig.2 according to 5 degrees.

We detect W_{500} to Fig.5(a) to use two detectors respectively, and the Fig.5(b) and (c) are their output results.

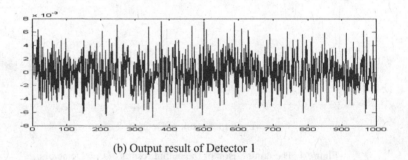

(b) Output result of Detector 1

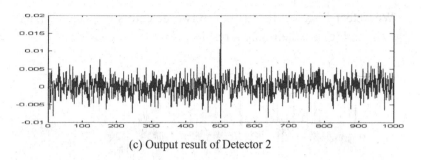

(c) Output result of Detector 2

Figure 5. The comparison of the output results of two Detectors.

From the Fig.5(b) and (c) we know that Detector 1 can't detect W_{500} correctly, and Detector 2 can generate a higher the peak value in 500 position. This show that Detector 2 is not sensitive to rotation, it has the very strong anti-rotation ability. This is because the projection characteristic of digital image is internal characteristic of this image, and its existence don't depend on the pixel position. Therefore Detector 2 is not sensitive to rotation attack.

3.4. Test of Anti-Translation Attack

Fig.6(a) is a result image when Fig.2 is translated 3 pixel rightwards and downward respectively.

(a) This is an image which is obtained by translating Fig.2

We detect W_{500} to Fig.6(a) to use two detectors respectively, and the Fig.6(b) and (c) are their output results.

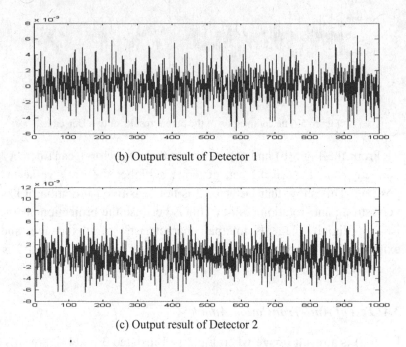

(b) Output result of Detector 1

(c) Output result of Detector 2

Figure 6. The comparison of the output results of two Detectors.

From the Fig.6(b) and (c) we know that Detector 1 can't detect W_{500} correctly, are Detector 2 can generate a higher the peak value in 500 position. This show that Detector 2 is not sensitive to translation, it has the very strong anti-translation ability. Its reason is the same with Detector 2 has the very strong anti-rotation ability.

3.5. *Test of Anti-Other Attack*

For two detectors, the other attacks, such as filtering, JPEG compression *etc*, are tested. By these experiments we know that, for these attacks, two detectors can't detect W_{500} correctly. This show that performance of Detector 2 isn't more superior than Detector 1's in the aspects of resisting filtering and JPEG compression *etc*.

4. Conclusion

In this paper, the blind watermark detection is realized partly by orthogonal projection sequence of digital image. By experiment we find that the blind watermark detector, the normalized correlation value is calculated by orthogonal projection sequence of digital image, has the good robustness to Gaussian noise attack, rotation attack, and translation attack. It points out a new way for designing the better blind watermark detector.

References

1. M.D. Swanson, M. Kobayashi, and A.H. Tewfik. Multimedia data-embedding and watermarking technologies, *Proceedings of the IEEE*, p.1064-1087, 86 (1998).
2. F. Hartung, and M. Kutter. Multimedia watermarking techniques, *Proceedings of the IEEE*, p.1079-1107, 87 (1999).
3. Stirmark Package, http://www.cl.com.uk/~fapp2/watermarking/stirmark
4. Q. Sun, J. Wu, R. Deng. Recovering modified watermarked image with reference to original image, *In Proceedings of SPIE: Security and Watermarking of Multimedia Contents*, 3657 (1999).
5. J.J.K.O Ruanaidh and T. Pun. Rotation, scale and translation invariant spread spectrum digital image watermarking, *Signal Processing*, p. 303-317, 66(1998).
6. M. Alghoniemy, A. Tewfik. Image watermarking by moment invariants, *In Proceedings of ICIP*, (2000).
7. R. Caldelli, M. Barni, F. Bartolini, A. Piva. Geometric-invariant robust watermarking through constellation matching in the frequency domain, *In Proceedings of ICIP*, (2000).
8. J.S.F. Hartung, B. Girod. Spread spectrum watermarking: Malicious attacks and counter-attacks, *In Proceedings of SPIE: Security and Watermarking of Multimedia Contents*, 3657(1999).
9. M. K. Hu. Visual Pattern Recognition by Moment Invariants. *IRE Trans. Information Theory*, IT-8, p. 179-187, (1962).
10. Ron N. Bracewell. *The Fourier Transform and Its Applications*, New York: McGraw-Hill Book Company, (1965).
11. I.J.Cox., J.Killian, F.Thomson, and T.Shamoon. Secure Spread Spectrum Watermarking for Multimedia. *IEEE Transaction on Image Processing*, p.1673-1687, 6 (1997).
12. P. Moulin and E. Delp. A mathematical approach to watermarking and data hiding. In Proc. *IEEE ICIP*, Thessaloniki, Greece, (2001).
13. Tzafestas, S.G. Walsh Functions in Signal and Systems Analysis and Design. New York: Van Nostrand Reinhold, (1985).

CHAPTER 10

SELF-SUPERVISED ADAPTATION FOR ON-LINE SCRIPT TEXT RECOGNITION

Lionel Prevost and Loïc Oudot

Universit Pierre et Marie Curie
LISIF / PARC BC 252
4 Place Jussieu, 75252 Paris Cedex 05, France

We have recently developed in our lab a text recognizer for on-line texts written on a touch-terminal. We present in this paper several strategies to adapt this recognizer in a self-supervised way to a given writer and compare them to the supervised adaptation scheme. The baseline system is based on the activation-verification cognitive model. We have designed this recognizer to be writer-independent but it may be adapted to be writer-dependent in order to increase the recognition speed and rate. The classification expert can be iteratively modified in order to learn the particularities of a writer. The best self-supervised adaptation strategy is called prototype dynamic management and gets good results, close to those of the supervised methods. The combination of supervised and self-supervised strategies increases accuracy again. Results, presented on a large database of 90 texts (5,400 words) written by 38 different writers are very encouraging with an error rate lower than 10 %.

10.1. Introduction

Recently, handheld devices like PDAs, mobiles phones, e-books or tablet PC have became very popular. In opposition to classical personal computers, they are small, keyboard-less and mouse-less. Therefore, electronic pen is very attractive as pointing and handwriting device. Such a device is at the frontier of two research fields: man-machine interface and handwriting recognition.

In this paper, we focus on the problem of handwriting recognition for handheld devices with large screen on which we can write texts. For such an application, recognition rate should be very high otherwise it should discourage all the possible users. With the last handwriting recognizers on the market (Microsoft Windows XP Tablet Edition, Apple Ink, myScript...,) the recognition rate has became acceptable but is not high enough. The major problem for these recognizers is the vast variation in personal writing style. Updating the parameters of a writer-independent recognizer to transform it into a writer-dependent recognizer with a higher accuracy can solve this difficulty. The systems listed above are not able to adapt themselves to a given writer. We can get better recognition rates if we adapt a writer-independent recognizer with an adequate architecture and transform it quickly in a writer-dependent system. However, it should not be forgotten that the use of a pen as input modality has to be user friendly. So, the training step must be as shorter as possible or - better - totally hidden for the user.

Traditional adaptation technics require the writer intervention (the so-called supervised adaptation). We propose in this article several self-supervised adaptation scheme that we compare to the already existing techniques like supervised adaptation.

The article is organized as follows. In section 2, we present a review of the various techniques of adaptation. In section 3, we describe the writer-independent baseline system. In section 4, we describe the different adaptation strategies. In section 5, we present a combination between self-supervised and supervised methods to achieve very good results. Finally, conclusions and prospects are given in section 6.

10.2. Literature review

The idea of writer adaptation was revealed by researches in the field of perceptive psychology. It has been shown that, in the case of a hardly readable writer, it is easier to read a word if we have already read other words written by the same person. This phenomenon is called the graphemic priming effect.[1] Thus, we learn the user writing characteristics from the words we can read, and then, we use this new knowledge to read the remaining words.

In the literature, we consider two adaptation strategies: systems where the adaptation step takes place once first before use (called off-line) and systems with continuous adaptation (on-line).

Most systems[2–5] using an off-line adaptation scheme need a labeled database of the writer. These examples are use to make a supervised training of the system. Thus, the system learns the characteristics of this particular writer before being used.

On the other hand, the following systems evolve continuously during use.

The on-line handwriting recognition and adaptation system of[6] uses a supervised incremental adaptation strategy. The baseline system uses a single MLP with 72 outputs (62 letters and 10 punctuation marks). An adaptation module, at the output of the MLP modifies its output vector. This adaptation module is a RBF

(*Radial Basis Function*) network. The user informs the system of the classification error, giving the letter label, and the RBF is re-trained (modification of the existing kernels or addition of a new one).

Two other systems use a TDNN (*Time Delay Neural Network*) as classifier instead of the MLP. This TDNN is trained on an omni-writer database and the output layer of this network is replaced either by a k-nn classifier in[7] or by a discriminating classifier in.[8] During the adaptation step, the TDNN is fixed and the output classifier is trained, in order to learn mis-recognized characters.

The system described in[9] is very close to our system but is dedicated to isolated alphanumeric character recognition. The k-nn classifier uses the Dynamic Time Warping algorithm to compare the unknown characters to a prototype database. The writer adaptation consists in adding the mis-classified characters in this database. Moreover, useless prototypes can be removed from the database to avoid an excessive growth of this latter.

There are also a lot of works on adaptation in off-line character recognition and other pattern recognition fields including speech recognition.[10] For example, in,[11] the authors adapt the Hidden Markov Models (HMM) first trained on a large database with a small database of the particular writer.

Based on the results of all these studies, we can notice that model-based classifier (MBC) like k-nn have better ability to learn particular patterns than machine learning classifier (MLC) like HMM, MLP or GMM (Gaussian Mixture Model). MBC need very few samples to learn a new pattern (sometime one sample is enough) and, as this learning consists in adding the new sample in the classifier database, they are not time consuming. But the database size tends to increase significantly, so the classification time and the memory needed, increase linearly with this size. On the other hand, MLC need more samples and are time consuming to re-estimate their parameters. But after the training, the size and the classification time remain the same.

10.3. Writer independent baseline system

For the experiments, we collected a large text database written by 38 different writers. Each writer wrote an average of 150 words for a total of 5,400 words and 26,000 letters. A human expert labeled all the texts. We present in this paper some iterative adaptation strategies: the performances of the system improve continuously with the amount of data. Thus, we will study the evolution of the recognition rate on three ranges corresponding respectively to 50, 100 and 150 words used for the adaptation. Some other writers who have written less than 50 words are kept to constitute the text training database for the tuning of the writer independent system.[12]

We use for adaptation a lexicon containing the 8,000 most frequent words of the French language. Our system is also able to handle very large lexicons (some 200,000 words) as shown in the following. The complete analysis speed is about 6 words per second (P4 1,8GHz Matlab) and a small amount of memory is required (about 500Ko including the system program, the 8K lexicon and the database).

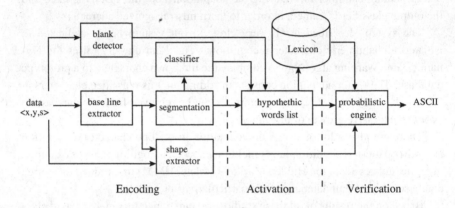

Fig. 10.1.   Baseline system.

The writer independent baseline system is presented in figure 10.1. It is based on the activation-verification cognitive model described by Paap in 1982.[13] The system consists of a set of three neural encoding experts[12] that extract geometrical and morphological informations in the input data (*i.e.* strokes)

The first expert gives informations about the **shape** of the strokes (size of ascender and descender...). We compare the bounding box of the stroke with the estimated height and positioning of medium letters in the line.

The second expert gives us **segmentation** informations like between-letter, within-letter and within-word separation between two consecutive strokes. The input of the neural network is a 32 features vector composed of absolute and relative measurement of the two strokes. We use a *forward backward sequential selection* (FBSS algorithm described in[14]) to keep the most relevant features.

The last expert is the **character classifier**. It is a k-nn classifier and it uses an omni-writer prototype database. This database was created by using an automatic clustering algorithm[15] starting from the 60,000 samples of UNIPEN database[16] (corpus Train-R01/V07). This algorithm is well fitted to heterogeneous character classes with highly variable densities. It overcomes the classical problems of clustering (prototype optimal number, initialization ...). It works on labeled examples of a given class and try to optimize the within-class variance by combining two stages: a sub-optimal unsupervised research of prototypes followed by an adaptation stage using vector quantization. After clustering, the prototype database contains some 3,000 stroke prototypes for the 62 classes (26 upper-case letters, 26 lower-case letters and 10 digits). Each sample represents a given character allograph (for single-stroke characters) or a part of the allograph (for multi-stroke characters). An allograph is a specific handwriting feature. It includes on the one hand characters with the same static representation (i.e. the same image) but written with variable dynamics (number of strokes, senses, direction ...) and on the other hand, the different handwriting model for a given character : cursive, hand-printed, mixed ... When an unknown character has to be classified, it is first divided into strokes. Then, each stroke is compared with a prototype subset producing a distance vector. The distance of the unknown data to each character class is the sum of all the distance vectors (over the number of strokes). The nearest-neighbor criterion is then applied to find the winning class.

All these experts provide probabilistic information at the stroke level. For each expert, we also compute a confusion matrix on the training data, in order to evaluate prior probabilities. We use the Bayesian rule to re-estimate posterior probabilities by combining this latter with prior knowledge. The segmentation probabilities are used to construct the smallest and most relevant segmentation tree of a line of text. The classifier probabilities are used to activate a list of hypothetical words in the lexicon for each segmentation in the tree. A probabilistic engine that combines all the available probabilities evaluates the likelihood of each hypothetic word in this list. We call this information the *probability of lexical reliability* (PLR). We used dynamic programming in the segmentation tree where each node has a PLR in order to get the best re-transcription of the line.

We evaluate this lexicon driven recognizer on differently lexicon size on the whole text database used for adaptation (figure 10.2, graph Omni). We also add some allographes from the text database into the classifier prototype database to turn the system into a multi-writer recognizer (figure 10.2, graph Multi). Even if the recognition rate is not so high, we can notice the very good ability to manipulate very big lexicon. We loose less than 5 % of the recognition rate when we use a 187,000 words lexicon comparing with a 400 words lexicon (4675 times smaller). Finally, we achieve a word error rate of 25 % in a writer-independent frame with a 8,0000 words lexicon.

10.4. Writer adaptation strategies

The baseline system recognition is writer-independent. Its prototype dataset (the so-called WI database) should cover all the writing styles. Each prototype corresponds to a particular shape of a whole letter (*i.e.* allograph). Experimental results show that it covers at least the most common writing styles. We also remark that storing character samples taken from the text database in the prototypes database (multi-writer system) improves greatly the recognition rate. There are, at least, two situations that reduce the recognition rate.

- Missing allograph: the allograph is missing in the prototype database and it must be stored (added) in this set.
- Confusing allograph: for a given writer, the prototype is confusing or erroneous and it must be removed from the prototype database.

Model-based classifier can be adapted very easily and quickly to new writing styles, just by storing new character samples in the writer dependent (WD) database (when these latter miss) and, if needed, by inactivating existing prototypes (when they are confusing). The system specialization on a given user – by registration of his personal features – makes it writer-dependent and increases its accuracy. The comparison of classification hypothesis with either the labeled data (supervised adaptation) or the lexical hypothesis (self-supervised adaptation) detects classification errors. The misclassified characters can be stored in the writer-dependent (WD) database, using the lexical hypothesis as a label.

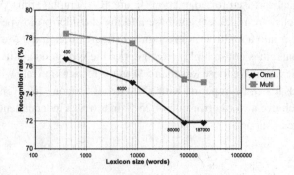

Fig. 10.2.   Recognition rate vs lexicon size.

10.4.1. *Supervised adaptation*

Before comparing the accuracy of self-supervised adaptation strategies, we start by studying supervised technics. We use the labels of the text database and the real text segmentation to carry out supervised adaptation. Note that when we know the text segmentation, our writer-independent recognizer does not have to build a segmentation tree and so the word error rate is about 5 %. The supervised adaptation acts as follow. Characters of the text are classified one after the other. The classification hypothesis (the best answer, top_1, of the character classifier) is compared with the label. If they do not match, the mis-recognized character is stored in the user personal database (figure 10.3). We consider two approaches: the *text* approach where the characters are added at the end of the analysis of the text and the *line* approach where the characters are added at the end of the analysis of each line. The results (table 10.1) show the improvement of the recognition rate due to the writer adaptation of the handwriting recognition system when the segmentation of the text in words and letters is known. We present the word error rate (WER) after 50, 100, and 150 analyzed words.

Fig. 10.3.   Supervised addition of prototypes in the user database.

As we know the labels and the text segmentation (it is not realistic just an interesting case study), we achieve an awesome word recognition rate of 99 % that proves the necessity of applying adaptation strategies to recognition systems. The WDDBS show the amount of prototypes added in the WD database regarding to the WI database size. The *line* approach allows a faster improvement of the recognition rate and adds fewer prototypes to the user database than the *text* approach. When we add characters after a full text analysis, we can add several similar prototypes (and the average number of added prototypes increases). On the other hand, the *line* approach, adds the first prototype of a mis-recognized character. Thanks to this new sample, the following similar characters are correctly classi-

Table 10.1. Supervised adaptation: Word error rate WER and WD database size WDDBS (known segmentation). *min* is the result on the best writer, *max* is the result on the worst writer and *mean* is the result on the overall text database (8k lexicon).

	WER			WDDBS
Words	50	100	150	
Baseline system		5 %		100 %
Text appr.: min	0 %	0 %	0 %	+3 %
mean	1.3 %	1.1 %	0.6 %	+6 %
max	10 %	5.1 %	4.5 %	+9 %
Line Appr.: min	0 %	0 %	0 %	+2 %
mean	**1.1 %**	**0.7 %**	**0.4 %**	**+4 %**
max	6.2 %	5.2 %	3.7 %	+8 %

fied, so they do not need to be stored in the prototypes database. So, the number of added prototypes is smaller in the *line* approach than in the *text* approach and we select the first strategy for the following works. Due to the architecture of the recognition system, it is not possible to study a *word* approach, where we made the adaptation after each analyzed words. It seems logical to think that a *word* approach should perform better than the *line* approach but the difference should not be enough to change completely the results obtained with the *line* approach.

From a perceptive point of view, the prototype storing imitates – at the letter level – the priming repetition effect noticed at the word level: the initial presentation of a word reduces the amount of information necessary to its future identification and this identification is performed faster. Nevertheless, activating WD prototypes is not sufficient to perform perfect classification, even with a great amount of labeled data. Some added characters will generate mis-classification and new errors will appear. It seems necessary to inactivate – or even delete – some WI prototypes.

10.4.2. *Self-supervised adaptation*

In self-supervised adaptation, we use the recognizer in a real framework, *i.e.* the data labels and the text segmentation are not known (our reference system achieve a word error rate of 25 % on a 8,000 words lexicon, see figure 10.2). Moreover, self-supervised adaptation must be completely hidden to the writer which should not be solicited by the system. Now, the classifier hypothesis and the lexical hypothesis are compared to find which prototypes must be stored in the user database.

Fig. 10.4. Self-Supervised adaptation method. Addition of prototypes in the user database.

10.4.2.1. *Systematical activation (SA)*

In the systematical activation strategy, we consider that the lexical analyzer is "perfect". Therefore, when an error (difference between the classification hypothesis and the lexical hypothesis) occurs, the corresponding character is stored in the user personal database. Due to the lexical analyzer errors cumulated with the segmentation errors, some prototypes are stored in bad classes (figure 10.4). These errors introduce many new classification errors. The performances of the recognition system after adaptation is just a little bit better than those of the baseline system (table 10.2).

10.4.2.2. *Conditional activation (CA)*

As the previous strategy is not really accurate, it seems necessary to study the behavior of the lexical analyzer in order to store only useful prototypes. We saw that the recognition engine estimates for each word a *probability of lexical reliability (PLR, section 10.3)*. This PLR reflects the probability of error of the lexical analyzer for this word. The conditional activation strategy is described in the following. If, for a given word, the PLR is greater than α (*i.e.* we have good confidence in this word), then the mis-classified characters of this word are added to the user database. We determined the α parameter on the text training database by minimizing the Bayesian error between the PLR distributions of well-corrected words and words which were not well corrected by lexical analysis. We obtained an α of 0.015 and we show in table 10.2 the result of the conditional activation.

The CA strategy is more accurate than the SA strategy as it reduces considerably the false additions of prototypes (see the small growth of the user database). Moreover, with the CA strategy the error rate decreases continuously over the time. After 150 words of adaptation, the error rate decreases of about 8 %.

Table 10.2. Systematic and conditional activation: Word error rate WER and WD database size WDDBS (8k lexicon).

	WER			WDDBS
Words	50	100	150	
Baseline system	25 %			100 %
SA strategy: min	0 %	1.9 %	2 %	+2 %
mean	25 %	23 %	23 %	+6 %
max	53 %	73 %	51 %	+14 %
CA strategy: min	0 %	0 %	2 %	+1 %
mean	**22 %**	**20 %**	**17 %**	**+2 %**
max	71 %	58 %	43 %	+3 %

10.4.2.3. *Dynamic management (DM)*

This method has two goals. As seen previously, using lexical hypothesis as a reference may add confusing or erroneous prototypes, even when conditional activation is applied. Dynamic management is used to recover from those prototypes that contribute more often to incorrect than correct classifications. Inactivation methods are also used to prune the prototype set and speed-up the classification.[9] Each prototype (of the WI database as of the WD database) has an initial adequacy ($Q_0 = 1000$). This adequacy is modified during the recognition of the text according to the usefulness of the prototype in the classification process, by comparing the classification hypothesis and the lexical hypothesis. Let us consider the prototype i of the class j, three parameters are necessary for the dynamic management:

- **G** : Rewards (+) the prototype i when it performs **G**ood classification (classification and lexical hypotheses are the same).
- **M** : Penalizes (-) the prototype i when it performs **M**is-classification (classification and lexical hypotheses are different).
- **U** : Penalizes (-) for all the **U**seless prototypes of the class j.

The three parameters act differently. The U parameter is used to reduce the adequacy of the useless prototypes for a given writer. As the baseline recognizer is writer-independent, it needs many prototypes (an average of 40 prototypes per class) to model a character class but only a few ones will be useful for a given user. This parameter eliminates the prototypes that are not used during a long time. The value of U defines this life "time". The M parameter is used to penalize strongly erroneous prototypes. The value of this parameter must be bigger than the value of U because erroneous prototypes are much more troublesome than useless prototypes. By preserving only these two parameters, all the prototypes should disappear. Thus, it is necessary to reward good prototypes. To achieve it, the G parameter is used to increase the adequacy of any prototype activated during the classification and validated by the lexical analyzer. The equation (10.1) describes the evolution of the prototype adequacy. Where F_j is the frequency of the class j in the French language. These three parameters are mutually exclusive *i.e.* on each occurrence, only one parameter is activated. When $Q^i_j = 0$, the prototype is removed from the database. If these parameters are finely tuned, the system should inactivate quickly erroneous prototypes while preserving only the useful writer prototypes. After an exhaustive search of the parameters (G, M, U) the optimal triplet is (30, 200, 8) and does not depend of the lexicon size used for the lexical analysis. Moreover, we can change their values by $\pm 20\ \%$ without changing the results. A complete analysis of these three parameters can be found on.[14]

$$Q^i_j(n+1) = Q^i_j(n) + [G(n) - M(n) - U(n)]/F_j \qquad (10.1)$$

The dynamic management combined with the conditional activation strategy is very efficient as it greatly reduces the size of the database while preserving the recognition rate of the conditional activation strategy (table 10.3). Even with a very large lexicon of more than 187,000 words, this self-supervised adaptation technique is very accurate and allows us to increase the recognition rate of about 7 %.

Table 10.3. Dynamic management: Word error rate WER and WD database size WDDBS after 150 adaptation words for two different lexicon sizes.

	WER		WDDBS
	8k words	187k words	
Baseline system	25 %	28 %	100 %
DM strategy	**17 %**	**21 %**	**-80 %**

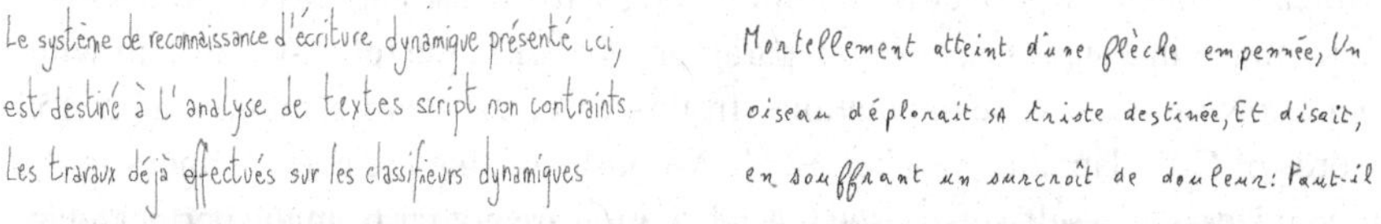

Fig. 10.5. Best recognition rate writer (99 %) and worst writer (70 %).

Now, let us focus on the evolution of the adequacy of some prototypes (figure 10.6). For some writers, the WI prototypes are sufficient. For the class 'a', 2 prototypes are used and thus the adequacy of the 45 others decreases. For the class 's', 4 prototypes are useful (the writer has probably an unstable writing, see figure 10.5) and the 36 others are inactivated. For another writer (class 's' and 'e'), WD prototypes (in bold) are necessary. For the class 's', at the beginning, a WI prototype is used and after some 15 occurrences, a WD prototype is added (the writer gets familiar with the handheld device and the pen). Another WD prototype is stored after some 35 occurrences (the user writes faster perhaps and changes his way of writing). After 150 adaptation words, the size of the prototype database was reduced by 80 %.

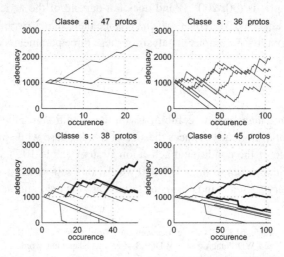

Fig. 10.6. Prototypes adequacy evolution vs. occurrence. Thin lines are WI prototypes and bold lines are WD prototypes.

10.5. Supervised / self-supervised combination

We can simulate a perfect adaptation strategy if we use the prototype database determined in a supervised way in paragraph 10.4.1 in the reference system without knowing the text segmentation. In this case, the word error rate after 150 words of CA adaptation reaches 12 %. We just saw that the performances of the recognizer with a self-supervised CA adaptation are not far from the perfect adaptation (17 % against 12 %). It seems interesting to introduce some labelled data (*i.e.* soliciting the user to enter the real word) in the self-supervised adaptation scheme to achieve better results. So, it becomes a combination of supervised and self-supervised adaptation called semi-supervised strategy.

Soliciting the user for writing 150 words is much too constraining. On the other hand, asking him (her) to write some words is acceptable, especially if the recognition rate is largely improved. This last combination consists in carrying out a supervised adaptation of the system on some known words and then uses the self-supervised dynamic management adaptation strategy (table 10.4). Asking the user to write a sentence of 30 words decreases the error rate to 10 % which is even better than supervised adaptation performed alone (12 %)! We guess these very interesting results are due to the fact that, in supervised adaptation, we do not use the dynamic management of the prototypes.

Table 10.4.   Word error rate (WER) in semi-supervised adaptation

Words for supervised adapt.	WER	
	After supervised adapt.	After 100 words more (DM)
0	25 %	20 %
10	24 %	17 %
20	24 %	12 %
30	24 %	10 %
50	23 %	9 %

10.6. Conclusions & Future works

In this paper, we have shown that model-based classifiers are easy to adapt. Thanks to their structure, they can learn new writings styles, by activating new prototypes and inactivating erroneous ones. We first present a supervised adaptation strategy. It is very accurate but not user-friendly as it needs to be supervised by the writer. Then we try to hide the adaptation process and present several self-supervised strategies. The conditional activation scheme is the more accurate as it focuses on reliable words alone. The prototype dynamic management increases both recognition rate (from 75 % to 83 %) and classification speed (close to twice). This process automatically transforms a writer-independent database into a writer-dependent database of very high quality and compactness. Finally, combining supervised and self-supervised improves again the system accuracy (more than 90

It would be interesting to evaluate a semi-supervised strategy where the user is solicited only in the ambiguous cases. We have also to adapt the parameters of the segmentation expert, which actually is the biggest source of error.

References

1. M. Taft, *Reading and mental lexicon*. (Erlbaum Edition, 1991).
2. H. Li. *Traitement de la variabilité et développement de systèmes robustes pour la reconnaissance de l'écriture manuscrite en-ligne*. PhD thesis, UPMC Paris 6, (2002).
3. L. Schomaker, E. H. Helsper, H.-L. Teulings, and G. H. Abbink, Adaptive recognition of online, cursive handwriting, *6th ICOHD*. **1**, 19–21, (1993).
4. A. Brakensiek, A. Kosmala, and G. Rigoll, Comparing adaptation techniques for on-line handwriting recognition, *ICDAR*. **1**, 486–490, (2001).
5. S. D. Connel and A. K. Jain, Writer adaptation of online handwriting models, *IEEE Transaction PAMI*. **24**(3), 329–346, (2002).
6. J. C. Platt and N. P. Matić, A constructive RBF network for writer adaptation, *Advances in Neural Information Processing Systems, 9*. **1**, 765–771, (1997).
7. I. Guyon, D. Henderson, P. Albrecht, Y. L. Cun, and J. Denker, *Writer independent and writer adaptative neural network for on-line character recognition*. (S. Impedovo, From Pixels to Featuress III, Elsevier, 1992).
8. N. Matić, I. Guyon, J. Denker, and V. Vapnik, Writer-adaptation for on-line handwritten character recognition, *ICDAR*. **1**, 187–191, (1993).
9. V. Vuori, J. Laaksonen, and J. Kangas, Influence of erroneous learning samples on adaptation in on-line handwriting recognition, *Pattern Recogntion*. **35**(4), 915–926, (2002).
10. L. Wang and P. Woodland, Mpe-based discriminative linear transform for speaker adaptation, *ICASSP*. (2005).
11. A. Vinciarelli and S. Bengio, Writer adaptation techniques in HMM based off-line cursive script recognition, *Pattern Recognition Letters*. **23**(8), 905–916, (2002).
12. L. Oudot, L. Prevost, and M. Milgram, An activation-verification model for on-line texts recognition, *IWFHR*. **1**, 9–13, (2004).
13. K. Paap, S. L. Newsome, J. E. McDonald, and R. W. Schvaneveldt, An activation-verification model for letter and word recognition: The word superiority effect, *Psychological Review*. **89**, 573–594, (1982).
14. L. Oudot. *Fusion d'informations et adaptation pour la reconnaissance de textes manuscrits dynamiques*. PhD thesis, UPMC Paris 6, (2003).
15. L. Prevost and M. Milgram, Modelizing character allographs in omni-scriptor frame: a new non-supervised algorithm, *Pattern Recognition Letters*. **21**(4), 295–302, (2000).
16. I. Guyon, L. Schomaker, R. Plamondon, M. Liberman, and S. Janet, UNIPEN project of on-line data exchange and recognizer benchmarks, *ICPR'94*. pp. 29–33, (1994).

CHAPTER 11

COMBINING MODEL-BASED AND DISCRIMINATIVE APPROACHES IN A MODULAR TWO-STAGE CLASSIFICATION SYSTEM: APPLICATION TO ISOLATED HANDWRITTEN DIGIT RECOGNITION

Jonathan Milgram, Robert Sabourin and Mohamed Cheriet

Laboratoire d'Imagerie, de Vision et d'Intelligence Artificielle
École de Technologie Supérieure, Université du Québec
1100, rue Notre-Dame Ouest, Montréal, Canada, H3C-1K3
http://www.livia.etsmtl.ca

The motivation of this work is based on two key observations. First, the classification algorithms can be separated into two main categories: discriminative and model-based approaches. Second, two types of patterns can generate problems: ambiguous patterns and outliers. While, the first approach tries to minimize the first type of error, but cannot deal effectively with outliers, the second approach, which is based on the development of a model for each class, make the outlier detection possible, but are not sufficiently discriminant. Thus, we propose to combine these two different approaches in a modular two-stage classification system embedded in a probabilistic framework. In the first stage we estimate the posterior probabilities with a model-based approach and we re-estimate only the highest probabilities with appropriate Support Vector Classifiers (SVC) in the second stage. Another advantage of this combination is to reduce the principal burden of SVC, the processing time necessary to make a decision and to open the way to use SVC in classification problem with a large number of classes. Finally, the first experiments on the benchmark database MNIST have shown that our dynamic classification process allows to maintain the accuracy of SVCs, while decreasing complexity by a factor 8.7 and making the outlier rejection available.

1. Introduction

The principal objective of a pattern recognition system is to minimize classification errors. However, another important factor is the capability to estimate a confidence measure in the decision made by the system. Indeed, this type of measure is essential to be able to make no decision when the result of classification is uncertain. From this point of view, it is necessary to distinguish two categories of problematic patterns. The first one relates to ambiguous data which may cause confusion between several classes and the second category consists of data not belonging to any class: the outliers.

Furthermore, most classification algorithms can be divided into two main categories denoted as discriminative and model-based approaches. The former tries to split the feature space into several regions by decision surfaces, whereas the latter is based on the development of a model for each class along with a similarity measure between each of these models and the unknown pattern (see Fig. 1). Different terms are used in literature to refer it, generative method[2], density model[18], approach by modeling[23] or model-based classifier[21].

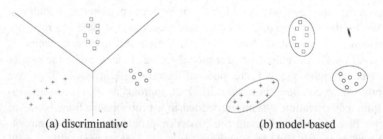

(a) discriminative   (b) model-based

Figure 1. Two types of classification approaches.

Thus, as is shown by Liu *et al.*[18], the discriminative classifiers are more accurate in classifying ambiguous data, but not suitable for outlier detection, whereas model-based approaches are able to reject outliers but not effective in classifying ambiguous patterns. Considering this, the authors propose to hybridize the two types of approaches internally or to combine them externally. In a more recent paper[19], the same authors have tested an internal fusion of the two approaches. Their method improves the accuracy of the model-based approach by using discriminative learning. However, even though their classifier is more accurate, it is not as accurate as the best discriminative approaches such as support vector classifiers.

Hence, in this paper, we propose to combine a model-based approach with support vector classifier (SVC). This classification system should give high accuracy and strong outlier resistance. The idea is to develop a two-stage classification system. At the first stage, a model-based approach can directly classify patterns that are recognized with high confidence, reject outliers or insulate those classes in conflict. Then, if conflict is detected, the appropriate SVCs will make better decision at the second stage. Another advantage of this combination is to reduce the main burden of SVC: the processing time necessary to make a decision.

Thus, the proposed system is a multiple classifiers combination, which is a widely studied domain in classification.[4,9,13,14,15] Although a number of similar ideas related to two-stage classification to treat ambiguity were introduced in recent papers,[1,5,8,21,22,24] our classification system remains different and original. Indeed, the idea of multiple classifiers combination to treat ambiguity is presented by Gunes *et al.*,[8] but the proposed system combine only different model-based classifiers and is only tested on 2D artificial data. On the other hand, the combination of model-based and discriminative approaches is proposed by several authors[5,8,21,22] but their motivations are different. In the approach proposed by Francesconi *et al.*,[5] the model-based approach is used in a second stage to slightly improve the rejection capability of the MLP used at the first stage. Prevost *et al.*[21] use only a few MLPs to improve the accuracy of the first classifier, which used a reduced number of prototypes. Ragot & Anquetil[22] use fuzzy decision trees to improve significantly a first system based on fuzzy clustering, but their combination is not as accurate as SVC. Concerning the use of SVCs in a second stage of classification to improve the accuracy two different approaches are proposed.[1,24] Bellili *et al.*[1] take into account the problem of complexity of SVCs, but in the first-stage they use MLP which is another discriminative approach. Furthermore, their system does not make decisions at the first-stage and always uses one SVC, and never more than one, which limits the performance of the system. Vuurpijl *et al.*[24] propose several elaborate strategies for detecting conflicts. However, they do not take into account the problem of complexity. Indeed, the first-stage uses a complex ensemble of classifiers. Moreover, the results of their two-stage system are not compared to a full SVCs system. Thus, if the use of SVCs can improve the accuracy of the ensemble of classifier used in the first stage, would it then be better to use a full SVCs system?

Moreover, we embed our system within a probabilistic framework, because as mentioned by Platt: "The output of a classifier should be a calibrated posterior probability to enable post-processing".[20] Indeed, this type of confidence measure is essential in many application, when the classifier only contributes a small part of the final decision or if it is preferable to make no decision when the result of classification is uncertain. So, in the first stage, we estimate the probabilities with a model-based approach and re-estimate only the highest probabilities with appropriate SVCs in the second stage. Thus, to compare the quality of the probabilities estimate by the different methods, we use the Chow's rule to evaluate their error-reject tradeoff. Indeed, as it is shown by Fumera *et al.*,[6] this rule provides the optimal error-reject tradeoff only if the posterior probabilities of the data classes are exactly known. But, in real applications, such probabilities are affected by significant estimate errors. In consequence, the better the probabilities estimate is, the better the error-reject tradeoff is.

This paper is organized as follows: Section 2 presents the model-based approach, while the section 3 presents its combination with discriminative approach. Section 4 summarizes our experimental results and the last section concludes with some perspectives.

2. Model-based approach

One of the main advantages of this type of approach is the modularity. Indeed the training process is computationally cheap because the model of each class is learned independently. Thus, it is well scalable to large category problems such as Chinese character recognition.[12] On the other hand, this also facilitates the increment/decrement of categories without re-training all categories.

2.1. Characterization of the pattern recognition problem

Although this type of approach is not very discriminant, it can be used to characterize the problem of pattern recognition. Thus, three cases can be considered during testing:

- A single similarity measure is significant. The pattern can be directly classified.

- Several similarity measures are comparable. It is an ambiguous pattern and it is better to use a discriminative approach to make decision.

- All similarity measures are unsignificant. The pattern can be considered as an outlier.

An artificial toy example with only 2 features is presented in Fig. 2 to show how this type of classifier is able to detect outliers and ambiguous patterns. The ideal similarity measure of each class is represented by level line in (a) and (b). Thus, we can see that it is possible to use it to make new interesting measures. Indeed, in this simple example with two classes, the maximum of the two similarity measures shown in (c) can be used to detect outlier, whereas the minimum shown in (d) can be used to detect conflict.

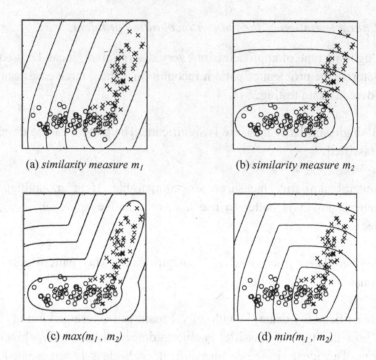

(a) *similarity measure m_1*   (b) *similarity measure m_2*

(c) *max(m_1, m_2)*   (d) *min(m_1, m_2)*

Figure 2. Use of model-based approach to detect outliers (c) and ambiguous patterns (d).

2.2. *Modeling data with hyperplanes*

To start, we make the assumption that each class is composed of a single cluster in the feature space and that data distributions are Gaussian in nature. Then, a classical Bayesian approach consists to use parametric methods to model each class statistically based on data means and covariance, which can be used in quadratic discriminant functions to make decision. But, Kimura *et al.*[12] showed that quadratic discriminant functions are very sensitive to the estimation error of the covariance matrix. Thus, in many applications with a large number of features, it is preferable to regularize the covariance matrix. Another improvement proposed by Kimura *et al.*[12] is to neglect the nondominant eigenvectors, because the estimation errors in the nondominant eigenvectors are much greater than those of the dominant eigenvectors.

With the same idea, it is possible to model each class ω_j with a hyperplane defined by the mean vector μ_j, and the matrix Ψ_j which contains the k first eigenvectors ϕ_j^i extracted from the covariance matrix Σ_j. Then, the measure of the similarity (or dissimilarity) used is the projection distance on the hyperplane:

$$d_j(x) = \left\| x - f_j(x) \right\|^2 . \tag{1}$$

Thus, given a data point x of the feature space, the membership to the class ω_j can be evaluated by the square of the Euclidean distance d_j from the point x to its projection on the hyperplane:

$$f_j(x) = \left((x - \mu_j)\Psi_j \right)\Psi_j^T + \mu_j . \tag{2}$$

Finally, it is possible to reformulate the projection distance to reduce the complexity of calculation:

$$d_j(x) = \left\| x - \mu_j \right\|^2 - \sum_{i=1}^{k} \left\{ (x - \mu_j)\phi_j^i \right\}^2 . \tag{3}$$

The Fig. 3 shows a simple example of projection distance, where each class is modeled by its principal axis ($k = 1$) and the data point x is projected on $f_1(x)$ and $f_2(x)$.

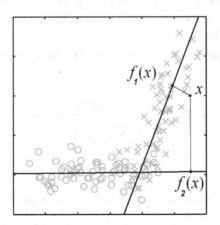

Figure 3. 2D example of projection distance.

Although it would be preferable to bound the hyperplanes with the intention to close the decision surface, when the feature space is very large and bounded, it seems that the probability that a pattern is far away from the training data and close to the hyperplane is very low. Thus, Kimura *et al.*[11] showed that the accuracy obtained by the projection distance method is very close to the accuracy of a three layer autoassociative neural networks with sigmoid function on the hidden layer, which guaranties to close the decision surface.[7]

Furthermore, this method requires the optimization of only one parameter: the number k of eigenvectors used. But, as we can see in section 4.1, this parameter is crucial for classification. Thus, if k is too small, the models are not precise so we loose too much information. In fact, while $k = 0$, each class is model by a simple prototype that is the mean vector μ_j of training data. On the other hand, if the value of k is too large, the models are not discriminative. At worst, if $k = d$, where d is the dimension of the input pattern, the hyperplane embeds all the points of the feature space. Hence, for all point x, the projection distance will be null.

2.3. *Estimate posterior probability*

Thus, if the processed pattern is not an outlier, we can estimate posterior probability in the first stage of our system. Then, if we suppose that the distribution of the projection distances between the margins is exponential, we can use the softmax function to map projection distance to posterior probability:

$$\hat{P}_f(\omega_j \mid x) = \frac{\exp(-\alpha\, d_j(x))}{\sum_{j'=1}^{c} \exp(-\alpha\, d_{j'}(x))}. \tag{4}$$

3. Combination with discriminative approach

Thereafter, if a pattern is considered as ambiguous in the first stage of our system, we use appropriate discriminative experts to re-estimate only the most significant posterior probabilities in the second stage.

3.1. *Conflict detection*

The first step is to detect the patterns that may cause confusion. Bellili *et al.*[1] and Prevost *et al.*[21] consider that conflict involves only two classes and they use appropriate experts, to reprocess all samples,[1] or just the samples rejected by the first classifier.[21] However, we consider that conflict may involve more than two classes. Hence, it is preferable to use a dynamic number of classes in conflict. With this intention, we determine the list of p classes $\{\omega_{\ell(1)}, \ldots, \omega_{\ell(p)}\}$ of which the posterior probabilities estimated in the first stage are higher than a threshold ε. Thus, $\ell(j)$ is the index of the j th class that verifies:

$$\hat{P}_f(\omega_{\ell(j)} \mid x) > \varepsilon. \tag{5}$$

Then, if p is superior to one, we use in the second stage the appropriate discriminative expert to re-estimate the posterior probabilities of the p classes. Finally, this parameter controls the tolerance level of the first stage of classification and consequently the classifying cost. Indeed, the smaller the threshold ε is, the larger the number p will tend to be. If ε is too large, then we never use the second stage of classification. But, if ε is too small, then the system uses unnecessary discriminative classifiers.

3.2. *Use of Support Vector Classifiers*

A recent benchmarking of state-of-the-art techniques for handwritten digit recognition[19] has shown that Support Vector Classifier (SVC) gives higher accuracy than classical neural classifiers like Multi Layer Perceptron (MLP) or Radial Basis Function (RBF) networks. However, thanks to the improvement of the computing power and the development of new learning algorithms, it is now possible to train SVC in real world applications. Thus, we choose to use SVC in the second stage of our system. Also, if an SVC can possibly make good decisions, these output values are uncalibrated. But, a simple solution is proposed by Platt[20] to map the SVC outputs into posterior probabilities. Given a training set of instance-label pairs $\{(x_k, y_k) : k = 1, \ldots, n\}$, where $y_k \in \{1, -1\}$ and $x_k \in \Re^d$, the unthresholded output of an SVC is

$$f(x) = \sum_{k=1}^{n} y_k \alpha_k K(x_k, x) + \beta,$$ (6)

where the samples with non-zero Lagrange multiplier α_k are called support vectors (SVs).

Since the class-conditional between the margins are apparently exponential the authors suggest to fit an additional sigmoid function (Equ. 7) to estimate probabilities.

$$\hat{P}(y = 1 \mid x) = \frac{1}{1 + \exp(af(x) + b)}$$ (7)

The parameter a and b are derived by minimizing the negative log likelihood of the training data, which is a cross-entropy function:

$$-\sum_{k=1}^{n} \left(t_k \log\left(\hat{P}(y_k = 1 \mid x_k) \right) + (1 - t_k) \log\left(1 - \hat{P}(y_k = 1 \mid x_k) \right) \right),$$ (8)

where $t_k = \dfrac{y_k + 1}{2}$ denotes the probability target.

Then, to solve this optimization problem, the author uses a model-trust minimization algorithm based on the Levenberg-Marquardt algorithm. But, in a recent note[17] it is shown that there are two problems in the pseudo-code provided by Platt.[20] One is the calculation of the objective value, and the other is the implementation of the optimization algorithm. Therefore, the authors propose another minimization algorithm more reliable, based on a simple Newton's method with backtracking line search. Thus, we use this second algorithm to fit additional sigmoid function and estimate posterior probabilities.

Furthermore, SVC is a binary classifier, so it is necessary to combine several SVCs to solve a multi-class problem. A most classical method is the "one against all" strategy in which one SVC per class is constructed. Each classifier is trained to distinguish the examples in a single class from the examples in all remaining classes. Although this strategy is very accurate, it seems better to use in the second stage of our system a "pairwise coupling" approach, which consists to construct a classifier for each pair of classes. Indeed, this strategy is more modular and as reported by Chang & Lin,[3] although we have to train as many as c(c-1)/2 classifiers, as each problem is easier, the total training time of "pairwise coupling" may not be more than that of the "one against all" method. Furthermore, if we use "one against all" SVCs in the second stage, we are obliged to calculate the distances of a large number of SVs belonging to the implausible classes, which increases the classifying cost. Thus, we choose to use a "pairwise coupling" approach and we apply the "Resemblance Model" proposed by Hamamura *et al.*[10] to combine posterior probability of each pairwise classifier into posterior probability of multi-class classifier. Then, since prior probabilities are all the same, posterior probabilities can be estimated by

$$\hat{P}(\omega_j \mid x) = \frac{\prod_{j' \neq j} \hat{P}(\omega_j \mid x \in \omega_{j,j'})}{\sum_{j''=1}^{c} \prod_{j' \neq j''} \hat{P}(\omega_{j''} \mid x \in \omega_{j'',j'})}, \qquad (9)$$

where $\omega_{j,j'}$ denotes the union of classes ω_j and $\omega_{j'}$.

3.3. Re-estimate posterior probabilities

Finally, as we can see in Fig. 4, we use only $p(p-1)/2$ SVCs to re-estimate only the most significant posterior probabilities. In consequence, the final probabilities are not homogeneous, since they can be estimated by different approaches. However, it is not an important drawback. Indeed, when p is superior to one, the first stage estimates only the smallest probabilities, which are negligible, and in this case the second stage estimates all the remaining probabilities. These p significant probabilities are obtained by

$$\hat{P}_s(\omega_{\ell(j)} \mid x) = \frac{\prod_{j''=1, j'' \neq j}^{p} \hat{P}_s(\omega_{\ell(j)} \mid x \in \omega_{\ell(j), \ell(j'')})}{\sum_{j'=1}^{p} \prod_{j''=1, j'' \neq j'}^{p} \hat{P}_s(\omega_{\ell(j')} \mid x \in \omega_{\ell(j'), \ell(j'')})} \times \left(1 - \sum_{j'=p+1}^{c} \hat{P}_f(\omega_{\ell(j')} \mid x) \right), \quad (10)$$

where the first term is related to the second stage, while the second term is related to the first stage. The objective of this second term is to maintain the sum of all the probabilities equal to one.

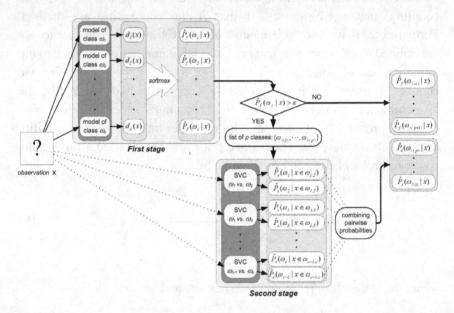

Figure 4. Overview of our two-stage classification system.

4. Experimental results

To evaluate our method, we chose a classical pattern recognition problem: isolated handwritten digit recognition. Thus, in our experiments, we used a well-known benchmark database. The MNIST (Modified NIST) dataset[a] was extracted from the NIST special database SD3 and SD7. The original binary images were normalized into 20×20 grey-scale images with aspect ratio preserved and the normalized images

---

[a] available at http://yann.lecun.com/exdb/mnist/

were centered by center of mass in 28×28 images. Some sample images of this database are shown in Fig. 5.

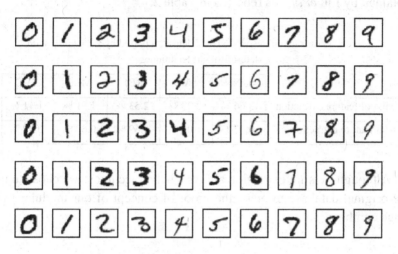

Figure 5. Sample images of MNIST dataset.

The learning dataset contains 60,000 samples and 10,000 others are used for testing. Moreover, we have divided the learning database into two subsets. The first 50,000 samples have been used for training and the next 10,000 for validation. Finally, the number of samples per class for each subset is reported in the Table 1.

Table 1. Number of samples per class in the three subset of the MNIST database.

	ω_1	ω_2	ω_3	ω_4	ω_5	ω_6	ω_7	ω_8	ω_9	ω_{10}
training	4932	5678	4968	5101	4859	4506	4951	5175	4842	4988
validation	991	1064	990	1030	983	915	967	1090	1009	961
test	980	1135	1032	1010	982	892	958	1028	974	1009

Several papers dealt with the MNIST database. The best result mentioned in the original paper[16] is obtained by the convolutional neural network LeNet-5 (0.95% of error rate on the test dataset). More recently, a benchmarking of state-of-the-art techniques[19] has shown that SVC with

8-direction gradient features gives the highest accuracy reported at this day (0.42% of error rate on the test dataset). A short summary of results obtained by Liu *et al.*[19] is reported in Table 2.

Table 2. Error rate on the MNIST test dataset reported by Liu *et al.*[19] with state-of-the-art techniques.

	k-NN	LVQ	RBF	MLP	SVC
without feature extraction	3.66 %	2.79 %	2.53 %	1.91 %	1.41 %
with feature extraction	0.97 %	1.05 %	0.69 %	0.60 %	0.42 %

Although, feature extraction allows a better accuracy, we chose to use the original database to make the proof of concept of our modular two-stage combination.

4.1. *Model-based approach*

Initially, we must fix the dimensionality of the hyperplane models. For this purpose, we chose to use the same value of k for all hyperplanes, because it is not trivial to find the optimal values of each hyperplane. Furthermore, we think that it is not a problem to use a suboptimal solution because the second stage is here to refine classification. Finally, we use the validation dataset to find the better value of k and we can see in Fig. 6 that this parameter strongly influences the accuracy of the classification. Consequently, we use $k = 25$ and we obtain an error rate of 4.09 % on the test dataset. For comparison, we obtain an error rate of 7.06 % with the quadratic discriminant function. Indeed, because the data have many singular directions, we are forced to add an important constant ($\lambda = 0.4$).

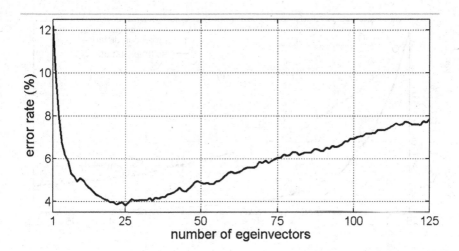

Figure 6. Effect of the dimensionality of the hyperplane models.

Thereafter, the α parameter of the softmax function (Equ. 4) is chosen to minimize the cross entropy error on the validation dataset. We obtain the best result with α = 5.6. We can notice in Fig. 7 that the use of the softmax function improves significantly the error-reject tradeoff of the model-based and that half of the examples with the highest confidence levels are correctly classified.

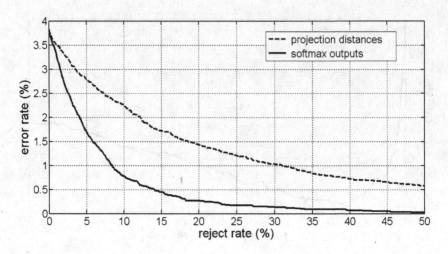

Figure 7. Error-reject tradeoff of the model-based approach on the validation dataset.

Finally, even though the reliability of the proposed model-based approach is not very high, it should be able to characterize the pattern recognition problem. Indeed, as we can see below, the three cases considered in section 2.1 can be observed in real application like isolated digit recognition:

- A single projection distance is very small. The pattern can be considered as **unambiguous** and the posterior probabilities can be directly estimated (see Fig. 8).

- Several projection distances are small. The pattern can be considered as **ambiguous** and it is preferable to re-estimate the posterior probabilities with the discriminative approach (see Fig. 13).

- All projection distances are high. The pattern can be considered as **outlier** and can be rejected (see Fig. 9).

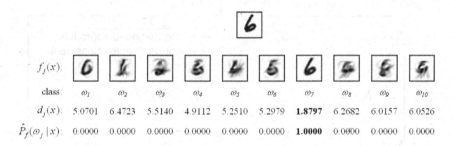

Figure 8. Example of unambiguous pattern (8,400th sample of the test dataset).

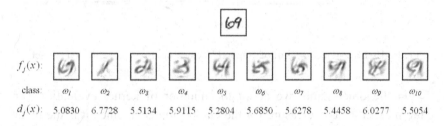

Figure 9. Example of outlier (generated with the 12th and 13th sample of the test dataset).

4.2. Support Vector Classifiers

The training and testing of all SVCs are performed with the LIBSVM software.[3] We use the C-SVC with a Gaussian kernel $K(x_k, x) = \exp(-\gamma \|x_k - x\|^2)$. The penalty parameter C and the kernel parameter γ are empirically optimized by trial and error. Then, we have chosen parameters that minimize the error rate on the validation dataset. Finally, we used $C = 10$ and $\gamma = 0.0185$ and we obtain an error rate of 1.48 % on the test dataset, which is comparable with those reported by Liu *et al.*[19] when no discriminative features are extracted. Moreover, as we can see in Fig. 10 the SVCs estimate better probabilities than model-based approach.

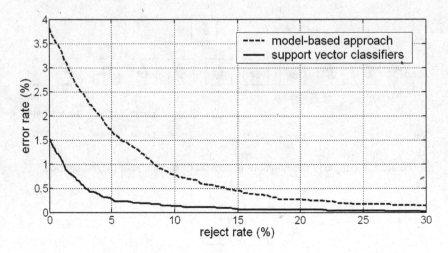

Figure 10. Error-reject tradeoff of Support Vector Classifiers on validation dataset.

On the other hand, we adopt the number of kernel evaluation per pattern (KEPP) as a measure for the classifying cost, since it is the main cause of the computation effort during the test phase. Thus, our ensemble of 45 SVCs requires 11,118 KEPPs to make decision.

4.3. *Two-stage classification system*

As we can see on Table 3, after the first stage of classification the label of the data is not always in the first two classes, which justifies the choice of a dynamic number of classes in conflict.

Table 3. Ranking distibution of the label obtained with the model-based approach on the validation dataset.

ranking of the label	1	2	3	> 3
% of the dataset	96.18	2.50	0.76	0.56

According to the application constraints, it is necessary to make a compromise between accuracy and complexity. The threshold ε of Equ. 5

controls this tradeoff. Then, the validation dataset can be used to fix this parameter according to the constraints fixed by the application.

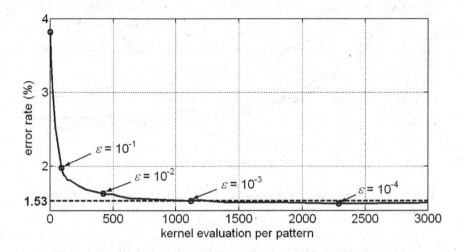

Figure 11. Accuracy-complexity tradeoff on the validation dataset.

As we can see in Fig. 11, while using a threshold of 10^{-3}, it is possible to obtain exactly the same error rate of 1.53% than with the full "pairwise coupling" ensemble. Moreover, the use of a smaller threshold ($\varepsilon = 10^{-4}$) allows a slightly better error-reject tradeoff (see Fig. 12), but the number of KEPP is multiplied by two.

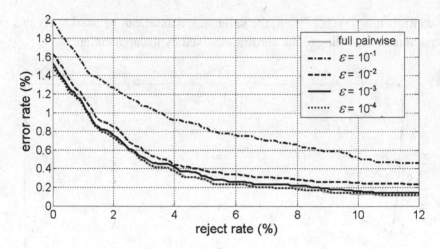

Figure 12. Error-reject tradoff of our two-stage classification system on the validation dataset.

For this reason, we fix the tolerance threshold ε at 10^{-3}, which seems a good tradeoff between accuracy and complexity. The Fig. 13 shows an example of ambiguous pattern. We can see in dark the posterior probability efficiently re-estimated by the second stage. Thus, if we had used $\varepsilon = 10^{-4}$, we would have obtained for this example a number $p = 7$ of classes in conflict and we would have used 21 SVCs to re-estimate posterior probabilities.

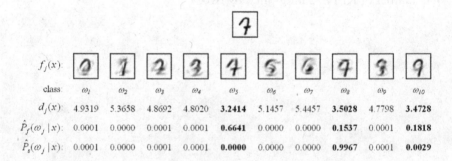

Figure 13. Example of ambiguous pattern (5,907th sample of the test dataset).

Also, while the number p of SVCs used is dynamic, it is interesting to observe the distribution of p (Fig. 15). Hence, we can see that with our threshold of 10^{-3}, the half of the examples are processed without SVC, which confirms the previous remark related to Fig. 7.

Finally, our two-stage system uses a mean of 1,120.1 KEPP and obtained on the test dataset an error rate of 1.50 %, which is comparable to the result of the full "pairwise coupling" ensemble (1.48 %). The analysis of these 150 errors reported in Fig.14, shows that only one error is due to the first stage, which classify directly 4,890 test samples.

Figure 14. The 150 errors obtained on the test dataset (label - > decision).

Moreover, as we can see in Fig.15, it is necessary to use more than one SVC to resolve conflict. This fact shows that the first level is not effective enough.

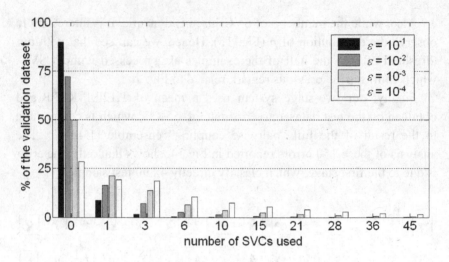

Figure 15. Distribution of the number p of SVCs used to classify the validation dataset.

5. Conclusions and perspectives

We have presented a new classification architecture that has several interesting properties for application to pattern recognition. It combines the advantages of a model-based classifier, in particular modularity and efficient rejection of outliers, with the high accuracy of SVC. Moreover, it greatly reduces the decision time related to the SVC, which is very important in the majority of real pattern recognition systems.

The results on the MNIST database show that the use of the first stage to estimate probabilities allows to reduce the classifying cost by a factor 8.7, while preserving the accuracy of the full "pairwise coupling" ensemble (see Table 4). Indeed, if we express the computational complexity in number of floating point operations (FLOPs), a kernel evaluation requires 2,355 FLOPs and a projection distance evaluation requires 81,510 FLOPs. Thus, the computational cost necessary to classify a pattern is approximately 26.2 MFLOPs with the full "pairwise coupling" ensemble, only 0.4 MFLOPs with the model-based approach and an average of 3.0 MFLOPs with our dynamic two-stage process.

Table 4. Error-reject tradeoff of the three approaches on the test dataset.

error rate (%)		0.5	0.4	0.3	0.2	0.1
reject rate (%)	model-based approach	12.68	13.74	16.97	20.01	28.59
	our two-stage system	3.31	3.99	4.94	6.57	9.85
	full "pairwise coupling"	3.29	4.00	5.13	6.34	9.55

Furthermore, while this implementation is only a proof of concept, several aspects can be improved in future works. Indeed, the model-based approach used in the first stage is not accurate. Thus, the use of a mixture of hyperplanes to model each class instead of one single hyperplane per class should improve significantly the accuracy of the first stage. Then, it will be interesting to test the capability of model-based approach to reject outliers. With this intention, we propose to generate a database of artificial outliers like "touching digit" shown in Fig. 9.

In addition, to improve the generalization performance, as shown by Liu *et al.*,[19] it is preferable to extract discriminative features. For example, 8-direction gradient features allows to reduce the error-rate to only 0.4 %. On the other hand, it will be interesting to train local SVC only with training data rejected by the first stage.

To conclude, the modularity of the proposed architecture open the way to use SVC to resolve classification problems with a large number of classes. Indeed, we can use the first stage, which are suited for this type of problems, to evaluate the possible conflict and we construct only the appropriate SVCs.

References

1. A. Bellili, M. Gilloux and P. Gallinari, An MLP-SVM combination architecture for offline handwritten digit recognition, *International Journal on Document Analysis and Recognition*, 5(4), 244-252 (2003).
2. C.M. Bishop, Generative versus Discriminative Methods, in Computer Vision, invited keynote talk at *International Conference on Pattern Recognition* (2004).
3. C.-C. Chang and C.-J. Lin, LIBSVM : a library for support vector machines (2001).

4. V. Di Lecce, G. Dimauro, A. Guerriero, S. Impedovo, G. Pirlo and A. Salzo, Classifier combination: the role of a-priori knowledge, *International Workshop on Frontiers in Handwriting Recognition*, 143-152 (2000).
5. E. Francesconi, M. Gori, S. Marinai and G. Soda, A serial combination of connectionist-based classifiers for OCR, *International Journal on Document Analysis and Recognition*, 3(3), 160-168 (2001).
6. G. Fumera, F. Roli and G. Giacinto, Reject option with multiple thresholds, *Pattern Recognition*, 33(12), 2099-2101 (2000).
7. M. Gori and F. Scarselli, Are Multilayer Perceptrons Adequate for Pattern Recognition and Verification ? *IEEE transaction on Pattern Analysis and Machine Intelligence*, 20(11), 1121-1132 (1998).
8. V. Gunes, M. Ménard and P. Loonis, Fuzzy clustering with ambiguity for multi-classifiers fusion: Clustering-Classification Cooperation. *EUSFLAT-ESTYLF Joint Conference*, 505-508 (1999).
9. V. Gunes, M. Ménard, P. Loonis and S. Petit-Renaud, Combination, cooperation, and selection of classifiers, *International Journal of Pattern Recognition and Artificial Intelligence*, 17(8), 1303-1324 (2003).
10. T., Hamamura, H. Mizutani and B. Irie, A multiclass classification method based on multiple pairwise classifiers. *International Conference on Document Analysis and Recognition*, 809-813 (2003).
11. F. Kimura, S. Inoue, T. Wakabayashi, S. Tsuruoka and Y. Miyake, Handwritten numeral recognition using autoassociative neural networks, *International Conference on Pattern Recognition*, 166-171 (1998).
12. F. Kimura, K. Takashina, S. Tsuruoka and Y. Miyake, Modified Quadratic Discriminant functions and the Application to Chinese Character Recognition, *IEEE transaction on Pattern Analysis and Machine Intelligence*, 9(1), 149-153 (1987).
13. J. Kittler, M. Hatef, R.P.W. Duin, and J. Matas (1998) On combining classifiers, *IEEE transaction on Pattern Analysis and Machine Intelligence*, 20(3), 226-239.
14. L.I. Kuncheva, J.C. Bezdek and R.P.W. Duin, Decision templates for multiple classifier fusion: an experimental comparison. *Pattern Recognition*, 34(2), 299-314 (2001).
15. L. Lam, Classifier Combinations: Implementations and Theoretical Issues, *Multiple Classifier Systems, volume 1857 of Lecture Notes in Computer Science*, 77-86 (2000).
16. Y. LeCun, L. Bottou, Y. Bengio and P. Haffner, Gradient-based learning applied to document recognition. *Proceedings of IEEE*, 86(11), 2278-2324 (1998).
17. H.-T Lin, C.-J. Lin and R.C. Weng, *A note on Platt's probabilistic outputs for support vector machines*. Technical report, Department of computer science and information engineering, National Taiwan University (2003).
18. C.-L. Liu, H. Sako and H. Fujisawa, Performance evaluation of pattern classifiers for handwritten character recognition, *International Journal on Document Analysis and Recognition*, 191-204 (2002).

19. C.-L. Liu, K. Nakashima, H. Sako and H. Fujisawa, Handwritten digit recognition: benchmarking of state-of-the-art techniques, *Pattern Recognition*, 36(10), 2271-2285 (2003).

20. J.C. Platt, Probabilities for SV Machines, *Advances in Large Margin Classifiers*, MIT Press, 61-74 (1999).

21. L. Prevost, C. Michel-Sendis, A. Moises, L. Oudot and M. Milgram, Combining model-based and discriminative classifiers: application to handwritten character recognition, *International Conference on Document Analysis and Recognition*, 31-35 (2003).

22. N. Ragot and E. Anquetil, A generic hybrid classifier based on hierarchical fuzzy modeling: Experiments on on-line handwritten character recognition, *International Conference on Document Analysis and Recognition*, 963-967 (2003).

23. H. Schwenk, The diabolo classifier, *Neural Computation*, 10(8), 2175-2200 (1998).

24. L. Vuurpijl, L. Schomaker and M. Van Erp, Architectures for detecting and solving conflicts: two-stage classification and support vector classifiers, *International Journal on Document Analysis and Recognition*, 5(4), 213-223 (2003).

CHAPTER 12

LEARNING MODEL STRUCTURE FROM DATA: AN APPLICATION TO ON-LINE HANDWRITING

Henri Binsztok and Thierry Artières

LIP6, Université Paris VI
104, av du Président Kennedy
75016 Paris, France

We present a learning strategy for Hidden Markov Models that may be used to cluster handwriting sequences or to learn a character model by identifying its main writing styles. Our approach aims at learning both the structure and parameters of a Hidden Markov Model (HMM) from the data. A byproduct of this learning strategy is the ability to cluster signals and identify allograph. We provide experimental results on artificial data that demonstrate the possibility to learn from data HMM parameters and topology. For a given topology, our approach outperforms in some cases that we identify standard Maximum Likelihood learning scheme. We also apply our unsupervised learning scheme on on-line handwritten signals for allograph clustering as well as for learning HMM models for handwritten digit recognition.

12.1. Introduction

This paper deals with on-line handwriting signals clustering and Hidden Markov Models (HMM) structure learning. These two problems may be closely related and are of interest in the field of on-line handwriting processing and recognition. Clustering on-line signals is useful for determining allograph automatically, identifying writing styles, discovering new handwritten shapes, etc. HMM structure learning may help to automatically handle allograph when designing an on-line handwriting recognition system. The standard way to learn HMM model is indeed only semi-automatic and requires manual tuning, especially for the HMM topology. Learning HMM models involves learning the structure (topology) and the parameters of the model. Usually, learning consists in first choosing a structure and then in automatically learning the model parameters from training data. Learning parameters is generally achieved with Maximum Likelihood optimization (EM algorithm). Learning of model structure is then implicitly performed manually through successive trials. A fully automatic method would open new perspectives and allow designing easily new recognition engines for any kind of language, characters or drawings.

Fundamentally, we seek to develop learning algorithms for Markovian systems and focus on the learning of mixture models for typical writing styles; it is then very close to model-based clustering. Such techniques were studied in speech recognition. [LB93] proposed an algorithm that uses probabilistic grammatical inference techniques, which specifically addresses speech variability. A few techniques have been proposed for related tasks within the Handwriting Recognition community, e.g. automatic identification of writing styles, writer identification. For example, [NHP03] proposed a probabilistic approach to define clusters: For each handwritten character, an approach is used to learn the probabilities that a character belongs to a given cluster. The use of HMM for clustering handwritten characters was tackled by [PC00], but their approach depends on initialization so that some supervised information is needed to achieve good performance. Also, [VS97] proposed an interesting hierarchical approach. Besides, more generic approaches have been proposed for sequence clustering, for example [Smy97] presented an algorithm to cluster sequences into a predefined number of clusters, along with a preliminary method to find the numbers of clusters through cross-validation using a Monte Carlo measure. This theoretical approach relies on iterative reestimation of parameters via an instance of the EM algorithm, which requires careful initialization. Furthermore, the structure of the model is limited to a mixture model of fixed-length left-right HMM, which may not model correctly sequences of varying length in the data.

Our goal is to define a learning algorithm for HMM that meets two main requirements. First, the resulting model should describe well the training data. Second, the model should allow identifying sets of similar sequences corresponding to allograph or writing styles. However, the methods discussed above are most often adapted to the task and too restrictive to meet such requirements. Besides, there has been some more generic works dealing with HMM topology learning. Most of these approaches suggest starting by building a complex initial model covering all training data then to simplify it iteratively [Omo92, Bra99, SO93]. In [Bra99], the simplification is based on entropic prior probabilities of the transitions between states, and some transition probabilities converge towards 0, thus simplifying the structure of the model. In [SO93], pair of states from the initial HMM are merged iteratively as long as the loss of likelihood is not too significant. Both approaches, being generic, meet the first requirement but not the second.

We chose to build upon the work from [SO93] and to adapt this method to our goals by restricting the HMM to belong to the class of mixtures of left-right HMMs. As in [SO93] we focus in our work on learning discrete HMM. The learning consists in two steps. In a first step, a global HMM is built from training data, using a procedure to build a left-right HMM from each training sequence. We propose in this step an original procedure for initializing emission probability distribution from the data and discuss its interest with respect to the Maximum Likelihood strategy used in [SO93]. This initial global HMM is then iteratively simplified by removing one left-right HMM in the mixture at a time. This ensures that at any step, the global HMM belongs to the class of mixtures of left-right HMM, which in particular allows performing clustering. This study is an extension of our previous work [BAG04] with new original contributions related mainly to the iterative simplification algorithm and to extended results on different databases.

We first present our unsupervised learning algorithm. First, we detail the building of the initial HMM (section 2). Then, we describe the iterative simplification algorithm applied to this initial model (section 3). The application of our algorithm to cluster sequences and to learn character models in a recognition engine is explained in section 4. The remaining of the paper is dedicated to experiments. We present experimental databases in section 5 and evaluate the emission probability distribution estimation in section 5. The two next sections present experimental results on the two databases for clustering (section 7) and classification (section 8).

12.2. Building an initial HMM from training data

The main idea for building an initial global HMM covering all training data relies on the build of a left-right HMM from one training sequence. We first detail this idea, then we discuss how to build the global HMM.

Let $D = \{x_1, ..., x_n\}$ be a set of training sequences (e.g. a number of handwriting signals corresponding to a character). Each training sequence x_i, whose length is noted l_i, is a sequence of symbols $x_i = \left(s_1^i, s_2^i, ..., s_{l_i}^i\right)$ where each symbol s_j^i belongs to a finite *alphabet* Σ.

12.2.1. *Building a left-right HMM from a training sequence*

We detail first the structure of a left-right HMM built from a training sequence. Then we discuss its parameters, i.e. emission probability distributions and transition probabilities. We aim at building, from an original training sequence, a HMM that models well (i.e. gives high likelihood to) sequences that are close to the original sequence and that models other sequences badly.

12.2.1.1. *HMM structure*

The HMM built from a training sequence $x = (s_1, ..., s_l)$ of length l is a left-right HMM with l states, one for each symbol in x. According to this procedure, there exists a natural correspondence between any state and a particular symbol in Σ. This step is illustrated in Figure 1 where a training sequence of length 3 is used to build a three-states left-right HMM.

As we detail next, the emission probability distribution in a state of such a HMM is determined from the associated symbol in Σ. This ensures that the HMM will score well only sequences that are close to the original sequence.

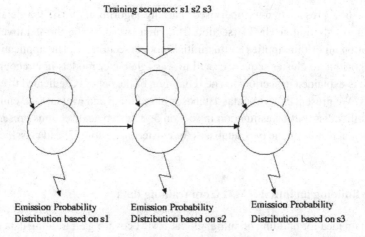

Fig. 12.1. *Building a left-right HMM from a training sequence.*

12.2.1.2. *Parameters*

Parameters of an HMM are transition probabilities, emission probabilities and initial state probabilities. Initial state probabilities are completely determined by our choice of left-right HMM (there is only one initial state). Besides, transition probabilities are well known to be a bad approximation of duration in states and we did not learn these here. We seek to use explicit duration models in the future. In the present work, transition probabilities are uniform: 0.5 for both the transition from a state to itself and to the following state.

We explain now how emission probability distributions associated to the states of this HMM are defined; it is based on the correspondence between states and symbols in Σ discussed in previous section.

An optimal solution, from the Maximum Likelihood point of view (i.e. leading to the maximum likelihood of the training sequence), would be to define emission probability of a symbol s in a state equal to 1 if the state corresponds to symbol s and 0 otherwise. There are a few other smoother solutions. Basically, we want that the emission probability distribution in a state that corresponds to a symbol s gives a high probability to symbols that are similar to s. [SO93] suggests learning emission probability distributions with a standard Maximum Likelihood criterion using an EM algorithm. However, this strategy did not appear relevant to us since training is delicate insofar as it requires to find a good initialization. Assume we have 1000 training sequences, each of length 10, with the alphabet size $|\Sigma|$ equal to 50. We therefore have 10 000 symbols to estimate 1000x10 emission probability distributions. If we choose to estimate all probability distributions without sharing parameters, we would have to estimate 10 000 probability distributions, each defined on Σ with 50 parameters. This is practically impossible to achieve with only 10 000 observed symbols in the training set. The solutions proposed in the literature rely on prior information about parameters and particularly about probability density functions [SO93]. The solution we propose may also be viewed as a use of prior information about these parameters, but this prior knowledge is in our case gained from the training data.

Recall that, according to the procedure used to build an initial global HMM, each state of this HMM is associated to a symbol in Σ. We chose to share emission probability distributions between all states that correspond to a same symbol in Σ so that there are only $|\Sigma|$ probability distributions to estimate. For instance, if the first state and the last state of a left-right HMM correspond to the same stroke s, both states will share the same emission probability distribution. In the above context our strategy requires estimating only 2500 parameters (50 distributions, each one defined with 50 parameters with an alphabet of size 50) from the same number of observations, 10000. In addition, we will show later in our experiments that a Maximum Likelihood Estimation scheme is not necessarily an optimal method for clustering.

These $|\Sigma|$ emission probability distributions are estimated by countings from D, and are based on a similarity measure between symbols in Σ. It is a heuristic method and it is not warranted to be a good approximation of emission probability distributions in all cases. However, it allows to capture efficiently, at least qualitatively, the similarity between symbols and has shown interesting experimental behavior.

We consider as similar two strokes which appear in the same context: Let x be any sequence of strokes ($x \in \Sigma^*$), and let $P_x(s)$ be the probability of seeing stroke s after sequence x. An estimate for $P_x(s)$ may be computed by counting on D:

$$P_x(s) = \frac{w(\mathrm{xs})}{w(x)}$$

where $w(x)$ represents the number of occurrences of the subsequence x in D.

We may then characterize a stroke s by a *profile* defined as the following distribution, where Σ^* is the set of strings on Σ :

$$P_s = \{P_x(s), x \in \Sigma^*\}$$

The idea is that two symbols with similar profiles, i.e. appearing with the same frequency in the same contexts (sequence of symbols in Σ) should be very similar. This distribution may be approximated on D by:

$$P_s = \{P_x(s), x \in \mathrm{sub}_c(D)\}$$

where $sub(D)$ stands for all subsequences of length c (the context length) in the training sequences in D.

We then define the similarity κ between two strokes $(s_1, s_2) \in \Sigma^2$ by the correlation between the *profiles* P_{s_1} and P_{s_2}:

$$\kappa(s_1, s_2) = \mathrm{corr}(P_{s1}, P_{s_2})$$

Finally, the emission probability distribution, b_s, in a state corresponding to a symbol s is computed by normalizing the above similarities:

$$b_s(s') = \frac{\kappa(s,s')}{\sum\limits_{u \in \Sigma} \kappa(s,u)}, \forall s' \in \Sigma$$

12.2.2. *Building the initial global HMM*

Once every training sequence x_i in D has been transformed into a left-right HMM λ_i, a global initial model M_0 is defined as a mixture of all these left-right HMM with uniform priors. This model implements a probabilistic model on symbol sequences:

$$P(x|M_0) = \sum_{i=1}^{n} w_i P(x|\lambda_i)$$

where x is an observed sequence, λ_i the ith left-right HMM built from x_i and for each i, $w_i = \frac{1}{n}$.

This HMM gives high likelihood to all training sequences in D and gives low likelihood to any sequence that is far from every sequence in D. To sum up ideas for the building of the global HMM, Figure 2 illustrates the procedure for a set of 3 training sequences $D=\{abba, aab, bacca\}$ with an alphabet $\Sigma=\{a,b,c\}$. It is a mixture of three left-right HMMs, each one corresponding to a training sequence. In this construction, each state of the HMM is naturally associated to a symbol in Σ. Probability density functions (p.d.f.) in all states are defined according to this association; for instance states associated to symbol a use a p.d.f. pa.

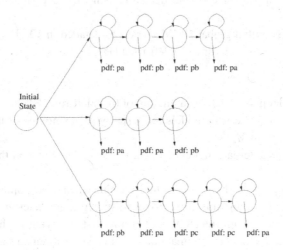

Fig. 12.2.   *Illustration of the building of a global HMM from a training set of three training sequences.*

A major difference between our work and previous works lies in these p.d.f., pa, pb and pc. In [SO93], the global HMM that is built maximizes the likelihood of training data. It has the same topology, but p.d.f. are somehow Dirac functions. This means that the p.d.f. associated to symbol a, pa, would be [1 0 0], pb would be [0 1 0]. That means the only possible observation in a state associated to symbol a would be a, the only one possible observation in a state associated to symbol b would be b etc. In our case, p.d.f. are estimated from the data through the computation of a similarity measure between symbols in Σ. This allows, as we will describe next, to design an iterative simplification procedure for the initial global HMM based on a simple likelihood criteria.

12.3. Iterative simplification algorithm

The general idea of the algorithm is to iteratively merge the two *closest* left-right HMM in the global model, M, so that, at the end only typical left-right HMM remain, each one may be viewed as a model of an allograph. However, in order to keep a limited set of emission p.d.f., hence a limited number of parameters, we do not actually merge left-right HMMs but we rather remove less significant left-right HMMs. The principle of the algorithm is then to *select* the best models from the initial mixture model. The iterative simplification algorithm relies on a maximum likelihood criterion and is summed up below:

1. For each sequence of the database, build the corresponding left-right HMM.

2. Build the initial global HMM model as detailed in §3. Using n training data sequences, M is a mixture of n left-right HMM.

$k=0$.

3. Loop:

At the kth loop, model M_k is a mixture of $(n-k)$ left-right HMM.

(a) Build $(n-k)$ alternate models for M_{k+1} by removing one of the $(n-k)$ left-right components of M_k.

(b) Select the alternate model that maximizes the likelihood of the all training data in D.

Several stop criteria may be used to determine when to stop simplification. In the context of clustering, this corresponds to strategies for determining the good number of clusters. Unfortunately, it does not exist satisfying methods to determine automatically such an optimal number of clusters; it remains an open problem. In the present implementation, the stop criterion is satisfied when a given number of left-right HMMs is obtained. However we will show experimentally that the likelihood decreases sharply when a right number of clusters is reached. This suggests that standard strategies can provide effective hints to determine automatically a correct number of left-right HMMs.

12.4. Using the approach for clustering and for classification

Our algorithm leads to a model M that is a mixture of a limited number of left-right HMM, which are the most significant to model the whole training data. Such an approach may be used for two different tasks.

First, it may be used for clustering sequences, when viewing each element of the mixture (a left-right HMM) as a model of a given cluster. This may be of interest to identify writing styles, for example to cluster writers according to the way they write some characters.

Consider that M is a mixture of N left-right HMM, with $N<<n$:

$$P(x|M_0) = \sum_{i=1}^{N} w_i P(x|\lambda_i)$$

Then, for a given sequence x, posterior probabilities of clusters given x may be computed with:

$$P(i^{\text{th}}\text{cluster}/x) = \frac{w_i P(x|\lambda_i)}{\sum\limits_{i=1}^{N} w_i P(x|\lambda_i)}$$

This allows to assign any sequence x to a particular cluster using a Bayes rule, i.e. a maximum posterior probability rule.

Second, the approach may be used to learn character models. For example, we will provide experimental results for the task of digit classification. In these experiments, the algorithm is run independently on the training data for each character, leading to a HMM whose topology and parameters are fully learned from training data. This is an interesting procedure to design, with less manual tuning, a new recognition engine for a particular set of symbols or characters.

12.5. Experimental databases

We apply our approach to two sets of data. In a first series of experiments we use artifical data generated by a set of HMMs. These experiments, being based on generated data, allow to control the task complexity and thus allow a deep investigation of the behavior of our method. In a second series of experiments, we used real on-line handwritten signals from the Unipen database [GSP94+]. We present now these databases.

12.5.1. *Artificial data*

Our artificial data are generated by HMMs, which have already been used in [LK00] to investigate HMM topology learning strategies. Note that we will not compare our approach with their results since these results were only visual.

We used in this study the same HMMs as in [LK00]. There are four discrete HMMs operating over an alphabet Σ of 16 symbols noted 'A' to 'P'. Each HMM

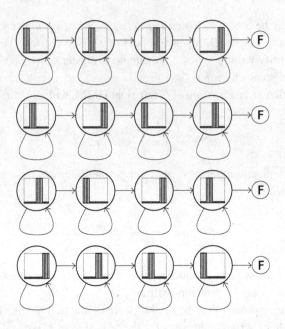

Fig. 12.3.   *The four generating HMMs for the artificial datasets. F represents the final state; the emission p.d.f. shown correspond to the easy dataset.*

Table 12.1.   Statistical details about the two artifical datasets.

	Average Length	Min. Length	Max. Length	Bayes Error	Noise Ratio	Parameters
Set *easy*	40.23	7	122	0.7%	13.6%	$a = 0.22$ $b = 0.01$
Set *hard*	42.34	6	109	13.4%	66.7%	$a = 0.150$ $b = 0.034$

is a 5 states left-right model: 4 emitting states and a final state. Self-transition probabilities equal 0.9 so that the expected length of sequences is 40. Each state has a high probability a of emitting 4 symbols (either 'A' to 'D', 'E' to 'H', 'I' to 'L' or 'M' to 'P') and a low probability b of emitting the 12 others symbols. Figure **3** represents the states of the HMMs. One may tune the complexity of the learning task by varying parameters of the generation process, namely a and b (note that a and b are linked since $4a + 12b = 1$). Of course, recovering the generative HMM models from generated data is easier as a increases.

Two datasets of 1000 sequences were generated from this set of 4 HMMs. The first set is labelled *easy*, with $a = 0.22$. The second set is labelled *hard*, with $a = 0.15$. Table 1 shows statistical details for these two datasets.

12.5.2. *On-line handwritten signals*

We carried out our experiments on on-line handwritten digits written by about 100 writers, extracted from the Unipen database [GSP94+]. The rough on-line signal is a temporal sequence of pen coordinates and is first preprocessed as in [AG02] using a kind of direction coding. A handwritten signal is represented as a sequence of symbols that are *strokes*; each stroke is characterized by a direction and a curvature. The strokes belong to a finite dictionary Σ of 36 elementary *strokes*, including 12 straight lines in directions uniformly distributed between 0 and 360°, 12 convex curves and 12 concave curves. This set of elementary strokes is illustrated in Figure 4.

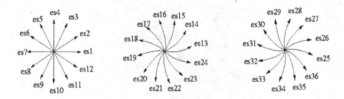

Fig. 12.4.   *Set Σ of 36 fixed elementary strokes used to represent handwriting signals — from left to right: 12 straight lines (named es_1 to es_{12}), 12 convex strokes (named es_{13} to es_{24}), and 12 concave strokes (named es_{25} to es_{36}).*

At the end of the preprocessing step, an on-line handwritten signal is represented as a sequence of symbols belonging to the alphabet Σ. This representation is computed through dynamic programming [AG02]. Such a sequence of strokes represents the shape of the signal and may be efficiently used for recognition.

We used several subsets of the database: 1000 samples of digits '0' and '9', 1000 samples of all ten digits, and about 6000 samples of all ten digits for classification.

12.6. **Probability density function estimation**

We investigate here the quality of our method for estimating emission probability distributions.

12.6.1. *Artificial data*

As the topology of the generating HMMs suggests, there is a close similarity
between the first four symbols 'A' to 'D', etc. Therefore, the artificial datasets are
useful to test the validity of our estimation model.

Figure 5 shows the estimated emission probability distributions for the *easy*
dataset in matrix form. The dimensions of the matrix are 16x16. The jth column of
the matrix corresponds to the emission probability distribution in a state associated
to the jth symbol. The pixel at the intersection of the ith row and j^{th} column is the
probability of observing the ith symbol in a state corresponding to the jth symbol
in Σ ; Gray levels are proportional to probabilities (white = close to 1, black =
close to 0).

We see that our estimation model captures well the information at the symbol
level with the *easy* dataset.

Fig. 12.5.   *Similarities between symbols inferred from the easy dataset, with context length 1. The jth
column of the matrix corresponds to the emission probability distribution in a state associated to the
j^{th} symbol.*

Figure 6 represents the estimation of emission laws associated to symbols from
the *hard* dataset. We have used three different context lengths c (see section 3.1.2).
The number of training sequences being limited the estimation of emission probabilities naturally tend to 1 for $\kappa(s_1,s_1)$ and 0 for $\kappa(s_1,s_2), s_2 \neq s_1$ when c
increases. Therefore, a context length $c=1$ provides best estimation results in our
experiments since it does not introduce artefacts.

12.6.2. *Handwritten signals*

Figure 7 represents two sets of emission probabilities distributions over alphabet
Σ of 36 elementary strokes in the same matrix form as above. The dimensions
of the matrixes are then 36x36. The pixel at the intersection of the ith row and j^{th}

Fig. 12.6. *Similarities between symbols of the alphabet inferred from the hard dataset, with different context lengths (from left to right: 1, 2, 3).*

column is the probability of observing the ith stroke in a state corresponding to the jth stroke in Σ.

The left matrix has been tuned manually according to prior knowledge [AG02] while the right matrix is estimated with the method presented in section §2.1.2. As may be seen, there are strong correlations between these two matrices, which shows that our estimation method allows capturing efficiently, from the training database D, the similarity between symbols.

Fig. 12.7. *36x36 matrices representing probability distributions of states associated to strokes of Σ. The matrix on the left has been tuned manually using prior knowledge and the matrix on the right has been learned from the data using the procedure in §2.1.2.*

12.7. Clustering experiments

We present here experimental results for the sequences clustering task. We first discuss the evaluation criteria. And then we present a benchmark method, with which we compare our approach. Finally, we present experiments on artifical data and on handwritten signals.

12.7.1. *Evaluation criteria*

Evaluating unsupervised methods (e.g. clustering) is still an open problem. This is not a problem for artificial data experiments since we do have an ideal labeling information for these data (we know which HMM generated each sequence). This is more problematic for the handwritten signals since we do not have any label information about allographs. Then, for these data, we chose to perform clustering experiments on databases including signals of various but close digits (e.g. '0' and '9'). This allows an objective evaluation of clustering using the available label information.

Hence, we evaluated clustering results in the following way: After learning of a mixture of left-right HMM from the data, all sequences in the database are clustered using these left-right HMMs as cluster models. We then use criteria relying on a labeling of samples with class information (e.g. digits) to evaluate the clustering results.

A few criteria may be used to evaluate clustering [SKK00]. Among these, we chose the *precision* measure that is also used in classification. In the following, we name *clusters* the result of our clustering and *classes* the labeling of the data. For a cluster j, P_{ij} is the probability that an element of the cluster j belongs to class i. This probability is estimated by counting: Let n_j be the number of sequences in cluster j and n the total number of sequences in the data. We note $\max_i$ the maximum of all possible values for i. Then:

$$precision = \sum_j \frac{n_j}{n} \max_i P_{ij}$$

12.7.2. *Benchmark method*

In order to give more insights of our approach, labelled **BAG** in the figures, we provide some comparative results using a standard learning scheme for HMM parameters, based on the CEM algorithm (stochastic EM). It is a variant of the EM algorithm that may outperform EM in unsupervised learning, especially when dealing with too few data to estimate the likelihood correctly [CD88].

For each number of clusters K, we learn a HMM, whose topology is a mixture of left-right HMMs. We use this HMM to perform clustering, using a Maximum Likelihood estimation scheme. To use such a learning strategy, one has to define first the topology of the model and then to initialize parameters (emission probability distributions). We have investigated two ways to do this. The first one, named **CEM1**, is based on a k-means like algorithm and a distance between sequences [REFF]. The second approach, named **CEM2**, uses the global HMM obtained with our method after a number of iterations (n-K). It may be seen as an upper-bound of Maximum Likelihood estimation performance since this initialization is, as we will show experimentally, already a good solution.

12.7.3. *Experiments on artificial data*

First, we investigate the clustering performance of our approach and compare this to CEM reestimation (CEM2). This favours the CEM approach, since the main problem for the latter is to find a correct initialization. On the *easy* dataset, as may be seen in Figure 8, our approach outperforms CEM and its performance is close to the Bayes error of classification, though the learning is totally unsupervised. With the *easy* dataset, we also see that the likelihood function shows an inflexion point for the "good" number of clusters, i.e. the number of HMMs that generated the data. This allows to easily detect the correct number of clusters.

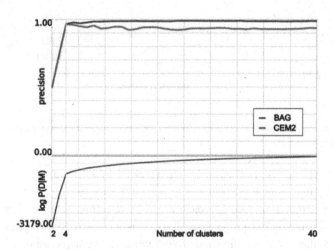

Fig. 12.8. *Above, Performance on the easy dataset comparing our approach (BAG) to CEM2, an EM reestimation of the model learned with our approach (above). Below, logarithm of the likelihood, showing an inflexion point for 4 clusters, which corresponds to the number of HMMs that generated the data.*

A look to cluster models reveals that our approach correctly identifies the *best shortest sequences* that are typical for each model. Our analysis is that the strength of our approach is to correctly identify the most typical sequences in the data, and use them as cluster models. Furthermore, we can stress that, given the high probability of self-transition (0.9), there is a high tendency to have in the data much longer sequences that there are number of states in the generating models. Therefore, to minimize the probability of having a misrepresentative state in the cluster models, the shorter the sequence, the more likely it is to have only "good" states. But there are also fewer short sequences present in the data.

The *hard* dataset provides weaker results, which is logical, given the high noise ratio. Figure 9 shows the clustering results for all three approaches (BAG, CEM1 and CEM2). There is no clear tendency between BAG and CEM1: CEM1 gives better results for a low number of clusters, our approach gives better results for a high number of clusters.

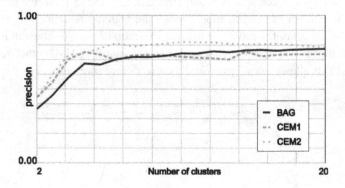

Fig. 12.9.   *Performance on the hard dataset, comparing our approach (BAG) to the CEM1 and CEM2 clustering approaches.*

For CEM2, we used our approach (BAG) as the initialization of the CEM clustering algorithm and CEM2 provides better results. We can explain this using our previous interpretation: Our approach works by selecting the most representative sequences of the model in the data. Indeed, as we could check by a deep look at the data, there is simply no single fully representative sequence of each model, since the noise ratio is very high in the *hard* dataset. Therefore, the selected cluster models contain some "bad" states, and our approach can not modify the left-right HMMs which are part of the model, whereas the CEM reestimation does.

In the next section, we will look to our real world application – handwritten digit clustering and classification – to see how our approach compares, and whether there exists at least some good sequences in the data in a real-world application.

12.7.4. *Experiments on on-line handwritten signals*

In a first series of experiments, we used 100 samples of digits '0' and '9' whose drawings are very similar. As an illustration, the resulting clusters from one experiment using our model are drawn in Figure 10: The discovered clusters are homogeneous (including either '0' or '9' samples). The two clusters for digit '0' include indeed slightly different drawings since samples from the smaller set are drawn the other way round. In this figure, the drawing is generated from our model representation; therefore, characters do not display as nicely as the fine-grained original representation.

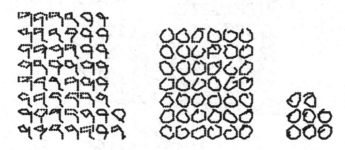

Fig. 12.10.   *The three discovered clusters for a database of on-line handwriting samples of digits '0' and '9'.*

To demonstrate the ability of our approach to discover allographs, we applied our clustering approach to 500 samples of handwritten digit '2'. Since we do not have any allograph labeled database, it is difficult to define an interesting evaluation criteria, but we show the resulting clusters (Figure 11). One may recognize some typical allograph of this digit: drawn in 'Z' shape, upper round, lower round, etc. We note however that the cluster limits are not always well defined and some examples could be affected to different clusters. This visual evaluation is completed by more quantitative results next.

To further validate our approach, we performed another comparison on a set of 1000 samples of the ten digits. Figure 12 compares the performance of our approach with emission probability distributions tuned by hand (cf. §6 and Figure 7) or estimated using the technique detailed in §2.1.2.

The graphs are labeled "BAG (Fix)" and "BAG (Est)". Results (using the precision measure defined in §7.1) are given as a function of the number of clusters identified (i.e. all along the iterative learning algorithm of §3, as the number of clusters decreases). In addition to these two systems we provide results obtained

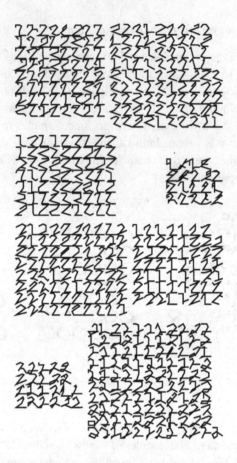

Fig. 12.11.   *Visualization of allograph of handwritten digit '2' with 8 clusters.*

with the benchmark method (CEM2). Hence, at each step of the simplification algorithm, i.e. for any number of clusters, the resulting models M are re-estimated
with the CEM algorithm. Graph "CEM2 (Fix)" use the model learned with manually tuned emission probability distributions, while "CEM2 (Est)" use the model
using distributions estimated from the data.

For example, for 20 clusters, our approach leads to about 86% accuracy with
tuned emission probability distributions and to 83% with estimated emission probability distributions. These two systems when re-estimated using a CEM optimization lead respectively to 80% and 74% accuracy.

As may be seen, whatever the number of clusters, CEM re-estimation lowers
the performance, although it maximizes the likelihood. Note that, assuming that

there are, in average, two allographs per digit, we are mostly interested here in the performance for about 20 clusters; i.e. a perfect automatic method would find the 20 clusters that would represent all allographs. The reason for the ineffectiveness of CEM reestimation scheme is not clear. However, we think that our learning strategy is naturally more adapted to discover typical cluster of sequences. The reason lies in that a left-right HMM built from a training sequence, as detailed in section §2.1 cannot handle much variability around the original training sequence. Thus it leads to compact and homogeneous clusters. At the opposite, performing CEM re-estimation may result in less specific left-right HMM, thus in less precise clusters. These results answer the question we left open in section 6.1. Our approach depends on its ability to find typical sequences in the data. Indeed, in our real application, there are at least some characters that are well recorded and associated to a given handwritten character.

At last, we conducted an experiment using 1000 samples of the letters 'a' and 'd', which are often confused in online handwriting systems. Whereas the precision is only 60% for 2 clusters, it jumps to 95% for 5 clusters, which constitutes a rather acceptable approximation of the number of allograph for these two characters.

Preceding results show that clustering is indeed a difficult task since for a reasonable number of clusters (20) precision does not exceed 85% whereas classification results on such handwriting signals may reach about 95% [AG02]. However, our unsupervised approach outperforms benchmark methods provided there are enough clusters while performance falls sharply when the number of clusters decreases.

12.8. Classification experiments

We present here experiments on learning character models for classification tasks. In this section, we use our learning algorithm to learn, for every digit, a digit model that is a mixture of left-right HMM. Experiments were performed on a bigger subset of Unipen, about 6000 samples of the ten digits (from '0' to '9') with 800 samples for training and the remaining for test. Recognition rates are displayed in Figure 13 as a function of the number of left-right HMMs in a character model. Without simplification of the initial HMMs (i.e. about 80 left-right HMM per digit) the classification accuracy reaches an asymptotic performance of 92.5%. By learning a model for each digit, we can achieve same or better performance while simplifying the models up to 7 left-right HMM per digit in average.

Note that these performance do not match state of the art recognition rates [Rat03]. The main reason is that we did not model specific parameters of hand-

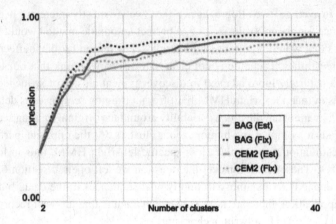

Fig. 12.12. *Clustering performance using our approach (BAG) and CEM2. The red graph BAG (Est) corresponds to the model using estimated emission probability distributions; the blue graph BAG (Fix) corresponds to the model using manually tuned emission probability distributions. Green (CEM2 (Est)) and yellow (CEM2 (Fix)) graphs correspond to the re-estimation of the two models BAG (Est) and BAG (Fix).*

writing recognition (i.e. duration model and pen-up moves) to keep the generality of our approach. However, in sight of these shortcomings, our results appear promising since we obtain the same level of performance than by using the approach described in [MSAG03].

12.9. Conclusion

We presented a model-based approach to cluster sequences that we tackled through unsupervised HMM learning. We proposed to learn, from the data, the structure and parameters of a global HMM that is a mixture of left-right HMMs. This structure seems much appropriate for sequence clustering and allograph identification. The learning consists in building from data an initial mixture model of left-right HMMs that cover all training data and then simplifying it by removing iteratively the less significant left-right HMM. This algorithm relies on an original estimation of emission probability distributions. We provide experimental results on artificial data that show that our approach is efficient for learning HMM topology. Furthermore, we obtained an unexpected and interesting result: for a fixed HMM topology our approach may outperform Maximum Likelihood re-estimation in some cases. We also applied our approach to clustering and classification of on-line handwritten digits. These results confirm the ones obtained on

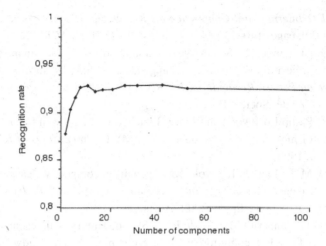

Fig. 12.13.   *Recognition rate (for digit recognition) as a function of the number of components (left-right HMMs) per digit model.*

artificial data. Furthermore, clustering as well as classification results are promising, showing for instance that it is possible to learn complete character models from the data without any manual tuning of model topology.

References

[AG02] Thierry Artières and Patrick Gallinari. Stroke level HMMs for on-line handwriting recognition. In *8th International Workshop on Frontiers in Handwriting Recognition (IWFHR-8)*, Niagara, August 2002, pages 227-232.

[BAG04] Henri Binsztok, Thierry Artières, Patrick Gallinari: A Model-Based Approach to Sequence Clustering. *European Conference on Artificial Intelligence* (ECAI 2004). Valencia, Spain. Pages 420-424.

[Bra99] M. Brand. Structure learning in conditional probability models via an entropic prior and parameter extinction. *Neural Computation*, 11:1155–1182, 1999.

[CD88] Gilles Celeux and Jean Diebolt. A random imputation principle: the stochastic em algorithm. *Technical report, Rapport de recherche de l'INRIA-Rocquencourt*, 1988.

[CGS00] Igor V. Cadez, Scott Gaffney, and Padhraic Smyth. A general probabilistic framework for clustering individuals and objects. In Raghu Ramakrishnan, Sal Stolfo, Roberto Bayardo, and Ismail Parsa, editors, *Proceedings of the 6th ACM*

SIGKDD International Conference on Knowledge Discovery and Data Mining (KDD-00), pages 140–149, N. Y., August 20–23 2000. ACM Press.

[GSP94] I. Guyon, L. Schomaker, R. Plamondon, M. Liberman, and S. Janet. Unipen project of on-line data exchange and benchmarks. In *International Conference on Pattern Recognition, ICPR'94*, pages 29–33, Jerusalem, Israel, 1994. IEEE Computer Society Press.

[LB93] Philip Lockwood and Marc Blanchet. An algorithm for the dynamic inference of hidden markov models (DIHMM). In *Proceedings of ICASSP*, pages 251–254, 1993.

[LK00] M. H. Law, J. T. Kwok. Rival penalized competitive learning for model-based sequence clustering. *International Conference of Pattern Recognition, ICPR'00*, Barcelona, Spain, 2000. Pages 2195-2198.

[MSAG03] Sanparith Marukatat, Rudy Sicard, Thierry Artières, and Patrick Gallinari. A flexible recognition engine for complex on-line handwritten character recognition. In *7th International Conference on Document Analysis and Recognition (ICDAR 2003)*, Edinbourgh, Scotland, August 2003, pages 1048-1052.

[NHP03] Ali Nosary, Laurent Heutte, and Thierry Paquet. Unsupervised writer adaptation applied to handwritten text recognition. *Pattern Recognition*, 37:385–388, 2003.

[Omo92] Stephen M. Omohundro. Best-first model merging for dynamic learning and recognition. In John E. Moody, Steve J. Hanson, and Richard P. Lippmann, editors, *Advances in Neural Information Processing Systems*, volume 4, pages 958–965. Morgan Kaufmann Publishers, Inc., 1992.

[PC00] M. Perrone and S. Connell. K-means clustering for hidden markov models. In *In Proceedings of the Seventh International Workshop on Frontiers in Handwriting Recognition*, pages 229–238, Amsterdam, Netherlands, September 2000.

[Rat03] Eugene H. Ratzlaff. Methods, report and survey for the comparison of diverse isolated character recognition results on the unipen database. In *Seventh International Conference on Document Analysis and Recognition*, Edinburgh, Scotland, August 2003, pages 623-628.

[SKK00] M. Steinbach, G. Karypis, and V. Kumar. A comparison of document clustering techniques. *KDD Workshop on Text Mining*, 2000.

[Smy97] Padhraic Smyth. Clustering sequences with hidden markov models. In Michael C. Mozer, Michael I. Jordan, and Thomas Petsche, editors, *Advances in Neural Information Processing Systems*, volume 9, page 648. The MIT Press, 1997.

[Spe03] Speed Terry. Statistical analysis of gene expression microarray data, Terry Speed Ed.

[SO93] Andreas Stolcke and Stephen Omohundro. Hidden Markov Model induction by bayesian model merging. In Stephen José Hanson, Jack D. Cowan, and C. Lee Giles, editors, *Advances in Neural Information Processing Systems*, volume 5, pages 11–18. Morgan Kaufmann, San Mateo, CA, 1993.

[VS97] L. Vuurpijl and L. Schomaker. Finding structure in diversity: A hierarchical clustering method for the categorization of allographs in handwriting. *International Conference on Document Analysis and Recognition* 1997. Pages 387-393.

CHAPTER 13

SIMULTANEOUS AND CAUSAL APPEARANCE LEARNING AND TRACKING

J. Melenchón, I. Iriondo and L. Meler

Communications and Signal Theory Department,
Enginyeria La Salle, Universitat Ramon Llull,
Pg. Bonanova 8, 08022, Barcelona, Spain
E-mail: {jmelen, iriondo, lmeler}@salle.url.edu

A novel way to learn and track simultaneously the appearance of a previously non-seen face without intrusive techniques can be found in this article. The presented approach has a causal behaviour: no future frames are needed to process the current ones. The model used in the tracking process is refined with each input frame thanks to a new algorithm for the simultaneous and incremental computation of the singular value decomposition (SVD) and the mean of the data. Previously developed methods about iterative computation of SVD are taken into account and an original way to extract the mean information from the reduced SVD of a matrix is also considered. Furthermore, the results are produced with linear computational cost and sublinear memory requirements with respect to the size of the data. Finally, experimental results are included, showing the tracking performance and some comparisons between the batch and our incremental computation of the SVD with mean information.

13.1. Introduction

The last years have witnessed extraordinary advances in computer and communications technology, leading to an increasing availability of information and processing capabilities of multimedia data.[1,2] This fact is resulting in a higher and wider demand for easier access to information.[3] On one hand, this information is mainly stored in digital format, so its acces is limited to the user's ability to communicate with computers. On the other hand, it has been remarked the great expressive power of the natural language used in human-human communication, as well as its intrinsic multimodal features.[4] Consequently, the acces to digital information could be carried out using this natural language: reducing the necessity of knowing a specific way to interact with the computer and taking advantage of its expressive features. Moreover, multimodal interfaces with an audio visual system like a talking head could be used in order to speak to the user in natural language. As a result, talking heads used in multimodal interfaces seem to be a proper solution for making acces to information easier and more pleasing for human users.

As explained in,[4] multimodal input analysis is necessary when working with multimodal interfaces and relies on interaction devices e.g. facial trackers. Some non-intrusive visual trackers can be used in this sheme because they retain information regarding to position, scale, orientation and appearance of the tracked element, e.g.[5-9] Nevertheless, the whole sequence is needed by these algorithms to be processed off-line (they have a non-causal behaviour); as a result, a real time implementation of these methods is impossible, even without considering their computational cost. This temporal restriction is caused by the computation of a Singular Value Decomposition (SVD) over the whole observed data. Moreover, memory resources are greatly affected by this fact, limiting the duration of the observed sequence. Incremental SVD computation techniques as[10,11] and[12] may be useful in this case, but they do not take into consideration the mean of the data, which is crucial in the classification of the different gestures. Fortunately, this is taken into account in[13] and.[14] By one hand, the work presented in[13] does not does not propose a method to extract the mean information from a given SVD and it can only update the SVD from two other known SVD. By the other hand, Skočaj presented in[14] a method with a similar performance to the one achieved in this paper, but he focused on incremental Principal Component Analysis rather than incremental SVD.

In this paper, a new method for updating both SVD and mean information as well as extracting the mean of the data contained in a given SVD without increasing the cost order of either time or memory is presented in Sect. 13.2. The application of this new method is carried out in Sect. 13.3 by a causal algorithm for the tracking and learning of the facial appearance of a person. Experimental results are given in Sect. 13.4 and concluding remarks are explained in Sect. 13.5.

13.2. Incremental SVD with Mean Update

13.2.1. *Fundamentals*

The singular value decomposition of matrix $M_{p \times q} = [m_1 \cdots m_q]$ is given by:

$$M_{p \times q} = U_{p \times p} \Sigma_{p \times q} V_{q \times q}^T \qquad (13.1)$$

where $U = [u_1 \cdots u_p]$ and $V = [v_1 \cdots v_q]$ are orthonormal matrices; u_i are the eigenvectors of MM^T and span the column space of M; v_i are the eigenvectors of $\mathbf{M}^T\mathbf{M}$ and span the row space of $\mathbf{M}$; and $\mathbf{\Sigma}$ is a diagonal matrix with the singular values of either $\mathbf{MM}^T$ and $\mathbf{M}^T\mathbf{M}$ in descending order. Notice that if $\mathbf{M}$ is a rank r matrix, where $r \leq p$ and $r \leq q$, its corresponding $\mathbf{\Sigma}$ has only r non-null singular values and Eq. (13.1) can be rewritten as the *thin SVD*: $\mathbf{M}_{p \times q} = \mathbf{U}_{p \times r}\mathbf{\Sigma}_{r \times r}\mathbf{V}_{q \times r}^T$. By the other hand, let $\mathbf{C}_{r \times q} = \mathbf{U}_{p \times r}^T\mathbf{M}_{p \times q}$ be the projections of the columns of $\mathbf{M}$ over the eigenspace spanned by $\mathbf{U}$. Using the *thin SVD* expression the projections matrix $\mathbf{C} = [\mathbf{c}_1 \cdots \mathbf{c}_q]$ can be written also as $\mathbf{C}_{r \times q} = \mathbf{\Sigma}_{r \times r}\mathbf{V}_{q \times r}^T$.

In other fields, like classification problems pointed by,[13] a more suitable representation of $\mathbf{M}$ can be achieved including mean information $\overline{\mathbf{m}} = \frac{1}{q}\sum_{i=1}^{q}\mathbf{m}_i$ in Eq. (13.1), which has to be computed and substracted previously from $\mathbf{M}$ in order to be able to generate the SVD of $\mathbf{M} - \overline{\mathbf{m}} \cdot \mathbf{1}$:

$$\mathbf{M}_{p \times q} = \mathbf{U}_{p \times r}\mathbf{\Sigma}_{r \times r}\mathbf{V}_{q \times r}^T + \overline{\mathbf{m}}_{p \times 1}\mathbf{1}_{1 \times q}. \tag{13.2}$$

13.2.2. *Updating SVD*

Assuming an existing SVD Eq. (13.1), if new columns $\mathbf{I}_{p \times c} = [\mathbf{I}_1 \cdots \mathbf{I}_c]$ are added in order to obtain a new matrix $\mathbf{M}'_{p \times (q+c)} = [\mathbf{M}_{p \times q}\ \mathbf{I}_{p \times c}]$, the SVD of $\mathbf{M}'$ can be updated from Eq. (13.1) using methods like[11] and,[12] achieving:

$$\mathbf{M}'_{p \times (p+c)} = \mathbf{U}'_{p \times r'}\mathbf{\Sigma}'_{r' \times r'}\mathbf{V}'^T_{(q+c) \times r'}. \tag{13.3}$$

Otherwise, if the representation of $\mathbf{M}'$ is chosen to be as Eq. (13.2) and $\overline{\mathbf{m}}'$ is set to $\frac{1}{q+c}(\sum_{k=1}^{q}\mathbf{m}_k + \sum_{l=1}^{c}\mathbf{I}_l)$ the SVD becomes:

$$\mathbf{M}'_{p \times (q+c)} = \mathbf{U}'_{p \times r'}\mathbf{\Sigma}'_{r' \times r'}\mathbf{V}'^T_{(q+c) \times r'} + \overline{\mathbf{m}}'_{p \times 1}\mathbf{1}_{1 \times (q+c)}. \tag{13.4}$$

Starting from Eq. (13.2) and matrix $\mathbf{I}$, Eq. (13.4) can be obtained using the method proposed by[13] if the SVD of $\mathbf{I}$ is previously computed and q and c are known beforehand. A new method for updating both the SVD and the mean using only the new observations and previous factorization is presented in Sect. 13.2.3.

13.2.3. *Updating SVD and Mean*

Beginning with an existing factorization of $\mathbf{M}_i$ as in Eq. (13.5), it is desired to obtain the SVD and mean of $\mathbf{M}_f$ shown in Eq. (13.6):

$$\mathbf{M}_i = \mathbf{U}_i\mathbf{\Sigma}_i\mathbf{V}_i^T + \overline{\mathbf{m}}_i\mathbf{1}. \tag{13.5}$$

$$\mathbf{M}_f = [\mathbf{M}_i\ \mathbf{I}] = \mathbf{U}_f\mathbf{\Sigma}_f\mathbf{V}_f^T + \overline{\mathbf{m}}_f\mathbf{1}. \tag{13.6}$$

Defining $\hat{\mathbf{M}}_i$ Eq. (13.7) and centering new columns $\mathbf{I}$ around $\overline{\mathbf{m}}_i$ Eq. (13.8), it can be written:

$$\hat{\mathbf{M}}_i \quad = \mathbf{M}_i - \overline{\mathbf{m}}_i \mathbf{1} = \mathbf{U}_i \mathbf{\Sigma}_i \mathbf{V}_i^T . \tag{13.7}$$

$$[\mathbf{M}_i \ \mathbf{I}] - \overline{\mathbf{m}}_i \mathbf{1} = \mathbf{U}_f \mathbf{\Sigma}_f \mathbf{V}_f^T + \overline{\mathbf{m}}_f \mathbf{1} - \overline{\mathbf{m}}_i \mathbf{1} . \tag{13.8}$$

$$[\mathbf{M}_i - \overline{\mathbf{m}}_i \mathbf{1} \ \ \mathbf{I} - \overline{\mathbf{m}}_i \mathbf{1}] = \mathbf{U}_f \mathbf{\Sigma}_f \mathbf{V}_f^T + (\overline{\mathbf{m}}_f - \overline{\mathbf{m}}_i) \, \mathbf{1} . \tag{13.9}$$

$$\left[\hat{\mathbf{M}}_i \ \hat{\mathbf{I}} \right] \qquad = \mathbf{U}_t \mathbf{\Sigma}_t \mathbf{V}_t^T . \tag{13.10}$$

The new columns $\mathbf{I}_{\mathbf{p} \times \mathbf{c}}$ (see sect. 13.2.2) will be known through this paper as the *update block*. Note that Eq. (13.10) is the updated SVD from Eq. (13.7) when some new observations $\hat{\mathbf{I}}$ are added. This update can be done as[12] suggests:

$$\left[\hat{\mathbf{M}}_i \ \hat{\mathbf{I}} \right] = [\mathbf{U}_i \ \mathbf{Q}_i] \begin{bmatrix} \mathbf{\Sigma}_i & \mathbf{U}_i^T \hat{\mathbf{I}} \\ 0 & \mathbf{Q}_i^T \hat{\mathbf{I}} \end{bmatrix} \begin{bmatrix} \mathbf{V}_i^T & 0 \\ 0 & 1 \end{bmatrix} =$$

$$= [\mathbf{U}_i \ \mathbf{Q}_i] \mathbf{U}_d \mathbf{\Sigma}_d \mathbf{V}_d^T \begin{bmatrix} \mathbf{V}_i^T & 0 \\ 0 & 1 \end{bmatrix} = \mathbf{U}_t \mathbf{\Sigma}_t \mathbf{V}_t^T \tag{13.11}$$

where QR-decomposition is done to $\hat{\mathbf{I}} - \mathbf{U}_i \mathbf{U}_i^T \hat{\mathbf{I}} = \mathbf{Q}_i \mathbf{R}_i$ to obtain an orthogonal basis $\mathbf{Q}_i$ for the reconstruction error. Next, the *mean update algorithm* can be executed starting from the knowledge of $\mathbf{V}_t^T = \hat{\mathbf{V}}_t^T + \overline{\mathbf{v}}_t \mathbf{1}$, where $\overline{\mathbf{v}}_t = \frac{1}{q+c} \sum_{k=1}^{q+c} \mathbf{v}_k$:

$$\left[\hat{\mathbf{M}}_i \ \hat{\mathbf{I}} \right] = \mathbf{U}_t \mathbf{\Sigma}_t \hat{\mathbf{V}}_t^T + \mathbf{U}_t \mathbf{\Sigma}_t \overline{\mathbf{v}}_t \mathbf{1} = \mathbf{U}_t \mathbf{\Sigma}_t \hat{\mathbf{V}}_t^T + \overline{\mathbf{m}}_t \mathbf{1} . \tag{13.12}$$

$$\left[\hat{\mathbf{M}}_i \ \hat{\mathbf{I}} \right] = \mathbf{U}_t \mathbf{\Sigma}_t \mathbf{R}_v^T \mathbf{Q}_v^T + \overline{\mathbf{m}}_t \mathbf{1} = \mathbf{U}_f \mathbf{\Sigma}_f \mathbf{V}_u^T \mathbf{Q}_v^T + \overline{\mathbf{m}}_t \mathbf{1} = \mathbf{U}_f \mathbf{\Sigma}_f \mathbf{V}_f^T + \overline{\mathbf{m}}_t \mathbf{1} \tag{13.13}$$

$$\left[\hat{\mathbf{M}}_i \ \hat{\mathbf{I}} \right] + \overline{\mathbf{m}}_i \mathbf{1} = \mathbf{U}_f \mathbf{\Sigma}_f \mathbf{V}_f^T + \overline{\mathbf{m}}_t \mathbf{1} + \overline{\mathbf{m}}_i \mathbf{1} . \tag{13.14}$$

$$[\mathbf{M}_i \ \mathbf{I}] = \mathbf{U}_f \mathbf{\Sigma}_f \mathbf{V}_f^T + \overline{\mathbf{m}}_f \mathbf{1} . \tag{13.15}$$

It is assumed $\mathbf{Q}_v \mathbf{R}_v$ as the QR-decomposition of $\hat{\mathbf{V}}_t$, $\mathbf{U}_f \mathbf{\Sigma}_f \mathbf{V}_u^T$ as the SVD of $\mathbf{U}_t \mathbf{\Sigma}_t \mathbf{R}_v^T$ and $\overline{\mathbf{m}}_f = \overline{\mathbf{m}}_t + \overline{\mathbf{m}}_i$. Note that Eq. (13.15) and Eq. (13.6) are the same expression.

13.2.4. *Mean Extraction from a Given SVD*

The previous method can also be used to extract the mean information from an existing SVD, e.g. trying to express $\mathbf{S} = \mathbf{U}_t \mathbf{\Sigma}_t \mathbf{V}_t^T$ as $\mathbf{S} = \mathbf{U}_f \mathbf{\Sigma}_f \mathbf{V}_f^T + \overline{\mathbf{s}} \cdot \mathbf{1}$ setting $\left[\hat{\mathbf{M}}_i \ \hat{\mathbf{I}} \right] = \mathbf{S}$ and $\overline{\mathbf{m}}_t = 0$ in Eq. (13.12) to Eq. (13.15).

Table 13.1. Resource order requirements of the proposed *mean update algorithm*.

Operation	Comp. cost	Mem. requirements
$\mathbf{V}_{q\times r}^{T} - \left(\frac{1}{q}\sum_{k=1}^{q}(\mathbf{v}_k)_{r\times 1}\right)\mathbf{1}_{1\times q} \rightarrow \hat{\mathbf{V}}_{q\times r}^{T}$	$O\left(qr\right)$	$O\left(qr+r\right)$
$\hat{\mathbf{V}}_{q\times r} \rightarrow (\mathbf{Q}_v)_{q\times r}(\mathbf{R}_v)_{r\times r}$	$O\left(qr^2\right)$	$O\left(qr+r^2\right)$
$(\mathbf{U}_i)_{p\times r}(\mathbf{\Sigma}_i)_{r\times r}(\mathbf{R}_v^T)_{r\times r} \rightarrow \mathbf{T}_{p\times r}$	$O\left(pr^2+r^3\right)$	$O\left(pr+r^2\right)$
$\mathbf{T}_{p\times r} \rightarrow (\mathbf{U}_f)_{p\times r}(\mathbf{\Sigma}_f)_{r\times r}(\mathbf{V}_u^T)_{r\times r}$	$O\left(pr^2\right)$	$O\left(pr+r^2\right)$
$(\mathbf{V}_f)_{q\times r} \rightarrow (\mathbf{Q}_v)_{q\times r}(\mathbf{V}_u)_{r\times r}$	$O\left(qr^2\right)$	$O\left(qr+r^2\right)$
Totals, assuming $p \gg r$ and $g \gg r$	$O\left(qr^2+pr^2\right)$	$O\left(pr+qr\right)$

13.2.5. *Time and Memory Complexity*

The mean update presented in section 13.2.3 does not increase the order of resources required in methods of incremental SVD developed in[10–14]. The computational cost becomes $O\left(qr^2+pr^2\right)$ and the memory complexity is $O\left(pr+qr\right)$, as shown in Table 13.1.

13.3. On-the-Fly Face Training

In this paper, *On-the-fly Face Training* is defined as the process of learning the photo-realistic facial appearance model of a person observed in a sequence in a rigorous causal fashion. This fact means that it is not necessary to take into account subsequent images when adding the information of the current one, which is considered only once. Note that the facial appearance is learnt in the same order as the captured images, allowing a real-time learning capability in near future, as computational resources are constantly being increased.

13.3.1. *Data Representation*

An N image sequence $\mathbf{S} = [\mathbf{I}_1 \cdots \mathbf{I}_N]$ and a set of four masks $\mathbf{\Pi} = \{\pi^1, \ldots, \pi^4\}$, attached to four facial elements (like mouth, eyes or foerehead), are given. For each image $\mathbf{I}_t$, its specific mouth, eyes and forehead appearance are extracted using $\mathbf{\Pi}$, obtaining four observation vectors $\mathbf{o}_t^r$ (see Fig. 13.1). Therefore, four observation matrices $\mathbf{O}^r$ can be obtained from the application of the set of masks $\mathbf{\Pi}$ over the sequence $\mathbf{S}$. Dimensionality reduction of $\mathbf{O}^r$ can be achived using SVD:[15] $\mathbf{O}^r = [\mathbf{o}_1^r \cdots \mathbf{o}_N^r] = \mathbf{U}^r \mathbf{\Sigma}^r (\mathbf{V}^r)^T + \overline{\mathbf{o}}^r \mathbf{1}_{1\times N}$, where $\overline{\mathbf{o}}^r = \frac{1}{N}\sum_{k=1}^{N}\mathbf{o}_k^r$. Note that facial element appearances can be parameterized as $\mathbf{C}^r = \mathbf{\Sigma}^r (\mathbf{V}^r)^T$ (see Sect. 13.2.1). In the example proposed in this paper, faces composed of 41205 pixels could be codified with 35 coefficients, representing a reduction of more than 99.9% without any loss of perceptual quality (see Fig. 13.2).

13.3.2. Training Process

One major drawback of the parametrization presented in section 13.3.1 consists in the image alignment of the sequence.[5] Unless all face images through the whole sequence have the same position, ghoslty results may appear and suboptimal dimensionality reduction will be achieved. The tracking scheme presented in this paper combines simultaneously both processes of learning and alingment.

First of all, the four masks π^r are manually extracted from the first image I_1 of sequence S and the first observation vectors $o_1^1, \ldots, o_1^4$ are obtained. Next, the corresponding alignment coefficients a_1 are set to 0; they represent the affine transformation used to fit the masks onto the face on each frame.[5] Using the tracking algorithm presented in[7] over the second image I_2, observations $o_2^1, \ldots, o_2^4$ and alignment coefficients a_2 are stored. At this point, each facial element r can be factorized as $[o_1^r \, o_2^r] = O_2^r = U_2^r \Sigma_2^r (V_2^r)^T + \overline{o}_2^r = U_2^r (C_2^r)^T + \overline{o}_2^r$, where the current mean observation is generated by $\overline{o}_2^r = 0'5 o_1^r + 0'5 o_2^r$, the eigenvectors of $O_2^r (O_2^r)^T$ are found in U_2^r and the texture parametrization of the r-th facial element in images I_1 and I_2 is obtained in C_2^r. Once this initialization is done, the *On-the-fly Training Algorithm* (Figure 13.3) can be executed. Besides, only those columns of U_{t+1}^r and V_{t+1}^r whose values of Σ_{t+1}^r exceed a threshold τ are considered, keeping only those eigenvectors with enough information. The value of τ decreases from $0,5$ to $0,5 \cdot 10^{-3}$ in the first images (1 seconds at 25 im/s) in order to allow better face localization when almost no information is known about its appearance.[14] Notice that alignment parameters a can be used to extract gestural information in a multimodal input system.[16]

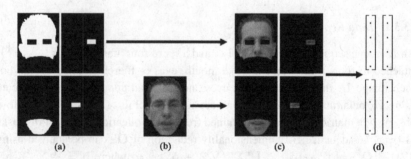

(a)　　　　　　(b)　　　　　　(c)　　　　　　(d)

Fig. 13.1.　(a) Masks π^r. (b) Image I_t. (c) Regions R_t^r, obtained from the application of each mask π^r over image I_t. (d) Vectors o_t^r related to the defined regions.

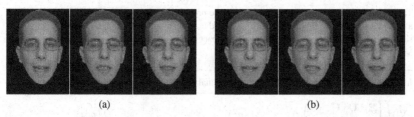

(a)   (b)

Fig. 13.2. (a) Three observed frames of a subject's face. (b) The same synthesized frames after learning the appearance model of this person.

On-the-Fly Training Algorithm

In: $\mathbf{U}_2, \mathbf{\Sigma}_2, \mathbf{V}_2, \bar{\mathbf{o}}_2$, alignment coefficients $\mathbf{a}_2$ and set of four masks $\mathbf{\Pi}$
1. Set $k = 2$
2. Using $\mathbf{U}_k, \mathbf{\Sigma}_k, \mathbf{V}_k, \bar{\mathbf{o}}_k, \mathbf{a}_k$ and $\mathbf{\Pi}$, the images of the new update block are aligned, generating L observation vectors $\mathbf{o}_{k+1}^r$ and alignment information $\mathbf{a}_{k+1}$ for each image.
3. Obtain $\mathbf{U}_{k+1}, \mathbf{\Sigma}_{k+1}, \mathbf{V}_{k+1}$ and $\bar{\mathbf{o}}_{k+1}$ from $\mathbf{U}_k, \mathbf{\Sigma}_k, \mathbf{V}_k, \bar{\mathbf{o}}_k$, and $\mathbf{o}_{k+1}$ Eq. (13.4)-Eq. (13.8).
4. Trim $\mathbf{U}_{k+1}$ and $\mathbf{V}_{k+1}$ according to $\mathbf{\Sigma}_{k+1}$.
5. Set $k = k + 1$ and go to Step 2 until there is no more new images.

Out: $\mathbf{U}_f, \mathbf{\Sigma}_f, \mathbf{V}_f, \bar{\mathbf{o}}_f$ and alignment coefficients $\mathbf{a}_f$ for each image.

13.3.3. Cost Analysis

In this section, the computational cost and memory requirements of the incremental computation of matrices $\mathbf{U}_f$, $\mathbf{\Sigma}_f$ and $\mathbf{V}_f$ and vector $\bar{\mathbf{o}}_f$ of the previous *On-the-fly algorithm* is presented in table 13.2. As could be seen in the previous section, this incremental process consists of successive SVD and data mean

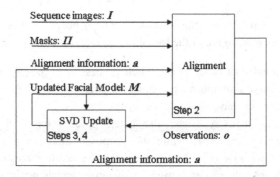

Fig. 13.3. Block diagram of the *On-the-fly Training Algorithm*.

Table 13.2. Resource order requirements of the proposed SVD and mean update algorithm over a matrix $\mathbf{O}_{p \times q}$ using update block size c and the s eigenvectors corresponding to the largest s singular values of $\mathbf{O}_{p \times q}$. To obtain more compact expressions, value $n = s + c$ has been used. Value k identifies the iteration number.

Id. Operation	Computational cost	Memory requirements
$\mathrm{SVD}\left(\begin{bmatrix} \boldsymbol{\Sigma}_k & \mathbf{U}_k^T \hat{\mathbf{i}} \\ \mathbf{0} & \mathbf{Q}_k^T \hat{\mathbf{i}} \end{bmatrix}_{n \times n} \right)$	$O\left(n^2\right)$	$O\left(n^2\right)$
$\left[\mathbf{U}_k \ \mathbf{Q}_k \right]_{p \times n} \cdot \left(\mathbf{U}_d \right)_{n \times n}$	$O\left(pn^2\right)$	$O\left(pn\right)$
$\left(\mathbf{V}_d^T \right)_{n \times n} \cdot \begin{bmatrix} \mathbf{V}_k^T & \mathbf{0} \\ \mathbf{0} & 1 \end{bmatrix}_{n \times (kc+c)}$	$O\left((kc+c)\,n^2\right)$	$O\left((kc+c)\,n\right)$
Mean update	$O\left(s^2\left(p+kc+c\right)\right)$	$O\left(s\left(p+kc+c\right)\right)$
Total	$O\left(q\left(\frac{s^2}{c}+n\right)(n+p+q)\right)$	$O\left(n\left(p+q+s\right)+c^2\right)$

updates, explained in section 13.2.3 to achieve a final factorization of the whole observation matrix $\mathbf{O}$:

$$\mathbf{O}_{p \times q} = \left(\mathbf{U}_f \right)_{p \times s} \left(\boldsymbol{\Sigma}_f \right)_{s \times s} \left(\left(\mathbf{V}_f \right)_{q \times s} \right)^T + \bar{\mathbf{o}}_{p \times 1} \cdot \mathbf{1}_{1 \times q}. \tag{13.16}$$

The value s consists in the number of eigenvectors kept in matrices $\mathbf{U}_{k+1}$ (step 4 of the *On-the-fly algorithm*). Also, it must be noted that he update block size is specified by c. In this analysis, we presuppose that $p > q$, $q > s$ and $q > c$. Moreover, if additional considerations are taken into account for the values of c and s, particular cost functions can be described as follows:

- When c and s are of small order of magnitude (o.o.m.) compared to q, the lowest computational cost is obtained: $O\left(sq\left(p+q\right)\right)$.
- If only c has small o.o.m., the computational cost becomes the highest one: $O\left(qs\frac{s}{c}\left(s+p+q\right)\right)$.
- For small o.o.m of s only, the computational cost becomes $O\left(qc\left(c+p+q\right)\right)$.
- When all c,s,p and q are of the same o.o.m., $O\left(q\left(s+c\right)\left(s+c+p+q\right)\right)$.

The computational cost order of the batch process is $O\left(pq\left(p+q\right)\right)$, which is higher than the first assumption and slightly higher than the two last ones. Note that the two last cases have also a similar cost.

Regarding to memory costs, the batch process has memory requirements of order $O\left(q^2 + sp\right)$, while the proposed incremental approach has $O\left((c+s)\left(p+q+s\right)+c^2\right)$. As can be noted, for small values of c and s the presented approach achieves great memory reduction and do not increase its order in the other cases.

13.4. Experimental Results

In this section, the performance of our incremental algorithm is shown. First, tracking results are specified in section 13.4.1, showing a comparison between the presented algorithm and its previous version. Next, precision results about incremental SVD with mean update are presented in section 13.4.2. Finally, in section 13.4.2.2 execution time is put in correspondence with the cost analysis obtained from section 13.3.3.

13.4.1. *On-the-Fly Training Algorithm*

The *On-the-fly Training Algorithm* has been tested over a short sequence and a long one, both recorded at a frame rate of 25 im/s. The short sequence consists of 316 images and it has been used to compare the results obtained from our *On-the-fly Training Algorithm* and its previous non-causal version.[7] Achieving the same quality in the results (see Fig. 13.4), the presented algorithm has reduced the execution time about 66% with respect to[7] and has required about 7 Mbytes in front of the 200 Mbytes consumed by[7] (see the comparison in Fig. 13.5). Later, if we focus on the long sequence (10000 frames), its processing requirements were impossible to met with the non-causal algorithm[7] because its huge memory cost of 6000 Mbytes, although massive storage systems (e.g. hard drives) were used; the *On-the-fly Training Algorithm* reduced the memory requirements to 17 Mbytes with a processing time of a little more than 10 hours (using a 2GHz processor) (see Fig. 13.5).

(a)   (b)

Fig. 13.4. Output tracking results of the learning process for: (a) the *On-the-fly Training Algorithm* and (b) the non-causal algorithm.

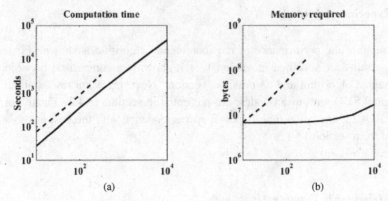

Fig. 13.5.   Solid line represents the *On-the-fly Training Algorithm* performance while the dashed one belongs to the non-causal algorithm presented in.[7] (a) Computation time in seconds. (b) Memory used in bytes.

13.4.2. *Incremental SVD and Mean Computation*

In this section, the goodness of the results given by the proposed incremental SVD and mean update algorithm (sect. 13.2.3) is analyzed and compared to the ideal performance offered by the batch solution.

13.4.2.1. *Precision comparisons*

Some experiments have been developed in order to test the analysis shown in the previous section (13.3.3). Two video sequences have been recorded and the face has been aligned in each one using our *On-the-fly training algorithm*. Starting from these aligned observations set stored columnwise in every O^k, we have factorized it using both the batch SVD process and our incremental SVD with mean update algorithm (sect. 13.2.3), obtaining two approximations of the form:

$$O^k_{p \times q} \approx U^k_{p \times s} \Sigma^k_{s \times s} \left(V^k_{q \times s} \right)^T + \bar{o}^k_{p \times 1} \cdot 1_{1 \times q}. \tag{13.17}$$

$$O^k_{p \times q} \approx \hat{U}^k_{p \times s} \hat{\Sigma}^k_{s \times s} \left(\hat{V}^k_{q \times s} \right)^T + \hat{o}^k_{p \times 1} \cdot 1_{1 \times q}. \tag{13.18}$$

where matrices U^k, Σ^k and V^k are the trimmed version of the thin-SVD of $\hat{O}^k = O^k - \bar{o}^k \cdot 1$ and $\bar{o}^k$ is the mean column of O^k; matrices $\hat{U}^k$, $\hat{\Sigma}^k$ and $\hat{V}^k$ and vector $\hat{o}^k$ are the corresponding ones when obtained with the incremental approach presented in section 13.2.3. This incremental process has been executed with different sizes of update block c and different threshold τ (sect. 13.3.2); the higher the threshold, the lesser eigenvalues kept in the model (with a non-linear case specific relation $s = f(c, \tau, k)$). Next, we define:

$$e_b(c, \tau) = \sum_{\forall k} \left\| \mathbf{M}_{p \times q}^k - \mathbf{U}_{p \times s}^k \mathbf{\Sigma}_{s \times s}^k \left(\mathbf{V}_{q \times s}^k \right)^T - \bar{\mathbf{o}}_{p \times 1}^k \cdot \mathbf{1}_{1 \times q} \right\|_2 . \quad (13.19)$$

$$e_i(c, \tau) = \sum_{\forall k} \left\| \mathbf{M}_{p \times q}^k - \hat{\mathbf{U}}_{p \times s}^k \hat{\mathbf{\Sigma}}_{s \times s}^k \left(\hat{\mathbf{V}}_{q \times s}^k \right)^T - \hat{\mathbf{o}}_{p \times 1}^k \cdot \mathbf{1}_{1 \times q} \right\|_2 . \quad (13.20)$$

Function e_b is shown in fig. 13.6(a) and e_i is represented in fig. 13.6(b). Following the reduction and compression of matrices theorem found in,[15] it can be assured that $e_b(c, \tau) \leq e_i(c, \tau)$ for any c and τ. Figure 13.6(c) represents the relative error as a function of c and τ. This relative error is measured as $\frac{e_i(c, \tau) - e_b(c, \tau)}{e_b(c, \tau)}$ and, as can be observed, all three figures achieve its lowest value when both c and τ have low values (1-5 and 0.001, respectively).

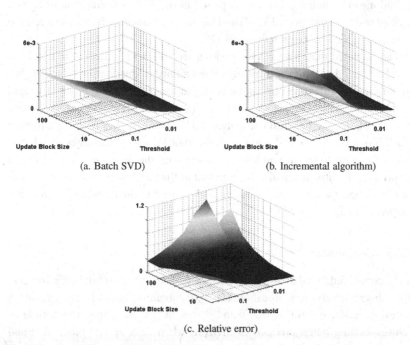

(a. Batch SVD)   (b. Incremental algorithm)

(c. Relative error)

Fig. 13.6.   Error between the original data matrix **O** and the factorization obtained by our incremental SVD and mean update algorithm.

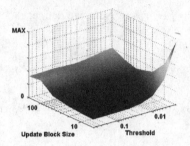

Fig. 13.7. Execution time of the algorithm with different number of eigenvectors and update block size.

13.4.2.2. Execution time

We have measured the execution time of both the batch and our incremental computation process done in section 13.4.2.1. The execution time of our incremental SVD and mean update algorithm is depicted in fig. 13.7 as a function of update block size and treshold (sect. 13.3.2) and has been obtained as the mean execution time related to the observation matrices O^k.

It can be noted that the analysis made in sect. 13.3.3 is reflected in fig. 13.7. It must be noted that the fastest results (about a third of the computation time belonging to the batch approach) can be achieved for small update block sizes and large threshold, which translates in taking into account few (1-2) eigenvectors. By the other hand, the heaviest computational load corresponds to the assumption of small block size (1-5) and low threshold (0.001), which translates to a larger number of eigenvectors (30) and further overcomes the computation time of the batch process. Finally, it can also be seen that as the block size grows, the computational cost becomes more independent with respect to the threshold (or number of eigenvector kept).

13.4.2.3. Conclusions

It can be concluded that the best alternative consists in using a small block size (*i.e.* 1-10) with a relatively small threshold (*i.e.* 0.01, obtaining about 10 eigenvectors); it achieves a relative error of less than 10^{-3} with half the computation time of the corresponding batch process. Moreover, when both update block size and threshold are small enough ($\tau = 0.001$, obtaining more than 30 eigenvectors, and $c = 1$), the incremental SVD and mean update algorithm achieves the best performance but with the heaviest computational load. By the other hand, the fastest option, achieved with small update block size and high threshold ($\tau = 0.1$,

$c = 1$), offers a poor precision compared to the previous cases. Finally, if we increase the update block size ($c > 10$), both computational and precision results also get worse.

13.5. Concluding Remarks

In this paper, a new method for extracting the mean of an existing SVD is presented, without increasing either the cost order of memory or time. This fact has allowed us to offer an incremental computation of SVD preserving a zero data mean, which has been analyzed and compared with the batch approach. The precision offered by our method is high enough to allow photorealistic reconstructions of observed face images using half the computation time of the non-incremental processes. Fields that can benefit from it can be, *e.g.*: classification problems, where the mean information is used to center the data; incremental computation of covariation matices, which need to be centered around its mean; causal construction of eigenspaces, where the principal components of the data are included, as well as the mean information. With respect to the latter, the *On-the-fly Algorithm* is presented in this work. Given an image sequence and a set of masks, this algorithm is capable of generating a separate eigenspace for each facial element (learning all their appearance variations due to changes in expression and visual utterances) and effectively tracking and aligning them. Furthermore, longer sequences than previous methods[5,7] can be processed with the same visual accuracy when no ilumination changes appear. Finally, we plan to add more robustness to this algorithm using methods like[5] and more work will be done in order to achieve real time perfomance, so specific appearance models can be obtained as a person is being recorded.

References

1. E. André, *The generation of multimedia presentations*, A Handbook of Natural Language Processing: techniques and applications for the processing of language as text, R. Dale, H. Misl and H. somers, Eds., Marcel Dekker Inc., 305–327, (2000).
2. S. Robbe-Reiter, N. Carbonell and P. Dauchy, *Expression constraints in multimodal human-computer interaction*, Intelligent User Interfaces, 225–228, (2000).
3. C. Stephanidis, *Towards universal acces in the disappearing computer environment*, UPGRADE, 4(1) 53–59:(2003).
4. E. André. *Natural language in multimedia/multimodal systems*, Handbook of Computational Linguistics, R. Miktov, Ed., Oxford Univ. Press, 650–669, (2003).
5. F. de la Torre and M. Black, *Robust parameterized component analysis: Theory and applications to 2d facial modeling*, ECCV, 654–669, (2002).

6. T. Ezzat, G. Geiger and T. Poggio, *Trainable videorealistic speech animation*, ACM SIGGRAPH, San Antonio, Texas, 225–228, (2002).

7. J. Melenchón, F. de la Torre, I. Iriondo, F. Alías, E. Martínez and Ll. Vicent, *Text to visual synthesis with appearance models*, ICIP, vol. I, 237–240, (2003).

8. D. Cosker, D. Marshall, P. Rosin and Y. Hicks, *Video realistic talking heads using hierarchical non-linear speech-appearance models*, Mirage, France, (2003).

9. B.J. Theobald , J.A. Bangham, I. Matthews and G.C. Cawley, *Near-videorealistic synthetic talking faces: Implementation and evaluation*, Speech Communication Journal, (2004).

10. M. Gu and S.C. Eisenstat, *A Stable and fast algorithm for updating the singular value decomposition* Tech. Rep. YALEU/DCS/RR-966, New Haven, (1993).

11. S. Chandrasekaran, B. Manjunath, Y. Wang, J. Winkeler and H. Zhang, *An eigenspace update algorithm for image analysis*, GMIP, **59**(5):321–332, (1997).

12. M. Brand, *Incremental singular value decomposition of uncertain data with missing values*, ECCV, I:707–ff, (2002).

13. P.M. Hall, D.R. Marshall and R. Martin, *Adding and substracting eigenspaces with eigenvalue decomposition and singular value decomposition*. ICV, **20**(13-14):1009–1016, (2002).

14. D. Scočaj, *Robust Subspace Approaches to Visual Learning and Recognition*, Ph.D. dissertation, University of Ljubljana, Faculty of computer and information science, Ljubljana, (2003).

15. M. Kirby, *Geometric Data Analysis: An Empirical Approach to Dimensionality Reduction and the Study of Patterns*, John Wiley & Sons Inc., (2001).

16. F. Keates and P. Robinson, *Gestures and multimodal input. Behaviour and Information Technology*, Taylor and Francis Ltd., **18**(1):35–42, (1999).

CHAPTER 14

A COMPARISON FRAMEWORK FOR WALKING
PERFORMANCES USING *aSpaces*

Jordi Gonzàlez[†], Javier Varona[+], F. Xavier Roca[*] and Juan J. Villanueva[*]

† *Institut de Robòtica i Informàtica Industrial (UPC-CSIC), Edifici U, Parc Tecnològic de Barcelona, 08028 Barcelona, Spain*
* *Centre de Visió per Computador & Dept. d'Informàtica, Universitat Autònoma de Barcelona (UAB), 08193 Bellaterra, Spain*
+ *Dept. Matemàtiques i Informàtica & Unitat de Gràfics i Visió, Universitat de les Illes Balears (UIB), 07071 Palma de Mallorca, Spain*

In this paper, we address the analysis of human actions by comparing different performances of the same action executed by different actors. Specifically, we present a comparison procedure applied to the walking action, but the scheme can be applied to other different actions, such as bending, running, etc. To achieve fair comparison results, we define a novel human body model based on joint angles, which maximizes the differences between human postures and, moreover, reflects the anatomical structure of human beings. Subsequently, a human action space, called *aSpace*, is built in order to represent each performance (i.e., each predefined sequence of postures) as a parametric manifold. The final human action representation is called *p–action*, which is based on the most characteristic human body postures found during several walking performances. These postures are found automatically by means of a predefined distance function, and they are called *key-frames*. By using key-frames, we *synchronize* any performance with respect to the *p–action*. Furthermore, by considering an arc length parameterization, independence from the speed at which performances are played is attained. Consequently, the *style* of human walking is successfully analysed by establishing the differences of the joints between a male and a female walkers.

14.1. Introduction

Computational models of action style are relevant to several important application areas.[1] On the one hand, it helps to enhance the qualitative description provided by a human action recognition module. Thus, for example, it is important to generate style descriptions which best characterize an specific agent for identification purposes. Also, the style of a performance can help to establish ergonomic evaluation and athletic training procedures. Another application domain is to enhance the human action library by training different action models for different action styles, using the data acquired from a motion capture system. Thus, it should be possible to re-synthesize human performances exhibiting different postures.

In the literature, the most studied human action is *walking*. Human walking is a complex, structured, and constrained action, which involves to maintain the balance of the human body while transporting the figure from one place to another. The most exploited characteristic is the cyclic nature of walking, because it provides uniformity to the observed performance. In this paper, we propose to use a human action model in the study of the *style* inherent in human walking performances, such as the gender, the walking pace, or the effects of carrying load, for example.

Specifically, we show how to use the *aSpace* representation presented in[2] to establish a characterization of the walking style in terms of the gender of the walker. The resulting characterization will consist of a description of the variation of specific limb angles during several performances played by agents of different gender. The aim is to compare performances to derive motion differences between female and male walkers.

14.2. Related Work

Motion capture is the process of recording live movement and translating it into usable mathematical terms by tracking a number of key points or regions/segments in space over time and combining them to obtain a 3-D representation of the performance.[3]

By reviewing the literature, we distinguish between two different strategies for human action modeling based on motion capture data, namely *data-driven* and *model-driven*. Data-driven approaches build detailed descriptions of recorded actions, and develop procedures for their adaption and adjustment to different characters.[4] Model-driven strategies search for parameterized representations controlled by few parameters:[5] computational models provide compactness and facilities for an easy edition and manipulation. Both approaches are reviewed next.

Data-driven procedures do care of specific details of motion: accurate movement descriptions are obtained by means of motion capture systems, usually optical. As a result, a large quantity of unstructured data is obtained, which is difficult to be modified while maintaining the *essence* of motion.[6,7] Inverse Kinematics (IK) is a well-known technique for the correction of one human posture.[8,9] However, it is difficult to apply IK over a whole action sequence while obeying spatial constraints and avoiding motion discontinuities. Consequently, current effort is centered on Motion Retargetting Problem,[10,11] i.e. the development of new methods for the edition of recorded movements.

Model-driven methods search for the main properties of motion: the aim is to develop computational models controlled by a reduced set of parameters.[12] Thus, human action representations can be easily manipulated for its re-use. Unfortunately, the development of action models is a difficult task, and complex motions are hard to be composed.[13]

Human action modeling can be based on Principal Component Analysis (PCA).[2,14–17] PCA computes an orthogonal basis of the samples, the so-called eigenvectors, which control the variation along the maximum variance directions. Each principal component is associated to a mode of variation of the shape, and the training data can be described as a linear combination of the eigenvectors. The basic assumption is that the training data generates a single cluster in the shape eigenspace.[18]

Following this strategy, we use a PCA-based space to emphasize similarities between the input data, in order to describe motion according to the gender of the performer. In fact, this space of reduced dimensionality will provide discriminative descriptions about style characteristics of motion.

14.3. Defining the Training Samples

In our experiments, an optical system was used to provide real training data to our algorithms. The system is based on six synchronized video cameras to record images, which incorporates all the elements and equipment necessary for the automatic control of cameras and lights during the capture process. It also includes an advanced software pack for the reconstruction of movements and the effective treatment of occlusions.

Consequently, the subject first placed a set of 19 reflective markers on the joints and other characteristic points of the body, see Fig. 14.1.(a) and (b). These markers are small round pieces of plastic covered in reflective material. Subsequently, the agent is placed in a controlled environment (i.e., controlled illumination and reflective noise), where the capture will be carried out. As a result, the accurate 3-D positions of the markers are obtained for each recorded posture $\mathbf{p}_s$, 30 frames per second:

$$\mathbf{p}_s = (x_1, y_1, z_1, ..., x_{19}, y_{19}, z_{19})^T. \qquad (14.1)$$

An action will be represented as a sequence of postures, so a proper body model is required. In our experiments, not all the 19 markers are considered to model human actions. In fact, we only process those markers which correspond

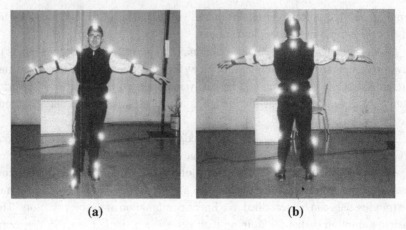

(a)   **(b)**

Fig. 14.1.   Procedure for data acquisition. Figs. **(a)** and **(b)** shows the agent with the 19 markers on the joints and other characteristic points of its body.

to the joints of a predefined human body model. The body model considered is composed of twelve rigid body parts (hip, torso, shoulder, neck, two thighs, two legs, two arms and two forearms) and fifteen joints, see Fig. 14.2.**(a)**. These joints are structured in a hierarchical manner, where the root is located at the hips, see Fig. 14.2.**(b)**.

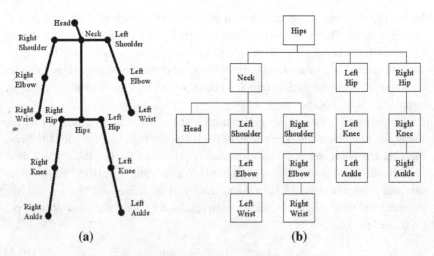

(a)   **(b)**

Fig. 14.2.   **(a)** Generic human body model represented using a stick figure similar to[19], here composed of twelve limbs and fifteen joints. **(b)** Hierarchy of the joints of the human body model.

We next represent the human body by describing the elevation and orientation of each limb using three different angles which are more natural to be used for limb movement description.[20] We consider the 3-D polar space coordinate system which describes the orientation of a limb in terms of its elevation, latitude and longitude, see Fig. 14.3. As a result, the twelve independently moving limbs in the 3-D polar space have a total of twenty-four rotational DOFs which correspond to thirty-six absolute angles.

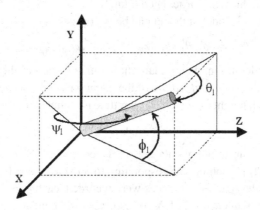

Fig. 14.3. The polar space coordinate system describes a limb in terms of the elevation ϕ_l, latitude θ_l, and longitude ψ_l.

So we compute the 3-D polar angles of a limb (i.e., elevation ϕ_l, latitude θ_l, and longitude ψ_l) as:

$$\phi_l = \tan^{-1}\left(\frac{y_i - y_j}{\sqrt{(x_i - x_j)^2 + (z_i - z_j)^2}}\right),$$

$$\theta_l = \tan^{-1}\left(\frac{x_i - x_j}{\sqrt{(y_i - y_j)^2 + (z_i - z_j)^2}}\right),$$

$$\psi_l = \tan^{-1}\left(\frac{z_i - z_j}{\sqrt{(x_i - x_j)^2 + (y_i - y_j)^2}}\right), \tag{14.2}$$

where denominators are also prevented to be equal to zero. Using this description, angle values lie between the range of $\left[-\frac{\pi}{2}, \frac{\pi}{2}\right]$, and the angle discontinuity problem is avoided.

Note that human actions are constrained movement patterns which involve to move the limbs of the body in a particular manner. That means, there is a relationship between the movement of different limbs while performing an action. In order to incorporate this relationship into the human action representation, we consider the hierarchy of Fig. 14.2.(b) in order to describe each limb with respect to its parent. That means, the relative angles between two adjacent limbs are next computed using the absolute angles of Eq. (14.2). Consequently, by describing the the human body using the relative angles of the limbs, we actually model the body as a hierarchical and articulated figure.

As a result, the model of the human body consists of thirty-six relative angles:

$$\Delta_s = (\phi_1', \theta_1', \psi_1', \phi_2', \theta_2', \psi_2', ..., \phi_{12}', \theta_{12}', \psi_{12}')^T. \tag{14.3}$$

Using this definition, we measure the *relative motion* of the human body. In order to measure the *global motion* of the agent within the scene, the variation of the (normalized) height of the hip u_s over time is included in the model definition:

$$x_s = (u_s, \Delta_s)^T. \tag{14.4}$$

Therefore, our training data set A is composed of r sequences $A = \{H_1, H_2, ..., H_r\}$, each one corresponding to a cycle or *stride* of the *aWalk* action. Three males and three females were recorded, each one walking five times in circles. Each sequence H_j of A corresponds to f_j human body configurations:

$$H_j = \{x_1, x_2, ..., x_{f_j}\}, \tag{14.5}$$

where each x_i of dimensionality $n \times 1$ stands for the 37 values of the human body model described previously. Consequently, our human performance analysis is restricted to be applied to the variation of these twelve limbs.

14.4. The *aWalk aSpace*

Once the learning samples are available, we compute the *aSpace* representation Ω of the *aWalk* action, as detailed in.[2] In our experiments, the walking performances of three females and two males were captured to collect the training data set. For each walker, near 50 *aWalk* cycles have been recorded. As a result, the training data is composed of near 1500 human posture configurations per agent, thus resulting 7500 3D body postures for building the *Walk aSpace*. From Eq. (14.5), the training data set A is composed of the acquired human postures:

$$A = \{x_1, x_2, ..., x_f\}, \tag{14.6}$$

where f refers to the overall number of training postures for this action:

$$f = \sum_{j=1}^{r} f_j. \tag{14.7}$$

The mean human posture $\bar{\mathbf{x}}$ and the covariance matrix Σ of $\mathbf{A}$ are calculated. Subsequently, the eigenvalues Λ and eigenvectors $\mathbf{E}$ of Σ are found by solving the eigenvector decomposition equation.

We preserve major linear correlations by considering the eigenvectors $\mathbf{e}_i$ corresponding to the largest eigenvalues λ_i. Fig. 14.4 shows the three eigenvectors associated to the three largest eigenvalues, which correspond to the most relevant modes of change of the human posture in the *aWalk aSpace*. As expected, these modes of variation are mainly related to the movement of legs and arms.

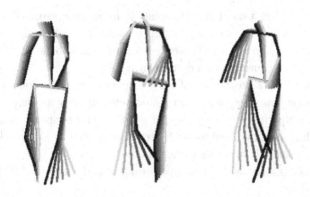

Fig. 14.4.   The three most important modes of variation of the *aWalk aSpace*.

So, by selecting the first m eigenvectors, $\{\mathbf{e}_1, \mathbf{e}_2, ..., \mathbf{e}_m\}$, we determine the most important modes of variation of human body during the *aWalk* action.[15] The value for m is commonly determined by eigenvalue thresholding. Consider the overall variance of the training samples, computed as the sum of the eigenvalues:

$$\lambda_T = \sum_{k=1}^{n} \lambda_k. \tag{14.8}$$

If we need to guarantee that the first m eigenvectors actually model, for example, 95% of the overall variance of the samples, we choose m so that:

$$\frac{\sum_{k=1}^{m} \lambda_k}{\lambda_T} \geq 0.95. \tag{14.9}$$

The individual contribution of each eigenvector determines that 95% of the variation of the training data is captured by the thirteen eigenvectors associated to the thirteen largest eigenvalues. So the resulting *aWalk aSpace* Ω is defined as the combination of the eigenvectors $\mathbf{E}$, the eigenvalues $\mathbf{\Lambda}$ and the mean posture $\bar{\mathbf{x}}$:

$$\Omega = (\mathbf{E}, \mathbf{\Lambda}, \bar{\mathbf{x}}). \tag{14.10}$$

14.5. Parametric Action Representation: the *p–action*

Using the *aWalk aSpace*, each performance is represented as a set of points, each point corresponding to the projection of a learning human posture $\mathbf{x}_i$:

$$\mathbf{y}_i = [\mathbf{e}_1, ..., \mathbf{e}_m]^T (\mathbf{x}_i - \bar{\mathbf{x}}). \tag{14.11}$$

Thus, we obtain a set of discrete points $\mathbf{y}_i$ in the action space that represents the action class Ω. By projecting the set of human postures of an *aWalk* performance $\mathbf{H}_j$, we obtain a cloud of points wich corresponds to the projections of the postures exhibited during such a performance.

We consider the projections of each performance as the control values for an interpolating curve $\mathbf{g}_j(p)$, which is computed using a standard cubic-spline interpolation algorithm.[21] The parameter p refers to the temporal variation of the posture, which is normalized for each performance, that is, $p \in [0, 1]$. Thus, by varying p, we actually move along the manifold.

This process is repeated for each performance of the learning set, thus obtaining r manifolds:

$$\mathbf{g}_j(p), \qquad p \in [0, 1], j = 1, ..., r. \tag{14.12}$$

Afterwards, the mean manifold $\mathbf{g}(p)$ is obtained by interpolating between these means for each index p. This performance representation is not influenced by its duration, expressed in seconds or number of frames. Unfortunately, this resulting parametric manifold is influenced by the fact that any subject performs an action in the way he or she is used to. That is to say, the extreme variability of human posture configurations recorded during different performances of the *aWalk* action affects the mean calculation for each index p. As a result, the manifold may comprise abrupt changes of direction.

A similar problem can be found in the computer animation domain, where the goal is to generate virtual figures exhibiting smooth and realistic movement. Commonly, animators define and draw a set of specific frames, called *key frames* or *extremes*, which assist the task of drawing the intermediate frames of the animated sequence.

Likewise, our goal is set to the extract the most characteristic body posture configurations which will correspond to the set of key-frames for that action. From a probabilistic point of view, we define characteristic postures as the least likely body postures exhibited during the action performances. As the *aSpace* is built based on PCA, such a space can also be used to compute the action class conditional density $P(\mathbf{x}_j|\mathbf{\Omega})$.

We assume that the *Mahalanobis distance* is a sufficient statistic for characterizing the likelihood:

$$d(\mathbf{x}_j) = (\mathbf{x}_j - \bar{\mathbf{x}})^T \Sigma (\mathbf{x}_j - \bar{\mathbf{x}}). \tag{14.13}$$

So, once the mean manifold $\mathbf{g}(p)$ is established, we compute the likelihood values for the sequence of pose-ordered projections that lie in such a manifold.[22,23] That is, we apply Eq. (14.13) for each component of the manifold $\mathbf{g}(p)$. Local maxima of this function correspond to locally maximal distances or, in other words, to the least likely samples, see Fig. 14.5.

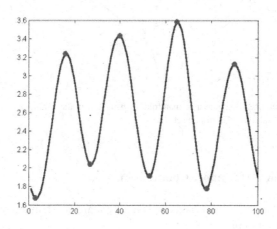

Fig. 14.5.   Distance measure after pose ordering applied to the points of the mean manifold in the *aWalk aSpace*. Maxima (i.e., the key-frames) also correspond to important changes of direction of the manifold.

Since each maximum of the distance function corresponds to a key-frame $\mathbf{k}_i$, the number of key-frames k is determined by the number of maxima. Thus, we obtain the set of time-ordered key-frames for the *aWalk* action:

$$\mathbf{K} = \{\mathbf{k}_1, \mathbf{k}_2, ..., \mathbf{k}_k\}, \qquad \mathbf{k}_i \in \mathbf{g}(p). \tag{14.14}$$

Once the key-frame set $\mathbf{K}$ is found, the final human action model is represented as a parametric manifold $\mathbf{f}(p)$, called *p–action*, which is built by interpolation between the peaks of the distance function defined in Eq. (14.13). We refer the reader to[2] for additional details. Fig. 14.6 shows the final *aWalk* model $\mathbf{\Gamma}$, defined as the combination of the *aWalk aSpace* Ω, the key-frames $\mathbf{K}$ and the *p–action* $\mathbf{f}$:

$$\Gamma = (\Omega, \mathbf{K}, \mathbf{f}).\qquad(14.15)$$

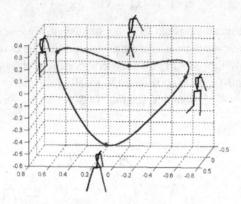

Fig. 14.6.   Prototypical performance manifold, or *p–action*, in the *aWalk aSpace*. Depicted human postures correspond to the key-frame set.

14.6. Human Performance Comparison

In order to compare performances played by male and female agents, we define two different training sets:

$$\mathbf{H}^{W_M} = \{\mathbf{x}_1, \mathbf{x}_2, ..., \mathbf{x}_{f_M}\},$$
$$\mathbf{H}^{W_F} = \{\mathbf{x}_1, \mathbf{x}_2, ..., \mathbf{x}_{f_F}\},\qquad(14.16)$$

that is, the set human postures exhibited during several *aWalk* performances for a male and a female agent, respectively.

Next, we project the human postures of $\mathbf{H}^{W_M}$ and $\mathbf{H}^{W_F}$ in the *aWalk aSpace*, as shown in Fig. 14.7. The cyclic nature of the *aWalk* action explains the resulting circular clouds of projections. Also, note that both performances do not *intersect*, that is, they do not exhibit the same set of human postures. This is due to the high variability inherent in human performances. Consequently, we can *identify* a posture as belonging to a male or female walker.

However, the scope of this paper is not centered on determining a *discriminative* procedure between generic male and female walkers. Instead, we look for a

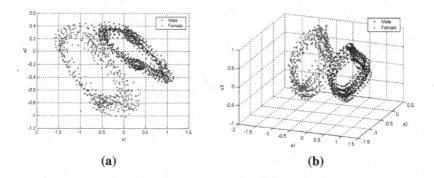

(a)   **(b)**

Fig. 14.7.   Male and female postures projected in the *aWalk aSpace*, by considering two **(a)** and three **(b)** eigenvectors for the *aSpace* representation.

comparison procedure to subsequently *evaluate* the variation of the angles of specific agents while performing the same action, in order to derive a characterization of the action *style*.

Following the procedure described in the last section, we use the projections of each walker to compute the performance representation for the male Γ^{W_M} and female Γ^{W_F} agents:

$$\Gamma^{W_M} = (\Omega, \mathbf{K}^{W_M}, \mathbf{f}^{W_M}),$$
$$\Gamma^{W_F} = (\Omega, \mathbf{K}^{W_F}, \mathbf{f}^{W_F}), \tag{14.17}$$

where $\mathbf{f}^{W_M}$ and $\mathbf{f}^{W_F}$ refer to the male and female *p–actions*, respectively. These manifolds have been obtained by interpolation between the key-frames of their respective key-frame set, i.e., $\mathbf{K}^{W_M}$ and $\mathbf{K}^{W_F}$. Fig. 14.8 shows the resulting *p–action* representations in the *aWalk aSpace* Ω.

14.7.   Arc length Parameterization of *p–actions*

In order to compare the human posture variation for both performances, we sample both *p–actions* to describe each manifold as a sequence of projections:

$$\mathbf{f}^{W_M}(\mathbf{p}) = [\ \mathbf{y}_1^{W_M}, \mathbf{y}_2^{W_M}, ..., \mathbf{y}_{q_M}^{W_M}\ ],$$
$$\mathbf{f}^{W_F}(\mathbf{p}) = [\ \mathbf{y}_1^{W_F}, \mathbf{y}_2^{W_F}, ..., \mathbf{y}_{q_F}^{W_F}\ ], \tag{14.18}$$

where q_M and q_F refer to the number of projections considered for performance comparison. However, the sampling rate of both *p–actions* should be established in order to attain independence from the speed at which both performances have

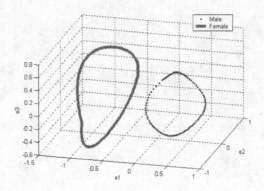

Fig. 14.8.   Male and female performance representations in the *aWalk aSpace*.

been played. Thus, synchronization of recorded performances is compulsory to allow comparison.

Speed control is achieved by considering the distance along a curve of interpolation or, in other words, by establishing a reparameterization of the curve by arc length.[24] Thus, once the *aWalk p–action* is parameterized by arc length, it is possible to control the speed at which the manifold is traversed.

Subsequently, the key-frames will be exploited for synchronization: the idea of synchronization arises from the assumption that any performance of a given action should present the key-frames of such an action. Therefore, the key-frame set is considered as the reference postures in order to adjust or *synchronize* any new performance to our action model. Subsequently, by considering the arc length parameterization, the aim is to sample the new performance and the *p–action* so that the key-frames are equally spaced in both manifolds.

Therefore, both *p–actions* are parameterized by arc length and, subsequently, the synchronization procedure described in[25] is applied: once the key-frames establish the correspondences for $\mathbf{f}^{W_M}$ and $\mathbf{f}^{W_F}$, we modify the rate at which the male and female *p–actions* are sampled, so that their key-frames coincide in time with the key-frames of the *aWalk p–action*.

14.8. Experimental Results

Once the male and female *p–actions* are synchronized, the angle variation for different limbs of the human body model can be analysed. Fig. 14.9.(a), (b), (c), and (d) show the evolution of the elevation angle for four limbs of the human body model, namely the shoulder, torso, left arm, and right thigh, respectively.

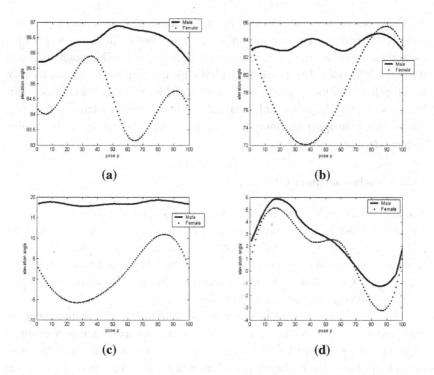

Fig. 14.9.   The elevation variation for the shoulder (**a**), torso (**b**), left arm (**c**), and right thigh (**d**) limbs are depicted for a male and a female walker.

By comparing the depicted angle variation values of both walkers, several differences can be observed. The female walker moves her shoulder in a higher degree than the male shoulder. That is, the swing movement of the shoulder is more accentuated for the female. Also, the female bends the torso in a higher inclination degree. Therefore, the swing movement of the shoulder and torso for the male agent is less pronounced. The female walker also exhibits an emphasized swing movement in her left arm. On the contrary, the male agent does not show a relevant swing movement for his left arm. As expected, when the left arm swings backward, the right thigh swings forward, and vice versa. When comparing the angle variation of the right thigh for both walkers, few dissimilarities can be derived. In fact, most differences between the male and the female performances have been found in the elevation values of the limbs corresponding to the upper part of the human body.

These results are also supported by other authors such as,[26] which explicitly differentiate walking modeling into upper and lower body. Thus, the lower body is usually concentrated in locomotion, that is, modeling the walking motion so that it is physically valid. This is usually achieved by applying inverse kinematics. On the other hand, the movement of the upper body adds reality and naturalness to the human walking, which is mainly attained by means of interpolation techniques. Afterwards, both upper and lower body motion should be synchronized to creating a natural looking walking.

14.9. Conclusions and Future Work

Summarizing, a comparison framework has been presented which allows to evaluate the variation of the angles of specific human body limbs for different agents while performing the same action. This analysis of human actions helps to determine those human body model parameters which best characterize an specific action style. Consequently, a suitable characterization of the action *style* can be built by analyzing the resulting angle values.

The procedure presented in this work is restricted to differentiate between male and female walkers, but it can be enhanced to compare their performances instead. Thus, future work will be addressed to evaluate not only the differences of walking, but of the performances of other actions in order to derive different style attributes such as the mood or fatigue of the performer, and even for injury detection when such an injury affects an action performance.

As a result of synchronization, differences between a performance and the prototypical action will be studied to analyze the resulting angle variation curves. Such differences could be associated with natural language terms related to speed, naturalness, or suddenness, for example. These terms could be used to enhance the description of a recognized action. Additionally, as a result of comparison, a parameterization of the differences between the joint angles will be established, in order to further parameterize the action style. Furthermore, using this characterization about action styles, human action recognition procedures will be enhanced by deriving style attributes about recognized performances, thus deriving richer motion descriptions. Also, we plan to enhance human action synthesis procedures by incorporating restrictions about predefined action styles, which the virtual agent should obey while reproducing the requested action. Therefore, small details of motion will be added to the resulting synthesized sequence.

Acknowledgements

This work has been supported by EC grants IST-027110 for the HERMES project and IST-045547 for the VIDI-Video project, and by the Spanish MEC under projects TIN2006-14606 and DPI-2004-5414. Jordi Gonzlez also acknowledges the support of a Juan de la Cierva Postdoctoral fellowship from the Spanish MEC.

References

1. J. Davis and A. Bobick. The representation and recognition of movement using temporal templates. In *Proceedings of IEEE Conference on Computer Vision and Pattern Recognition (CVPR'97)*, pp. 928–934, San Juan, Puerto Rico, (1997).
2. J. Gonzàlez, X. Varona, F. Roca, and J. Villanueva. *aSpaces*: Action spaces for recognition and synthesis of human actions. In *Proc. Second International Workshop on Articulated Motion and Deformable Objects (AMDO 2002)*, pp. 189–200, Palma de Mallorca, Spain, (2002).
3. F. Perales, A. Igelmo, J. Buades, P. Negre, and G.Bernat. Human motion analysis & synthesis using computer vision and graphics techniques. Some applications. In *IX Spanish Symposium on Pattern Recognition and Image Analysis*, vol. 1, pp. 271–277, Benicassim, Spain (16-18 May, 2001).
4. M. Gleicher and N. Ferrier. Evaluating video-based motion capture. In *Proceedings of Computer Animation*, pp. 75–80, Geneva, Switzerland (June, 2002).
5. R. Boulic, N. Magnenat-Thalmann, and D. Thalmann, A global human walking model with real-time kinematics personification, *The Visual Computer.* **6**(6), 344–358, (1990).
6. D. Thalmann and J. Monzani. Behavioural animation of virtual humans : What kind of law and rules? In ed. I. C. Press, *Proc. Computer Animation 2002*, pp. 154–163, (2002).
7. M. Unuma, K. Anjyo, and R. Takeuchi. Fourier principles for emotion-based human figure animation. In *Proceedings of SIGGRAPH 95*, pp. 91–96 (August, 1995).
8. R. Boulic, R. Mas, and D. Thalmann, A robust approach for the center of mass position control with inverse kinetics, *Journal of Computers and Graphics.* **20**(5), 693–701, (1996).
9. M. Gleicher, Retargetting motion to new characters, *Computer Graphics, Proceedings of ACM SIGGRAPH 85*. pp. 33–42, (1998).
10. M. Gleicher, Comparing constraint-based motion editing methods, *Graphical Models.* pp. 107–134, (2001).
11. Z. Popović and A. Witkin. Physically based motion transformation. In *Proceedings of ACM SIGGRAPH 99*, pp. 11–20 (August, 1999).
12. N. Badler, C. Phillips, and B. Webber, *Simulating Humans. Computer Graphics Animation and Control.* (Oxford University Press, 1993).
13. K. Perlin and A. Goldberg. Improv: a system for scripting interactive actors in virtual worlds. In *Proceedings of ACM SIGGRAPH 96*, pp. 205–216, (1996).

14. A. Baumberg and D. Hogg, Generating spatio temporal models from examples, *Image and Vision Computing*. **14**, 525–532, (1996).

15. R. Bowden. Learning statistical models of human motion. In *Proceedings of the IEEE Workshop on Human Modeling, Analysis and Synthesis*, pp. 10–17, (2000).

16. P. Glardon, R. Boulic, and D. Thalmann. Pca-based walking engine using motion capture data. In *Computer Graphics International*, pp. 292–298, Crete, Greece, (2004).

17. N. Troje, Decomposing biological motion: a framework for analysis and synthesis of human gait patterns, *Journal of Vision*. **2**, 371–387, (2002).

18. T. Heap and D. Hogg, Extending the point distribution model using polar coordinates, *Image and Vision Computing*. **14**, 589–599, (1996).

19. J. Cheng and M. Moura, Capture and represention of human walking in live video sequences, *IEEE Transactions on Multimedia*. **1**(2), 144–156, (1999).

20. D. Ballard and C. Brown, *Computer Vision*. (Prentice-Hall, Englewood Cliffs, NJ, 1982).

21. W. Press, B. Flannery, S. Teukolsky, and W. Vetterling, *Numerical Recipes in C*. (Cambridge University Press, Cambridge, 1988).

22. H. Borotschnig, L. Paletta, M. Prantl, and A. Pinz, Appearance-based active object recognition, *Image and Vision Computing*. **18**, 715–727, (2000).

23. H. Murase and S. Nayar, Visual learning and recognition of 3-D objects from appearance, *International Journal of Computer Vision*. **14**, 5–24, (1995).

24. B. Guenter and R. Parent, Computing the arc length of parametric curves, *IEEE Computer Graphics and Applications*. **10**(3), 72–78 (May, 1990).

25. J. Gonzàlez, J. Varona, F. Roca, and J. Villanueva. A human action comparison framework for motion understanding. In *Artificial Intelligence Research and Developments. Frontiers in Artificial Intelligence and Applications*, vol. 100, pp. 168–177. IOS Press, (2003).

26. K. Ashida, S. Lee, J. Allbeck, H. Sun, N. Badler, and D. Metaxas. Pedestrians: Creating agent behaviors through statistical analysis of observation data. In *Proceedings of Computer Animation*, pp. 84–92, Seoul, Korea, (2001).

CHAPTER 15

DETECTING HUMAN HEADS WITH THEIR ORIENTATIONS

Akihiro Sugimoto[†], Mitsuhiro Kimura* and Takashi Matsuyama*

† *National Institute of Informatics*
Chiyoda, Tokyo 1018430, Japan
E-mail: sugimoto@nii.ac.jp
* *Graduate School of Informatics, Kyoto University*
Kyoto 6068501, Japan

We propose a two-step method for detecting human heads with their orientations. In the first step, the method employs an ellipse as the contour model of human-head appearances to deal with wide variety of appearances. Our method then evaluates the ellipse to detect possible human heads. In the second step, on the other hand, our method focuses on features inside the ellipse, such as eyes, the mouth or cheeks, to model facial components. The method evaluates not only such components themselves but also their geometric configuration to eliminate false positives in the first step and, at the same time, to estimate face orientations. Our intensive experiments show that our method can correctly and stably detect human heads with their orientations.

15.1. Introduction

Automatically detecting and tracking people and their movements is important in many applications such as in– and out-door surveillance, distance learning, or interfaces for human-computer interaction.[2,4,6–9] In particular, the human face is a key object of interest for visual discrimination and identification. A tremendous amount of research has been made for detecting human heads/faces and for recognizing face orientations/expressions (see Refs.[3] and[23] for surveys). Most existing methods in the literatures, however, focus on only one of these two. Namely, methods to detect human heads/faces (see Refs.[1,12,19,20] and,[24] for example) do not estimate orientations of the detected heads/faces, and methods to recognize face orientations/expressions (see Refs.[10,14,15,18] and,[21] for example) assume that human faces in an image or an image sequence have been already segmented.

Recently, a visual object detection framework was proposed and applied to face detection.[16,17] Though the framework is capable of processing images rapidly with achieving high detection rate, it focuses on rapidly detecting human faces as rectangle regions and does not pay any attention to the contours of their appearances.

To build a fully automated system that recognizes human faces from images, it is essential to develop robust and efficient algorithms to detect human heads and, at the same time, to identify face orientations. Given a single image or a sequence of images, the goal of automatic human-face recognition is to detect human heads/faces and estimate their orientations regardless of not only their positions, scales, orientations, poses, but also individuals, background changes and lighting conditions.

This paper proposes a two-step method for detecting human heads and, at the same time, for estimating face orientations by a monocular camera. In the both steps, we employ models of the human-head contour and face orientations to enhance robustness and stableness in detection. We also introduce model evaluation with only image-features robust against lighting conditions, i.e., the gradient of intensity and texture.

In the first step, our method employs an ellipse as the contour model of human-head appearances to deal with wide variety of appearances. The ellipse is generated from one ellipsoid based on the camera position with its angle of depression in the environment. Our method then evaluates the ellipse over a given image to detect possible human heads. In evaluation of an ellipse, two other ellipses are generated inside and outside of the ellipse, and the gradient of intensity along the perimeter of the three ellipses is used for accurate detection of human-head appearances.

In the second step, on the other hand, our method focuses on facial components such as eyes, the mouth or cheeks to generate inner models for face-orientation estimation. Based on the camera position with its angle of depression, our method projects the facial components on the ellipsoid onto the ellipse to generate inner models of human-head appearances. Our method then evaluates not only such components themselves but their geometric configuration to eliminate false positives in the first step and, at the same time, to estimate face orientations. Here the Gabor-Wavelets filter, which is verified its robustness and stableness against changes in scale, orientation and illumination, is used for detecting features representing the facial components.

Consequently, our method can correctly and stably detect human heads and estimate face orientations even under environments such as illumination changes or face-orientation changes. Our intensive experiments using a face-image database and real-situation images show the effectiveness of the proposed method.

15.2. Contour model for human-head appearances

The model-based approach is inevitable to enhance stableness against environment changes. This is because features detected from images without any models often generate false positives in recognition.

15.2.1. *Human head and its appearances*

Human beings have almost the same contour in shape of the head and an ellipse approximates the appearance of the contour. These observations remain invariant against changes in face orientation. We, therefore, model the contour of human-head appearances by the ellipse.[1,12,19]

An ellipse has five parameters in the image (Fig. 15.1): the 2D coordinates (x, y) of the ellipse center, the length a of the semiminor axis, the oblateness r, and the slant ψ of the ellipse.

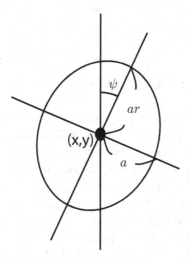

Fig. 15.1.   Geometric model of human-head appearances.

These parameters of the ellipse change depending on the angle of depression of a camera even though human heads are in the same pose. In particular, the change in oblateness is outstanding. To investigate this change in oblateness, we introduce an ellipsoid to the human-head model in 3D. We assume that the ellipsoid is represented in the world coordinates by

$$x^2 + y^2 + \frac{z^2}{r^2} = 1, \tag{15.1}$$

where $r \geq 1$. We then derive an ellipse as the contour model of human-head appearances depending on the angle of depression of the camera (Fig. 15.2).

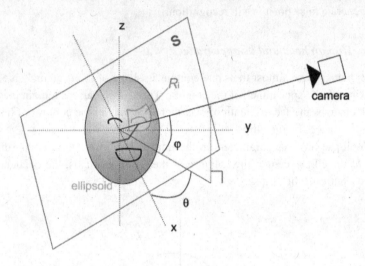

Fig. 15.2.   Human-head model.

When we set up a camera with any angle of depression, the ellipsoid (15.1) is observed as an ellipse. The length of the semiminor axis of the ellipse is always one. The length of the semimajor axis, on the other hand, is between one and r depending on the angle of depression of the camera.

Now we determine the oblateness, r' ($1 \leq r' \leq r$), of the ellipse observed by a camera with φ angle of depression providing that the distance of the camera position from the ellipsoid is large enough. We consider the ellipse obtained through the projection of (15.1) onto the $xz-$plane and its tangential line ℓ (Fig. 15.3).

We see that the ellipse, the projection of (15.1) onto the $xz-$plane, is represented by

$$x^2 + \frac{z^2}{r^2} = 1. \tag{15.2}$$

Let its tangential line with slant φ from the $x-$axis be

$$z = \sin \varphi x + b, \tag{15.3}$$

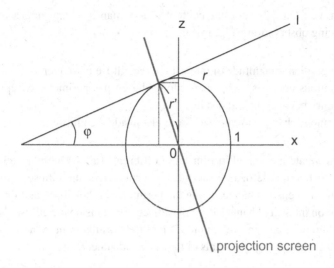

Fig. 15.3.   Projection of the ellipsoid onto the xz−plane.

where b is the z-intercept. Combining (15.2) and (15.3), we can compute b. We then have the coordinates of their contact point, from which it follows that

$$r' = \sqrt{\frac{r^4 + \tan^2 \varphi}{r^2 + \tan^2 \varphi}}.$$

This relates φ, i.e., the angle of depression of the camera, with r', i.e., the oblateness of the ellipse representing the contour of human-head appearances. We dynamically compute the oblateness of the ellipse from the camera position based on this relationship.

15.2.2.   *Evaluation of contour model*

When we are given an ellipse in the image, how to evaluate the goodness of the ellipse to recognize as a human-head appearance is a difficult problem. Employing image features invariant under changes in environment is indispensable.

Color information is widely used there. Color information is robust against scale changes but sensitive to changes in illumination. To overcome this problem, eliminating the luminance from color information and evaluating chromaticity is proposed.[1,13,19] The effectiveness of this approach is, however, limited.

We employ, in this paper, the gradient of intensity in evaluating an ellipse to identify whether it is an applicant of human-head appearances. This is because the gradient of intensity is robust against illumination changes.

When we fit an ellipse to the contour of a human-head appearance, we have the following observations (Fig. 15.4):

- Great gradient magnitude of intensity at the ellipse perimeter.
- Continuous changes in intensity along the ellipse perimeter except for the boundary between hair and skin.
- Continuous changes in intensity from just inside the ellipse.

We thus evaluate a given ellipse in three different ways. One is evaluation on the gradient magnitude of intensity at the perimeter of the ellipse. Another is evaluation on intensity changes along the perimeter of the ellipse and the other is evaluation on intensity changes from the adjacent part inside the ellipse. Introducing these three aspects in evaluation of an ellipse results in more accurately and more robustly obtaining applicants of human-head appearances.

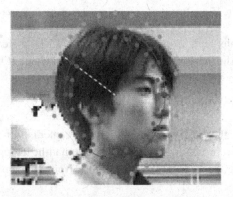

Fig. 15.4.   The (red) ellipse representing a human-head appearance.

For evaluating an ellipse, we construct two other ellipses (Fig. 15.5). One is a smaller size ellipse with the identical center and the other is a larger size ellipse with the identical center. In Fig. 15.5, the red ellipse is to be evaluated and the blue ellipse is the smaller size one and the green is the larger size one. We denote by $orbit(i)$ the intensity of the intersection point of the (red) ellipse to be evaluated and ray i whose end point is the ellipse center. We remark that we have N rays with the same angle-interval and they are sorted by the angle from the horizontal axis in the image. $outer(i)$ and $inner(i)$ are defined in the same way for the cases of the larger size ellipse (green ellipse) and the smaller size ellipse (blue ellipse), respectively.

We now have the following function evaluating the (red) ellipse.

$$f(p) = k\frac{1}{N} \sum_{i=1}^{N} \{G(i) - O(i) - I(i)\},\qquad (15.4)$$

where p is the parameter vector representing the red ellipse and

$$G(i) = |outer(i) - orbit(i)|,\qquad (15.5)$$
$$O(i) = |orbit(i) - orbit(i-1)|,\qquad (15.6)$$
$$I(i) = |orbit(i) - inner(i)|.\qquad (15.7)$$

Note that k is the constant making the value dimensionless.[1] (15.5), (15.6), and (15.7) evaluate the gradient magnitude of intensity at the ellipse perimeter, intensity changes along the ellipse perimeter and intensity changes from just inside the ellipse, respectively. Ellipses having a small value of (15.4) are then regarded as applicants of human-head appearances. We remark that our ellipse evaluation is effective even if a face region is darker than the surrounding background. This is because our evaluation is based on not intensity itself but the gradient magnitude of intensity.

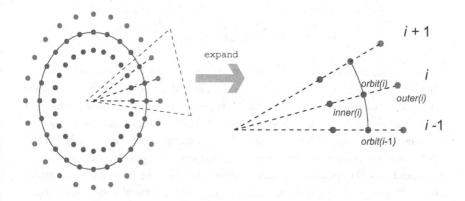

Fig. 15.5.   Evaluation of the ellipse (red: the ellipse to be evaluated).

In the next section, we evaluate the applicants of human-head appearances based on features inherent in the human face to recognize as a human-head appearance and, at the same time, to identify the face orientation.

15.3. Inner models for face orientations

We investigate inside the ellipse in more detail to detect human heads and face orientations providing that applicants of the human heads are already detected as ellipses. In detection, these pre-obtained applicants facilitate determination of parameters such as scale or direction.

15.3.1. *Facial components*

Eyebrows, eyes, the mouth, the nose and cheeks are the features inherent in the human face. Here we focus on eyes, the mouth and cheeks, and characterize textures around such facial components. We remark that textures are robust against illumination changes.

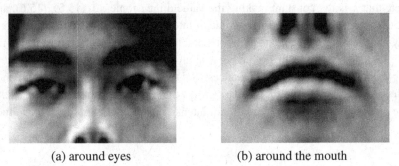

(a) around eyes   (b) around the mouth

Fig. 15.6.   Textures around facial components.

In oriental countries, we observe around eyes (1) a dark area due to eyebrows, (2) a bright area due to eyelids, and (3) a dark area due to the pupil (see Fig. 15.6 (a)). These are observations along the vertical direction of the human face and these characterize the texture of an eye area. We also observe that the eye area is symmetrical with respect to the pupil. As for an area around the mouth, on the other hand, we observe (1) a bright area due to the upper lip, (2) a dark area due to the mouth, and (3) a bright area due to the lower lip (see Fig. 15.6 (b)). In addition, the mouth area is also symmetrical with respect to the vertical center of the face. These observations characterize the texture of a mouth area. We see no complex textures in a cheek area. These observations are almost invariant and stable under changes in illumination, in face-orientation and in scale.

The geometric configuration of the facial components, i.e., the relative position between eyes, the mouth and cheeks is also invariant. Combining the characteristic of textures of the facial components with their geometric configuration enables us to stably recognize human heads/faces.

For each applicant of human-head appearances, we detect the facial components with their geometric configuration to verify whether it is a human-head appearance. We remark that we can easily identify the scale in detecting facial components since we have already obtained applicants of human-head appearances in terms of ellipses.

15.3.2. *Detecting facial components using Gabor-Wavelets*

In detecting facial feature points described in the previous section, the Gabor-Wavelets filter is most promising in robustness and stableness against illumination changes.[5,11,14,15,22] We thus use Gabor-Wavelets to extract the facial feature points, eyes, the mouth and cheeks, as a set of multi-scale and multi-orientation coefficients.

Applying the Gabor-Wavelets filter to a point (x_0, y_0) of a given image $f(x, y)$ can be written as a convolution

$$\psi(x_0, y_0, \sigma, \omega, \phi) = \iint dx dy f(x, y) G(x - x_0, y - y_0, \sigma, \omega, \phi)$$

with Gabor kernel $G(x, y, \sigma, \omega, \phi)$s where G is formulated in Ref.[11] by

$$G(x, y, \sigma, \omega, \phi) = \kappa e^{\frac{-1}{4\pi\sigma^2}(\tilde{x}^2 + \tilde{y}^2)} e^{j\omega\tilde{x}}.$$

Here

$$\begin{bmatrix} \tilde{x} \\ \tilde{y} \end{bmatrix} = \begin{bmatrix} \cos\phi & \sin\phi \\ -\sin\phi & \cos\phi \end{bmatrix} \begin{bmatrix} x \\ y \end{bmatrix}, \quad \kappa = \frac{1}{4\pi^2\sigma^2}, \quad j = \sqrt{-1}.$$

σ, ω, ϕ are the parameters representing the scale, frequency and orientation, respectively. Note that $(\tilde{x}, \tilde{y})$ is obtained by rotating image point (x, y) by ϕ.

Figure 15.7 shows an example of a set of Gabor-Wavelets. (a) is the real part of the Gabor kernel with $\sigma = 3.0, \omega = 0.5°, \phi = 0°$, and (b) is the kernels with the same scale, different orientations and frequencies.

We can selectively apply the Gabor-Wavelets filter to particular locations. In addition, we can easily specify scales, frequencies, and orientations in the application of the Gabor-Wavelets filter. In other words, we can apply the Gabor-Wavelets filter to specific regions in the image, i.e., pre-obtained applicants of human-head appearances, with selective parameters in scale, frequency, and orientation to extract a feature vector. This is because we have already detected applicants of human-head appearances in terms of ellipses (we have already roughly estimated a size of a human-head appearance). This reduces the computational cost in recognizing human-head appearances in the practical sense.

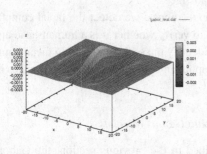

(a) Real-part of a kernel   (b) Kernels with different orientations

Fig. 15.7.   Gabor kernels.

We characterized in Section 15.3.1 textures around eyes and the mouth along the vertical direction of the human face. To detect these textures we only have to select the parameters in the Gabor-Wavelets filter so that the filter detects the textures along the semimajor axis of the ellipse. Points with maximal values in the response ellipse-region can be eyes and those with minimal values can be a mouth. The area with no singularity, on the other hand, can be cheeks.

15.3.3. *Inner models of head appearances with facial components*

We generate here inner models of human-head appearances based on the ellipsoid (15.1). As shown in Fig. 15.2, area R_i on the ellipsoid denoting a facial component such as an eye or a mouth is projected onto the plane when it is viewed from the camera with direction (θ, φ), where θ is the rotation angle toward the camera from the front of the face and φ is the angle of depression of the camera. The projected area then enables us to identify the location of the facial component in the human-head appearance. Hence, we can generate the inner models of human-head appearances. We remark that we can measure φ in advance when we set up a camera in the environment.

We consider plane S that goes though the origin and whose normal vector is identical with the viewing line of the camera (Fig. 15.8). Let $D = (k, l, m)^\top$ be the unit normal vector of plane S. S is then expressed by $kx + ly + mz = 0$. It is easy to see that k, l and m are expressed in terms of θ and φ:

$$k = \cos \varphi \cos \theta,$$
$$l = \cos \varphi \sin \theta,$$
$$m = \sin \varphi.$$

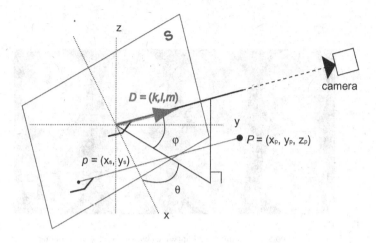

Fig. 15.8.   Geometry in deriving an inner model.

Letting p be the foot of the perpendicular from a 3D point P onto S, we can easily relate P and p by

$$p = \begin{pmatrix} X_S^\top \\ Y_S^\top \end{pmatrix} P.$$

Here $X_S^\top, Y_S^\top$ are the orthogonal unit vectors in 3D representing the coordinates in S:

$$X_S = \frac{1}{\sqrt{1 - m^2}} \begin{pmatrix} l \\ -k \\ 0 \end{pmatrix}, \quad Y_S = \frac{m}{\sqrt{1 - m^2}} \begin{pmatrix} -k \\ -l \\ \frac{1 - m^2}{m} \end{pmatrix}.$$

In this way, when depression angle φ and rotation angle θ are specified, we can project a facial area of the ellipsoid onto the image plane to obtain an inner model of the human-head appearance that represents the facial components with their geometric configuration.

Figure 15.9 shows the inner models of human-head appearances with $\varphi = 0$ (upper: $\theta = 0°, 30°, 60°, 90°$, lower: $\theta = 180°, 270°, 300°, 330°$). R_1 and R_2 denote the eye areas. R_3 denotes the mouth area, and R_4 and R_5 denote the cheek areas.

To the response ellipse-region of the Gabor-Wavelets filter, we apply the inner model matching to detect human-head appearances and face orientations. To be more concrete, if we find eyes, a mouth and cheeks in a response ellipse, we then identify that the ellipse is a human-head appearance and that the orientation of

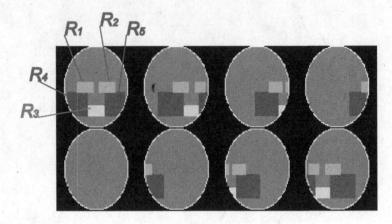

Fig. 15.9.   Inner models of human-head appearances with the facial components.

the matched inner-model is the face orientation of the appearance. Otherwise, we identify that the ellipse is not a human-head appearance and eliminate the ellipse.

15.4. Algorithm

Based on the discussion above, we describe here the algorithm for detecting human-head appearances with face orientations.

To reduce the computational cost in generating applicants of human-head appearances, we introduce the coarse-to-fine sampling of the parameters representing ellipses. Namely, we first coarsely sample points in the parameter space for the ellipse and then minutely sample the area around the points that are selected based on plausibility of the human-head appearance. Moreover, in the coarse sampling, we fixate parameters depending only on poses of a human head to enhance position identification of the human head. In the fine sampling, we sample all the parameters. The following algorithm effectively detects human heads and, at the same time, estimates their orientations.

Step 1: Capture an image.
Step 2: Search applicants of human heads in the image.

    2.1: (**Coarse sampling**): randomly sample position parameters, i.e., (x, y, a), in the parameter space representing the ellipses that are generated from (15.1); let $\{p_i\}$ be the sampled set.

    2.2: Evaluate each entry of $\{p_i\}$ by (15.4); let $\{p_{i*}\}$ be the set of samples whose scores of f in (15.4) are less than a given threshold.

2.3: **(Fine sampling):** more minutely sample points in the area around each entry of $\{p_{i*}\}$ (more specifically, more minutely sample parameters (x, y, a, r, ψ) around each entry of (x_{i*}, y_{i*}, a_{i*}) where (x_{i*}, y_{i*}, a_{i*}) is the position parameters of $\{p_{i*}\}$); let $\{p_j^*\}$ be the sampled set. (Note that $\{p_j^*\}$ is applicants of human-head appearances.)

Step 3: To each entry of $\{p_j^*\}$, generate inner models of human-head appearances.

Step 4: Apply the Gabor-Wavelets filter to each entry of $\{p_j^*\}$ to detect facial feature points.

Step 5: To each p_j^*, apply the matching with the corresponding inner models.

Step 6: If p_j^* matches one of its corresponding inner models with a high score, then recognize p_j^* as a human-head appearance and the face orientation as that of the matched inner-model. If p_j^* does not match any of its corresponding inner models with a high score, then eliminate p_j^*.

We remark that iterating the steps above enables us to track human heads with their orientations. Though introducing a transition model of motion to our detection algorithm leads to more effective tracking, it is beyond the scope of this paper.

15.5. Experimental evaluation

15.5.1. *Evaluation on face orientations using a face-image database*

We first evaluated our algorithm using a face-image database. The database contains face images of 300 persons with the ages ranging uniformly from 15 to 65 years old including men and women. Each person is taken his/her face images from different directions as shown in Fig. 15.10. To each face image in the database, attached is the ground truth of the direction from which the image is taken.

We used 9600 $(= 32 \times 300)$ face images in the database where 32 directions are used in taking images of each person: the angles of depression of the camera were $\varphi = 0°$, 15°, 30°, 45° and the rotation angles with respect to the horizontal axis, i.e., face orientations, were 0°, 30°, 60°, 90°, 180°, 270°, 300°, 330°. Fig. 15.11 shows samples of the face images of one person in the database.

We applied our algorithm to the 9600 images to detect face orientations. Table 15.1 shows the recognition rates of the estimated face-orientations.

Table 15.1 shows that face orientations are in general recognized with high scores. We see low accuracy in orientations with 90° and 270°. This is because

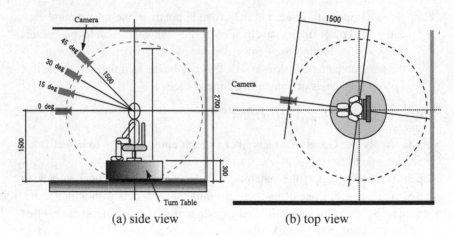

(a) side view   (b) top view

Fig. 15.10.   Parameters in obtaining a face-image database.

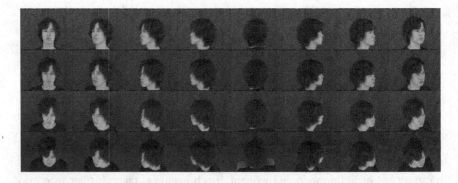

Fig. 15.11.   Sample images of the face-image database (with 0° of depression).

one eye and one cheek do not appear in the face with such orientations and thus
the inner model matching becomes unstable. We also see that accuracy becomes
higher as the angle of depression of the camera becomes smaller. The small angle
of depression of the camera means that the face is captured from the horizontal
direction of the face and that the facial components clearly appear in the image.
It is understood that clearly appearing facial components improves the estimation
accuracy of face orientations. A large angle of depression, on the other hand,
causes great changes not only in human-head appearance but also in face appearance. Handling such great changes with our models has limitation. This is because
we generate a contour model and inner models of human-head appearances from

Table 15.1. Recognition accuracy for different face orientations (%).

angles of depression	face orientations							
	0°	30°	60°	90°	180°	270°	300°	330°
0°	84.7	86.3	83.7	31.0	97.0	34.7	80.0	79.3
15°	64.7	86.3	75.3	27.7	97.7	21.0	71.7	71.7
30°	23.7	75.3	70.3	14.0	99.0	10.0	51.0	51.7
45°	17.7	61.7	51.0	16.0	94.7	8.3	27.0	27.0

only one ellipsoid. On the other hand, we see that face images from the orientation with 180°, back images of human heads, are recognized stably and accurately independent of the change in angle of depression. This is due to stableness of the Gabor-Wavelets filter in face-feature detection.

15.5.2. Evaluation in the real situation

Secondly, we evaluated the performance of our method in the real situation. We conducted two kinds of experiments here. One focused on human-head detection using real images and the other focused on ellipse evaluation in human-head detection. In both cases, we found the robustness and the efficiency of our method.

15.5.2.1. Human-head detection in the real situation

We here apply our method to real images to see its effectiveness.

We set up a camera with about 2m height and with about 20° angle of depression. Then, under changing lighting conditions one person turns round in front of the camera with changing his face orientations and walks for about 10 seconds. The distance from the camera to the person was about 1.5m. To the 100 captured images, we applied our method to detect human-head appearances and face orientations.

Figure 15.12 shows examples of the captured images with frame numbers. The ellipses detected as a human-head appearance are superimposed on the frames where their colors denote face orientations. We see that appearances of human heads are fairly large in the images.

We observed that human heads are incorrectly detected in several images. In such images, ellipses are detected in the background. This is party because of existing objects in the background; in fact, ellipses are easy to be detected in the background used in this experiment. Nevertheless, human-head appearances are detected correctly and accurately in the rest of the all images.

To quantitatively evaluate the correctness in detection, we first manually fitted

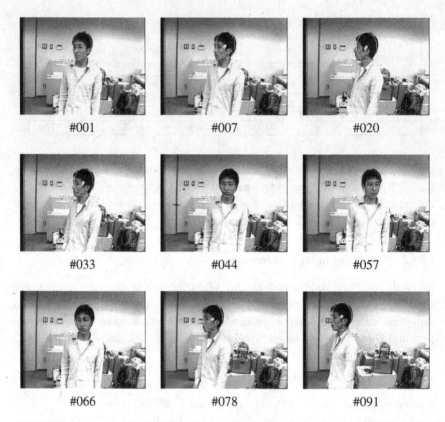

Fig. 15.12. Images (with frame numbers) and detected human heads (colors means orientations).

an ellipse onto the head appearance in each image to obtain the true ellipse as the reference. We then computed the distance (the position error) between the center of the detected ellipse and that of the true ellipse. We also computed the ratio (the size error) of the semiminor length of the detected ellipse to that of the true ellipse. These results are shown in Fig.15.13. The average and the standard deviation of errors in position were respectively, 8.85pixels and 22.4pixels. Those in size were, on the other hand, 0.0701 and 0.0485, respectively. Note that difference of the size errors from 1.0 was employed in this computation.

We see that our method for detecting human heads and face orientations is practical overall in the real situation.

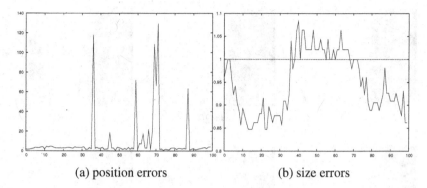

(a) position errors   (b) size errors

Fig. 15.13.   Errors in human head detection.

15.5.2.2. *Effectiveness of human-head evaluation*

We here focus on evaluation of ellipses in human-head detection and show effectiveness of our ellipse evaluation.

We set up a camera with 1.8m height and with about 0° angle of depression. We generated the situation in which under changing lighting conditions one person walks around in front of the camera with distance between about 2m and 4m for 20 seconds. 200 images were captured during the time. To the captured images, we applied our method to detect human-head appearances and face orientations.

Figure 15.14 shows examples of the captured images with frame numbers. The ellipses detected as a human-head appearance are superimposed on the frames. Colors of the ellipses denote face orientations. We see that in this experiment appearances of human heads are small in the images.

We again verified that human-head appearances are detected almost correctly and accurately in all the images in spite of changes in illumination. To see the performance of our method, we evaluated the accuracy of the detected human-head appearances. We first fitted an ellipse onto the head appearance in each image by hand to obtain the true ellipse as the reference. We introduced two kinds of evaluation to the ellipse that was recognized as the human-head appearance: one is the accuracy of the center and the other is the accuracy of the semiminor length. We computed the distance (the position error) between the center of the detected ellipse and that of the true ellipse. We also computed the ratio (the size error) of the semiminor length of the detected ellipse to that of the true ellipse. These results are shown in Figs. 15.15 and 15.16. We remark that the same evaluation was applied to the method (called the *simple-evaluation method* (cf. Refs.[1] and[19])) where the ellipse is evaluated only by (15.5), i.e., the gradient

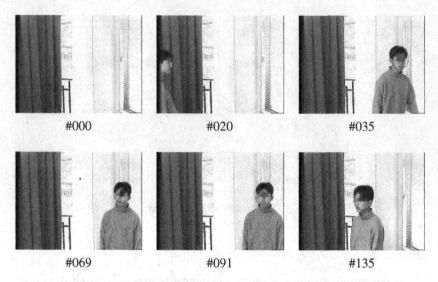

Fig. 15.14.   Examples of detected human heads (colors means orientations).

magnitude of intensity at the ellipse perimeter. For the position error and the difference of the size error from 1.0, the average and standard deviation over the image sequence were calculated, which is shown in Table 15.2.

Figures 15.15, 15.16 and Table 15.2 show the effectiveness of our method. Superiority of our method to the simple-evaluation method indicates that introducing the smaller- and larger-size ellipses to ellipse evaluation improves the accuracy in detecting the positions of human-head appearances.

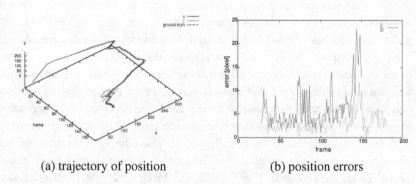

(a) trajectory of position   (b) position errors

Fig. 15.15.   Position errors in human-head detection (a: our method, b: simple evaluation).

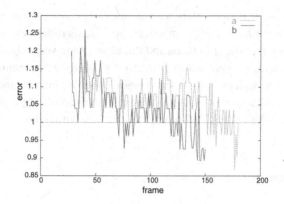

Fig. 15.16.   Size errors in human-head detection (a: our method, b: simple evaluation).

15.6. Conclusion

We proposed a two-step method for detecting human heads and estimating face orientations by a monocular camera. In the both steps, we employ models of the human-head contour and face orientations to enhance robustness and stableness in detection. We also introduced model evaluation with only image-features robust against lighting conditions.

The first step employs an ellipse as the contour model of human-head appearances to deal with wide variety of appearances. The ellipse was generated from one ellipsoid based on a camera position with its angle of depression in the environment. We then evaluated the ellipse over a given image to detect possible human-head appearances where we generated two other ellipses inside and outside of the ellipse to improve accuracy in detection of human-head appearances.

The second step, on the other hand, focuses on facial components such as eyes, the mouth or cheeks to generate inner models for face-orientation estimation. We evaluated not only such components themselves but also their geometric configuration to eliminate false positives in the first step and, at the same time,

Table 15.2.   Errors in detecting the human head.

error		our method	simple evaluation
position	mean [pixels]	3.250	6.401
	standard deviation [pixels]	1.950	4.386
size	mean	0.0762	0.0617
	standard deviation	0.04489	0.04877

to estimate face orientations. Here we used the Gabor-Wavelets filter in detecting features representing the facial components because its robustness and stableness against changes in scale, orientation and illumination are verified.

Consequently, our method can correctly and stably detect human heads and estimate face orientations even under changes in face orientation and in illumination. Our intensive experiments showed the effectiveness of the proposed method. Incorporating wider variety of face orientations into our method is left for future work.

Acknowledgements

The authors are thankful to Naoya Ohnishi for helping to perform an experiment in the real situation. The facial data in this paper are used permission of Softopia Japan, Research and Development Division, HOIP Laboratory. It is strictly prohibited to copy, use, or distribute the facial data without permission. This work is in part supported by Grant-in-Aid for Scientific Research of the Ministry of Education, Culture, Sports, Science and Technology of Japan under the contract of 13224051.

References

1. S. Birchfield: Elliptical Head Tracking Using Intensity Gradients and Color Histograms, *Proc. of CVPR*, pp. 232–237, 1998.
2. T. J. Cham and J. M. Rehg: A Multiple Hypothesis Approach to Figure Tracking, *Proc. of CVPR*, Vol. 2, pp. 239–245, 1999.
3. R. Chellappa, C. L. Wilson and S. Sirohey: Human and Machine Recognition of Faces, A Survey, *Proc. of IEEE*, **83** (1995), pp. 705–740.
4. Y. Cui, S. Samarasekera, Q. Huang and M. Greiffenhagen: Indoor Monitoring via the Collaboration between a Peripheral Sensor and a Foveal Sensor, *Proc. of the IEEE Workshop on Visual Surveillance*, pp. 2–9, 1998.
5. G. Donato, M. S. Bartlett, J. C. Hager, P. Ekman and T. J. Sejnowski: Classifying Facial Actions, *IEEE Trans. on PAMI*, **21** (1999), 10, pp. 974–989.
6. L. Davis, S. Fejes, D. Harwood, Y. Yacoob, I. Hariatoglu and M. J. Black: Visual Surveillance of Human Activity, *Proc. of the 3rd ACCV*, Vol.2, pp. 267–274, 1998.
7. D. M. Gavrila: The Visual Analysis of Human Movement: A Survey, *Computer Vision and Image Understanding*, **73** (1999), 1, pp. 82–98.
8. I. Haritaoglu, D. Harwood and L. S. Davis: W^4S: A Real-Time System for Detecting and Tracking People in $2\frac{1}{2}$D, *Proc. of the 5th ECCV*, Vol. 1, pp. 877–892, 1998.
9. I. Haritaoglu, D. Harwood and L. S. Davis: An Appearance-based Body Model for Multiple People Tracking, *Proc. of the 15th ICPR*, Vol. 4, pp. 184–187, 2000.
10. T. -K. Kim, H. Kim, W. Hwang, S. -C. Kee and J. Kittler: Independent Component Analysis in a Facial Local Residue Space, *Proc. of CVPR*, 2003.

11. T. S. Lee: Image Representation Using 2D Gabor Wavelets, *IEEE Trans. on PAMI*, **18** (1996), 10, pp. 959–971.
12. A. Sugimoto, K. Yachi and T. Matsuyama: Tracking Human Heads Based on Interaction between Hypotheses with Certainty, *Proc. of the 13th Scandinavian Conf. on Image Analysis*, (J. Bigun and T. Gustavsson eds: *Image Analysis*, Lecture Notes in Computer Science, Vol. 2749, Springer), pp. 617–624, 2003.
13. M. Swain and D. Ballard: Color Indexing, *Int. J. of Computer Vision*, **7** (1991), 1, pp. 11–32.
14. Y. Tian, T. Kanade and J. F. Cohn: *Recognizing Facial Actions by Combining Geometric Features and Regional Appearance Patterns*, CMU-RI-TR-01-0, Robotics Institute, CMU, 2001.
15. Y. Tian, T. Kanade and J. F. Cohn: Evaluation of Gabor-Wavelets Based Facial Action Unit Recognition in Image Sequences of Increasing Complexity, *Proc. of the 5th Int. Conf. on Automatic Face and Gesture Recognition*, pp. 229–234, 2002.
16. P. Viola and M. Jones: Rapid Object Detection using a Boosted Cascade of Simple Features, *Proc. of CVPR*, Vol. I, pp. 511-518, 2001.
17. P. Viola and M. Jones: Robust Real-Time Face Detection, *Int. J. of Computer Vision*, Vol. 57, No. 2, pp. 137–154, 2004.
18. Y. Wu and K. Toyama: Wide-Range, Person- and Illumination-Insensitive Head Orientation Estimation, *Proc. of the 4th IEEE Int. Conf. on Automatic Face and Gesture Recognition*, pp. 183–188, 2000.
19. K. Yachi, T. Wada and T. Matsuyama: Human Head Tracking using Adaptive Appearance Models with a Fixed-Viewpoint Pan-Tilt-Zoom Camera *Proc. of the 4th IEEE Int. Conf. on Automatic Face and Gesture Recognition*, pp. 150–155, 2000.
20. Z. Zeng and S. Ma: Head Tracking by Active Particle Filtering, *Proc. of the 5th IEEE Int. Conf. on Automatic Face and Gesture Recognition*, pp. 89–94, 2002.
21. L. Zhang and D. Samaras: Face Recognition under Variable Lighting using Harmonic Image Exemplars, *Proc. of CVPR*, 2003.
22. Z. Zhang, M. Lyons, M. Schuster and S. Akamatsu: Comparison between Geometry-based and Gabor-Wavelets-based Facial Expression Recognition using Multi-layer Perception, *Proc. Int. Workshop on Automatics Face and Gesture Recognition*, pp. 454–459, 1998.
23. W. Y. Zhao, R. Chellappa, A. Rosenfeld and P. J. Phillips: *Face Recognition: A Literature Survey*, CAR-TR-984, UMD, 2000.
24. S. Zhou, V. Krueger and R. Chellappa: Face Recognition from Video: A Condensation Approach, *Proc. of the 5th IEEE Int. Conf. on Automatic Face and Gesture Recognition*, pp. 221–226, 2002.

CHAPTER 16

PRIOR KNOWLEDGE BASED MOTION MODEL REPRESENTATION

Angel D. Sappa[†], Niki Aifanti[*], Sotiris Malassiotis[*] and Michael G. Strintzis[*]

[†] *Computer Vision Center, Edifici O, Campus UAB,*
08193 Bellaterra - Barcelona, Spain
[*] *Informatics & Telematics Institute, 1st Km Thermi-Panorama Road,*
Thermi-Thessaloniki, Greece

This paper presents a new approach for human walking modeling from monocular image sequences. A kinematics model and a walking motion model are introduced in order to exploit prior knowledge. The proposed technique consists of two steps. Initially, an efficient feature point selection and tracking approach is used to compute feature points' trajectories. Peaks and valleys of these trajectories are used to detect *key frames*—frames where both legs are in contact with the floor. Secondly, motion models associated with each joint are locally tuned by using those key frames. Differently than previous approaches, this tuning process is not performed at every frame, reducing CPU time. In addition, the movement's frequency is defined by the elapsed time between two consecutive key frames, which allows handling walking displacement at different speed. Experimental results with different video sequences are presented.

16.1. Introduction

3D human body representations opens a new and attractive field of applications, from more realistic movies to interactive environments. Unfortunately, it is not possible to completely recover 3D information from 2D video sequences when no other extra information is given or can be estimated (i.e., intrinsic and extrinsic camera parameters should be provided to compute the real 3D data up to a scale). However, since several video sequences are populated with objects with known structure and motion such as humans, cars, etc, prior knowledge would arguably aid the recovery of the scene. Prior knowledge in the form of kinematics constraints (average size of an articulated structure, degrees of freedom (DOFs) for each articulation), or motion dynamics (physical laws ruling the objects' movements), is a commonplace solution to handle the aforementioned problem.

In this direction, our work is devoted to depth augmentation of common human walking video sequences. Although this work is only focused on walking modeling, which is the most frequent type of locomotion of persons, other kinds of cyclic movement could also be modeled with the proposed approach (e.g., movements such as running or climbing down/upstairs).

3D motion models are required for applications such as: intelligent video surveillance, pedestrian detection for traffic applications, gait recognition, medical diagnosis and rehabilitation, human-machine interface.[1] Due to the widely interest it has generated, 3D human motion modeling is one of the most active area within the computer vision community.

In this paper a new approach to cope with the problem of human walking modeling is presented. The main idea is to search for a particular kinematics configuration throughout the frames of the given video sequence, and then to use the extracted information in order to tune a general motion model. Walking displacement involves the *synchronized* movements of each body part—the same is valid for any cyclic human body displacement (e.g., running, jogging). In this work, a set of curves, obtained from anthropometric studies,[2] is used as a coarse walking model. These curves need to be individually tuned according to the walking attitude of each pedestrian. This tuning process is based on the observation that although each person walks with a particular style, there is an instant in which every human body structure achieves the same configuration. This instant happens when both legs are in contact with the floor. Then, the open articulated structure becomes a closed structure. This closed structure is a rich source of information useful to tune most of the motion model's parameters. The outline of this work is as follows. Related works are presented in the next section. The proposed technique is described in section 16.3. Experimental results using different video sequences are presented in section 16.4. Conclusions and further improvements are given in section 16.5.

16.2. Previous Works

Vision-based human motion modeling approaches usually combine several computer vision processing techniques (e.g., video sequence segmentation, object tracking, motion prediction, 3D object representation, model fitting, etc). Different techniques have been proposed to find a model that matches a walking displacement. These approaches can be broadly classified into monocular or multi camera approaches.

A multicamera system was proposed by.[3] It consists of a stereoscopic technique able to cope not only with self-occlusions but also with fast movements and poor quality images. This approach incorporates physical forces to each rigid part of a kinematics 3D human body model consisting of truncated cones. These forces guide each 3D model's part towards a convergence with the body posture in the image. The model's projections are compared with the silhouettes extracted from the image by means of a novel approach, which combines the Maxwell's demons algorithm with the classical ICP algorithm. Although stereoscopic systems provide us with more information for the scanned scenes, 3D human motion systems with only one camera-view available is the most frequent case.

Motion modeling using monocular image sequences constitutes a complex and challenging problem. Similarly to approach,[3] but in a 2D space and assuming a segmented video sequence is given as an input,[4] proposes a system that fits a projected body model with the contour of a segmented image. This boundary matching technique consists of an error minimization between the pose of the projected model and the pose of the real body—all in a 2D space. The main disadvantage of this technique is that it needs to find the correspondence between the projected body parts and the silhouette contour, before starting the matching approach. This means that it looks for the point of the silhouette contour that corresponds to a given projected body part, assuming that the model posture is not initialized. This problem is still more difficult to handle in those frames where self-occlusions appear or edges cannot be properly computed.

Differently than the previous approaches, the aspect ratio of the bounding box of the moving silhouette has been used in.[5] This approach is able to cope with both lateral and frontal views. In this case the contour is studied as a whole and body parts do not need to be detected. The aspect ratio is used to encode the pedestrian's walking way. However, although shapes are one of the most important semantic attributes of an image, problems appear in those cases where the pedestrian wears clothes not so tight or carries objects such as a suitcase, handbag or backpack. Carried objects distort the human body silhouette and therefore the aspect ratio of the corresponding bounding box.

In order to be able to tackle some of the problems mentioned above, some authors propose simplifying assumptions. In[6] for example, tight-fitting clothes with sleeves of contrasting colors have been used. Thus, the right arm is depicted with a different color than the left arm and edge detection is simplified especially in case of self-occlusions.[7] proposes an approach where the user selects some points on the image, which mainly correspond to the joints of the human body. Points of interest are also marked in[8] using infrared diode markers. The authors present a physics-based framework for 3D shape and non-rigid motion estimation based on the use of a non-contact 3D motion digitizing system. Unfortunately, when a 2D video sequence is given, it is not likely to affect its content afterwards in such a way. Therefore, the usefulness of these approaches is restricted to cases where access in making the sequence is possible.

Recently, a novel approach based on feature point selection and tracking was proposed in.[9] This approach is closely related to the technique proposed in this work. However, a main difference is that in[9] feature points are triangulated together and similarity between triangles and body parts is studied, while in the current work, feature point's trajectories are plotted on the image plane and used to detect key frames. Robustness in feature point based approaches is considerably better than in those techniques based on silhouette, since silhouette does not only depend on walking style or direction but also on other external factors such as those mentioned above. Walking attitude is easier captured by studying the spatio-temporal motion of feature points.

16.3. The Proposed Approach

We may safely assume that the center of gravity of a walking person moves with approximately constant velocity. However, the speed of other parts of the body fluctuates. There is one instant per walking cycle (without considering the starting and ending positions) in which both feet are in contact with the floor, in other words with null velocity. This happens when the pedestrian changes from one pivot foot to the other. At that moment the articulated structure (Fig. 16.1) reaches the maximum hip angles. Frames containing these configurations will be called *key frames* and can be easily detected by extracting static points (i.e., pixels defining the boundary of the body shape contained in the segmented frames that remain static at least in three consecutive frames) through the given video sequence. Information provided by these frames is used to tune motion model parameters. In addition, the elapsed time between two consecutive key frames defines the duration of a half walking period—indirectly the speed of the movement. Motion models are tuned and used to perform the movement from the current key frame to the next one. This iterative process is applied until all key frames are covered by the walking model (input video sequence).

Human motion modeling based on tracking of point features has recently been used in.[9] Human motion is modeled by the joint probability density function of the position and velocity of a collection of body parts, while no information about kinematics or dynamics of the human body structure is considered. This technique has been tested only on video sequences containing pedestrians walking on a plane orthogonal to the camera's viewing direction.

Assuming that a segmented video sequence is given as an input (in the current implementation some segmented images were provided by the authors of[10] and others were computed by using the algorithm presented in[11]) the proposed technique consists of two stages. In the first stage feature points are selected and tracked throughout the whole video sequence in order to find key frames' positions. In the second stage a generic motion model is locally tuned by using kinematics information extracted from the key frames. The main advantage comparing with previous approaches is that matching between the projection of the 3D model and the body silhouette image features is not performed at every frame (e.g., hip tuning is performed twice per walking cycle). The algorithm's stages are fully described below together with a brief description of the 3D representation used to model the human body.

16.3.1. *Body Modeling*

Modeling the human body implies firstly the definition of a 3D articulated structure, which represents the body's biomechanical features; and secondly the definition of a motion model, which governs the movement of that structure.

Several 3D articulated representations have been proposed in the literature. Generally, a human body model is represented as a chain of rigid bodies, called links, interconnected to one another by *joints*. Links are generally represented by means of sticks,[7] polyhedron,[12] generalized cylinders[13] or superquadrics.[6] A joint interconnects two links by means of rotational motions about the axes. The number of independent rotation parameters defines the DOFs associated with that joint.

Considering that a human body has about six hundred muscles, forty just for a hand, the development of a highly realistic model is a computational expensive task, involving a high dimensionality problem. In computer vision, where models with only medium precision are required, articulated structures with less than thirty degrees of freedom are generally adequate. (e.g.[3,6]). In this work, an articulated structure defined by 16 links is initially considered. This model consists of 22 DOF, without modeling the palm of the hand or the foot and using a rigid head-torso approximation (four for each arm and leg and six for the torso, which are three for orientation and three for position). However, in order to reduce the complexity, a simplified model of 12 DOF has been finally chosen. This simplification assumes that in walking, legs' and arms' movements are contained in parallel planes (see illustration in Fig. 16.1). In addition, the body orientation is always orthogonal to the floor, thus the orientation is reduced to only one DOF. Hence, the final model is defined by two DOF for each arm and leg and four for the torso (three for the position plus one for the orientation).

The simplest 3D articulated structure is a stick representation with no asso-

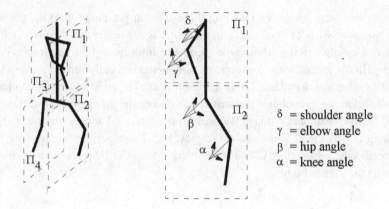

δ = shoulder angle
γ = elbow angle
β = hip angle
α = knee angle

Fig. 16.1.   Simplified articulated structure defined by 12 DOFs, arms and legs rotations are contained in planes parallel to the walking's direction.

ciated volume or surface. Planar 2D representations, such as a cardboard model, have been also widely used. However, volumetric representations are preferred in order to generate more realistic models. Volumetric representations such as parallelepipeds, cylinders, or superquadrics have been extensively used. For example,[3] proposes to model a person by means of truncated cones (arms and legs), spheres (neck, joints and head) and right parallelepipeds (hands, feet and body). Most of these shapes can be modeled by means of superquadrics.[14] Superquadrics are a compact and accurate representation generally used to model human body parts. Through this work the articulated structure will be represented by 16 superquadrics, see Fig. 16.2 ([15]). A superquadric surface is defined by the following parametric equation:

$$x(\theta, \phi) = \begin{bmatrix} \alpha_1 \cos^{\epsilon_1}(\theta) \cos^{\epsilon_2}(\phi) \\ \alpha_2 \cos^{\epsilon_1}(\theta) \sin^{\epsilon_2}(\phi) \\ \alpha_3 \sin^{\epsilon_1}(\theta) \end{bmatrix} \qquad (16.1)$$

where $(-\pi/2) \leq \theta \leq (\pi/2)$, $-\pi \leq \phi \leq \pi$. The parameters α_1, α_2 and α_3 define the size of the superquadric along the x, y and z axis respectively, while ϵ_1 is the squareness parameter in the latitude plane and ϵ_2 is the squareness parameter in the longitudinal plane. Furthermore, superquadric shapes can be deformed with tapering, bending and cavities. In our model, the different body parts are represented with superquadrics tapered along the y-axis. The parametric equation is

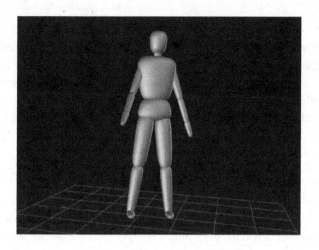

Fig. 16.2.   Illustration of a 22 DOF model built with superquadric.

then written as:

$$x'(\theta, \phi) = \begin{bmatrix} (\frac{t_1}{\alpha_2} x_2 + 1) x_1 \\ (\frac{t_3}{\alpha_2} x_2 + 1) x_3 \end{bmatrix} \tag{16.2}$$

where $-1 \leq t_1, t_3 \leq 1$ are the tapering parameters and x_1, x_2 and x_3 are the elements of the vector in equation 16.1. Parameters α_1, α_2 and α_3 were defined in each body part according to anthropometric measurements. An example can be seen in Fig. 16.2.

The movements of the limbs are based on a hierarchical approach (the torso is considered the root) using Euler angles. The body posture is synthesized by concatenating the transformation matrices associated with the joints, starting from the root.

16.3.2. *Feature Point Selection and Tracking*

Feature point selection and tracking approaches were chosen because they allow capturing the motion's parameters by using as prior knowledge the kinematics of the body structure. In addition, point-based approaches seem to be more robust in comparison with silhouette based approaches. Next, a brief description of the techniques used is given.

16.3.2.1. Feature Point Selection

In this work, the feature points are used to capture human body movements and are selected by using a corner detector algorithm. Let $I(x,y)$ be the first frame of a given video sequence. Then, a pixel (x,y) is a corner feature if at all pixels in a window W_S around (x,y) the smallest singular value of G is bigger than a predefined σ; in the current implementation W_S was set to 5×5 and $\sigma = 0.05$. G is defined as:

$$G = \begin{bmatrix} \Sigma I_x^2 & \Sigma I_x I_y \\ \Sigma I_x I_y & \Sigma I_y^2 \end{bmatrix} \tag{16.3}$$

and (I_x, I_y) are the gradients obtained by convolving the image I with the derivatives of a pair of Gaussian filters. More details about corner detection can be found in.[16] Assuming that at the beginning there is no information about the pedestrian's position in the given frame, and in order to enforce a homogeneous feature sampling, input frames are partitioned into 4 regular tiles (2×2 regions of 240×360 pixels each in the illustration presented in Fig. 16.3).

16.3.2.2. Feature Point Tracking

After selecting a set of feature points and setting a tracking window W_T (3×3 in the current implementation) an iterative feature tracking algorithm has been used.[16] Assuming a small interframe motion, feature points are tracked by minimizing the sum of squared differences between two consecutive frames.

Points, lying on the head or shoulders, are the best candidates to satisfy the aforementioned assumption. Most of the other points (e.g., points over the legs, arms or hands, are missed after a couple of frames). Fig. 16.3(top) illustrates feature points detected in the first frame of the video sequence used in.[17] Fig. 16.3($bottom - left$) depicts the trajectories of the feature points when all frames are considered. On the contrary, Fig. 16.3($bottom - right$) shows the trajectories after removing static points. In the current implementation we only use one feature point's trajectory. Further improvements could be to merge feature points' trajectories in order to generate a more robust approach.

16.3.3. Motion Model Tuning

The outcome of the previous stage is the trajectory of a feature point (Fig. 16.4(top)) consisting of peaks and valleys. Firstly, the first-order derivative of the curve is computed to find peaks' and valleys' positions by seeking the positive-to-negative zero-crossing points. Peaks correspond to those frames where the

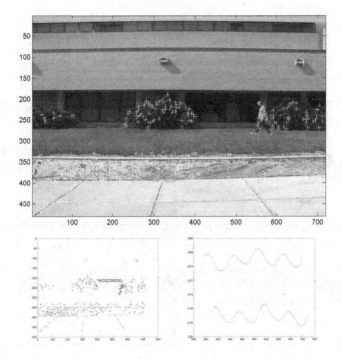

Fig. 16.3. (*top*) Feature points from the first frame of the video sequence used in.[17] (*bottom−left*) Feature points' trajectories. (*bottom−right*) Feature points' trajectories after removing static points.

pedestrian reaches the maximum height, which happens in that moment of the half walking cycle when the hip angles are minimum. On the contrary, the valleys correspond to those frames where the two legs are in contact with the floor and then, the hip angles are maximum. So, the valleys are used to find key frames, while the peaks are used for footprint detection. The frames corresponding to each valley of Fig. 16.4(*top*) are presented in Fig. 16.4(*middle*) and (*bottom*). An interesting point of the proposed approach is that in this video sequence, in spite of the fact that the pedestrian is carrying a folder, key frames are correctly detected and thus, the 3D human body configuration can be computed. On the contrary, with an approach such as,[4] it will be difficult since the matching error will try to minimize the whole shape (including folder).

After detecting key frames, which correspond to the valleys of the trajectory, it is necessary to define also the footprints of the pedestrian throughout the sequence. In order to achieve this, body silhouettes were computed using an image segmentation algorithm.[11] For some video sequences the segmented images were

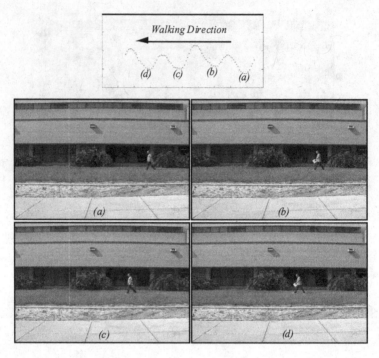

Fig. 16.4. (*top*) A single feature point's trajectory. (*middle* and *bottom*) Key frames associated with the valleys of a feature point's trajectory.

provided by.[10] Footprint positions are computed as follows.

Throughout a walking displacement sequence, there is always, at least, one foot in contact with the ground, with null velocity (pivot foot). In addition, there is one instant per walking cycle in which both feet are in contact with the floor (both with null velocity). The foot that is in contact with the floor can be easily detected by extracting its defining *static points*. A point is considered as a static point $spt^F_{(i,j)}$ in frame F, if it remains as a boundary point $bp^F_{(i,j)}$ (silhouette point, Fig. 16.5(*left*)) in at least three consecutive frames—value computed experimentally $spt^F_{(i,j)} \Rightarrow (bp^{F-1}_{(i,j)}, bp^F_{(i,j)}, bp^{F+1}_{(i,j)})$.

The result of the previous stage is a set of static points distributed along the pedestrian's path. Now, the problem is to cluster those points belonging to the same foot. Static points defining a single footprint are easily clustered by studying the peaks' positions in the feature point's trajectory. All those static points in a neighborhood of $F \pm 3$ from the frame corresponding to a peak position (F) will be clustered together and will define the same footprint (fp_i). Fig. 16.5(*right*) shows an illustration of static points detected after processing consecutive frames.

Fig. 16.5. (*left*) Five consecutive frames used to detect static points. (*right*) Footprints computed after clustering static points generated by the same foot (peaks in a feature point's trajectory (Fig. 16.4(*top*)).

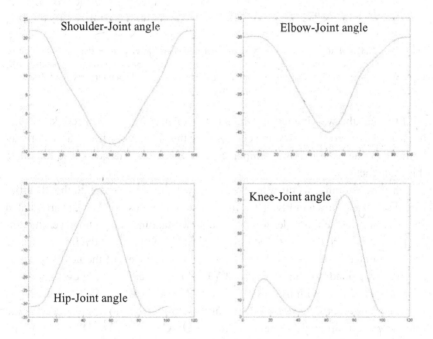

Fig. 16.6. Motion curves of the joints at the shoulder, elbow, hip and knee (computed from[2]).

As it was introduced above, key frames are defined as those frames where both feet are in contact with the floor. At every key frame, the articulated human body structure reaches a posture with maximum hip angles. In the current implementation, hip angles are defined by the legs and the vertical axis containing the hip joints. This maximum value, together with the maximum value of the hip motion model (Fig. 16.6) are used to compute a scale factor κ. This factor is utilized to adjust the hip motion model to the current pedestrian's walking. Actually, it is

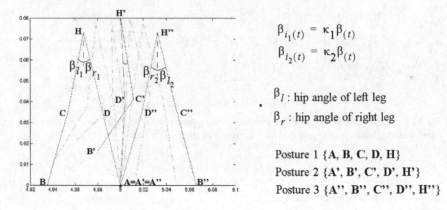

$$\beta_{i_1(t)} = \kappa_1 \beta_{(t)}$$

$$\beta_{i_2(t)} = \kappa_2 \beta_{(t)}$$

β_l : hip angle of left leg

β_r : hip angle of right leg

Posture 1 {A, B, C, D, H}
Posture 2 {A', B', C', D', H'}
Posture 3 {A'', B'', C'', D'', H''}

Fig. 16.7. Half walking cycle executed by using scale factors (κ_1, κ_2) over the hip motion curve presented in Fig. 16.6 (knee motion curve is not tuned at this stage). Spatial positions of points (**D**, **H**, **C** and **B**) are computed by using angles from the motion curves and trigonometric relationships.

used for half the walking cycle, which does not start from the current key frame but from a quarter of the walking cycle before the current key frame until halfway to the next one. The maximum hip angle in the next key frame is used to update this scale factor.

This local tuning, within a half walking cycle, is illustrated with the 2D articulated structure shown in Fig. 16.7, from Posture 1 to Posture 3. A 2D articulated structure was chosen in order to make the understanding easier, however the tuning process is carried out in the 3D space. The two footprints of the first key frame are represented by the points **A** and **B**, while the footprints of the next key frame are the corresponding points **A''** and **B''**. During this half walking cycle one foot is always in contact with the floor (so points **A = A' = A''**), while the other leg is moving from point **B** to point **B''**. In halfway to **B''**, the moving leg crosses the other one (null hip angle values). Points **C**, **C'**, **C''** and **D**, **D'**, **D''** represent the left and right knee, while the points **H**, **H'**, **H''** represent the hip joints.

Given the first key frame, the scale factor κ_1 is computed and used to perform the motion ($\beta_{i_{1(t)}}$) through the first quarter of the walking cycle. The second key frame (**A''**, **B''**) is used to compute the scale factor κ_2. At each iteration of this half walking cycle, the spatial positions of the points **B**, **C**, **D** and **H** are calculated using the position of point **A**, which remains static, the hip angles of Fig. 16.6 scaled by the corresponding factor κ_i and the knee angles of Fig. 16.6. The number of frames in between the two key frames defines the sampling rate of the motion curves presented on Fig. 16.6. This allows handling variations in the walking speed.

Fig. 16.8. (*top*) Three different frames of the video sequence used in.[17] (*bottom*) The corresponding 3D walking models.

Fig. 16.9. Input frames of two video sequences (240×320 each).

As aforementioned, the computed factors κ_i are used to scale the hip angles. The difference in walking between people implies that all the motion curves should be modified by using an appropriate scale factor for each one. In order to estimate these factors an error measurement (registration quality index: RQI) is introduced. The proposed RQI measures the quality of the matching between the projected 3D model and the corresponding human silhouette. It is defined as: $RQI = overlappedArea/totalArea$, where total area consists of the surface of the projected 3D model plus the surface of the walking human figure less the overlapped area, while the overlapped area is defined by the overlap of these two surfaces. Firstly, the algorithm computes the knee scale factor that maximizes the RQI values. In every iteration, an average RQI is computed for all the sequence. In order to speed up the process the number of frames was subsampled.

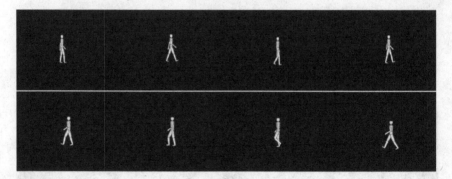

Fig. 16.10. 3D models corresponding to the frames presented in Fig. 16.9 (*top*) and (*bottom*) respectively.

Afterwards, the elbow and shoulder scale factors are estimated similarly. They are computed simultaneously using an efficient search method.

16.4. Experimental Results

The proposed technique has been tested with video sequences used in[17] and,[10] together with our own video sequences. Despite that the current approach has been developed to handle sequences with a pedestrian walking over a planar surface, in a plane orthogonal to the camera direction, the technique has been also tested with an oblique walking direction (see Fig. 16.11) showing encouraging results. The video sequence used as an illustration throughout this work consists of 85 frames of 480×720 pixels each, which have been segmented using the technique presented in.[11] Some of the computed 3D walking models are presented in Fig. 16.8(*bottom*), while the original frames together with the projected boundaries are presented in Fig. 16.8(*top*).

Fig. 16.9(*top*) presents a few frames of a video sequence defined by 103 frames (240×320 pixels each), while Fig. 16.9(*bottom*) corresponds to a video sequence defined by 70 frames (240×320 pixels each). Although the speed and walking style is considerably different, the proposed technique can handle both situations. The corresponding 3D models are presented in Fig. 16.10(*top*) and (*bottom*) respectively.

Finally, the proposed algorithm was also tested on a video sequence, consisting of 70 frames of 240×320 pixels each, containing a diagonal walking displacement (Fig. 16.11). The segmented input frames have been provided by the authors of.[10] Although the trajectory was not on a plane orthogonal to the camera direction, feature point information was enough to capture the pedestrian's attitude.

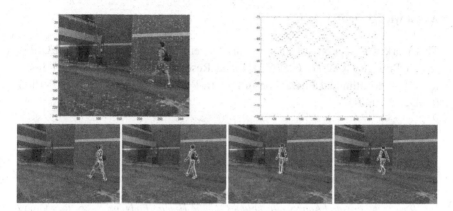

Fig. 16.11. $(top - left)$ Feature points of the first frame. $(top - right)$ Feature points' trajectories. $(bottom)$ Some frames illustrating the final result (segmented input has been provided by[10]).

16.5. Conclusions and Future Work

A new approach towards human motion modeling has been presented. It exploits prior knowledge regarding a person's movement as well as human body kinematics constraints. At this paper only walking has been modeled. Although constraints about walking direction and planar surfaces have been imposed, we expect to extend this technique in order to include frontal and oblique walking directions.[18] A preliminary result has been presented in Fig. 16.11.

Modeling other kinds of human body cyclic movements (such as running or going up/down stairs) using this technique constitutes a possible extension and will be studied. In addition, the use of a similar approach to model the displacement of other articulated beings (animals in general[19]) will be studied. Animal motion (i.e., cyclic movement) can be understood as an open articulated structure, however, when more than one extremity is in contact with the floor, that structure becomes a closed kinematics chain with a reduced set of DOFs. Therefore a motion model could be computed by exploiting these particular features.

Further work will also include the tuning of not only motion model's parameters but also geometric model's parameters in order to find a better fitting. In this way, external objects attached to the body (like a handbag or backpack) could be added to the body and considered as a part of it.

Acknowledgements

This work was supported in part by the Government of Spain under MEC Research Project TRA2007-62526/AUT and Research Program Consolider Ingenio 2010: Multimodal Interaction in Pattern Recognition and Computer Vision (CSD2007-00018).

References

1. A. Sappa, N. Aifanti, N. Grammalidis, and S. Malassiotis, *Advances in Vision-Based Human Body Modeling*, In eds. N. Sarris and M. Strintzis, *3D Modeling and Animation: Synthesis and Analysis Techniques for the Human Body*, pp. 1–26. Idea-Group Inc., (2004).
2. K. Rohr, *Human Movement Analysis Based on Explicit Motion Models*, In eds. M. Shah and R. Jain, *Motion-Based Recognition*, pp. 171–198. Kluwer Academic Publisher, (1997).
3. Q. Delamarre and O. Faugeras, 3D articulated models and multi-view tracking with physical forces, *Computer Vision and Image Understanding.* **81**(3), 328–357 (March, 2001).
4. H. Ning, T. Tan, L. Wang, and W. Hu, Kinematics-based tracking of human walking in monocular video sequences, *Image and Vision Computing.* **22**(5), 429–441 (May, 2004).
5. L. Wang, T. Tan, W. Hu, and H. Ning, Automatic gait recognition based on statistical shape analysis, *IEEE Transactions on Image Processing.* **12**(9), 1120–1131 (September, 2003).
6. D. Gavrila and L. Davis. 3-D model-based tracking of humans in action: a multi-view approach. In *Proc. IEEE Int. Conf. on Computer Vision and Pattern Recognition*, pp. 73–80, San Francisco, USA (June, 1996).
7. C. Barron and I. Kakadiaris. Estimating anthropometry and pose from a single camera. In *Proc. IEEE Int. Conf. on Computer Vision and Pattern Recognition*, pp. 669–676, Hilton Head Island, USA (June, 2000).
8. D. Metaxas and D. Terzopoulos, Shape and nonrigid motion estimation through physics-based synthesis, *IEEE Transactions on Pattern Analysis and Machine Intelligence.* **15**(6), 580–591 (June, 1993).
9. Y. Song, L. Goncalves, and P. Perona, Unsupervised learning of human motion, *IEEE Transactions on Pattern Analysis and Machine Intelligence.* **25**(7), 814–827 (July, 2003).
10. S. Jabri, Z. Duric, H. Wechsler, and A. Rosenfeld. Detection and location of people in video images using adaptive fusion of color and edge information. In *Proc. 15th. Int. Conf. on Pattern Recognition*, Barcelona, Spain (September, 2000).
11. C. Kim and J. Hwang, Fast and automatic video object segmentation and tracking for content-based applications, *IEEE Trans. on Circuits and Systems for Video Technology.* **12**(2), 122–129 (February, 2002).
12. M. Yamamoto, A. Sato, S. Kawada, T. Kondo, and Y. Osaki. Incremental tracking of

human actions from multiple views. In *Proc. IEEE Int. Conf. on Computer Vision and Pattern Recognition*, Santa Barbara, CA, USA (June, 1998).

13. I. Cohen, G. Medioni, and H. Gu. Inference of 3D human body posture from multiple cameras for vision-based user interface. In *World Multiconference on Systemic, Cybernetics and Informatics*, Orlando, Florida, USA (July, 2001).

14. F. Solina and R. Bajcsy, Recovery of parametric models from range images: The case for superquadrics with global deformations, *IEEE Transactions on Pattern Analysis and Machine Intelligence*. **12**(2), 131–147 (February, 1990).

15. A. Sappa, N. Aifanti, S. Malassiotis, and M. Strintzis. Monocular 3D human body reconstruction towards depth augmentation of television sequences. In *Proc. IEEE Int. Conf. on Image Processing*, Barcelona, Spain (September, 2000).

16. Y. Ma, S. Soatto, J. Kosecká, and S. Sastry, *An Invitation to 3-D Vision: From Images to Geometric Models*. (Springer-Verlag, New York, 2004).

17. P. Phillips, S. Sarkar, I. Robledo, P. Grother, and K. Bowyer. Baseline results for the challenge problem of human id using gait analysis. In *Proc. IEEE Int. Conf. on Automatic Face and Gesture Recognition*, Washington, USA (May, 2002).

18. L. Wang, T. Tan, H. Ning, and W. Hu, Silhouette analysis-based gait recognition for human identification, *IEEE Transactions on Pattern Analysis and Machine Intelligence*. **25**(12), 1505–1518 (December, 2003).

19. P. Schneider and J. Wilhelms. Hybrid anatomically based modeling of animals. In *IEEE Computer Animation'98*, Philadelphia, USA (June, 1998).

CHAPTER 17

COMBINING PARTICLE FILTER AND POPULATION-BASED METAHEURISTICS FOR VISUAL ARTICULATED MOTION TRACKING

Juan José Pantrigo[†], Ángel Sánchez[†], Antonio S. Montemayor[†] and Kostas Gianikellis[*]

[†]Dpto. de Ciencias de la Computación. Universidad Rey Juan Carlos.
c/ Tulipán s/n. 28933. Móstoles. Spain
E-mail: {juanjose.pantrigo, angel.sanchez, antonio.sanz}@urjc.es
[*]Dpto. de Didáctica de la Actividad Musical, Plástica y Corporal. Universidad de Extremadura. Av Universidad s/n. 10071. Cáceres. Spain
E-mail: kgiannik@unex.es

Visual tracking of articulated motion is a complex task with high computational costs. Because of the fact that articulated objects are usually represented as a set of linked limbs, tracking is performed with the support of a model. Model-based tracking allows determining object pose in an effortless way and handling occlusions. However, the use of articulated models generates a multidimensional state-space and, therefore, the tracking becomes computationally very expensive or even infeasible.

Due to the dynamic nature of the problem, some sequential estimation algorithms like particle filters are usually applied to visual tracking. Unfortunately, particle filter fails in high dimensional estimation problems such as articulated objects or multiple object tracking. These problems are called *dynamic optimization problems*. Metaheuristics, which are high level general strategies for designing heuristics procedures, have emerged for solving many real world combinatorial problems as a way to efficiently and effectively exploring the problem search space. Path relinking (PR) and scatter search (SS) are evolutionary metaheuristics successfully applied to several hard optimization problems. PRPF and SSPF algorithms respectively hybridize both, particle filter and these two population-based metaheuristic schemes.

In this paper, We present and compare two different hybrid algorithms called Path Relinking Particle Filter (PRPF) and Scatter Search Particle Filter (SSPF), applied to 2D human motion tracking. Experimental results show the proposed algorithms increase the performance of standard particle filters.

17.1. Introduction

Automatic visual analysis of human motion is an active research topic in Computer Vision and its interest has been growing in the last decade.[1-4] Analysis and synthesis of human motion has numerous applications. In Visual Surveillance, gait recognition has been used for controlling the access of persons to restricted areas.[1] In Advanced User Interfaces, visual analysis of human movement is applied in detecting human presence and interpreting human behaviour.[1] Human motion analysis in Medicine can be employed to characterize and diagnose certain types of disorders.[4] Finally, visual analysis of human movement is also used in Biomechanics, studying human body behavior subject to mechanical loads in three main areas: medical, sports and occupational.

Human body is usually represented as a set of limbs linked one to each other at joints.[5] Most studies in human motion analysis are based on articulated models that properly describe the human body.[2,5-7] Model-based tracking allows extracting body posture in an effortless way and handling occlusions.

2D contour representation of human body is relevant in the extraction of the human body projection in the image plane. In this description, human body segments are similar to 2D ribbons or blobs. In the work by Ju[6] a cardboard people model was proposed. Human body segments were modelled by planar patches. Leung and Yang[8] used a 2D ribbons with U-shaped edge segments. Rohr[5] proposed a 2D motion model in which a set of analytically motion curves represented the postures.

One particular pose of the subject can be expressed as a single point in a state-space. In this multidimensional space each axis represents a degree of freedom (DOF) of a joint in the model. Thus, all possible solutions to the pose estimation problem are represented as points in this state-space. The goal of the model is to connect the state-space with the 2D image space. This is achieved by creating a set of synthetic model images and comparing them to measurements taken at each frame of the video sequence thus obtaining a similarity frame estimate. Low level features such as blobs (silhouette), edges (contours), colour and movement have been widely used in diverse approaches.[2]

There are several methods for the comparison between synthetic data and frame measurements. A usual approach, given by a Kalman Filter, predicts just one state and estimates the difference between the synthetic data and the measurements data.[2] Another approach, given by a Particle Filter algorithm, predicts the most likely states using a multiple hypothesis framework. The Particle Filter (PF) algorithm, (also termed as Condensation algorithm) enables the modelling of a stochastic process with an arbitrary probability density function (pdf), by approximating it numerically with a set of points (particles) in a process state-space.[9]

The problem with using an articulated model for human body representation is the high dimensionality of the state-space and the high computational effort it supposes.[10] Also, in the Condensation approach, the number of required particles grows with the size of the state-space, as demonstrated in.[11] To address this difficulty, several optimized PF algorithms have been proposed. They use different strategies to improve their performance. Deutscher[10,12] developed an algorithm termed Annealed Particle Filter (APF) for tracking people. This filter works well for full-body models with 30 DOFs. Partitioned Sampling[11] (PS) is a statistical approach to tackle hierarchical search problems. PS consists by dividing the state space into two or more partitions, and sequentially applying the stated dynamic model for each partition followed by a weighted resampling stage. Ning[13] use learned motion models and motion constraints integrated into a dynamic model to concentrate factored sampling in the areas of state-space with most posterior information.

Optimization problems consist of the search for a "best" configuration of a set of variables to achieve some goals. Metaheuristics are a kind of approximate general methods that can be applied to solve complex optimization problems. Metaheuristics try to combine basic heuristic methods in higher level frameworks aimed at efficiently and effectively exploring a search space.[14]

Due to the dynamic nature of the problem, sequential estimation algorithms are usually applied to visual tracking. Unfortunately, particle filter are not effective in high dimensional estimation problems such as articulated objects or multiple object tracking. These problems can be seen as a sequence of optimization problems, and they are called *dynamic optimization problems*. In order to avoid the limitations to the particle filters, we propose a general framework to develop hybrid optimization algorithms which combine both sequential estimation algorithms and population-based metaheuristics.

In this paper we consider two different instances of this method: *Path Relinking Particle Filter* (PRPF) and *Scatter Search Particle Filter* (SSPF). These algorithms are inspired by the Path Relinking and the Scatter Search Metaheuristics proposed by Glover.[15,16] These algorithms hybridizes both Particle Filter (PF) and Population-based Metaheuristic (PBM) frameworks in two different stages. In the PF stage, a particle set is propagated and updated to obtain a new particle set. In PBM stage, an optimized subset (called RefSet) from the particle set is selected, according to quality and diversity criteria, and new solutions are constructed using different combination methods.

We have applied the PRPF and SSPF algorithms to 2D human pose estimation in different movement tracking activities such as running and jumping. Experimental results show that the proposed algorithms increase the performance of standard particle filters by improving the quality of the estimate, adapting the computational load to problem constraints and reducing the number of required evaluations of the weighting function.

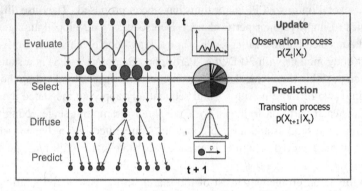

Fig. 17.1.   Particle Filter scheme

17.2. Particle Filters

Sequential Monte Carlo algorithms (also called Particle Filters) are a special class of filters in which theoretical distributions on the state-space are approximated by simulated random measures[17] (also called particles). The state-space model consists of two processes: (i) an observation process $p(Z_t|X_t)$, where X denotes the system state vector and Z is the observation vector, and (ii) a transition process $p(X_t|X_{t-1})$). Assuming that observations $\{Z_0, Z_1, \ldots, Z_t\}$ are sequentially measured in time, the goal is the estimation the new system state $\{\chi_0, \chi_1, \ldots, \chi_t\}$ at each time step. In the framework of Sequential Bayesian Modelling, posterior pdf is estimated in two stages:

(i) Evaluation: posterior pdf $p(X_t|Z_t)$ is computed using the observation vector Z_t:

$$p(X_t|Z_t) = \frac{p(Z_t|X_t)p(X_t|Z_{t-1})}{p(Z_t)} \tag{17.1}$$

(ii) Prediction: the posterior pdf $p(X_t|Z_{t-1})$ is propagated at time step t using the Chapman-Kolmogorov equation:

$$p(X_t|Z_{t-1}) = \int p(X_t|X_{t-1})p(X_{t-1}|Z_{t-1})dX_{t-1} \tag{17.2}$$

A predefined system model is used to obtain an updated particle set.

In Figure 17.1 an outline of the Particle Filter scheme is shown. The aim of the PF algorithm is the recursive estimation of the posterior pdf $p(X_t|Z_t)$, that constitutes a complete solution to the sequential estimation problem. This pdf is represented by a set of weighted particles $\{(x_t^0, p_t^0), \ldots, (x_t^N, p_t^N)\}$, where the weights $p_t^n = p(Z_t|X_t = x_t^n)$ are normalized.

PF algorithm starts by setting up an initial population X_0 of N particles using a known pdf. The measurement vector Z_t at time step t, is obtained from the system and particle weights Π_t are computed using a fitness function. Weights are normalized and a new particle set X_t^* is selected. As particles with larger weight values can be chosen several times, a diffusion stage is applied to avoid the loss of diversity in X_t^*. Finally, particle set at time step $t+1$, X_{t+1}, is predicted using the motion model. A pseudocode of a general PF is detailed in.[18,19]

Therefore, Particle Filters can be seen as algorithms handling the particles evolution. Particles in PF move according to the state model and are multiplied or died according to their weights or fitness values as determined by the pdf.[17]

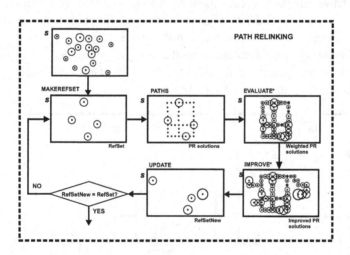

Fig. 17.2.   Path Relinking scheme

17.3. Population-Based Metaheuristics

Metaheuristics are a kind of approximate algorithm which basically tries to combine basic heuristic methods in higher level frameworks aimed at efficiently exploring a search space.[14] Metaheuristics are applied successfully in optimization problems, which consist of the search for a "best" configuration of a set of variables to achieve some goals. Population-based metaheuristics (PBM) are algorithms that works with a set of solution at the same time.[14] Thus, this kind of methods perform search processes which describe the refinement of a set of solutions in the search space. This section is devoted to present the considered population-based metaheuristics.

17.3.1. *Path Relinking*

Path Relinking[15,16] (PR) is an evolutionary metaheuristic in the context of the combinatorial optimization problems. PR constructs new high quality solutions by combining other previous solutions based on the exploration of paths connecting them. To yield better solutions than the original ones, PR starts from a given set of elite candidates, called $RefSet$ (short for "Reference Set"). These solutions are selected through a search process and are ordered according to their corresponding qualitative values. New candidates are then generated, exploring trajectories that connect solutions in the $RefSet$. The metaheuristic starts with two of these solutions x' and x'', and it generates a path $x' = x(l), x(2), \ldots, x(r) = x''$ in the neighbourhood space that leads toward the new sequence. In order to produce better quality solutions, it is convenient to add a local search optimization phase. In Figure 17.2 an outline of the PR is shown.

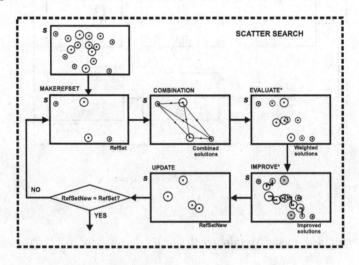

Fig. 17.3. Scatter Search scheme

17.3.2. *Scatter Search*

Scatter Search[20,21] (SS) is a population-based metaheuristic that provides unifying principles for recombining solutions based on generalized path construction in Euclidean spaces. In other words, SS systematically (never randomly) generates disperse set of points (solutions) from a chosen set of reference points throughout weighted combinations. This concept is introduced as the main mechanism to generate new trial points on lines jointing reference solutions. SS metaheuristic has been successfully applied to several hard combinatorial problems. A recent review of this method can be found in.[21]

In Figure 17.3 an outline of the SS is shown. SS procedure starts by choosing a solutions subset (called $RefSet$) from a set S of $PopSize = |S|$ initial feasible ones. The solutions in $RefSet$ are obtained by choosing the h best solutions and the r most diverse ones in S. Then, new solutions are generated by making combinations of solution subsets (pairs typically) from $RefSet$. The resulting solutions, called trial solutions, can be infeasible. In that case, repairing methods are used to transform these solutions into feasible ones. In order to improve the solution fitness, a local search from trial solutions is performed. SS ends when the new generated solutions do not improve the $RefSet$ quality.

17.4. Particle Filter and Population-Based Metaheuristics Hybrid Algorithms

Visual tracking of articulated motion is a complex task with high computational costs. Due to the dynamic nature of the problem, sequential estimation algorithms are usually applied to visual tracking. Unfortunately, particle filter fails in high dimensional estimation problems such as articulated objects or multiple object tracking. These problems can be seen as a sequence of optimization problems, and they are called *dynamic optimization problems*. In our opinion, dynamic optimization problems deals with optimization and prediction tasks. This assumption is supported by the fact that the optimization method for changing conditions needs from adaptive strategies. On the other hand, in dynamic optimization problems it is not good enough to predict, and high quality solutions must be found.

Therefore, it could be not too appropriate to use optimization procedures in the prediction stage. Analogously, sequential estimation algorithms are well-suited in prediction stages, but they are not good enough for solving dynamic optimization problems. Then, dynamic optimization problems needs from both, optimization and prediction tasks. The key question is how to hybridize these two kinds of algorithms to obtain a new one which combines both techniques. In order to answer this question, two different hybrid algorithm called *Path Relinking Particle Filter* (PRPF) and *Scatter Search Particle Filter* (SSPF) are presented in this section.

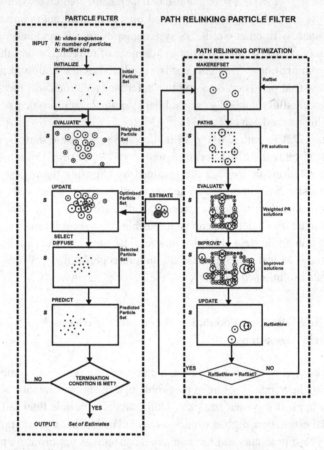

Fig. 17.4. Path Relinking Search Particle Filter scheme. Weight computation is required during EVALUATE and IMPROVE stages (*)

17.4.1. *Path Relinking Particle Filter*

Path Relinking Particle Filter (PRPF) algorithm was introduced in[19] to be applied to estimation problems in sequential processes that can be expressed using the state-space model abstraction. PRPF integrates both Path Relinking (PR) and Particle Filter (PF) frameworks in two different stages:

• In the *Particle Filter stage*, a particle (solution) set is propagated over the time and updated with measurements to obtain a new one. This stage is focused on the evolution of the best solutions found in previous time steps. The main aim for using PF is to avoid the loss of needed diversity in the solution set.

- In the *Path Relinking stage*, a fixed number of solutions from the particle set are selected and combined to obtain better ones. This stage is devoted to improve the quality of a set of good solutions in such a way that the final solution is also improved.

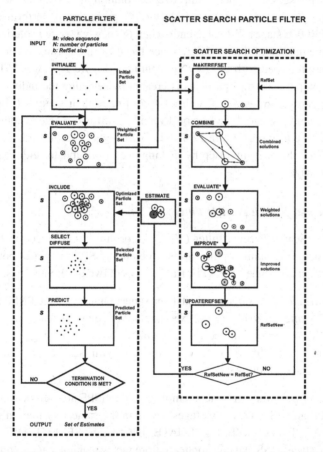

Fig. 17.5.   Scatter Search Particle Filter scheme. Weight computation is required during EVALUATE and IMPROVE stages (*)

Figure 17.4 shows a graphical template of the PRPF method. Dashed lines separate the two main components in the PRPF scheme: PF and PR optimization, respectively. PRPF starts with an initial population of N particles drawn from a known pdf (Figure 17.4: INITIALIZE stage). Each particle represents a possible solution of the problem. Particle weights are computed using a weighting function and a measurement vector (Figure 17.4: EVALUATE stage). PR stage is later applied improving the best obtained solutions of the particle filter stage. A $RefSet$ is created selecting the b ($b \ll N$) best particles (Figure 17.4: MAKEREFSET stage). New solutions are generated and evaluated by exploring trajectories that connect all possible pairs of particles in the $RefSet$ (Figure 17.4: PATHS and EVALUATE stages). In order to improve the solution fitness, a local search from some of the generated solutions within the PR procedure is performed (Figure 17.4: IMPROVE stage). PR stage ends when the new generated solutions do not improve the quality of the $RefSet$. Once the PR stage is finished, the "worst" particles are replaced with the $RefSet$ solutions (Figure 17.4: UPDATE stage). Then, a new population of particles is created by selecting the individuals from the whole particle set with probabilities according to their weights (Figure 17.4: SELECT stage). To avoid the loss of diversity, a diffusion stage is applied to the particles of the new set (Figure 17.4: DIFFUSE stage). At the end, particles are projected into the next time step by making use of the update rule (Figure 17.4: PREDICT stage).

17.4.2. *Scatter Search Particle Filter*

The Scatter Search Particle Filter (SSPF) algorithm is introduced in this paper to be applied to dynamic optimization problems. SSPF integrates both Scatter Search (SS) and Particle Filter (PF) frameworks in two different stages.

- The *Particle Filter stage* proceed in the same manner as in the PRPF algorithm
- In the *Scatter Search stage*, a fixed number of solutions from the particle set are selected and combined to obtain better ones. This stage is devoted to improve the quality of a set of good solutions in such a way that the final solution is also improved.

Figure 17.5 shows a graphical template of the SSPF algorithm. Dashed lines separate PF and SS stages. PF stages works in the same way than in the PRPF (Figure 17.5: INITIALIZE, EVALUATE, INCLUDE, SELECT, DIFFUSE and PREDICT stages). SS stage is applied before the evaluation stage to improve the best obtained solutions of the particle filter. A $RefSet$ is created selecting a subset of b ($b \ll N$) particles from the particle set (Figure 17.5: MAKEREFSET stage). This subset is composed by the $b/2$ best solutions and the $b/2$ most diverse ones of the particle set. New solutions are generated and evaluated, by combining all possible pairs of particles in the $RefSet$ (Figure 17.5: COMBINE and

EVALUATE stages). To improve the solution fitness, a local search from each new solution is performed (Figure 17.5: IMPROVE stage). Worst solutions in the *RefSet* are replaced when there are better ones (Figure 17.5: UPDATEREFSET stage). SS stage ends when new generated solutions *RefSetNew* do not improve the quality of the *RefSet*. Once the SS stage is finished, the "worst" particles in the particle set are replaced with the *RefSetNew* solutions (Figure 17.5: IN-CLUDE stage) and subsequent filter stages are performed (Figure 17.5: SELECT, DIFFUSE and PREDICT stages).

17.4.3. *PRPF and SSPF Main Features*

The SSPF and PRPF algorithms are centered on a delimited region of the state-space in which it is highly probable to find new better solutions than the initial ones. PRPF increases the performance of general PF by improving the quality of the estimate, adapting computational load to constraints and reducing the number of required evaluations of the particle weighting function.

PF performs two tasks over the set $S(t)$ to obtain the solution set $S(t+1)$: selecting the best solutions and predicting new solutions from the best ones. Firstly, the selection procedure selects particles with larger weight values more likely than those with lower weights. Secondly, PF performs a prediction procedure over these best solutions to obtain the set $S(t+1)$. In this way, PF beats to problem changes by predicting the best solution time evolution. As results, solutions in $S(t+1)$ will be closer to global optimum than another ones obtained randomly. On the other hand, a diffusion procedure is applied to the selected solutions to include diversity in the set $S(t+1)$.

To summarize, the main advantages of the PRPF and SSPF hybrid algorithms are:

- Hybrid estimator quality is improved with respect to PF and the required number of evaluations for the weighting function is also reduced. This is due to the fact that PRPF and SSPF search is not performed randomly like in a general particle filter.
- Both hybrid algorithms are time-adaptive since the number of evaluations of the weighting function changes in each time step. If the initial solutions in the *RefSet* are far away one from each other, paths connecting solutions become long enough, and the number of explored solutions increases.
- The number of individuals in the particle filter does not change during the algorithm execution. PRPF algorithm reduces the total required number of evaluations of the weighting function when increasing the number of total time steps.

Population-based Metaheuristics (PBM) and PF are related in such a way that when the PBM improves, the PF performance also improves and vice versa. PF allows parameter tuning in order to adjust the quality and the diversity of the set S, used by PBM. On the other hand PBM improves the quality of the particle set allowing the better estimation of the pdf, by including $RefSet$ solutions in the set S. This fact yields to a highly configurable algorithm. The main considered hybrid algorithm parameters are:

- The size of the particle set N is the number of particles in the particle set. There should be enough particles to support a set of diverse solutions, avoiding the loss of diversity in the particle set. Thus, N influences on the performance of the SS stage. The value of N depends on the problem instance complexity.
- The size of the reference set b is the number of solutions in the $RefSet$. A typical $RefSet$ size value recommended[21] is $b = 10$.
- The diffusion stage is applied to avoid the loss of diversity in S. It is performed by applying a random displacement with maximum amplitude A. This amplitude A is a measure of the diversity produced in the new particle set. Therefore, A influences the performance of the SS by tuning the diversity of the initial solution set, and hence, the diversity of the $RefSet$.

17.5. Models for Human Pose Estimation

Each one of the involved models in our framework is detailed in this section. A geometrical model is required to link solutions in the state-space with $2D$ image feature extraction. Observation and system models respectively define the observation and transition processes in the state-space model abstraction.

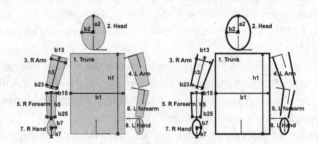

Fig. 17.6.   Proposed blob (left) and edge (right) configuration for human upper-body model

17.5.1. *Geometrical Model*

We use an a priori $2D$ geometrical model to represent the observed subject. It consists of a hierarchical set of articulated limbs. This model stores geometrical (time-independent) parameters describing the body components. Figure 17.6 illustrates the proposed blobs and edge models for upper-body tracking. As shown in the experiments section, this model can be easily extended to describe the whole human body.

Table 17.1.   Limb properties in a human upper-body model.

	Trunk	Head	Right Arm	Right Forearm	Right Hand
Identifier	1	2	3	5	7
Shape	T	E	T	T	E
Level	1	2	2	3	4
Father	-	1	1	3	5
Size	$[h1, b1, b1]$	$[a2, b2]$	$[h1, b13, b23]$	$[h1, b15, b25]$	$[a7, b7]$
Position	-	$[0, h1 + \Delta]$	$[-b1/2, h1 - b12/2]$	$[0, h3]$	$[0, h5]$

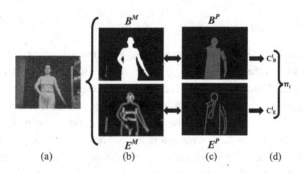

Fig. 17.7.   Observation process: (a) initial image, (b) feature extraction, (c) particle prediction and (d) particle weight computation

Body limbs are represented by a set of trapezium-shaped (trunk, arms, legs, and feet) and ellipse-shaped (head and hands) ribbons which are connected by joints. Size of trapeziums (T) is described by three parameters: one for the length and two for the axes. Size of ellipses (E) is described by two axes. Each limb is jointed with a father limb except trunk. Position and orientation of each body part is described in his father frame. The coordinate system for the body parts are

Fig. 17.8. Visual model adjustment for a subject performing planar movements (frames 10, 20, 30, 40 and 50) using (a) PRPF, (b) SSPF and (c) one-layered PF .

aligned with the natural axes. The origin of a coordinate system is located at the point in which each limb is jointed with his father limb. The level of the limb is related to the distance from the body center, and it is useful to calculate position and orientation of body parts in the global reference system. Several examples of limb descriptions in the proposed model are shown in Table 17.1.

Particles store time-dependent values relating to limb positions, orientations and velocities. The state x_t^i of a particle (x_t^i, π_t^i) in an eight-limb model is described as:

$$[x_1, y_1, \theta_1, \theta_2, \theta_3, \theta_4, \theta_5, \theta_6, \theta_7, \theta_8, \dot{x}_1, \dot{y}_1, \dot{\theta}_1, \dot{\theta}_2, \dot{\theta}_3, \dot{\theta}_4, \dot{\theta}_5, \dot{\theta}_6, \dot{\theta}_7, \dot{\theta}_8] \quad (17.3)$$

where x and y are the spatial positions, θ_i is the i limb orientation in the father's system of reference and $\dot{x}$, $\dot{y}$ and $\dot{\theta}$ represents the first derivative of its corresponding variable. The goal of the geometrical model is to relate solutions in the multi-dimensional state-space with the 2D image features. Thus, the method predicts the pose of the model for the next frame and creates synthetic edge and blobs images. Note that these parameters are defined with respect to the camera view point. Features, those extracted from each frame in the video sequence and those predicted by the PRPF and SSPF algorithms, are compared in order to obtain a corresponding similarity measure. This similarity value is iteratively used to establish the weights of the different particles for the following frame during the tracking stage.

17.5.2. Observation Model and Weighting Function

The observation model specifies the image features to be extracted. To construct the weighting function it is necessary to use adequate image features. In controlled environments, edges and silhouette are relatively easy to extract from both, the

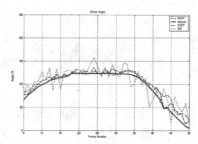

Fig. 17.9. Right elbow angle estimation in frontal movement shown in Figure 17.8 using PRPF, SSPF, One-Layered PF and manual digitizing

image and the geometrical model. Continuous edges extracted from a human image usually provide a good measure of visible body limbs. However, they are sensitive to noise. A region-based feature such as silhouette has the advantage over edges of being less sensitive to noise.[2] On the other hand, details may be lost in the extraction of silhouettes. In order to overcome these difficulties both a silhouette and an edge based model are used.

Figure 17.7 represents the observation process that leads to the particle weights computation. Continuous edges extracted from a human image usually provide a good measure of visible body limbs. A Canny edge method is used in this work, although any other edge detector could be employed. The resulting human body edges are then smoothed using a convolution operation. This produces a pixel map E^M in which each pixel is set to a value related to its proximity to an edge. Another pixel map E^P is built extracting edges produced by the geometrical model of the configuration predicted by the ith particle, for each pixel j in the pixel map. Similarly, a background subtraction was used to obtain human silhouette. Two pixel maps B^M and B^P are built and compared to compute the corresponding values of C_j^B. Differences between these two maps are computed by:

$$\forall i \in \{1, \ldots, N_{particles}\}, \forall j \in \{1, \ldots, N_{pixel}\} \rightarrow C_E^i = \sum_j |E_j^M - E_j^P|$$

(17.4)

$$\forall i \in \{1, \ldots, N_{particles}\}, \forall j \in \{1, \ldots, N_{pixel}\} \rightarrow C_B^i = \sum_j |B_j^M - B_j^P|$$

(17.5)

Finally, edges and blobs coefficients are combined to obtain i^{th} particle weight

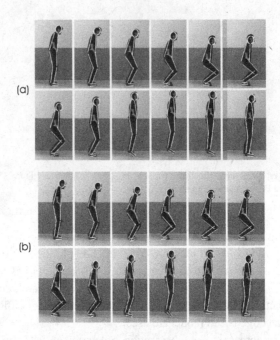

Fig. 17.10.   Visual model adjustment for a jumping man using (a) PRPF and (b) SSPF

at each frame using an exponential weighting function as follows:

$$\forall i \in \{1, \ldots, N_{particles}\} \rightarrow \pi^i = e^{-\alpha(C_E^i + C_B^i)} \qquad (17.6)$$

where α is an experimental parameter which allow us to tune the influence of peaks in the weighting function. This weighting function give a measure of the model fitting quality, so that larger weights mean better fits.

17.5.2.1. System Model

The system model describes the temporal update rule for the system state.[9] The tracked object state consists of a given number of spatial (linear or angular) coordinates and the corresponding velocities, deriving in a first-order motion model. Two excitation forces, F and G, that are modeled by random Gaussian variables with zero mean and normal deviation σ_F and σ_G respectively allow changes in the object state (position and velocity). The value of σ_F and σ_G depend on expected changes in the position and velocity of the tracked object. The update rule used in

Fig. 17.11.   Visual model adjustment for a running man using (a) PRPF and (b) SSPF

this work is performed by these two equations:

$$x_{t+\Delta t} = x_t + \dot{x}_t \Delta t + F_x$$
$$\dot{x}_{t+\Delta t} = \dot{x}_t + G_x \qquad (17.7)$$

where x represents some spatial (linear or angular) variable, Δt is the time step and F_x and G_x are random Gaussian variables with zero mean and normal deviation σ_F and σ_G, respectively.

17.6. Experimental Results

To analyze the performance of the proposed model-based PRPF and SSPF algorithms, people performing different activities were recorded in several scenarios. These algorithms were implemented using MATLAB 6.1. Figure 17.8 shows the model adjustment for a subject performing planar movements. Upper-body model consists of eight limbs. A visual comparison leads to a very good estimation between the PRPF and SSPF results. Right elbow angle estimation using PRPF, SSPF are compared against the One-Layered Particle FIlter (1LPF) and manual digitizing curves in Figure 17.9. One-layered Particle Filter algorithm is an improved version of classical Particle Filter. A description of this algorithm can be found in.[12]

Table 17.2 shows the mean values of several angles from frontal (Figure 17.8) and jump (Figure 17.10) sequences. In order to give a measure of the performance

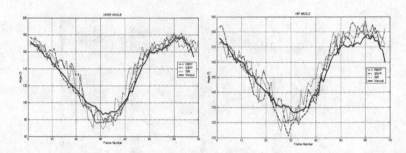

Fig. 17.12.   Right hip (left) and knee (right) angle estimation in the jump sequence shown in Figure 17.10 using PRPF ($N_{part}/frame$ = 2838), SSPF ($N_{part}/frame$ = 1626), 1LPF ($N_{part}/frame$ = 4000) and manual digitizing

of three methods, we calculate a performance factor (P_f) given by

$$P_f = \frac{1}{N_{part} * MSE/fr} \tag{17.8}$$

where N_{part} is the number of particles and MSE/fr is the mean square error per frame. P_f increases when N_{part} or MSE/fr decrease. Thus, a greater value of p indicates greater performance of the approach. Table 17.3 shows the P_f obtained for one-layered PF, PRPF and SSPF in absolute and relative terms. In these experiments SSPF obtain the best performance factor.

Table 17.2. $MSE/frame$ values with respect to manual digitizing and $N_{part}/frame$ of one-layered PF, PRPF and SSPF for two motion sequences

	SEQUENCES	1LPF	PRPF	SSPF
	$N_{part}/frame$	1600	1363	999
Jump	Knee Angle (MSE/fr)	10.53	5.10	8.72
(Figure 17.10)	Hip Angle (MSE/fr)	6.81	5.15	5.86
Frontal	$N_{part}/frame$	4000	2401	1626
Movement	Right Elbow Angle (MSE/fr)	17.43	8.27	7.99
(Figure 17.8)	Left Elbow Angle (MSE/fr)	45.22	11.31	8.67

Figure 17.11 shows a runner tracked with a ten limbs body model using PRPF and SSPF algorithm. Both sequences demonstrate an accurate model adjustment. Right arm is not included into the geometrical model because it remains completely occluded during most video sequence. Figure 17.10 shows the same countermovement jump sequence tracked by PRPF and SSPF. A full-body model formed by only five limbs is employed. Selected non-consecutive frames are

Table 17.3.   Performance Factor obtained for 1LPF, PRPF and SSPF for two motion sequences

SEQUENCES		1LPF	PRPF	SSPF	$\frac{PRPF}{1LPF}$	$\frac{SSPF}{1LPF}$
Jump	P_f Knee Angle	5.9×10^{-5}	1.4×10^{-4}	1.1×10^{-4}	2.4	1.9
	P_f Hip Angle	9.2×10^{-5}	1.4×10^{-4}	1.7×10^{-4}	1.5	1.9
Frontal Movement	P_f Right Elbow Angle	1.4×10^{-5}	5.0×10^{-5}	1.2×10^{-5}	3.5	8.7
	P_f Left Elbow Angle	5.5×10^{-6}	3.7×10^{-5}	1.1×10^{-4}	6.7	20.8

shown in both figures. Right knee (left) and hip (right) angle estimation using PRPF, SSPF, 1LPF and manual digitizing curves are shown in Figure 17.12.

17.7. Conclusion

The main contribution of this work is the application of the Path Relinking Particle Filter (PRPF) and the Scatter Search Particle Filter (SSPF) algorithms to the model-based human motion tracking. Both algorithms were originally developed for general dynamic optimization and complicated sequential estimation problems. Experimental results have shown that PRPF and SSPF frameworks can be very efficiently applied to the 2D human pose estimation problem. We have estimated a performance factor taking into account the number of particles and the MSE of the corresponding methods against the manual digitizing. By means of this factor we observe that the SSPF algorithm has the best performance hit in terms of MSE and computational load. The proposed geometrical human model is flexible and easily adaptable to the different analyzed human motion activities. However, it depends on the view-point and it is only suitable for planar movements. In this way, quite energetic planar activities such as running and jumping in different environment have been effectively tracked.

References

1. L. Wang, H. Weiming, and T. Tieniu, Recent developments in human motion analysis, *Pattern Recognition*. **36**(3), 585–601, (2003).
2. B. Moeslund and E. Granum, A survey on computer vision-based human motion capture, *Computer Vision and Image Understanding*. **81**(3), 231–268, (2001).
3. D. Gavrila, The visual analysis of human movement: a review, *Computer Vision and Image Understanding*. **73**(1), 82–98, (1999).

4. I. Kakadiaris, R. Sharma, and M. Yeasin, Editorial introduction to the special issue on human modelling, analysis and syntesis, *Machine Vision and Applications*. **14**, 197 – 198, (2003).

5. K. Rohr. Human movement analysis based on explicit motion models. In *Motion-based Recognition*, pp. 171–198, (1997).

6. S. Ju, M. Black, and Y. Yaccob. Cardboard people: a parameterized model of articulated image motion. In *IEEE Int. Conf. on Automatic Face and Gesture Recognition*, vol. 1, pp. 38–44, (1996).

7. S. Wachter and H. Nagel, Tracking persons in monocular image sequences, *Computer Vision and Image Understanding*. **74**(3), 174 – 192, (1999).

8. M. Leung and Y. Yang, First sight: a human body outline labeling system, *IEEE Transactions on Pattern Analysis and Machine Intelligence*. **17**(4), 359 – 377, (1995).

9. D. Zotkin, R. Duraiswami, and L. Davis., Joint audio-visual tracking using particle filters, *EURASIP journal on Applied Signal Processing*. **2002**(11), 1154–1164, (2002).

10. J. Deutscher, A. Blake, and I. Reid. Articulated body motion capture by annealed particle filtering. In *Proc. of the IEEE Conf. on CVPR*, vol. 2, pp. 126–133, (2000).

11. J. MacCormick and A. Blake. Partitioned sampling, articulated objects and interface-quality hand tracking. In *Proceedings of the $7^t h$ European Conference on Computer Vision*, vol. 2, pp. 3–19, (2000).

12. J. Deutscher and I. Reid, Articulated body motion capture by stochastic search, *International Journal on Computer Vision*. **61**(2), 185–205, (2005).

13. H. Ning, T. Tan, L. Wang, and W. Hu, People tracking based on motion model and motion constraints with automatic initialization, *Pattern Recognition*. **37**, 1423–1440, (2004).

14. C. Blum and A. Roli, Metaheuristics in combinatorial optimization: Overview and conceptual comparison, *ACM Computing Surveys*. **35**(3), 268–308, (2003).

15. F. Glover, M. Laguna, and R. Mart. Scatter search and path relinking: Foundations and advanced designs. In *New Optimization techniques in Engineering*, (2003).

16. F. Glover. A template for scatter search and path relinking. In *Artificial Evolution, Lecture Notes in Computer Science*, pp. 14–53, (1998).

17. J. Carpenter, P. Clifford, and P. Fearnhead. Building robust simulation-based filters for evolving data sets. Technical report, University of Oxford, Dept. of Statistics, (1999).

18. S. Arulampalam, S. Maskell, N. Gordon, and T. Clapp, A tutorial on particle filters for on-line nonlinear/non-gaussian bayesian tracking, *IEEE Trans. on Signal Processing*. **50**(2), 174–188, (2002).

19. J. Pantrigo, A. Sánchez, K. Gianikellis, and A. Duarte. Path relinking particle filter for human body pose estimation. In *SSPR/SPR*, pp. 653–661, (2004).

20. F. Glover and G. Kochenberger, *Handbook of metaheuristics*. (Kluwer Academic Publishers, 2002).

21. M. Laguna and R. Marti, *Scatter Search methodology and implementations in C*. (Kluwer Academic Publishers, 2003).

CHAPTER 18

EAR BIOMETRICS BASED ON GEOMETRICAL FEATURE EXTRACTION

Michał Choraś

Institute of Telecommunications, University of Technology & LS
85-796, Bydgoszcz, Poland,
E-mail: chorasm@utp.edu.pl

Biometrics identification methods proved to be very efficient, more natural and easy for users than traditional methods of human identification. In fact, only biometrics methods truly identify humans, not keys and cards they posses or passwords they should remember.

The future of biometrics will surely lead to systems based on image analysis as the data acquisition is very simple and requires only cameras, scanners or sensors. More importantly such methods could be passive, which means that the user does not have to take active part in the whole process or, in fact, would not even know that the process of identification takes place. There are many possible data sources for human identification systems, but the physiological biometrics seem to have many advantages over methods based on human behaviour. The most interesting human anatomical parts for such passive, physiological biometrics systems based on images acquired from cameras are face and ear. Both of those methods contain large volume of unique features that allow to distinctively identify many users and will be surely implemented into efficient biometrics systems for many applications.

The article introduces to ear biometrics and presents its advantages over face biometrics in passive human identification systems. Then the geometrical method of feature extraction from human ear images in order to perform human identification is presented.

1. Introduction

Personal identification has lately become a very important issue in a still evolving network society. Most of the traditional identification methods, which are widespread in the commercial systems, have very many disadvantages. Well known methods like entering Personal Identification Number (PIN), typing logins and passwords, displaying identification cards or using specific keys require users to take active part in the process of identification. Moreover, those traditional methods are unreliable because it is hard to remember all the PIN-s and passwords, and it is fairly easy to loose ID cards and keys. The other drawback is the lack of security, as the cards and keys are often stolen, and passwords can be cracked.

Biometrics methods easily deal with those problems since users are identified by who they are, not by something they have to remember or carry with them. The passive methods of biometrics do not require any action from users and can take place even without their knowledge.

There are many known methods of human identification based on image analysis. In general, those biometrics methods can be divided into behavioural and physiological regarding the source of data, and can be divided into passive and invasive biometrics, regarding the way the data is acquired (Figure 1).

The first class is based on the behavioural features of human actions and it identifies people by how they perform something. The most popular of such methods is voice verification. Other methods are basically based on the dynamics of specific actions like making the signature, typing on the keyboard and simply moving or walking. Those methods are not that natural and they require users to take part in the process of identification by repeating specific actions, every time they are examined.

Physiological (anatomical) biometrics methods are based on the physiological features of humans thus they measure and compare features of specific parts of human body in the process of identification. So far the main interest is in the head and the hand with face, eye and fingerprint features being the most important discriminants of human identity.

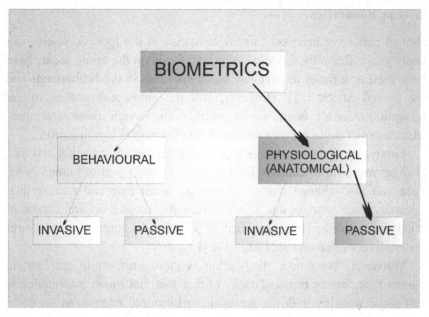

Figure 1. Biometrics methods.

The major advantage of physiological biometrics is that it is passive and the implemented systems work only with the acquired images of specific body parts. All the user has to do is to place his/her face or ear in front of the camera or alternatively touch the sensor with his/her fingers and wait for the identification process to take place.

Some systems can even verify the identity of humans even without their cooperation and knowledge, which is actually the future of biometrics. Crowd-surveillance, monitoring of public places like airports or sports arenas are the most important applications that need such solutions. Possible passive methods include popular and well-examined face recognition, but one of the most interesting novel approaches to human passive identification is the use of ear as the source of data [7].

2. Ear Biometrics

Human ears have been used as major feature in the forensic science for many years. Recently so called earprints, found on the crime scene, have been used as a proof in over few hundreds cases in the Netherlands and the United States [12]. However, still the automated system of ear recognition hasn't been implemented even though there are many advantages of using ear as a source of data for person identification.

Firstly, ear does not change considerably during human life, and face changes more significantly with age than any other part of human body. Face can also change due to cosmetics, facial hair and hair styling. Secondly, face changes due to emotions and expresses different states of mind like sadness, happiness, fear or surprise. In contrast, ear features are relatively fixed and unchangeable [14].

Moreover, the colour distribution is more uniform in ear than in human face, iris or retina. Thanks to that fact, not much information is lost while working with the greyscale or binarized images, as we do in our method.

Figure 2 presents two more aspects of ear identification. Firstly, ear is one of our sensors, therefore it is usually visible (not hidden underneath anything) to enable good hearing. Ear is also smaller than face, which means that it is possible to work faster and more efficiently with the images with the lower resolution.

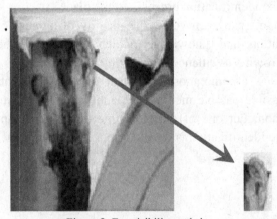

Figure 2. Ear visibility and size.

In the process of acquisition, in contrast to face identification systems, ear images cannot be disturbed by glasses, beard nor make-up. However, occlusion by hair or earrings is possible, but in access control applications, making ear visible is not a problem for user and takes just single seconds (Figure 3).

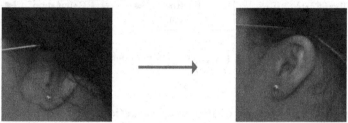

Figure 3. Ear visibility can be easily achieved in applications allowing interaction with the user (for example access control systems).

The first, manual method, used by Iannarelli in the research in which he examined over 10000 ears and proved their uniqueness, was based on measuring the distances between specific points of the ear [14]. The major problem in ear identification systems is discovering automated method to extract those specific, key points. Another well-known method by Burge and Burger [4,5] was based on building neighbourhood graph from Voronoi diagrams of the detected edges. Hurley et al. [13] introduced a method based on energy features of the image. They proposed to perform force field transformation in order to find energy lines, wells and channels. Another method used by Victor at al. [22], in the experiment comparing ear and face properties in order to successfully identify humans in various conditions, was based on PCA. Their work proved that ear images are a very suitable source of data for identification and their results for ear images were not significantly different from those achieved for face images. The method, however, was not fully automated, since the reference points had to be manually inserted into images. Another approach presented by Moreno et al. [20] was based on macrofeatures extracted by compression networks.

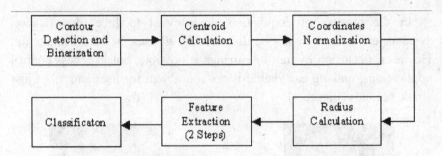

Figure 4. The block diagram of our method.

3. Geometrical Method of Feature Extraction

We propose a straightforward method to extract features needed to classification. Our method represents the geometrical approach, but it is automated and no manual operations are needed. After experiments we concluded that geometrical features representing shapes of ear contours are more suitable for ear images than texture, colour or global features.

Our method is divided into image normalization, contour extraction (edge detection), calculation of the centroid, coordinates normalization and 2 steps of geometrical feature extraction, as described in the next section. We treat the centroid as the specific point in our method, even though it is not a specific point within the ear topology.

Our method consists of the following steps (Figure 4):
- contour detection,
- binarization,
- coordinates normalization,
- feature extraction (2 steps),
- classification.

3.1. Contour Detection

First we perform the edge detection step. In our case it is a crucial operation, since it is obvious that lines are the most prominent features that could be obtained from the ear image, and our goal is to detect major outer and inner curves of the earlobe. We tested many known methods as Canny operator, Sobel filters and CWT (Complex Wavelets) but we propose another method, which proved to be most convenient in our experiments.

We propose to use the local method which examines illumination changes within the chosen window $n \times n$. We usually use 3×3 window and we divided the image into many overlapping regions of that size.

For each of those regions we calculated mean μ and standard deviation σ of the pixel intensity values in 8-pixel neighbourhood.

$$\mu = \frac{1}{n^2} \sum_{i=1}^{n} \sum_{j=1}^{n} I(i,j) \tag{1}$$

$$\sigma = \sqrt{\frac{1}{n^2} \sum_{i=1}^{n} \sum_{j=1}^{n} \left(I(i,j) - \mu\right)^2} \tag{2}$$

Then we perform decision if the centre pixel of the examined region belongs to the line or to the background. For the maximum value of the pixel intensity I_H, and the minimum value of the pixel intensity in the region I_L, we calculate the difference $S(i,j)$ such as:

$$S(i,j) = I_H - I_L \tag{3}$$

and we compare it to certain threshold value. Even though thresholding is one of the basic operations of image processing, there is always the major problem in selecting appropriate threshold value.

We propose the usage of mean and standard deviation of pixel intensities in calculation of the threshold value $T(i,j)$ used in contour detection as given in equation 4:

$$T(i,j) = \mu - k\sigma \tag{4}$$

where k is a certain value.

Then the rule for the contour detection is:

$$g(i,j) = \begin{cases} 1 & if & S(i,j) \geq T(i,j) \\ 0 & if & S(i,j) < T(i,j) \end{cases} \tag{5}$$

In result we obtain the binary image $g(i,j)$ with the detected contours. Moreover, the constant k allows to adjust and change the sensivity of the edge detection algorithm [9].

An example of the edge detection algorithm is shown in the Figure 5.

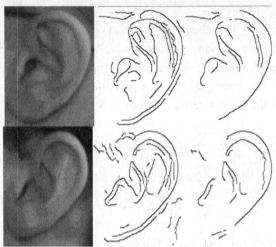

Figure 5. Result of edge detection algorithm for two different values of k.

3.2. Normalization

Given the binary image $g(i,j)$, we search for the centroid which later becomes the reference point for feature extraction. We obtain centroid such as:

$$I = \frac{\sum_i \sum_j ig(i,j)}{\sum_i \sum_j g(i,j)}, J = \frac{\sum_i \sum_j jg(i,j)}{\sum_i \sum_j g(i,j)} \tag{6}$$

Because the features for a recognition algorithm should be invariant to ear translation and scale change, the coordinates normalization is performed. Therefore we normalize coordinates, such that the centroid becomes the centre of the image. Suppose that the image with pixel coordinates (i, j) undergoes geometric transformations to produce an invariant image with coordinates (x, y). This transformation may be expressed as:

$$[x, y, z] = [i, j, 1] \begin{bmatrix} 1 & 0 & 0 \\ 0 & 1 & 0 \\ -I & -J & 1 \end{bmatrix} \begin{bmatrix} \dfrac{1}{\sigma_i} & 0 & 0 \\ 0 & \dfrac{1}{\sigma_j} & 0 \\ 0 & 0 & 1 \end{bmatrix} \begin{bmatrix} \cos\beta & \sin\beta & 0 \\ -\sin\beta & \cos\beta & 0 \\ 0 & 0 & 1 \end{bmatrix} \quad (7)$$

where:
I, J – centroid,
σ_i, σ_j - standard deviation of i and j respectively:

$$\sigma_i = \sqrt{\dfrac{\sum_i \sum_j i^2 g(i,j)}{\sum_i \sum_j g(i,j)} - I^2}, \sigma_j = \sqrt{\dfrac{\sum_i \sum_j j^2 g(i,j)}{\sum_i \sum_j g(i,j)} - J^2} \quad (8)$$

Furthermore, our method is also invariant to rotation as all the rotated images of the same object have the same centroid. That is the major reason that we chose the centroid of the image to be the reference point in the feature extraction algorithm. Such approach allows the successful processing of RST queries.

3.3. *Feature Extraction*

There are many possible geometrical methods of feature extraction and shape description such as Fourier Descriptors, Delaunay Triangles and methods based on combination of angles and distances as parameters. We propose a 2 step-method that is based on number of pixels that have the same radius in a circle with the centre in the centroid and on the contour topology. The algorithm for the first step of feature extraction is presented below:

1. we create a set of circles with the centre in the centroid (Figure 6)
2. number of circles N_r is fixed and unchangeable

3. we create circles in such a manner that the corresponding radiuses are α pixels longer from the previous radius
4. since each circle is crossed by the contour image pixels we count the number of intersection pixels l_r
5. next we calculate all the distances d between neighbouring pixels, we proceed in the counter-clockwise direction
6. we build the feature vector that consists of all the radiuses with the corresponding number of pixels belonging to each radius and with the sum of all the distances between those pixels $\sum d$

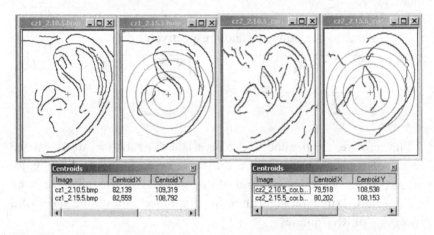

Figure 6. Binary ear images with the extracted edges (2 values of k) and with the centroid marked with a cross. Circles represent the radius values for calculation of number of pixels intersecting each circle. The table below shows the centroid values for each binary image.

The algorithm for *Nr=3* is symbolically presented in the Figure 7.

Figure 7. The symbolic representation of our algorithm for $N_r = 3$.

The general rule for forming the first vector is presented below:

$$V = \left\{ \left[r_{\min}, l_{r\min}, \sum d_{r\min} \right] \cdots \left[r_{\max}, l_{r\max}, \sum d_{r\max} \right] \right\} \qquad (9)$$

where:

r – radius length,

l_r – number of intersection points for each radius,

$\sum d$ – sum of all the distances between the intersection points for the considered radius.

Then in order to enhance the distinctiveness of the extracted features, we build the second vector in the second step of feature extraction. Once again we base upon the created circles with the centre in the centroid. Hereby, we propose to extract the characteristic points for each contour in the normalized coordinates.

For each contour line the characteristic points are:

- contour endings,
- contour bifurcations,
- all the points that cross the created circles (those points are already extracted by the previous algorithm).

In each contour we check the topological properties of every pixel. For each contour pixel g_o we use 3×3 window as in Figure 8 (left). When $g_0 = 1$, the connected number N_c^8 of g_0 is defined as:

$$N_c^8(g_o) = \sum_{k=S} \left(\bar{g}_k - \bar{g}_k \, \bar{g}_{k+1} \, \bar{g}_{k+2} \right), \tag{10}$$

where $S = (1,3,5,7)$ and $\bar{g}_k = g_k - 1$.

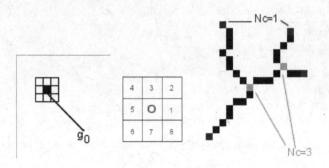

Figure 8. Characteristic points detection algorithm.

We search for the contour beginning in the area A, such that: $r_i \geq A > r_{i-1}$. We begin the search for $r_i = r_{max}$, which means that we start our algorithm in the most outer circle. Then we search in all other circles heading towards the centre in the centroid. If we come across any point with $N_c^8 = 1$, we check if it is already stored in the feature vector and if not, we store it as the ending point and we trace its contour. Points with $N_c^8 = 1$ and $N_c^8 > 2$ are the ear contour endings and the contour bifurcation points respectively. Those points are marked as E and B in the Figure 9.

For each contour we also extract the intersections with the circles created earlier. For each contour intersecting the circles we store all the intersections coordinates i and the number of such intersections N_I as presented in Figure 9 (right) and Eq. 11.

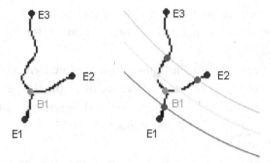

Figure 9. The symbolic representation of the second step of feature extraction algorithm.

The general rule for forming the second vector for each contour is presented below. First we store the number of endings, bifurcations and intersection points, and then we store all the coordinates of those points, for all the extracted and traced contours. For C contours in a given image we obtain:

$$F = \{ \left[(N_E, N_B, N_I)(e_1, \cdots, e_{N_E}, b_1, \cdots, b_{N_B}, i_1, \cdots, i_{N_I}) \right]_1 \cdots$$

$$\cdots \left[(N_E, N_B, N_I)(e_1, \cdots, e_{N_E}, b_1, \cdots, b_{N_B}, i_1, \cdots, i_{N_I}) \right]_C \} \qquad (11)$$

where:
N_E - number of endings in each contour,
N_B - number of bifurcations in each contour,
N_I - number of points intersecting the circles,
e – coordinates of endings,
b - coordinates of bifurcations,
i - coordinates of intersections in each contour.

4. Classification

For each image stored in the database we have two vectors F_{ref} and V_{ref}. For each input ear, we acquire many images under different angles to the camera.

The algorithm for recognition of an input image is following:

1. for the fixed number of circles, the feature vectors V and F of the input image are obtained

2. for each radius, we search the database feature vectors V_{ref} that have the same number of intersections l_r for the corresponding radiuses

3. the vectors with the number of intersections $(l_r \pm \delta)$ are also accepted, allowing the difference of δ pixel on each circle

4. in the next step we check if the difference within the distance sum $\sum d$ for all the extracted vectors is less than a certain threshold value

5. if none of the vectors V_{ref} are found for the input image, the input image is rejected

6. if the number of intersecting points l_r is accepted and the difference within the distance sum $\sum d$ is less than a certain threshold value we check the contour-topology vector F

7. we first search for the same triples (N_E, N_B, N_I) of the input contour-topology vector F with the reference contour vectors F_{ref}

8. then for the images with the same triples (N_E, N_B, N_I) we check if the coordinates of the stored points are the same

9. if the corresponding coordinates of those vectors refer to the same points, the algorithm finds the winner of classification.

5. Experimental Results and Future Work

We perform our experiments on our own database of collected ear images. At the moment of writing, the database consists of over 240 images, but we are still adding more ear images of different type. For each person included in the experiments, we collected 2 left ear images, first with the camera perpendicular to the head and the second, with the camera within the specified angle of 30 degrees. Now, analogically to face recognition systems, we collect larger database of ear images, which contains 20 different views for each person (5 orientations, 2 scales, 2 illuminations).

We divided the database to several sets of images concerning their quality and degree of complexity. So far we have only experimented with images of very high quality and with the ideal conditions of recognition, without illumination changes (Figure 10). For such "easy" images from our database we obtained error-free recognition.

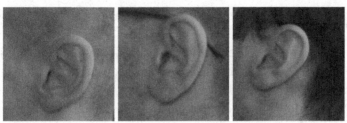

Figure 10. Some examples of "easy" ear images from our database.

In further experiments we work with the "difficult" images and with the changing conditions of the image acquisition. In order to achieve satisfactory results with such complex images (Figure 11) we are improving the contour detection algorithm, so that long, straight line-contours of glasses and artificial contours of earrings and hair are eliminated before applying feature extraction algorithm. Moreover, we work on the algorithm selecting only the most significant ear contours. We eliminate contours that are short in comparison to the longest contour detected in the ear image.

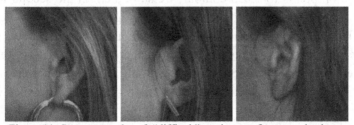

Figure 11. Some examples of "difficult" ear images from our database.

We also think that the feature vectors should be enriched with more geometrical features in order to better distinguish ear identity. We are testing some new geometrical parameters describing shapes of ear contours and we compare their effectiveness in ear identification.

Moreover, we search for other than geometrical features describing ear images, such as energy and shape parameters. We try to discover, which features are the most significant in determining ear identity, so that we will be able to weight them properly in the process of building hybrid vectors of features of different types.

6. Conclusions

In the article we proposed a human identification method based on human ear images. We proposed invariant geometrical method in order to extract features needed to classification. First we perform contour detection algorithm, then coordinates normalization. Thanks to placing the centre of the new coordinates system in the centroid, our method is invariant to rotation, translation and scaling, which will allow RST queries. The centroid is also a key reference point in the feature extraction algorithm, which is divided into 2 steps. In the first step, we create circles centred in the centroid and we count the number of intersection points for each radius and the sum of all the distances between those points. All those points are stored in the first feature vector corresponding to the radiuses. In the second step, we use the created circles, but hereby we count the intersection points for each contour line. Moreover, while tracing the contour lines, we detect the characteristic points like endings and bifurcations. Together with the intersection points for each contour, we store them in the second feature vector corresponding to contour topology. Then we perform classification, basing on the simple comparison between the input image feature vectors, and all the vectors from the database. So far we have obtained very good results, however we still continue our research in order to improve our method and add more parameters to the feature vectors.

We believe that human ear is a perfect source of data for passive person identification in many applications. In a growing need for security in various public places, ear biometrics seem to be a good solution, since ears are visible and its images can be easily taken, even without the knowledge of the examined person. Then the robust feature extraction method can be used to determine personality of some individuals, for instance terrorists at the airports and stations. Access control to various buildings and crowd surveillance are among other possible applications.

Ear biometrics can be also used to enhance effectiveness of other well-known biometrics, by its implementation in multimodal systems. Since most of the methods have some drawbacks, recently, the idea of building multimodal (hybrid) biometrics systems is gaining lot of attention [11,16]. Due to its advantages, ear biometrics seem to be a good choice to support well known methods like voice, hand or face identification.

References

1. Ashbourn J., Biometrics - Advanced Identity Verification, Springer-Verlag 2000.
2. Beveridge J.R., She R., Draper B.A., Givens G.H., Parametric and Nonparametric Methods for the Statistical Evaluation of Human Id Algorithms, Workshop on Evaluation Methods in Computer Vision, 2001.
3. Bowman E., Everything You Need to Know about Biometrics, Technical Report, Identix Corporation, 2000.
4. Burge M., Burger W., Ear Biometrics, Johannes Kepler University, Linz, Austria 1999.
5. Burge M., Burger W., Ear Biometrics for Machine Vision, 21 Workshop of the Austrian Association for Pattern Recognition, Hallstatt, 1997.
6. Canny J., A Computational Approach to Edge Detection, IEEE Trans. on Pattern Analysis and Machine Intelligence, vol. 8, no. 6, 679-698, 1986.
7. Choraś M., Human Identification Based on Image Analysis – New Trends, Proc. Int. IEEE Workshop Signal Processing'03, pp. 111-116, Poznan 2003.
8. Choraś M., Human Ear Identification Based on Image Anlysis, in L. Rutkowski et al. (Eds): Artificial Inteligence and Soft Computing, ICAISC 2004, 688-693, LNAI 3070, Springer-Verlag 2004.
9. Choraś M., Feature Extraction Based on Contour Processing in Ear Biometrics, IEEE Workshop on Multimedia Communications and Services, MCS'04, 15-19, Cracow.
10. Danielsson P. E., Ye Q. Z., Rotation-Invariant Operators Applied to Enhancement of Fingerprints, Proc. 8th ICPR, Rome 1988.
11. Hong L, Jain A.K., Pankanti S., Can Multibiometrics Improve Performance?, Proc. of AutoID'99, 59-64, 1999.
12. Hoogstrate A.J., Heuvel van den H., Huyben E., Ear Identification Based on Surveillance Camera's Images, Netherlands Forensic Institute, 2000.
13. Hurley D.J., Nixon M.S., Carter J.N., Force Field Energy Functionals for Image Feature Extraction, Image and Vision Computing Journal, vol. 20, no. 5-6, 311-318, 2002.

14. Iannarelli A., Ear Identification, Forensic Identification Series, Paramont Publishing Company, California 1989.
15. Jain A., Bolle R., Pankanti S., Biometrics: Personal Identification in Networked Society, Kluwer Academic Publishers, 1999.
16. Jain A.K., Ross A., Multibiometric Systems, Comm. ACM, Special Issue on Multimodal Interfaces, vol. 47, no. 1, 34-40, 2004.
17. Jain L. C., Halici U., Hayashi I., Lee S. B., Tsutsui S., Intelligent Biometric Techniques in Fingerprint and Face Recognition, CRC Press International Series on Computational Intelligence, 1999.
18. Kouzani A.Z., He F., Sammut K., Towards Invariant Face Recognition, Journal of Information Sciences 123, Elsevier 2000.
19. Lai K., Chin R., Deformable Contours: Modeling and Extraction, IEEE Trans. on Pattern Analysis and Machine Intelligence, vol. 17, no. 11, 1084-1090, 1995.
20. Moreno B., Sanchez A., Velez J.F., On the Use of Outer Ear Images for Personal Identification in Security Applications, IEEE Conf. On Security Technology, 469-476, 1999.
21. Safar M., Shahabi C., Sun X., Image Retrieval By Shape: A Comparative Study, University of Southern California, November 1999.
22. Victor B., Bowyer K.W., Sarkar S., An Evaluation of Face and Ear Biometrics, Proc. of Intl. Conf. on Pattern Recognition, I: 429-432, 2002.
23. Zhang D., Automated Biometrics – Technologies and Systems, Kluwer Academic Publishers, 2000.

CHAPTER 19

IMPROVEMENT OF MODAL MATCHING IMAGE OBJECTS IN DYNAMIC PEDOBAROGRAPHY USING OPTIMIZATION TECHNIQUES

João Manuel R. S. Tavares[*] and Luísa Ferreira Bastos[+]

* *Laboratório de Óptica e Mecânica Experimental, Instituto de Engenharia Mecânica e Gestão Industrial / Departamento de Engenharia Mecânica e Gestão Industrial, Faculdade de Engenharia da Universidade do Porto, Rua Dr. Roberto Frias, s/n, 4200-465, Porto, PORTUGAL E-mail: tavares@fe.up.pt, url: www.fe.up.pt/~tavares*

+ *Laboratório de Óptica e Mecânica Experimental, Instituto de Engenharia Mecânica e Gestão Industrial, Rua Dr. Roberto Frias, s/n, 4200-465, Porto, PORTUGAL E-mail: lbastos@fe.up.pt*

This paper presents an improved approach for matching objects represented in dynamic pedobarography image sequences, based on finite element modeling, modal analysis and optimization techniques.

In this work, the determination of correspondences between objects data points is improved by using optimization techniques and, because the number of data points of each object is not necessary the same, a new algorithm to match the excess points is also proposed. This new matching algorithm uses a neighbourhood criterion and can overcome some disadvantages of the usual "one to one" matching.

The considered approach allows the determination of correspondences between 2D or 3D objects data points, and is here apply in dynamic pedobarography images.

1. Introduction

In several areas of Computational Vision, one of the main problems consists in the determination of correspondences between objects represented in different images, and on the computation of robust canonical descriptors that can be used for their recognition.

In this paper, is presented a methodology to address the above problem, based on an approach initially proposed by Sclaroff[1, 2], and in this work improved by using optimization algorithms in the matching phase. A new algorithm to determine the correspondences between excess models nodes is also proposed, and can be used when the objects to be matched are represented by different number of data points. With this new algorithm, we can successfully overcome some disadvantages of the usual "one to one" matching as, for example, loss of information along image sequences.

The application of the proposed matching methodology on deformable objects represented in dynamic pedobarography image sequences leads to very promising results, and will be discussed in this paper.

The following sections present a brief introduction to the background problem, the dynamic pedobarography principle, the used object models, the proposed matching methodology, experimental results obtained on deformable objects represented in dynamic pedobarography images and some conclusions.

1.1. Background

There is an eigen methods class[2] that derives its parameterization directly from objects data shape. Some of these techniques also try to determine, explicitly and automatically, the correspondences between characteristic points sets, while others try to match images using more global approaches instead of local ones. Each eigen method decomposes the object deformation in an orthogonal and ordered base.

Usually, solution methods for the matching problem include several restrictions that prevent inadequate matches according to some criteria, as for example: order[3, 4]; rigidity[3, 4]; unicity[5]; visibility[6]; and proximity[2]. Some of these methods are image correlation (it is presumed that the images are similar)[7], point proximity[8], and smoothness of disparity fields[3].

The matching problem can also be interpreted as an optimization problem, in which the objective function can, for example, depend on any criteria mentioned in the previous paragraph, and the restrictions considered must form a non-empty space of possible solutions. To solve this optimization problem, it can be used dynamic programming[3], graphs[4] and convex minimization[7]. Non-optimal approaches include, for example, greedy algorithms[9], simulated annealing[10], relaxation[5], etc.

To determine correspondences between two objects, Belongie[11] considered shapes context, and a similar optimization technique to the one used in this work. Although shape description algorithms have usually a higher computational efficiency, the modeling methodology considered in this work as the major advantage of attributing a physical behaviour to each object to be matched, through the consideration of a virtual elastic material.

2. Dynamic Pedobarography

Pedobarography refers to measuring and visualizing the distribution of pressure under the foot sole. The recording of pedobarographic data along the duration of a step, in normal walking conditions, permits the dynamic analysis of the foot behavior. This introduction of the time dimension augments the potential of this type of clinical examination as an auxiliary tool for diagnostics and therapy planning[12].

The basic pedobarography system consists of a transparent plate trans-illuminated through its borders in such a way that the light is internally reflected. The plate is covered on its top by a single or dual thin layer of soft porous plastic material where the pressure is applied (see Fig. 1).

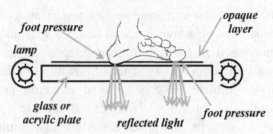

Figure 1. Basic (pedo)barography principle.

When observed from below, in the absence of applied pressure the plate is dark. However, when pressure is applied on top of the plastic layer, the plate displays bright areas that correspond to the light crossing the plate after reflection on the plastic layer. This reflection occurs due to the alteration of the local relation of light refraction indices resulting from the depletion of the air interface between the glass plate and the plastic layer. A good choice of materials and an adequate calibration of the image acquisition system, allow a nearly proportional relation between the local pressure and the observed brightness.

Using a practical setup as the one represented in Fig. 2, a time sequence of pressure images can be captured. Fig. 3 shows thirteen images of a captured sample sequence; as can be verified, the image data is very dense, as opposed to other measuring methods, and very rich in terms of the information it conveys on the interaction between the foot sole and the flat plate.

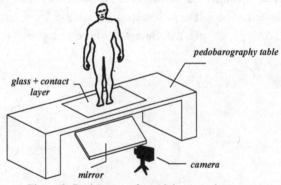

Figure 2. Basic setup of a pedobarography system.

3. Object Models

In the initial stages of the work, the object contours in each image were extracted and the matching process was oriented to the contours' pixels[2,13]. A practical difficulty arising from this approach is the possible existence of more than one contour for the object represented in each image (i. e. see Fig. 7). To find the correspondence between each contours pair along the image sequence, two possible solutions were considered: i) use of a Kalman filtering (see[13], for example) approach to estimate and track the location of the contours' centroids along the image sequence; ii) use of a measure of the deformation energy necessary to align each contour pairs, selecting the lower energy pairs.

However, an additional problem is still present: the possibility that along the image sequence various contours will merge or split. In order to accommodate this possibility, a new model has been developed, similar to the one used in various applications working with controlled environment, such as in face analysis and recognition[14, 15]: The brightness level of each pixel is considered as the third coordinate of a 3D surface point. The resulting single surface model solves the two aforementioned problems.

The use of the surface model, also simplifies the consideration of isobaric contours, which are important in pedobarographic analysis, either for matching contours of equal pressure along the time sequence or for matching contours of different pressure in a single image[12, 13].

The following sections describe the object models used in this work and briefly describe their construction. Each model has its own advantages and shortcomings; for every particular problem, the best choice must be made[12, 13].

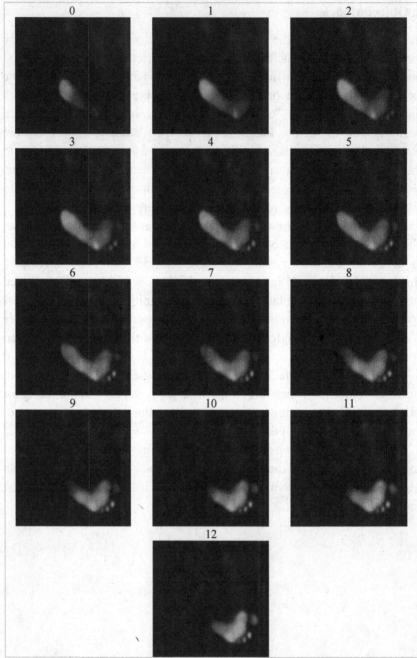

Figure 3. Example of a captured sequence composed by thirteen images.

3.1. Contour Model

To determine the correspondence among two contours were used two modeling approaches:

- For each contour is used a single 2D Sclaroff's isoparametric finite element. In building this type of element, no previous ordering of the data points is required and Gaussian functions are used as interpolations functions. The method to determine the mass and stiffness matrices for this 2D element is described in[1], for example.

- For each contour is built a finite elements model using linear axial finite elements (see Fig. 4). For this type of discretisation a previous ordering of the contour data points is required. The matrix formulation for these finite elements can be found in[16], for example.

To determine in each image the contour pixels, are used standard image processing and analysis techniques; namely, thresholding, edge enhancement, hysteresis line detection and tracking[2]. For example, Fig. 6 and 7 show the intermediate result and the final contours obtained from the image of Fig. 5.

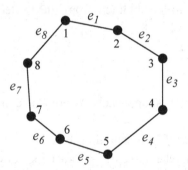

Figure 4. Modeling a contour by using a set e_i of axial finite elements.

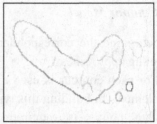

Figure 5. Image (negated) where contours must be found.

Figure 6. Result image after edge enhancement.

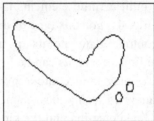

Figure 7. Contours obtained by a line detection and tracking algorithm[2].

The sampled contours obtained from the thirteen images shown in Fig. 3 are presented in Fig. 8.

3.2. Surface Model

For the surface model, two approaches were also considered:

- A single 3D Sclaroff's isoparametric finite element is used for each surface to be matched. Again, it must be noticed that there is no requirement for previous ordering of the surface nodes. The matrix building for these finite elements can be found in[1].
- Each surface model is built by using linear axial finite elements (see Fig. 9). The previous ordering of the surface data points is required. The matrix formulation for these finite elements can be found in[16], for example.

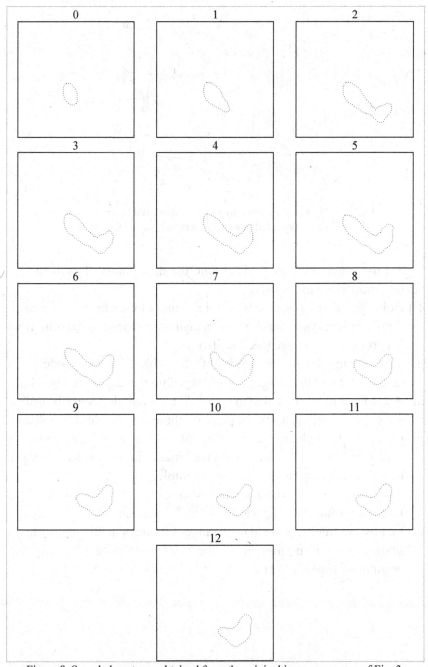

Figure 8. Sampled contours obtained from the original image sequence of Fig. 3.

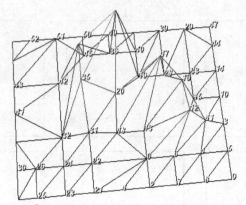

Figure 9. Modeling a surface by using a set of axial finite elements.
(Each node is connected to its neighbors through axial elements.)

The used methodology to determine the data points of each surface can be summarized as follows:

(i) Noise pixels (that is, pixels with brightness lower than a calibration threshold level) are removed and a Gaussian-shaped smoothing filter is applied to the image (see Fig. 10);

(ii) The circumscribing rectangle of the object to be modeled is determined and the image is sampled within that area (see Fig. 11);

(iii) A 2D Delaunay triangulation (see[25, 26], for example) is performed on the sampled points, using the point brightness as the third coordinate;

(iv) In order to reduce the number of nodes used, and thus the computational cost, the triangular mesh is simplified using a decimation algorithm (see[25, 26], for example);

(v) To reduce the high frequency noise associated to the mesh, is used a Laplacian smoothing algorithm (see[25, 26], for example);

(vi) Finally, in order to have similar ranges of values in all coordinates, a scale change is performed on the third coordinate (derived from brightness) (see Fig. 12).

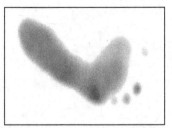

Figure 10. Image (negated) after noise removal and Gaussian filtering.

Figure 11. Object sampling.

Figure 12. Resulting surface.

The surfaces obtained from the original images presented in Fig. 3 are visible in Fig. 13. The original images with identification (ID) 0 (zero) and 1 (one) were not considered.

3.3. Isobaric Contour Model

As in the two previous models, the approaches used to match isobaric contours are:

- A single Sclaroff's isoparametric finite element, either 2D or 3D, is used to model each contour.
- A set of linear axial finite elements are used to build each contour model.

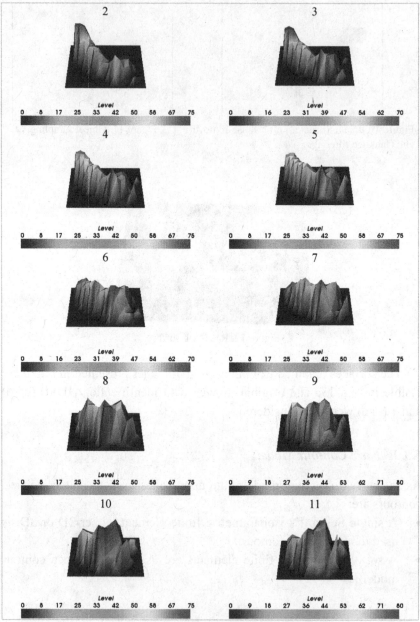

Figure 13. Surfaces obtained from the last eleven images of the example sequence (continue).

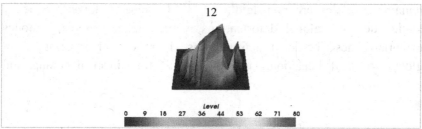

Figure 13. Surfaces obtained from the last eleven images of the example sequence (conclusion).

The isobaric contours are extracted from the correspondent surface, beforehand obtained using the procedures described in the previous section (see Fig. 14).

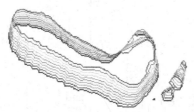

Figure 14. Ten isobaric contours extracted from the surface of Fig. 12.

4. Matching Methodology

Fig. 15 displays a diagram of the adopted physical matching methodology. The locations of the objects data points in each image, $X = [X_1 \ldots X_m]$, are used as the nodes of a finite elements model made of an elastic material. Next, the eigenmodes $\{\phi\}_i$ of the model are computed, providing an orthogonal description of the object and its natural deformations, ordered by frequency. Using a matrix based notation, the eigenvectors matrix $[\Phi]$ and the eigenvalues diagonal matrix $[\Omega]$ can be written as in equation (1) for 2D objects and as in equation (2) for 3D objects.

The eigenvectors, also called shape vectors[1, 2, 16, 17], describe how each vibration mode deforms the object by changing the original data point locations: $X_{deformed} = X + a\{\phi\}_i$. The first three (in 2D) or six (in 3D) vibration modes are the rigid body modes of translation and rotation; the remaining modes are non-rigid[1, 2, 16, 17]. In general, lower frequency modes describe global deformations, while higher frequency modes essentially describe local deformations. This type of ordering, from global to local behaviour, is quite useful for object matching and recognition.

$$[\Phi] = \left[\{\phi\}_1 | \cdots | \{\phi\}_{2m}\right] = \begin{bmatrix} \{u\}_1^T \\ \vdots \\ \{u\}_m^T \\ \{v\}_1^T \\ \vdots \\ \{v\}_m^T \end{bmatrix} \text{ and } [\Omega] = \begin{bmatrix} \omega_1^2 & & 0 \\ & \ddots & \\ 0 & & \omega_{2m}^2 \end{bmatrix}, \quad (1)$$

$$[\Phi] = \left[\{\phi\}_1 | \cdots | \{\phi\}_{3m}\right] = \begin{bmatrix} \{u\}_1^T \\ \vdots \\ \{u\}_m^T \\ \{v\}_1^T \\ \vdots \\ \{v\}_m^T \\ \{w\}_1^T \\ \vdots \\ \{w\}_m^T \end{bmatrix} \text{ and } [\Omega] = \begin{bmatrix} \omega_1^2 & & 0 \\ & \ddots & \\ 0 & & \omega_{3m}^2 \end{bmatrix}. \quad (2)$$

The eigenmodes also form an orthogonal, object-centred coordinate system for the location of the data points, i.e., the location of each point is uniquely described in terms of each eigenmode displacement. The transformation between the Cartesian image coordinates and the modal coordinates system is achieved through the eigenvectors matrix of the physical model.

Two sets of data points, for example, corresponding to the objects represented in two different images of a sequence, are to be compared in the modal eigenspace. The main idea is that the low order modes of two similar objects will be very close, even in the presence of an affine transformation, a non-rigid deformation, a local shape variation, or noise.

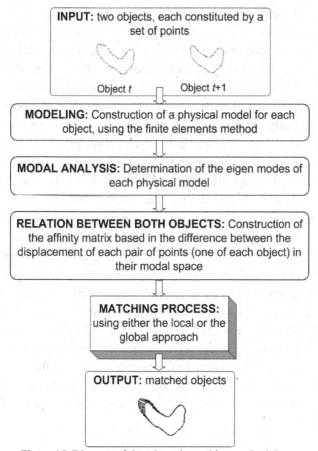

Figure 15. Diagram of the adopted matching methodology.

Using the above concept, data correspondence is obtained by modal matching. In this work, two matching search procedures are considered: (i) a local search or (ii) a global search. Both search strategies consider an affinity matrix $[Z]$, constructed from the Euclidian distance between the characteristic vectors of each physical model, whose elements are, for 2D and for 3D, respectively:

$$Z_{ij} = \left\| \{u\}_{t,i} - \{u\}_{t+1,j} \right\|^2 + \left\| \{v\}_{t,i} - \{v\}_{t+1,j} \right\|^2, \qquad (3)$$

$$Z_{ij} = \left\| \{u\}_{t,i} - \{u\}_{t+1,j} \right\|^2 + \left\| \{v\}_{t,i} - \{v\}_{t+1,j} \right\|^2 + \left\| \{w\}_{t,i} - \{w\}_{t+1,j} \right\|^2. \qquad (4)$$

The local search strategy was proposed in the original modal matching methodology[1, 2, 13], and basically it consists in seeking each row of the affinity matrix for its lowest value, considering the associated correspondence if, and only if, that value is also the lowest of the related column. With this search philosophy, the models nodes are considered as independent entities and so the original object structure is ignore.

As previously referred, the matching problem considering only matches of type "one to one" and objects with equal number of data points can be considered as a classical assignment problem, which is a particular case of an optimization problem[18, 20]. In the formulation of this type of problem is assumed that: the number of data points of both objects is the same, n; it is known the assignment cost, Z_{ij}, of each pair of points (i, j), where i is a point of object t and j is a point of object $t+1$. As the notation tries to evidence, this assignment cost is equal to the element in line i and column j of the affinity matrix, $[Z]$.

The assignment problem initially appeared to mathematically formulate problems in which n jobs/works must be distributed by n tasks, with the restriction that each job/work had to be assigned to one, and only one, task and vice-versa, subject to the minimization of the global assignment cost. In this work, the jobs/works are the data points of the object t and the tasks are the data points of the object $t+1$. So, for the mathematical formulation of this matching problem, let's consider:

$$x_{ij} = \begin{cases} 1 & \text{if point } i \text{ of } t \text{ is assigned to point } j \text{ of } t+1 \\ 0 & \text{otherwise} \end{cases}, \quad (5)$$

with i, $j = 1, 2, ..., n$. Next expressions follow the typical structure of a mathematical programming problem, with an objective function and a set of restrictions in the problem's variables:

$$\text{minimize } f = \sum_{i=1}^{n} \sum_{j=1}^{n} Z_{ij} x_{ij}, \quad (6)$$

$$\text{subject to } \sum_{j=1}^{n} x_{ij} = 1, \text{ with } i = 1, 2, ..., n, \quad (7)$$

$$\sum_{i=1}^{n} x_{ij} = 1, \text{ with } j = 1, 2, ..., n, \quad (8)$$

$$and \ x_{ij} \in \{0,1\}, \forall i,j \ . \tag{9}$$

In equation (6), the function f takes the value of the assignment total cost. The first restriction (7), forces each data point in object t to be assigned to one, and only one, data point in object $t+1$. The second restriction (8), forces each data point in object $t+1$ to be assigned to one, and only one, data point in object t. The third and last restriction (9), forces the problem's variables, x_{ij} $(i,j = 1,2,...,n)$, to take one of the two possible values $\{0,1\}$.

To solve the assignment (matching) problem we considered three algorithms: the *Hungarian* method[18, 19]; the *Simplex* method for flow problems[18, 21]; and the *LAPm* algorithm[18, 22]. The *Hungarian* method is the most well known method for the resolution of the assignment problem. The *Simplex* method for flow problems solves problems with less rigid restrictions than the assignment problem, but where this last can be included as a special case. The *LAPm* method is a considerably recent algorithm developed to solve classical assignment problems.

Once the optimal global matching solution is found, as in the original local matching procedure, the matches that exceed a pre-established matching threshold level are eliminated from that solution. The relevance of this restriction is higher with this global matching approach, because a solution of the assignment problem always has the maximum number of matches of type "one to one", due to the problem's restrictions.

Case the number of data points of the two objects to be matches are different, with the usual matching restriction that allows only matches of type "one to one", will necessarily exist data points that will not be matched. The solution found was initially add fictitious points to the model with fewer data points; this way, we solve the optimization problem requirement of the affinity matrix be necessarily square. Then, after the optimization phase, we have some real objects data points, the excess points, matched with the fictitious elements previously add. Finally, these excess points are matched adequately with real objects data points, using a neighbourhood and an affinity criterion, as follows:

- For each excess point, the developed algorithm fits it between its matched nearest neighbours;

- From the correspondences of those neighbours in the other object, it is determined the best correspondence for the excess point, minimizing the costs and considering that the neighbours must remain as so and that there must not exist crossed matches;
- As in the optimization phase, the obtained matches will only be considered as good matches if, and only if, the pre-established matching threshold level is respected.

With this solution, for the excess objects data points are allowed matches of type "one to many" or vice versa.

Note that, for all the used methodologies in the matching framework it is not considered any additional information about the original image sequence neither about the represented objects.

5. Results

The presented matching methodology was integrated in a generic software platform for deformable objects[2, 23], previous developed using *Microsoft Visual C^{++}*, the *Newmat*[24] library for matrix computation and the *VTK - The Visualization Toolkit*[25, 26] for 3D visualization, mesh triangulation, simplification and smoothing, and for isobaric contours extraction.

This section presents some experimental results obtained on objects extracted from dynamic pedobarography images, using the adopted matching methodology. First, are presented results considering contour, then surface, and finally isocontour models. In all cases, the object pairs considered were just selected for example purposes.

All the results presented in this section, were obtained considering in the objects modeling the Sclaroff's isoparametric finite element and rubber as the virtual elastic material, and using 25% of the models vibration modes in the matching phase.

5.1. Contour Object Matching

Considering the pairs of contours with ID 2/3, 3/4 and 10/11, previously presented in Fig. 8, using the matching methodology adopted, we obtain the matches shown in Fig. 16, 17, and 18, respectively. In these figures, the contours data points, and also the matched pairs, are connected for better visualization.

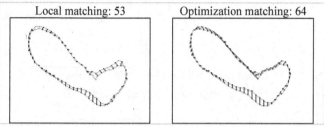

Figure 16. Matches obtained between contours with ID 2 (64 nodes) and 3 (64 nodes).

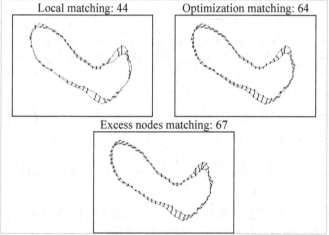

Figure 17. Matches obtained between contours with ID 3 (64 nodes) and 4 (67 nodes).

The matches found between the contours extracted from the last eleven images (ID 2 to 12) of the example sequence, are present in Fig. 19. The number and the percentage of matches obtained during the same sequence are indicated in Table 1.

The results obtained using the local search strategy, were in range of 50.2% to 82.8% and present all good quality; instead, the optimization search procedure had always 100% of matching success, and in generally the found matches also have good quality and the excess nodes were reasonably matched.

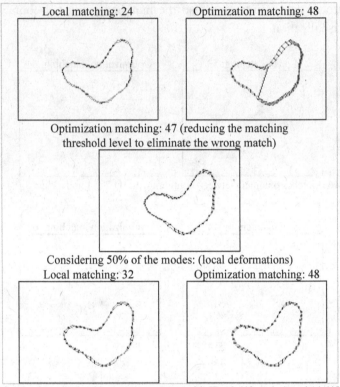

Figure 18. Matches obtained between contours with ID 10 (48 nodes) and 11 (48 nodes).

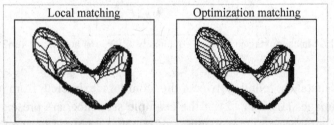

Figure 19. Matches obtained between all eleven contours (from ID 2 to 12).

One important remark is the use of the same methodology parameters for all matching cases. If the parameters were adjusted for each contour pair, the results could be improved. In the same way, the matching threshold level was chosen to allow all the established matches, avoiding the rejection of the less adequate matches (see Fig. 18, for example).

Table 1. Number (N° Match) and percentage of matches (% Match) obtained between the contours extracted from the last eleven images (ID 2 to 12) of the example sequence.

contours ID	N° Nodes	N° Match	% Match	N° Match	% Match	N° Match
		Local		*Optimization*		*Excess Nodes*
2, 3	64/64	53	82,8%	64	100%	
3, 4	64/67	44	68,8%	64	100%	67
4, 5	67/67	55	82,1%	67	100%	
5, 6	67/64	47	73,4%	64	100%	67
6, 7	64/58	46	79,3%	58	100%	64
7, 8	58/51	30	58,8%	51	100%	58
8, 9	51/50	33	66,0%	50	100%	51
9, 10	50/48	26	54,2%	48	100%	50
10, 11	48/48	24	50,0%	48	100%	
11, 12	48/46	25	54,3%	46	100%	48

5.2. Surface Matching

The matches found between the surfaces models with ID 2/3, 4/5 and 11/12, each one build from the correspondent image of the example sequence, using the adopted matching methodology, are shown in the Fig. 20, 21, and 22, respectively. In these figures, the matched nodes are connected for better viewing and two different views are presented.

The number and the percentage of matches obtained considering the surfaces models build from the last eleven images of the example sequence are indicated in Table 2.

The results of the local search strategy were in range of 33.3% to 87.8%, and, attending to the high objects deformation, we can consider that the found matches have good quality. In other hand, the search strategy based on optimization techniques had always 100%, and generally the matches present also good quality.

As in the contour case, all the parameters of the matching methodology were considered constant along the sequence.

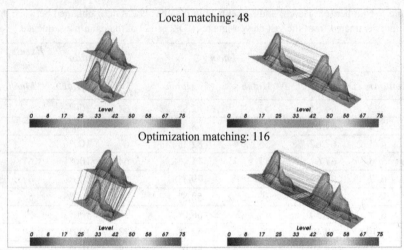

Figure 20. Matches obtained between surfaces with ID 2 (116 nodes) and 3 (131 nodes).

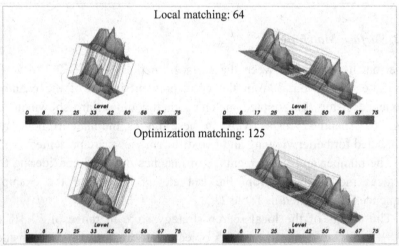

Figure 21. Matches obtained between surfaces with ID 4 (131 nodes) and 5 (125 nodes).

5.3. Isocontour Matching

Using the proposed matching methodology to establish the correspondences between the isocontours with ID 1/2, 4/5, and 6/7, all extracted from the image with ID 6 of the example sequence, were obtained the matches shown in Fig. 23, 24, and 25, respectively. As in the surface case, in these figures the matched nodes are connected and two different views are presented.

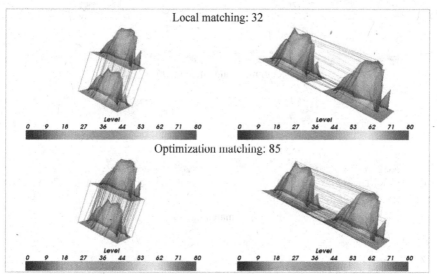

Figure 22. Matches obtained between surfaces with ID 11 (99 nodes) and 12 (85 nodes).

Table 2. Number (Nº Match) and percentage of matches (% Match) obtained with the surfaces build from the last eleven images of the example sequence.

| Surfaces ID | Nº Nodes | Local | | Optimization | |
		Nº Match	% Match	Nº Match	% Match
2, 3	116/131	48	41,3%	116	100%
3, 4	131/131	115	87,8%	131	100%
4, 5	131/125	64	51,2%	125	100%
5, 6	125/109	67	61,5%	109	100%
6, 7	109/107	51	47,7%	107	100%
7, 8	107/96	32	33,3%	96	100%
8, 9	96/98	52	54,1%	96	100%
9, 10	98/95	56	58,9%	95	100%
10, 11	95/99	52	54,7%	95	100%
11, 12	99/85	32	37,4%	85	100%

The matches found considering eleven isocontours extracted from the same image (with ID 6) of the example sequence are shown in Fig. 26.

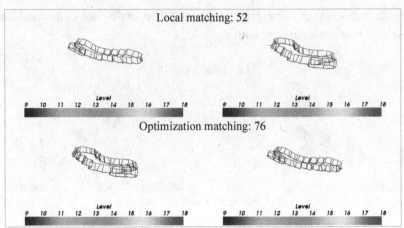

Figure 23. Matches obtained between isocontours with ID 1 (76 nodes) and 2 (76 nodes).

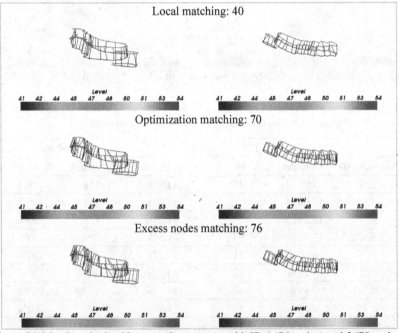

Figure 24. Matches obtained between isocontours with ID 4 (76 nodes) and 5 (70 nodes).

The number and the percentage of the obtained matches considering the referred eleven isocontours are indicated in Table 3.

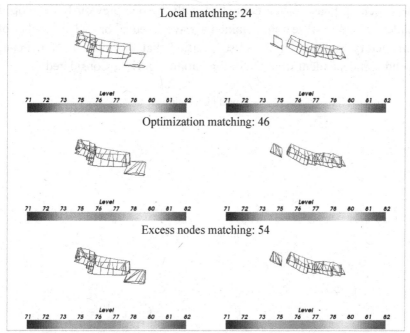

Figure 25. Matches obtained between isocontours with ID 6 (54 nodes) and 7 (46 nodes).

Using the local search strategy, the results obtained were in range of 50.0% to 94.1%, and the matches found could be considered of good quality. Instead, the search based on optimization techniques had always 100% of matching success, and in generally the matches found have also good quality and the excess nodes were reasonably matched.

As in the contour and surface cases, the matching results obtained could be improved if the parameters of the adopted methodology were adjusted for each isocontour pair.

6. Conclusions

The several experimental tests carried through this work, some reported in this paper, allow the presentation of some observations and conclusions.

The physical methodology proposed, for the determination of correspondences between two objects, using optimization techniques on the matching phase, when compared with the one previously developed that considers local search, obtained always an equal or higher number of satisfactory matches. It was also verified that the number of matches found is independent from the optimization algorithm considered.

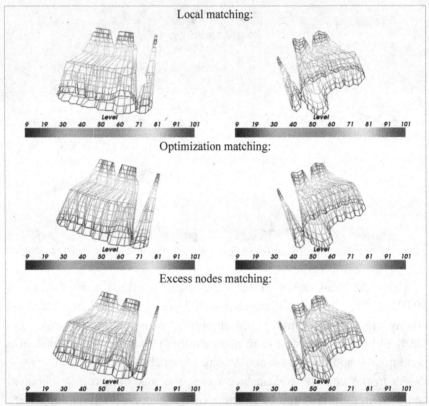

Figure 26. Matches obtained between the eleven isocontours extracted from the image with ID 6 of the example sequence.

In some experimental cases, in order to obtain a higher number of satisfactory matches using the local search strategy, the parameters of the physical methodology had to be carefully chosen. In those same cases, the application of the optimization strategy in the matching phase, beyond the good quality of the matches found, revealed less sensible to the methodology parameters. This suggests that using the proposed global search strategy in the matching phase, the adopted physical methodology become easier to handle and also more adjustable to different kinds of applications.

Table 3. Number (N° Match) and percentage of matches (% Match) obtained with the eleven isocontours extracted from the image with ID 6 of the example sequence.

Isocontours ID	N° Nodes	Local N° Match	% Match	Optimization N° Match	% Match	Excess Nodes N° Match
1, 2	76/76	52	68,4%	76	100%	
2, 3	76/74	58	78,4%	74	100%	76
3, 4	74/76	50	67,6%	74	100%	76
4, 5	76/70	40	57,1%	70	100%	76
5, 6	70/54	32	59,3%	54	100%	70
6, 7	54/46	24	52,2%	46	100%	54
7, 8	46/38	22	57,9%	38	100%	46
8, 9	38/34	17	50,0%	34	100%	38
9, 10	34/34	32	94,1%	34	100%	
10, 11	34/34	17	50,0%	34	100%	

To have satisfactory matching results in some of the examples considered, when compared with the local search strategy, the global search strategy always required an inferior number of eigenvectors in the affinity matrix construction. This suggests that the total computational effort of the global matching methodology can be reduced if optimization techniques are considered.

In terms of execution time, the optimization algorithm that uses the *Hungarian* method showed to be of low efficiency. In the several experimental examples performed, the *Simplex* algorithm for flow problems revealed the most efficient among the optimization algorithms considered. The execution time of *LAPm* algorithm was higher than the Simplex algorithm for flow problems, even being a more specific algorithm for this type of problems. This can be dew to the interval in which lay the elements of the affinity matrix, [0; 1], since when this algorithm was tested in [27] it revealed the most efficient when the considered interval was [1; 100].

In the several experimental tests performed considering contour objects, the implemented algorithm for the determination of correspondences of the excess data points always finds satisfactory matches. That allows us to conclude that the referred algorithm can become an interesting base for the development of new solutions for the determination of matches of type "one to many" and vice versa, and that should be ported to more complex objects (i. e., surfaces).

The experimental results shown in this paper, confirm that the proposed physical methodology can satisfactory match objects represented in dynamic pedobarography images, and that the use of the pixel brightness values as a third Cartesian coordinate is very satisfactory, both in terms of its interpretation as pressure, and in solving the problems associated to merging or the splitting of objects.

Acknowledgments

This work was partially done in the scope of project "Segmentation, Tracking and Motion Analysis of Deformable (2D/3D) Objects using Physical Principles", with reference POSC/EEA-SRI/55386/2004, financially supported by *FCT – Fundação para a Ciência e a Tecnologia* from Portugal.

References

1. S. E. Sclaroff and A. Pentland, "Modal Matching for Correspondence and Recognition", *IEEE Transactions on Pattern Analysis and Machine Intelligence*, vol. 17, pp. 545-561, 1995.
2. J. M. R. S. Tavares, PhD Thesis, "Análise de Movimento de Corpos Deformáveis usando Visão Computacional", in *Faculdade de Engenharia da Universidade do Porto*, Portugal, 2000.
3. Y. Ohta and T. Kanade, "Stereo by Intra- and Inter-Scanline Search using Dynamic Programming", *IEEE Transactions on Pattern Analysis and Machine Intelligence*, vol. 7, pp. 139-154, 1985.
4. S. Roy and I. J. Cox, "A Maximum-Flow Formulation of the N-camera Stereo Correspondence Problem", presented at *International Conference on Computer Vision (ICCV'98)*, Bombay, India, 1998.

5. S. Gold, A. Rangarajan, C. P. La, S. Pappu and E. Mjolsness, "New algorithms for 2D and 3D point matching: pose estimation and correspondence", *Pattern Recognition*, vol. 31, pp. 1019-1031, 1998.

6. C. Silva, PhD Thesis, "3D Motion and Dense Structure Estimation: Representation for Visual Perception and the Interpretation of Occlusions", in *Instituto Superior Técnico: Universidade Técnica de Lisboa*, Portugal, 2001.

7. J. L. Maciel and J. P. Costeira, "A Global Solution to Sparse Correspondence Problems", *IEEE Transactions on Pattern Analysis and Machine Intelligence*, vol. 25, pp. 187-199, 2003.

8. Z. Zhang, "Iterative Point Matching for Registration of Free-Form Curves", *INRIA*, Technical Report RR-1658, April 1992.

9. M. S. Wu and J. J. Leou, "A Bipartite Matching Approach to Feature Correspondence in Stereo Vision", *Pattern Recognition Letters*, vol. 16, pp. 23-31, 1995.

10. J. P. P. Starink and E. Backer, "Finding Point Correspondences using Simulated Annealing", *Pattern Recognition*, vol. 28, pp. 231-240, 1995.

11. S. Belongie, J. Malik and J. Puzicha, "Shape Matching and Object Recognition using Shape Context", *IEEE Transactions on Pattern Analysis and Machine Intelligence*, vol. 24, pp. 509-522, 2002.

12. A. J. Padilha, L. A. Serra, S. A. Pires and A. F. N. Silva, "Caracterização Espacio-Temporal de Pressões Plantares em Pedobarografia Dinâmica", *FEUP/INEB*, Internal Report, 1995.

13. J. M. R. S. Tavares, J. Barbosa and A. Padilha, "Matching Image Objects in Dynamic Pedobarography", presented at *11th Portuguese Conference on Pattern Recognition (RecPad'00)*, Porto, Portugal, 2000.

14. T. F. Cootes and C. J. Taylor, "Modelling Object Appearance Using The Grey-Level Surface", presented at *British Machine Vision Conference (BMVC'94)*, 1994.

15. B. Moghaddam, C. Nastar and A. P. Pentland, "Bayesian Face Recognition using Deformable Intensity Surfaces", *MIT Media Laboratory*, Technical Report N° 371, 1996.

16. K.-J. Bathe, Finite Element Procedures, *Prentice Hall*, 1996.

17. S. Graham Kelly, Fundamentals of Mechanical Vibrations, *McGraw-Hill*, 1993.

18. L. F. Bastos and J. M. R. S. Tavares, "Optimization in Modal Matching for Correspondence of Objects Nodal Points", presented at *7th Portuguese Conference on Biomedical Engineering (BioEng'2003)*, Fundação Calouste Gulbenkian, Lisboa, Portugal, 2003.

19. F. S. Hillier and G. J. Lieberman, Introduction to Operations Research. *Mcgraw-Hill*, 1995.

20. L. F. Bastos, MSc Thesis, "Optimização da Determinação das Correspondências entre Objectos Deformáveis no Espaço Modal", in *Faculdades de Engenharia e Ciências: Universidade do Porto*, Portugal, 2003.

21. A. Löbel, "MFC - A Network Simplex Implementation", *Konrad-Zuse-Zentrum für Informationstechnik Berlin*, Division Scientific Computing, Department Optimization, 2000.
22. A. Volgenant, "Linear and Semi-Assignment Problems: A Core Oriented Approach", *Computers and Operations Research*, vol. 23, pp. 917-932, 1996.
23. J. M. R. S. Tavares, J. Barbosa and A. Padilha, "Apresentação de um Banco de Desenvolvimento e Ensaio para Objectos Deformáveis", *Revista Electrónica de Sistemas de Informação*, vol. 1, 2002.
24. R. Davies, Newmat, A matrix library in C++, 2005.
25. The VTK User's Guide, *Kitware Inc.*, 2003.
26. W. Schroeder, K. Martin and B. Lorensen, The Visualization Toolkit, 3rd Edition, *Kitware Inc*, 2002.
27. M. Dell'Amico and P. Tooth, "Algorithms and Codes for Dense Assignment Problems: The State of The Art", *Discrete Applied Mathematics*, 100, pp. 17-48, 2000.

CHAPTER 20

TRAJECTORY ANALYSIS FOR SPORT AND VIDEO SURVEILLANCE

Y. Lopez de Meneses, P. Roduit* [+], F. Luisier and J. Jacot*

Laboratoire de Production Microtechnique (LPM)
[+] *Swarm-Intelligent System Group (SWIS)*
Ecole Polytechnique Fédérale de Lausanne, 1015 Lausanne, Switzerland
E-mail: pierre.roduit@epfl.ch.

In video surveillance and sports analysis applications, object trajectories offer the possibility of extracting rich information on the underlying behavior of the moving targets. To this end we introduce an extension of Point Distribution Models (PDM) to analyze the object motion in their spatial, temporal and spatiotemporal dimensions. These trajectory models represent object paths as an average trajectory and a set of deformation modes, in the spatial, temporal and spatiotemporal domains. Thus any given motion can be expressed in terms of its modes, which in turn can be ascribed to a particular behavior.

The proposed analysis tool has been tested on motion data extracted from a vision system that was tracking radio-guided cars running inside a circuit. This affords an easier interpretation of results, because the shortest lap provides a reference behavior. Besides showing an actual analysis we discuss how to normalize trajectories to have a meaningful analysis.

20.1. Introduction

Object tracking at frame-rate on standard desktop computers has been rendered possible by faster and cheaper hardware (cameras, frame-grabbers, processors). This has sprung up many applications in video surveillance,[1] sports analysis,[2] human-machine interfaces,[3] robotics,[4] and ethology.[5,6] Since tracking data is now relatively easy to acquire,[7] it is necessary to process it and to extract meaningful information for higher-level tasks such as behavior analysis or sportsmen performance evaluation.

This project intends to develop new analysis tools to characterize the gestures or motions of sportsmen by means of their trajectories or the trajectories of their extremities. To this end, we intend to use deformable templates to build meaningful models of a set of trajectories. These deformable models should allow to describe variations around an average or reference trajectory. Point Distribution Models (PDMs)[8] are one kind of deformable templates of particular interest because of their statistical meaning and simple mathematical expression. They have been applied to model object shapes. However a trajectory is more than a geometric shape; it comprises also temporal information that can be of key importance in some analyses. This paper proposes an adaptation of Point Distribution Models to analyze trajectories in their spatial, temporal and spatiotemporal dimensions.

This paper is organized as follows. In the next section, Point Distribution Models will be succinctly presented together with the adaptations introduced to model temporal information. Section 20.3 will describe the experiments we have conducted with trajectories from radio-controlled cars and a discussion will close the paper.

20.2. Point Distribution Models for Trajectories

A trajectory can be represented as an ordered set of points π in space and time. Without loss of generality we shall consider trajectories lying on a plane and hence, given a set of trajectories, the ith point in the kth trajectory can be written as

$$\pi_i^k = \left[x_i^k \ y_i^k \ t_i^k\right]^T, \tag{20.1}$$

where x_i^k, y_i^k are the spatial coordinates and t_i^k is in the temporal dimension. The kth trajectory, τ_k, made up of N points $\pi_1^k \ldots \pi_N^k$, is then written as

$$\tau_k = \left[x_1^k \ldots x_N^k \ y_1^k \ldots y_N^k \ t_1^k \ldots t_N^k\right]^T. \tag{20.2}$$

As described in,[8] each trajectory in the set can be described as the superposition of an average or reference trajectory and a linear combination of deformation modes:

$$\tau_k = \overline{\tau} + P \cdot B_k, \tag{20.3}$$

where $P = [p_1 \ p_2 \ldots p_r]$ is the matrix of eigenvectors of the covariance matrix

$$S = \frac{1}{K-1} \sum_{i=1}^{K} (\tau_i - \overline{\tau})(\tau_i - \overline{\tau})^T = P \cdot \Lambda \cdot P^{-1} \tag{20.4}$$

and K is the number of trajectories available in the training set and $r = \min(3N, K) - 1$ is the number of degrees of freedom in the set.

The computation of matrix P from a set of representative trajectories is known as Principal Component Analysis (PCA)[9] or Karhunen-Love Transform (KLT). It provide the r vectors $[p_1 \ldots p_r]$ or eigenshapes that define a set of orthogonal deformations. These deformations indicate the directions, relative to the mean shape, in which the trajectory points π_i^k are found to be moving. Generally only the M most important or energetic modes ($M \leq r$) are retained, where their energy is defined by the associated eigenvalue λ_i in matrix Λ.

In equation (20.3), B_k is a vector of deformation coefficients defined as

$$B_k = \begin{bmatrix} b_1^k \ b_2^k \ldots b_r^k \end{bmatrix}^T , \tag{20.5}$$

that indicates the contribution of each deformation mode p_i toward the actual shape. For a given trajectory τ_k this contribution B_k is computed as

$$B_k = P^{-1}(\tau_k - \bar{\tau}). \tag{20.6}$$

Vector B_k provides a signature of the trajectory in deformation space. Similar trajectories should have resembling signatures, and since signatures provide a more compact description of trajectories —that is the whole point in using models— they are more convenient for classification tasks.

20.2.1. *Outlier detection*

However, if a given trajectory is very different from the ones in the training set, it will require a large amount of deformation to fit the resulting model. Therefore the deformation coefficients B_k can be used to detect outlier trajectories by using Hotelling's T^2 statistic,[10] which is a multivariate analogue of the t-distribution. To use this statistic, the deformation modes have to be normalized so that they all have the same unit variance. Mathematically it means that we define a new set of normalized modes and coefficients

$$\tilde{P} = P\Lambda^{-\frac{1}{2}} \tag{20.7}$$

$$\tilde{B}_k = \Lambda^{-\frac{1}{2}} B_k. \tag{20.8}$$

where Λ is the diagonal matrix that contains the eigenvalues of the covariance matrix. In this normalized space we can define for each trajectory a scalar value

$$T_k^2 = \tilde{B}_k^T \tilde{B}_k = \sum_{j=1}^{M} (\tilde{b}_j^k)^2 \tag{20.9}$$

where M is the number of principal modes retained. This scalar T_k^2 is the Mahalanobis distance of the trajectory, and it can be interpreted as the normalized deformation energy of the related trajectory. If deformation coefficients b_j^k in the training set were normally distributed, then $(1 - \alpha)\%$ of times the deformation energy would be bounded by the scalar

$$T^2_{\alpha,M,K} = \frac{M \cdot (K-1)}{K - M} F_{M,K-M;\alpha} \qquad (20.10)$$

where $F_{M,K-M;\alpha}$ stands for the Fisher distribution with M and $K-M$ degrees of freedom and $(1 - \alpha)\%$ confidence interval. Therefore a trajectory can be defined as statistically conforming to the set if

$$T^2_k \leq T^2_{\alpha,M,K}. \qquad (20.11)$$

20.2.2. Analysis of temporal information

Trajectories can be analyzed in their spatial, temporal or spatiotemporal dimension by projecting them into the corresponding subspaces. If taken only in their spatial dimensions they become geometric shapes as in the original PDM formulation.[8] If they are projected into the time dimension they provide a temporal profile and can also be analyzed with the same methodology.

A spatiotemporal analysis requires measuring spatial and temporal deformation modes combined, but the variance present in the spatial and temporal components is generally different by orders of magnitude, which means that spatial deformation modes can be "masked" by temporal deformation modes. To avoid this problem, instead of applying the PCA on the covariance matrix, the correlation matrix is used, that is, the difference components are normalized with respect to their variance:

$$\tilde{X}_k = \frac{1}{\sigma_x}[x^k_1 \dots x^k_N]^T \qquad (20.12)$$

$$\tilde{Y}_k = \frac{1}{\sigma_y}[y^k_1 \dots y^k_N]^T \qquad (20.13)$$

$$\tilde{t}_k = \frac{1}{\sigma_t}[t^k_1 \dots t^k_N]^T \qquad (20.14)$$

where σ_x stands for the standard deviation of the x component.

20.3. Experiments

We have applied the analysis described above to a series of trajectories extracted from a vision system that was tracking radio-guided cars running inside a circuit, shown in figure 20.1(a).

This was a playful demonstrator installed during the public festivities for the EPFL's 150th anniversary. Spectators had the possibility of racing 2 cars for about

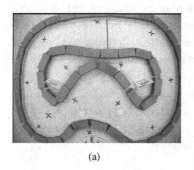
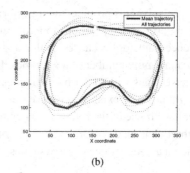

(a)   (b)

Fig. 20.1. On the left, the circuit used for the radio-controlled cars, with the cross markings used for camera calibration purposes. On the right the spatial profile of a set of trajectories for one player (9 trajectories). The average trajectory is indicated with a thicker line.

3 minutes, which implied typically 8-9 laps, which will be the trajectories under study (cf. figure 20.1(b)).

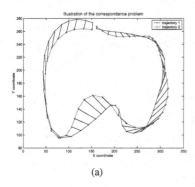
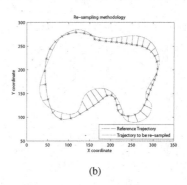

(a)   (b)

Fig. 20.2. On the left the problem of correspondence between the points in two trajectories is shown. On the right, the selected resampling technique is shown: trajectories are resampled along orthogonal lines to the points in a reference trajectory.

Before being analyzed, trajectories have to be preprocessed to meet some requirements imposed by PDMs, such as that they all should have the same number of points. The simplest way is to perform a temporal resampling, whereby each trajectory is fitted by a cubic spline[11] and resampled with a uniform sampling rate on the time axis, but this approach leads to a correspondence problem between points in two trajectories, as shown in figure 20.2(a).

To solve this problem the trajectories are fitted to cubic splines and resampled along orthogonal positions to a reference trajectory (cf. figure 20.2(b)). The reference trajectory is chosen so that it is smooth enough to afford the resampling of the maximum number of trajectories. Indeed, if the trajectory has many bends, the intersections with the orthogonal lines might not respect the original order or they might not even exist. In any case, sensitivity analysis has shown that, for this data set, the choice of the reference trajectory does not have a noticeable impact on the subsequent modes. Once the trajectories are resampled they can be superposed and an average trajectory and modes can be computed.

20.3.1. Purely-spatial analysis

To perform a purely-spatial analysis we deal only with the x_i^k and y_i^k coordinates of the trajectory, removing the temporal values t_i^k. Equation (20.2) becomes

$$\tau_k = \left[x_1^k \ldots x_N^k \, y_1^k \ldots y_N^k \right]^T \tag{20.15}$$

and the analysis is performed as in the original PDM formulation,[8] providing information about the spatial shape of the trajectories.

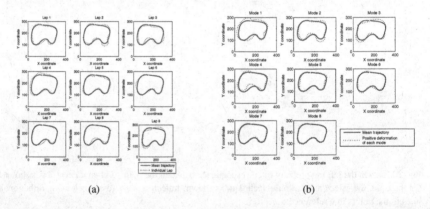

(a)   (b)

Fig. 20.3. On the left side each individual lap is plotted together with the average trajectory $\bar{\tau}$. The right image shows the synthetic trajectory corresponding to each mode p_j with its greatest contribution $\max_k(b_j^k)$ found in the set.

Figure 20.3(a) shows the individual laps together with the average trajectory $\bar{\tau}$. Figure 20.3(b) represents the different modes of the spatial analysis. Each mode is plotted with a coefficient corresponding to the greatest contribution $\max_k(b_j^k)$

found in the set. The modes are ordered by decreasing amount of shape variation (energy). The cumulative energy is plotted in figure 20.4(a), where it can be seen that the first 4 modes contain 85% of the energy in the training set. The last mode can be neglected.

The spatial representation of each mode can be directly linked to the trajectories. Figure 20.4(b) shows mode 2 with different amounts of deformation by generating synthetic trajectories $\tau = \bar{\tau} + B \cdot P$ with a deformation vector $B = [0 \ d \ 0 \ 0 \ 0 \ 0 \ 0 \ 0]$ where only the second component is nonzero. It can be interpreted that this 2nd mode encodes the variability in the way the bottom curves are negotiated, and most particularly the bottom-right curve. Indeed lap 2, which has a variation in that same curve, shows the greatest contribution from mode 2, as seen in figure 20.5(a). A similar relationship can be seen between mode 3 and lap 9. However, the most occurring source of variation, mode 1, represents the global variation among trajectories that follow the inner wall or the outer wall of the circuit.

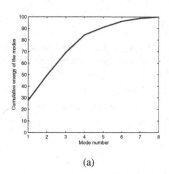

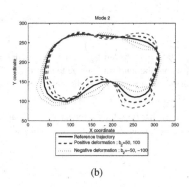

(a)   (b)

Fig. 20.4. On the left, the cumulative energy of the deformation modes $Ce(j) = \sum_{i=1}^{j} \lambda_i / \sum_{k=1}^{r} \lambda_k$. It can be seen that that 85% of the total energy is contained in the first 4 modes. The right image shows some synthetic trajectories corresponding to mode 2: $\tau = \bar{\tau} + B \cdot P$ with $B = [0 \ d \ 0 \ 0 \ 0 \ 0 \ 0 \ 0]$ and $d = -100, -50, 0, 50, 100$. It can be interpreted that this 2nd mode seems to encode mainly the variations in the way the bottom-right curve is negotiated.

The outlier-detection procedure presented in section 20.2.1 can be used to investigate trajectories that stand out because they are too different from the original set. This difference can be related to higher efficiency (faster laps) or lower efficiency (slower laps). In figure 20.5(b) we plot each trajectory in the 2D space defined by the two first components of their normalized deformation vector $\tilde{B}_k$, as given in equation (20.8). In this 2D space, the upper limit of statistically acceptable deformation with a 90% confidence level is given by $T^2_{0.1,2,9} = 7.45$. This is plotted as a circle of radius $\sqrt{7.45} = 2.73$, because in that case equations (20.9) and (20.11) become

$$T^2_k = (\tilde{b}^k_1)^2 + (\tilde{b}^k_2)^2 < T^2_{0.1,2,9} = 7.45 \tag{20.16}$$

It can be seen from figure 20.5(b) that none of the trajectories are statistically outliers, although trajectories 2 and 3 do stand out. Indeed, trajectory 2 happens to be the slowest one.

(a)

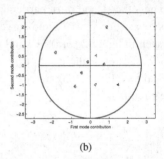

(b)

Fig. 20.5. On the left figure, the contribution of each mode to the different trajectories is plotted. A great contribution from a mode to a trajectory implies that the shape of the mode can be found in the shape of the trajectory. On the right figure the normalized deformation vector $\tilde{B}_k = [\tilde{b}^k_1 \; \tilde{b}^k_2]$ for the two first modes is plotted on a circle of radius $\sqrt{T^2_{0.1,2,9}} = 2.73$ (cf. equation 20.10). In this case, no outlier has been found. Indeed the original variability is so high that none of the trajectories can be considered as an outlier.

20.3.2. *Spatiotemporal analysis*

The resampling described in section 20.3 also involves the temporal component of trajectories. Indeed, a time component can be interpolated for each point on a given trajectory orthogonal to the points on the reference trajectory. This interpolation provides a series of spatiotemporal curves, shown in figure 20.6(a). After normalizing the trajectory data as explained in section 20.2.2, they are next decomposed into several deformation modes. Figure 20.6(b) shows the first mode with the highest amplitude present in the training set. It can be seen that this synthetic curve, which is the highest contribution of the first mode in the trajectory set, corresponds to a slower trajectory —it finishes later than the average trajectory. It has a jump in the time dimension, indicating that the car has been stopped, probably due to a collision.

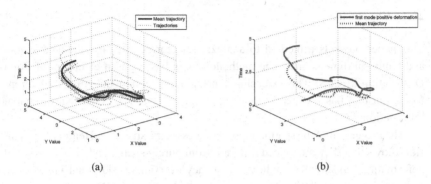

(a)   (b)

Fig. 20.6.   The left figure shows the trajectories in spatiotemporal dimension superposed together with the mean trajectory. The right figure plots the shape of the maximum contribution of the first mode, showing that it produces a more jumpy, slower trajectory.

In their spatiotemporal domain, the trajectories that have been analyzed seem to have a smaller number of deformation modes. Indeed, the first mode, pictured above, accounts for 80% of the total energy in the set (see figure 20.7(a)). From figure 20.7(b) it can be seen that mode 1 contributes the most, with a positive coefficient, to trajectory or lap 2. So much so that the corresponding coefficient $\tilde{b}_1^2$ is greater than the expected threshold $\sqrt{T_{0.1,1,9}^2}$, as per eq. (20.10), indicating that the second trajectory is a statistical outlier. It is indeed this trajectory that happens to be the slowest in the set.

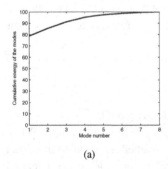
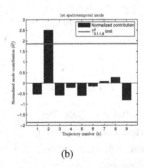

(a)   (b)

Fig. 20.7.   The left figure shows the cumulative energy in the spatiotemporal analysis of the trajectory set. The first deformation mode accounts for 80% of the total energy. The right figure shows the normalized deformation coefficients $\tilde{b}_1^k$ corresponding to the first mode in the spatiotemporal analysis of the trajectory set.

20.4. Conclusion

This paper presents a method to analyze trajectories in their combined spatial and temporal dimensions. The methodology is based on an extension of Point Distribution Models. This extension is needed to accommodate time-domain information that has a different dynamic range and variance than that of spatial information.

The projection of the spatiotemporal modes on the spatial and temporal dimension shows that they are indeed different from purely spatial and purely temporal deformation modes. This indicates that they do contain additional information compared to shape PDMs. However, compared to spatial PDMs, the interpretation of the resulting modes is much more complicated, because the data are richer. Some relationship can be found with the slowest trajectory in the set, because it has a longer temporal profile. Part of the interpretation problem lies in the fact that the underlying driver's style or behavior is unknown. It would therefore be desirable to apply the methodology on trajectories of known behavior such as those produced by a given stochastic differential equation or a robot, or on a more applied way, on the trajectories of a reduced number of expert pilots.

This project has also shown the importance of preprocessing the data and has provided a solution for the problem at hand, car trajectories in a closed circuit. This implies that the beginning and end of each trajectory was clearly defined (a lap), but this might not be always so easy, particularly in open spaces. The same applies for the time-domain information, because lap times were comparable quantities from lap to lap and they contained the relevant information (to analyze the driver's style.) In other applications, instantaneous velocity might be a more relevant information. Thus the choice of temporal features deserves further research.

20.4.1. *Perspectives*

To better correlate the analyzed trajectories with the observed behaviors, we have started a collaborative project with the Swarm-Intelligent Systems group (SWIS), a research team at the EPFL focusing on collective embedded systems involving multi-robot platforms. The point is that mobile robots provide an experimental platform the behavior of which can be programmed and yet provide a natural variability to their trajectories. From the roboticists' point of view, trajectory analysis tools such as the one described in this paper, provide a means of quantifying the robot's behavior and hence predict their performance (in terms of time, energy, work done) for tasks where trajectories play a role.

The first work to be done is to recreate the circuit experiment with mobile robots and to generate a huge number of trajectories, in order to classify the different behaviors. This experiment could demonstrate the validity of these first results.

Acknowledgments

The continuation of this project is supported by the Swiss National Science Foundation grant "Trajectory Analysis and Behavioral Identification in Multi-Robot Systems", No. 200021–105565.

References

1. N. Johnson and D. Hogg, Learning the distribution of object trajectories for event recognition, *Image and Vision Computing.* **14**(8), 609–615, (1996).
2. N. N. Gehrig, V. Lepetit, and P. Fua. Golf club visual tracking for enhanced swing analysis tools. In *British Machine Vision Conference*, Norwich, UK (September, 2003).
3. A. F. Bobick and J. W. Davis, The recognition of human movement using temporal templates, *IEEE Transactions on Pattern Analysis and Machine Intelligence.* **23**(3), 257–267, (2001). URL citeseer.nj.nec.com/bobick01recognition. html.
4. R. Vaughan, N. Sumpter, J. Henderson, A. Frost, and S. Cameron, Experiments in automatic flock control, *Robotics and Autonomous Systems.* **31**, 109–117, (2000).
5. R. Jeanson, S. Blanco, R. Fournier, J. Deneubourg, V. Fourcassie, and G. Theraulaz, A model of animal movements in a bounded space, *Journal of Theoretical Biology.* **225**, 443–451 (Dec, 2003).
6. Z. Khan, T. Balch, and F. Dellaert. Efficient Particle Filter-Based Tracking of Multiple Interacting Targets Using an MRF-based Motion Model. In *Proceedings of the 2003 IEEE/RSJ International Conference on Intelligent Robots and Systems (IROS'03)*, (2003).
7. T. Moeslund and E. Granum, A survey of computer vision-based human motion capture, *Computer Vision and Image Understanding.* **81**(3), 231–268, (2001).
8. T. Cootes, C. Taylor, and D. Cooper, Active shape-models - their training and applications, *Computer Vision and Image Understanding.* pp. 38–59, (1995).
9. J. Jackson, Principal components and factor analysis: part I, *Journal of Quality Technology.* **12**(4), 201–213 (October, 1980).
10. D. Montgomery, *Introduction to statistical quality control.* (Wiley, New York, 2001), 4th edition.
11. M. Unser, Splines: A perfect fit for signal and image processing, *IEEE Signal Processing Magazine.* **16**(6), 22–38 (November, 1999).

CHAPTER 21

AREA AND VOLUME RESTORATION IN ELASTICALLY DEFORMABLE SOLIDS

Micky Kelager, Anders Fleron and Kenny Erleben

Department of Computer Science, University of Copenhagen, DIKU
Universitetsparken 1, 2100 Copenhagen Ø, Denmark
E-mail: micky@kelager.dk - afleron@knights.dk - kenny@diku.dk

This paper describes an improvement of a classical energy-based model to simulate elastically deformable solids. The classical model lacks the ability to prevent the collapsing of solids under influence of external forces, such as user interactions and collision. A thorough explanation is given for the origins of instabilities, and extensions that solve the issues are proposed to the physical model. Within the original framework of the classical model a complete restoration of area and volume is introduced. The improved model is suitable for interactive simulation and can recover from volumetric collapsing, in particular upon large deformation.

1. Introduction

Deformable objects seem to have gained increasing interest during recent years. Part of this success comes from a desire to interact with objects that resemble those in real life, which all seem to be deformable at some level. The next step in interactive applications, such as computer games, is a more expansive integration of complex physical objects such as deformable objects. Because CPUs and GPUs today are both advanced and powerful, it is possible to simulate and animate deformable objects interactively.

This paper builds on work done by Terzopoulos et al. in 1987 [16], which focused on a generic model for simulating elastically deformable objects. The application is mainly objects of a very soft nature due to the elastic properties of the constraint structure. In this model problems with keeping integrity arise when simulating deformable solids. We will explain the origins of the instabilities that cause the solids to collapse. An introduction of area and volume restoration to the model is made that deal with the integrity issues. The result is an improved model that is suitable for a satisfactory simulation of solids.

1.1. Background

In 1987 Terzopoulos et al. presented a continuum model for simulating elastic curves, surfaces, and solids [16], which pioneered the field of computer graphics by introducing physically-based simulation. In the following year the model was extended to include both rigid and deformable components, which made the objects appear less elastic [17]. Concepts such as viscoelasticity, plasticity, and fracture were also added into the model [15].

In [1] a modified Conjugate Gradient method with integrated contact forces is used to increase performance with collision handling. In [18] energy-based preservation of distance, surface area, and volume were introduced, which is similar to the way we use area and volume restoration in this paper.

In the area of geometrical approaches Provot used a relaxation-based method back in 1995 [13] to solve a system of constraints, and gained significant performance improvements. In [2] the relaxation-based method was introduced into in the impulse-based domain. In [7, 20] the iterative SHAKE and RATTLE methods from molecular dynamics were introduced into the area of physically-based simulation and animation. Both methods are based on the Verlet integration scheme.

For better visual results of large deformations, stiffness warping [10] was used to separate the rotational element from the deformable motion. The stiffness warping method was extended in [11] to include plasticity, fracture, and a new method for cracking in a coupled mesh.

In [6] integrity problems upon large deformations were handled by using a finite element method. It was done by using a diagonalization procedure within the tetrahedral mesh, which meant that the method could handle extreme cases such as inverted elements. This resembles the volume restoring technique that we are using in this paper.

1.2. Motivation

The physically-based model for simulating elastically deformable objects, presented in [16], is capable of describing deformable curves, surfaces and volumes. The method is still of interest today because it is firmly based on Newtonian mechanics. Many recent methods primarily use geometry-based procedures to achieve performance when imitating the complex behavior of deformable objects [10, 18, 11]. Physically accurate models convey a more believable behavior and with the increase in processing power they become more relevant.

The integrity problems that are inherent in the original model make it unsuitable for simulating deformable solids in practice. Restoration of integrity is important to give a realistic impression to people who interact with them. With the restoration the objects will be forced to seek toward their original volume size. This should not be confused with volume preservation, which insures that the overall volume of the object never changes. The extensions are achieved by using concepts from the framework of the original model, with the price of a constant increase of calculations per particle.

1.3. Overview

In section 2 we revisit the theory of elastically deformable models, with focus on solids. The theory serves as a foundation for understanding the following sections. Section 3 reveals and explains the instabilities of the classical model. In section 4 we introduce our improvements to area and volume restoration, and in section 5 we extend the model with the ability to resist collapsing. In section 6 we present the results of our improvements and perform comparisons visually between the improved and the classical model.

2. Elastically Deformable Solids

The theory of deformable models is based on elasticity theory. From physical laws [16] have extrapolated a model that governs the movements of elastically deformable objects.

A point in a solid is described by the intrinsic coordinates $\mathbf{a} = [a_1, a_2, a_3]$. A deformable solid is thought of as having a natural rest state, where no elastic energy is inherent. When the solid is deformed, it takes on a different shape than its rest shape, and distances between nearby points are either stretched or compressed with the deformation. This ultimately creates elasticity that results in internal forces that will seek to minimize the elastic energy. The deformation will evolve over time and can be described by the time-varying positional vector function $\mathbf{r}(\mathbf{a}, t) = \left[r_1(\mathbf{a}, t), r_2(\mathbf{a}, t), r_3(\mathbf{a}, t) \right]$, which is defined in 3-dimensional Euclidian space. The evolving deformation is independent of the rigid body motion of the solid. The equations governing the motion of particles in a deformable solid are obtained from Newtonian mechanics, and given by

$$\frac{\partial}{\partial t}\left(\mu \frac{\partial \mathbf{r}}{\partial t} \right) + \gamma \frac{\partial \mathbf{r}}{\partial t} + \frac{\delta \varepsilon (\mathbf{r})}{\delta \mathbf{r}} = \mathbf{f}(\mathbf{r}, t), \tag{1}$$

where $\mathbf{r}(\mathbf{a}, t)$ is the position of the particle, $\mathbf{a}$, at time t, $\mu(\mathbf{a})$ is the mass density, $\gamma(\mathbf{a})$ is the damping density, and the right hand side represents the sum of externally applied forces. The third term on the left hand side of (1) is called a variational derivative and represents the internal elastic energy. $\varepsilon(\mathbf{r})$ is a functional that measures the potential energy that builds up when the solid is deformed.

2.1. Energy of Deformation

A method is needed to measure the deformation energies that arise when a solid deforms. For this task, we use differential geometry. It is convenient to look at arc-lengths on curves, running along the intrinsic directions of the solid. A way of measuring the directions is specified by the metric tensor also known as the first fundamental form,

$$G_{ij}\left(\mathbf{r(a)}\right)=\frac{\partial\mathbf{r}}{\partial a_i}\cdot\frac{\partial\mathbf{r}}{\partial a_j}, \quad 1\le i,j\le 3, \tag{2}$$

which is a symmetric tensor. The diagonal of the tensor represents length measurements along the coordinate directions from the particle in question. The off-diagonal elements represent angle measurements between the coordinate directions. When measuring deformation energy in a solid, we are interested in looking at the change of the shape, with respect to the natural rest shape, which is described by G_{ij}^0. The energy of deformation, $\varepsilon(\mathbf{r})$, can be described by the weighted Hilbert-Schmidt matrix norm of the difference between the metric tensors in the deformed and rest states,

$$\varepsilon(\mathbf{r})=\int_\Omega S\left(\mathbf{r(a},t)\right)da_1da_2da_3, \quad \text{where} \quad S(\mathbf{r})=\sum_{i,j=1}^{3}\eta_{ij}\left(G_{ij}-G_{ij}^0\right)^2, \tag{3}$$

where Ω is the domain of the deformable solid and $\boldsymbol{\eta}$ is a user defined tensor that weights each of the coefficients of the metric. By using the Euler-Lagrange equation from variational calculus on $S(\mathbf{r})$ in (3) a minimizing term for the energy is obtained

$$\frac{\delta S}{\delta\mathbf{r}}=-\sum_{i,j=1}^{3}\partial_{a_i}\left(\alpha_{ij}\mathbf{r}_{a_j}\right), \quad \text{where} \quad \alpha_{ij}=\eta_{ij}\left(\mathbf{r}_{a_i}\cdot\mathbf{r}_{a_j}-G_{ij}^0\right). \tag{4}$$

The $\boldsymbol{\alpha}$-tensors represent the comparison between the deformed state and the rest state of the solid. When an element in $\boldsymbol{\alpha}$ becomes positive, it means that the corresponding constraint has been stretched and it converges to its rest length by shrinking. Likewise, when an element becomes negative, the constraint has been compressed and it converges to its rest length by growing.

2.2. Discretization

The deformable object is continuous in the intrinsic coordinates. To allow an implementation of deformable solids, the object is discretized into a regular 3D grid structure, where grid nodes represent the particles which will make up a solid. The grid has three principal directions called l, m, and n. Particles in the grid are uniformly distributed with spacings in each of the three directions, given by h_1, h_2, and h_3. The number of particles in each of the directions are designated L, M, and N.

The model requires that derivatives are calculated in the intrinsic directions of the object. For this purpose we use finite difference operations to achieve the desired derivative approximations [3]. Replacing the derivatives with the corresponding difference operators yields the discrete equation for the elastic force $\mathbf{e}$,

$$\mathbf{e}[l,m,n] = \sum_{i,j=1}^{3} -D_i^-(\mathbf{p})[l,m,n],\qquad(5)$$

where

$$\mathbf{p}[l,m,n] = \alpha_{ij}[l,m,n]D_j^+(\mathbf{r})[l,m,n],$$

where the superscripts $+$ and $-$ designates forward and backward differences, respectively. The tensor field $\boldsymbol{\alpha}$ is also discretized using finite differencing,

$$\alpha_{ij}[l,m,n] = \eta_{ij}[l,m,n]\left(D_i^+(\mathbf{r})[l,m,n]\cdot D_j^+(\mathbf{r})[l,m,n] - G_{ij}^0[l,m,n]\right).\qquad(6)$$

To solve the equations for all particles at the same time, the values in the positional grid, $\mathbf{r}$, and the energy grid, $\mathbf{e}$, can be unwrapped into LMN-dimensional vectors, $\underline{\mathbf{r}}$ and $\underline{\mathbf{e}}$. With these vectors, the entire system of equations can be written as

$$\underline{\mathbf{e}} = \mathbf{K}(\underline{\mathbf{r}})\underline{\mathbf{r}},\qquad(7)$$

where $\mathbf{K}(\underline{\mathbf{r}})$ is an $LMN \times LMN$ sized stiffness matrix, which has desirable computational properties such as sparseness and bandedness. We introduce the diagonal $LMN \times LMN$ mass matrix $\mathbf{M}$, and damping matrix $\mathbf{C}$, assembled from the corresponding discrete values of $\mu[l,m,n]$ and $\gamma[l,m,n]$, respectively. The equations of the elastically deformable objects (1) can now be expressed in grid vector form, by the coupled system of second-order ordinary differential equations,

$$\mathbf{M}\frac{\partial^2 \underline{\mathbf{r}}}{\partial t^2} + \mathbf{C}\frac{\partial \underline{\mathbf{r}}}{\partial t} + \mathbf{K}(\underline{\mathbf{r}})\underline{\mathbf{r}} = \underline{\mathbf{f}}.\qquad(8)$$

With these equations it is possible to implement real-time dynamic simulations of deformable solids. To evolve the solid through time we use the semi-implicit integration method described in [16]. The time

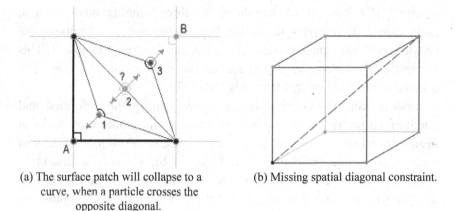

(a) The surface patch will collapse to a curve, when a particle crosses the opposite diagonal.

(b) Missing spatial diagonal constraint.

Figure 1. Constraint instabilities.

derivatives in (8) can be approximated by second and first order central differencing [3]. Further more the desirable properties of the stiffness matrix indicate that a relaxation method, such as the conjugate gradient [14], can be utilized.

3. Instabilities

Notions from differential geometry are used as a tool to measure deformation of an elastic object. For solids the 3×3 metric tensors are sufficient to distinguish between the shapes of two objects. However, the metric tensor of a solid is not sufficient to compute the complex particle movements of a deformed solid, seeking towards its resting shape. The discrete off-diagonal components of (2) are the cosine to the angle between directions through the dot product,

$$\mathbf{v} \cdot \mathbf{w} = |\mathbf{v}||\mathbf{w}|\cos\theta, \quad 0 \le \theta \le \pi . \tag{9}$$

The angle between two vectors is not dependent on their mutual orientation, as verified by the domain of θ in (9). This leads to problems with area restoration on the sides of grid cubes. Figure 1(a) illustrates this instability. The bold lines and the angle between them form the natural condition. If particle A is moved towards particle B, it will only be forced back towards its resting position when $0 < \theta < \pi$, as depicted in case 1. If $\theta = \pi \vee \theta = 0$ then the elastic force is ambiguously defined, as in case 2. If the particle reaches beyond the opposite diagonal, the elasticity will now push particle A into B, as illustrated in case 3. This is clearly a problem, as it can reduce the surface into a curve. The original model [16] suffers from this instability.

Internal constraints are enforced by comparing the deformed and undeformed metric tensors, which means that the model only looks at distances and angles between adjacent particles. As a result of the lack of spatial constraints, as depicted on Figure 1(b), volumetric instability issues arise. This leads to problems with solids not being able to restore their original volume. It turns out that the volume restoration problem is more significant than the problem with area restoration, and has a bigger impact on object integrity.

4. Improvements

To handle the integrity instabilities of the discrete grid cubes we extend the elasticity constraints in order to improve their ability to prevent collapsing. Basically, the extension will be done by both replacing and adding new constraints. The metric tensor is redesigned to stabilize the area restoration while we introduce a new spatial diagonal metric to handle volume restoration.

4.1. Improved Area Restoration

Area restoration concerns 2 dimensions, thus in the following we will focus on the metric tensor for deformable surfaces. For a surface, the tension constraints on a given particle are the four constraints given by the comparison between its 2×2 metric tensors $\mathbf{G}$ and $\mathbf{G}^0$. The comparison between the diagonal elements defines the length constraints along the intrinsic coordinate directions. The comparison between the off-diagonal elements represents pairs of angular constraints between two intrinsic directions, which imply resistance to shearing within the local particle structure. Since $G_{ij} = G_{ji}$ the idea is to replace the pair of angular constraints with two diagonal length constraints. These constraints will reach from the particle at $[m,n]$ to the diagonally

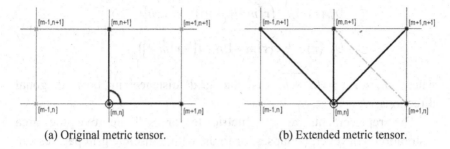

(a) Original metric tensor.   (b) Extended metric tensor.

Figure 2. (a) The angular constraints are replaced by (b) two new diagonal constraints that will define the angular constraints implicitly.

opposite particles at $[m+1, n+1]$ and $[m-1, n+1]$, as depicted in Figure 2. The diagonal length constraints will implicitly work as angular constraints that can account for all 360 degrees. The directions along the new constraints will be considered as new intrinsic directions, a_{d1} and a_{d2}. Writing out $S(\mathbf{r})$ in (3), for the case of surfaces, with the new directions yields

$$S(\mathbf{r}) = \sum_{i=1}^{2} \eta_{ii} \left(\mathbf{r}_{a_i} \cdot \mathbf{r}_{a_i} - G_{ii}^0 \right) + \eta_{12} \left(\mathbf{r}_{a_{d1}} \cdot \mathbf{r}_{a_{d1}} - G_{12}^0 \right) + \eta_{21} \left(\mathbf{r}_{a_{d2}} \cdot \mathbf{r}_{a_{d2}} - G_{21}^0 \right), \quad (10)$$

where the elements G_{12}^0 and G_{21}^0 now holds the rest states of the new diagonal constraints. Using variational calculus on (10) results in the following discretization for the elastic force $\mathbf{e}$,

$$\mathbf{e}[m,n] = -\sum_{i=1}^{2} D_i^{-}(\mathbf{p})[m,n] - D_{d1}^{-}(\mathbf{p}_1)[m,n] - D_{d2}^{-}(\mathbf{p}_2)[m,n], \quad (11)$$

where

$$\begin{aligned}
\mathbf{p}[m,n] &= \eta_{ii}[m,n]D_i^{+}(\mathbf{r})[m,n], \\
\mathbf{p}_1[m,n] &= \eta_{12}[m,n]D_{d1}^{+}(\mathbf{r})[m,n], \\
\mathbf{p}_2[m,n] &= \eta_{21}[m,n]D_{d2}^{+}(\mathbf{r})[m,n].
\end{aligned} \quad (12)$$

Notice that new difference operators arise with the new directions. These operators work exactly as the operators in the original directions. E.g. the new first order forward difference operators on the positional field $\mathbf{r}$ becomes

$$D_{d1}^+ (\mathbf{r}) = h_{d1}^{-1} \left(\mathbf{r}[m+1, n+1] - \mathbf{r}[m,n] \right)$$

$$\text{and} \qquad (13)$$

$$D_{d2}^+ (\mathbf{r}) = h_{d2}^{-1} \left(\mathbf{r}[m-1, n+1] - \mathbf{r}[m,n] \right),$$

where $h_{d1} = h_{d2} = \sqrt{h_1^2 + h_2^2}$ is the grid distance in both diagonal directions.

The replacements to the metric tensor will improve the area restoration. However, collapses, or folds, within discrete grid patches can occur if $\eta_{12} + \eta_{21} < \eta_{11} + \eta_{22}$, thus choosing $\boldsymbol{\eta}$ wisely is important.

The improvements to the metric tensor for surfaces can likewise be applied to deformable solids in a straight forward manner. The off-diagonal elements of the 3×3 metric tensor contain pair-wise expressions of the angular constraints between two of the three directions. These pairs can each be replaced by two diagonal length constraints. The extended metric tensor for solids will now span area restoration in the three directions of a discrete grid cube. When the extended metric tensor is applied to all particles of the deformable solid, the result will be that all grid patches have gained the desired area restoration.

4.2. Volume Restoration

Area restoration can keep grid cube patches from collapsing. However, this is not always enough to keep the cubes from collapsing. If a particle is being forced along its spatial diagonal, the result of the area restoration will normally push the particle back to its relative point of origin. Yet, if the force is strong enough to push the particle beyond the center of the cube, the area restoration will still succeed, but the restoring of the grid patches will now push the particle further along the diagonal. This is an analogy to the instability problem discussed in section 3.

To implement volume restoration, we introduce the spatial diagonal metric, $\mathbf{V}$, which is a 2×2 tensor. The four elements of $\mathbf{V}$ represent length constraints that will be spatially diagonal, meaning they will span grid cubes volumetrically, as depicted in Figure 3(a),

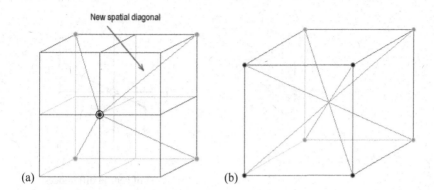

New spatial diagonal

(a)   (b)

Figure 3. Spatial length constraints for solids. (a) The four constraints reach out from the center. (b) The constraint contribution from four particles on a single cube patch renders symmetric behavior.

$$\mathbf{V} \equiv \begin{bmatrix} D_{v1}^+ \cdot D_{v1}^+ & D_{v2}^+ \cdot D_{v2}^+ \\ D_{v3}^+ \cdot D_{v3}^+ & D_{v4}^+ \cdot D_{v4}^+ \end{bmatrix}, \tag{14}$$

where $D_{v1..4}^+ (\mathbf{u})$ are the four new first order forward difference operators along the new spatial diagonal directions. The spatial diagonal constraints can be chosen to favor any directions, as long as the contributions from the four particles on a grid cube patch will end up covering the cube symmetrically, as depicted in Figure 3(b).

The difference operators are designed similarly to the two dimensional case in (13). To implement volume restoration into the model, the discrete elastic force $\mathbf{e}[l,m,n]$ must be extended to contain the contributions provided by the spatial diagonal metric. This can likewise be shown to be as straight forward as the addition of the extended metric tensor.

5. Implosions

With the improved area and volume restorations we can restore the shape of the discrete grid cubes after deformation. This is an important improvement towards keeping the integrity of a deformable solid intact. Another integrity issue still exists since a simulated solid is still unable to prevent implosions. We define an implosion as when grid cubes enter

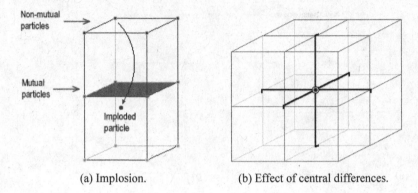

(a) Implosion.   (b) Effect of central differences.

Figure 4. (a) Grid cube implosion is avoided using (b) Central differences that bind adjacent grid cubes together.

their adjacent grid cubes through non-mutual particles, as depicted in Figure 4(a). Implosions happen upon large deformation, which typically are caused by heavy external forces, e.g. reaction to collisions and aggressive user interactions. Implosions can also be described as internal self-intersections, thus self-intersection detection can be utilized as a tool to prevent implosions. For details on the area of self-intersection we recommend papers such as [5, 9, 19, 8].

We seek a mechanism that binds adjacent grid cubes together, in such a way that if implosions occur, we can disperse self-intersecting cubes. This is not a method that can prevent self-intersections, but it can restore the integrity of the solid upon implosions. We can reuse the constraint system that we have been working with so far, and thus reduce the computational cost and memory use significantly, compared to the extra load we would introduce into the system, if we had implemented a standard self-intersection detection algorithm.

We introduce the pillar tensor $\mathbf{P}$, which is based upon the discrete metric tensor $\mathbf{G}$, but extended to use first order central difference operators. For reasons of clarity we will limit $\mathbf{P}$ only to use the length constraints along the diagonal,

$$\mathbf{P}[l,m,n] = \begin{bmatrix} D_1^2(\mathbf{r}) & 0 & 0 \\ 0 & D_2^2(\mathbf{r}) & 0 \\ 0 & 0 & D_3^2(\mathbf{r}) \end{bmatrix}, \tag{15}$$

where

$$D_1(\mathbf{u})[l,m,n] = (2h_1)^{-1}(\mathbf{u}[l+1,m,n] - \dot{\mathbf{u}}[l-1,m,n]),$$
$$D_2(\mathbf{u})[l,m,n] = (2h_2)^{-1}(\mathbf{u}[l,m+1,n] - \mathbf{u}[l,m-1,n]), \tag{16}$$
$$D_3(\mathbf{u})[l,m,n] = (2h_3)^{-1}(\mathbf{u}[l,m,n+1] - \mathbf{u}[l,m,n-1]).$$

The effect of using central difference operators results in a convincing way to bind adjacent grid cubes together, see Figure 4(b). The pillar tensor is yet another addition to the extended elasticity term and is handled exactly the same way as the area and volume restorations. Since every grid particle will be extended with the contribution of the pillar tensor, the combined range of **P** will overlap all grid cubes along the intrinsic directions. The effect of using the pillar tensor is that grid cubes will repel each other in situations of overlapping.

In some cases of extreme external forces the pillar contribution is not enough to completely prevent grid cubes from overlapping. This is due to the sum of external forces is exceeding the internal elastic forces. One way to handle this is to strengthen the overall weight of the pillar tensor. However, as this can lead to numerical instabilities, the pillar tensor can implement the missing off-diagonal elements from the extended metric. To further prevent implosions an additional tensor can be added that implements a central difference spatial diagonal metric.

6. Results

We have implemented the original model from [16] with our improvements of area and volume restoration and with the simple prevention of implosion, as described in section 4 and 5, respectively. The implementation is publicly available from [4]. Experiments have revealed that the effects of the spatial diagonal metric do not always succeed satisfactorily in moving particles back to their natural location.

In some situations new energy equilibriums arise unnaturally. We have realized that the constraints from the area restoration can work against the volume restoration. To counteract this problem, we have simply squared the constraint forces of the spatial diagonal metric tensors, to make sure they prevail. In general this means that volume restoration should have a higher precedence than area restoration, which in turn should have a higher precedence than distance restoration. Numerical instabilities tend to occur when too large parameter values are used, such as particle mass, time step, and constraint strength. This is likely a problem with the semi-implicit integrator.

We have performed visual comparisons between the original and our improved model to show the advantage of handling the integrity instabilities. In Figure 5, still frames of a small box that is influenced by gravity and collides with a plane are compared frame to frame between the two models. Primarily due to the lack of volume restoration, the constraints of the original model simply cannot keep the shape of the discrete grid cubes. In Figure 6 we compare two rubber balls with different particle mass. The rubber ball in Figure 6(a) is simulated using the original model and fails to maintain its integrity, thus the ball collapses on itself. The rubber ball in Figure 6(b) is simulated using the improved model with the same parameters, and the integrity of the ball is now strong enough to stay solid. In Figure 7, a test of how well the two models can recover from a sudden aggressive deformation is performed. The original model fails its attempt at complete recovery, whereas the improved model actually performs its recovery convincingly.

The improved model enables real-time simulation of situations that are impossible with the original model. In Figure 8, a soft solid is depicted. The solid has been constrained to the ground, and in three of the top corners. Pulling the free top corner downwards results in a large deformation and renders convincing material buckling. In Figure 9, the true strength of the pillar tensor contribution is illustrated, showing an effect of inflation. First the overall constraint strength is at a minimum and is then increased in the following frames. In Figure 10, a soft solid is constrained to the ground, and being twisted by its top face. The sides of the deformable solid skew as expected of a soft body like pudding. In

Figure 11, a large water lily is deformed when resting on pearls. The improved model performs a great job in keeping the water lily fluffy.

7. Conclusion

The original model presented in [16] for simulating elastically deformable solids turned out to be insufficient for achieving realism. Even extremely modest external forces applied to the solids would ruin their integrity. In this paper we have shown how replacements to the metric tensor can be implemented to improve area restoration, and how to implement the missing volume restoration. Furthermore we have shown how to handle internal self-intersection using the framework from the original model. Even though the original model is dated back to 1987 it is still competitive in the field of physically-based simulation. Visual comparisons have revealed that our improvements to the model provide deformable solids with the ability to keep their integrity, and thus the ability to handle large deformations in real-time without collapsing. Our improved model is a viable alternative to other methods for simulating deformable solids.

Interesting challenges for future work include using unstructured meshes instead of the regular 3D grid. However, this will complicate the use of finite difference operators when approximating derivatives. Working with solids gives the occasion to use tetrahedral meshes and the finite element method. The problem of generating tetrahedral meshed from closed 2D manifolds can be solved using the approach described in [12]. The advantage of the regular grid approach, taken by this model, compared to using a tetrahedral mesh is that fewer elements are needed to represent the deformable solid. It is also possible that other integration procedures can perform better in terms of numerical stability and thus an analysis of this field might be beneficial.

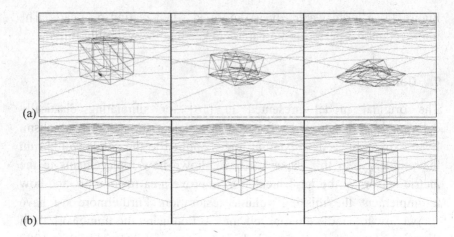

Figure 5. A small box is influenced by gravity and collides with a plane. (a) The three stills illustrate the original model, and (b) the frames from the improved model are shown.

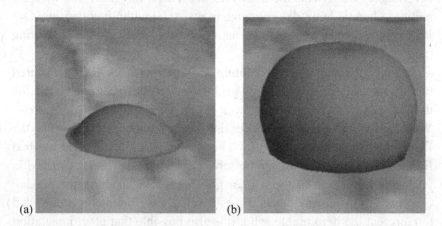

Figure 6. Rubber balls. (a) Illustrates the situation from the original model, where the ball is unable to maintain its integrity, (b) the same situation is depicted, but simulated using the improved model.

(a) Original Model.   (b) Improved Model.

Figure 7. A wooden box is heavily lifted in one corner.

Figure 8. Large deformation results in convincing material buckling.

Figure 9. Constraint strength is increased interactively and yields the effect of inflation.

Figure 10. Twisting the pudding renders skewing.

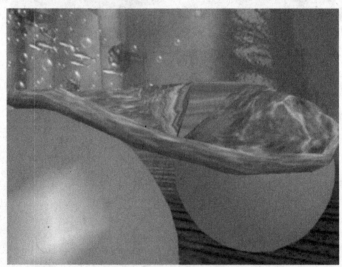

Figure 11. Fluffy water lily modeled using an ellipsoid solid.

References

1. D. Baraff and A. Witkin. "Large Steps in Cloth Simulation". *Proceedings of the Annual ACM SIGGRAPH'98 Conference*, ACM Press, Vol. 33, pp. 43-54, 1998.
2. R. Bridson, R. Fedkiw, and J. Anderson. "Robust Treatment of Collisions, Contact and Friction for Cloth Animation". *In Proceedings of ACM SIGGRAPH 2002*, pp. 594-603, 2002.
3. D. Eberly. *Derivative Approximation by Finite Differences*. Magic Software, Inc., January 21, 2003.
4. K. Erleben, H. Dohlmann, J. Sporring, and K. Henriksen. *The OpenTissue project*. Department of Computer Science, University of Copenhagen, DIKU, November 2003, http://www.opentissue.org
5. B. Heidelberger, M. Teschner, and M. Gross. "Detection of Collisions and Self-collisions Using Image-space Techniques". *In Proceeding of WSCG'04*, University of West Bohemia, Czech Republic, pp. 145-152, 2004.
6. G. Irving, J. Teran, and R. Fedkiw. "Invertible Finite Elements for Robust Simulation of Large Deformation". *ACM SIGGRAPH/Eurographics Symposium on Computer Animation (SCA)*, pp. 131-140, 2004.
7. T. Jakobsen. "Advanced Character Physics". *In Proceedings of Game Developer's Conference 2001*, 2001.
8. D. L. James and D. K. Pai. "BD-Tree: Output-Sensitive Collision Detection for Reduced Deformable Models". *In Proceedings ACM SIGGRAPH 2004*, pp. 393-298, 2004.
9. T. Larsson and T. Akenine-Möller. "Collision Detection for Continuously Deforming Bodies". *In Eurographics 2001*, pp. 325-333, 2001.
10. M. Müller, J. Dorsey, L. McMillan, R. Jagnow, and B. Cutler. "Stable Real-Time Deformations". *In Proceedings of ACM SIGGRAPH 2002*, pp 49-54, 2002.
11. M. Müller and M. Gross. "Interactive Virtual Materials". *In Proceedings of Graphics Interface (GI 2004)*, pp 239-246, 2004.
12. M. Müller and M. Teschner. "Volumetric Meshes for Real-Time Medical Simulations". *In Proceedings of BVM*, pp. 279-283, 2003.
13. Provot, X. "Deformation constraints in a mass-spring model to describe rigid cloth behavior". *In Graphics Interface 1995*, pp. 147–154, 1995.
14. J. R. Shewchuk. *An Introduction to the Conjugate Gradient Method Without the Agonizing Pain*. Carnegie Mellon University, 1994.
15. D. Terzopoulos and K. Fleischer. "Modeling Inelastic Deformation: Viscoelasticity, Plasticity, Fracture". *In Computer Graphics*, Volume 22, Number 4, August 1988, pp. 269-278, 1988.
16. D. Terzopoulos, J. C. Platt, A. H. Barr, and K. Fleischer. "Elastically Deformable Models". *Computer Graphics*, volume 21, Number 4, July 1987, pp 205-214, 1987.

17. D. Terzopoulos and A. Witkin. "Physically-Based Models with Rigid and Deformable Components". *In Proceedings of Graphics Interface '88*, pp.146-154, 1988.
18. M. Teschner, B. Heidelberger, M. Müller, and M. Gross. "A Versatile and Robust Model for Geometrically Complex Deformable Solids". *In Proceedings of Computer Graphics International*, June 16-19 2004, pp 312-319, 2004.
19. G. van den Bergen. "Efficient Collision Detection of Complex Deformable Models using AABB Trees". *Journal of Graphics Tools 2(4)*, pp. 1–14, 1998.
20. J. M. Wagenaar. *Physically Based Simulation and Visualization, A particle-based approach*. Ph.D. Thesis, The Mærsk Mc-Kinney Møller Institute for Production Technology, 2001.

CHAPTER 22

HAND TRACKING AND GESTURE RECOGNITION FOR HUMAN-COMPUTER INTERACTION

Cristina Manresa-Yee, Javier Varona, Ramon Mas and Francisco J. Perales

Unidad de Gráficos y Visión por Computador
Departamento de Matemáticas e Informática
Universitat de les Illes Balears
Edificio Anselm Turmeda, Crta. Valldemossa km 7.5
07122 - Palma de Mallorca - Spain,
E-mail: cristina.manresa@uib.es

The proposed work is part of a project that aims for the control of a videogame based on hand gesture recognition. This goal implies the restriction of real-time response and unconstrained environments. In this paper we present a new algorithm to track and recognise hand gestures for interacting with videogames. This algorithm is based on three main steps: hand segmentation, hand tracking and gesture recognition from hand features. For the hand segmentation step we use the colour cue due to the characteristic colour values of human skin, its invariant properties and its computational simplicity. To prevent errors from hand segmentation we add a second step, hand tracking. Tracking is performed assuming a constant velocity model and using a pixel labeling approach. From the tracking process we extract several hand features that are fed to a finite state classifier which identifies the hand configuration. The hand can be classified into one of the four gesture classes or one of the four different movement directions. Finally, the system's performance evaluation results are used to show the usability of the algorithm in a videogame environment.

22.1. Introduction

Nowadays, the majority of human-computer interaction (HCI) is based on mechanical devices such as keyboards, mouses, joysticks or gamepads. In recent years there has been a growing interest in methods based on computational vision due to its ability to recognise human gestures in a natural way.[1] These methods use the images acquired from a camera or from a stereo pair of cameras as input. The main goal of these algorithms is to measure the hand configuration in each time instant.

To facilitate this process many gesture recognition applications resort to the use of uniquely coloured gloves or markers on hands or fingers.[2] In addition, using a controlled background makes it possible to locate the hand efficiently, even in real-time.[3] These two conditions impose restrictions on the user and on the interface setup. We have specifically avoided solutions that require coloured gloves or markers and a controlled background because of the initial requirements of our application. It must work for different people, without any complement on them and also for unpredictable backgrounds.

Our application uses images from a low-cost web camera placed in front of the work area, where the recognised gestures act as the input for a computer 3D videogame. The players, rather than pressing buttons, must use different hand gestures that our application should recognise. This fact, increases the complexity since the response time must be very fast. Users should not appreciate a significant delay between the instant they perform a gesture or motion and the instant the computer responds. Therefore, the algorithm must provide real-time performance for a conventional processor. Most of the known hand tracking and recognition algorithms do not meet this requirement and are inappropriate for visual interface. For instance, particle filtering-based algorithms can maintain multiple hypotheses at the same time to robustly track the hands but they need high computational demands.[4] Recently, several contributions for reducing the complexity of particle filters have been presented, for example, using a deterministic process to help the random search.[5] Also in Bretzner et al.,[6] we can see a multi-scale colour feature for representing hand shape and particle filtering that combines shape and colour cues in a hierarchical model. The system has been fully tested and seems robust and stable. To our knowledge the system runs at about 10 frames/second and does not consider several hand states. However, these algorithms only work in real-time for a reduced size hand and in our application, the hand fills most of the image. In Ogawara et al.,[7] shape reconstruction is quite precise, a high DOF model is considered, and in order to avoid self-occlusions infrared orthogonal cameras are used. The authors propose to apply this technique using a colour skin segmentation algorithm.

In this paper we propose a real-time non-invasive hand tracking and gesture recognition system. In the next sections we explain our method which is divided in three main steps. The first step is hand segmentation, the image region that contains the hand has to be located. In this process, the use of the shape cue it is possible, but they vary greatly during the natural hand motion.[8] Therefore, we choose skin-colour as the hand feature. The skin-colour is a distinctive cue of hands and it is invariant to scale and rotation. The next step is to track the position and orientation of the hand to prevent errors in the segmentation phase. We use a pixel-based tracking for the temporal update of the hand state. In the last step we use the estimated hand state to extract several hand features to define a deterministic process of gesture recognition. Finally, we present the system's performance evaluation results that prove that our method works well in unconstrained environments and for several users.

22.2. Hand Segmentation Criteria

The hand must be located in the image and segmented from the background before recognition. Colour is the selected cue because of its computational simplicity, its invariant properties regarding to the hand shape configurations and due to the human skin-colour characteristic values. Also, the assumption that colour can be used as a cue to detect faces and hands has been proved useful in several publications.[9,10] For our application, the hand segmentation has been carried out using a low computational cost method that performs well in real time. The method is based on a probabilistic model of the skin-colour pixels distribution. Then, it is necessary to model the skin-colour of the user's hand. The user places part of his hand in a learning square as shown in Fig. 22.1. The pixels restricted in this area will be used for the model learning. Next, the selected pixels are transformed from the RGB-space to the HSL-space and the chroma information is taken: hue and saturation.

Fig. 22.1. Application interface and skin-colour learning square.

We have encountered two problems in this step that have been solved in a pre-processing phase. The first one is that human skin hue values are very near to red colour, that is, their value is very close to 2π radians, so it is difficult to learn the distribution due to the hue angular nature that can produce samples on both limits. To solve this inconvenience the hue values are rotated π radians. The second problem in using HSL-space appears when the saturation values are close to 0, because then the hue is unstable and can cause false detections. This can be avoided discarding saturation values near 0.

Once the pre-processing phase has finished, the hue, h, and saturation, s, values for each selected pixel are used to infer the model, that is, $\mathbf{X} = (\mathbf{x}_1, \ldots, \mathbf{x}_n)$, where n is the number of samples and a sample is $\mathbf{x}_i = (h_i, s_i)$. A Gaussian model is chosen to represent the skin-colour probability density function. The values for the parameters of the Gaussian model (mean, μ, and covariance matrix, Σ) are computed from the sample set using standard maximum likelihood methods.[11] Once they are found, the probability that a new pixel, $\mathbf{x}$, is skin can be calculated as

$$P(\mathbf{x}) = \frac{1}{\sqrt{(2\pi)^2 |\Sigma|}} \exp -\frac{1}{2}(\mathbf{x} - \mu)\Sigma^{-1}(\mathbf{x} - \mu)^T. \tag{22.1}$$

Finally, we obtain the blob representation of the hand by applying a connected components algorithm to the probability image, which groups pixels into the same blob. The system is robust to background changes and low light conditions. If the system gets lost, you can initialise it again by going to the hand start state. Fig. 22.2 shows the blob contours found by the algorithm for different environment conditions where the system has been tested.

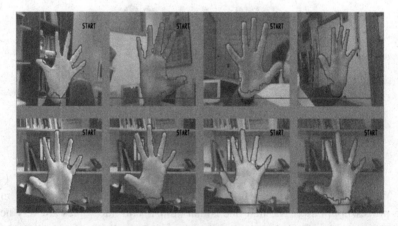

Fig. 22.2.   Hand contours for different backgrounds (1st row) and different light conditions (2nd row).

22.3. Tracking Procedure

USB cameras are known for the low quality images they produce. This fact can cause errors in the hand segmentation process. In order to make the application robust to these segmentation errors we add a tracking algorithm. This algorithm tries to maintain and propagate the hand state over time.

We represent the hand state in time t, s_t, by means of a vector, $s_t = (p_t, w_t, \alpha_t)$, where $p = (p_x, p_y)$ is the hand position in the 2D image, the hand size is represented by $w = (w, h)$, where w is the hand width and h is the hand height in pixels, and, finally, α is the hand's angle in the 2D image plane. First, from the hand state in time t we built an hypothesis of the hand state, $h = (p_{t+1}, w_t, \alpha_t)$, for time $t + 1$ applying a simple second-order autoregressive process to the position component

$$p_{t+1} - p_t = p_t - p_{t-1} \qquad (22.2)$$

Equation (22.2) expresses a dynamical model of constant velocity. Next, if we assume that at time t, M blobs have been detected, $B = \{b_1, \ldots, b_j, \ldots, b_M\}$, where each blob b_j corresponds to a set of connected skin-colour pixels, the tracking process has to set the relation between the hand hypothesis, h, and the observations, b_j, over time.

In order to cope with this problem, we define an approximation to the distance from the image pixel, $x = (x, y)$, to the hypothesis h. First, we normalize the image pixel coordinates

$$n = R \cdot (x - p_{t+1}), \qquad (22.3)$$

where R is a standard 2D rotation matrix about the origin, α is the rotation angle, and $n = (n_x, n_y)$ are the normalized pixel coordinates. Then, we can find the crossing point, $c = (c_x, c_y)$, between the hand hypothesis ellipse and the normalized image pixel as follows

$$\begin{aligned} c_x &= w \cdot \cos(\theta), \\ c_y &= h \cdot \sin(\theta), \end{aligned} \qquad (22.4)$$

where θ is the angle between the normalized image pixel and the hand hypothesis. Finally, the distance from an image pixel to the hand hypothesis is

$$d(x, h) = \|n\| - \|c\|. \qquad (22.5)$$

This distance can be seen as the approximation of the distance from a point in the 2D space to a normalized ellipse (normalized means centred in origin and not rotated). From the distance definition of Eq. (22.5) it turns out that its value is equal or less than 0 if x is inside the hypothesis h, and greater than 0 if it is outside. Therefore, considering the hand hypothesis h and a point x belonging to a blob b, if the distance is equal or less than 0, we conclude that the blob b supports the existence of the hypothesis and it is selected to represent the new hand state. This tracking process could also detect the presence or the absence of the hand in the image.[12]

22.4. Gesture Recognition

Our gesture alphabet consists in four hand gestures and four hand directions in order to fulfil the application's requirements. The hand gestures correspond to a fully opened hand (with separated fingers), an opened hand with fingers together, a fist and the last gesture appears when the hand is not visible, in part or completely, in the camera's field of view. These gestures are defined as *Start*, *Move*, *Stop* and the *No-Hand* gesture respectively. Also, when the user is in the *Move* gesture, he can carry out *Left*, *Right*, *Front* and *Back* movements. For the *Left* and *Right* movements, the user will rotate his wrist to the left or right. For the *Front* and *Back* movements, the hand will get closer to or further from the camera. Finally, the valid hand gesture transitions that the user can carry out are defined in Fig. 22.3.

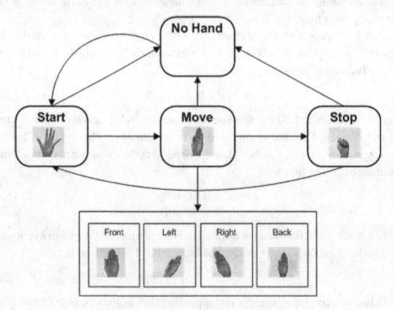

Fig. 22.3.   Gesture alphabet and valid gesture transitions.

The process of gesture recognition starts when the user's hand is placed in front of the camera's field of view and the hand is in the *Start* gesture, that is, the hand is fully opened with separated fingers. In order to avoid fast hand gesture changes that were not intended, every change should be kept fixed for a number of predefined frames, if not the hand gesture does not change from the previous recognised gesture.

To achieve this gesture recognition, we use the hand state estimated in the tracking process, that is, $\mathbf{s} = (\mathbf{p}, \mathbf{w}, \alpha)$. This state can be viewed as an ellipse approximation of the hand where $\mathbf{p} = (p_x, p_y)$ is the ellipse centre and $\mathbf{w} = (w, h)$ is the size of the ellipse in pixels. To facilitate the process we define the major axis length as M and the minor axis length as m. In addition, we compute the hand's blob contour and its corresponding convex hull using standard computer vision techniques. From the hand's contour and the hand's convex hull we can calculate a sequence of contour points between two consecutive convex hull vertices. This sequence forms the so-called convexity defect (i.e., a finger concavity) and it is possible to compute the depth of the ith-convexity defect, d_i. From these depths it is possible to compute the depth average, $\bar{d}$, as a global hand feature, see Eq. 22.6, where n is the total number of convexity defects in the hand's contour, see Fig. 22.4.

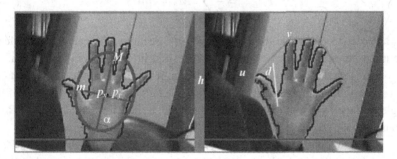

Fig. 22.4. Extracted features for the hand gesture recognition. In the right image, u and v indicate the start and the end points of the convexity defect, the depth, d, is the distance from the farthermost point of the convexity defect to the convex hull segment.

$$\bar{d} = \frac{1}{n} \sum_{i=0}^{n} d_i. \tag{22.6}$$

The first step of the gesture recognition process is to model the *Start* gesture. The average of the depths of the convexity defects of an opened hand with separated fingers is larger than in an open hand with no separated fingers or in a fist. This feature is used for differentiating the next hand gesture transitions: from

Stop to *Start*; from *Start* to *Move*; and from *No-Hand* to *Start*. However, first it is necessary to compute the *Start* gesture feature, T_{start}. Once the user is correctly placed in the camera's field of view with the hand widely opened the skin-colour learning process is initiated. The system also computes the Start gesture feature for the n first frames,

$$T_{start} = \frac{1}{2n} \sum_{t=0}^{n} \overline{d}(t). \qquad (22.7)$$

Once the *Start* gesture is identified, the most probable valid gesture change is the *Move* gesture. Therefore, if the current hand depth is less than T_{start} the system goes to the *Move* hand gesture. If the current hand gesture is *Move* the hand directions will be enabled: *Front, Back, Left* and *Right*.

If the user does not want to move in any direction, he should set his hand in the *Move* state. The first time that the *Move* gesture appears, the system computes the *Move* gesture feature, T_{move}, that is an average of the approximated area of the hand for n consecutive frames,

$$T_{move} = \frac{1}{n} \sum_{t=0}^{n} M(t) \cdot m(t). \qquad (22.8)$$

In order to recognise the *Left* and *Right* directions, the calculated angle of the fitted ellipse is used. To prevent non desired jitter effects in orientation, we introduce a predefined constant T_{jitter}. Then, if the angle of the ellipse that circumscribes the hand, α, satisfies $\alpha > T_{jitter}$, *Left* orientation will be set. If the angle of the ellipse that circumscribes the hand, α, satisfies $\alpha < -T_{jitter}$, *Right* orientation will be set.

In order to control the *Front* and *Back* orientations and to return to the *Move* gesture the hand must not be rotated and the *Move* gesture feature is used to differentiate these movements. If $T_{move} \cdot C_{front} < M \cdot m$ succeeds the hand orientation will be *Front*. The *Back* orientation will be achieved if $C_{back} > m/M$.

The *Stop* gesture will be recognised using the ellipse's axis. When the hand is in a fist, the fitted ellipse is almost like a circle and m and M are practically the same, that is, when $C_{stop} > M - m$.

C_{front}, C_{back} and C_{stop} are predefined constants established during the algorithm performance evaluation. Finally, the *No-Hand* state will appear when the system does not detect the hand, the size of the detected hand is not large enough or when the hand is in the limits of the camera's field of view. The next possible hand state will be the *Start* gesture and it will be detected using the transition procedure from *Stop* to *Start* explained earlier on.

Some examples of gesture transitions and the recognised gesture results can be seen in Fig. 22.5. These examples are chosen to show the algorithm robustness for different lighting conditions, hand configurations and users. We realize that a correct learning of the skin-colour is very important. If not, some problems with the detection and the gesture recognition can be encountered. One of the main problems with the use of the application is the hand control, maintaining the hand in the camera's field of view and without touching the limits of the capture area. This problem has been shown to disappear with user's training.

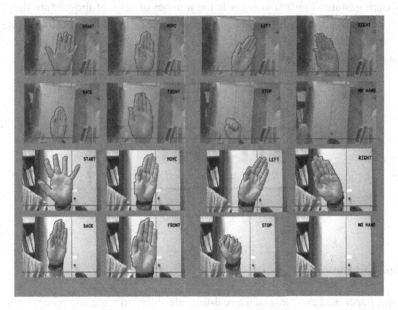

Fig. 22.5.   Gesture recognition examples for different lighting conditions, users and hand configurations.

22.5. System's Performance Evaluation

In this section we describe the accuracy of our hand tracking and gesture recognition algorithm. The application has been implemented in Visual C++ using the OpenCV libraries.[13] The application has been tested on a Pentium IV running at 1.8 GHz. The images have been captured using a Logitech Messenger WebCam with USB connection. The camera provides 320x240 images at a capture and processing rate of 30 frames per second.

For the performance evaluation of the hand tracking and gesture recognition, the system has been tested on a set of 40 users. Each user has performed a pre-defined set of 40 gestures and therefore we have 1600 gestures to evaluate the application results. It is natural to think that the system's accuracy will be measured controlling the performance of the desired user movements for managing the videogame. This sequence included all the application's possible states and transitions. Figure 22.6 shows the performance evaluation results. These results are represented using a bidimensional matrix with the application states as columns and the number of appearances of the gesture as rows. The columns are paired for each gesture: the first column is the number of tests of the gesture that has been correctly identified; the second column is the total number of times that the gesture has been carried out. As it can be seen in Fig. 22.6, the hand recognition gesture works fine for a 98% of the cases.

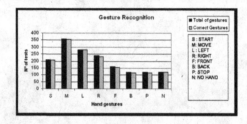

Fig. 22.6.   System's performance evaluation results.

22.6. Conclusions

In this paper we have presented a real-time algorithm to track and recognise hand gestures for human-computer interaction within the context of videogames. We have proposed an algorithm based on skin colour hand segmentation and tracking for gesture recognition from extracted hand morphological features. The system's performance evaluation results have shown that the users can substitute traditional interaction metaphors with this low-cost interface.

The experiments have confirmed that continuous training of the users results in higher skills and, thus, better performances. Also the system has been tested in indoor laboratory with changing background scenario and low light conditions. In these cases the system run well, with the logical exception of similar skin background situations or several hands intersecting in the same space and time. The system must be improved to discard bad classifications situations due to the segmentation procedure. But, in this case, the user can restart the system only going to the Start hand state.

Acknowledgements

The projects TIC2003-0931 and TIC2002-10743-E of MCYT Spanish Government and the European Project HUMODAN 2001-32202 from UE V Program-IST have subsidized this work. Besides, Dr. J. Varona acknowledges the support of a Ramon y Cajal fellowship from the Spanish MEC.

References

1. V.I. Pavlovic, R. Sharma, T.S. Huang. Visual interpretation of hand gestures for human-computer interaction: a review, *IEEE Pattern Analysis and Machine Intelligence*, **19**(7), 677–695, (1997).
2. R. Bowden, D. Windridge, T. Kadir, A. Zisserman, M. Brady. A Linguistic Feature Vector for the Visual Interpretation of Sign Language. In: *Proc. European Conference on Computer Vision (ECCV04)*, vol. 1, pp. 391–401, LNCS3022, Springer-Verlag, (2004).
3. J. Segen, S. Kumar. Shadow gestures: 3D hand pose estimation using a single camera. In: *Proc. of the Computer Vision and Pattern Recognition Conference (CVPR99)*, vol. 1, 485, (1999).
4. M. Isard, A. Blake. ICONDENSATION: Unifying low-level and high-level tracking in a stochastic framework. In: *Proc. European Conference on Computer Vision (ECCV98)*, pp. 893–908, (1998).
5. C. Shan, Y. Wei, T. Tan, F. Ojardias. Real time hand tracking by combining particle filtering and mean shift. In: *Proc. Sixth IEEE Automatic Face and Gesture Recognition (FG04)*, pp. 229–674, (2004).
6. L. Bretzner, I. Laptev, T. Lindeberg. Hand Gesture Recognition using Multi-Scale Colour Features, Hierarchical Models and Particle filtering. In: *Proc. Fifth IEEE International Conference on Automatic Face and Gesture Recognition (FRG02)*, (2002).
7. K. Ogawara, K. Hashimoto, J. Takamtsu, K. Ikeuchi. Grasp Recognition using a 3D Articulated Model and Infrared Images. In: *Proc. Intelligent Robots and Systems (IROS03)*, vol. 2, pp. 1590–1595, (2003).
8. T. Heap, D. Hogg. Wormholes in shape space: tracking through discontinuous changes in shape. In: *Proc. Sixth International Conference on Computer Vision (ICCV98)*, pp. 344–349, (1998).
9. G.R. Bradski. Computer video face tracking for use in a perceptual user interface. *Intel Technology Journal*, Q2'98, (1998).
10. D. Comaniciu, V. Ramesh. Robust detection and tracking of human faces with an active camera. In: *Proc. of the Third IEEE International Workshop on Visual Surveillance*, pp. 11–18, (2000).
11. C.M. Bishop. *Neural Networks for Pattern Recognition*. Clarendon Press, (1995).

12. J. Varona, J.M. Buades, F.J. Perales. Hands and face tracking for VR applications. *Computers & Graphics*, **29**(2), 179–187, (2005).
13. G.R. Bradski, V. Pisarevsky. Intel's Computer Vision Library. In: *Proc of IEEE Conference on Computer Vision and Pattern Recognition (CVPR00)*, vol. 2, pp. 796–797, (2000).

CHAPTER 23

A NOVEL APPROACH TO SPARSE HISTOGRAM IMAGE
LOSSLESS COMPRESSION USING JPEG2000

Marco Aguzzi and Maria Grazia Albanesi

Dipartimento di Informatica e Sistemistica, Università degli Studi di Pavia, Via Ferrata 1, Pavia, Italy
E-mail: marco.aguzzi@unipv.it

In this paper a novel approach to the compression of sparse histogram images is proposed. First, we define a sparsity index which gives hints on the relationship between the mathematical concept of matrix sparsity and the visual information of pixel distribution. We use this index to better understand the scope of our approach and its preferred field of applicability, and to evaluate the performance. We present two algorithms which modify one of the coding steps of the JPEG2000 standard for lossless image compression. A theoretical study of the gain referring to the standard is given. Experimental results on well standardized images of the literature confirm the expectations, especially for high sparse images.

23.1. Introduction

The JPEG2000[1–8] started its standard formalization in 1997 and became an ISO standard in late 2000, confirming itself as the new reference point for researches in the field of still image compression. Among several innovations, the use of wavelets instead of DCT (Discrete Cosine Transform) (first appeared on,[9] based on Fourier analysis, which was used by JPEG[10,11] standard) allows multiresolution processing, preservation of spatial locality information and adaptivity on the image content. JPEG2000 obtains better results in terms of compression ratios, image quality and flexibility according to user demands. The JPEG2000 coding scheme is quite similar in philosophy to the EZW[12] and SPIHT[13] algorithms, even if it uses different data structures. Furthermore, the architectural design of the JPEG2000 allows several degrees of freedom aimed at tailoring the processing toward specific needs.

In literature, there are several proposal of approaches that modify only the coder (thus preserving the standard compatibility[14–26]) or both the coder and the decoder. Our approach belongs to the second group and the gain over the standard will be motivated from a theoretical point of view (by definition of a gain function, see Section 4.2) and by the experimental results. A very brief and preliminary version of our algorithms has been described in;[27] here we give a fully review of new experiments to validate our approach, and we add new considerations about comparison to JPEG 2000, PNG, and JPEG-LS. In fact we present concepts, theory and results about two novel algorithms which can be used to enhance performance (in terms of compression ratio) of lossless compression of images[28–32] coded with JPEG2000 standard. In particular, the proposed algorithms modify the compression chain in the bit-plane encoding step, allowing adaptations particularly suited for sparse histogram images, for which the gain is at its best. For completeness sake, a brief introduction of JPEG2000 is given in Section 23.2; Section 23.3 gives the basis to understand the theory of the work through an original definition of histogram sparsity concept. Section 23.4 describes the two algorithms. Experimental results are fully reported in Section 23.4.1.1 and 23.4.1.3 for the first proposal, and in Section 23.4.2.2 for the second one. Conclusions (Section 23.5) and suggestions for further works end the paper.

23.2. JPEG2000 Overview

In order to fully understand the proposed algorithms for a modified JPEG2000 encoder, a brief introduction of the standard is presented: a block system level description of the compression chain is given (for further details the reader can refer to the corresponding literature[2,4,7]). In Figure 23.1 a black-box scheme of JPEG2000 compression chain is depicted, showing at which point our algorithms introduce modifications.

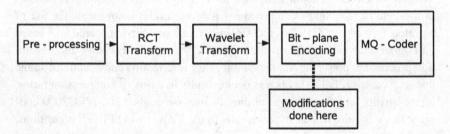

Fig. 23.1.   JPEG2000 compression chain at a system level: in the proposed algorithms, modifications occur in bit-plane encoding block.

23.2.1. Preprocessing

By referring to Figure 23.1, the first stage of JPEG2000 compression chain involves a resampling of pixel values to obtain symmetry around zero: if s_i is the ith sample of an input image (of size $D = V * H$, where V and H are the vertical and horizontal dimensions, respectively), and bps is the bit per sample rate, this is done through relation in Equation 23.1:

$$\forall i \in [0, D - 1] \; s_i^\star = s_i - 2^{bps-1} \tag{23.1}$$

so that $\forall i \in [0, D - 1]$ the old samples s_i are in the range $[0, 2^{bps} - 1]$ while the new ones $s_i^\star$ in $[-2^{bps-1}, 2^{bps-1} - 1]$. This operation enhances the decorrelation among samples and helps in making statistical assumption on the sample distribution.

23.2.2. Wavelet transform

The choice of the wavelet kernel[12,33–37] is one of the points that makes JPEG2000 different from the standard JPEG. This kind of transform can produce highly decorrelated coefficients, although preserving spatial locality, which makes them the ideal input for an image compression algorithm. The advantages that JPEG2000 takes from wavelet transform are: a) the coefficients produced are resolution correlated, thus enabling the use of multiresolution analysis, and b) a smooth area of an image will produce small magnitude coefficients, while a sharp shaped one will give high magnitude ones; the second property allows an adaptive coding based on spatial locality.

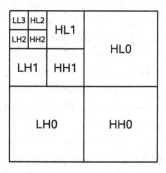

Fig. 23.2.   Wavelet decomposition of image I, organized in subbands.

The two wavelet transforms used in JPEG2000 coding chain are LeGall 5/3 and Daubechies 9/7.[38] The characteristics of the former (good approximation property and the shortest biorthogonal filters available) lead it to be used for loss-less compression, while the latter (good orthogonality, despite of a non optimal smoothness) is more suitable for the lossy one. In order to reduce computational load, instead of using the original Mallat multiresolution scheme[39] the wavelet decomposition is carried out using a lifting scheme.[40] Starting from the origi-nal image I, the coefficients produced by the multiresolution computation of the wavelet transform are organized in bands (conventionally referred to as LL, HL, LH and HH) and levels, depicted in Figure 23.2.

23.2.3. *Coefficient coding*

The coefficient coding is composed into several functional units, described in the current section (Figure 23.3). The first one, called Tier-1, processes wavelet co-

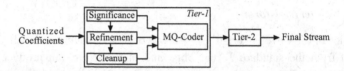

Fig. 23.3.   The coefficient coding block of JPEG2000 compression chain.

efficients and generates a bitstream; the second one, called Tier-2, organizes the bitstream according to user specifications. In Tier-1, after the wavelet coefficients have been computed, the whole subsequent processing is organized into non over-lapping code-blocks of (typically 64 by 64) coefficients; each code block is passed to the coding chain independently. This creates the input for $EBCOT$[41] algorithm. The main idea behind this algorithm is to code coefficients "by difference" be-tween two sets: significant and non significant ones, the big effort is toward local-izing the non significant (which occurs with a higher probability) area of blocks: in this way the position of significant coefficients is easily determined. This fun-damental idea of EZW is implemented in JPEG2000 by bit-plane coding (Figure 23.4(a)) in which a particular scan order of coefficient inside each code block is applied (Figure 23.4(b)).

The implementation is slightly different from the original EZW because thresholding is abandoned and the significance of a coefficient is determined in bit-plane scanning according to the bare value of the bit and the relationship with neighborhood coefficients. The bit-plane scan unit is called *stripe*, which is four bits high and as wide as the code block (Figure 23.4(b)). For simplicity, we call a single column of a stripe a *quadruplet*: this term will be used further in the paper. The bit-plane coding is implemented in a sequence of three passes called *signif-*

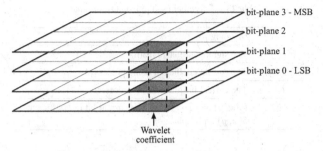

(a) A wavelet coefficient viewed over four different bit-planes.

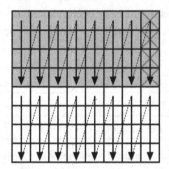

(b) Two stripes are shown with scan order within a bit-plane in a code block. The first stripe has been shaded in dark gray, and a single quadruplet has been "crossed".

Fig. 23.4.   Organization and scan order of wavelet coefficients.

icance, *refinement* and *cleanup*: each sequence is executed on every bit plane, starting from the MSB to the LSB.

23.2.3.1. *Significance pass*

In this pass each stripe is scanned, bit by bit, to decide if a coefficient is significant or not. For clarity sake, the symbols that will be used are presented in Table 23.1 (here, x and y identify the current position in the block). If the current coefficient $b(x, y)$ has not already been marked as significant ($\sigma(x, y) = 0$) and its neighborhood (Figure 23.5) contains at least one significant coefficient, the value v is conveyed to the MQ-coder (see Figure 23.3) and the corresponding $\sigma(x, y)$ is updated (one if v is equal to one, zero otherwise). If v is equal to one, the sign of the coefficient will be conveyed too. If the coefficient $b(x, y)$ has already been marked

Table 23.1.   Symbol used in EBCOT summary.

Symbol	Meaning
$\sigma(x,y)$	The significance state matrix
$b(x,y)$	The current coefficient being processed
bp	The current bit-plane being processed
v	($b(x,y)$ and $1 << bp$) The current bit of coefficient $b(x,y)$ on bit-plane bp

as significant ($\sigma(x,y) = 1$), the bit v will be processed in the refinement pass. If the current coefficient has not already been marked as significant ($\sigma(x,y) = 0$) and its neighborhood does not contain any significant coefficient, the cleanup pass will take care of it.

$b(x-1,y-1)$	$b(x,y-1)$	$b(x+1,y-1)$
$b(x-1,y)$	$\bullet$	$b(x+1,y)$
$b(x-1,y+1)$	$b(x,y+1)$	$b(x+1,y+1)$

Fig. 23.5.   The 8 connected neighborhood of a coefficient $b(x,y)$.

23.2.3.2. *Refinement pass*

This second pass is used to convey the magnitude of coefficients that have already been found significant ($\sigma(x,y) = 1$) in previous passes, conveying v.

23.2.3.3. *Cleanup pass*

This pass takes care of processing all the coefficients discarded by the two previous passes. It scans for every quadruplet: if all the four quadruplet coefficients have ($\sigma=0$) and their neighborhoods do not contain any significant coefficient and they do not become significant in the current bit-plane (all v are equal to zero) a bit zero is conveyed together with the corresponding context (this configuration has been called *non significant quadruplet*). If all the four quadruplet coefficients have $\sigma = 0$ and their neighborhoods do not contain any significant coefficient but at least one v value is equal to one, a string is conveyed to identify the position of the first $v = 1$ and the remaining coefficients are coded according to the standard significance pass policy. This particular configuration will be referred to as *half quadruplet*. If at least one of the four quadruplet coefficients have $\sigma = 1$, the whole quadruplet is coded as if it were on a significance pass.

When starting the chain on most significant bit plane, the significance and refinement pass have no effect on bitstream generation because the first actual σ matrix update is performed in the first cleanup pass.

23.2.4. *MQ-coder*

Referring to Figure 23.3, this part takes the values produced either by *significance*, *refinement* or the *cleanup* passes and generates the stream accordingly to a half context, half arithmetic coder. Instead of using a totally arithmetic coder,[42] some previously defined probability context are used to empower the codeword production. The contexts have been defined for each pass according to probability model of the bitstream. For example, in the *significance* and *refinement* passes the choice of the context depends upon the corresponding band of the coefficient and the eight connected neighborhood configuration of the currently processed bit (a reference regarding the approach of MQ-coder can be found in[43]).

23.2.5. *Tier-2 coder*

Tier-2 coder is the second part of *EBCOT* algorithm. The bitstream produced by each code block from the previous step is now organized into layers: this is done with a sort of multiplexing and ordering the bitstreams associated to code blocks and bit-planes. A *layer* is a collection of some consecutive bit-plane coding passes from all code blocks in all subbands and in all components.[1] The quality of the image can be tuned in two ways: with the same levels of resolution but varying the number of layers, one can perceive an image in its original size with different level of degradation (typically in the form of blurring artifacts); with the same number of layers, but varying the levels of resolution, the image is perceived always at the same quality, but in different sizes, obviously smaller for less resolution levels.

The compressed data, now organized in layers, are then organized into packets, each of them composed by a header, containing important information about how the packet has been built, and a body. This kind of organization of the final codestream is done for a better control of the produced quality and for an easier parsing that will be done by a decoder.

23.3. Toward the Proposed Algorithms

The first of the two proposed algorithms makes modifications on the *significance* and *refinement* passes, while the second one works only on the *cleanup* pass;

before explaining those in details, the concept of sparse histogram images is addressed in order to understand the approach of the work. The aim of this study is to find an intuitive relation between the term "sparse histogram" and its visual meaning; therefore, we propose a novel sparsity index definition. For clarity, the index is composed by two terms, which are defined as follows. Let us take the set T defined as:

$$T \equiv \{t \mid t \in [0, 2^{bps} - 1]\} \tag{23.2}$$

where bps is the bit per sample of the image and $\sharp T$ will denote the cardinality of T. In this work, 256 gray levels images are taken into account, so bps will be normally set to 8. We define the function $H(t)$ as the histogram of a given image, that is, for each image tone t, $H(t)$ is equal to the number of occurrences of the tone t in the image. Let's define a threshold th as the mean value of a normalized version of $H(t)$ (the normalization of $H(t)$ is done on the maximum value of $H(t)$, so that for every image the histogram values are in the range $[0, 1]$), which visually is a discriminant between an image having some gray tones more prevalent than other, or having all the gray tones playing more or less the same role. Basing upon the histogram function, we define a sparsity index as the sum of two terms:

$$\mathcal{I} = A + B \tag{23.3}$$

The computation of A and B is explained in the following paragraphs.

23.3.1. *The sparsity index: First term computation*

The first term of the sparsity index is defined as follows: from Equation 23.2, taking into account the set

$$T' \equiv \{t \mid H(t) < th\} \tag{23.4}$$

we define A as

$$A = \frac{\sharp T'}{\sharp T} \tag{23.5}$$

that is, the ratio between the number of image tones t that have a histogram value below that threshold and the total number of image tones.

23.3.2. *The sparsity index: Second term computation*

Starting from $H(t)$, we define m_1 (Figure 23.6(a)) as

$$m_1 = \max(H(t)) \tag{23.6}$$

and $\bar{t}$ as

$$\bar{t} \quad | \quad H(\bar{t}) = m_1 \tag{23.7}$$

From 23.6 and 23.7, we modify $H(t)$ to produce $H_\star$ defined as:

$$H_\star = \begin{cases} H(t) \ \forall t \neq \bar{t} \\ 0 \quad \text{if } t = \bar{t} \end{cases} \tag{23.8}$$

The same operations are performed on $H_\star$, so (Figure 23.6(b)):

$$m_2 = \max(H_\star(t)) \tag{23.9}$$

and $\bar{\bar{t}}$

$$\bar{\bar{t}} \quad | \quad H_\star(\bar{\bar{t}}) = m_2 \tag{23.10}$$

If there is an ambiguity in the choice of $\bar{t}$ and $\bar{\bar{t}}$, we consider the values of $\bar{t}$ and $\bar{\bar{t}}$ that minimize the distance $|\bar{t} - \bar{\bar{t}}|$ (Figure 23.6(c)). So, the second term (B) is defined as follows:

$$B = \frac{|\bar{t} - \bar{\bar{t}}|}{\sharp T - 1} \tag{23.11}$$

In order to better highlight the sparsity index boundaries, two synthetic images have been created: in image 23.7(a) the number of pixels is equal to the number of gray scale tones, in image 23.7(b) only the two most distant tones (e.g. black and white) have been used.

When the sparsity index is calculated for the first image (23.7(a)), called "Smooth", its histogram is a constant function of value 1 over all the image tones: so we have

$$th = 1 \text{ (the only histogram value)} \tag{23.12}$$

and, from Equation 23.5

$$A = \frac{0}{\sharp T} = 0 \text{ (no tone is below the threshold)} \tag{23.13}$$

For B term, we have (see Equation 23.11):

$$B = \frac{1}{\sharp T - 1} \text{ (each maximum is one-tone far from its neighbor)} \tag{23.14}$$

therefore, from Eqs. 23.3, 23.13, and 23.14 we have

$$\mathcal{I} = 0 + \frac{1}{\sharp T - 1} = 0.003922 \tag{23.15}$$

Taking into account the second image (23.7(b)), called "Hard", its histogram consists of only two peaks at the edge of the graph ($t = 0$ and $t = \sharp T - 1$), both of

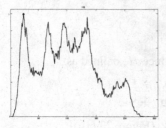 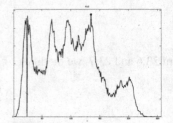

(a) The image histogram $H(t)$ with m_1 high-
lighted by a rounded dot.

(b) The image histogram $H_\star(t)$ with m_2 high-
lighted by a rounded dot.

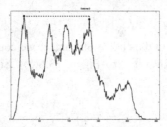

(c) The image histogram and the distance $|\bar{t} - \bar{\bar{t}}|$
indicated by the dashed line.

Fig. 23.6.   The steps of the computation of the second term B as in Equation 23.11.

(a) "Smooth"   (b) "Hard"

Fig. 23.7.   Test images for sparsity index boundaries evaluation. (a) sparsity index is equal to 0 and
(b) is equal to 2.

value $\sharp T/2$ (this height of the peaks is valid only in this case for a "Hard" image
measuring 16 by 16 pixels; in the most general case, for a V*H image, the peak
height is (V*H)/2). For image "Hard" we have (using the normalized version of
$H(t)$, the two $\sharp T/2$ peaks normalize to 1):

$$th = (1 + 0 + \ldots + 0 + 1)\frac{1}{\sharp T} = \frac{2}{\sharp T} \qquad (23.16)$$

and (Equation 23.5):

$$A = \frac{\sharp T - 2}{\sharp T} \qquad (23.17)$$

(all the tones but the two at the very edge of the histogram are below the threshold, which is small but strictly positive.) For B term, we have (Equation 23.11):

$$B = \frac{|0 - (\sharp T - 1)|}{\sharp T - 1} \text{ (the two tones are at the maximum distance)} \qquad (23.18)$$

therefore, from Eqs. 23.3, 23.17, and 23.18 we have

$$\mathcal{I} = \frac{\sharp T - 2}{\sharp T} + 1 = 1.992188 \qquad (23.19)$$

In Table 23.2 is shown a list of images from literature in increasing order, according to the sparsity index. In order to give the reader a visual feedback

Table 23.2. Test images in increasing order according to the sparsity index (Equation 23.3).

Name	zelda	mandrill	bride	bird	peppers	camera	barb	mehead	mountain	boat	lena
Id	21	13	4	2	17	5	1	14	16	3	11
Unique Colors	187	226	256	145	230	247	221	256	110	224	230
$\mathcal{I}$	0.47	0.52	0.55	0.61	0.65	0.66	0.66	0.72	0.72	0.75	0.96

	frog	squares	montage	slope	fractalators	text	library-1	circles	crosses	jpf
Id	10	19	15	18	9	20	12	6	7	8
Unique Colors	102	4	251	248	6	2	221	4	2	2
$\mathcal{I}$	0.97	1.18	1.61	1.67	1.69	1.69	1.69	1.83	1.84	1.84

for sparsity index $\mathcal{I}$ we present (Figure 23.8), three examples from the tested images, showing also, with a solid line, the corresponding threshold th: the first one is *zelda* (Figure 23.8(a)), the least sparse ($\mathcal{I}$=0.473), with its histogram, then an intermediate case with *lena* (Figure 23.8(b)) ($\mathcal{I}$=0.955), and finally, the most sparse case with *crosses* (Figure 23.8(c)) ($\mathcal{I}$=1.835).

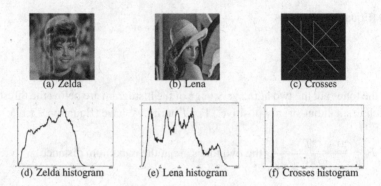

(a) Zelda   (b) Lena   (c) Crosses

(d) Zelda histogram   (e) Lena histogram   (f) Crosses histogram

Fig. 23.8.   Reading the figures columnwise, for each column the couple picture-histogram is presented.

23.4. The Two Proposals

23.4.1. *First algorithm: Stripe lengthening*

The first algorithm proposed in this paper addresses the first part of *Tier-1* encoder, the *significance* and the *refinement* passes: recalling that bit coefficients are encoded in groups of four by four (the quadruplets), the aim is to reduce changing context overhead by making quadruplets (and, consequently, stripes) longer; therefore, we call it "stripe lengthening". We expect that, by lengthening the stripe, the number of context changes is reduced; this is particularly true for images with a higher sparseness, because their characteristics are likely to change less often than other kind of images. For this reason, we expect better result for images with a higher index $\mathcal{I}$. The lengthening is the same in *significance* and *refinement* pass (while the *cleanup* pass is performed with the original length 4): in fact, it would not be coherent to group coefficients in two different ways in the same encoding process. The reason why we choose to leave the cleanup pass with its original stripe length of 4 bits is that we prefer to have the two modifications distinguished; moreover, it does not make sense using longer stripe in the cleanup pass when the second modification is active: the longer the stripe, the shorter the quadruplet series.

In order to perform the modification of the algorithm to the encoding process, two variables (pointers) have been used to keep track of the current quadruplets and to identify the beginning of the next one and they are properly initialized according to the new stripe length. The original JPEG2000 quadruplet length was fixed to 4 (hence the name). In our algorithm, we test the encoder over various quadruplet lengths; the range varies from 5 to the block height, but in the experimental results here reported only significant values are considered, namely 8, 16 and 32. We have implemented the algorithm in a way that it is fully compatible with the source code Jasper[44] in which the piece of code regarding each quadruplet bit was repeated four times. As we have parameterized the length, we embodied such code in a counter based loop which cycles until the quadruplet length counter becomes zero. The implementation of the stripe lengthening requires a corresponding modification of the decoder structure, in order to couple correctly coder and decoder. Various combinations of resolution levels and stripe lengths have been evaluated; first we present the results of the experiments for single combinations (*stripe length-resolution level* - Figure 23.9(a)-23.11(b)), then three overall graphs will be shown in order to give a general overview of the combinations.

23.4.1.1. *Single combination experiments*

The bar graphs (see Figure 23.9(a) and 23.9(b)) have on the X-axis an image identifier (for space reason it could not be possible to put the whole image name (see Table 23.2)), and on the Y-axis a ratio R defined as

$$R = 1 - \frac{P}{O} \tag{23.20}$$

where P is the encoded file size obtained using the encoder modified by this proposal and O is the size regarding the original JPEG2000 encoder. The formula in Equation 23.20 has been adopted in order to give an immediate visual feedback: if the bar is above the ordinate of value 0, the modified encoder works better (the file is smaller) than the original one, the contrary otherwise. In Figure 23.9 graphs relative to 8 bit long stripes with 2 and 6 levels of resolution are presented.

The most remarkable results (between 7% and 8% gain) are obtained at 2 levels of resolution, while, using 6 levels, the situation becomes worse (around 1.1%) and just few images (always the sparse histogram ones) can perform well. The performance decay when the number of wavelet decomposition levels increase because the code blocks will be smaller, as dictated by the wavelet transform. Therefore, stripe lengthening will work in a smaller number of areas (if the stripe length is greater than the code block, the stripe is truncated to the code block dimension) and its application will have less relevance.

In the subsequent Figures (23.10 and 23.11) plots are as follows: for stripes length of 16 and 32 bits two graphs, regarding 2 and 6 levels of resolutions, are depicted. Therefore, the algorithm introduces enhancement at lower levels of resolutions, where JPEG2000 has a lower compression ratio.

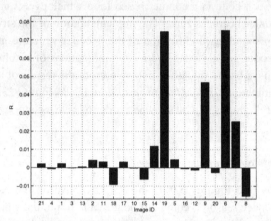

(a) Two levels of resolution. Best gain about 8%

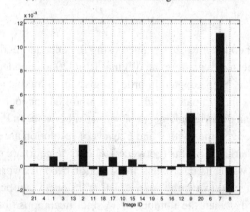

(b) Six levels of resolution. Best gain about 1.1%

Fig. 23.9.   Single combination graphs for stripe length equal to 8 bit for each image, the R value (Equation 23.20) shows the gain of our coder compared to JPEG2000. Images are ordered increasingly according to sparsity.

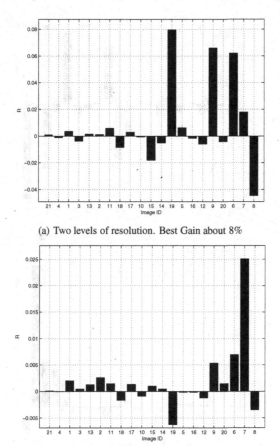

(a) Two levels of resolution. Best Gain about 8%

(b) Six levels of resolution. Best Gain about 2.5%

Fig. 23.10.   Single combination graphs for stripe lengths equal to 16 bit: for each image, the R value (Equation 23.20) shows the gain of our coder compared to JPEG2000. Images are ordered increasingly according to sparsity.

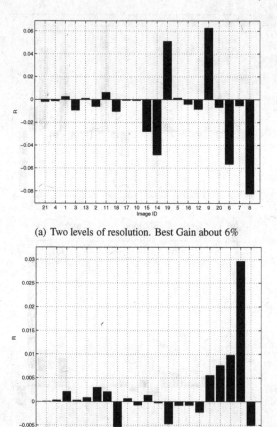

(a) Two levels of resolution. Best Gain about 6%

(b) Six levels of resolution. Best Gain about 3%

Fig. 23.11.   Single combination graphs for stripe length equal to 32 bit: for each image, the R value (Equation 23.20) shows the gain of our coder compared to JPEG2000.

23.4.1.2. Overall graphs

As an overall example, the values of R obtained at the various levels of resolution are depicted in Figures 23.12-23.14. Besides, the mean value of R, computed over 3 - 6 levels of resolution, is reported in the graph. In the graph of Figure 23.13 the best results are obtained; from the next one (Figure 23.14) there is no more reason to further increase the stripe length because the ratio become significantly less than zero, meaning that the original coder is performing better than the modified one. In Figures 23.15(a) and 23.15(b) overall mean graphs are proposed. In the first one the mean is over the stripes, while in the second the mean is over the resolution levels.

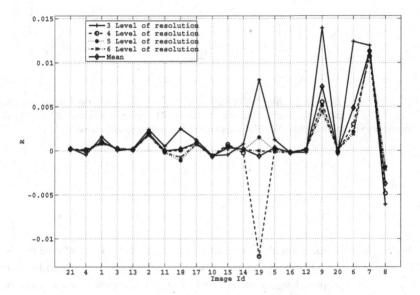

Fig. 23.12.   Overall graph for stripe length equal to 8 bit: for each image, the R value (Equation 23.20) shows the gain of our coder compared to JPEG2000. The best gain is in term of 8% of the file size coded with standard JPEG2000. The images are sorted by their sparsity value.

From the several experiments one thing is clearly noticeable: almost all of the image files with a high sparsity index are significantly smaller when processed by our algorithm at a low level of resolution: the behavior does not follow the trend of JPEG2000 encoder, which obtains better results with more resolution levels. It is otherwise important to notice that in each graph the best performances are

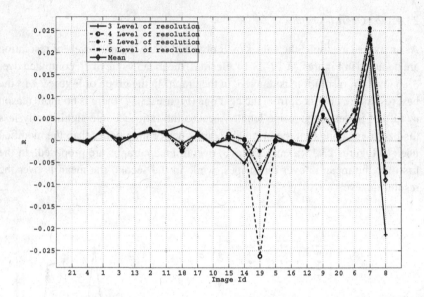

Fig. 23.13. Overall graph for stripe length equal to 16 bit: for each image, the R value (Equation 23.20) shows the gain of our coder compared to JPEG2000. The best gain is in term of 8% of the file size coded with standard JPEG2000. The images are sorted by their sparsity value.

always given by images with a high degree of sparseness, in accordance to what we supposed at the beginning of the work. Another approach has been followed in the second proposed algorithm, which is almost resolution - independent, but still preserving the biased behavior toward sparse histogram images. Observing that there is a better margin for improvement when the resolution level is low but standard JPEG2000 level of resolution is 5, to justify the use of less levels of resolution and the stripe lengthening, we compare the execution times of standard algorithm with no stripe lengthening and 5 levels of resolution to the use of 8 bit stripe lengthening and 2 levels of resolution. As Figure 23.16(a) shows, despite the fact that this comparison is not so favorable for the modified algorithm in terms of compression, execution times are always lower or at most equal to the standard algorithm. If we compare the size, our modification is better for sparse histogram images (Figure 23.16(b).)

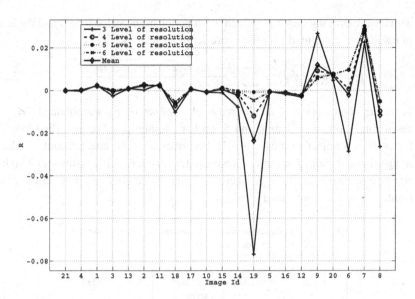

Fig. 23.14.   Overall graph for stripes height equal to 32 bit: for each image, the R value (Equation 23.20) shows the gain of our coder compared to JPEG2000. The best gain is in term of 6% of the file size coded with standard JPEG2000. The images are sorted by their sparsity value.

23.4.1.3. *Comparison to other compression algorithms*

Several articles in literature[6,45] show that JPEG2000 now is one of the most promising and well performing format for compression of still images; even if some formats perform better in some cases, JPEG2000 characteristics and versatility justify our choice of having JPEG2000 as our main comparison term. Moreover, as we consider lossless compression only, we consider also JPEG-LS[46] as the "optimum" comparison term. However, we want to give an idea of possible comparisons to other approaches by taking also into consideration another compression algorithm: the choice has been directed to PNG[47] format, because it is one of the most recent image format that has achieved popularity on the Web. In this section, a comparison table (Table 23.3) among the obtained compression ratios of Standard JPEG2000, stripe lengthening, JPEG-LS, and the PNG format is given. From the experimental results (summarized in Table 23.3), we point out that the performance of our algorithm, when applied to sparse histogram images (from *text* to *fpf*), are between standard JPEG2000 and JPEG-LS. It is interesting to study the effect of multiresolution and stripe length choice over the compression ratio; so, in order to find the best stripe length and level of resolution, we define an improving factor F (which is a function of the stripe length and the level of resolution) computed over the entire set of 21 images:

$$F(stripe, level) = \sum_{i=1}^{21} \frac{size_{standard} - size_{modified}^{stripe,level}}{size_{uncompressed}} \qquad (23.21)$$

From the computation of all the reasonable values of F, we obtained the best result for 32 bit stripe length and 5 levels of resolution. We underline that the factor F is a objective measure only, and does not take into account whatever image characteristic. F computation mediates between highly positive and highly negative results in each image; therefore, there is no contradiction between this result and the ones presented in Figures 23.12-23.14.

Table 23.3. Comparison of the compression ratios obtained from lossless JPEG2000, stripe lengthening (8 bit stripe and 2 levels of resolution), JPEG-LS, and PNG.

Image	JPEG2000	8 bit stripe - 2 levels	PNG	JPEG-LS
zelda	2.00	1.89	1.88	2.00
bridge	1.34	1.33	1.35	1.38
barb	1.72	1.66	1.51	1.69
boat	1.82	1.77	1.73	1.88
mandrill	1.31	1.30	1.28	1.33
bird	2.22	2.13	2.02	2.31
lena	1.69	1.65	1.59	1.75
slope	6.02	3.82	5.60	5.09
peppers	1.73	1.67	1.65	1.78
frog	1.28	1.27	1.33	1.32
montage	2.70	2.54	2.72	2.94
mehead	3.78	3.39	4.02	4.89
squares	50.52	31.14	99.52	103.77
camera	1.76	1.72	1.71	1.86
mountain	1.19	1.19	1.21	1.25
library-1	1.40	1.40	1.56	1.57
fractalators	3.80	3.65	11.15	6.03
text	1.91	2.01	27.81	4.91
circles	8.84	9.30	35.49	52.46
crosses	7.67	8.21	32.48	20.77
fpf	7.50	8.57	43.18	64.10

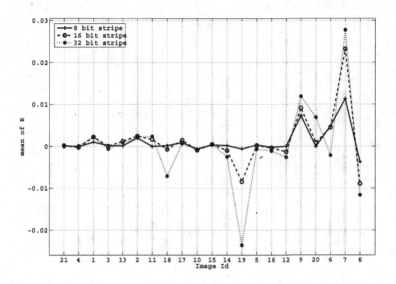

(a) Mean over stripe length.

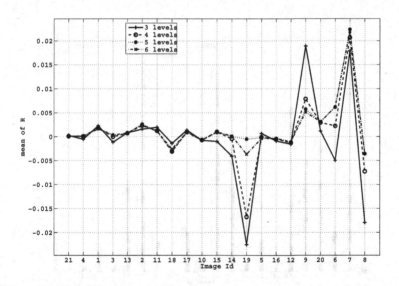

(b) Mean over resolution levels.

Fig. 23.15.   On top, the mean of R value is computed over different stripe lengths of 8, 16, and 32 pixels with 3-6 Level of resolution; on bottom, the mean is computed over 3 - 6 Resolution Level with a different stripe lengths of 8, 16, and 32 pixels.

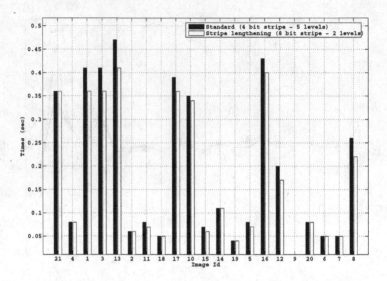

(a) Time comparison. The computation time is always lower (at most equal) than the one obtained with the standard encoder, and this behavior is more prominent in the high sparsity region.

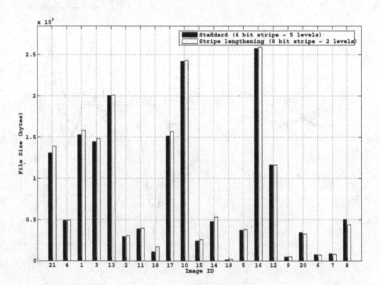

(b) Size comparison. Our algorithm works better on images with a high sparsity index.

Fig. 23.16. Comparison between a 5 level standard JPEG2000 against a 2 level (stripe 8) modified algorithm.

23.4.2. Second algorithm: SuperRLC

23.4.2.1. Theoretical considerations

The second proposal focuses on the last part of Tier-1 coder, which is the *cleanup* pass. Recalling the concepts exposed in section 23.2.3.3, pointing at the fact that each completely non significant quadruplet is conveyed with one bit, a possible improvement is the following: instead of coding quadruplets with one bit each, we use a binary word for every set of consecutive non significant quadruplets. The binary word length is fixed throughout the whole encoding process. The gain is higher as the number of consecutive non significant quadruplets increases. At the end of the *cleanup* pass, it is possible to identify on the current bit-plane different series of non significant quadruplet, each of them has a different length.

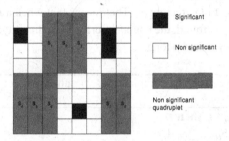

Fig. 23.17.   Different groups of quadruplets. From this block it can be figured out eight single quadruplets, s_1 through s_8. Here we have S_3 with $\sharp S_3$ equal to 2, and S_2 with $\sharp S_2$ equal to 1.

Before attempting a non trivial modification to the coder, it is important to see how this is going to affect its behavior (a good introduction on statistic has been taken from[48]). In this explanation the concept of non significant consecutive quadruplets will be addressed many times, so in the following we refer it to as *nscq*. A pictorial view of what is explained below is given in Figure 23.17. Let us define a set S_j containing all *nscq*s with the same length j, with j varying in the range $[1, j_{MAX}]$, where j_{MAX} is the longest group of *nscq* that could be found. The length of a single *nscq* will be referred to as $l(nscq)$. Another index that has to be defined is k_{MAX}, which is the maximum number of *nscq* that can be sent to the MQ-coder in only one binary word, as explained later. So j_{MAX} depends on the current coefficients of the bit-plane in the running encoding process, while k_{MAX} (we have $k_{MAX} \leq j_{MAX}$) depends on the actual length of the binary word: referring to the length as W we have $k_{MAX} = 2^W - 1$. If the length of the current *nscq* is less than k_{MAX}, the *nscq* is entirely coded, otherwise it is treated as two shorter *nscq*. This process affects the values of $\sharp S$ (we use $\sharp S$ referring to

$\sharp S_j \forall j$). The following equations describe the process in detail referring to how $\sharp S$ is modified. Using the remainder function

$$r(x, y) = \left(x - \left\lfloor \frac{x}{y} \right\rfloor y \right) \qquad (23.22)$$

and setting p and q as

$$p = r(l(nscq), k_{MAX}) \qquad (23.23)$$

$$q = \left\lfloor \frac{l(nscq)}{k_{MAX}} \right\rfloor$$

the computation of $\sharp S$ comes to as described by Algorithm 23.1 (for clarity, $\sharp S$ values are expressed in percentage). That means that when a *nscq* with its length greater than k_{MAX} is found, the encoder performs in this way: it conveys q series k_{MAX} long and one series p long.

Algorithm 23.1 Cardinality computation. p and q are computed in Equation 23.23.

---

if $l(nscq) \le k_{MAX}$ **then**

$\quad \sharp S_{l(nscq)} = \sharp S_{l(nscq)} + 1$

else

$\quad \sharp S_{k_{MAX}} = \sharp S_{k_{MAX}} + q$

$\quad \sharp S_p = \sharp S_p + 1$

end if

Applying the $\sharp S$ computation to Lena image, Figure 23.18 presents the results of the histogram of the $\sharp S$ computation. The explanation of a high value in the case $j = 31$ is quite straightforward: the last bin of the histogram counts all not significant sequences composed by 31 quadruplets. Hence, all sequences composed by more than 31 (in this case) quadruplets will score a point for the bin in the r position, and q point for the bin in the 31st position. Due to this reason, the last bin takes a value higher than the others.

Figure 23.20(a) shows the same histogram computation for image Crosses.

The $\sharp S$ refers to a particular choice of k_{MAX}, depending on W. Its computation ends the implementation of modified cleanup pass. However, as we are interested into an evaluation of the actual gain, (referring to the standard JPEG2000 cleanup pass) we can study the behavior of $\sharp S$ varying the upper limit of $l(nscq)$. Therefore, we have recalculated $\sharp S$ values for k varying from 1 to k_{MAX}. To do

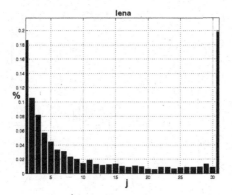

Fig. 23.18.   Cardinality computation for *nscq*s (Image Lena).

this a new $\sharp S$ (named $\sharp S'$) is computed in this way:

$$\forall k \leq k_{MAX} \ \sharp S'_k = \sum_{i=1}^{k_{MAX}} \sharp S_z \text{ where } z = \max(k_{MAX}, k \cdot i) \qquad (23.24)$$

So now $\sharp S'$ contains the probability distribution as if j_{MAX} (that is, the maximum of $l(nscq)$) could assume all the values in the range $1,\ldots k_{MAX}$. Knowing from Equation 23.24 the entire probability distribution, it is interesting to give an estimation of the acquired gain versus the original coder. We defined a gain function G as

$$G(k, k_{MAX}) = \frac{k}{1 + \log_2(k_{MAX} + 1)} \qquad (23.25)$$

in which the numerator represents the bits used by the original coder and the denominator the bits used by the modified one. Function G (Equation 23.25) is used to weight the quadruplets probability distribution leading to (assuming that k_{MAX} is fixed):

$$\sharp S'_\star(k) = G(k)\sharp S'_k - 1 \qquad (23.26)$$

In Figure 23.19 is presented the final graph that shows $\sharp S'_\star$ (Equation 23.26). The meaning of this function $\sharp S'_\star$ is an evaluation of $\sharp S'(k)$ weighted by the gain function G, thus giving an estimation of the gain toward JPEG2000 standard coder for each admissible value of consecutive quadruplet series. We point out that in Equation 23.26, the term -1 introduces a shift; therefore if values of $\sharp S'_\star$ (Figure 23.19) are greater than zero it means a positive gain. Apart from an initial irregular shape, the function in Figure 23.19 shows a stable gain for a maximum $l(nscq)$ greater than 16. From this point on, our algorithm performs better. This Figure refers to

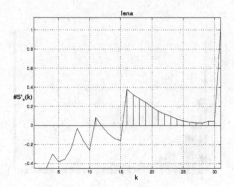

Fig. 23.19. The weighted histogram $\sharp S'_\star(k)$ (Equation 23.26) shows the gain in terms of bit number with respect to the original coder JPEG2000 as a function of quadruplet series length (Image Lena).

Lena, but the same behavior is confirmed (or even better) for the other images: as an example, in Figure 23.20(b) the function in Equation 23.26 is plotted for image "crosses". For completeness, we have computed the gain for all the other test images. The final measure of how much using the *SuperRLC* is convenient is given by:

$$M = \sum_{i=1}^{k_{MAX}} \sharp S'_{\star_i} \tag{23.27}$$

Equation 23.27 computes in fact the integral function of the weighted histogram (Equation 23.26), measuring the positive gain area. M values are reported in Table 23.4. It is important to remind that this is not an overall gain, but it is just set up for bits sent by the cleanup pass to the final stage of Tier-1, the *MQ-coder*.

23.4.2.2. *Comparisons with other images and the sparsity index*

"Lena" is a well - known standard image for compression evaluation; however we present here the results about other interesting cases: as regards *Crosses* image, which has a sparsity index of 1.835 against the 0.955 of Lena, the tracking of $\sharp S$ during the encoding process is as depicted in Figure 23.20(a). The distribution follows the sparsity: while in the *lena* case a smaller $\sharp S$ was more probable, this time the plot shows a clear need of a longer quadruplets series length ($\sharp S$). The graphic, depicted in Figure 23.20(b), overtakes more strongly the gain equal to one, and the measure given by Equation 23.27 is equal to 10.2347, against - 0.3694 for Lena. In Table 23.4 all integral values associated to each image have been reported. Referring to Table 23.2 for sparsity indices, the values of M grow

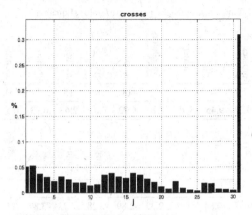

(a) Cardinality computation for *nscqs*.

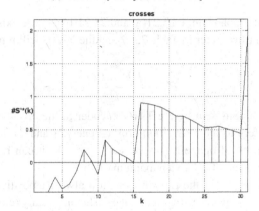

(b) The weighted $\sharp S'_\star(k)$ (Equation 23.26) shows the gain in terms of bit number respect to the original coder JPEG2000 as a function of quadruplet series length

Fig. 23.20.   Cardinality computation and weighted $\sharp S'_\star(k)$ for image Crosses.

following, with few exceptions, the sparsity order. More generally, for all the images, there is always a value $\overline{k}$ for which our algorithm outperforms JPEG2000 $\forall k > \overline{k}$.

23.4.2.3. *Overall comparison to JPEG2000*

In this part, the computation of the ratio between all the bits (from significance, refinement, and cleanup) sent by original JPEG2000 and SuperRLC coder is plotted. As an example, two cases for W value equal to 5 and 6, respectively are

Table 23.4.　Images and their M value (Equation 23.27)

Name	crosses	circles	squares	fractalators	slope	fpf	montage	camera	mehead	bird	barb
Image ID	7	6	19	9	18	8	15	5	14	2	1
M	10.23	9.45	8.78	7.78	6.72	5.08	2.63	0.93	0.51	0.49	0.18

Name	lena	boat	peppers	zelda	library-1	mandrill	mountain	text	bridge	frog
Image ID	11	3	17	21	12	13	16	20	4	10
M	-0.37	-0.84	-0.89	-2.32	-2.89	-3.28	-3.32	-3.84	-4.05	-5.08

shown. For each graph (Figure 23.21(a) and 23.21(b)), the X-axis will report the usual image identifier (refer to Table 23.2) and the Y-axis will report the quantity R' defined as:

$$R' = \frac{|BP - BO|}{D} \tag{23.28}$$

where BP are the bits sent by the Tier-1 encoder to the *MQ-coder* in the RLC method, BO refers to the JPEG2000 original encoder and D is the size of the original uncompressed image file expressed in bit. As it can be seen, the gain goes from a minimum of 2% to a maximum of 15%.

For these values of W, the experiments show always a positive gain, which is more impressive for sparse histogram images. The only really relevant exceptions are for images 12 and 20 (*text* and *library-1*, respectively), which do not follow the behavior dictated by their sparseness; as it could be clearly seen (Figure 23.22(a) and 23.22(b)), these two images have nothing in common with the other images with sparse histogram, that is, their structure is so significantly different (a text document and a compound image) which justifies their anomalous behavior. We underline the fact that also image 8 is a text image, but it performs quite well. Moreover, the simple fact that an image represents a text is not discriminant. The reason is that image 8 is really a sparse image with a constant white background and a foreground (the text) which is spatially distributed in a very sparse way. We mean that in the case of image 8, "sparsity" is not only on grey level distribution, but also on the geometrical disposition inside the image. This does not hold for the second text image (12), where the background is not constant and the text is an automated list. By carefully observing the plots of Figure 23.21, a further comment about image 10 (frog) is mandatory. Image 10, despite its index $\mathcal{I}$, has a value of

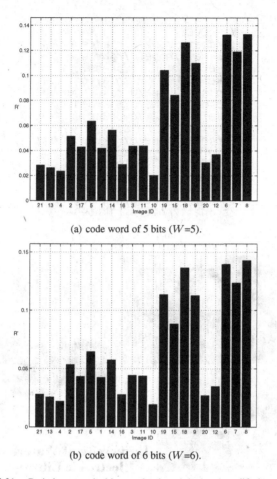

(a) code word of 5 bits (W=5).

(b) code word of 6 bits (W=6).

Fig. 23.21.   Ratio between the bits sent by the original and modified encoder.

R' (Equation 23.28) significantly smaller than image 11 and 19, and we explain this fact by observing that the "frog" image is a highly textured one, because the subject (the animal) is so close to the camera that the spatial disposition of pixels is more similar to a texture than a tipical object on a background.

We prefer to consider R' (Equation 23.28) as a performance index, rather that comparing the bare file sizes at the end of the entire compress chain, because: a) we are interested into exploring the positive effects of our modifications on the significance, refinement, and cleanup group (where they effectively occur); b) we want to exclude any possible effects of the arithmetic coder, which follows in the chain.

```
MT-LEVEL
{spinet}/home/u/rjkroeger/vf
{spinet}/home/u/rjkroeger/vf
Makefile        compress.c    fi
Makefile~       display.c     fr
{spinet}/home/u/rjkroeger/vf
{spinet}/home/u/rjkroeger/vf
Makefile        compress.c    fi
Makefile~       display.c     fr
{spinet}/home/u/rjkroeger/vf
Makefile        display.c     im
Makefile~       fileio.c      im
compress.c      fractal.h     im
{spinet}/home/u/rjkroeger/vf
{spinet}/home/u/rjkroeger/vf
{spinet}/home/u/rjkroeger/vf
```

(a) The *text* image.

University Map and Design Library

Davis Centre Library

Dana Porter Library

**University of Waterloo
Electronic Library**

(b) The *library-1* image.

Fig. 23.22.   Figures for which the behavior does not follow the general trend.

23.4.2.4. *Technical details*

The project has been developed on a Celeron 1.5Ghz, 512Mb RAM, using Microsoft Visual C[49] for JPEG2000 codec and Matlab[50] for presenting the results in a convenient way. The codec is Jasper version from 1.400 to 1.600, of which a guide can be found in Jasper User Manual[44] and implements a JPEG2000 coder fully reviewed by the creator of Jasper M.D. Adams.[5]

23.5. Conclusions

In this paper, we have presented two algorithms for modifying all the three passes of JPEG2000 Tier-1 coder, that is significance, refinement, and cleanup. Theoretical studies have been reported in order to classify the images according to the concept of sparsity and to compute the saving of conveyed bits. The best results are for high sparsity images: assuming the spatial preservation of wavelet coefficients, it has come to mind that longer stripe would have grouped better the (scarce) significant zones in this kind of images. The first algorithm, stripe lengthening, shows significant gain at low levels of resolution on the overall file size respect to the standard. The second algorithm, *SuperRLC*, has the advantage of being independent on the levels of resolution; experiments confirm that it gives a relevant gain on bits conveyed to the MQ-coder respect to the standard JPEG2000. Future works will regard a modification of the arithmetic coder in order to adapt the probability context to the statistics of the new conveyed symbols. We would like to use the same approach as[51] to extend the arithmetic coder contexts in order to evaluate if it is possible to capture the efficiency of the new bitstream generated by our algorithm.

References

1. M. Rabbani and D. Santa Cruz. The JPEG2000 still-image compression standard. In *Proceedings of IEEE International Conference on Image Processing*, Thessaloniki, Greece (Oct., 2001). Course given at conference.
2. A. N. Skodras, C. A. Christopoulos, and T. Ebrahimi, JPEG2000: The upcoming still image compression standard, *Pattern Recognition Letters*. **22**, 1337–1345, (2001).
3. M. W. Marcellin, M. J. Gormish, A. Bilgin, and M. P. Boliek. An overview of JPEG-2000. In *Proc. IEEE Data Compression Conference (DCC'00)*, pp. 523–541, Snowbird, UT (Mar., 2000).
4. D. Taubman, E. Ordentlich, M. Weinberg, and G. Seroussi, Embedded block coding in JPEG 2000, *Signal Processing: Image Communication*. **17**, 49–72, (2002).
5. M. D. Adams. The JPEG2000 still image compression standard. Technical report, ISO/IEC JTC 1/SC 29/WG 1 N 2412 (Dec., 2002).
6. M. Charrier, D. Santa Cruz, and M. Larsson. JPEG 2000, the next millenium compression standard for still images. In *Proc. of the IEEE International Conference on Multimedia Computing and Systems (ICMCS'99)*, pp. 131–132, Florence, Italy (June, 1999).
7. ISO/IEC. 15444-1:2000 information technology - JPEG2000 - image coding system - part 1: Core coding system, (2000).
8. D. S. Taubman and M. W. Marcellin, *JPEG2000: Image compression fundamentals, standards, and practice*. (Kluwer International Series In Engineering and Computer Science, 2002).

9. N. Ahmed, T. Natarajan, and K. R. Rao, Discrete cosine transform, *IEEE Trans. Computers.* **C-23**, 90–93 (Jan., 1974).

10. G. K. Wallace, The JPEG still picture compression standard, *Communications of the ACM.* **34**(4), 30–44, (1991).

11. ISO/ITU. ISO 10918 information technology – digital compression and coding of continuous-tone still images: Requirements and guidelines, (1994).

12. J. M. Shapiro, Embedded image coding using zerotree of wavelet coefficients, *IEEE Trans. Signal Processing.* **41**, 3445–3462 (Dec., 1993).

13. A. Said and W. A. Pearlman, A new fast and efficient image codec based on set partitioning in hierarchical trees, *IEEE Transactions on Circuits and Systems for Video Technology.* **6**, 243–250 (June, 1996).

14. E. Ardizzone, M. La Cascia, and F. Testa. A new algorithm for bit rate allocation in JPEG 2000 tile encoding. In *Proc. IEEE International Conference on Image Analysis and Processing (ICIAP'03)*, pp. 529–534, Mantua, Italy (Sept., 2003).

15. T.-H. Chang, L.-L. Chen, C.-J. Lian, H.-H. Chen, and L.-G. Chen. Computation reduction technique for lossy JPEG 2000 encoding through ebcot tier-2 feedback processing. In *Proc. IEEE International Conference on Image Processing (ICIP'02)*, pp. 85–88, Rochester, NY (June, 2002).

16. S. Battiato, A. Buemi, G. Impoco, and M. Mancuso. Content - dependent optimization of JPEG 2000 compressed images. In *Proc. IEEE International Conference on Consumer Electronics (ICCE'02)*, pp. 46–47, Los Angeles, CA (June, 2002).

17. K. C. B. Tan and T. Arslan. An embedded extension algorithm for the lifting based discrete wavelet transform in JPEG 2000. In *Proc. IEEE Internation Conference on Acoustic, Speech, and Signal Processing (ICASSP'02)*, pp. 3513–3516, Orlando, FL (May, 2002).

18. M. Kurosaki, K. Munadi, and H. Kiya. Error concealment using layer structure for JPEG 2000 images. In *Proc. IEEE Asia-Pacific Conference on Circuit and Systems (APCCS'02)*, pp. 529–534 (Oct., 2002).

19. L. Aztori, A. Corona, and D. Giusto. Error recovery in JPEG 2000 image transmission. In *Proc. IEEE International Conference on Acoustic, Speech, and Signal Processing (ICASSP'01)*, pp. 364–367, Salt Lake City, UT (May, 2001).

20. Y. M. Yeung, O. C. Au, and A. Chang. Successive bit - plane allocation technique for JPEG2000 image coding. In *Proc. IEEE International Conference on Acoustic Speech*, pp. 261–264, Hong Kong, China (Apr., 2003).

21. G. Pastuszak. A novel architecture of arithmetic coder in JPEG2000 based on parallel symbol encoding. In *Proceedings of the IEEE International Conference on Parallel Computing in Electrical Engineering*, pp. 303–308 (Sept., 2004).

22. T. Tillo and G. Olmo, A novel multiple description coding scheme compatible with the JPEG2000 decoder, *IEEE Signal Processing Letters.* **11**(11), 908–911 (Nov., 2004).

23. W. Du, J. Sun, and Q. Ni, Fast and efficient rate control approach for JPEG2000, *IEEE Transactions on Consumer Electronics.* **50**(4), 1218 – 1221 (Nov., 2004).

24. K. Varma and A. Bell. Improving JPEG2000's perceptual performance with weights based on both contrast sensitivity and standard deviation. In *Proceedings of the IEEE International Conference on Acoustics, Speech, and Signal Processing*, vol. 3, pp. 17–21 (May, 2004).

25. T. Kim, H. M. Kim, P.-S. Tsai, and T. Acharya, Memory efficient progressive rate-

distortion algorithm for JPEG 2000, *IEEE Transaction on Circuits and Systems for Video Technology.* **15**(1), 181–187 (Jan., 2005).

26. K. Vikram, V. Vasudevan, and S. Srinivasan, Rate-distortion estimation for fast JPEG2000 compression at low bit-rates, *IEE Electronics Letters.* **41**(1), 16–18 (Jan., 2005).

27. M. Aguzzi. Working with JPEG 2000: two proposals for sparse histogram images. In *Proc. IEEE International Conference on Image Analysis and Processing (ICIAP'03)*, pp. 408–411, Mantua, Italy (Sept., 2003).

28. P. J. Ferreira and A. J. Pinho, Why does histogram packing improve lossless compression rates?, *IEEE Signal Processing Letters.* **9**(8), 259–261 (Aug., 2002).

29. A. J. Pinho, An online preprocessing technique for improving the lossless compression of images with sparse histograms, *IEEE Signal Processing Letters.* **9**(1), 5–7 (Jan., 2002).

30. A. J. Pinho. On the impact of histogram sparseness on some lossless image compression techniques. In *Proceedings of the IEEE International Conference on Image Processing*, pp. 442–445, (2001).

31. A. J. Pinho. A comparison of methods for improving the lossless compression of images with sparse histogram. In *Proceedings of IEEE International Conference on Image Processing*, pp. 673–676, (2002).

32. A. J. Pinho, An online preprocessing technique for improving the lossless compression of images with sparse histograms, *IEEE Signal Processing Letters.* **9**, 5–7, (2002).

33. C. K. Chui, A. K. Chan, and C. S. Liu, *An Introduction To Wavelets.* (Academic Press, San Diego, CA, 1991).

34. M. Vetterli and J. Kovačević, *Wavelets And Subband Coding.* (Prentice Hall, 1995).

35. G. Strang and T. Nguyen, *Wavelets and filters banks.* (Wellsley-Cambridge Press, Wellsley, MA, 1997).

36. I. Daubechies, *Ten lectures on wavelets.* Number 61 in CBMS Lecture, (SIAM, 1992).

37. P. N. Topiwala, *Wavelet Image and Video Compression.* (Kluwer Academic Publisher, Norwell, MA, 1998).

38. M. Unser and T. Blu, Mathematical properties of the JPEG2000 wavelet filters, *IEEE Trans. Image Processing.* **12**, 1080–1090 (Sept., 2003).

39. S. G. Mallat, A theory for multiresolution signal decomposition: the wavelet representation, *IEEE Transaction on Pattern Analysis and Machine Intelligence.* **11**(7), 674–693 (July, 1989).

40. K. Andra, C. Chakrabarti, and T. Acharya. Efficient implementation of a set of lifting based wavelet filters. In *Proc. IEEE International Conference on Acoustic, Speech, and Signal Processing (ICASSP'01)*, pp. 1101–1104, Salt Lake City, UT (May, 2001).

41. D. Taubman, High performance scalable image compression with EBCOT, *IEEE Trans. Image Processing.* **9**, 1158–1170 (July, 2000).

42. I. H. Witten, R. M. Neal, and J. G. Cleary, Arithmetic coding for data compression, *Communication of the ACM.* **30**(6), 520–540 (June, 1987).

43. M. J. Slattery and J. L. Mitchell, The qx-coder, *IBM Journal of Research and Development, Data compression technology in* ASIC *cores.* **42**(6), (1998).

44. M. D. Adams. *Jasper software reference manual* (Oct., 2002). URL http://www.ece.uvic.ca/~mdadams/jasper/jasper.pdf.

45. D. Santa-Cruz and T. Ebrahimi. An analitical study of JPEG2000 functionalities. In

Proceedings of the IEEE International Conference on Image Processing, vol. 2, pp. 49–52 (Sept., 2000).

46. M. Weinberger, G. Seroussi, and G. Sapiro. The loco-i lossless image compression algorithm: Principles and standardization into jpeg-ls. Technical report, HP Labs, (2000).

47. ISO/IEC. 15948:2004 information technology - computer graphics and image processing - portable network graphics (png): Functional specification. Technical report, ISO/IEC, (2004).

48. S. Haykin, *An Introduction to Analog and Digital Communications*. (John Wiley & Sons, 1991).

49. B. W. Kerninghan and D. M. Ritchie, *The C Programming Language* (ANSI C). (Prentice Hall, 1988).

50. The Mathworks Staff, *Using Matlab*. (The Mathworks, Inc., Natick, MA, 2000).

51. Z. Liu and L. Karam, Mutual information-based analysis of JPEG2000 contexts, *IEEE Transaction on Image Processing*. **14**(4), 411–422 (Apr., 2005).

CHAPTER 24

GENETIC PROGRAMMING FOR OBJECT DETECTION: A TWO-PHASE APPROACH WITH AN IMPROVED FITNESS FUNCTION

Mengjie Zhang*, Urvesh Bhowan and Bunna Ny

*School of Mathematics, Statistics and Computer Science,
Victoria University of Wellington, PO Box 600, Wellington, New Zealand
E-mail: mengjie.zhang@mcs.vuw.ac.nz[†]*

This paper describes two innovations that improve the efficiency and effectiveness of a genetic programming approach to object detection problems. The approach uses genetic programming to construct object detection programs that are applied, in a moving window fashion, to the large images to locate the objects of interest. The first innovation is to break the GP search into two phases with the first phase applied to a selected subset of the training data, and a simplified fitness function. The second phase is initialised with the programs from the first phase, and uses the full set of training data with a complete fitness function to construct the final detection programs. The second innovation is to add a program size component to the fitness function. This approach is examined and compared with a neural network approach on three object detection problems of increasing difficulty. The results suggest that the innovations increase both the effectiveness and the efficiency of the genetic programming search, and also that the genetic programming approach outperforms a neural network approach for the most difficult data set in terms of the object detection accuracy.

24.1. Introduction

Object detection and recognition tasks arise in a very wide range of applications,[1–7] such as detecting faces from video images, finding tumours in a database of x-ray images, and detecting cyclones in a database of satellite images. In many cases, people (possibly highly trained experts) are able to perform the classification task well, but there is either a shortage of such experts, or the cost of people is too high. Given the amount of data that needs to be detected, automated object detection systems are highly desirable. However, creating such automated systems

---

*Corresponding author.
[†]Corresponding email address.

that have sufficient accuracy and reliability turns out to be very difficult.

Genetic programming (GP) is a relatively recent and fast developing approach to automatic programming.[8,9] In GP, solutions to a problem are represented as computer programs. Darwinian principles of natural selection and recombination are used to evolve a population of programs towards an effective solution to specific problems. The flexibility and expressiveness of computer program representation, combined with the powerful capabilities of evolutionary search, makes GP an exciting new method to solve a great variety of problems.

There have been a number of reports on the use of genetic programming in object detection.[10–16] The approach we have used in previous work[15,16] is to use a single stage approach (referred to as *the basic GP approach* here), where the GP is directly applied to the large images in a moving window fashion to locate the objects of interest. Past work has demonstrated the effectiveness of this approach on several object detection tasks.

While showing promise, this genetic programming approach still has some problems. One problem is that the training time was often very long, even for relatively simple object detection problems. A second problem is that the evolved programs are often hard to understand or interpret. We have identified two causes of these problems: the programs are usually quite large and contain much redundancy, and the cost of the fitness function is high. We believe that the size and redundancy of the programs contributes to the long training times and may also reduce the quality of the resulting detectors by unnecessarily increasing the size of the search space and reducing the probability of finding an optimal detector program. Evaluating the fitness of a candidate detector program in the basic GP approach involves applying the program to each possible position of a window on all the training images, which is quite expensive. An obvious solution is to apply the program to only a small subset of the possible window positions, but it is not obvious how to choose the subset. A poor choice could bias the evolution towards programs that are sub-optimal on the real data.

The goal of this paper is to investigate a study on improving GP techniques for object detection (rather than investigate an application of GP for object detection). Specifically, we investigate two innovations on the basic GP approach to address the problems described above. The first is to split the GP evolution into two phases, using a different fitness function and just a subset of the training data in the first phase. The second is to augment the fitness function in the second phase by a component that biases the evolution towards smaller, less redundant programs. We consider the effectiveness and efficiency of this approach by comparing it with the basic GP approach. We also examine the comprehensibility of the evolved genetic programs.

The rest of the paper is organised as follows. Section 24.2 gives some essential background of object detection and recognition and GP related work to object detection. Section 24.3 describes the main aspects of this approach. Section 24.4 describes the three image data sets and section 24.5 presents the experimental results. Section 24.6 draws the conclusions and gives future directions.

24.2. Background

This section provides some essential background, including a brief overview of the object recognition and detection with related methods, and a brief overview of related work in GP to object detection and recognition and image analysis.

24.2.1. *Object Detection/Recognition and Related Methods*

The term *object detection* here refers to the detection of small objects in large images. This includes both *object classification* and *object localisation*. *Object classification* refers to the task of discriminating between images of different kinds of objects, where each image contains only one of the objects of interest. *Object localisation* refers to the task of identifying the positions of all objects of interest in a large image. The object detection problem is similar to the commonly used terms *automatic target recognition* and *automatic object recognition*.

Traditionally, most research on object recognition involves four stages: *preprocessing, segmentation, feature extraction* and *classification*.[17,18] The preprocessing stage aims to remove noise or enhance edges. In the segmentation stage, a number of coherent regions and "suspicious" regions which might contain objects are usually located and separated from the entire images. The feature extraction stage extracts domain specific features from the segmented regions. Finally, the classification stage uses these features to distinguish the classes of the objects of interest. The features extracted from the images and objects are generally domain specific such as high level relational image features. Data mining and machine learning algorithms are usually applied to object classification.

Object detection and recognition has been of tremendous importance in many application domains. These domains include military applications,[10,19,20] shape matching,[2] human face and visual recognition,[1,5,21,22] natural scene recognition,[4] agricultural product classification,[23] handwritten character recognition,[24,25] medical image analysis,[26] postal code recognition,[27,28] and texture classification.[29]

Since the 1990s, many methods have been employed for object recognition. These include different kinds of neural networks,[28,30-33] genetic algorithms,[34,35] decision trees,[36] statistical methods such as Gaussian models and

Naive Bayes,[36,37] support vector machines,[36,37] genetic programming,[13,22,38,39] and hybrid methods.[40-42]

24.2.1.1. *Performance Evaluation*

Object detection performance is usually measured by *detection rate* and *false alarm rate*. The detection rate (DR) refers to the number of small objects correctly reported by a detection system as a percentage of the total number of actual objects in the image(s). The false alarm rate (FAR), also called false alarms per object,[43] refers to the number of non-objects incorrectly reported as objects by a detection system as a percentage of the total number of actual objects in the image(s). Note that the detection rate is between 0 and 100%, while the false alarm rate may be greater than 100% for difficult object detection problems.

24.2.2. *GP Main Characteristics: GP vs GAs*

GP is an approach to automatic programming, in which a computer can construct and refine its own programs to solve specific tasks. First popularised by Koza[9] in 1992, GP has become another main genetic paradigm in evolutionary computation (EC) in addition to the well known *genetic algorithms* (GAs).

Compared with GAs, GP has a number of characteristics. While the standard GAs use bit strings to represent solutions, the forms evolved by GP are generally trees or tree-like structures. The standard GA bit strings use a fixed length representation while the GP trees can vary in length. While the GAs use a binary alphabet to form the bit strings, the GP uses alphabets of various sizes and content depending on the problem domain. These trees are made up of internal nodes and leaf nodes, which have been drawn from a set of primitive elements that are relevant to the problem domain. Compared with a bit string to represent a given problem, the trees can be much more flexible.

24.2.3. *GP Related Work to Object Detection*

Since the early 1990s, there has been only a small amount of work on applying genetic programming techniques to object classification, object detection and other image recognition problems. This in part reflects the fact that genetic programming is a relatively young discipline compared with, say, neural networks and genetic algorithms.

In terms of the number of classes in object classification, there are two categories: *binary classification problems*, where there are only two classes of objects to be classified, and *multi-class classification problems*, where more than two classes of images are involved. While GP has been widely applied to binary classification problems,[10,38,44,45] it has also been applied to multi-class classification problems.[15,16,22,46-48]

In terms of the representation of genetic programs, different forms of genetic programs have been developed in GP systems for object classification and image recognition. The main program representation forms include tree or tree-like or numeric expression programs,[8,46,48,49] graph based programs,[8] linear GP,[50] linear-graph GP,[51] and grammar based GP.[52]

The use of GP in object/image recognition and detection has also been investigated in a variety of application domains. These domains include military applications,[10,45] English letter recognition,[24] face/eye detection and recognition,[22,39,53] vehicle detection[13,38] and other vision and image processing problems.[9,12,14,54-56]

Since the work to be presented in this paper focuses on the use of genetic programming techniques for object detection, table 24.1 lists the recent research to overview the GP related work based on the applications and the first authors.

24.3. The Approach

24.3.1. *Overview of the Approach*

Figure 24.1 shows an overview of this approach, which has two phases of learning and a testing procedure. In the first learning phase, the evolved genetic programs were initialised randomly and trained on object examples cut out from the large images in the training set. This is just an object classification task, which is simpler than the full object detection task. This phase therefore uses a fitness function which maximises classification accuracy on the object cutouts.

In the second phase, a second GP process is initialised with the programs generated by the first phase, and trained on the full images in the training set by applying the programs to a square input field ("window") that was moved across the images to detect the objects of interest. This phase uses a fitness function that maximises *detection* performance on the large images in the training set. In the test procedure, the best refined genetic program is then applied to the entire images in the test set to measure object detection performance. The process of the second phase and the GP testing procedure are shown in figure 24.2.

Because the object classification task is simpler than the object detection task, we expect the first phase to be able to find good genetic programs much more rapidly and effectively than the second phase. Also, the fitness function is much easier to evaluate, so that a more extensive evolution can be performed in the same time. Although simpler, the object classification task is closely related to

Table 24.1. Object recognition and detection related work based on genetic programming.

Problems	Applications	Authors	Source
Object Detection	Orthodontic landmark detection	Ciesielski et al.	57
	Ship detection	Howard et al.	38
	Mouth detection	Isaka	58
	Small target detection	Benson	11
	Vehicle detection	Howard et al.	13
	Medical object detection	Zhang et al.	15,48
Object Classification	Tank detection	Tackett	10,45
	Letter recognition	Andre	24
		Koza	49
	Face recognition	Teller et al.	22
	Small target classification	Stanhope et al.	59
		Winkeler et al.	39
	Shape recognition	Teller 7et al.	47
	Eye recognition	Robinson et al.	53
	Texture classification	Song et al.	29,44,60–62
	Medical object classification	Loveard et al.	46,63
	Shape and coin recognition	Zhang et al.	64
Other Vision Problems	Edge detection	Lucier et al.	65
	San Mateo trail	Koza	9
	problem	Koza	66
	Image analysis	Howard et al.	54
		Poli	67
	Model Interpretation	Lindblad et al.	14
	Stereoscopic Vision	Graae et al.	12
	Image compression	Nordin et al.	55

the detection task, so we believe that the genetic programs generated by the first phase are likely to be very good starting points for the second phase, allowing the more expensive evolutionary process to concentrate its effort in the more optimal part of the search space.

Since the number of possible programs increases exponentially with the size of the programs, the difficulty of finding an optimal program also increases with the size of the programs. In the second phase, we added a program size component to the fitness function to bias the search towards simpler functions, which we expected would increase both the efficiency and the effectiveness of the evolutionary search. It will also have a tendency to remove redundancy (since a program with redundancy will be less fit than an equivalent program with the redundancy removed), making the programs more comprehensible.

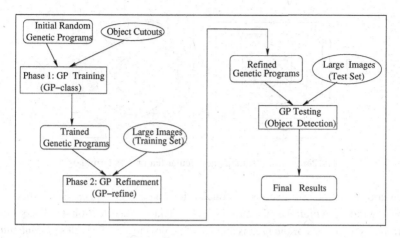

Fig. 24.1. An overview of the two phase GP approach.

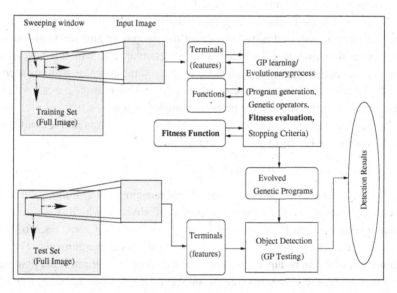

Fig. 24.2. The second phase of GP training (GP-refine) and the GP testing procedure.

24.3.2. *Terminal Set and Function Set*

For object detection problems, terminals generally correspond to image features. Instead of using global features of an entire input image window, we used a number of statistical properties of local square and circular region features as terminals, as shown in figure 24.3. The first terminal set consists of the means and

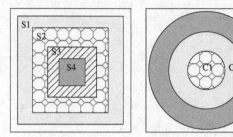

Fig. 24.3.   Local square and circular features as terminals.

standard deviations of a series of concentric square regions centred in the input image window, which was used in the *shape* data set (see section 4). The second terminal set consists of the means and standard deviations of a series of concentric circular regions, which was used in the two coin data sets. For each terminal set, we also used a random constant as an additional terminal.

Notice that these features are certainly not the best for these particular problems. However, our goal is to investigate the two-phase and the program size ideas rather than finding good features for a particular task, which is beyond the scope of this paper. Accordingly, instead of using some complex features such as the SIFT features,[7,68] haar wavelets and orientation histogram features,[1] we used these simple features to keep the problem complexity low.

In the function set, the four standard arithmetic operators and a conditional operator were used to form the non-terminal nodes:

$$FuncSet = \{+, -, *, /, if\}$$

The $+$, $-$, and $*$ operators have their usual meanings — addition, subtraction and multiplication, while / represents "protected" division which is the usual division operator except that a divide by zero gives a result of zero. Each of these functions takes two arguments. The *if* function takes three arguments. The first argument, which can be any expression, constitutes the condition. If the first argument is positive, the *if* function returns its second argument; otherwise, it returns its third argument. The *if* function allows a program to contain a different expression in different regions of the feature space, and allows discontinuous programs, rather than insisting on smooth functions.

24.3.3. *Object Classification Strategy*

The output of a genetic program is a floating point number. Generally genetic programs can perform one class object detection tasks quite well where the division between positive and negative numbers of a genetic program output corresponds to the separation of the objects of interest (of a single class) from the background (non-objects). However, for multiple class object detection problems, where three or more classes of objects of interest are involved, the standard genetic programming classification strategy mentioned above cannot be directly applied.

In this approach, we used a different strategy called *program classification map*, as shown in equation 24.1, for the multiple class object detection problems.[48] Based on the output of an evolved genetic program, this map can identify which class of the object located in the current input field belongs to. In this map, m refers to the number of object classes of interest, v is the output value of the evolved program and T is a constant defined by the user, which plays a role of a threshold.

$$
\text{Class} = \begin{cases}
background, & v \leq 0 \\
\text{class 1}, & 0 < v \leq T \\
\text{class 2}, & T < v \leq 2T \\
\cdots & \cdots \\
\text{class i}, & (i-1) \times T < v \leq i \times T \\
\cdots & \cdots \\
\text{class m}, & v > (m-1) \times T
\end{cases}
\tag{24.1}
$$

24.3.4. *Fitness Functions*

We used two fitness functions for the two learning phases. In the first phase, we used the classification accuracy directly as the fitness function to maximise object classification accuracy. In the second phase, we used a more complex fitness function to be described below to maximise object detection accuracy.

The goal of object detection is to achieve both a high detection rate and a low false alarm rate. In genetic programming, this typically needs either a multi-objective fitness function or a single-objective fitness function that can integrate the effects of the multiple objectives.

While a real multi-objective fitness function can be used for object detection as in,[69] the GP community typically takes the latter approach — usually uses a single-objective fitness function that can reflect the effects of the multiple objectives for a particular problem such as object detection.[13,16,38,70] An example existing fitness function of this kind used in our previous work[16] (and similar ideas also used in other work[13,38,70]) is:

$$
fitness(DR, FAR) = W_d * (1 - DR) + W_f * FAR
\tag{24.2}
$$

where DR is the Detection Rate (the number of small objects correctly reported by a detection system as a percentage of the total number of actual objects in the images) and FAR is the False Alarm Rate (also called *false alarms per object*, the number of non-objects incorrectly reported as objects by a detection system as a percentage of the total number of actual objects in the images). The parameters W_d, W_f reflect the relative importance between the detection rate and the false alarm rate.

Although such a fitness function accurately reflects the performance measure of an object detection system, it is not smooth. In particular, small improvements in an evolved genetic program may not be reflected in any change to the fitness function. The reason is the clustering process that is essential for the object detection — as the sliding window is moved over a true object, the program will generally identify an object at a cluster of window locations where the object is approximately centered in the window. It is important that the set of positions is clustered into the identification of a single object rather than the identification of a set of objects on top of each other.

Suppose we obtained two genetic programs from the population. Program 1 incorrectly identified a large cluster of locations as an object and Program 2 identified a smaller cluster of locations (as shown in figures 24.4 (b) and (c)). In terms of object detection, the program 2 was clearly better than program 1 since program 2 only produced six false alarm pixels but program 1 produced 18 false alarm pixels. However, the above fitness function grouped the two clusters of different numbers of false alarm pixels as the same number (which is two) of false positives for both programs. Thus the two programs have exactly the same FAR since both of them have two false positives. Accordingly, a fitness function based solely on DR and FAR cannot correctly rank these two programs, which means that the evolutionary process will have difficulty for selecting better programs. To deal with this problem, the False Alarm Area (FAA, the number of false alarm pixels which are not object centres but are incorrectly reported as object centres before clustering) was added to the fitness function.

Another problem of using this fitness function is that some genetic programs evolved are very long. When a short program and a long program produce the same detection rate and the same false alarm rate, the GP system will randomly choose one for reproduction, mutation or crossover during the evolutionary process. If the long programs are selected, the evolution for the rest of the learning process will be slow. More importantly, the good building blocks in these long programs will have a much greater chance to be destroyed than in the short programs (Gedanken experiment in GP[8]), which could lead to poor solutions by the evolutionary process. This is mainly because this fitness function does not include any hints about the size of programs.

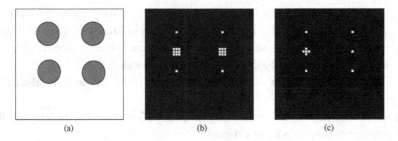

Fig. 24.4. Sample object detection maps. (a) Original image; (b) Detection map produced by Program 1; (c) Detection map produced by program 2.

24.3.4.1. *The new fitness function*

To smooth the fitness function so that small improvement in genetic programs could be reflected and to consider the effect of program size, we added two measures, *false alarm area* and *program size* to the fitness function.

The new fitness of a genetic program is calculated as follows.

(1) Apply the program as a moving $n \times n$ window template (n is the size of the input image window) to each of the training images and obtain the output value of the program at each possible window position, as shown in Figure 24.2. Label each window position with the 'detected' object according to the object classification strategy. Call this data structure a detection map.

(2) Find the centres of *objects of interest only* by the following clustering process:

- Scan the detection map from the up-left corner "pixel by pixel" for detected *objects of interest* (those "pixels" marked as the "background" class are skipped). When an object of a class of interest at a particular location is encountered, mark that location point as the centre of the object and skip pixels in $n/2 \times n/2$ square to right and below this location. In this way, all the locations ("pixels") considered "detected objects" by the genetic program within the square of then $n/2 \times n/2$ size will be "clustered" as a single object. The square size $n/2 \times n/2$ was chosen as half of the moving sweeping window size in order not to miss any detected object. This process will continue in the right cross and down directions until all the locations in the detection map are scanned or skipped. The locations marked by this process are considered the centres of the objects for the classes of interest detected by the genetic program.

(3) Match these detected objects with the known locations of each of the desired/target objects and their classes. Here, we allow location error of

$TOLERANCE$ pixels in the x and y directions. We have used a value of 2 for $TOLERANCE$. For example, if the coordinates of a known object centre are *(21, 19)* and the coordinates of a detected object centre are *(22, 21)*, we consider that the object has been correctly located.

(4) Calculate the detection rate DR, the false alarm rate FAR, and the false alarm position FAA of the evolved program.

(5) Count the size of the program by adding the number of terminals and the number of functions in the program.

(6) Compute the fitness of the program according to equation 24.3.

$$fitness = K_1 \cdot (1 - DR) + K_2 \cdot FAR + K_3 \cdot FAP + K_4 \cdot ProgSize \quad (24.3)$$

where K_1, K_2, K_3, and K_4 are constant weighting parameters which reflect the relative importance between detection rate, false alarm rate, false alarm area, and program size.

We expect that the new fitness function can reflect both small and large improvement in genetic programs and can bias the search towards simpler functions. We also expected this would increase both the efficiency and the effectiveness of the evolutionary search. It will also have a tendency to reduce redundancy, making the programs more comprehensible.

Notice that adding the program size constrain to the fitness function is a kind of *parsimony pressure* technique.[71–73] Early work on this issue resulted in diverse opinions: some researchers think using parsimony pressure could improve performance,[72] while some others thinks this could lead to premature convergence.[73] Although our approach is different from the early work, it might still face a risk of early convergence. Therefore, we used a very small weight (K_4) for the program size in our fitness function relative to K_1 and K_2 (see table 24.2).

24.3.5. *Parameters and Termination Criteria*

In this system, we used tree structures and Lisp S-expressions to represent genetic programs.[9] The ramped half-and-half method[8,9] was used for generating the programs in the initial population and for the mutation operator. The proportional selection mechanism and the reproduction,[48] crossover and mutation operators[8] were used in the learning process.

Important parameter values used in the experiments are shown in table 24.2. These parameter values were obtained using the existing heuristics in GP plus some minor effort on empirical search via experiments.

The learning/evolutionary process is run for a fixed number (*max-generations*) of generations, unless it finds a program that solves the problem perfectly (100%

Table 24.2. Parameters used for GP training for the three databases.

Parameter Kind	Parameter Name	Shape	Coins	Heads/tails
Search	population-size	800	1000	1600
	initial-max-depth	2	2	5
	max-depth	6	7	8
Parameters	max-generations	50	150	200
	input-size	20×20	72×72	62×62
Genetic	reproduction-rate	2%	2%	2%
	cross-rate	70%	70%	70%
Parameters	mutation-rate	28%	28%	28%
Fitness	T	100	80	80
	K1	5000	5000	5000
	K2	100	100	100
Parameters	K3	10	10	10
	K4	1	1	1

detection rate and no false alarms), or there is no increase in the fitness for 10 generations, at which point the evolution is terminated early.

24.4. Image Data Sets

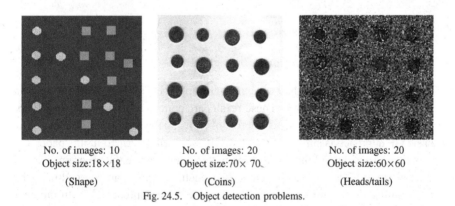

No. of images: 10   No. of images: 20   No. of images: 20
Object size:18×18   Object size:70× 70.   Object size:60×60

(Shape)   (Coins)   (Heads/tails)

Fig. 24.5.   Object detection problems.

We used three data sets in the experiments. Example images are given in figure 24.5. These data sets provide object detection problems of increasing difficulty. Data set 1 (Shape) was generated to give well defined objects against a uniform background. The pixels of the objects were generated using a Gaussian generator with different means and variances for different classes. There are two classes of small objects of interest in this database: circles and squares. Data set

2 (Coins) was intended to be somewhat harder and consists of scanned images of New Zealand coins. There are two object classes of interest: the 5-cent coins and 10-cent coins. These coins are a mixture of head up or tail up and accordingly has a greater variance than data set 1. The objects in each class have a similar size but are located at arbitrary positions and with different rotations. Since the sizes of the two classes (5-cent coins vs 10-cent coins) are quite different, it should not be very difficult to distinguish between the two classes. Data set 3 (Heads/tails) also contains two object classes of interest, but the detection task is significantly more difficult. The task is detecting the head side and the tail side of New Zealand 5 cent coins. The coins are placed in different locations with significantly different orientations. In addition, the background was generated using a Gaussian generator with the same mean (100) but a very large standard deviation (120), making the background more complex. Given the low resolution (75pt) of the images, this detection task is actually very difficult — even humans cannot distinguish the classes perfectly.

In the experiments, we used one, three, and five images as the training set and used five, ten and ten images as the test set for the *Shape, Coins*, and *Heads/tails* data sets, respectively. To avoid the "lucky partitioning" of the these data set, the partitioning process of training and test sets was randomly repeated ten times for each of the three data sets and the average results are reported in the next section.

24.5. Results and Discussion

24.5.1. *Object Detection Results*

The detection results of the two phase GP approach for the three image data sets are shown in table 24.3. These results are compared with the basic GP approach[15,74] and a neural network approach[75,76] using the same set of features. The basic GP approach is similar to the new GP approach described in this paper, except that it uses the old fitness function without considering the program size and false alarm areas (equation 24.2) and that genetic programs are learned from the full training images directly, which is a single stage approach.[15,74] In the neural network approach,[75,76] a three layered feed forward neural network is trained by the back propagation algorithm[77] without momentum using an online learning scheme and fan-in factors.[78] For all the three approaches, the experiments are repeated 50 times and the average results on the *test set* are presented in this section.

As can be seen from table 24.3, all the three approaches achieved ideal results for the shape and the Coins data sets, reflecting the fact that the detection problems

Table 24.3. Object detection results achieved by different approaches.

Image Data Set		Shape	Coins	Heads/tails	
				heads	tails
Best Detection Rate(%)		100	100	100	100
Best False Alarm Rate (%)	Two-phase GP Approach	0	0	0	55
	Basic GP Approach	0	0	0	100
	Neural Networks	0	0	9.4	134.1

in the two data sets are relatively easy and that the two terminal sets are appropriate for the two data sets (note that other terminal sets did not achieve ideal results,[74] but this is beyond the scope of this paper). For the difficult Heads/tails data set, none of the three methods resulted in ideal performance. However, the two phase GP approach described in this paper achieved the best performance.

Notice also that both GP approaches achieved better results than the neural network approach on this data set using the same set of features. However, this might be partially because the features used here carried intrinsic bias towards the neural network approach and/or partially because the neural networks were not tuned, pruned or optimised.[30,69] While further discussion here on this topic is beyond the goal of this paper, we are interested in carrying out further investigation in the future.

24.5.2. *Training Time and Program Size*

Although both of the GP approaches achieved better results than the neural networks overall, the time spent on the training/refining process are quite different. For the *Coins* data set, for example, the basic GP approach used 17 hours on average to find a good genetic program, whereas the two phase GP approach used only 11 hours on average. For the *Heads/tails* data set, the two phase GP approach found good programs after 23 hours on average (of which the first phase only took only two to three minutes). The basic GP approach, on the other hand, took an average of 45 hours. The first phase is so fast because the size of the training data set is small, and the task of discriminating the classes of objects (when centered in the input window) is quite simple. However, the programs it finds appear to be very good starting points for the more expensive second phase, which enables the evolution in the second phase to concentrate its search in a much more promising part of the search space.

In addition, the sizes of the programs (the number of terminals plus the number of functions in a program) evolved by the two phase GP approach were also found to be shorter than those evolved by the basic GP approach. For the *Coins* data set, for example, the program size in the two phase GP approach averages 56 nodes, in contrast to 107 nodes for the basic GP approach. Both the good initial programs and the bias towards smaller programs would contribute to this result; we will investigate which of the factors is the most important for object detection in the future.

24.5.3. *Comprehensibility of Genetic Programs*

To check the effectiveness of the new fitness function at improving the comprehensibility of the programs, an evolved genetic program in the *shape* data set is shown below:

$$\text{(/ (if (/ (- }F_{4\mu}\text{ T) }F_{4\mu}\text{) }F_{3\mu}\text{ (* (- }F_{4\mu}\text{ }F_{2\mu}\text{) }F_{1\sigma}\text{)) (/ }F_{4\mu}\text{ }F_{4\mu}\text{))}$$

This program detector can be simplified as follows:

$$\text{(if (- }F_{4\mu}\text{ T) }F_{3\mu}\text{ (* (- }F_{4\mu}\text{ }F_{2\mu}\text{) }F_{1\sigma}\text{))}$$

where $F_{i\mu}$ and $F_{i\sigma}$ are the mean and standard deviation of region i (see figure 24.3, left) of the window, respectively, and T is a predefined threshold. This program can be translated into the following rule:

```
if (F_{4μ} > T) then
   value = F_{3μ};
else
   value = (F_{4μ} - F_{2μ}) * F_{1σ};
```

If the sweeping window is over the background only, $F_{4\mu}$ would be smaller than the threshold (100 here), the program would execute the "else" part. Since $F_{4\mu}$ is equal to $F_{2\mu}$ in this case, the program output will be zero. According to the classification strategy — object classification map, this case would be correctly classified as *background*. If the input window contains a portion of an object of interest and some background, $F_{4\mu}$ would be smaller than $F_{2\mu}$, which results in a negative program output, corresponding to class *background*. If $F_{4\mu}$ is greater than the threshold T, then the input window must contain an object of interest, either for *class1* or for *class2*, depending the value of $F_{3\mu}$.

While this program detector can be relatively easily interpreted and understood, the programs obtained using the old fitness function are generally hard to interpret due to the length of the programs and the redundancy. By carefully designing the fitness function to constrain the program size, the evolved genetic programs appear to be more comprehensible.

24.6. Conclusions

Rather than investigating an application of GP for object detection, the goal of this paper is to investigate a study on improving GP techniques for object detection. The goal has been successfully achieved by developing a two phase GP approach and a new fitness function with constraints on program size. We investigated the effectiveness and efficiency of the two phase GP approach and the comprehensibility of genetic programs evolved using the new fitness function. The approach was tested on three object detection problems of increasing difficulty and achieved good results.

We developed a two phase approach to object detection using genetic programming. Our results suggest that the two phase approach is more effective and more efficient than the basic GP approach. The new GP approach also achieved better detection accuracy than a neural network approach on the second coin data set using the same set of features. While a detailed comparison between the two approaches is beyond the goal of this paper, we are interested in doing further investigation in the future.

We modified the fitness function by including a measure of program size. This resulted in genetic program detectors that were better quality and more comprehensible. It also reduced the search computation time.

Although this approach considerably shortens the training times, the training process is still relatively long. We intend to explore better classification strategies and add more heuristics to the genetic beam search to the evolutionary process.

While the programs evolved by the two phase GP approach with the new fitness function are considerably shorter than the basic GP approach, they usually still contain some redundancy. Although we suspect that this redundancy reduces the efficiency and the effectiveness of the evolutionary search, it is also possible that redundancy plays an important role in the search. We are experimenting with simplification of the programs during the evolutionary process to remove the redundancy, and will be exploring whether it reduces training speed and improves program quality.

This paper was focused on improving GP techniques rather than investigating applications of GP on object detection. However, it would be interesting to test the new GP approach developed in this paper on some more difficult, real world object detection tasks such as those in the Caltech 101 data set and the retina data set in the future.

Acknowledgements

This work was supported in part by the national Marsden Fund of Royal Society of New Zealand (05-VUW-017) and the University Research Fund (7/39) at Victoria University of Wellington.

References

1. F. Schwenker, A. Sachs, G. Palm, and H. Kestler. Orientation histograms for face recognition. In eds. S. F. and M. S., *Artificial neural Networks in Pattern Recognition*, vol. 4087, *LNAI*, pp. 253–259, Berlin Heidelberg New York, (2006). Springer Verlag. URL http://neuro.informatik.uni-ulm.de/basilic/Publications/2006/SSPK06.
2. A. C. Berg, T. L. Berg, and J. Malik. Shape matching and object recognition using low distortion correspondence. In *Proceedings of 2005 IEEE Computer Society Conference on Computer Vision and Pattern Recognition (CVPR), Volume 1,*, pp. 26–33. IEEE Computer Society Press, (2005).
3. A. D. Holub, M. Welling, and P. Perona. Combining generative models and fisher kernels for object class recognition. In *Tenth IEEE International Conference on Computer Vision (ICCV), Volume 1*, pp. 136–143. IEEE Computer Society Press, (2005).
4. S. Lazebnik, C. Schmid, and J. Ponce. Beyond bags of features: Spatial pyramid matching for recognizing natural scene categories. In *Proceedings of 2006 IEEE Computer Society Conference on Computer Vision and Pattern Recognition (CVPR), Volume 2*, pp. 2169–2178. IEEE Computer Society Press (June, 2006).
5. H. Zhang, A. Berg, M. Maire, and J. Malik. Svm-knn: Discriminative nearest neighbor classification for visual category recognition. In *Proceedings of 2006 IEEE Computer Society Conference on Computer Vision and Pattern Recognition (CVPR), Volume 2*, pp. 2126–2136. IEEE Computer Society Press (June, 2006).
6. J. Mutch and D. G. Lowe. Multiclass object recognition with sparse, localized features. In *Proceedings of 2006 IEEE Computer Society Conference on Computer Vision and Pattern Recognition (CVPR), Volume 1*, pp. 11–18. IEEE Computer Society Press (June, 2006).
7. D. G. Lowe. Object recognition from local scale-invariant features. In *ICCV*, pp. 1150–1157, (1999).
8. W. Banzhaf, P. Nordin, R. E. Keller, and F. D. Francone, *Genetic Programming: An Introduction on the Automatic Evolution of computer programs and its Applications.* (San Francisco, Calif. : Morgan Kaufmann Publishers; Heidelburg : Dpunkt-verlag, 1998). Subject: Genetic programming (Computer science); ISBN: 1-55860-510-X.
9. J. R. Koza, *Genetic programming : on the programming of computers by means of natural selection.* (Cambridge, Mass. : MIT Press, London, England, 1992).
10. W. A. Tackett. Genetic programming for feature discovery and image discrimination. In ed. S. Forrest, *Proceedings of the 5th International Conference on Genetic Algorithms, ICGA-93*, pp. 303–309, University of Illinois at Urbana-Champaign (17-21 July, 1993). Morgan Kaufmann.
11. K. Benson. Evolving finite state machines with embedded genetic programming for

automatic target detection within SAR imagery. In *Proceedings of the 2000 Congress on Evolutionary Computation CEC00*, pp. 1543–1549, La Jolla Marriott Hotel La Jolla, California, USA (6-9 July, 2000). IEEE Press. ISBN 0-7803-6375-2.

12. C. T. M. Graae, P. Nordin, and M. Nordahl. Stereoscopic vision for a humanoid robot using genetic programming. In eds. S. Cagnoni, R. Poli, G. D. Smith, D. Corne, M. Oates, E. Hart, P. L. Lanzi, E. J. Willem, Y. Li, B. Paechter, and T. C. Fogarty, *Real-World Applications of Evolutionary Computing*, vol. 1803, *LNCS*, pp. 12–21, Edinburgh (17 Apr., 2000). Springer-Verlag. ISBN 3-540-67353-9.

13. D. Howard, S. C. Roberts, and C. Ryan. The boru data crawler for object detection tasks in machine vision. In eds. S. Cagnoni, J. Gottlieb, E. Hart, M. Middendorf, and G. Raidl, *Applications of Evolutionary Computing, Proceedings of EvoWorkshops2002: EvoCOP, EvoIASP, EvoSTim*, vol. 2279, *LNCS*, pp. 220–230, Kinsale, Ireland (3-4 Apr., 2002). Springer-Verlag.

14. F. Lindblad, P. Nordin, and K. Wolff. Evolving 3d model interpretation of images using graphics hardware. In *Proceedings of the 2002 IEEE Congress on Evolutionary Computation, CEC2002*, Honolulu, Hawaii, (2002).

15. M. Zhang and V. Ciesielski. Genetic programming for multiple class object detection. In ed. N. Foo, *Proceedings of the 12th Australian Joint Conference on Artificial Intelligence (AI'99)*, pp. 180–192, Sydney, Australia (December, 1999). Springer-Verlag Berlin Heidelberg. Lecture Notes in Artificial Intelligence (LNAI Volume 1747).

16. M. Zhang, P. Andreae, and M. Pritchard. Pixel statistics and false alarm area in genetic programming for object detection. In ed. S. Cagnoni, *Applications of Evolutionary Computing, Lecture Notes in Computer Science, LNCS Vol. 2611*, pp. 455–466. Springer-Verlag, (2003).

17. T. Caelli and W. F. Bischof, *Machine Learning and Image Interpretation*. (Plenum Press, New York and London, 1997). ISBN 0-306-45761-X.

18. E. Gose, R. Johnsonbaugh, and S. Jost, *Pattern Recognition and Image Analysis*. (Prentice Hall PTR, Upper Saddle River, NJ 07458, 1996). ISBN 0-13-236415-8.

19. A. Howard, C. Padgett, and C. C. Liebe. A multi-stage neural network for automatic target detection. In *1998 IEEE World Congress on Computational Intelligence – IJCNN'98*, pp. 231–236, Anchorage, Alaska, (1998). 0-7803-4859-1/98.

20. Y. C. Wong and M. K. Sundareshan. Data fusion and tracking of complex target maneuvers with a simplex-trained neural network-based architecture. In *1998 IEEE World Congress on Computational Intelligence – IJCNN'98*, pp. 1024–1029, Anchorage, Alaska (May, 1998). 0-7803-4859-1/98.

21. D. Valentin, H. Abdi, and O'Toole, Categorization and identification of human face images by neural networks: A review of linear auto-associator and principal component approaches, *Journal of Biological Systems*. **2**(3), 413–429, (1994).

22. A. Teller and M. Veloso. A controlled experiment : Evolution for learning difficult image classification. In eds. C. Pinto-Ferreira and N. J. Mamede, *Proceedings of the 7th Portuguese Conference on Artificial Intelligence*, vol. 990, *LNAI*, pp. 165–176, Berlin (3–6 Oct., 1995). Springer Verlag. ISBN 3-540-60428-6.

23. P. Winter, W. Yang, S. Sokhansanj, and H. Wood. Discrimination of hard-to-pop popcorn kernels by machine vision and neural network. In *ASAE/CSAE meeting*, Saskatoon, Canada (Sept., 1996). Paper No. MANSASK 96-107.

24. D. Andre. Automatically defined features: The simultaneous evolution of 2-

dimensional feature detectors and an algorithm for using them. In ed. K. E. Kinnear, *Advances in Genetic Programming*, pp. 477–494. MIT Press, (1994).

25. Y. LeCun, L. Bottou, Y. Bengio, and P. Haffner. Gradient-based learning applied to document recognition. In *Intelligent Signal Processing*, pp. 306–351. IEEE Press, (2001).

26. B. Verma. A neural network based technique to locate and classify microcalcifications in digital mammograms. In *1998 IEEE World Congress on Computational Intelligence – IJCNN'98*, pp. 1790–1793, Anchorage, Alaska, (1998). 0-7803-4859-1/98, IEEE.

27. Y. LeCun, L. D. Jackel, B. Boser, J. S. Denker, H. P. Graf, I. Guyon, D. Henderson, R. E. Howard, and W. Hibbard, Handwritten digit recognition: application of neural network chips and automatic learning, *IEEE Communications Magazine*. pp. 41–46 (November, 1989).

28. D. de Ridder, A. Hoekstra, and R. P. W. Duin. Feature extraction in shared weights neural networks. In *Proceedings of the Second Annual Conference of the Advanced School for Computing and imaging, ASCI*, pp. 289–294, Delft (June, 1996).

29. A. Song, T. Loveard, and V. Ciesielski:. Towards genetic programming for texture classification. In *Proceedings of the 14th Australian Joint Conference on Artificial Intelligence*, pp. 461–472. Springer Verlag, (2001).

30. R. D. Reed and R. J. M. II, *Neural Smithing: Supervised Learning in Feedforward Artificial Neural Networks*. (Cambridge, MA: The MIT Press, 1999). ISBN 0-262-18190-8.

31. M. R. Azimi-Sadjadi, D. Yao, Q. Huang, and G. J. Dobeck, Underwater target classification using wavelet packets and neural networks, *IEEE Transactions on Neural Networks*. 11(3), 784–794 (May, 2000).

32. C. Stahl, D. Aerospace, and P. Schoppmann. Advanced automatic target recognition for police helicopter missions. In ed. F. A. Sadjadi, *Proceedings of SPIE Volume 4050, Automatic Target Recognition X* (April, 2000). [4050-30].

33. T. Wessels and C. W. Omlin. A hybrid system for signature verification. In *Proceedings of the IEEE-INNS-ENNS International Joint Conference on Neural Networks (IJCNN'00), Volume V*, Como, Italy (July, 2000).

34. J. Bala, K. D. Jong, J. Huang, H. Vafaie, and H. Wechsler, Using learning to facilitate the evolution of features for recognising visual concepts, *Evolutionary Computation*. 4(3), 297–312, (1997).

35. J.-S. Huang and H.-C. liu, Object recognition using genetic algorithms with a Hopfield's neural model, *Expert Systems with Applications*. 13(3), 191–199, (1997).

36. S. Russell and P. Norvig, *Artificial Intelligence, A modern Approach*. (Prentice Hall, 2003), 2nd edition.

37. M. H. Dunham, *Data Mining: Introductory and Advanced Topics*. (Prentice Hall, 2003).

38. D. Howard, S. C. Roberts, and R. Brankin, Target detection in SAR imagery by genetic programming, *Advances in Engineering Software*. 30, 303–311, (1999).

39. J. F. Winkeler and B. S. Manjunath. Genetic programming for object detection. In eds. J. R. Koza, K. Deb, M. Dorigo, D. B. Fogel, M. Garzon, H. Iba, and R. L. Riolo, *Genetic Programming 1997: Proceedings of the Second Annual Conference*, pp. 330–335, Stanford University, CA, USA (13-16 July, 1997). Morgan Kaufmann.

40. P. G. Korning, Training neural networks by means of genetic algorithms working

on very long chromosomes, *International Journal of Neural Systems.* **6**(3), 299–316 (September, 1995).

41. V. Ciesielski and J. Riley. An evolutionary approach to training feed forward and recurrent neural networks. In eds. L. C. Jain and R. K. Jain, *Proceedings of the Second International Conference on Knowledge Based Intelligent Electronic Systems*, pp. 596–602, Adelaide (Apr., 1998).

42. X. Yao and Y. Liu, A new evolutionary system for evolving artificial neural networks, *IEEE Transactions on Neural Networks.* **8**(3), 694–713 (May, 1997). URL citeseer.ist.psu.edu/yao96new.html.

43. M. V. Shirvaikar and M. M. Trivedi, A network filter to detect small targets in high clutter backgrounds, *IEEE Transactions on Neural Networks.* **6**(1), 252–257 (Jan, 1995).

44. A. Song, V. Ciesielski, and H. Williams. Texture classifiers generated by genetic programming. In eds. D. B. Fogel, M. A. El-Sharkawi, X. Yao, G. Greenwood, H. Iba, P. Marrow, and M. Shackleton, *Proceedings of the 2002 Congress on Evolutionary Computation CEC2002*, pp. 243–248. IEEE Press, (2002). ISBN 0-7803-7278-6.

45. W. A. Tackett. *Recombination, Selection, and the Genetic Construction of Computer Programs.* PhD thesis, Faculty of the Graduate School, University of Southern California, Canoga Park, California, USA (April, 1994).

46. T. Loveard and V. Ciesielski. Representing classification problems in genetic programming. In *Proceedings of the Congress on Evolutionary Computation*, vol. 2, pp. 1070–1077, COEX, World Trade Center, 159 Samseong-dong, Gangnam-gu, Seoul, Korea (27-30 May, 2001). IEEE Press. ISBN 0-7803-6657-3. URL http://goanna.cs.rmit.edu.au/~toml/cec2001.ps.

47. A. Teller and M. Veloso. PADO: Learning tree structured algorithms for orchestration into an object recognition system. Technical Report CMU-CS-95-101, Department of Computer Science, Carnegie Mellon University, Pittsburgh, PA, USA, (1995).

48. M. Zhang, V. Ciesielski, and P. Andreae, A domain independent window-approach to multiclass object detection using genetic programming, *EURASIP Journal on Signal Processing, Special Issue on Genetic and Evolutionary Computation for Signal Processing and Image Analysis.* **2003**(8), 841–859, (2003).

49. J. R. Koza, *Genetic Programming II: Automatic Discovery of Reusable Programs.* (Cambridge, Mass. : MIT Press, London, England, 1994).

50. W. Kantschik, P. Dittrich, M. Brameier, and W. Banzhaf. Meta-evolution in graph GP. In eds. R. Poli, P. Nordin, W. B. Langdon, and T. C. Fogarty, *Genetic Programming, Proceedings of EuroGP'99*, vol. 1598, *LNCS*, pp. 15–28, Goteborg, Sweden (26-27 May, 1999). Springer-Verlag. ISBN 3-540-65899-8.

51. W. Kantschik and W. Banzhaf. Linear-graph GP—A new GP structure. In eds. E. Lutton, J. A. Foster, J. Miller, C. Ryan, and A. G. B. Tettamanzi, *Proceedings of the 4th European Conference on Genetic Programming, EuroGP 2002*, vol. 2278, pp. 83–92, Kinsale, Ireland (3-5, 2002). Springer-Verlag. URL http://citeseer.nj.nec.com/kantschik02lineargraph.html.

52. P. A. Whigham. Grammatically-based genetic programming. In ed. J. P. Rosca, *Proceedings of the Workshop on Genetic Programming: From Theory to Real-World Applications*, pp. 33–41, Tahoe City, California, USA (9 July, 1995). URL http://citeseer.ist.psu.edu/whigham95grammaticallybased.html.

53. G. Robinson and P. McIlroy. Exploring some commercial applications of genetic programming. In ed. T. C. Fogarty, *Evolutionary Computation, Volume 993, Lecture Note in Computer Science*. Springer-Verlag, (1995).

54. D. Howard, S. C. Roberts, and C. Ryan. Evolution of an object detection ant for image analysis. In ed. E. D. Goodman, *2001 Genetic and Evolutionary Computation Conference Late Breaking Papers*, pp. 168–175, San Francisco, California, USA (9-11 July, 2001).

55. P. Nordin and W. Banzhaf. Programmatic compression of images and sound. In eds. J. R. Koza, D. E. Goldberg, D. B. Fogel, and R. L. Riolo, *Genetic Programming 1996: Proceedings of the First Annual Conference*, pp. 345–350, Stanford University, CA, USA, (1996). MIT Press.

56. R. Poli. Genetic programming for feature detection and image segmentation. In ed. T. C. Fogarty, *Evolutionary Computing*, number 1143 in Lecture Notes in Computer Science, pp. 110–125. Springer-Verlag, University of Sussex, UK (1-2 Apr., 1996). ISBN 3-540-61749-3.

57. V. Ciesielski, A. Innes, S. John, and J. Mamutil. Understanding evolved genetic programs for a real world object detection problem. In eds. M. Keijzer, A. Tettamanzi, P. Collet, J. I. van Hemert, and M. Tomassini, *Proceedings of the 8th European Conference on Genetic Programming*, vol. 3447, *Lecture Notes in Computer Science*, pp. 351–360, Lausanne, Switzerland (30 Mar. - 1 Apr., 2005). Springer. ISBN 3-540-25436-6.

58. S. Isaka. An empirical study of facial image feature extraction by genetic programming. In ed. J. R. Koza, *the Genetic Programming 1997 Conference*, pp. 93–99. Stanford Bookstore, Stanford University, CA, USA (July, 1997). Late Breaking Papers.

59. S. A. Stanhope and J. M. Daida. Genetic programming for automatic target classification and recognition in synthetic aperture radar imagery. In eds. V. W. Porto, N. Saravanan, D. Waagen, and A. E. Eiben, *Evolutionary Programming VII: Proceedings of the Seventh Annual Conference on Evolutionary Programming*, vol. 1447, *LNCS*, pp. 735–744, Mission Valley Marriott, San Diego, California, USA (25-27 Mar., 1998). Springer-Verlag. ISBN 3-540-64891-7.

60. A. Song. *Texture Classification: A Genetic Programming Approach*. PhD thesis, Department of Computer Science, RMIT University, Melbourne, Australia, (2003).

61. A. Song and V. Ciesielski. Texture analysis by genetic programming. In *Proceedings of the 2004 IEEE Congress on Evolutionary Computation*, pp. 2092–2099, Portland, Oregon (20-23 June, 2004). IEEE Press. ISBN 0-7803-8515-2.

62. A. Song and V. Ciesielski. Fast texture segmentation using genetic programming. In eds. R. Sarker, R. Reynolds, H. Abbass, K. C. Tan, B. McKay, D. Essam, and T. Gedeon, *Proceedings of the 2003 Congress on Evolutionary Computation CEC2003*, pp. 2126–2133, Canberra (8-12 Dec., 2003). IEEE Press. ISBN 0-7803-7804-0.

63. T. Loveard. *Genetic Programming for Classification Learning Problems*. PhD thesis, RMIT University, School of Computer Science and Information Technology, (2003).

64. M. Zhang and W. Smart. Multiclass object classification using genetic programming. In eds. G. R. Raidl, S. Cagnoni, J. Branke, D. W. Corne, R. Drechsler, Y. Jin, C. Johnson, P. Machado, E. Marchiori, F. Rothlauf, G. D. Smith, and G. Squillero, *Applications of Evolutionary Computing, EvoWorkshops2004: EvoBIO, EvoCOMNET, Evo-*

HOT, EvoIASP, EvoMUSART, EvoSTOC, vol. 3005, *LNCS*, pp. 367–376, Coimbra, Portugal (5-7 Apr., 2004). Springer Verlag.

65. B. J. Lucier, S. Mamillapalli, and J. Palsberg. Program optimisation for faster genetic programming. In *Genetic Programming – GP'98*, pp. 202–207, Madison, Wisconsin (July, 1998).

66. J. R. Koza. Simultaneous discovery of reusable detectors and subroutines using genetic programming. In ed. S. Forrest, *Proceedings of the 5th International Conference on Genetic Algorithms, ICGA-93*, pp. 295–302, Morgan Kauffman, (1993).

67. R. Poli. Genetic programming for image analysis. In eds. J. R. Koza, D. E. Goldberg, and D. B. F. a nd Rick L. Riolo, *Genetic Programming 1996: Proceedings of the First Annual Conference*, pp. 363–368, Stanford University, CA, USA (28–31, 1996). MIT Press.

68. D. G. Lowe, Distinctive image features from scale-invariant keypoints., *International Journal of Computer Vision.* **60**(2), 91 110, (2004).

69. A. Gepperth and S. Roth, Applications of multi-objective structure optimization., *Neurocomputing.* **69**(7-9), 701–713, (2006).

70. M. E. Roberts and E. Claridge. Cooperative coevolution of image feature construction and object detection. In eds. X. Yao, E. Burke, J. A. Lozano, J. Smith, J. J. Merelo-Guervós, J. A. Bullinaria, J. Rowe, P. T. A. Kabán, and H.-P. Schwefel, *Parallel Problem Solving from Nature - PPSN VIII*, vol. 3242, *LNCS*, pp. 902–911, Birmingham, UK (18-22 Sept., 2004). Springer-Verlag. ISBN 3-540-23092-0. doi: doi:10.1007/b100601. URL http://www.cs.bham.ac.uk/~mer/papers/ppsn-2004.pdf.

71. P. W. H. Smith. Controlling code growth in genetic programming. In eds. R. John and R. Birkenhead, *Advances in Soft Computing*, pp. 166–171, De Montfort University, Leicester, UK, (2000). Physica-Verlag. ISBN 3-7908-1257-9. URL http://www.springer-ny.com/detail.tpl?ISBN=3790812579.

72. R. Dallaway. Genetic programming and cognitive models. Technical Report CSRP 300, School of Cognitive & Computing Sciences, University of Sussex,, Brighton, UK, (1993). In: Brook & Arvanitis, eds., 1993 The Sixth White House Papers: Graduate Research in the Cognitive & Computing Sciences at Sussex.

73. T. Soule and J. A. Foster, Effects of code growth and parsimony pressure on populations in genetic programming, *Evolutionary Computation.* **6**(4), 293–309 (Winter, 1998).

74. U. Bhowan. A domain independent approach to multi-class object detection using genetic programming. Master's thesis, BSc Honours research project/thesis, School of Mathematical and Computing Sciences, Victoria University of Wellington, (2003).

75. M. Zhang and V. Ciesielski. Using back propagation algorithm and genetic algorithm to train and refine neural networks for object detection. In eds. T. Bench-Capon, G. Soda, and A. M. Tjoa, *Proceedings of the 10th International Conference on Database and Expert Systems Applications (DEXA'99)*, pp. 626–635, Florence, Italy (August, 1999). Springer-Verlag. Lecture Notes in Computer Science, (LNCS Volume 1677).

76. B. Ny. Multi-cclass object classification and detection using neural networks. Master's thesis, BSc Honours research project/thesis, School of Mathematical and Computing Sciences, Victoria University of Wellington, (2003).

77. D. E. Rumelhart, G. E. Hinton, and R. J. Williams. Learning internal representations by error propagation. In eds. D. E. Rumelhart, J. L. McClelland, and the PDP research group, *Parallel distributed Processing, Explorations in the Microstructure of Cognition, Volume 1: Foundations*, chapter 8. The MIT Press, Cambridge, Massachusetts, London, England, (1986).
78. Y. LeCun, B. Boser, J. S. Denker, D. Henderson, R. E. H. W. Hubbard, and L. D. Jackel. Handwritten zip code recognition with a back-propagation network. In ed. D. S. Touretzky, *Advances in Neural Information Processing Systems*, vol. 2. Morgan Kaufmann, San Mateo, CA, (1990).

CHAPTER 25

ARCHITECTURAL SCENE RECONSTRUCTION FROM SINGLE OR MULTIPLE UNCALIBRATED IMAGES

Huei-Yung Lin[*], Syuan-Liang Chen[†], and Jen-Hung Lin[‡]

Department of Electrical Engineering,
National Chung Cheng University,
168 University Road, Min-Hsiung,
Chia-Yi 621, Taiwan, R.O.C.

In this paper we present a system for the reconstruction of 3D models of architectural scenes from single or multiple uncalibrated images. The partial 3D model of a building is recovered from a single image using geometric constraints such as parallelism and orthogonality, which are likely to be found in most architectural scenes. The approximate corner positions of a building are selected interactively by a user and then further refined automatically using Hough transform. The relative depths of the corner points are calculated according to the perspective projection model. Partial 3D models recovered from different viewpoints are registered to a common coordinate system for integration. The 3D model registration process is carried out using modified ICP (iterative closest point) algorithm with the initial parameters provided by geometric constraints of the building. The integrated 3D model is then fitted with piecewise planar surfaces to generate a more geometrically consistent model. The acquired images are finally mapped onto the surface of the reconstructed 3D model to create a photo-realistic model. A working system which allows a user to interactively build a 3D model of an architectural scene from single or multiple images has been proposed and implemented.

25.1. Introduction

3D reconstruction of real scenes is one of the most challenging tasks in computer vision.[7] In this work we have focused on the reconstruction of 3D models of architectural scenes. One major difference between the 3D reconstruction of ar-

---

[*]The corresponding author, E-mail:lin@ee.ccu.edu.tw
[†]Syuan-Liang Chen is now with NewSoft Technology Corporation, Taipei 114, Taiwan. R.O.C.
[‡]Jen-Hung Lin is now with Machvision Inc., Hsinchu 30076, Taiwan, R.O.C.

chitectural scenes and general objects is that the former contains easily detectable man-made features such as parallel lines, orthogonal lines, corners, etc. These features are important cues for finding the 3D structure of a building. Most research on architectural scene reconstruction in the photogrammetry community has concentrated on 3D reconstruction from aerial images.[2,8] Due to long-range photography, aerial images are usually modeled as orthographic projection. Although the orthographic projection model is easier for aerial images, one major drawback is that most of the 3D reconstruction of architectural scenes can only be done on the roofs of the buildings. On the other hand, the perspective projection model is usually needed for close-range photography, which is capable of reconstructing the complete (360 degrees) 3D model of an architectural scene.

3D models of architectural scenes have important application areas such as virtual reality (VR) and augmented reality (AR). Both applications require photo-realistic 3D models as input. A photo-realistic model of a building consists not only the 3D shape of the building (geometric information) but also the image texture on the outer visible surface of the building (photometric information). The geometric and photometric information can be acquired either by range data and intensity images, or by the intensity images recorded by a camera. Allen *et al*[1,9] created 3D models of historic sites using both range and image data. They first built the 3D models from range data using a volumetric set intersection method. The photometric information was then mapped onto those models by registering features from both the 3D and 2D data sets. To accurately register the range and intensity data, and reduce the overall complexity of the models, they developed range data segmentation algorithms to identify planar regions and determine linear features from planar intersections. Dick *et al*[5] recovered 3D models from uncalibrated images of architectural scenes. They proposed a method which exploited the rigidity constraints usually seen in the indoor and outdoor architectural scenes such as parallelism and orthogonality. These constraints were then used to calibrate the intrinsic and extrinsic parameters of the cameras through projection matrix using vanishing points.[3] The Euclidean models of the scene were reconstructed from two images from arbitrary viewpoints.

In this work, we develop a system for 3D model reconstruction of architectural scenes from one or more uncalibrated images. The input images can be taken from off-the-shelf digital cameras and the camera parameters for 3D reconstruction are estimated from the structure of the architectural scene. The feature points (such as corners) in the images are selected by a user interactively through a graphical user interface. The selected image points are then refined automatically using Hough transform to obtain more accurate positions in subpixel resolution. For a given set of corner points, various constraints such as parallelism, orthogonality, coplanarity are enforced to create a 3D model of the building. Partial 3D models reconstructed from different viewpoints are then registered to a common coordinate system to create a complete 3D model. The texture information is finally mapped onto the building to create a photo-realistic 3D model.

25.2. Camera Model and Parameter Estimation

The most commonly used camera model is the pinhole camera model. In this model the projection from a point (X_i, Y_i, Z_i) in Euclidean 3-space to a point (x_i, y_i) in the image plane can be represented in homogeneous coordinates by

$$
s \begin{bmatrix} x_i \\ y_i \\ 1 \end{bmatrix} = \begin{bmatrix} m_{11} & m_{12} & m_{13} & m_{14} \\ m_{11} & m_{22} & m_{23} & m_{24} \\ m_{31} & m_{32} & m_{33} & m_{34} \end{bmatrix} \begin{bmatrix} X_i \\ Y_i \\ Z_i \\ 1 \end{bmatrix}
\tag{25.1}
$$

where s is an arbitrary scale factor, and the 3×4 matrix

$$
\mathbf{M} = \begin{bmatrix} m_{11} & m_{12} & m_{13} & m_{14} \\ m_{11} & m_{22} & m_{23} & m_{24} \\ m_{31} & m_{32} & m_{33} & m_{34} \end{bmatrix}
\tag{25.2}
$$

is the perspective projection matrix of the camera. The perspective projection matrix can be further decomposed into the intrinsic camera parameters and the relative pose of the camera:

$$
\mathbf{M} = \mathbf{K}[\mathbf{R} \; \mathbf{t}]
\tag{25.3}
$$

The 3×3 matrix $\mathbf{R}$ and 3×1 vector $\mathbf{t}$ are the relative orientation and translation with respect to the world coordinate system, respectively. The intrinsic parameter matrix $\mathbf{K}$ of the camera is a 3×3 matrix and usually modeled as

$$
\mathbf{K} = \begin{bmatrix} f_x & \gamma & u_0 \\ 0 & f_y & v_0 \\ 0 & 0 & 1 \end{bmatrix}
\tag{25.4}
$$

where (u_0, v_0) is the principal point (the intersection of the optical axis with the image plane), γ is a skew parameter related to the characteristic of the CCD array, and f_x and f_y are scale factors. Thus, Eq. (25.1) can be rewritten as

$$
s\mathbf{p} = \mathbf{K}[\mathbf{R} \; \mathbf{t}]\mathbf{P}
\tag{25.5}
$$

where $\mathbf{P}$ is a 3D point and $\mathbf{p}$ is the corresponding image point (in homogeneous coordinates).

The correctness of reconstructed 3D model depends on the accuracy of camera parameters. Classical camera calibration methods[10] rely on fixed calibration patterns. In this work, the primary goal is to reconstruct 3D models of architectural scenes. Since the man-made structures usually contain parallelepipeds, parallelism and orthogonality will be used for camera parameter estimation. Consider a parallelepiped shown in Fig. 25.1, which resembles the visible surface of a building. Two planes $\mathbf{P}_0\mathbf{P}_1\mathbf{P}_4\mathbf{P}_2$ and $\mathbf{P}_0\mathbf{P}_2\mathbf{P}_5\mathbf{P}_3$ are determined by the six points, $\mathbf{P}_0$, $\mathbf{P}_1$, $\mathbf{P}_2$, $\mathbf{P}_3$, $\mathbf{P}_4$ and $\mathbf{P}_5$. Assume the corresponding image points are $\mathbf{p}_0$, $\mathbf{p}_1$, $\mathbf{p}_2$, $\mathbf{p}_3$, $\mathbf{p}_4$, $\mathbf{p}_5$, then we have

$$s_i\mathbf{p}_i = \mathbf{K}[\mathbf{R}\mathbf{P}_i + \mathbf{t}] \tag{25.6}$$

for $i = 0, 1, \cdots, 5$ by Eq. (25.5).

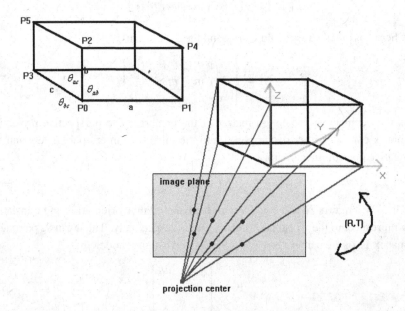

Fig. 25.1.   Parallelepiped and a pinhole camera model

As shown in,[4] for a given parallelepiped in 3D space, if the three angles between its adjacent edges, θ_{ab}, θ_{bc}, θ_{ca}, and the image points of the six points of its two adjacent faces are available, then the pose of the parallelepiped, intrinsic parameters of the camera and the size of the parallelepiped can be determined by solving polynomial equations of at most fourth degree. For a special case that θ_{ab},

θ_{bc} and θ_{ca} are right angles, the equation can be further simplified to a linear system. Thus, the camera parameters can be found if the corner points of a building are identified. Furthermore, the focal length of the camera can be estimated and used for 3D model reconstruction in the next section.

25.3. Three-Dimensional Model Reconstruction

25.3.1. *Reconstruction Algorithm*

Chen *et al*[4] showed that for any given parallelogram in 3D space with known image coordinates of four corner points, the relative depths of the four corner points can be determined. If we consider the four points $\mathbf{P}_0$, $\mathbf{P}_1$, $\mathbf{P}_2$ and $\mathbf{P}_3$, which forms a parallelogram as shown in Fig. 25.1, then $\mathbf{P}_0 + \mathbf{P}_4 = \mathbf{P}_1 + \mathbf{P}_2$ by the property of parallelogram in any world coordinate. Thus, we have

$$s_0 \begin{bmatrix} u_0 \\ v_0 \\ 1 \end{bmatrix} = A \begin{bmatrix} s_1 \\ s_4 \\ s_2 \end{bmatrix} \tag{25.7}$$

where A is given by

$$\begin{bmatrix} u_1 & -u_4 & u_2 \\ v_1 & -v_4 & v_2 \\ 1 & -1 & 1 \end{bmatrix} \tag{25.8}$$

with the corresponding image points $\mathbf{p}_i = (u_i, v_i)$ for $i = 0, 1, 2, 4$. If the three points $\mathbf{p}_1$, $\mathbf{p}_2$, $\mathbf{p}_4$ are not collinear, then A is nonsingular. Thus, the relative depths, s_1/s_0, s_4/s_0, s_2/s_0, of the 3D points are given by

$$\begin{bmatrix} s_1/s_0 \\ s_4/s_0 \\ s_2/s_0 \end{bmatrix} = A^{-1} \begin{bmatrix} u_0 \\ v_0 \\ 1 \end{bmatrix} \tag{25.9}$$

if the corresponding image points are not collinear.

The above algorithm calculates the relative depths of the object points, i.e., s_1/s_0, s_4/s_0, s_2/s_0, from their corresponding image points $\mathbf{p}_1$, $\mathbf{p}_4$, $\mathbf{p}_2$ with respect to $\mathbf{p}_0$. Only the depth information is not sufficient for shape recovery since the 3D model of the object contains x and y direction information as well. Thus, we use the known focus length of the camera (obtained from camera parameter estimation described in the previous section) to constraint the relative positions of the 3D points. That is, the focus length of the camera is used as a factor to scale the displacement in the x and y directions with respect to the depth of the 3D point.

For example, suppose $\mathbf{P}_0$ and $\mathbf{P}_1$ are two 3D points, then we have

$$\mathbf{P}_0 \sim s_0 \mathbf{p}_0 \tag{25.10}$$

$$\mathbf{P}_1 \sim s_1 \mathbf{p}_1 \tag{25.11}$$

by the perspective projection. The ratio of $\mathbf{P}_1$ to $\mathbf{P}_0$ is given as

$$\frac{\mathbf{P}_1}{\mathbf{P}_0} \approx \frac{s_1 \mathbf{P}_1}{s_0 \mathbf{P}_0} = \frac{s_1 [u_1 \; v_1 \; 1]^T}{s_0 [u_0 \; v_0 \; 1]^T} . \tag{25.12}$$

In the above equation, the z direction information is lost in the image coordinate system. To recover the 3D shape of the object, the z coordinate of $\mathbf{P}_0$ is fixed as the focal length of the camera (in pixel), i.e., $z = f$ or $\mathbf{P}_0 = [u_0 \; v_0 \; f]^T$. Now, if $\mathbf{P}_0$ is used as a reference point as shown in Fig. 25.1, then we have

$$\mathbf{P}_i = \frac{s_i}{s_0} \begin{bmatrix} u_i \\ v_i \\ f \end{bmatrix} \tag{25.13}$$

for $i = 1, 2, 4$.

25.3.2. *Registration and Pose Estimation*

The goal of model registration is to combine two or more partial 3D models acquired from different viewpoints to a complete 3D models. Usually the registration or pose estimation involve finding the rotation matrix and translation vector for the transformation between two different coordinate systems. For any given two partial 3D models of an object, the overlapping parts are used to identify the corresponding 3D points for the two models. The corresponding 3D points are then used to find the rotation matrix and translation vector.

Suppose there are two sets of 3D points to be registered. More precisely, if we want to find the rotation matrix and translation vector for the data sets, $\{\mathbf{x}_1, \mathbf{x}_2, ..., \mathbf{x}_n\}$ and $\{\mathbf{y}_1, \mathbf{y}_2, ..., \mathbf{y}_n\}$, where $\mathbf{x}_i$ and $\mathbf{y}_i$ are the corresponding points, for $i = 1, ..., n$. Then the relationship between $\mathbf{x}_i$ and $\mathbf{y}_i$ can be written as

$$\mathbf{y}_i = \mathbf{R}\mathbf{x}_i + \mathbf{t} \tag{25.14}$$

Let the correlation matrix for the two data sets be

$$C = \sum_{i=1}^{n} w_i \mathbf{x}_i \mathbf{y}_i^T \tag{25.15}$$

To find the rotation matrix $\mathbf{R}$, singular value decomposition technique is used to rewrite $\mathbf{C}$ as $\mathbf{C} = \mathbf{UDV}^T$ by Eq. (25.15). Since the rotation matrix must satisfy $\mathbf{RR}^T = \mathbf{I}$, we have

$$\mathbf{R} = \mathbf{U} \begin{bmatrix} 1 & 0 & 0 \\ 0 & 1 & 0 \\ 0 & 0 & \det(\mathbf{UV}^T) \end{bmatrix} \mathbf{V}^T \qquad (25.16)$$

by Eq. (25.15). Finally, the translation vector $\mathbf{t}$ can be calculated by

$$\mathbf{t} = \bar{\mathbf{y}} - \mathbf{R}\bar{\mathbf{x}} \qquad (25.17)$$

where $\bar{\mathbf{x}}$ and $\bar{\mathbf{y}}$ are the centroids of the two data sets, respectively.[6]

25.3.3. *Model Optimization*

In this work, the 3D model is reconstructed using parallelism and orthogonality of an architectural scene. Thus, selecting feature points (edge points) which form parallel or perpendicular lines is an important issue. In the implementation, a graphical user interface is provided such that the user can manually select the corner points. Since the selected points are not always accurate enough (for example, subpixel resolution is not possible and the selection can be affected by the radial distortion of the camera), an automatic corner detection algorithm is applied on the neighborhood of the selected points. Hough transform is then carried out to find more accurate positions in subpixel resolution. For the images captured with short focal length, the lens radial distortion parameter is approximated by line fitting and then used for image distortion correction.

To use parallelism, orthogonality constraints and force four corner points to be coplanar to create an optimized 3D model, we first find the plane equations for the coplanar points, say A, B, C, D, using least squared fitting. Then the four points are projected on the plane as points A', B', C', D'. Parallelism and orthogonality constraints are applied on the above four points to obtain the points A'', B'', C'', D'' which form a rectangle. After the coplanar four points are determined, similar arguments apply to the planar surfaces which are parallel and orthogonal to each other in order to satisfy the geometric constraints.

If the roof of a building contains different geometric primitives rather than rectangles (e.g., triangles or trapezoids), parallelism and orthogonality constraints cannot be directly applied. In this case, a 3D model of the lower part of the building is first reconstructed as a "base-model", which typically contains two perpendicular planar surfaces. The roof (i.e., upper part) of the building is then reconstructed using coplanarity, parallelism and equidistance constraints on the image points corresponding to the roof and the 3D points on the base-model. Commonly

Fig. 25.2.   Graphics user interface

used equidistance constraints include the same length of the left and right sides of a triangle, and the same length of the diagonals of a trapezoid.

25.4. Experimental Results

The described algorithms are tested on a number of objects for the indoor environment and outdoor architectural scenes. As shown in Fig. 25.2, a graphics user interface is developed to assist users to select approximate corner points interactively for 3D model reconstruction. The first experiment is the 3D reconstruction of a building. Fig. 25.2 shows the three images taken from different viewpoints. The images are used to create the partial 3D shapes of the object individually. For each image, the corner points are selected manually by a user and the positions are automatically refined by Hough transform. The reconstructed partial 3D models with texture information using the acquired images are shown in Fig. 25.3. The

Fig. 25.3.   Partial 3D shapes of the first experiment

complete 3D model after registration and integration is shown in Fig. 25.4. Although plane fitting has been done on the object surface, rendering with triangular mesh still cause some visual distortions.

For the structures of the objects containing non-rectangular surface patches, camera parameters and the "base-models" are first obtained from the lower part of the objects. Additional image points associated with the upper part of the object are then added with coplanarity and equidistance constraints. Fig. 25.6 shows the reconstructed partial 3D models from the corresponding single input images shown in Fig. 25.5. We have tested the proposed 3D model reconstruction approach on six outdoor architectural scenes and four indoor objects. The small scale objects in the laboratory environment usually give better reconstruction results mainly because of the controlled illumination conditions and the larger focal length used for image acquisition. For the outdoor building reconstruction, careful selections of the initial corner points are mandatory since the images might contain more complicate background scenes. Furthermore, the lens distortion has to be modeled for even close-range photography with short focal length. Since the evaluation of the final reconstruction result is usually based on the texture information of the object, novel views are best synthesized on the viewpoints closer to the original acquired images.

25.5. Conclusion and Future Research

In this paper, we have presented a 3D model reconstruction system for architectural scenes using one or more uncalibrated images. The images can be taken from off-the-shelf digital cameras. The feature points for 3D model reconstruction are selected by a user interactively through a graphical user interface. For a given set of corner points from one viewpoint, parallelism, orthogonality and coplanarity constraints are applied to obtain the partial 3D shape of the building. The complete (360 degrees) 3D model of the building is obtained by registering the partial

Fig. 25.4.   Complete 3D model of the first experiment

Fig. 25.5.   Input images of the second experiment

Fig. 25.6.   Partial 3D shapes of the second experiment

3D models to a common coordinate system. Future research will focus on using additional geometric constraints to create more detailed 3D models of architectural scenes. Whenever it is possible, texture mapping which contains occluding objects such as trees will be avoided by using the images captured from different viewpoints.

Acknowledgments

The support of this work in part by the National Science Council of Taiwan, R.O.C. under Grant NSC-93-2218-E-194-024 is gratefully acknowledged.

References

1. P.K. Allen, I. Stamos, A. Troccoli, B. Smith, M. Leordeanu, Y.C. Hsu, 3D Modeling of Historic Sites Using Range and Image Data, *IEEE International Conference on Robotics and Automation*, pp. 145-150, (2003).
2. C. Baillard and A. Zisserman, Automatic Reconstruction of Piecewise Planar Models from Multiple Views, *IEEE Computer Vision and Pattern Recognition*, vol. II, pp. 559-565, (1999).
3. B. Caprile and V. Torre, Using Vanishing Points for Camera Calibration, *International Journal of Computer Vision*, pp. 127-140, March, (1990).
4. C. Chen, C. Yu, and Y. Hung, New Calibration-free Approach for Augmented Reality based on Parameterized Cuboid Structure, *International Conference on Computer Vision*, pp. 30-37, (1999).
5. A.R. Dick, P.H.S. Torr, and R. Cipolla, Automatic 3D Modelling of Architecture, *British Machine Vision Conference*, pp. 372-381, (2000).
6. K. Kanatani, *Geometric Computation for Machine Vision*, Oxford Science Publications, (1993).
7. E. Trucco and A. Verri, *Introductory Techniques for 3-D Computer Vision*,Prentice Hall, (1998).
8. T. Moons, D. Frere, J. Vandekerckhove, L.J.V. Gool, Automatic modelling and 3D reconstruction of urban house roofs from high resolution aerial imagery", *European Conference on Computer Vision*, vol. I, pp. 410–425, (1998).
9. I. Stamos and P.K. Allen, 3-D Model Construction using Range and Image Data, *IEEE Computer Vision and Pattern Recognition*, vol. I, pp. 531–536, (2000).
10. R.Y. Tsai, A Versatile Camera Calibration Technique for High-Accuracy 3D Machine Vision Metrology Using Off-the-Shelf TV Cameras and Lenses, *IEEE Trans. Robotics and Automation*, **3**(4), pp. 323–344, (1987).

CHAPTER 26

SEPARATING RIGID MOTION FOR CONTINUOUS SHAPE EVOLUTION

Niels Chr. Overgaard and Jan Erik Solem

Applied Mathematics Group, School of Technology and Society, Malmö University, Sweden,
E-mail: nco@ts.mah.se

A method is proposed for the construction of descent directions for the minimization of energy functionals defined for plane curves. The method is potentially useful in a number of image analysis problems, such as image registration and shape warping, where the standard gradient descent curve evolutions are not always feasible. The descent direction is constructed by taking a weighted average of the three components of the gradient corresponding to translation, rotation, and deformation. Our approach differs from previous work in the field by the use of implicit representation of curves and the notion of normal velocity of a curve evolution. Thus our theory is morphological and well suited for implementation in the level set framework.

26.1. Introduction

Gradient descent curve evolutions occur frequently in image analysis applications. One popular example is the geodesic active contours.[1] Geodesic active contours is an example of *shape optimization* where curves are evolved to fit some form of data such as, for instance, image edges. Other examples are *shape analysis* applications such as shape warping and shape statistics. Shape statistics is often used as prior information in e.g. segmentation, cf.[5,10]

Traditionally, shape analysis has been performed by studying the variation of landmarks on the curves, cf. e.g.[4] The drawback of this approach is that landmarks are often very hard to find automatically. Performing analysis directly on the continuous curve overcomes this problem, but then registration of the shapes becomes much harder. Here we propose a method that has the potential of solving this registration problem. Also, a correct warping between shapes has the potential of solving the difficult "landmark correspondence" problem. In Section 26.4

we successfully apply the proposed method to both these problems.

In this paper we introduce a geometric procedure for decomposing any curve evolution into *translation, rotation and deformation*. This is useful for many applications and gives a way of modifying gradient flows. The decomposition is achieved by introducing orthogonal projections of the normal velocity of the evolution onto the subspaces generated by translations and rotations. Our investigation is inspired by the work in,[3] where this type of decompositions were first studied. However, our method differs from theirs in that we use *normal velocities* which gives a geometric theory well suited for level set implementation, whereas[3] use vector-valued velocities allowing for tangential re-parametrization. This may seem like a small difference, but it turns out that the actual projections used are very different. We also show that the projected evolution still gives descent directions for the energy functional. It should be noted that similar questions have already been considered for deformable models working with elastic energy expressions for parametrized curves, surfaces, and bodies, see e.g.,.[12] However, here we focus on methods that can be incorporated into the level set framework.

The present paper is an extended version of an earlier work[8] which has been presented at the 18th International Conference on Pattern Recognition in Hong Kong, August 2006.

26.2. Level Sets, Normal Velocity, and L^2-Gradient Descent

A simple closed curve Γ can be represented as the zero level set of a function $\phi : \mathbf{R}^2 \to \mathbf{R}$ as

$$\Gamma = \{\mathbf{x} \in \mathbf{R}^2 \; ; \; \phi(\mathbf{x}) = 0\} \; . \tag{26.1}$$

The sets $\Omega^{\text{int}} = \{\mathbf{x} \; ; \; \phi(\mathbf{x}) < 0\}$ and $\Omega^{\text{ext}} = \{\mathbf{x} \; ; \; \phi(\mathbf{x}) > 0\}$ are called the *interior* and the *exterior* of Γ, respectively. Geometric quantities such as the outward unit normal $\mathbf{n}$ and the curvature κ can be expressed in terms of ϕ as

$$\mathbf{n} = \frac{\nabla\phi}{|\nabla\phi|} \quad \text{and} \quad \kappa = \nabla \cdot \frac{\nabla\phi}{|\nabla\phi|} \; . \tag{26.2}$$

The function ϕ is usually called the level set function for Γ, cf. e.g.[7]

A curve evolution, that is, a time dependent curve $t \mapsto \Gamma(t)$, can be represented by a time dependent level set function $\phi : \mathbf{R}^2 \times \mathbf{R} \to \mathbf{R}$ as $\Gamma(t) = \{\mathbf{x} \in \mathbf{R}^2 \; ; \; \phi(\mathbf{x}, t) = 0\}$. Let us consider the kinematics of curve evolutions. In the implicit representation, it does not make sense to "track" points on an evolving curve, as there is no way of knowing the tangential motion of points on $\Gamma(t)$. The important notion is instead that of *normal velocity*. The normal velocity of a curve evolution $t \mapsto \Gamma(t)$ is the scalar function defined by

$$v(\Gamma) = \frac{d}{dt}\Gamma(t) := -\frac{\partial\phi(\mathbf{x},t)/\partial t}{|\nabla\phi(\mathbf{x},t)|} \qquad (\mathbf{x} \in \Gamma(t)) \ . \qquad (26.3)$$

The normal velocity is independent of the curve representation (and the choice of level set function ϕ) and is therefore a geometric quantity of the evolution. The set of normal velocities at Γ is a linear space. It can be endowed with a natural scalar product and a corresponding norm, cf.,[11]

$$\langle v, w \rangle_\Gamma = \int_\Gamma v(\mathbf{x})w(\mathbf{x})\,d\sigma \quad \text{and} \quad \|v\|_\Gamma^2 = \langle v, v \rangle_\Gamma \ , \qquad (26.4)$$

where v, w are normal velocities and $d\sigma$ is the curve length element. In the following we therefore denote the linear space of normal velocities at Γ by $L^2(\Gamma)$.

The scalar product (26.4) is important in the construction of *gradient descent flows* for functionals $E(\Gamma)$ defined on a "manifold" M of admissible curves Γ. Let the Gâteaux derivative of $E(\Gamma)$ at Γ is denoted by $dE(\Gamma)v$, for any normal velocity v, and suppose that there exists a vector $\nabla E(\Gamma) \in L^2(\Gamma)$ such that

$$dE(\Gamma)v = \langle \nabla E(\Gamma), v \rangle_\Gamma \quad \text{for all } v \in L^2(\Gamma) \ . \qquad (26.5)$$

Then $\nabla E(\Gamma)$ is called the L^2-*gradient* of E at Γ. We make two remarks concerning this notion. First of all, not every functional $E = E(\Gamma)$ has an L^2-gradient, not even when the Gâteaux derivative exists. A concrete example is the Kimmel-Bruckstein functional, $E(\Gamma) = \int_\Gamma |\mathbf{w} \cdot \mathbf{n}|\,d\sigma$, for the optimal alignment of a curve Γ to a given vector field $\mathbf{w} = \mathbf{w}(\mathbf{x}) : \mathbf{R}^2 \to \mathbf{R}^2$. It was shown in[9] that this functional has a well-defined Gâteaux derivative, however this derivative contains terms with Dirac δ's which cannot be expressed using the scalar product defined in (26.4). Secondly, if the L^2-gradient does exist, then it is uniquely determined. This is essentially a consequence of the fact that any smooth function $v : \Gamma \to \mathbf{R}$ may be considered to be the normal velocity of some curve evolution which passes through Γ at $t = 0$, see [11, Lemma 2], so that $C^\infty(\Gamma)$ is dense in $L^2(\Gamma)$. Then, if $\tilde{\nabla}E(\Gamma)$ is "another" gradient for E at Γ, then $\langle \tilde{\nabla}E - \nabla E, v \rangle_\Gamma = 0$ for all normal velocities, by the definition of the gradient in (26.5), hence for all $v \in L^2(\Gamma)$ by density. In particular, we can take $v = \tilde{\nabla}E - \nabla E$ so that $\|\tilde{\nabla}E - \nabla E\|_\Gamma^2 = 0$, which proves the uniqueness assertion.

The gradient descent flow for the problem of minimizing $E(\Gamma)$ is defined as the solution of the following initial value problem

$$\frac{d}{dt}\Gamma(t) = -\nabla E(\Gamma(t)), \qquad \Gamma(0) = \Gamma_0, \qquad (26.6)$$

where Γ_0 is an initial contour specified by the user.

Let us mention that in[3] the kinematic entity corresponding to our normal velocity v in (26.3) is a vector valued function $\mathbf{v} : \Gamma \to \mathbf{R}^2$ given by $\mathbf{v} = v\mathbf{n}$. Consequently the L^2-scalar product used there is defined, via the Euclidean scalar product in $\mathbf{R}^2$, as $(\mathbf{v}, \mathbf{w})_\Gamma = \int_\Gamma \mathbf{v}^T \mathbf{w}\, d\sigma$. While $\langle v, w \rangle_\Gamma = (\mathbf{v}, \mathbf{w})_\Gamma$, for any pair of normal velocities, the difference in choice of scalar products actually makes a difference when rigid motions are considered, as we shall in the following sections.

26.3. Decomposition of Evolutions

Let $E(\Gamma)$ be an energy functional defined on the manifold M of admissible curves. Again, we want to minimize $E(\Gamma)$. Instead of using the gradient descent evolution defined by (26.6), we search along the path of another evolution $t \mapsto \Gamma(t)$ defined by

$$\frac{d}{dt}\Gamma(t) = v(\Gamma(t)), \qquad \Gamma(0) = \Gamma_0, \tag{26.7}$$

where the normal velocity $v = v(\Gamma)$ is a descent direction for $E(\Gamma)$. The construction of $v(\Gamma)$ is based on an idea presented in.[3] The L^2-gradient $\nabla E = \nabla E(\Gamma)$, is decomposed into three components $\Pi_T \nabla E$, $\Pi_R \nabla E$, and $\Pi_D \nabla E$. Here $\Pi_T \nabla E$ and $\Pi_R \nabla E$ are the orthogonal projections of ∇E onto the subspaces of normal velocities at Γ generated by translations and rotations, respectively. $\Pi_D \nabla E$ is defined as the residual $\Pi_D \nabla E = \nabla E - \Pi_T \nabla E - \Pi_R \nabla E$. The right-hand side in (26.7) is defined as a convex combination of these components,

$$v = -(\mu_1 \Pi_T \nabla E + \mu_2 \Pi_R \nabla E + \mu_3 \Pi_D \nabla E), \tag{26.8}$$

where the weights $\mu_1, \mu_2, \mu_3 \geq 0$ satisfy $\mu_1 + \mu_2 + \mu_3 = 1$.

Note that if we choose $\mu_3 = 0$ in (26.8), then the curve evolution (26.7) becomes a rigid motion; it changes the position and orientation of the initial contour Γ_0 without changing its shape. Hence the residual component $\Pi_D \nabla E$ may be interpreted as the part of ∇E responsible for the *deformation* of the contour shape. Also, note that if $\mu_1 = \mu_2 = \mu_3 = 1/3$, then $v = -\frac{1}{3}\nabla E$, so, apart from a time scaling, we recover the original gradient descent evolution (26.6).

26.3.1. *The Projection onto Translations*

We now show how the projections Π_T is constructed. Let Γ be a fixed contour, $\mathbf{v} \in \mathbf{R}^2$ an arbitrary vector, and define a curve evolution $t \mapsto \Gamma(t)$ as the translation of Γ,

$$\Gamma(t) = \{\mathbf{x} + t\mathbf{v}; \mathbf{x} \in \Gamma\}. \tag{26.9}$$

It is easy to see that the normal velocity of the evolution in (26.9) is given by

$$v_T = \mathbf{n}^T \mathbf{v}. \tag{26.10}$$

Inspired by this we define the following subspace of $L^2(\Gamma)$:

$$L_T = L_T(\Gamma) := \{v \in L^2(\Gamma); v = \mathbf{n}^T \mathbf{v} \text{ for some } \mathbf{v} \in \mathbf{R}^2\}. \tag{26.11}$$

The elements of L_T are exactly the the normal velocities which come from pure translation motions. Notice that $\dim L_T = 2$, because L_T has the normal velocities $v_1 = \mathbf{n}^T \mathbf{v}_1, v_2 = \mathbf{n}^T \mathbf{v}_2$ as a basis, whenever $\mathbf{v}_1, \mathbf{v}_2$ is a basis for $\mathbf{R}^2$. Now, define $\Pi_T = \Pi_T(\Gamma)$ as the orthogonal projection in $L^2(\Gamma)$ onto L_T. Clearly, the identity

$$\Pi_T v_T = v_T \tag{26.12}$$

holds because v_T, given by (26.10), belongs to L_T. We can use this identity to find an explicit formula for Π_T. Multiply v_T by $\mathbf{n}$ and integrate over Γ, then (26.10) implies that

$$\int_\Gamma v_T \mathbf{n} \, d\sigma = \int_\Gamma (\mathbf{n}^T \mathbf{v}) \mathbf{n} \, d\sigma = \left[\int_\Gamma \mathbf{n} \mathbf{n}^T \, d\sigma \right] \mathbf{v}. \tag{26.13}$$

We call the matrix $S := \int_\Gamma \mathbf{n} \mathbf{n}^T \, d\sigma$ appearing on the right-hand side the *structure tensor* for the curve Γ. S is clearly positive semi-definite;

$$\mathbf{w}^T S \mathbf{w} = \int_\Gamma \mathbf{w}^T \mathbf{n} \mathbf{n}^T \mathbf{w} \, d\sigma = \int_\Gamma (\mathbf{n}^T \mathbf{w})^2 \, d\sigma \geq 0, \tag{26.14}$$

for any $\mathbf{w} \in \mathbf{R}^2$. However, more is true:

Proposition 1 *The structure tensor S is positive definite, in particular S is invertible.*

Proof: Suppose $\mathbf{w}_0^T S \mathbf{w}_0 = 0$ for some $\mathbf{w}_0 \in \mathbf{R}^2$, then it follows from (26.14) that $\int_\Gamma (\mathbf{n}^T \mathbf{w}_0)^2 \, d\sigma = 0$, so that $\mathbf{n}^T \mathbf{w}_0 = 0$ identically on Γ. This implies that $\mathbf{n}$ is constant along Γ, which is clearly impossible if Γ is a closed curve. This contradiction shows that S must be positive definite. $\square$

We remark that the above results is invalid for one-dimensional curves in three of more space dimensions. In fact, the above proof breaks down of we consider a planar curve in three dimensions and take $\mathbf{w}_0$ normal to the plane in question.

By the proposition and (26.13) the translation vector $\mathbf{v}$ corresponding to the normal velocity v_T can be reconstructed: $\mathbf{v} = \left[\int_\Gamma \mathbf{n} \mathbf{n}^T \, d\sigma \right]^{-1} \int_\Gamma v_T \mathbf{n} \, d\sigma$. Using (26.10) we then get

$$v_T = \mathbf{n}^T \mathbf{v} = \mathbf{n}^T \left[\int_\Gamma \mathbf{n} \mathbf{n}^T \, d\sigma \right]^{-1} \int_\Gamma v_T \mathbf{n} \, d\sigma. \tag{26.15}$$

Comparing this identity to (26.12) suggests that Π_T is given by

$$\Pi_T v = \mathbf{n}^T \mathbf{v} = \mathbf{n}^T \left[\int_\Gamma \mathbf{n}\mathbf{n}^T \, d\sigma \right]^{-1} \int_\Gamma v\mathbf{n} \, d\sigma \ , \qquad (26.16)$$

for all normal velocities $v \in L^2(\Gamma)$. This is indeed true, as it is easily checked that the operator Π defined by the right hand-side of (26.16) is self-adjoint ($\Pi^* = \Pi$) and idempotent ($\Pi^2 = \Pi$), hence an orthogonal projection. Moreover, (26.15) shows that L_T is contained in the range of Π, and since the dimension of Π's range is two, it follows that $\Pi = \Pi_T$ as claimed in (26.16).

26.3.2. The Projection onto Rotations

Next, we derive a formula for the projection Π_R. Consider rotations in the plane; the rotation of Γ about a point $\mathbf{x}_0 \in \mathbf{R}^2$ with angular velocity ω is given by

$$\Gamma(t) = \{R(t)(\mathbf{x} - \mathbf{x}_0) + \mathbf{x}_0 : \mathbf{x} \in \Gamma\}, \qquad (26.17)$$

where $R(t) = \left[\begin{smallmatrix} \cos(\omega t) & -\sin(\omega t) \\ \sin(\omega t) & \cos(\omega t) \end{smallmatrix} \right]$. The corresponding normal velocity at $t = 0$ is given by

$$v_R = \omega \mathbf{n}^T (\hat{\mathbf{x}} - \hat{\mathbf{x}}_0) \qquad (\mathbf{x} \in \Gamma) \ . \qquad (26.18)$$

Here we have defined $\hat{\mathbf{x}} = \left[\begin{smallmatrix} 0 & -1 \\ 1 & 0 \end{smallmatrix} \right] \mathbf{x} = R'(0)\mathbf{x}$. Now, set

$$L_R = \{v \in L^2(\Gamma); v = \omega \mathbf{n}^T (\hat{\mathbf{x}} - \hat{\mathbf{x}}_0) \text{ for some } \omega \in \mathbf{R}\}.$$

Clearly $\dim L_R = 1$ for any fixed $\mathbf{x}_0$. The orthogonal projection onto L_R is given by the formula

$$\Pi_R v = \frac{\mathbf{n}^T (\hat{\mathbf{x}} - \hat{\mathbf{x}}_0) \int_\Gamma v\mathbf{n}^T (\hat{\mathbf{x}} - \hat{\mathbf{x}}_0) \, d\sigma}{\int_\Gamma |\mathbf{n}^T (\hat{\mathbf{x}} - \hat{\mathbf{x}}_0)|^2 \, d\sigma} \ . \qquad (26.19)$$

Again it is easy to check that $\Pi_R^* = \Pi_R$ and $\Pi_R^2 = \Pi_R$.

The point $\mathbf{x}_0$ in (26.19) is chosen such that the two subspaces L_T and L_R are orthogonal, or equivalently, $\Pi_T \Pi_R = \Pi_R \Pi_T = 0$. Using (26.16) and (26.19) it is easy to see that $\mathbf{x}_0$ must satisfy the following vector relation $\int_\Gamma \left[\mathbf{n}^T (\hat{\mathbf{x}} - \hat{\mathbf{x}}_0) \right] \mathbf{n} \, d\sigma = 0$, hence

$$\hat{\mathbf{x}}_0 = \left[\int_\Gamma \mathbf{n}\mathbf{n}^T \, d\sigma \right]^{-1} \int_\Gamma (\mathbf{n}^T \hat{\mathbf{x}})\mathbf{n} \, d\sigma, \qquad (26.20)$$

where the structure tensor for Γ appears again. Since L_T and L_R are now orthogonal, it follows that the residual $\Pi_D = I - \Pi_T - \Pi_R$ (I denoting the identity operator) is also an orthogonal projection. The range of Π_D is interpreted as the space of normal velocities which are responsible for deformations of the initial contour.

We end this section with some two important observations. The first observation implies that the normal velocity constructed in (26.8) is in fact a descent direction for the functional $E(\Gamma)$.

Proposition 2 *If* Π *is an orthogonal projection in* $L^2(\Gamma)$, *and the normal velocity* $v(\Gamma) = -\Pi\nabla E(\Gamma)$ *is not identically zero on* Γ. *Then* $v(\Gamma)$ *is a descent direction for* $E(\Gamma)$.

Proof: Let $t \mapsto \Gamma(t)$ be the curve evolution which solves (26.7) with $v(\Gamma)$ given by the formula in the proposition, then the claim follows from the following simple calculation:

$$\frac{d}{dt}E(\Gamma) = \langle \nabla E(\Gamma), v(\Gamma)\rangle_\Gamma$$

$$= \langle \nabla E(\Gamma), -\Pi\nabla E(\Gamma)\rangle_\Gamma = -\|\Pi\nabla E(\Gamma)\|_\Gamma^2 < 0,$$

where we have used that $\Pi^2 = \Pi$, $\Pi^* = \Pi$, and $v(\Gamma) \neq 0$. $\qquad\square$

The second observation is related to the fact that the projection methods described above can be applied to any energy functional E with a well-defined L^2-gradient ∇E. For instance we may apply the method to the *arc length-* and *enclosed area* functionals:

$$E_\circ(\Gamma) := \int_\Gamma d\sigma \ , \quad \text{and} \quad E_\bullet(\Gamma) := \int_{\Omega^{\text{int}}} dx \ ,$$

respectively. Since the values of $E_\circ(\Gamma)$ and $E_\bullet(\Gamma)$ are invariant under translation and rotation, we would not expect these functionals to generate any rigid motion at all. In other words we expect the orthogonal projections onto $L_T(\Gamma)$ and $L_R(\Gamma)$ of the L^2-gradients

$$\nabla E_\circ(\Gamma) = \kappa \ , \quad \text{and} \quad \nabla E_\bullet(\Gamma) = 1 \ ,$$

to be zero. This expectation is easily verified by substituting the above gradients into the formulas (26.16) and (26.19) for the projections Π_T and Π_R, and use the basic identities $\int_\Gamma \kappa\mathbf{n}\,ds = 0$, $\int_\Gamma \mathbf{n}\,ds = 0$, and the definition (26.20) of the centre of rotation $\mathbf{x}_0$. $\qquad\bullet$

26.4. Experiments

In this section we apply the method of projections, introduced above, to some concrete examples. We consider two applications within shape analysis of curves: Continuous shape warping and registration of continuous shapes. All curves are

Fig. 26.1. The figure shows the contours of two copies of the same pigeon. The *symmetric difference* of the interiors of these contours is the shaded region, i.e., the set of points belonging to exactly one of the interiors.

represented implicitly as described in Section 26.2. The shapes are taken from the Kimia shape database.[6]

We will use the the gradient flow associated with the *area of symmetric differ-ence*, cf.,[2] between two shapes $\Gamma = \{\mathbf{x} \in \mathbf{R}^2 : \phi(\mathbf{x}) = 0\}$ and $\Gamma_0 = \{\mathbf{x} \in \mathbf{R}^2 : \phi_0(\mathbf{x}) = 0\}$ defined as

$$E_{\mathrm{SD}}(\Gamma) = E_{\mathrm{SD}}(\Gamma, \Gamma_0) = \frac{1}{2}\mathrm{area}(\Omega^{\mathrm{int}} \triangle \Omega_0^{\mathrm{int}}) \ , \qquad (26.21)$$

where $A \triangle B$ denotes the *symmetric difference of A and B*, defined as the set of points which is contained in exactly one of the sets A of B, cf. Figure 1. To find the gradient of the functional E_{SD}, we introduce the characteristic functions $\chi_{\Omega^{\mathrm{int}}}$ and $\chi_{\Omega_0^{\mathrm{int}}}$ of the interiors of Γ and Γ_0 respectively, and rewrite E as,

$$
\begin{aligned}
E_{\mathrm{SD}}(\Gamma) &= \frac{1}{2}\int_{\mathbf{R}^2}(\chi_{\Omega^{\mathrm{int}}} - \chi_{\Omega_0^{\mathrm{int}}})^2 \, d\mathbf{x} = \frac{1}{2}\int_{\mathbf{R}^2}(\chi_{\Omega^{\mathrm{int}}}^2 - 2\chi_{\Omega^{\mathrm{int}}}\chi_{\Omega_0^{\mathrm{int}}} + \chi_{\Omega_0^{\mathrm{int}}}^2) \, d\mathbf{x}\\
&= \frac{1}{2}\int_{\mathbf{R}^2}(\chi_{\Omega^{\mathrm{int}}} - 2\chi_{\Omega^{\mathrm{int}}}\chi_{\Omega_0^{\mathrm{int}}} + \chi_{\Omega_0^{\mathrm{int}}}) \, d\mathbf{x}\\
&= \int_{\Omega^{\mathrm{int}}}(\frac{1}{2} - \chi_{\Omega_0^{\mathrm{int}}}) \, d\mathbf{x} + \mathrm{const},
\end{aligned}
$$

since the target contour Γ_0 is held fixed. It is now easy to see that the correspond-ing L^2-gradient is given by the normal velocity $\nabla E_{\mathrm{SD}}(\Gamma) = \frac{1}{2} - \chi_{\Omega_0^{\mathrm{int}}}$ defined on Γ. In practice the characteristic functions are represented using continuous approximations of the Heaviside function, cf. e.g.[2]

26.4.1. *Continuous Shape Warping*

Here we show that the standard evolution from the symmetric difference gives a very un-intuitive motion when continuous shapes are warped from one shape to

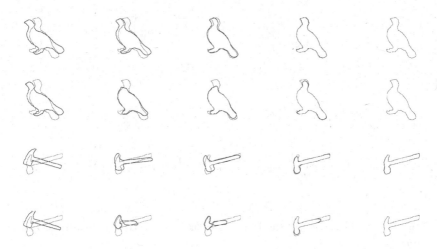

Fig. 26.2.   Examples of shape warping generated by minimizing the area of the symmetric difference between an evolving shape and the fixed target shape. The evolving shape is the black curve and the red curve is the target shape. The evolution is from left to right with the initial curve to the far left and the final curve to the far right. For each example, the top row corresponds to the evolution where the rigid motion projection is weighted higher than the deformation and the bottom row is the standard gradient descent flow. Notice that with the standard gradient descent flow, the intermediate shapes bear little or no resemblance to neither the initial nor the target shape. This problem can be solved using the weighted projected motion. The parameters used were $(\mu_1, \mu_2, \mu_3) = (0.3, 0.7, 0)$, initially, switching to $(\mu_1, \mu_2, \mu_3) = (0.1, 0.1, 0.8)$ at the end of the evolution.

another. This has also been noted for the case of using approximate Hausdorff distance in.[3] If the shapes are not perfectly aligned, the evolution will remove details of the initial shape to a smooth shape and then grow new details corresponding to the target shape. This gives practically useless intermediate shapes. If we instead partition the flow as in (26.8) and weight rotation and translation higher than deformation, we obtain a much more intuitive flow with the desired intermediate shapes. We illustrate this in Figure 26.2. For each example the top row corresponds to the evolution where rigid motion projection is weighted higher than deformation and the bottom row is the unchanged symmetric difference flow.

26.4.2. *Registration of Continuous Shapes*

Another important application is shape registration. Shape registration implies the alignment of shapes and is a crucial step if one is interested in computing shape statistics and analyze shape variation. In this case we turn off the deformation part

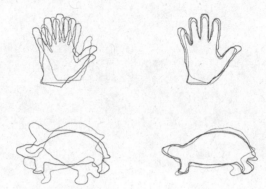

Fig. 26.3. Registration using the rigid part of the evolution. The initial shapes (**left**), shapes registered (**right**).

entirely and simply use the normal velocity

$$v(\Gamma) = -(\mu_1 \Pi_T \nabla E_{\text{SD}}(\Gamma) + \mu_2 \Pi_R \nabla E_{\text{SD}}(\Gamma)) \ . \tag{26.22}$$

Figure 26.3 shows some examples of this procedure where one curve is chosen as the target shape and all other shapes are evolved towards this curve using (26.22).

26.5. Conclusions

We have presented a method for decomposing *any* curve evolution into rigid motion and deformation. The method is applied to shape warping and registration problems with satisfying results. The theory is developed for use in the level set framework and is simple to implement. It is our opinion that problems of shape analysis, shape statistics and shape optimization should be studied in the continuum framework using the language of geometry and mathematical analysis. Many vision problems can then be formulated as variational problems, which are usually easy to interpret, and discretizations are introduced only at the point where the numerical solution of the derived equations are computed. This will facilitate the understanding and comparison of different methods in the field. The aim of this paper was to try to apply level set methods to standard problems in shape analysis of curves. Although the method presented here is far from perfect, and certainly not competitive with standard tools in the field, it may still be regarded as a small step in the direction of a continuum formulation of shape analysis.

References

1. V. Caselles, R. Kimmel, and G. Sapiro. Geodesic active contours. *Int. Journal of Computer Vision*, 1997.
2. T. F. Chan and W. Zhu. Level set based prior segmentation. Technical Report UCLA CAM Report 03-66, University of California at Los Angeles, 2003.
3. G. Charpiat, R. Keriven, J-P. Pons, and O. Faugeras. Designing spatially coherent minimizing flows for variational problems based on active contours. In *ICCV, Beijing, China*, 2005.
4. T. Cootes, C. Taylor, D. Cooper, and J. Graham. Active shape models – their training and application. *Computer Vision and Image Understanding*, 61(1):38–59, 1995.
5. D. Cremers and S. Soatto. A pseudo-distance for shape priors in level set segmentation. In *IEEE Workshop, Variational, Geometric and Level Set Methods in Computer Vision*, 2003.
6. Benjamin B. Kimia. *The Kimia shape data base.* http://www.lems.brown.edu/vision/software/.
7. S. J. Osher and R. P. Fedkiw. *Level Set Methods and Dynamic Implicit Surfaces.* Springer Verlag, 2002.
8. N. Chr. Overgaard and J. E. Solem. Separating rigid motion for continuous shape evolution. In *Proc. Int. Conf. on Pattern Recognition*, Supplemental volume, pages 1–4, Hong Kong, 2006.
9. N. Chr. Overgaard and J. E. Solem. An analysis of variational alignment of curves in images. In *Scale Space 2005*, LNCS 3459, pages 480–491, Springer-Verlag 2005.
10. M. Rousson and N. Paragios. Shape priors for level set representations. In *Proc. European Conf. on Computer Vision*. Springer, 2002.
11. J. E. Solem and N. Chr. Overgaard. A geometric formulation of gradient descent for variational problems with moving surfaces. In *Scale Space 2005*, LNCS 3459, pages 419–430, Springer-Verlag 2005.
12. D. Terzopoulos and A. Witkin. Physically based models with rigid and deformable components. *IEEE Comput. Graph. Appl.*, 8(6):41–51, 1998.

CHAPTER 27

A PDE METHOD TO SEGMENT IMAGE LINEAR OBJECTS WITH APPLICATION TO LENS DISTORTION REMOVAL

Moumen T. El-Melegy and Nagi H. Al-Ashwal

Electrical Engineering Department,
Assiut University, Assiut 71516, Egypt
moumen@aun.edu.eg

In this paper, we propose a partial differential equation based method to segment image objects, which have a given parametric shape based on energy functional. The energy functional is composed of a term that detects object boundaries and a term that constrains the contour to find a shape compatible with the parametric shape. While the shape constraints guiding the PDE may be determined from object's shape statistical models, we demonstrate the proposed approach on the extraction of objects with explicit shape parameterization, such as linear image segments. Several experiments are reported on synthetic and real images to evaluate our approach. We also demonstrate the successful application of the proposed method to the problem of removing camera lens distortion, which can be significant in medium to wide-angle lenses.

1. Introduction

Variational methods and partial differential equations (PDEs) are more and more being used to analyze, understand and exploit properties of images in order to design powerful application techniques, see for example [15, 16, 17]. Variational methods formulate an image processing or computer vision problem as an optimization problem depending on the unknown variables (which are functions) of the problem. When the optimization functional is differentiable, the calculus of variations provides a tool to find the extremum of the functional leading to a PDE whose steady state gives the solution of the imaging or vision problem. A very attractive property of these mathematical frameworks is to state well-posed problems to guarantee existence, uniqueness and regularity of solutions [16]. More recently, implicit level set based representations of a contour [9] have become a popular framework for image segmentation [10, 11, 1].

The integration of shape priors into PDE based segmentation methods has been a focus of research in past years [2, 3, 4, 5, 6, 7, 8, 12, 13, 14]. Almost all of these variational approaches address the segmentation of non-parametric shapes in images. They use training sets to introduce the shape prior to the problem formulation in such a way that only familiar structures of one given object can be recovered. They typically do not permit the segmentation of several instances of the given object. This may be attributed to the fact that a level set function is restricted to the separation of two regions. As soon as more than two regions are considered, the level set idea looses parts of its attractiveness. These level-set methods find their largest area of application in the segmentation of medical images. After all, none can expect to find two instances of a human heart in a patient's scanned chest images!

On the other hand, extracting image parametric shapes and their parameters is an important problem in several computer vision applications. For example, extraction of a line is a crucial problem in calculating lens distortion and matching in stereo pairs [18]. As such, our research has addressed the application of variational methods and PDEs to the extraction of linear shapes from images. To the best of our knowledge, we are not aware of any efforts, other than ours, in that regard. Towards this end, we associate the parameters of the linear shape within the energy functional of an evolving level set. While existing approaches do not consider the extraction of more than one object instance in an image, the case where they would fail, our formulation allows the segmentation of multiple linear objects from an image.

The basic idea of this paper is inspired by a level set formulation of Chan-Vese [1]. We introduce line parameters into a level set formulation of a Chan-Vese like functional in a way that permits the simultaneous segmentation of several lines in an image. The parameters of the line are not specified beforehand, they rather evolve in an unsupervised manner in order to automatically select the image regions that are linear and the parameters of each line are calculated. In particular, we will show that this approach allows detecting image linear segments while ignoring other objects. This simple, easy-to-implement method provides noise-robust results because it relies on a region-based driving flow.

Moreover we apply the proposed PDE-based level set method to the calibration and removal of camera lens distortion, which can be significant in medium to wide-angle lenses. Applications that require 3-D modelling of large scenes typically use cameras with such wide fields of view [18]. In such instances, the camera distortion effect has to be removed by calibrating the camera's lens distortion and subsequently undistorting the input image. One key feature of our method is that it integrates the extraction of image features needed for calibration and the computation of distortion parameters within one energy functional, which is minimized during level set evolution. Thus our approach, unlike most other nonmetric calibration methods [21, 22, 23], avoids the propagation of errors in feature extraction onto the computation stage. This results in a more robust computation even at high noise levels.

The organization of this paper is as follows: In Section 2, we briefly review a level set formulation of the piecewise-constant Mumford-Shah functional, as proposed in [1]. In Section 3, we augment this variational framework by a parametric term that affects the evolution of the level set function globally for one object in the image. In Section 4, we extend this in order to handle more than one parametric object. In Section 5 we describe several experiments to evaluate the proposed method. We apply this method to lens distortion removal in Section 6. The conclusions are presented in Section 7.

2. Region-Based Segmentation with Level Sets and PDEs

In [1] Chan and Vese detailed a level set implementation of the Mumford-Shah functional, which is based on the use of the Heaviside function as an indicator function for the separate phases. The Chan-Vese method used a piecewise-constant, region-based formulation of the functional, which allows the contour to converge to the final segmentation over fairly large distances, while local edge and corner information is well preserved. It can detect cognitive contours (which are not defined by gradients), and contours in noisy images.

According to the level-set framework a contour, C, is embedded in a single level set function $\phi : \Omega \to \Re$ such that:

$$
\begin{cases}
C = \{(x,y) \in \Omega : \phi(x,y) = 0\}, \\
inside\,(C) = \{(x,y) \in \Omega : \phi(x,y) > 0\}, \\
outside\,(C) = \{(x,y) \in \Omega : \phi(x,y) < 0\}.
\end{cases}
\tag{1}
$$

In the Mumford-shah model, a piecewise constant segmentation of an input image f is given by [1]:

$$
\begin{aligned}
E_{seg}(c_1,c_2,\phi) &= \mu \int_{\Omega} |\nabla H_\varepsilon(\phi)|\,dxdy + v \int_{\Omega} H_\varepsilon(\phi)\,dxdy \\
&+ \lambda_1 \int_{\Omega} |f - c_1|^2 H_\varepsilon(\phi)\,dxdy + \lambda_2 \int_{\Omega} |f - c_2|^2 (1 - H_\varepsilon(\phi))\,dxdy,
\end{aligned}
\tag{2}
$$

where c_1 and c_2 are the mean values of the image f inside and outside the curve defined as the zero-level set of ϕ, respectively, and $\mu, v, \lambda_1, \lambda_2$ are regularizing parameters to be estimated or chosen a priori. H_ε is the regularized Heaviside function defined as [1]

$$
H_\varepsilon(s) = \frac{1}{2}\left(1 + \frac{2}{\pi}\arctan\left(\frac{s}{\varepsilon}\right)\right).
\tag{3}
$$

so

$$
\delta_\varepsilon(s) = \frac{dH_\varepsilon}{ds} = \frac{1}{\pi}\frac{\varepsilon}{\varepsilon^2 + s^2}.
\tag{4}
$$

The regularized H_ε and δ_ε having a discretization with a support larger than zero permit the detection of interior contours – for example if one wants to segment a ring-like structure, starting from an initial contour located outside the ring.

The Euler-Lagrange equation for this functional is implemented in [1] by the following gradient descent:

$$\frac{\partial \phi}{\partial t} = \delta_\varepsilon(\phi) \left[\mu div \left(\frac{\nabla \phi}{|\nabla \phi|} \right) - v - \lambda_1 \left(f - c_1 \right)^2 + \lambda_2 (f - c_2)^2 \right], \qquad (5)$$

where the scalars c_1 and c_2 are updated with the level set evolution and given by:

$$c_1 = \frac{\int f(x,y) H_\varepsilon(\phi) dx dy}{\int H_\varepsilon(\phi) dx dy}, \qquad (6)$$

$$c_2 = \frac{\int f(x,y)(1 - H_\varepsilon(\phi)) dx dy}{\int (1 - H_\varepsilon(\phi)) dx dy}. \qquad (7)$$

Figure 1 illustrates the main advantages of this level set method. Minimization of the functional (2) is done by alternating the two steps of iterating the gradient descent for the level set function ϕ as given by (5) and updating the mean gray values for the two phases, as given in equations (6, 7). Implicit representation allows the boundary to perform splitting and merging.

3. PDE Method for Line Segmentation

Our goal here is to extend the energy functional (2) in order to force the level set to segment only the linear shapes. This is done by adding a term E_{Line} that measures how well the level set represents the line. The new energy functional becomes:

$$E = E_{Seg} + \alpha E_{Line}. \qquad (8)$$

To derive E_{Line} the line is represented by its polar coordinates:

$$\rho = x \cos \theta + y \sin \theta, \qquad (9)$$

where θ is the orientation of the normal to the line with the x axis, and ρ is the distance of the line from the origin. The square distance, r^2, of a point (x_1, y_1) from the line is obtained by plugging the coordinates of the point into (9):

$$r^2 = (x_1 \cos\theta + y_1 \sin\theta - \rho)^2 . \tag{10}$$

So we can express E_{Line} which minimizes the sum of distances between the points inside the zero level set and a line with parameters (ρ, θ):

$$E_{Line}(\rho, \theta, \phi) = \int_\Omega (\rho - x\cos\theta - y\sin\theta)^2 H_\varepsilon(\phi)dxdy . \tag{11}$$

If the points inside the zero level set represent a line, E_{Line} will tend to be zero.

Keeping ρ and θ constant and minimizing this energy functional (11) with respect to ϕ, we deduce the associated Euler-Lagrange equation for ϕ as

$$\frac{\partial E_{Line}}{\partial \phi} = \delta_\varepsilon(\phi)\left[(\rho - x\cos\theta - y\sin\theta)^2 \right]. \tag{12}$$

Keeping ϕ fixed and setting $\dfrac{\partial E_{Line}}{\partial \rho} = 0$, and $\dfrac{\partial E_{Line}}{\partial \theta} = 0$, it is straightforward to solve for the line's ρ and θ parameters as:

$$\rho = \bar{x}\cos\theta + \bar{y}\sin\theta , \tag{13}$$

where $\bar{x}$ and $\bar{y}$ represent the centroid of the region inside the zero level set and given by [26, 27]:

$$\bar{x} = \frac{\int_\Omega x\, H_\varepsilon(\phi)dxdy}{\int_\Omega H_\varepsilon(\phi)dxdy}, \bar{y} = \frac{\int_\Omega y H_\varepsilon(\phi)dxdy}{\int_\Omega H_\varepsilon(\phi)dxdy}, \tag{14}$$

and

$$\theta = \frac{1}{2}\arctan\left(\frac{a_2}{a_1 - a_3} \right), \tag{15}$$

where a_1, a_2 and a_3 are given by [26]

$$a_1 = \int_\Omega (x - \bar{x})^2 H_\varepsilon(\phi)dxdy , \tag{16}$$

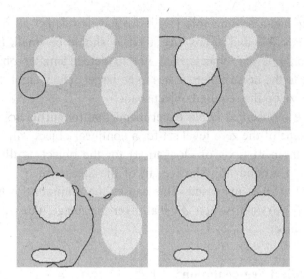

Figure 1. Evolution of the boundary for the Chan-Vese level set (with a single level set function). Due to the implicit level set representation, the topology is not constrained, which allows for splitting and merging of the boundary.

$$a_2 = 2 \int_\Omega (\dot{x} - \bar{x})(y - \bar{y}) H_\varepsilon(\phi) dx dy \ , \tag{17}$$

$$a_3 = \int_\Omega (y - \bar{y})^2 H_\varepsilon(\phi) dx dy \ . \tag{18}$$

The Euler-Lagrange equation for the total functional (8) can now be implemented by the following gradient descent:

$$\frac{\partial \phi}{\partial t} = \delta_\varepsilon(\phi) \left[\mu\, div\left((\frac{\nabla \phi}{|\nabla \phi|}) \right) - v - \lambda_1 (f - c_1)^2 \right.$$
$$\left. + \lambda_2 (f - c_2)^2 - \alpha(\rho - x\cos\theta - y\sin\theta)^2 \right], \tag{19}$$

where the scalars c_1, c_2, ρ, and θ are updated with the level set evolution according to Eqs. (6,7,13-18).

The weights λ_1 and λ_2 can be used to speed up the evolution towards the object boundaries, while μ and v regulate the zero level set. For example μ has a scaling role [1]; if we have to detect all or as many objects as possible and of any size, then μ should be small. If we have to detect only larger objects, and not to detect smaller objects (like points, due to the noise), then μ has to be larger. The weight α controls the emphasize on the required object shape.

It has been observed in our experiments that for sufficiently large α, the final shape of the zero level set for a nonlinear object will be the axis of second moment (axis of elongation) for the object as illustrated in Fig.2. To get around this, the weight of the area term, v, in (2), and consequently (8), is increased. This causes the minimum of the energy functional (8) to occur when $\phi < 0$ all over the image, thus ignoring the undesired object.

4. Multi-Object Segmentation

The previous method works only if there is one object in the image. If this object is linear, it will be detected, whereas other shapes are ignored. If there are more than one object, $H(\phi)$ will represent all those objects and Equations (13-18) will not be applicable. In this section we extend our method in order to perform multiple region segmentation based on fuzzy memberships that are computed by a Fuzzy C-mean algorithm (FCM) [19].

4.1. The Fuzzy C-mean Algorithm

The (FCM) generalizes the hard k-means algorithm to allow a point to partially belong to multiple clusters. Therefore, it produces a soft partition for a given dataset. If we assumed that $U[c \times n]$ is a membership matrix which contains the degree of membership for each cluster. Here, n denotes the number of patterns and c the number of clusters. In general the elements u_{ik} of the matrix U are in the interval $[0,1]$ and denote the degree of membership of the pattern $\mathbf{x}_k$ to the cluster c_i. The following condition must be satisfied

$$\sum_{i=1}^{c} u_{ik} = 1, \forall 1 \le k \le n. \tag{20}$$

Also if we assumed that $V = (v_1, v_2, \ldots, v_c)$ is a vector of cluster centre to be identified. The (FCM) attempts to cluster feature vectors by searching for local minima of the following objective function [19]:

$$J_m(U, v) = \sum_{i=1}^{c} \sum_{k=1}^{n} (u_{ik})^m D_{ik}, \qquad (21)$$

where the real number $m \in [0, \infty)$ is a weighting exponent on each fuzzy membership (typically taken equal to 2), D_{ik} is some measure of similarity between v_i and x_k or the attribute vectors and the cluster centers of each region. Minimization of J_m is based on the suitable selection of U and V using an iterative process through the following equations:

$$U_{ik} = \left(\sum_{j=1}^{c} \left(\frac{D_{ik}}{D_{jk}} \right)^{\frac{2}{(m-1)}} \right)^{-1} \forall i, k, \qquad (22)$$

$$v_i = \frac{\sum_{k=1}^{n} u_{ik}{}^m x_k}{\sum_{k=1}^{n} u_{ik}{}^m} \forall i. \qquad (23)$$

The algorithm stops when $u_{ik(\alpha)} - u_{ik(\alpha-1)} < \varepsilon$, or the maximum number of iteration has been reached. The (FCM) has several advantages. 1) It is unsupervised, 2) it can be used with any number of features and any number of classes and 3) it distributes the membership values in a normalized fashion. However, being unsupervised, it is not possible to predict ahead of time what type of clusters will emerge from the FCM.

4.2. Handling Multiple Objects

The FCM algorithm provides an initial segmentation of the image into a given number N of clusters. Let $u_i(x, y)$ denotes the membership of the pixel (x, y) in the i-th cluster. A level-set function, ϕ_i, is associated with each cluster, except for the cluster with largest number of pixels as it is assumed to be the background. Each ϕ_i is initialized such that:

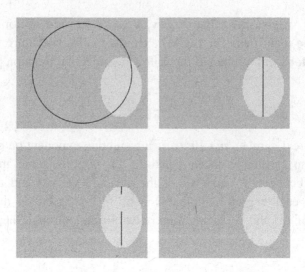

Figure 2. Evolution of the boundary for the level set under the functional (8). Due to the
E_{Line} term, the final shape of the boundary is the second moment axis of the object.
Increasing v causes smaller part of the object axis be detected. Further increase in v
leaves the nonlinear object undetected.

$$\begin{cases} \phi_i > 0, \forall (x,y) \in \{u_i(x,y) \geq 0.5\} \\ \phi_i < 0, \quad Otherwise \end{cases} \tag{24}$$

The term E_{Line} of the energy functional (8) is still given by (11),
whereas the term E_{seg} is now based on minimizing several level set
functions $\{\phi_i\}$:

$$E_{seg}(\phi) = \sum_{i=1}^{N-1} \left[\lambda \iint_\Omega [(1-u_i)H_\varepsilon(\phi_i) + u_i(1-H_\varepsilon(\phi_i))]dx \right.$$
$$\left. + \mu \int_\Omega |\nabla H_\varepsilon(\phi_i)|dx + v \int_\Omega H_\varepsilon(\phi_i)dx \right], \tag{25}$$

which can be simplified to

$$E_{seg}(\phi) = \sum_{i=1}^{N-1} \left[\lambda \int_{\Omega} (1 - 2u_i) H_\varepsilon(\phi_i) dx \right.$$

$$\left. + \mu \int_{\Omega} \left| \nabla H_\varepsilon(\phi_i) \right| dx + v \int_{\Omega} H_\varepsilon(\phi_i) dx \right], \tag{26}$$

where μ, λ are regularizing parameters to be estimated or chosen a priori. The functional (26) aims to maximize the total membership inside the isocontour of the zero level-set.

The Euler-Lagrange PDE for the new energy functional can now be implemented by the following gradient descent for each level set:

$$\frac{\partial \phi_i}{\partial t} = \delta_\varepsilon(\phi_i) \left[\mu div \left(\frac{\nabla \phi_i}{|\nabla \phi_i|} \right) - v - \lambda(1 - 2u_i) \right.$$

$$\left. - \alpha(\rho_i - x \cos \theta_i - y \sin \theta_i)^2 \right], \tag{27}$$

where the scalars ρ_i, and θ_i are updated with the level set evolution according to (13)-(18). The overall level set representation is eventually obtained from the final $\{\phi_i\}$ as $\max(\phi_i)$, for all i.

One problem however may arise if multiple disjoint objects belong to the same cluster (e.g., if they have the same color). Therefore after the initial clustering by the FCM algorithm, connected-component labeling is carried out on a hardened version of the result so objects within the same cluster are separated. Each object part is represented by an image that contains the membership information but with other twin object replaced by 0. Note that N in (26) will thus be increased accordingly.

We summarize the above scheme by the following algorithm outline:
- The input image is initially segmented into a number of clusters based on the FCM algorithm.
- Connected-component labelling is carried out on hardened version of each cluster, except the background, to separate the objects in that cluster.
- Construct an image for each initially detected object, this image contains the membership information of that object.

- Initial level-set is imposed for each object according to (24).
- Each level set is evolved based on (27). If the object is not linear, the isocontour of the zero level-set associated with this object will vanish.
- At the end of evolution, the final level set equals $\phi = \max\{\phi_i\}$, for all i. The remaining level sets, $\{\phi_i\}$, represent the linear objects. The parameters of the linear objects have been already calculated during the evolution according to (13)-(18).

This algorithm presents a simple, yet effective method to handle multiple objects in images. This is in contrast to existing methods that mostly did not consider this case. One of the few reported techniques that did consider it is the one by Brox et al. [25]. However, their method is rather complicated and not straight-forward to implement because they employed the combination of several ideas from multi-scale basis, a divide-and-conquer strategy, expectation-maximization principle and nonparametric Parzen density estimation.

5. Experimental Results

In order to evaluate the performance of the proposed technique on line segmentation, several experiments using synthetic and real images have been carried out. In the experiments, we choose the regularizing parameters as follows: $\alpha = 1$, $\lambda = 10$, $\mu = 0.5$, and $v = 10$. As our method is region-based segmentation it is robust in noisy images. This is demonstrated in Fig. 3. All lines have been successfully extracted from an image artificially corrupted with high noise with standard deviation $\sigma = 45$. Note that due to the shape constraints, our method again extracts only the lines and ignores other objects. For the sake of comparison, the result of the classical Hough transform applied to the same test image without noise, is shown in Fig. 3(c). Apparently, the level set method extracts only linear objects in the image, whereas Hough transform can also detect linear boundaries of objects (e.g., the box). However once the noise level in the image increases, Hough transform will face some problems. This is, because it depends largely on edge detection, it is sensitive to image noise, which may result in missing legitimate image lines when applied to the image in Fig. 3(a), as shown in Fig. 3(d).

We use the proposed method to extract intersected lines that have different colors; as shown in Fig. 4, which is a difficult problem for almost all existing level-set-based methods. Because of the lines intersections, the three lines could be treated as one object that would not become linear anymore. The initial level-sets based on the FCM output according to (24) are imposed on the image in Fig. 4(b). As shown in Fig. 4(c), the proposed method successfully segmented the lines, in spite of their intersections, and because of the shape-based term, other objects were discarded.

An example of a real image is illustrated in Fig. 5. The FCM output, shown in Fig. 5(b), treats lines and birds as the same object. This is clear in Fig. 5(c) where the initial level sets take the lines and birds as one object. The level sets correct this and successfully extract only the lines in Fig. 5(d), even in spite of the birds touching the lines. Another real example is considered in Fig. 6. The initial level set based on the FCM algorithm is shown in Fig. 6(b). The final result in Fig. 6(c) shows how our algorithm can extract only the linear objects and discard the others.

6. Application: Lens Distortion Removal

In this section we apply the variational-based method in the previous sections to calibrate lens distortion. We will focus in this section on recovering the radial component of lens distortion, as it is often the most prominent in images. Our approach is based on the analysis of distorted images of straight lines. We use a PDE-based level set method to find the lens distortion parameters that straighten these lines. One key advantage of this method is that it integrates the extraction of image distorted lines and the computation of distortion parameters within one energy functional which is minimized during level set evolution. Thus our approach, unlike most other nonmetric calibration methods [21, 22, 23], avoids the propagation of errors in feature extraction onto the computation stage. This results in a more robust computation even at high noise levels.

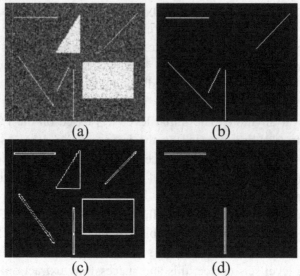

(a)   (b)

(c)   (d)

Figure 3. Extracted lines from highly noisy image (noise standard deviation = 45), (a) Input image, (b) The final result using our method, (c) Result of Hough transform on the noise-free image, (d) Result of Hough transform on the noisy image.

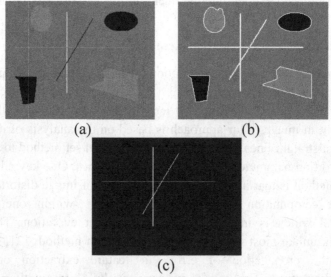

(a)   (b)

(c)

Figure 4. Extraction of intersected lines with different intensities. (a) The input image, (b) Initial level set based on FCM clustering , (c) Final result.

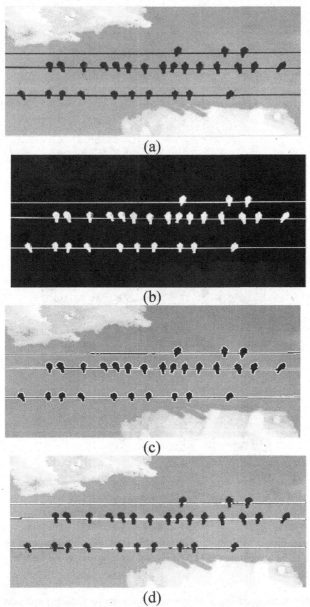

(a)

(b)

(c)

(d)

Figure 5. A real image "Birds on power lines". (a) Input image, (b) Hardened output of FCM algorithm, (c) Initial level set based on the output of FCM algorithm, (d) Final level set showed how our method excluded the birds.

(a)

(b)

(c)

Figure 6. A real image "A running track". (a) Input image, (b) Initial level set based on the output of FCM algorithm, (c) The final level set imposed on the image.

The closest work to ours is that of Kang [24]. He used the traditional snake to calculate the radial lens distortion parameters. However, his method is sensitive to the location of the initial contour, so the user should specify the position of the initial contour. In contrast, our level-set based method has some global convergence property that makes it not sensitive to the initial level set.

We start by giving briefly a standard model for lens distortion in camera lenses, and then we formulate our approach.

6.1. Camera Distortion Model

The standard model for the radial and decentering distortion [20, 21, 28] is mapping from the observable, distorted image coordinates, (x,y), to the unobservable, undistorted image plan coordinates, (x'',y''). Neglecting all coefficients other than the first radial distortion term, the model becomes:

$$
\begin{aligned}
x'' &= x + \hat{x}(\kappa r^2), \\
y'' &= y + \hat{y}(\kappa r^2),
\end{aligned}
\tag{28}
$$

$\hat{x} = x - c_x, \hat{y} = y - c_y, r^2 = \hat{x}^2 + \hat{y}^2$, and κ is the coefficient of radial distortion. r is the radius of an image point from the distortion center, defined as (c_x, c_y) above. The distortion centre is quite often located near the image centre [20, 22, 28]. Following previous works [24, 28] we assume the distortion centre to be the image centre. We thus seek to recover, κ, as it has the most dominating effect.

6.2. Our Approach

Our goal here is to use the energy functional (8) in order to force the level set to segment linear, or should-to-be-linear, objects from the image and simultaneously solve for the lens distortion parameter. The algorithm outlined in Section 4 is used here. However the E_{Line} term of the energy functional becomes

$$E_{Line}(\rho_i,\theta_i,\phi_i) = \int_\Omega \left(\rho_i - x'' \cos\theta_i - y'' \sin\theta_i\right)^2 H(\phi_i) dxdy , \quad (29)$$

which measures how well a level set presents a line in the undistorted image coordinates (x'',y''), with θ_i being the orientation of the normal to the line, and ρ_i being the distance to the line from the origin. Note that the undistorted coordinates are related to the given distorted image coordinates (x,y) via the distortion parameter κ as in (28). As for κ that minimizes the total energy functional E, we start with an initial guess κ^0 (in our implementation, we take it 0). Introducing an artificial time, t, κ is then updated according to the gradient decent rule $\frac{\partial \kappa}{\partial t} = -\frac{\partial E}{\partial \kappa}$,

where

$$\frac{\partial E}{\partial \kappa} = 2\alpha \sum_{i=1}^{N-1} \int_\Omega (x'' \cos\theta_i + y'' \sin\theta_i - \rho_i)$$
$$\left[(x - c_x)r^2 \cos\theta_i + (y - c_y)r^2 \sin\theta_i\right] H(\phi_i) dx \, dy \quad (30)$$

Note that κ is updated based on all level sets, but on the other hand each level set is updated by deducing the associated Euler-Lagrange equation for ϕ_i :

$$\frac{\partial \phi_i}{\partial t} = -\frac{\partial E}{\partial \phi_i} = \delta_\varepsilon(\phi_i) \left[\mu div\left((\frac{\nabla \phi_i}{|\nabla \phi_i|}) \right) -v - \lambda(1 - 2u_i) \right.$$
$$\left. -\alpha(\rho_i - x'' \cos\theta_i - y'' \sin\theta_i)^2 \right], \quad (31)$$

where the scalars ρ_i, θ_i, and κ are updated with the level set evolution according to (13, 15, 31). In the steady state the value of κ is the required lens distortion coefficient.

6.3. Experimental Results

The approach is applied to real images acquired by a cheap BenQ camera. To calibrate the radial lens distortion coefficient, we captured an image of a group of straight lines on a white paper; see Fig. 7(a). Such a calibration pattern is easily prepared (e.g., with just a printer) without any special construction overhead. Another sample image captured by the same camera is shown in Fig. 7(b). Both acquired images are 160×120 and have noticeable lens distortion. Our approach is then applied to the calibration image to recover the value of lens distortion parameter. Figs. 7(c-d) show the initial and final zero-level sets, respectively. Our method took less than a minute on P4 2.8GHz pc. The

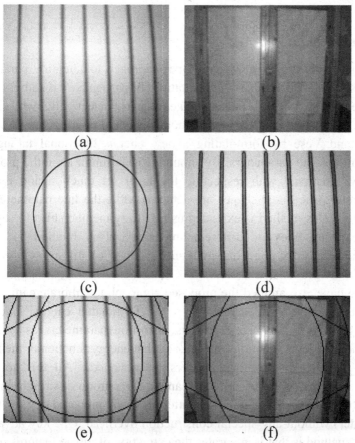

Figure 7. Lens distortion removal from a real images: (a) The calibration image which is used to get κ , (b) An input distorted image, (c) Initial zero level set, (d) Final zero level set (e) Calibration image undistorted, (f) Image in (b) undistorted using the obtained κ .

estimated κ is employed to remove the distortion from the original images taken by the camera, see Fig. 7(e-f). Clearly the should-to-be image lines are indeed mapped to straight lines in the resultant images. One may notice some artifacts (left intentionally) with the undistorted images due to the inverse mapping of the distortion model in (28), which can be fairly fixed, if desired, by doing some post-processing. Further experiments on synthetic data, [29], have shown that the accuracy of our proposed method remains within 0.1 pixels up to a high noise level of $\sigma \cong 35$.

7. Conclusions

We have presented a new variational approach to integrate parametric shapes into level set-based segmentation. In particular, we addressed the problem of extracting linear image objects, selectively, while other image objects are ignored. Our method is inspired by ideas introduced by Chan and Vese by formulating a new energy functional taking into account the line parameters. By simultaneously minimizing the proposed energy functional with respect to the level set function and the line parameters, the linear shapes are detected while the line parameters are obtained. This method is extended using Fuzzy memberships to segment simultaneous lines of different intensities. This method is shown experimentally to segment simultaneous lines of different intensities, even in images of large noise.

We have also applied the proposed approach to calibrate camera lens distortion. In order to achieve this, the formulated energy functional depends on the parameters of lens distortion parameters as well. By evolving the level functions minimizing that energy functional, the image lines and lens distortion parameters are obtained. All this approach needs is an image captured by the camera for a group of straight lines on a white paper. Such a calibration pattern is easily prepared (e.g., with just a printer) without any special construction overhead. One key advantage of our method is that it integrates the extraction of image features needed for calibration and the computation of distortion parameters; thus avoiding, unlike most other nonmetric calibration methods, the propagation of errors in feature extraction onto the computation stage.

Our future research is directed towards the segmentation of other parametric shapes from images, e.g., conics, which are of special importance in geometric computer vision. In addition, it is directed to incorporating more lens distortion parameters in order to be able to remove the distortion from severely-distorted images, such as in very-wide-view cameras, and to achieve more accurate calibration.

References

1. T. Chan and L. Vese, "Active contours without edges", *IEEE Trans. Image Processing*, 2001, pp. 266–277.
2. L. Staib and J. Duncan. "Boundary finding with parametrically deformable models", *IEEE Trans. on Patt. Anal. and Mach. Intel.*, pp. 1061–1075, 1992.
3. T. Cootes, A. Hill, C. Taylor, and J. Haslam, "Use of active shape models for locating structures in medical images", *Image and Vision Computing*, 1994, pp. 355–365.
4. M. Leventon, W. L. Grimson, and O. Faugeras, "Statistical shape influence in geodesic active contours", *in Proc. Conf. Computer Vis. and Pattern Recog.*, *volume 1*, Hilton Head Island, SC, June 13–15, 2000, pp. 316–323.
5. A. Tsai, A. Yezzi, W. Wells, C. Tempany, D. Tucker, A. Fan, E. Grimson, and A.. Willsky, "Model–based curve evolution technique for image segmentation", *in Conf. on Comp. Vision and Patt. Recog.*, Kauai, Hawaii, 2001, pp. 463–468.
6. D. Cremers, F. Tischhäuser, J. Weickert, and C. Schnörr, "Diffusion snakes: introducing statistical shape knowledge into the Mumford–Shah functional", *Int. J. of Comp. Vision*, 2002, pp.295–313.
7. D. Cremers, T. Kohlberger, and C. Schnörr, "Nonlinear shape statistics in Mumford–Shah based segmentation", in *A. Heyden et al., editors, Proc. of the Europ. Conf. on Comp. Vis.*, Copenhagen, May 2002, volume 2351 of LNCS, pp. 93–108.
8. M. Rousson and N. Paragios, "Shape priors for level set representations", *in A. Heyden et al., editors, Proc. of the Europ. Conf. on Comp. Vis.*, Copenhagen, May 2002, volume 2351 of LNCS, pp. 78–92.
9. S. Osher and J. Sethian, "Fronts propagation with curvature dependent speed: Algorithms based on Hamilton–Jacobi formulations", *J. of Comp. Phys.*, 1988, pp. 12–49.
10. V. Caselles, R. Kimmel, and G. Sapiro, "Geodesic active contours", *in Proc. IEEE Internat. Conf. on Comp. Vision*, Boston, USA, 1995, pp. 694–699.

11. S. Kichenassamy, A. Kumar, P. Olver, A. Tannenbaum, and A. Yezzi, "Gradient flows and geometric active contour models", *in Proc. IEEE International Conf. on Comp. Vision,* Boston, USA, 1995, pp. 810–815.

12. Y. Chen, S. Thiruvenkadam, H. Tagare, F. Huang, D. Wilson, and E. Geiser, "On the incorporation of shape priors into geometric active contours", *in IEEE Workshop on Variational and Level Set Methods, Vancouver,* CA, 2001, pp. 145–152.

13. D. Cremers, N. Sochen and C. Schnörr, "Towards recognition-based variational segmentation using shape priors and dynamic labeling" *in 4th Int. Conf. on Scale Space Theories in Computer Vision, Isle of Skye,* June 2003, LNCS Vol. 2695, pp. 388-400.

14. X. Pardo , V. Leboran and R. Dosil, "Integrating prior shape models into level-set approaches", *in Pattern Recognition Letters, Elsevier Science,* 2004, pp. 631–639.

15. S. Osher and R. Fedkiw, *Level set methods and dynamic implicit surfaces,* Springer-Verlag, USA, 2003.

16. S. Osher and N. Paragios, *Geometric level set methods in imaging, vision and graphics,* Springer Verlag, USA, 2003.

17. J. Sethian, *Level set methods and fast marching methods: evolving interfaces in computational geometry, fluid mechanisms, computer vision, and material science,* Cambridge University Press, 1999.

18. O. Faugeras, *Three dimensional computer vision: a geometric viewpoint,* Cambridge, MA: MIT Press, 1993.

19. J. C. Bezdek and P. F. Castelaz, "Prototype Classification and Feature Selection with Fuzzy Sets", IEEE Trans. On Systems, Man and Cybernetics vol. SMC-7, pp 87-92, 1977.

20. J.Weng, P. Cohen, and M. Herniou, "Camera calibration with distortion models and accuracy evaluation", *PAMI,* 14(10), Oct 1992.

21. F. Devernay and O. Faugeras, "Straight lines have to be straight: automatic calibration and removal of distortion from scenes of structured environments", *Machine Vision and Applications,* Vol. 1, 14-24, 2001.

22. B. Prescott and G. McLean, "Line-based correction of radial lens distortion", *Graphical Models and Image Processing,* 59(1):39–47, 1997.

23. R. Swaminathan and S. Nayar, "Non-metric calibration of wide-angle lenses and polycameras", *IEEE Trans. Pattern Analysis and Machine Intelligence (PAMI),* 22(10), Oct. 2000.

24. S. Kang, "Radial distortion snakes", *IAPR Workshop on Machine Vision Applications (MVA2000),* Tokyo, Japan, Nov. 2000, pp. 603-606.

25. T. Brox and J. Weickert, "Level Set Based Image Segmentation with Multiple Regions", *In Pattern Recognition,* Springer LNCS 3175, pp. 415-423, Tübingen, Germany, Aug. 2004.

26. R. Jain, R. Kasturi and B. Schunck, Machine vision, McGraw-Hill, USA, 1995.

27. D. Cremers, S. Osher, S. Soatto, "Kernel density estimation and intrinsic alignment for shape priors in level set segmentation", International Journal of Computer Vision, 69(3), pp. 335-351, 2006.

28. M. Ahmed and A. Farag, "Nonmetric calibration of camera lens distortion: differential methods and robust estimation", IEEE Trans. on image processing, vol. 14, no. 8, pp. 1215-1230, 2005.

29. M. El-Melegy and N. Al-Ashwal, "Lens distortion calibration using level sets", Lecture Notes in Computer Science, N. Paragios et al. (Eds.)., Springer-Verlag, Berlin, LNCS 3752, pp. 356 – 367, 2005.

CHAPTER 28

IMPROVED MOTION SEGMENTATION BASED ON SHADOW DETECTION

M. Kampel*, H. Wildenauer+, P. Blauensteiner* and A. Hanbury*

*Pattern Recognition and Image Processing Group, Vienna University of
Technology, Favoritenstr.9, A-1040 Vienna, Austria
E-mail: kampel@prip.tuwien.ac.at
+Automation and Control Institute, Vienna University of Technology,
Gusshausstr.27, A-1040 Vienna, Austria

In this paper, we discuss common colour models for background subtraction and problems related to their utilisation are discussed. A novel approach to represent chrominance information more suitable for robust background modelling and shadow suppression is proposed. Our method relies on the ability to represent colours in terms of a 3D-polar coordinate system having saturation independent of the brightness function; specifically, we build upon an Improved Hue, Luminance, and Saturation space (IHLS). The additional peculiarity of the approach is that we deal with the problem of unstable hue values at low saturation by modelling the hue-saturation relationship using saturation-weighted hue statistics. The effectiveness of the proposed method is shown in an experimental comparison with approaches based on RGB, Normalised RGB and HSV.

28.1. Introduction

The underlying step of visual surveillance applications like target tracking and scene understanding is the detection of moving objects. Background subtraction algorithms are commonly applied to detect these objects of interest by the use of statistical colour background models. Many present systems exploit the properties of the Normalised RGB to achieve a certain degree of insensitivity with respect to changes in scene illumination.

Hong and Woo[1] apply the Normalised RGB space in their background segmentation system. McKenna et al.[2] use this colour space in addition to gradient information for their adaptive background subtraction. The AVITRACK project[3] utilises Normalised RGB for change detection and adopts the shadow detection proposed by Horprasert et al.[4]

519

Beside Normalised RGB, representations of the RGB colour space in terms of 3D-polar coordinates (hue, saturation, and brightness) are used for change detection and shadow suppresion in surveillance applications. François and Medioni[5] suggest the application of HSV for background modelling for real-time video segmentation. In their work, a complex set of rules is introduced to reflect the relevance of observed and background colour information during change detection and model update. Cucchiara et al.[6] propose a RGB-based background model which they transform to the HSV representation in order to utilise the properties of HSV chrominance information for shadow suppression.

Our approach differs from the aforementioned in the way that we build upon the IHLS colour space, which is more suitable for background subtraction. Additionally, we propose the application of saturation-weighted hue statistics[7] to deal with unstable hue values at weakly saturated colours. Also, a technique to efficiently classify changes in scene illumination (e.g. shadows), modelling the relationship between saturation and hue has been devised.

The remainder of this paper is organised as follows: Section 28.2 reviews the Normalised RGB and the Improved Hue, Luminance and Saturation (IHLS) colour space. Furthermore it gives a short overview over circular colour statistics, which have to be applied on the hue as angular value. Section 28.3 presents how these statistics can be applied in order to model the background in image sequences. In Section 28.4 we describe metrics for the performance evaluation of our motion segmentation. The conducted experiments and their results are presented in Section 28.5. Section 28.6 concludes this paper and gives an outlook.

28.2. Colour Spaces

In this section, the Normalised RGB and IHLS colour spaces used in this paper are described. It also gives a short overview over circular colour statistics and a review of saturation weighted hue statistics.

28.2.1. Normalised RGB

The Normalised RGB space aims to separate the chromatic components from the brightness component. The red, green and blue channel can be transformed to their normalised counterpart by using the formulae

$$l = R + G + B, \quad r = R/l, \quad g = G/l, \quad b = B/l \qquad (28.1)$$

if $l \neq 0$ and $r = g = b = 0$ otherwise.[8] One of these normalised channels is redundant, since by definition r, g, and b sum up to 1.

Therefore, the Normalised RGB space is sufficiently represented by two chromatic components (e.g. r and g) and a brightness component l. From Kender[9] it is known that the practical application of Normalised RGB suffers from a problem inherent to the normalisation; namely, that noise (such as, e.g. sensor or compression noise) at low intensities results in unstable chromatic components. For an example see Figure 28.1. Note the artefacts in dark regions such as the bushes (top left) and the shadowed areas of the cars (bottom right).

Fig. 28.1. Examples of chromatic components. Lexicographically ordered - Image from the *PETS2001* dataset, it's normalised blue component b, normalised saturation (cylindrical HSV), IHLS saturation.

28.2.2. *IHLS Space*

The Improved Hue, Luminance and Saturation (IHLS) colour space was introduced in.[10] It is obtained by placing an *achromatic axis* through all the grey $(R = G = B)$ points in the RGB colour cube, and then specifying the coordinates of each point in terms of position on the achromatic axis (brightness), distance from the axis (saturation s) and angle with respect to pure red (hue θ^H). The IHLS model is improved with respect to the similar colour spaces (HLS, HSI, HSV, etc.) by removing the normalisation of the saturation by the brightness. This has the following advantages: (a) the saturation of achromatic pixels is always low and (b) the saturation is independent of the brightness function used. One may therefore choose any function of R, G and B to calculate the brightness.

It is interesting that this normalisation of the saturation by the brightness, which results in the colour space having the shape of a cylinder instead of a cone or double-cone, is usually implicitly part of the transformation equations from RGB to a 3D-polar coordinate space. This is mentioned in one of the first papers on this type of transformation,[11] but often in the literature the equations for a cylindrically-shaped space (i.e. with normalised saturation) are shown along with a diagram of a cone or double-cone (for example in[12,13]). Figure 28.1 shows a comparison of the different formulations of saturation. The undesirable effects created by saturation normalisation are easily perceivable, as some dark, colourless regions (eg., the bushes and the side window of the driving car) reach higher saturation values than their more colourfull surroundings. Also, note the artefacts resulting from the singularity of the saturation at the black vertex of the RGB-cube (again, the bushes and the two bottom right cars).

The following formulae are used for the conversion from RGB to hue θ^H, luminance y and saturation s of the IHLS space:

$$s = \max(R, G, B) - \min(R, G, B)$$
$$y = 0.2125R + 0.7154G + 0.0721B$$
$$cr_x = R - \frac{G + B}{2}, \ cr_y = \frac{\sqrt{3}}{2}(B - G)$$
$$cr = \sqrt{cr_x^2 + cr_y^2} \tag{28.2}$$
$$\theta^H = \begin{cases} \text{undefined} & \text{if } cr = 0 \\ \arccos\left(\frac{cr_x}{cr}\right) & \text{elseif } cr_y \leq 0 \\ 360° - \arccos\left(\frac{cr_x}{cr}\right) & \text{else} \end{cases}$$

where cr_x and cr_y denote the chrominance coordinates and $cr \in [0, 1]$ the chroma. The saturation assumes values in the range $[0, 1]$ independent of the hue angle (the maximum saturation values are shown by the circle on the chromatic plane in Figure 28.2). The chroma has the maximum values shown by the dotted hexagon in Figure 28.2. When using this representation, it is important to remember that the hue is undefined if $s = 0$, and that it does not contain much useable information when s is low (i.e. near to the achromatic axis).

28.2.3. Hue Statistics

In a 3D-polar coordinate space, standard (linear) statistical formulae can be utilised to calculate statistical descriptors for brightness and saturation coordinates. The hue, however, is an angular value, and consequently the appropriate

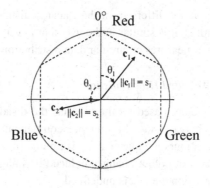

Fig. 28.2. The chromatic plane of the IHLS color space.

methods from circular statistics are to be used.

Now, let θ_i^H, $i = 1, \ldots, n$ be n observations sampled from a population of angular hue values. Then, the vector $\mathbf{h}_i$ pointing from $\mathbf{O} = (0, 0)^T$ to the point on the circumference of the unit circle, corresponding to θ_i^H, is given by the Cartesian coordinates $(\cos \theta_i^H, \sin \theta_i^H)^T$. [a]

The mean direction $\overline{\theta}^H$ is defined to be the direction of the resultant of the unit vectors $\mathbf{h_1}, \ldots, \mathbf{h_n}$ having directions θ_i^H. That is, we have

$$\overline{\theta}^H = \text{arctan2}\,(\mathcal{S}, \mathcal{C})\,, \tag{28.3}$$

where

$$\mathcal{C} = \sum_{i=1}^{n} \cos \theta_i^H, \quad \mathcal{S} = \sum_{i=1}^{n} \sin \theta_i^H \tag{28.4}$$

and $\text{arctan2}(y, x)$ is the four-quadrant inverse tangent function.

The mean length of the resultant vector

$$\overline{\mathcal{R}} = \frac{\sqrt{\mathcal{C}^2 + \mathcal{S}^2}}{n}. \tag{28.5}$$

is an indicator of the dispersion of the observed data. If the n observed directions θ_i^H cluster tightly about the mean direction $\overline{\theta}^H$ then $\overline{\mathcal{R}}$ will approach 1. Conversely, if the angular values are widely dispersed $\overline{\mathcal{R}}$ will be close to 0. The *circular variance* is defined as

$$\mathcal{V} = 1 - \overline{\mathcal{R}} \tag{28.6}$$

---

[a]Note that, when using the IHLS space (Eq. 28.3), no costly trigonometric functions are involved in the calculation of $\mathbf{h}_i$, since $cos(\theta_i^H) = cr_x/cr$ and $sin(\theta_i^H) = -cr_y/cr$.

While the circular variance differs from the linear statistical variance in being limited to the range $[0, 1]$, it is similar in the way that lower values represent less dispersed data. Further measures of circular data distribution are given in .[14]

28.2.4. *Saturation-Weighted Hue Statistics*

The use of statistics solely based on the hue has the disadvantage of ignoring the tight relationship between the chrominance components hue and saturation. For weakly saturated colours the hue channel is unimportant and behaves unpredictably in the presence of colour changes induced by image noise. In fact, for colours with zero saturation the hue is undefined.

As one can see in Figure 28.2, the chromatic components may be represented by means of Cartesian coordinate vectors $\mathbf{c}_i$ with direction and length given by hue and saturation respectively. Using this natural approach, we introduce the aforementioned relationship into the hue statistics by weighting the unit hue vectors $\mathbf{h}_i$ by their corresponding saturations s_i.

Now, let (θ_i^H, s_i), $i = 1, \ldots, n$ be n pairs of observations sampled from a population of hue values and associated saturation values. We proceed as described in Section 28.2.3, with the difference that instead of calculating the resultant of unit vectors, the vectors $\mathbf{c}_i$, which we will dub *chrominance vectors* throughout this paper, have length s_i.

That is, we weight the vector components in Eq. 28.4 by their saturations s_i

$$\mathcal{C}_s = \sum_{i=1}^{n} s_i \cos \theta_i^H, \quad \mathcal{S}_s = \sum_{i=1}^{n} s_i \sin \theta_i^H, \tag{28.7}$$

and choose the mean resultant length of the chrominance vectors (for other possible formulations see, e.g.[7]) to be

$$\overline{\mathcal{R}}_n = \frac{\sqrt{\mathcal{C}_s^2 + \mathcal{S}_s^2}}{n}. \tag{28.8}$$

Consequently, for the mean resultant chrominance vector we get

$$\overline{\mathbf{c}}_{\mathbf{n}} = (\mathcal{C}_s/n, \mathcal{S}_s/n)^T. \tag{28.9}$$

Here, the length of the resultant is compared to the length obtained if all vectors had the same direction and maximum saturation. Hence, $\overline{\mathcal{R}}_n$ gives an indication of the saturations of the vectors which gave rise to the mean of the chrominance vector, as well as an indication of the angular dispersion of the vectors. To test if a mean chrominance vector $\overline{\mathbf{c}}_{\mathbf{n}}$ is similar to a newly observed chrominance vector, we use the Euclidean distance in the chromatic plane:

$$D = \sqrt{(\overline{\mathbf{c}}_n - \mathbf{c}_o)^T (\overline{\mathbf{c}}_n - \mathbf{c}_o)}, \tag{28.10}$$

with $c_o = s_o h_o$. Here, h_o and s_o denote the observed hue vector and saturation respectively.

28.3. The IHLS Background Model

With the foundations laid out in Section 28.2.4 we proceed with devising a simple background subtraction algorithm based on the IHLS colour model and saturation-weighted hue statistics. Specifically, each background pixel is modelled by its mean luminance μ_y and associated standard deviation σ_y, together with the mean chrominance vector $\bar{c}_n$ and the mean Euclidean distance σ_D between $\bar{c}_n$ and the observed chrominance vectors (see Eq. 28.10).

On observing the luminance y_o, saturation s_o, and a Cartesian hue vector h_o for each pixel in a newly acquired image, the pixel is classified as foreground if:

$$|(y_o - \mu_y)| > \alpha\sigma_y \vee \|\bar{c}_n - s_o h_o\| > \alpha\sigma_D \qquad (28.11)$$

where α is the foreground threshold, usually set between 2 and 3.5.

In order to decide whether a foreground detection was caused by a moving object or by its shadow cast on the static background, we exploit the chrominance information of the IHLS space. A foreground pixel is considered as shaded background if the following three conditions hold:

$$y_o < \mu_y \ \wedge \ |y_o - \mu_y| < \beta\mu_y, \qquad (28.12)$$

$$s_o - \overline{\mathcal{R}}_n < \tau_{ds} \qquad (28.13)$$

$$\|h_o\overline{\mathcal{R}}_n - \bar{c}_n\| < \tau_h, \qquad (28.14)$$

where $\overline{\mathcal{R}}_n = \|\bar{c}_n\|$ (see Eq. 28.8,).

These equations are designed to reflect the empirical observations that cast shadows cause a darkening of the background and usually lower the saturation of a pixel, while having only limited influence on its hue. The first condition (Eq. 28.12) works on the luminance component, using a threshold β to take into account the strength of the predominant light source. Eq. 28.13 performs a test for a lowering in saturation, as proposed by Cucchiara et al.[6] Finally, the lowering in saturation is compensated by scaling the observed hue vector h_o to the same length as the mean chrominance vector $\bar{c}_n$ and the hue deviation is tested using the Euclidean distance (Eq. 28.14). This, in comparison to a check of angular deviation (see Eq. 28.31 or[6]), also takes into account the model's confidence in the learned chrominance vector. That is, using a fixed threshold τ_h on the Euclidean distance relaxes the angular error-bound in favour of stronger hue deviations at lower model saturation value $\overline{\mathcal{R}}_n$, while penalising hue deviations for high saturations (where the hue is usually more stable).

28.4. Metrics for Motion Segmentation

The quality of motion segmentation can in principle be described by two characteristics. Namely, the spatial deviation from the reference segmentation, and the fluctuation of spatial deviation over time. In this work, however, we concentrate on the evaluation of spatial segmentation characteristics. That is, we will investigate the capability of the error metrics listed below, to describe the spatial accuracy of motion segmentations.

- Detection rate (DR) and false alarm rate (FR)

$$DR = \frac{TP}{FN + TP} \tag{28.15}$$

$$FR = \frac{FP}{N - (FN + TP)} \tag{28.16}$$

where TP denotes the number of true positives, FN the number of false negatives, FP the number of false positives, and N the total number of pixels in the image.

- Misclassification penalty (MP)
  The obtained segmentation is compared to the reference mask on an object-by-object basis; misclassified pixels are penalized by their distances from the reference objects border.[15]

$$MP = MP_{fn} + MP_{fp} \tag{28.17}$$

with

$$MP_{fn} = \frac{\sum_{j=1}^{N_{fn}} d_{fn}^{j}}{D} \tag{28.18}$$

$$MP_{fp} = \frac{\sum_{k=1}^{N_{fp}} d_{fp}^{k}}{D} \tag{28.19}$$

Here, d_{fn}^{j} and d_{fp}^{k} stand for the distances of the jth false negative and k^{th} false positive pixel from the contour of the reference segmentation. The normalised factor D is the sum of all pixel-to-contour distances in a frame.

- Rate of misclassifications (RM)
  The average normalised distance of detection errors from the contour of a reference object is calculated using:[16]

$$RM = RM_{fn} + RM_{fp} \tag{28.20}$$

with

$$RM_{fn} = \frac{1}{N_{fn}} \sum_{j=1}^{N_{fn}} \frac{d_{fn}^j}{D_{diag}} \qquad (28.21)$$

$$RM_{fp} = \frac{1}{N_{fp}} \sum_{k=1}^{N_{fp}} \frac{d_{fp}^k}{D_{diag}} \qquad (28.22)$$

N_{fn} and N_{fp} denote the number of false negative and false positive pixels respectively. q D_{diag} is the diagonal distance within the frame.

- Weighted quality measure (*QMS*)
  This measure quantifies the spatial discrepancy between estimated and reference segmentation as the sum of weighted effects of false positive and false negative pixels.[17]

$$QMS = QMS_{fn} + QMS_{fp} \qquad (28.23)$$

with

$$QMS_{fn} = \frac{1}{N} \sum_{j=1}^{N_{fn}} w_{fn}(d_{fn}^j)d_{fn}^j \qquad (28.24)$$

$$QMS_{fp} = \frac{1}{N} \sum_{k=1}^{N_{fp}} w_{fp}(d_{fp}^k)d_{fp}^k \qquad (28.25)$$

N is the area of the reference object in pixels. Following the argument that the visual importance of false positives and false negatives is not the same, and thus they should be treated differently, the weighting functions w_{fp} and w_{fn} were introduced:

$$w_{fp}(d_{fp}) = B_1 + \frac{B_2}{d_{fp} + B_3} \qquad (28.26)$$

$$w_{fn}(d_{fn}) = C \cdot d_{fn} \qquad (28.27)$$

In our work for a fair comparison of the change detection algorithms with regard to their various decision parameters, receiver operating characteristics (ROC) based on detection rate (DR) and false alarm rate (FR) were utilised.

28.5. Experiments and Results

We compared the proposed IHLS method with three different approaches from literature. Namely, a RGB background model using either NRGB- (*RGB+NRGB*), or HSV-based (*RGB+HSV*) shadow detection, and a method relying on NRGB for both background modelling and shadow detection (*NRGB+NRGB*).

All methods were implemented using the *Colour Mean and Variance* approach to model the background.[18] A pixel is considered foreground if $|c_o - \mu_c| > \alpha\sigma_c$ for any channel c, where $c \in \{r, g, l\}$ for the Normalised RGB and $c \in \{R, G, B\}$ for the RGB space respectively. o_c denotes the observed value, μ_c its mean, σ_c the standard deviation, and α the foreground threshold.

The tested background models are maintained by means of exponentially weighted averaging[18] using different learning rates for background and foreground pixels. During the experiments the same learning and update parameters were used for all background models, as well as the same number of training frames.

For Normalised RGB (*RGB+NRGB, NRGB+NRGB*), shadow suppression was implemented based on Horprasert's approach.[3,4] Each foreground pixel is classified as shadow if:

$$l_o < \mu_l \wedge l_o > \beta\mu_l$$
$$|r_o - \mu_r| < \tau_c \wedge |g_o - \mu_g| < \tau_c \qquad (28.28)$$

where β and τ_c denote thresholds for the maximum allowable change in the intensity and colour channels, so that a pixel is considered as shaded background.

In the HSV-based approach (*RGB+HSV*) the RGB background model is converted into HSV (specifically, the reference luminance μ_v, saturation μ_s, and hue μ_θ) before the following shadow tests are applied. A foreground pixel is classified as shadow if:

$$\beta_1 \leq \frac{v_o}{\mu_v} \leq \beta_2 \qquad (28.29)$$

$$s_o - \mu_s \leq \tau_s \qquad (28.30)$$

$$|\theta_o^H - \mu_\theta| \leq \tau_\theta \qquad (28.31)$$

The first condition tests the observed luminance v_o for a significant darkening in the range defined by β_1 and β_2. On the saturation s_o a threshold on the difference is performed. Shadow lowers the saturation of points and the difference between images and the reference is usually negative for shadow points. The last condition takes into account the assumption that shading causes only small deviation of the hue θ_o^H.[6]

For the evaluation of the algorithms, three video sequences were used. As an example for a typical indoor scene *Test Sequence 1*, recorded by an AXIS-211 network camera, shows a moving person in a stairway. For this sequence, ground truth was generated manually for 35 frames. *Test Sequence 2* was recorded with the same equipment and shows a person waving books in front of a coloured background. For this sequence 20 ground truth frames were provided. Furthermore in *Test Sequence 3* the approaches were tested on 25 ground truth frames from the *PETS2001* dataset 1 (camera 2, testing sequence). Example pictures of the dataset can be found in Figure 28.3.

(a)   (b)   (c)

Fig. 28.3.   Evaluation dataset: *Test Sequence 1* (a), *Test Sequence 2* (b), *Test Sequence 3* (c).

For a dense evaluation, we experimentaly determined suitable ranges for all parameters and sub-sampled them in ten steps. Figure 28.7 shows the convex hulls of the points in ROC space obtained for all parameter combinations. We also want to point out that *RGB+HSV* was tested with unnormalised and normalised saturation; however, since the normalised saturation consistently performed worse, we omit the results in the ROC for clarity of presentation.

As one can see, our approach outperforms its competitors on *Test Sequence 1*. One reason for this is the insensitivity of the *RGB+NRGB* and *NRGB+NRGB* w.r.t. small colour differences at light, weakly saturated colours. *RGB+HSV*, however, suffered from the angular hue test reacting strongly to unstable hue values close to the achromatic axis. For conservative thresholds (i.e. small values for τ_c or τ_θ) all three approaches either detected shadows on the wall as foreground, or, for larger thresholds failed to classify the beige t-shirt of the person as foreground. Figure 28.4 shows output images from *Test Sequence 1*. We present the source image (a), the ground truth image (b), the resulting image from our approach (c), and the resulting images from the algorithms we compared with. I.a. it is shown that the shirt of the person in image (c) is detected with higher precision as in the images (d), (e), and (f), where it is mostly marked as shadow.

For *Test Sequence 2* the advantageous behaviour of our approach is even more evident. Although the scene is composed of highly saturated, stable colours, *RGB+NRGB* and *NRGB+NRGB* show rather poor results, again stemming from

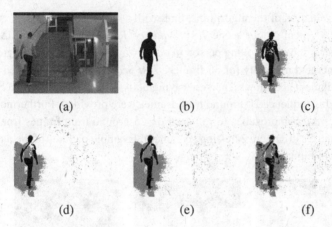

Fig. 28.4.   Output images *Test Sequence 1*: *Source Image* (a), *Ground Truth* (b), *Our Approach* (c), *RGB+NRGB* (d), *NRGB+NRGB* (e), *RGB+HSV* (f).

their insufficient sensitivity for bright colours. *RGB+HSV* gave better results, but could not take full advantage of the colour information. Similar hue values for the books and the background resulted in incorrectly classified shadow regions. Figure 28.5 shows output images from *Test Sequence 2*. Especially the lower left part of the images (c), (d), (e), and (f) visualizes a better performance of the IHLS approach.

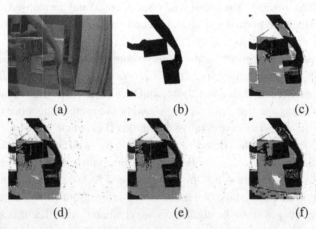

Fig. 28.5.   Output images *Test Sequence 2*: *Source Image* (a), *Ground Truth* (b), *Our Approach* (c), *RGB+NRGB* (d), *NRGB+NRGB* (e), *RGB+HSV* (f).

The *Test Sequence 3* sequence shows the problems of background modelling using NRGB already mentioned in Section 28.2. Due to the low brightness and the presence of noise in this scene, the chromatic components are unstable and therefore the motion detection resulted in an significantly increased number of false positives. *RGB+NRGB* and our approach exhibit similar performance (our approach having the slight edge), mostly relying on brightness checks, since there was not much useable information in shadow regions. *RGB+HSV* performed less well, having problems to cope with the unstable hue information in dark areas. Figure 28.6 shows output images *Test Sequence 3*.

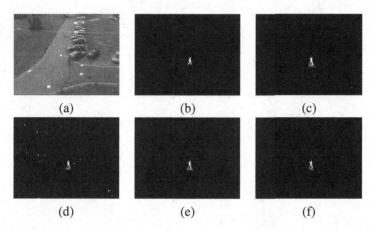

Fig. 28.6.   Output images *Test Sequence 3*: *Source Image* (a), *Ground Truth* (b), *Our Approach* (c), *RGB+NRGB* (d), *NRGB+NRGB* (e), *RGB+HSV* (f).

28.6. Conclusion

We proposed the usage of the IHLS colour space for change detection and shadow suppression in visual surveillance tasks. In the proposed framework, we advocate the application of saturation-weighted hue statistics to deal with the problem of the unstable hue channel at weakly saturated colours.

We have shown that our approach outperforms the approaches using Normalised RGB or HSV in several challenging sequences. Furthermore, our experiments have shown that it is not advisable to use NRGB for background modelling due to its unstable behaviour in dark areas.

One problem of our approach, however, is the fact that due to the use of saturation weighted hue statistics, it is impossible to tell whether a short chrominance vector in the background model is the result of unstable hue information or of a permanent low saturation. Although in the conducted experiments no impairments were evident, it is subject of further research in which cases this shortcom-

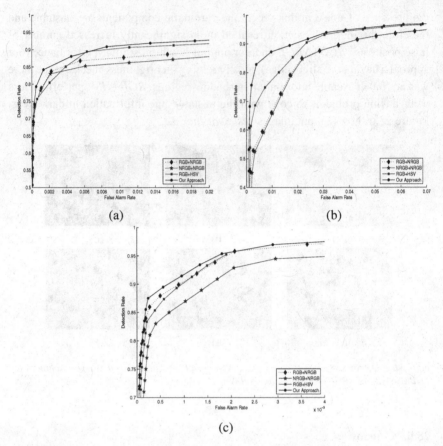

Fig. 28.7. Experimental results: ROCs for *Test Sequence 1* (a), *Test Sequence 2* (b), and *Test Sequence 3* (c).

ing poses a problem. Other fields of interest are the examination of alternatives to the Euclidean distance for the comparison of the chrominance vectors and an experimental in-depth-investigation of the shadow classification.

References

1. D. Hong and W. Woo. A Background Subtraction for Vision-based User Interface. In *4th International Conference on Information, Communications and Signal Processing and Fourth IEEE Pacific-Rim Conference on Multimedia*, pp. 263–267, (2003).
2. S. McKenna, S. Jabri, Z. Duric, H. Wechsler, and A. Rosenfeld, Tracking Groups of People, *Computer Vision and Image Understanding*. **80**(1), 42–56, (2000).
3. J. Ferryman, M. Borg, D. Thirde, F. Fusier, V. Valentin, F. Brémond, M. Thonnat,

J. Aguilera, and M. Kampel. Automated Scene Understanding for Airport Aprons. In *Australian Joint Conference on Artificial Intelligence*, pp. 593–503, Australia, (2005).

4. T. Horprasert, D. Harwood, and L. Davis. A Statistical Approach for Real-time Robust Background Subtraction and Shadow Detection. In *IEEE Conference on Computer Vision, FRAME-RATE Workshop*, (1999).

5. A. R. J. François and G. G. Medioni. Adaptive Color Background Modeling for Real-Time Segmentation of Video Streams. In *International Conference on Imaging Science, Systems, and Technology*, pp. 227–232, (1999).

6. R. Cucchiara, C. Grana, M. Piccardi, A. Prati, and S. Sirotti. Improving Shadow Suppression in Moving Object Detection with HSV Color Information. In *Intelligent Transport Systems*, pp. 334–339. IEEE, (2001).

7. A. Hanbury and W. G. Kropatsch. Colour Statistics for Matching in Image Databases. In *27th OEAGM Workshop*, pp. 221–228, Austria, (2003).

8. G. D. Finlayson, B. Schiele, and J. L. Crowley. Comprehensive Colour Image Normalization. In *5th European Conference on Computer Vision*, pp. 475–490, (1998).

9. J. R. Kender. Saturation, Hue and Normalized Colors: Calculation, Digitisation Effects, and Use. Technical report, Department of Computer Science, Carnegie Mellon University, (1976).

10. A. Hanbury. A 3D-polar coordinate colour representation well adapted to image analysis. In *13th Scandinavian Conference on Image Analysis*, pp. 804–811, (2003).

11. A. R. Smith, Color gamut transform pairs, *Computer Graphics.* **12**(3), 12–19, (1978).

12. R. C. Gonzalez and R. E. Woods, *Digital Image Processing.* (Prentice-Hall, Englewood Cliffs, NJ, 2002), 2nd edition.

13. D. Hearn and M. P. Baker, *Computer Graphics.* (Prentice Hall, Englewood Cliffs, NJ, 1997).

14. K. V. Mardia, *Statistics of Directional Data.* (Academic Press, London, UK, 1972).

15. C. Erdem and B. Sankur. Performance Evaluation Metrics for Object-Based Video Segmentation. In *10th European Signal Processing Conference, Tampere, Finnland*, pp. 917–920 (September, 2000).

16. T. Schlögl, C. Beleznai, M. Winter, and H. Bischof. Performance Evaluation Metrics for Motion Detection and Tracking. In *Proceedings of the International Conference on Pattern Recognition, Cambridge, UK*, vol. 4, pp. 519–522 (August, 2004).

17. P. Villegas and X. Marichal, Perceptually-Weighted Evaluation Criteria for Segmentation Masks in Video Sequences, *IEEE Transactions on Image Processing.* (8), 1092–1103 (August, 2004).

18. C. R. Wren, A. Azarbayejami, T. Darrel, and A. Pentland, Pfinder: Real-Time Tracking of the Human Body, *IEEE Transactions on Pattern Analysis and Machine Intelligence.* **19**(7), 780–785, (1997).

CHAPTER 29

SNAKECUT: AN INTEGRATED APPROACH BASED ON ACTIVE CONTOUR AND GRABCUT FOR AUTOMATIC FOREGROUND OBJECT SEGMENTATION

Surya Prakash, R. Abhilash and Sukhendu Das

Visualization and Perception Lab, Department of Computer Science and Engineering, Indian Institute of Technology Madras, Chennai-600 036, India.

Interactive techniques for extracting the foreground object from an image have been the interest of research in computer vision for a long time. This paper addresses the problem of an efficient, semi-interactive extraction of a foreground object from an image. Snake (also known as Active contour) and GrabCut are two popular techniques, extensively used for this task. Active contour is a deformable contour, which segments the object using boundary discontinuities by minimizing the energy function associated with the contour. GrabCut provides a convenient way to encode color features as segmentation cues to obtain foreground segmentation from local pixel similarities using modified iterated graph-cuts. This paper first presents a comparative study of these two segmentation techniques, and illustrates conditions under which either or both of them fail. We then propose a novel formulation for integrating these two complimentary techniques to obtain an automatic foreground object segmentation. We call our proposed integrated approach as "SnakeCut", which is based on a probabilistic framework. To validate our approach, we show results both on simulated and natural images.

29.1. Introduction

Interactive techniques for extracting the foreground object from an image have been the interest of research in computer vision for long time. Snake (Active contour)[1] and GrabCut[2] are two popular semi-automatic techniques, extensively used for foreground object segmentation. Active contour is a deformable contour, which segments the object using boundary discontinuities by minimizing the energy function associated with the contour. Deformation in contour is caused because of internal and external forces acting on it. Internal force is derived from the contour itself and external force is invoked from the image. The internal and external forces are defined so that the snake will conform to object boundary or other desired features within the image. Snakes are widely used in many applications such as segmentation,[3,4] shape modeling,[5] edge detection,[1] motion tracking[6] etc. Active contours can be classified as either *parametric active contours*[1,7] or *geometric active contours*,[8,9] according to their representation and implementation. In this work, we focus on using parametric active contours, which synthesize parametric curves within the image domain and allow them to move towards the desired image features under the influence of internal and external forces. The internal force serves to impose piecewise continuity and smoothness constraint, whereas external force pushes the snake towards salient image features like edges, lines and subjective contours.

GrabCut[2] is an interactive tool based on iterative graph-cut for foreground object segmentation in still images. GrabCut provides a convenient way to encode color features as segmentation cues to obtain foreground segmentation from local pixel similarities and global color distribution using modified iterated graph-cuts. GrabCut extends graph-cut to color images and to incomplete trimaps. GrabCut has been applied in many applications for the foreground extraction.[10–12]

Since Active Contour uses gradient information (boundary discontinuities) present in the image to estimate the object boundary, it can detect the object boundary efficiently but cannot penetrate inside the object boundary. It cannot remove any pixel present inside the object boundary which does not belong to a foreground object. Example of such case is the segmentation of an object with holes. On the other hand, GrabCut works on the basis of pixel color (intensity) distribution and so it has the ability to remove interior pixels which are not the part of the object. Major problem with the GrabCut is: if some part of the foreground object has color distribution similar to the image background, that part will also be removed in GrabCut segmentation. In the GrabCut algorithm,[2] missing foreground data is recovered by user interaction. This paper first presents a comparative study of these two segmentation techniques. We then present a semi-automatic technique based on the integration of Active Contour and Grab-Cut which can produce correct segmentation in cases where both Snake and Grab-Cut fail. We call our technique as "SnakeCut", which is based on integrating the outputs of Snake and GrabCut using a probabilistic framework. In SnakeCut, user needs to only specify a rectangle (or polygon) enclosing the foreground object. No post corrective editing is required in our approach. Proposed technique is used to segment a single object from an image.

Rest of the paper is organized as follows. In section 29.2, we briefly present Active Contour and GrabCut techniques which provides the theoretical basis for the paper. Section 29.3 compares the two techniques and discusses the limitations of both. In section 29.4, we present the SnakeCut algorithm, our proposed segmentation technique for foreground object segmentation. Section 29.5 presents some results on simulated and natural images. We conclude the paper in section 29.6.

29.2. Preliminaries

29.2.1. *Active Contour (Snake) Model*

A traditional active contour is defined as a parametric curve $\mathbf{v}(s) = [x(s), y(s)]$, $s \in [0, 1]$, which minimizes the following energy functional

$$E_{snake} = \int_0^1 \frac{1}{2}(\eta_1 |\mathbf{v}'(s)|^2 + \eta_2 |\mathbf{v}''(s)|^2) + E_{ext}(\mathbf{v}(s))ds \qquad (29.1)$$

where, η_1 and η_2 are weighting constants to control the relative importance of the elastic and bending ability of snake respectively. $\mathbf{v}'(s)$ and $\mathbf{v}''(s)$ are the first and second order derivatives of $\mathbf{v}(s)$, and E_{ext} is derived from the image so that it takes smaller values at the feature of interest such as edges, object boundaries etc. For an image $I(x, y)$, where (x, y) are spatial co-ordinates, typical external energy is defined as follows to lead snake towards step edges:[1]

$$E_{ext} = -|\nabla I(x, y)|^2 \qquad (29.2)$$

where, ∇ is gradient operator. For color images, we estimate the intensity gradient which takes the maximum of the gradients of R, G and B bands at every pixel, using:

$$|\nabla I| = \max(|\nabla R|, |\nabla G|, |\nabla B|) \qquad (29.3)$$

Figure 29.1(b) shows an example of intensity gradient estimation using the Eq. 29.3 for the image shown in Figure 29.1(a). Figure 29.1(d) shows the intensity gradient for the same input image estimated from its gray scale image (Figure 29.1(c)). The gradient obtained using Eq. 29.3 gives better edge information. A snake that minimizes E_{snake} must satisfy the following Euler equation[13]

$$\eta_1 \mathbf{v}''(s) - \eta_2 \mathbf{v}''''(s) - \nabla E_{ext} = \mathbf{0} \qquad (29.4)$$

where, $\mathbf{v}''(s)$ and $\mathbf{v}''''(s)$ are the second and fourth order derivatives of $\mathbf{v}(s)$. Eq. 29.4 can also be viewed as a force balancing equation, $\mathbf{F}_{int} + \mathbf{F}_{ext} = \mathbf{0}$ where, $\mathbf{F}_{int} = \eta_1 \mathbf{v}''(s) - \eta_2 \mathbf{v}''''(s)$ and $\mathbf{F}_{ext} = -\nabla E_{ext}$. $\mathbf{F}_{int}$, the internal force, is responsible for stretching and bending and $\mathbf{F}_{ext}$, the external force, attracts the snake towards the desired features in the image. To find the object boundary, Active Contour deforms so it can be represented as a time varying curve $\mathbf{v}(s, t) =$

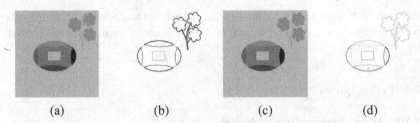

| (a) | (b) | (c) | (d) |

Fig. 29.1.   Gradient in color and gray scale images: (a) Input image, (b) Gradient image of (a) estimated using Eq. 29.3, (c) Gray scale image of the input image (a), (d) Gradient image of (c).

$[\mathbf{x}(s,t), \mathbf{y}(s,t)]$ where $s \in [0,1]$ is arc length and $t \in R^{+}$ is time. Dynamics of the contour in presence of external and internal forces can be governed by the following equation

$$\xi \mathbf{v}_t = \mathbf{F}_{int} + \mathbf{F}_{ext} \tag{29.5}$$

where, $\mathbf{v}_t$ is the partial derivative of $\mathbf{v}$ $w.r.t.$ t and ξ being an arbitrary non-negative constant. The contour comes to rest when the net effect of the internal and external forces reaches zero, which eventually happens when deforming contour reaches the object boundary.

29.2.2. *GrabCut*

GrabCut[2] is an interactive tool based on iterative graph-cut for foreground extraction in still images. To segment a foreground object using GrabCut, user has to select an area of interest (AOI) with a rectangle to obtain the desired result. Grab-Cut extends the graph-cut based segmentation technique, introduced by Boykov and Jolly,[14] using color information. In this section, we briefly discuss about the GrabCut. For more details readers are advised to see.[2]

Consider image I as an array $\mathbf{z} = (z_1, ..., z_n, ..., z_N)$ of pixels, indexed by the single index n, where z_n is in RGB space. Segmentation of the image is expressed as an array of "opacity" values $\underline{\alpha} = (\alpha_1, ..., \alpha_n, ..., \alpha_N)$ at each pixel. Generally $0 \leq \alpha_n \leq 1$, but for hard segmentation, $\alpha_n \in \{0, 1\}$ with 0 for background and 1 for foreground. For the purpose of segmentation, GrabCut constructs two separate Gaussian mixture models (GMMs) to express the color distributions for the background and foreground. Each GMM, one for foreground and one for background, is taken to be a full-covariance Gaussian mixture with K components. In order to deal with the GMM tractability in an optimization framework, an additional vector $\mathbf{k} = (k_1, ..., k_n, ..., k_N)$ is taken, with $k_n \in \{1, ..., K\}$, assigning to each pixel a unique GMM component, which is either from the foreground or background according to $\alpha_n = 0$ or 1.

GrabCut defines an energy function **E** such that its minimum should correspond to a good segmentation, in the sense that it is guided both by the observed foreground and background GMMs and that the opacity is "coherent". This is captured by "Gibbs" energy in the following form:

$$\mathbf{E}(\underline{\alpha}, \mathbf{k}, \underline{\theta}, \mathbf{z}) = U(\underline{\alpha}, \mathbf{k}, \underline{\theta}, \mathbf{z}) + V(\underline{\alpha}, \mathbf{z}) \tag{29.6}$$

The data term U evaluates the fit of the opacity distribution $\underline{\alpha}$ to the data $\mathbf{z}$. It takes into account the color GMM models, defined as

$$U(\underline{\alpha}, \mathbf{k}, \underline{\theta}, \mathbf{z}) = \sum_n D(\alpha_n, k_n, \underline{\theta}, z_n) \tag{29.7}$$

where,

$$D(\alpha_n, k_n, \underline{\theta}, z_n) = -\log p(z_n | \alpha_n, k_n, \theta_n) - \log \pi(\alpha_n, k_n) \tag{29.8}$$

Here, $p(.)$ is a Gaussian probability distribution, and $\pi(.)$ are mixture weighting coefficients. Therefore, the parameters of the model are now $\underline{\theta} = \{\pi(\alpha, k), \mu(\alpha, k), \Sigma(\alpha, k); \alpha = 0, 1; k = 1..K\}$, where π, μ and Σ's represent the weights, means and covariances of the $2K$ Gaussian components for the background and the foreground distributions. In Equation 29.6, the term V is called the smoothness term and is given as follows:

$$V(\underline{\alpha}, \mathbf{z}) = \gamma \sum_{(m,n) \in R} \frac{1}{dist(m, n)} [\alpha_n \neq \alpha_m] exp(-\beta(\|z_m - z_n\|^2)) \tag{29.9}$$

where, $[\phi]$ denotes the indicator function taking values 0, 1 for a predicate ϕ, γ is a constant, R is the set of neighboring pixels, and $dist(.)$ is the Euclidian distance of neighboring pixels. This energy encourages coherence in the regions of similar color distribution.

Once the energy model is defined, segmentation can be estimated as a global minimum: $\widehat{\underline{\alpha}} = \arg\min_{\underline{\alpha}} \mathbf{E}(\underline{\alpha}, \underline{\theta})$. Energy minimization in GrabCut is done by using standard minimum cut algorithm.[14] Minimization follows an iterative procedure that alternates between estimation and parameter learning.

29.3. Comparison of Active Contour and GrabCut Methods

Active contour relies on the presence of intensity gradient (boundary discontinuities) in the image. So it is a good tool for the estimation of the object boundaries. But, since it cannot penetrate inside the object boundary, it is not able to remove

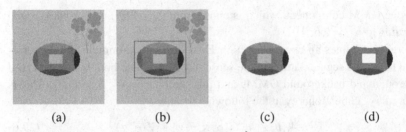

(a)   (b)   (c)   (d)

Fig. 29.2.   (a) Input image, elliptical object present in the image contains a rectangular hole at the center, (b) foreground initialization by user, (c) Active Contour segmentation result and (d) GrabCut segmentation result.

the undesired parts, say holes, present inside the object boundary. If an object has a hole in it, Active Contour will detect the hole as a part of the object. Figure 29.2(c) shows one such segmentation example of Active Contour for a synthetic image shown in Figure 29.2(a). Input image (Figure 29.2(a)) contains a foreground object with rectangular hole at the center, through which gray color background is visible. Segmentation result for this image (shown in Figure 29.2(c)), contains the hole included as a part of the detected object which is incorrect. Since Snake could not go inside, it has converted the outer background into white but retained the hole as gray. Similar erroneous segmentation result of Active Contour for a real image (shown in Figure 29.3(a)) is shown in Figure 29.3(b). One can see that segmentation output contains a part of the background region (e.g. grass patch between legs) along with the foreground object. Figure 29.4(b) shows one more erroneous Active Contour segmentation result for the image shown in Figure 29.4(a). Segmentation output contains some pixels in the interior part of the foreground object from the background texture region.

On the other hand, GrabCut considers global color distribution (with local pixels similarities) of the background and foreground pixels for segmentation. So it has the ability to remove interior pixels which are not a part of object. To segment the object using GrabCut, user draws a rectangle enclosing the foreground object. Pixels outside the rectangle are considered as background pixel and pixels inside the rectangle are considered as unknown. GrabCut estimates the color distribution for the background and the unknown region using separate GMMs. Then, it iteratively removes the pixels from the unknown region which belong to background. Major problem with the GrabCut is as follows. If some part of the object has color distribution similar to the image background then that part of foreground object is also removed in the GrabCut segmentation output. So GrabCut is not intelligent enough to distinguish between the desired and unnecessary pixels, while eliminating some of the pixels from the unknown region. Figure 29.2(d) shows one such

(a)   (b)   (c)

Fig. 29.3. (a) Soldier Image, (b) segmentation result of Active Contour, (c) segmentation result of GrabCut.

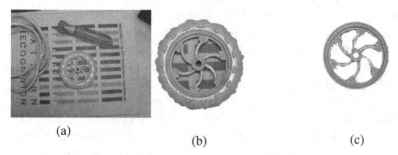

(a)   (b)   (c)

Fig. 29.4. (a) Image containing wheel, (b) segmentation result of Active Contour, (c) segmentation result of GrabCut.

segmentation result of GrabCut for the image shown in Figure 29.2(a), where the objective is to segment the object with a hole present in the image. Segmentation result does not produce the upper part of the object (shown in Green color in Figure 29.2(a)) near the boundary. This occurs because, in the original input image (Figure 29.2(a)), a few pixels with Green color were present as a part of the background region. Figure 29.3(c) presents a GrabCut segmentation result for a real world image shown in Figure 29.3(a). The objective in this case is to crop the soldier from the input image. GrabCut segmentation result for this input image does not produce the soldier's hat and the legs. In another real world image example in Figure 29.4(a), where the user targets to crop the wheel present in the image, GrabCut segmentation output (Figure 29.4(c)) does not produce the wheel's grayish green rubber part. This happened because of the presence of some objects with similar color in the background.

In GrabCut[2] algorithm, missing data of the foreground object is often recovered by user interaction. User has to mark the missing object parts as compulsory foreground. We present in this paper, an automatic foreground object segmentation technique based on the integration of Active Contour and GrabCut, which can produce accurate segmentation in situations where both or either of these techniques fail. We call our proposed technique as "SnakeCut". We present it in the next section.

29.4. SnakeCut: Integration of Active Contour and GrabCut

Active Contour works on the principle of intensity gradient, where the user initializes a contour around or inside the object for it to detect the boundary of the object easily. GrabCut, on the other hand, works on the basis of the pixel's color distribution and considers global cues for segmentation. Hence it can easily remove the unwanted part (parts from the background) present inside the object boundary. These two segmentation techniques use complementary information (edge and region based) for segmentation. In SnakeCut, we combine these complementary techniques and present an integrated method for superior object segmentation. Figure 29.5 presents the overall flow chart of our proposed segmentation technique. In SnakeCut, input image is segmented using the Active Contour and GrabCut separately. These two segmentation results are provided to the probabilistic framework of SnakeCut. This integrates the two segmentation results based on a probabilistic criterion and produces the final segmentation result.

Main steps of the SnakeCut algorithm are provided in Algorithm 29.1. The probabilistic framework used to integrate the two outputs is as follows. Inside the object boundary C_0 (detected by the Active Contour), every pixel z_i is assigned two probabilities: $P_c(z_i)$ and $P_s(z_i)$. $P_c(z_i)$ provides information about the pixel's nearness to the boundary, and $P_s(z_i)$ indicates how similar the pixel is to the background. Large value of $P_c(z_i)$ indicates that pixel z_i is far from the boundary and a large value of $P_s(z_i)$ specifies that the pixel is more similar to the background. To take the decision about a pixel belonging to foreground or background, we evaluate a decision function p as follows:

$$p(z_i) = \rho P_c(z_i) + (1 - \rho)P_s(z_i) \qquad (29.10)$$

where, ρ is the weight which controls the relative importance of the two techniques, and is learnt empirically. Probability P_c is computed from the distance transform (DT)[15] of the object boundary C_0. DT has been used in many computer vision applications.[16–19] It is given by the following equation:

$$I_d(z_i) = \begin{cases} 0, & \text{if } z_i \text{ lies on contour } C_0 \\ d, & \text{otherwise} \end{cases} \tag{29.11}$$

where, d is the Euclidian distance of pixel z_i to the nearest contour point. Figure 29.6(b) shows an example of DT image for the contour image shown in Figure 29.6(a). Distance transform values are first normalized in the range $[0, 1]$, before they are used for the estimation of P_c. Let, I_n be the normalized distance transform image of I_d and d_n be the DT value of a pixel z_i in I_n (i.e. $d_n = I_n(z_i)$). Probability P_c of z_i is estimated using the following fuzzy distribution function:

$$P_c(z_i) = \begin{cases} 0, & 0 \le d_n < a; \\ 2\left(\frac{d_n - a}{b - a}\right)^2, & a \le d_n < \frac{a+b}{2}; \\ 1 - 2\left(\frac{b - d_n}{b - a}\right)^2, & \frac{a+b}{2} \le d_n < b; \\ 1, & b \le d_n \le 1. \end{cases} \tag{29.12}$$

where, a and b are constants and $a < b$. When $a \ge b$ this becomes a step function with transition at $(a + b)/2$ from 0 to 1. Probability distribution function (Eq. 29.12) has been chosen in such way that the probability value P_c is small near the contour C_0 and large for points farther away. In this fuzzy function, a and b dictate the non-linear behavior of the function. The parameters a and b control the extents (distance from the boundary) to which the output response is considered from Snake and then onwards from that of GrabCut respectively. The extent of the points considered near the contour can be suitably controlled by choosing appropriate values of a and b. The value of P_c is zero (0) when the distance of the pixel from the boundary is in the range $[0..a]$, and one (1) in the range $[b..1]$ (all values normalized). For the values between $[a..b]$, we empirically found the smooth, non-linear S-shaped function to provide the best result. Figure 29.7 shows the effect of the interval $[a, b]$ on the distribution function.

Probability value P_s is obtained from the GrabCut segmentation process. GrabCut assigns likelihood values to each pixel in the image using the GMMs constructed for the foreground and background, which represent how likely a pixel belongs to the foreground or background. In our approach, after the segmentation of the object using GrabCut, the final background GMMs are used to estimate P_s. For each pixel z_i inside C_0, $D(z_i)$ is computed using Eq. 29.8 considering background GMMs. Normalized values of D between 0 and 1, for all the pixels inside C_0, define the probability P_s.

Using the decision function $p(z_i)$ estimated in Eq. 29.10 and an empirically estimated threshold T, GrabCut and Active Contour results are integrated using

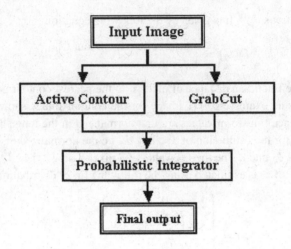

Fig. 29.5.   Flow chart of proposed SnakeCut technique.

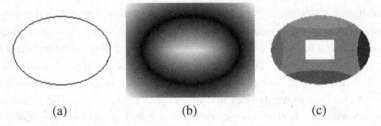

        (a)   (b)   (c)

Fig. 29.6.   Segmentation of image shown in Figure 29.2(a) using SnakeCut: (a) object boundary produced by Active Contour, (b) distance transform for the boundary contour shown in (a); (c) SnakeCut segmentation result.

the SnakeCut algorithm (refer Algorithm 29.1). In the integration process of the SnakeCut algorithm, segmentation output for a pixel is taken from the GrabCut result if $p > T$, otherwise it is taken from the Active Contour result. In our experiments, we empirically found $\rho = 0.5$ to give the best result, and $T = 0.7$, $a = 0.15$ and $b = 0.2$.

We demonstrate the integrated approach to the process of foreground segmentation with the help of a simulated example. Figure 29.6 shows the details of the SnakeCut technique for the segmentation of a foreground object present in the simulated image shown in Figure 29.2(a). Intermediate segmentation outputs produced by Active Contour and GrabCut for this image have been shown in Figures 29.2(c) & 29.2(d). These outputs are integrated by the SnakeCut algorithm. Fig-

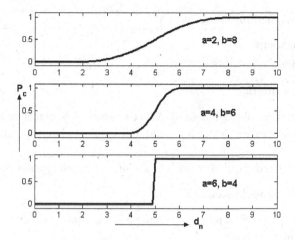

Fig. 29.7.   Effect of interval $[a, b]$ on the non-linearity of the fuzzy distribution function (Eq. 29.12). When $a < b$, transition from 0 (at a) to 1 (at b) is smooth. When $a \geq b$, we have a step function with the transition at $(a + b)/2$.

ure 29.6(a) shows the object boundary obtained by Active Contour for the object shown in Figure 29.2(a). Active Contour boundary is used to estimate the distance transform, shown in Figure 29.6(b), using Eq. 29.11. Probability values P_c and P_s are estimated for all the pixels inside the object boundary obtained by Active Contour as described above. SnakeCut algorithm is then used to integrate the outputs of Active Contour and GrabCut. Figure 29.6(c) shows the segmentation result of SnakeCut after integration of intermediate outputs (Figure 29.2(c) & 29.2(d)) obtained using Active Contour and GrabCut algorithms. Our proposed method is able to retain a part of the object which appears similar to background color and simultaneously eliminate the hole within the object.

To demonstrate the impact of the probability values P_c and P_s, and its impact on the decision making in SnakeCut algorithm, we use the soldier image (Figure 29.3(a)). We compute P_c, P_s and p values for a few points marked in the soldier image (Figure 29.8(a)) and then use SnakeCut algorithm to obtain the final segmentation decision. Values obtained for P_c, P_s and p are shown in Figure 29.8(b). Last column of the table shows the final decision taken by SnakeCut based on the estimated value of p.

Algorithm 29.1 Steps of SnakeCut

- Input I and output I_{sc}.
- All pixels of I_{sc} are initialized to zero.

A. Initial Segmentation

(1) Segment desired object in I using Active Contour. Say, object boundary identified by the Active Contour is C_0 and segmentation output of Active Contour is I_{ac}.

(2) Segment desired object in I using GrabCut. Say, segmentation output is I_{gc}.

B. Integration using SnakeCut

(1) Find set of pixels Z in image I, which lie inside contour C_0.

(2) For each pixel $z_i \in Z$,

   (a) Compute $p(z_i)$ using Eq. 29.10.

   (b) **if** $p(z_i) \leq T$ **then**
        $I_{sc}(z_i) = I_{ac}(z_i)$
     else
        $I_{sc}(z_i) = I_{gc}(z_i)$
     end if

Point	Pc	Ps	p	Output taken from
A	0.0026	0.6827	0.3426	Snake
B	1.0000	0.6601	0.8300	GrabCut
C	1.0000	0.6366	0.8183	GrabCut
D	0.0000	0.7300	0.3650	Snake
E	0.0000	0.5840	0.2922	Snake
F	1.0000	0.0000	0.5000	Snake

(a)   (b)

Fig. 29.8. Demonstration of the impact of P_c and P_s values on the decision making in Algorithm 29.1: (a) soldier image with a few points marked on it, (b) values of P_c, P_s and p, and the decision obtained using Algorithm 29.1. Values used for ρ and T are 0.5 and 0.7 respectively.

29.5. SnakeCut Segmentation Results

To extract a foreground object using SnakeCut, user draws a rectangle (or polygon) surrounding the object. This rectangle is used in the segmentation process

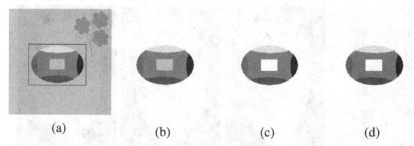

Fig. 29.9. Demonstration of a SnakeCut result on a synthetic image, where Snake fails and GrabCut works: (a) input image with foreground initialized by the user (object contains a rectangular hole at the center), (b) Snake segmentation result (incorrect, output contains the hole as a part of the object), (c) GrabCut segmentation result (correct, hole is removed), and (d) SnakeCut segmentation result (correct, hole is removed).

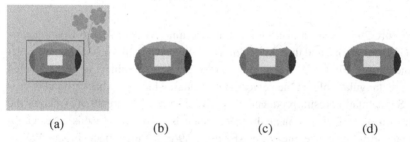

Fig. 29.10. Demonstration of a SnakeCut result on a synthetic image, where Snake works and Grab-Cut fails: (a) input image with foreground initialized by the user, (b) Snake segmentation result (correct), (c) GrabCut segmentation result (incorrect, upper green part of the object is removed), and (d) correct segmentation result produced by SnakeCut.

of Active Contour as well as GrabCut. Active Contour considers the rectangle as an initial contour and deforms it to converge on the object boundary. GrabCut uses the rectangle to define the background and unknown regions. Pixels outside the rectangle are taken as known background and those inside as unknown. GrabCut algorithm (using GMM based modeling and minimal cost graph-cut) iterates and converges to a minimum energy level producing the final segmentation output. Segmentation outputs of Active Contour and GrabCut are integrated using SnakeCut algorithm to obtain the final segmentation result. First, we present a few results of segmentation using SnakeCut on synthetic and natural images, where either Snake or GrabCut fails to work. This is followed by a few examples where both Snake and GrabCut techniques fail to perform correct segmentation, whereas integration of the outputs of these techniques using SnakeCut algorithm gives correct segmentation results.

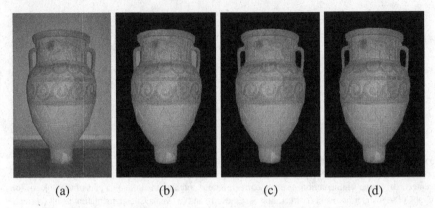

(a)   (b)   (c)   (d)

Fig. 29.11. Segmentation of real pot image: (a) input real image, (b) Active Contour segmentation result (incorrect), (c) GrabCut segmentation result (correct), and (d) SnakeCut segmentation result (correct, background pixels visible through the handles of the pot are removed).

Figure 29.9 shows a result on a synthetic image where Active Contour fails but GrabCut works, and their integration (*i.e.* SnakeCut) also produces the correct segmentation. Figure 29.9(a) shows an image where the object to be segmented has a rectangular hole (at the center) in it through which gray background is visible. Segmentation result produced by Active Contour (Figure 29.9(b)) shows the hole as a part of the segmented object which is incorrect. In this case, Grab-Cut performs correct segmentation (Figure 29.9(c)) of the object. Figure 29.9(d) shows the correct segmentation result produced by SnakeCut for this image. Figure 29.10 shows a result on another synthetic image where Active Contour works but GrabCut fails, and their integration (*i.e.* SnakeCut) produces the correct segmentation. Figure 29.10(a) shows an image where the object to be segmented has a part (upper green region) similar to the background (green flowers). Active contour, in this example, produces correct segmentation (Figure 29.10(b)) while GrabCut fails (Figure 29.10(c)). Figure 29.10(d) shows the correct segmentation result produced by SnakeCut for this image. Figure 29.11 presents a SnakeCut segmentation result on a real image. In this example, Active Contour fails but GrabCut performs correct segmentation. We see in Figure 29.11(b) that Active Contour segmentation result contains the part of the background (visible through the handles) which is incorrect. SnakeCut algorithm produces correct segmentation result which is shown in Figure 29.11(d).

In the examples presented so far, we have seen that only one among the two (Snake and GrabCut) techniques fail to perform correct segmentation. In these examples, either Snake is unable to remove holes from the foreground object or GrabCut is unable to retain the parts of the object which are similar to the back-

(a)   (b)

Fig. 29.12.   SnakeCut segmentation results of (a) soldier (for image in Figure 29.3(a)); and (b) wheel (for image in Figure 29.4(a)).

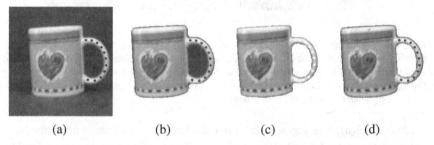

(a)   (b)   (c)   (d)

Fig. 29.13.   Segmentation of cup image: (a) input real image, (b) segmentation result produced by Snake (incorrect, as background pixels visible through the cup's handle are detected as a part of the object), (c) GrabCut segmentation result (incorrect, as spots present on the cup's handle are removed), and (d) correct segmentation result produced by SnakeCut.

ground. SnakeCut performs well in all such situations. We now present a few results on synthetic and real images, where SnakeCut performs well even when both Snake and GrabCut techniques fail to perform correct segmentation. Figure 29.12 presents two such SnakeCut results on real world images. Figure 29.12(a) shows the segmentation result produced by SnakeCut for the soldier image shown in Figure 29.3(a). This result is obtained by integrating the Active Contour and GrabCut outputs shown in Figures 29.3(b) and 29.3(c), without user interaction. Figure 29.12(b) shows the wheel segmentation result produced by SnakeCut, for the image shown in Figure 29.4(a). Intermediate Active Contour and GrabCut segmentation results for the wheel are shown in Figure 29.4(b) and 29.4(c).

Two more SnakeCut segmentation results are presented in Figures 29.13 and 29.14 for cup and webcam bracket images, where both Snake and GrabCut techniques fail to perform correct segmentation. The objective in the cup example

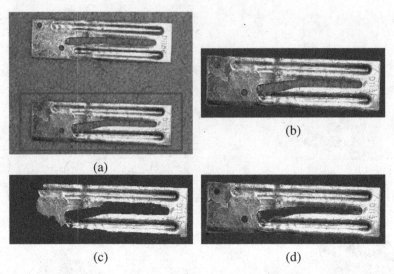

Fig. 29.14.   Segmentation of webcam bracket: (a) input real image where the objective is to segment the lower bracket present in the image, (b) Snake segmentation result (incorrect, as background pixels visible through the holes present in the object are detected as part of the foreground object), (c) Grab-Cut segmentation result (incorrect, as large portions of the bracket are removed in the result), and (d) correct segmentation result produced by SnakeCut.

(Figure 29.13(a)) is to segment the cup in the image. Cup's handle has some blue color spots similar to the background color. Snake and GrabCut results for this image are shown in Figure 29.13(b) and Figure 29.13(c) respectively. We can see that both these results are erroneous. Result obtained using Snake contains some part of the background which is visible through the handle. GrabCut has removed the spots in the handle since their color is similar to the background. Correct segmentation result produced by SnakeCut is shown in Figure 29.13(d). Objective in the webcam bracket example (Figure 29.14(a)) is to segment the lower bracket (inside the red contour initialized by the user) present in the image. Snake and GrabCut results for this image are shown in Figure 29.14(b) and Figure 29.14(c) respectively. We can see that both these results are erroneous. The result obtained using Snake contains some part of the background which is visible through the holes. GrabCut has removed large portions of the bracket. This is due to the similarity of the distribution of the metallic color of a part of another webcam bracket present in the background (it should be noted that the color distribution of the two webcam brackets are not exactly same due to different lighting effects). Correct segmentation result produced by SnakeCut is shown in Figure 29.14(d). We also observed a similar performance when the initialization was done around the upper bracket.

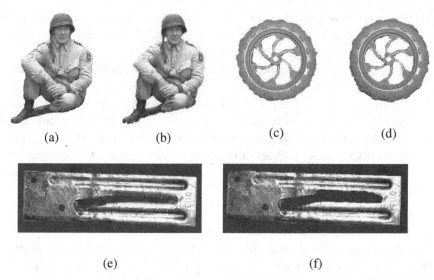

(a)   (b)   (c)   (d)

(e)   (f)

Fig. 29.15. Comparison of the results: (a) SnakeCut result for soldier, (b) GrabCut Output of soldier with user interaction (reproduced from[2]), (c) SnakeCut result for wheel, (d) GrabCut Output of wheel with user interaction, (e) SnakeCut result for webcam bracket, (f) GrabCut Output of webcam bracket with user interaction.

In Figure 29.15, we compare the automatic SnakeCut segmentation results of soldier (Figure 29.3(a)), wheel (Figure 29.4(a)) and webcam bracket (Figure 29.14(a)) images with the interactive GrabCut outputs. To obtain correct segmentation for these images with GrabCut, user interaction was necessary to obtain the results shown in Figures 29.15(b), 29.15(d) & 29.15(f). In case of soldier (Figure 29.15(b)), user marked the soldier's hat and legs as parts of the compulsory foreground. In case of wheel (Figure 29.15(d)) user marked the outer grayish green region of the wheel as a compulsory part of the foreground object and in case of webcam bracket (Figure 29.15(f)) user marked missing regions as compulsory parts of the foreground object. Segmentation results using SnakeCut were obtained without user interaction and are better than the results obtained by Grab-Cut with user's corrective editing. One can observe the smooth edges obtained at the legs of the soldier in Figure 29.15(a), unlike that in Figure 29.15(b). The same is true for Figure 29.15(c) and 29.15(e) (*w.r.t* Figures 29.15(d) and 29.15(f) respectively), which can be noticed after careful observation.

The presented approach takes advantage of Active Contour and GrabCut, and performs the correct segmentation in most cases where one or both of these techniques fail. However, the proposed technique (SnakeCut) was observed to have the following limitations:

(1) Since the SnakeCut relies on Active contours for regions near the object boundary, it fails when holes of the object (through which the background is visible) lie very close to the boundary.

(2) Since the Snake cannot penetrate inside the object boundary and detect holes, the proposed method of SnakeCut has to rely on the response of the GrabCut algorithm in such cases. This may result in a hazardous situation only when the GrabCut detects an interior part belonging to the object as a hole due to its high degree of similarity with the background. Since decision logic of SnakeCut relies on GrabCut response for interior parts of the object, it may fail in cases where GrabCut does not detect those parts of the object as foreground.

Figure 29.16 presents one such situation (using a simulated image) where SnakeCut fails to perform correct segmentation. Figure 29.16(a) shows a synthetic image where Active Contour works correctly (see Figure 29.16(b)) but GrabCut fails (see Figure 29.16(c)). GrabCut removes the central rectangular green part of the object in the segmented output, which may be perceived as a part of the object. We see in this case that SnakeCut also does not perform correct segmentation and removes the object's central rectangular green part from the segmentation result. SnakeCut thus fails when parts of the foreground object are far away from its boundary and very similar to the background.

The heuristic values of some of the parameters used in our algorithm, which were obtained empirically, were not so critical for accurate foreground object segmentation. The overall computational times required by SnakeCut on a P-IV, 3 GHz machine with 2 GB RAM, are given in Table 29.1 for some of the images.

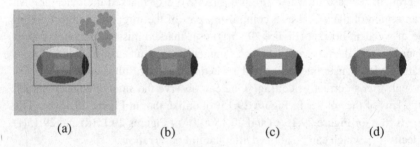

(a)   (b)   (c)   (d)

Fig. 29.16. Example where SnakeCut fails: (a) input image with foreground initialized by user, (b) Active Contour segmentation result (correct), (c) GrabCut segmentation result (incorrect), and (d) SnakeCut segmentation result (incorrect).

Table 29.1. Computational times for foreground object segmentation, required by Snake, GrabCut and SnakeCut for various images.

Image Name	Image Size (in pixels)	Time required (in seconds)			
		Snake (A)	GrabCut (B)	Integration time[a] (C)	SnakeCut (A+B+C)
Synthetic Image (Figure 29.2(a))	250 × 250	4	5	2	11
Soldier Image (Figure 29.3(a))	321 × 481	8	10	3	21
Wheel Image (Figure 29.4(a))	640 × 480	6	14	5	25
Synthetic Image (Figure 29.9(a))	250 × 250	4	5	2	11
Pot image (Figure 29.11(a))	296 × 478	6	7	4	17
Cup image (Figure 29.13(a))	285 × 274	5	7	3	15
Webcam bracket (Figure 29.14(a))	321 × 481	7	8	3	18

[a]time required to integrate Snake and GrabCut outputs using the probabilistic integrator.

29.6. Conclusion

In this paper, we have presented a novel object segmentation technique based on the integration of two complementary object segmentation techniques, namely Active Contour and GrabCut. Active Contour cannot remove the holes in the interior part of the object. GrabCut produces poor segmentation results in cases when the color distribution of some part of the foreground object is similar to background. Proposed segmentation technique, SnakeCut, based on a probabilistic framework, provides an automatic way of object segmentation, where the user has to only specify the rectangular boundary around the desired foreground object. Our proposed method is able to retain parts of the object which appears similar to background color and simultaneously eliminates holes with the object. We validate our technique with a few synthetic and natural images. Results obtained using SnakeCut are quite encouraging and promising. As an extension of this work, one can use geodesic Active Contour (which can intrinsically segment multiple objects) to make the technique suitable for the segmentation of multiple objects.

References

1. M. Kass, A. Witkin, and D. Terzopoulos, Snakes: Active contour models, *International Journal of Computer Vision*. **1**(4), 321–331 (January, 1988).
2. C. Rother, V. Kolmogorov, and A. Blake, GrabCut: Interactive foreground extraction using iterated graph-cuts, *ACM Transactions on Graphics*. **23**(3), 309–34, (2004).
3. F. Leymarie and M. D. Levine, Tracking deformable objects in the plane using an active contour model, *IEEE Transactions on Pattern Analysis and Machine Intelligence*. **15**(6), 617–634, (1993).
4. Surya Prakash and S. Das. External force modeling of snake using DWT for texture object segmentation. In *Proceedings of International Conference on Advances in Pattern Recognition, ICAPR' 07, January 2-4, 2007*, pp. 215–219, ISI Calcutta, India, (2007). World Scientific, Singapore.
5. D. Terzopoulos and K. Fleischer, Deformable models, *The Visual Computer*. **4**(6), 306–331, (1988).
6. D. Terzopoulos and R. Szeliski, *Tracking with Kalman Snakes*. (MIT Press, Cambridge, MA, 1992).
7. L. D. Cohen, On active contour models and balloons, *CVGIP: Image Understanding*. **53**(2), 211–218, (1991).
8. V. Caselles, F. Catte, and T. Coll, A geometric model for active contours, *Numerische Mathematik*. **66**, 1–31, (1993).
9. V. Caselles, R. Kimmel, and G. Saprio, Geodesic active contours, *International Journal of Computer Vision*. **22**(1), 61–79, (1997).
10. P. Deepti, R. Abhilash, and S. Das. Integrating linear subspace analysis and interactive graphcuts for content-based video retrieval. In *Proceedings of International Conference on Advances in Pattern Recognition, ICAPR' 07, January 2-4, 2007*, pp. 263–267, ISI Calcutta, India, (2007). World Scientific, Singapore.
11. A. Haasch, N. Hofemann, J. Fritsch, and G. Sagerer. A multi-modal object attention system for a mobile robot. In *Proceedings of IEEE/RSJ International Conference on Intelligent Robots and Systems, IROS 2005*, pp. 1499–1504, Edmonton, Alberta, Canada, (2005).
12. B. Moller, S. Posch, A. Haasch, J. Fritsch, and G. Sagerer. Interactive object learning for robot companions using mosaic images. In *Proceedings of IEEE/RSJ International Conference on Intelligent Robots and Systems, IROS 2005, 2-6 August, 2005*, pp. 2650–2655, Edmonton, Alberta, Canada, (2005).
13. L. E. Elsgolc, *Calculus of Variations*. (Pergamon Press, 1963).
14. Y. Boykov and M.-P. Jolly. Interactive graph-cuts for optimal boundary and region segmentation of objects in N-D images. In *Proceedings of International Conference on Computer Vision, ICCV' 01*, vol. 1, pp. 105–112, (2001).
15. H. Breu, J. Gil, D. Kirkpatrick, and M. Werman, Linear time euclidean distance algorithms, *IEEE Transactions on Pattern Analysis and Machine Intelligence*. **17**(5), 529–533, (1995).
16. D. W. Paglieroni, G. E. Ford, and E. M. Tsujimoto, The position-orientation masking approach to parametric search for template matching, *IEEE Transactions on Pattern Analysis and Machine Intelligence*. **16**(7), 740–747, (1994).
17. P. Tsang, P. Yuen, and F. Lam, Classification of partially occluded objects using

3-point matching and distance transformation, *Pattern Recognition.* **27**(1), 27–40, (1994).

18. M. Sanjay, S. Das, and B. Yegnanarayana. Robust template matching for noisy bitmap images invariant to translation and rotation. In *Indian Conference on Computer Vision, Graphics and Image Processing, December 21-23, 1998*, pp. 82–88, New Delhi, INDIA, (1998).

19. D.-J. Lee, J. Archibald, X. Xu, and P. Zhan, Using distance transform to solve real-time machine vision inspection problems, *Machine Vision and Applications.* **18**(2), 85–93, (2007).

CHAPTER 30

INTELLIGENT CCTV FOR MASS TRANSPORT SECURITY: CHALLENGES AND OPPORTUNITIES FOR VIDEO AND FACE PROCESSING

Conrad Sanderson, Abbas Bigdeli, Ting Shan, Shaokang Chen, Erik Berglund and Brian C. Lovell

NICTA, PO Box 10161, Brisbane QLD 4000, Australia

CCTV surveillance systems have long been promoted as being effective in improving public safety. However due to the amount of cameras installed, many sites have abandoned expensive human monitoring and only record video for forensic purposes. One of the sought-after capabilities of an automated surveillance system is "face in the crowd" recognition, in public spaces such as mass transit centres. Apart from accuracy and robustness to nuisance factors such as pose variations, in such surveillance situations the other important factors are scalability and fast performance. We evaluate recent approaches to the recognition of faces at large pose angles from a gallery of frontal images and propose novel adaptations as well as modifications. We compare and contrast the accuracy, robustness and speed of an Active Appearance Model (AAM) based method (where realistic frontal faces are synthesized from non-frontal probe faces) against bag-of-features methods. We show a novel approach where the performance of the AAM based technique is increased by side-stepping the image synthesis step, also resulting in a considerable speedup. Additionally, we adapt a histogram-based bag-of-features technique to face classification and contrast its properties to a previously proposed direct bag-of-features method. We further show that the two bag-of-features approaches can be considerably sped up, without a loss in classification accuracy, via an approximation of the exponential function. Experiments on the FERET and PIE databases suggest that the bag-of-features techniques generally attain better performance, with significantly lower computational loads. The histogram-based bag-of-features technique is capable of achieving an average recognition accuracy of 89% for pose angles of around 25 degrees. Finally, we provide a discussion on implementation as well as legal challenges surrounding research on automated surveillance.

30.1. Introduction

In response to global terrorism, usage and interest in Closed-Circuit Television (CCTV) for surveillance and protection of public spaces (such as mass transit facilities) is growing at a considerable rate. A similar escalation of the installed CCTV base occurred in London late last century in response to the continual bombings linked to the conflict in Northern Ireland. Based on the number of CCTV cameras on Putney High Street, it is "guesstimated"[1] that there are around 500,000 CCTV cameras in the London area and 4,000,000 cameras in the UK. This suggests that in the UK there is approximately one camera for every 14 people. However, whilst it is relatively easy, albeit expensive, to install increasing numbers of cameras, it is quite another issue to adequately monitor the video feeds with security guards. Hence, the trend has been to record the CCTV feeds without monitoring and to use the video merely for a forensic, or reactive, response to crime and terrorism, often detected by other means.

In minor crimes such as assault and robbery, surveillance video is very effective in helping to find and successfully prosecute perpetrators. Thus one would expect that surveillance video would act as a deterrent to crime. Recently the immense cost of successful terrorist attacks on soft targets such as mass transport systems has indicated that forensic analysis of video after the event is simply not an adequate response. Indeed, in the case of suicide bombings there is simply no possibility of prosecution after the event and thus no deterrent effect. A pressing need is emerging to monitor all surveillance cameras in an attempt to detect events and persons-of-interest.

One important issue is the fact that human monitoring requires a large number of people, resulting in high ongoing costs. Furthermore, such a personnel intensive system has questionable reliability due to the attention span of humans decreasing rapidly when performing such tedious tasks. A solution may be found in advanced surveillance systems employing computer monitoring of all video feeds, delivering the alerts to human responders for triage. Indeed such systems may assist in maintaining the high level of vigilance required over many years to detect the rare events associated with terrorism — a well-designed computer system is never caught "off guard". Because of this, there has been a significant rush in both the industry and the research community to develop advanced surveillance systems, sometimes dubbed as Intelligent CCTV (ICCTV). In particular, developing total solutions for protecting critical infrastructure has been on the forefront of R&D activities in this field [2–4].

Amongst the various biometric techniques for person identification, recognition via gait and faces appears to be the most useful in the context of CCTV. Our

(a)   (b)   (c)

Fig. 30.1. Several frames from CCTV cameras located at a railway station in Brisbane (Australia), demonstrating some of the variabilities present in real-life conditions: (a) varying face pose, (b) illumination from one side, (c) varying size and pose.

starting point is the robust identification of persons of interest, which is motivated by problems encountered in our initial real-world trials of face recognition technologies in public railway stations using existing cameras.

While automatic face recognition of cooperative subjects has achieved good results in controlled applications such as passport control, CCTV conditions are considerably more challenging. Nuisance factors such as varying illumination, expression, and pose can greatly affect recognition performance. According to Phillips *et al.* head pose is believed to be the hardest factor to model.[5] In mass transport systems, surveillance cameras are often mounted in the ceiling in places such as railway platforms and passenger trains. Since the subjects are generally not posing for the camera, it is rare to obtain a true frontal face image. As it is infeasible to consider remounting all the cameras (in our case more than 6000) to improve face recognition performance, any practical system must have effective pose compensation or be specifically designed to handle pose variations. Examples of real life CCTV conditions are shown in Figure 30.1.

A further complication is that we generally only have one frontal gallery image of each person-of-interest (e.g. a passport photograph or a mugshot). In addition to robustness and accuracy, scalability and fast performance are also of prime importance for surveillance. A face recognition system should be able to handle large volumes of people (e.g. peak hour at a railway station), possibly processing hundreds of video streams. While it is possible to setup elaborate parallel computation machines, there are always cost considerations limiting the number of CPUs available for processing. In this context, a face recognition algorithm should be able to run in real-time or better, which necessarily limits complexity.

Previous approaches to addressing pose variation include the synthesis of new images at previously unseen views,[6,7] direct synthesis of face model parameters[8] and local feature based representations.[9–11] We note in passing that while true

3D based approaches in theory allow face matching at various poses, current 3D sensing hardware has too many limitations,[12] including cost and range. Moreover unlike 2D recognition, 3D technology cannot be retrofitted to existing surveillance systems.

In,[7] Active Appearance Models (AAMs) were used to model each face, detecting the pose through a correlation model. A frontal image could then be synthesized directly from a single non-frontal image without the need to explicitly generate a 3D head model. While the AAM-based face synthesis allowed considerable improvements in recognition accuracy, the synthesized faces have residual artefacts which may affect recognition performance.

In,[8] a "bag of features" approach was shown to perform well in the presence of pose variations. It is based on dividing the face into overlapping uniform-sized blocks, analysing each block with the Discrete Cosine Transform (DCT) and modelling the resultant set of features via a Gaussian Mixture Model (GMM). The robustness to pose change was attributed to an effective insensitivity to the topology of the face. We shall refer to this method as the *direct bag-of-features*.

Inspired by text classification techniques from the fields of natural language processing and information retrieval, alternative forms of the "bag of features" approach are used for image categorisation in.[13–15] Rather than directly calculating the likelihood as in,[8] histograms of occurrences of "visual words" (also known as "keypoints") are first built, followed by histogram comparison. We shall refer to this approach as the *histogram-based bag-of-features*.

The research reported in this paper has four main aims: **(i)** To evaluate the effectiveness of a novel modification of the AAM-based method, where we explicitly remove the effect of pose from the face model creating pose-robust features. The modification allows the use of the model's parameters directly for classification, thereby skipping the computationally intensive and artefact producing image synthesis step. **(ii)** To adapt the histogram-based bag-of-features approach to face classification and contrast its properties to the direct bag-of-features method. **(iii)** To evaluate the extent of speedup possible in the both bag-of-features approaches via an approximation of the $\exp()$ function, and whether such approximation affects recognition accuracy. **(iv)** To compare the performance, robustness and speed of AAM based and bag-of-features based methods in the context of face classification under pose variations.

The balance of this paper is structured as follows. In Section 30.2 we overview the two bag-of-features methods. In Section 30.3 we overview the AAM-based synthesis technique and present the modified form. Section 30.4 is devoted to an evaluation of the techniques on the FERET and PIE datasets. A discussion of the results, as well as implementation and legal issues surrounding research on automated surveillance, is given in Section 30.5.

30.2. Bag-of-Features Approaches

In this section we describe two local feature based approaches, with both approaches sharing a block based feature extraction method summarised in Section 30.2.1. Both methods use Gaussian Mixture Models (GMMs) to model distributions of features, but they differ in how the GMMs are applied. In the first approach (*direct bag-of-features*, Section 30.2.2) the likelihood of a given face belonging to a specific person is calculated directly using that person's model. In the second approach (*histogram-based bag-of-features*, Section 30.2.3), a generic model (not specific to any person), representing "face words", is used to build histograms which are then compared for recognition purposes. In Section 30.2.4 we describe how both techniques can be sped up.

30.2.1. *Feature Extraction and Illumination Normalisation*

The face is described as a set of feature vectors, $X = \{\mathbf{x}_1, \mathbf{x}_2, \cdots, \mathbf{x}_N\}$, which are obtained by dividing the face into small, uniformly sized, overlapping blocks and decomposing each block[a] via the 2D DCT.[17] Typically the first 15 to 21 DCT coefficients are retained (as they contain the vast majority of discriminatory information), except for the 0-th coefficient which is the most affected by illumination changes.[9]

To achieve enhanced robustness to illumination variations, we have incorporated additional processing prior to 2D DCT decomposition. Assuming the illumination model for each pixel to be $\widehat{p}_{(x,y)} = b + c \cdot p_{(x,y)}$, where $p_{(x,y)}$ is the "uncorrupted" pixel at location (x, y), b is a bias and c a multiplier (indicating the contrast), removing the 0-th DCT coefficient only corrects for the bias. To achieve robustness to contrast variations, the set of pixels within each block is normalised to have zero mean and unit variance.

30.2.2. *Bag-of-Features with Direct Likelihood Evaluation*

By assuming the vectors are independent and identically distributed (i.i.d.), the likelihood of X belonging to person i is found with:

$$P(X|\lambda^{[i]}) = \prod_{n=1}^{N} P(\mathbf{x}_n|\lambda^{[i]}) = \prod_{n=1}^{N} \sum_{g=1}^{G} w_g^{[i]} \mathcal{N}\left(\mathbf{x}_n|\mu_g^{[i]}, \mathbf{\Sigma}_g^{[i]}\right) \qquad (30.1)$$

---

[a]While in this work we used the 2D DCT for describing each block (or patch), it is possible to use other descriptors, for example Gabor wavelets.[16]

where $\mathcal{N}(\mathbf{x}|\mu, \boldsymbol{\Sigma}) = (2\pi)^{-\frac{d}{2}}|\boldsymbol{\Sigma}|^{-\frac{1}{2}} \exp\left\{-\frac{1}{2}(\mathbf{x} - \mu)^T \boldsymbol{\Sigma}^{-1}(\mathbf{x} - \mu)\right\}$ is a multi-variate Gaussian function,[18] while $\lambda^{[i]} = \{w_g^{[i]}, \mu_g^{[i]}, \boldsymbol{\Sigma}_g^{[i]}\}_{g=1}^G$ is the set of parameters for person i. The convex combination of Gaussians, with mixing coefficients w_g, is typically referred to as a Gaussian Mixture Model (GMM). Its parameters are optimised via the Expectation Maximisation algorithm.[18]

Due to the vectors being treated as i.i.d., information about the topology of the face is in effect lost. While at first this may seem counter-productive, the loss of topology in conjunction with overlapping blocks provides a useful characteristic: the precise location of face parts is no longer required. Previous research has suggested that the method is effective for face classification while being robust to imperfect face detection as well as a certain amount of in-plane and out-of-plane rotations.[8,9,19]

The robustness to pose variations can be attributed to the explicit allowance for movement of face areas, when comparing face images of a particular person at various poses. Furthermore, significant changes of a particular face component (e.g. the nose) due to pose variations affect only the subset of face areas that cover this particular component.

30.2.3. *Bag-of-Features with Histogram Matching*

The technique presented in this section is an adaption of the "visual words" method used in image categorisation.[13–15] First, a training set of faces is used to build a generic model (not specific to any person). This generic model represents a dictionary of "face words" — the mean of each Gaussian can be thought of as a particular "face word". Once a set of feature vectors for a given face is obtained, a probabilistic histogram of the occurrences of the "face words" is built:

$$\mathbf{h}_X = \frac{1}{N}\left[\sum_{i=1}^N \frac{w_1 p_1(\mathbf{x}_i)}{\sum_{g=1}^G w_g p_g(\mathbf{x}_i)}, \sum_{i=1}^N \frac{w_2 p_2(\mathbf{x}_i)}{\sum_{g=1}^G w_g p_g(\mathbf{x}_i)}, \cdots, \sum_{i=1}^N \frac{w_G p_G(\mathbf{x}_i)}{\sum_{g=1}^G w_g p_g(\mathbf{x}_i)}\right]$$

where w_g is the weight for Gaussian g and $p_g(\mathbf{x})$ is the probability of vector $\mathbf{x}$ according to Gaussian g.

Comparison of two faces is then accomplished by comparing their corresponding histograms. This can be done by the so-called χ^2 distance metric,[20] or the simpler approach of summation of absolute differences:[21]

$$d(\mathbf{h}_A, \mathbf{h}_B) = \sum_{g=1}^G \left|\mathbf{h}_A^{[g]} - \mathbf{h}_B^{[g]}\right| \tag{30.2}$$

where $\mathbf{h}_A^{[g]}$ is the g-th element of $\mathbf{h}_A$. As preliminary experiments suggested that there was little difference in performance between the two metrics, we've elected to use the latter one.

Note that like in the direct method presented in the previous section, information about the topology of the face is lost. However, the direct method requires that the set of features from a given probe face is processed using all models of the persons in the gallery. As such, the amount of processing can quickly become prohibitive as the gallery grows[b]. In contrast, the histogram-based approach requires the set of features to be processed using only one model, potentially providing savings in terms of storage and computational effort.

Another advantage of the histogram-based approach is that the face similarity measurement, via Eqn. (30.2), is symmetric. This is not the case for the direct approach, as the representation of probe and gallery faces differs — a probe face is represented by a set of features, while a gallery face is represented by a model of features (the model, in this case, can be thought of as a compact approximation of the set of features from the gallery face).

30.2.4. *Speedup via Approximation*

In practice the time taken by the 2D DCT feature extraction stage is negligible and hence the bulk of processing in the above two approaches is heavily concentrated in the evaluation of the $\exp()$ function. As such, a considerable speedup can be achieved through the use of a fast approximation of this function.[22] A brief overview follows: rather than using a lookup table, the approximation is accomplished by exploiting the structure and encoding of a standard (IEEE-754) floating-point representation. The given argument is transformed and injected as an integer into the first 32 bits of the 64 bit representation. Reading the resulting floating point number provides the approximation. Experiments in Section 30.4 indicate that the approximation does not affect recognition accuracy.

30.3. Active Appearance Models

In this section we describe face modelling based on deformable models popularised by Cootes et al., namely Active Shape Models (ASMs)[23] and Active Appearance Models (AAMs).[24] We first provide a brief description of the two models, followed by pose estimation via a correlation model and finally frontal view synthesis. We also show that the synthesis step can be omitted by directly removing the effect of the pose from the model of the face, resulting in (theoretically)

---

[b]For example, assuming each model has 32 Gaussians, going through a gallery of 1000 people would require evaluating 32000 Gaussians. Assuming 784 vectors are extracted from each face, the number of exp() evaluations is around 25 million.

pose independent features.

30.3.1. *Face Modelling*

Let us describe a face by a set of N landmark points, where the location of each point is tuple (x, y). A face can hence be represented by a $2N$ dimensional vector:

$$\mathbf{f} = [\, x_1, x_2, \cdots, x_N, \ y_1, y_2, \cdots, y_N \,]^T . \qquad (30.3)$$

In ASM, a face shape is represented by:

$$\mathbf{f} = \overline{\mathbf{f}} + \mathbf{P}_s \mathbf{b}_s \qquad (30.4)$$

where $\overline{\mathbf{f}}$ is the mean face vector, $\mathbf{P}_s$ is a matrix containing the k eigenvectors with largest eigenvalues (of a training dataset), and $\mathbf{b}_s$ is a weight vector. In a similar manner, the texture variations can be represented by:

$$\mathbf{g} = \overline{\mathbf{g}} + \mathbf{P}_g \mathbf{b}_g \qquad (30.5)$$

where $\overline{\mathbf{g}}$ is the mean appearance vector, $\mathbf{P}_g$ is a matrix describing the texture variations learned from training sets, and $\mathbf{b_g}$ is the texture weighting vector.

The shape and appearance parameters $\mathbf{b}_s$ and $\mathbf{b}_g$ can be used to describe the shape and appearance of any face. As there are correlations between the shape and appearance of the same person, let us first represent both aspects as:

$$\mathbf{b} = \begin{bmatrix} \mathbf{W}_s \mathbf{b}_s \\ \mathbf{b}_g \end{bmatrix} = \begin{bmatrix} \mathbf{W}_s \mathbf{P}_s^T (\mathbf{f} - \overline{\mathbf{f}}) \\ \mathbf{P}_g^T (\mathbf{g} - \overline{\mathbf{g}}) \end{bmatrix} \qquad (30.6)$$

where $\mathbf{W}_s$ is a diagonal matrix which represents the change between shape and texture. Through Principal Component Analysis (PCA)[18] we can represent $\mathbf{b}$ as:

$$\mathbf{b} = \mathbf{P}_c \mathbf{c} \qquad (30.7)$$

where $\mathbf{P}_c$ are eigenvectors, $\mathbf{c}$ is a vector of appearance parameters controlling both shape and texture of the model, and $\mathbf{b}$ can be shown to have zero mean. Shape $\mathbf{f}$ and texture $\mathbf{g}$ can then be represented by:

$$\mathbf{f} = \overline{\mathbf{f}} + \mathbf{Q}_s \mathbf{c} \qquad (30.8)$$

$$\mathbf{g} = \overline{\mathbf{g}} + \mathbf{Q}_g \mathbf{c} \qquad (30.9)$$

where

$$\mathbf{Q}_s = \mathbf{P}_s \mathbf{W}_s^{-1} \mathbf{P}_{cs} \qquad (30.10)$$

$$\mathbf{Q}_g = \mathbf{P}_g \mathbf{P}_{cg} \qquad (30.11)$$

In the above, $\mathbf{Q}_s$ and $\mathbf{Q}_g$ are matrices describing the shape and texture variations, while $\mathbf{P}_{cs}$ and $\mathbf{P}_{cg}$ are shape and texture components of $\mathbf{P}_c$ respectively, i.e.:

$$\mathbf{P}_c = \begin{bmatrix} \mathbf{P}_{cs} \\ \mathbf{P}_{cg} \end{bmatrix} \tag{30.12}$$

The process of "interpretation" of faces is hence comprised of finding a set of model parameters which contain information about the shape, orientation, scale, position, and texture.

30.3.2. *Pose Estimation*

Following,[25] let us assume that the model parameter c is approximately related to the viewing angle, θ, by a correlation model:

$$\mathbf{c} \approx \mathbf{c}_0 + \mathbf{c}_c \cos(\theta) + \mathbf{c}_s \sin(\theta) \tag{30.13}$$

where $\mathbf{c}_0$, $\mathbf{c}_c$ and $\mathbf{c}_s$ are vectors which are learned from the training data. (Here we consider only head turning. Head nodding can be dealt with in a similar way).

For each face from a training set Ω, indicated by superscript $[i]$ with associated pose $\theta^{[i]}$, we perform an AAM search to find the best fitting model parameters $\mathbf{c}^{[i]}$. The parameters $\mathbf{c}_0$, $\mathbf{c}_c$ and $\mathbf{c}_s$ can be learned via regression from $\left(\mathbf{c}^{[i]}\right)_{i\in 1,\cdots,|\Omega|}$ and $\left(\left[1, \cos(\theta^{[i]}), \sin(\theta^{[i]})\right]\right)_{i\in 1,\cdots,|\Omega|}$, where $|\Omega|$ indicates the cardinality of Ω.

Given a new face image with parameters $\mathbf{c}^{[new]}$, we can estimate its orientation as follows. We first rearrange $\mathbf{c}^{[new]} = \mathbf{c}_0 + \mathbf{c}_c \cos(\theta^{[new]}) + \mathbf{c}_s \sin(\theta^{[new]})$ to:

$$\mathbf{c}^{[new]} - \mathbf{c}_0 = [\,\mathbf{c}_c\ \mathbf{c}_s\,] \left[\cos(\theta^{[new]})\ \sin(\theta^{[new]})\right]^T. \tag{30.14}$$

Let $\mathbf{R}_c^{-1}$ be the left pseudo-inverse of the matrix $[\,\mathbf{c}_c\ \mathbf{c}_s\,]$. Eqn. (30.14) can then be rewritten as:

$$\mathbf{R}_c^{-1}\left(\mathbf{c}^{[new]} - \mathbf{c}_0\right) = \left[\cos(\theta^{[new]})\ \sin(\theta^{[new]})\right]^T. \tag{30.15}$$

Let $[\,x_\alpha\ y_\alpha\,] = \mathbf{R}_c^{-1}\left(\mathbf{c}^{[new]} - \mathbf{c}_0\right)$. Then the best estimate of the orientation is $\theta^{[new]} = \tan^{-1}(y_\alpha/x_\alpha)$. Note that the estimation of $\theta^{[new]}$ may not be accurate due to land mark annotation errors or regression learning errors.

30.3.3. *Frontal View Synthesis*

After the estimation of $\theta^{[new]}$, we can use the model to synthesize frontal face views. Let $\mathbf{c}_{res}$ be residual vector which is not explained by the correlation model:

$$\mathbf{c}_{res} = \mathbf{c}^{[new]} - \left(\mathbf{c}_0 + \mathbf{c}_c \cos(\theta^{[new]}) + \mathbf{c}_s \sin(\theta^{[new]})\right) \tag{30.16}$$

To reconstruct at an alternate angle, $\theta^{[alt]}$, we can add the residual vector to the mean face for that angle:

$$\mathbf{c}^{[alt]} = \mathbf{c}_{res} + \left(\mathbf{c}_0 + \mathbf{c}_c \cos(\theta^{[alt]}) + \mathbf{c}_s \sin(\theta^{[alt]})\right) \tag{30.17}$$

To synthesize the frontal view face, $\theta^{[alt]}$ is set to zero. Eqn. (30.17) hence simplifies to:

$$\mathbf{c}^{[alt]} = \mathbf{c}_{res} + \mathbf{c}_0 + \mathbf{c}_c \tag{30.18}$$

Based on Eqns. (30.8) and (30.9), the shape and texture for the frontal view can then be calculated by:

$$\mathbf{f}^{[alt]} = \overline{\mathbf{f}} + \mathbf{Q}_s \mathbf{c}^{[alt]} \tag{30.19}$$

$$\mathbf{g}^{[alt]} = \overline{\mathbf{g}} + \mathbf{Q}_g \mathbf{c}^{[alt]} \tag{30.20}$$

Examples of synthesized faces are shown in Fig. 30.2. Each synthesized face can then be processed via the standard Principal Component Analysis (PCA) technique to produce features which are used for classification.[7]

30.3.4. *Direct Pose-Robust Features*

The bracketed term in Eqn. (30.16) can be interpreted as the mean face for angle $\theta^{[new]}$. The difference between $\mathbf{c}^{[new]}$ (which represents the given face at the estimated angle $\theta^{[new]}$) and the bracketed term can hence be interpreted as removing the effect of the angle, resulting in a (theoretically) pose independent representation. As such, $\mathbf{c}_{res}$ can be used directly for classification, providing considerable computational savings — the process of face synthesis and PCA feature extraction is omitted. Because of this, we're avoiding the introduction of imaging artefacts (due to synthesis) and information loss caused by PCA-based feature extraction.

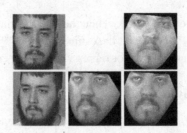

Fig. 30.2.   Top row: frontal view and its AAM-based synthesized representation. Bottom row: non-frontal view as well as its AAM-based synthesized representation at its original angle and $\theta^{[alt]} = 0$ (i.e. synthesized frontal view).

As such, the pose-robust features should represent the faces more accurately, leading to better discrimination performance. We shall refer to this approach as the *pose-robust features* method.

30.4. Evaluation

We are currently in the process of creating a suitable dataset for face classification in CCTV conditions (part of a separately funded project). As such, in these experiments we instead used subsets of the PIE dataset[26] (using faces at -22.5°, 0° and $+22.5^{\circ}$) as well as the FERET dataset[27] (using faces at -25°, -15°, 0°, $+15^{\circ}$ and $+25^{\circ}$).

To train the AAM based approach, we first pooled face images from 40 FERET individuals at -15°, 0°, $+15^{\circ}$. Each face image was labelled with 58 points around the salient features (the eyes, mouth, nose, eyebrows and chin). The resulting model was used to automatically find the facial features (via an AAM search) for the remainder of the FERET subset. A new dataset was formed, consisting of 305 images from 61 persons with successful AAM search results. This dataset was used to train the correlation model and evaluate the performances of all presented algorithms. In a similar manner, a new dataset was formed from the PIE subset, consisting of images for 53 persons.

For the synthesis based approach, the last stage (PCA based feature extraction from synthesized images) produced 36 dimensional vectors. The PCA subsystem was trained as per.[7] The pose-robust features approach produced 43 dimensional vectors for each face. For both of the AAM-based techniques, Mahalanobis distance was used for classification.[18]

For the bag-of-features approaches, in a similar manner to,[8] we used face images with a size of 64×64 pixels, blocks with a size of 8×8 pixels and an overlap of 6 pixels. This resulted in 784 feature vectors per face. The number of retained DCT coefficients was set to 15 (resulting in 14 dimensional feature vectors, as the 0-th coefficient was discarded). The faces were normalised in size so that the distance between the eyes was 32 pixels and the eyes were in approximately the same positions in all images.

For the direct bag-of-features approach, the number of Gaussians per model was set to 32. Preliminary experiments indicated that accuracy for faces at around 25° peaked at 32 Gaussians, while using more than 32 Gaussians provided little gain in accuracy at the expense of longer processing times.

For the histogram-based bag-of-features method, the number of Gaussians for the generic model was set to 1024, following the same reasoning as above. The generic model (representing "face words") was trained on FERET *ba* data (frontal

C. Sanderson et al.

Table 30.1. Recognition performance on the FERET pose subset.

Method	Pose			
	$-25°$	$-15°$	$+15°$	$+25°$
PCA	23.0	54.0	49.0	36.0
Synthesis + PCA	50.0	71.0	67.4	42.0
pose-robust features	**85.6**	88.2	88.1	66.8
Direct bag-of-features	83.6	93.4	**100.0**	72.1
Histogram bag-of-features	83.6	**100.0**	96.7	**73.7**

Table 30.2. Recognition performance on PIE.

Method	Pose	
	$-22.5°$	$+22.5°$
PCA	13.0	8.0
Synthesis + PCA	60.0	56.0
pose-robust features	83.3	80.6
Direct bag-of-features	**100.0**	90.6
Histogram bag-of-features	**100.0**	**100.0**

faces), excluding the 61 persons described earlier.

Tables 30.1 and 30.2 show the recognition rates on the FERET and PIE datasets, respectively. The AAM-derived pose-robust features approach obtains performance which is considerably better than the circuitous approach based on image synthesis. However, the two bag-of-features methods generally obtain better performance on both FERET and PIE, with the histogram-based approach obtaining the best overall performance. Averaging across the high pose angles ($\pm 25°$ on FERET and $\pm 22.5°$ on PIE), the histogram-based method achieves an average accuracy of 89%.

Table 30.3 shows the time taken to classify one probe face by the presented techniques (except for PCA). The experiments were performed on a Pentium-M machine running at 1.5 GHz. All methods were implemented in C++. The time taken is divided into two components: (1) one-off cost per probe face, and (2) comparison of one probe face with one gallery face.

The one-off cost is the time required to convert a given face into a format which will be used for matching. For the synthesis approach this involves an AAM search, image synthesis and PCA based feature extraction. For the pose-robust features method, in contrast, this effectively involves only an AAM search. For the bag-of-features approaches, the one-off cost is the 2D DCT feature extraction, with the histogram-based approach additionally requiring the generation of the "face words" histogram.

Table 30.3. Average time taken for two stages of processing: (1) conversion of a probe face from image to format used for matching (one-off cost per probe face), (2) comparison of one probe face with one gallery face, after conversion.

Method	Approximate time taken (sec)	
	One-off cost per probe face	Comparison of one probe face with one gallery face
Synthesis + PCA	1.493	< 0.001
pose-robust features	0.978	< 0.001
Direct bag-of-features	0.006	0.006
Histogram bag-of-features	0.141	< 0.001

The second component, for the case of the direct bag-of-features method, involves calculating the likelihood using Eqn. (30.1), while for the histogram-based approach this involves just the sum of absolute differences between two histograms (Eqn. (30.2)). For the two AAM-based methods, the second component is the time taken to evaluate the Mahalanobis distance.

As expected, the pose-robust features approach has a speed advantage over the synthesis based approach, being about 50% faster. However, both of the bag-of-features methods are many times faster, in terms of the first component — the histogram-based approach is about 7 times faster than the pose-robust features method. While the one-off cost for the direct bag-of-features approach is much lower than for the histogram-based method, the time required for the second component (comparison of faces after conversion) is considerably higher, and might be a limiting factor when dealing with a large set of gallery faces (i.e. a scalability issue).

When using the fast approximation of the $\exp()$ function, the time required by the histogram-based method (in the first component) is reduced by approximately 30% to 0.096, with no loss in recognition accuracy. This makes it over 10 times faster than the pose-robust features method and over 15 times faster than the synthesis based technique. In a similar vein, the time taken by the second component of the direct bag-of-features approach is also reduced by approximately 30%, with no loss in recognition accuracy.

30.5. Discussion

With an aim towards improving intelligent surveillance systems, in this paper we have made several contributions. We proposed a novel approach to Active Appearance Model based face classification, where pose-robust features are obtained without the computationally expensive image synthesis step. Furthermore, we've adapted a *histogram-based bag-of-features* technique (previously employed in image categorisation) to face classification, and contrasted its properties to a previously proposed *direct bag-of-features* method. We have also shown that the two bag-of-features approaches, both based on Gaussian Mixture Models, can be considerably sped up without a loss in classification accuracy via an approximation of the exponential function.

In the context of pose mismatches between probe and gallery faces, experiments on the FERET and PIE databases suggest that while there is merit in the AAM based methods, the bag-of-features techniques generally attain better performance, with the histogram-based method achieving an average recognition rate of 89% for pose angles of around 25 degrees. Furthermore, the bag-of-features approaches are considerably faster, with the histogram-based method (using the fast exp() function) being over 10 times quicker than the pose-robust features method.

We note that apart from pose variations, imperfect face localisation[19] is also an important issue in a real life surveillance system. Imperfect localisations result in translations as well as scale changes, which adversely affect recognition performance. To that end, we are currently extending the histogram-based bag-of-features approach to also deal with scale variations.

As mentioned in the introduction, the research presented here is motivated by application to real-life conditions. One of our "test-beds" intended for field trials is a railway station in Brisbane (Australia), which provides us with implementation and installation issues that can be expected to arise in similar mass-transport facilities. Capturing the video feed in a real-world situation can be problematic, as there should be no disruption in operational capability of existing security systems. The optimal approach would be to simply use Internet Protocol (IP) camera feeds, however, in many existing surveillance systems the cameras are analogue and often their streams are fed to relatively old digital recording equipment. Limitations of such systems can include low resolution, recording only a few frames per second, non-uniform time delay between frames, and proprietary codecs. To avoid disruption while at the same time obtaining video streams which are more appropriate for an intelligent surveillance system, it is useful to tap directly into the analogue video feeds and process them via dedicated analogue-to-digital video matrix switches.

The face recognition techniques were implemented with an aim to be fast as well as integrable into larger commercial intelligent surveillance systems. This necessitated the conversion of Matlab code into C++, which was non-trivial. Certain parts of the original code relied on elaborate functions and toolkits included with Matlab, which we had to re-implement. Furthermore, our experience also shows that while research code written by scientists/engineers (who are not necessarily professional programmers) might be sufficient to obtain experimental results which can be published, more effort is required to ensure the code is in a maintainable state as well as to guarantee that the underlying algorithm implementation is stable.

Apart from the technical challenges, issues in many other domains may also arise. Privacy laws or policies at the national, state, municipal or organisational level may prevent surveillance footage being used for research even if the video is already being used for security monitoring — the primary purpose of the data collection is the main issue here. Moreover, without careful consultation and/or explanation, privacy groups as well as the general public can become uncomfortable with security research. Some people may simply wish not to be recorded as they have no desire in having photos or videos of themselves being viewable by other people. Plaques and warning signs indicating that surveillance recordings are being gathered for research purposes may allow people to consciously avoid monitored areas, possibly invalidating results. Nevertheless, it is our experience that it is possible to negotiate a satisfying legal framework within which real-life trials of intelligent surveillance systems can take place.

Acknowledgements

NICTA is funded by the Australian Government's *Backing Australia's Ability* initiative, in part through the Australian Research Council. This project is supported by a grant from the Australian Government Department of the Prime Minister and Cabinet.

References

1. M. McCahill and C. Norris, *Urbaneye: CCTV in London*. (Centre for Criminology and Criminal Justice, University of Hull, UK, 2002).
2. G. Francisco, S. Roberts, K. Hanna, J.S., and Heubusch. Critical infrastructure security confidence through automated thermal imaging. In *Infrared Technology and Applications XXXII*, vol. SPIE 6206, (2006).
3. L. Fuentes and S. Velastin. From tracking to advanced surveillance. In *Proceedings of International Conference on Image Processing Conference (ICIP)*, vol. 3, pp. 121–124, (2003).
4. F. Ziliani, S. Velastin, F. Porikli, L. Marcenaro, T. Kelliher, A. Cavallaro, and P. Bruneaut. Performance evaluation of event detection solutions: the creds experience. In *Proceedings of IEEE Conference on Advanced Video and Signal Based Surveillance*, pp. 201–206, (2005).
5. P. Phillips, P. Grother, R. Micheals, D. Blackburn, E. Tabassi, and M. Bone. Face

recognition vendor test 2002. In *Proceedings of Analysis and Modeling of Faces and Gestures*, p. 44, (2003).

6. V. Blanz, P. Grother, P. Phillips, and T. Vetter. Face recognition based on frontal views generated from non-frontal images. In *Proc. IEEE Int. Conf. Computer Vision and Pattern Recognition*, vol. 2, pp. 454–461, (2005).

7. T. Shan, B. Lovell, and S. Chen. Face recognition robust to head pose from one sample image. In *Proc. 18th Int. Conf. Pattern Recognition (ICPR)*, vol. 1, pp. 515–518, (2006).

8. C. Sanderson, S. Bengio, and Y. Gao, On transforming statistical models for non-frontal face verification, *Pattern Recognition*. **39**(2), 288–302, (2006).

9. F. Cardinaux, C. Sanderson, and S. Bengio, User authentication via adapted statistical models of face images, *IEEE Transactions on Signal Processing*. **54**(1), 361–373, (2006).

10. S. Lucey and T. Chen. Learning patch dependencies for improved pose mismatched face verification. In *IEEE Conf. Computer Vision and Pattern Recognition*, vol. 1, pp. 909–915, (2006).

11. L. Wiskott, J. Fellous, N. Kuiger, and C. V. Malsburg, Face recognition by elastic bunch graph matching, *IEEE Trans. Pattern Analysis and Machine Intelligence*. **19** (7), 775–779, (1997).

12. K. Bowyer, K. Chang, and P. Flynn., A survey of approaches and challenges in 3D and multi-modal 3D+2D face recognition., *Computer Vision and Image Understanding*. **101**(1), 1–15, (2006).

13. G. Csurka, C. Dance, L. Fan, J. Willamowski, and C. Bray. Visual cetegorization with bags of keypoints. In *Workshop on Statistical Learning in Computer Vision (in conjunction with ECCV'04)*, (2004).

14. J. Sivic and A. Zisserman. Video google: A text retrieval approach to object matching in videos. In *Proceedings of 9th International Conference on Computer Vision (ICCV)*, vol. 2, pp. 1470–1477, (2003).

15. E. Nowak, F. Jurie, and B. Triggs. Sampling strategies for bag-of-features image classification. In *Computer Vision – ECCV 2006, Lecture Notes in Computer Science (LNCS)*, vol. 3954, pp. 490–503. Springer, (2006).

16. T. S. Lee, Image representation using 2D Gabor wavelets, *IEEE Trans. Pattern Analysis and Machine Intelligence*. **18**(10), 959–971, (1996).

17. R. Gonzales and R. Woods, *Digital Image Processing*. (Addison-Wesley, 1992).

18. R. Duda, P. Hart, and D. Stork, *Pattern Classification*. (Wiley, 2001), 2nd edition.

19. Y. Rodriguez, F. Cardinaux, S. Bengio, and J. Mariethoz, Measuring the performance of face localization systems, *Image and Vision Computing*. **24**, 882–893, (2006).

20. C. Wallraven, B. Caputo, and A. Graf. Recognition with local features: the kernel recipe. In *Proc. 9th International Conference on Computer Vision (ICCV)*, vol. 1, pp. 257–264, (2003).

21. T. Kadir and M. Brady, Saliency, scale and image description, *International Journal of Computer Vision*. **45**(2), 83–105, (2001).

22. N. Schraudolph, A fast, compact approximation of the exponential function, *Neural Computation*. **11**, 853–862, (1999).

23. T. Cootes and C. Taylor. Active shape models - 'smart snakes'. In *Proceedings of British Machine Vision Conference*, pp. 267–275, (1992).

24. T. Cootes, G. Edwards, and C. Taylor, Active appearance models, *IEEE Transactions on Pattern Analysis and Machine Intelligence*. **23**(6), 681–685, (2001).
25. T. Cootes, K. Walker, and C. Taylor. View-based active appearance models. In *Proceedings of 4th IEEE International Conference on Automatic Face and Gesture Recognition*, pp. 227–232, (2000).
26. T. Sim, S. Baker, and M. Bsat, The CMU pose, illumination, and expression database, *IEEE. Trans. Pattern Analysis and Machine Intelligence*. **25**(12), 1615–1618, (2003).
27. P. Phillips, H. Moon, S. Rizvi, and P. Rauss, The FERET evaluation methodology for face-recognition algorithms, *IEEE Trans. Pattern Analysis and Machine Intelligence*. **22**(10), 1090–1104, (2000).

AUTHOR INDEX

SUBJECT INDEX